Dear Jean,

Thank you for all your support.

Robert

NO CLAIM TO MERCY

Elizabeth Bain and Robert Baltovich,
A Suburban Mystery

DEREK FINKLE

VIKING

VIKING

Published by the Penguin Group

Penguin Books Canada Ltd, 10 Alcorn Avenue, Toronto, Ontario, Canada M4V 3B2

Penguin Books Ltd, 27 Wrights Lane, London W8 5TZ, England

Penguin Putnam Inc., 375 Hudson Street, New York, New York 10014, U.S.A.

Penguin Books Australia Ltd, Ringwood, Victoria, Australia

Penguin Books (NZ) Ltd, cnr Rosedale and Airborne Roads, Albany Aukland 1310, New Zealand

Penguin Books Ltd Registered Offices: Harmondsworth, Middlesex, England

First published 1998

10 9 8 7 6 5 4 3 2 1

CANADIAN CATALOGUING IN PUBLICATION DATA

Finkle, Derek
    No claim to mercy: Elizabeth Bain and Robert Baltovich, a suburban mystery

ISBN 0-670-87412-4

1. Baltovich, Robert. 2. Bain, Elizabeth, d. 1990. 3. Murder – Ontario – Scarborough. I. Title

HV6535.C33S38 1998   364.1´523´092   C96-932037-X

Visit Penguin Canada's website at www.penguin.ca

For my grandmother

Now they'd come so far
and they'd waited so long
just to end up caught in a dream
where everything goes wrong
where the darkness of night
holds back the light of the day
and you've got to stand and fight
for the price you pay
—Bruce Springsteen

Contents

—⊖—

Part 1 *First Love* 1

Part 2 *Through the Valley of the Shadow* 73

Part 3 *Closing in on the Heart* 157

Part 4 *Private Investigations* 267

Part 5 *No Claim to Mercy* 371

Part 6 *Fresh Evidence* 441

No
Claim to
Mercy

Part 1

—◦—

First Love

Now that the Christmas holidays were over, Elizabeth Bain found herself alone in her room, graced with a moment of solitude promising enough to begin writing her first diary entry of the new year. The festivities of the past week had simply heightened the usual incessant bustle at home. Twenty-two years old, she still lived with her parents, her two younger brothers, Mark and Paul, and her teenage sister, Cathy. If all went according to plan, she would graduate from university in another year and then she could finally move out and marry her boyfriend, Robert Baltovich. She had met him a few years earlier at the University of Toronto's satellite campus in the eastern suburb of Scarborough, where they had both grown up just a few miles apart. Rob, who also lived with his parents, was graduating in the spring. Maybe by the time she got her degree, they could afford a little apartment. Not a house, just an apartment. That would suit her just fine.

Liz wrote the date at the top of the page. Then, below at the left margin, the same salutation she used for every diary entry: "Dear Meg." She dreamed of having a daughter named Meg when she was married and imagined revising the whole diary one day, picking out all of the beautiful thoughts and making it into a story so that little Meg would always have something to remember her by.

January 2, 1990

Dear Meg,

I overdosed on laxatives and feel so sick as I write this. I am in a state of anxiety because I totally depend on enemas now. My exercise? I average two times a week. 25% raw vegetables, 1550 calories.

This last week has been hell. On Wednesday, Rob phoned me from school five times. He was angry, I know, but I kept telling everyone to say I wasn't home. Finally, at 3:30, he dropped by. He was sitting in the basement when I walked down and asked what he was doing. He said, "What is going on?" I said, "I don't want to talk to you right now. I'll talk to you later, when I feel I can speak rationally." He looked at me weird and said, "I don't want to go. I want you to tell me what is wrong." I said, firmly, "Well, you are going to have to leave because I'm not going to say anything until I can talk rationally. You can stay here—I'm going to my room." As I walked away, he called after me—"Liz, Liz, Elizabeth!" And he followed me up the stairs.

I said, "Don't follow me around the house like this." And I shut my bedroom door. He was still calling my name, loudly—"Elizabeth!" I opened the door because it was embarrassing. He was standing there, shaking, with his hands together like he was praying and he looked as if he was going to fall on his knees. The expression on his face—quite horrifying. We stood looking at each other for about a minute until I stepped out and took his hand and pulled him into my room. He sat on my bed, shaking, and I held him.

Five hours later, we came out. Both hurting inside and me feeling quite guilty. On Thursday, we went to a motel—he paid for sex.

At Roma's son's birthday on Saturday, he was a pure gentleman. Even in the car, when he should have yelled at me for being so cold—because of something that happened with my father—and then there was Sunday at the New Year's party. I spent most of the night in the loo with Mark's girlfriend, Nancy, crying about how badly he was treating her.

Over the last three days I've thought about how much shit I've taken from men and how much Rob is the only man who lets me walk all over him. He's so defenceless. So kind to me, yes, and I cry thinking about how lucky I am to have him surrender to me like that. Rob treats me like gold and very often I feel he's overdoing it. Like how, on Sunday, he offered to iron Evelyn's dress, and then said nothing about the sleazy outfit I wore. He gave a birthday card to Mom, a book to Tia Diana, and didn't even complain that I spent the night in the bathroom. Instead, he hugged me, kissed my neck, when I'd ignored him the whole night.

He didn't complain when Mark asked him to take Nancy home. He hugged me while I cried the whole night about Nancy and he sat there as if I hadn't already ruined the night for him. He spent another two hours consoling me in his car and then came the next day with a poem and a card to alleviate my pain. He asked Mom not to tell me he'd been here because he "wasn't supposed to see" me.

I am worried. He is trying too hard all of a sudden. I don't like having so much power over a man. I don't understand it at all when a man is so submissive. He's afraid of being alone but he doesn't realize how hard he's trying to keep me. It's unnecessary. One day he'll open his eyes and hate himself for it. He'll hate me too—for giving me power over him. No one should be so afraid of losing someone that they have to act that unnaturally. It won't last. It will not last. It will slowly kill him. There must be a woman who will love him unconditionally and he must believe it.

I don't believe that he's ever truly been intimate with a woman. Even though he has slept with others before me, he is uncomfortable about sex. He can't even refer to his genitals, or mine, or talk about making love without a squint. I can see the look on his face before the scene—it is almost a look of embarrassment. I don't understand. For me, he's my first, and it's understandable.

I am beginning to feel seriously ill from these laxatives. I know my running must improve and that I must start eating more raw vegetables.

But Rob has got to relax. Maybe this is a short phase. Perhaps I'm compensating for what happened on Wednesday. I don't know, but it isn't healthy. The motives definitely aren't healthy.

Liza

—◦—

Robert Baltovich: Last Kiss Good-bye

If you want to know about Tuesday, June 19, 1990, the day my girlfriend Liz disappeared, I should probably begin by telling you a little about the preceding Sunday, which was the last time I ever saw her. As I did just about every Sunday evening back then, I went to Major Video at Danforth and Midland to rent a movie. That night, I chose Honey, I Shrunk the Kids *and then drove to Kidbrooke, a group home for the physically and mentally handicapped where Liz was working part-time. When I rang the doorbell, I noticed that it took a while for someone to answer. The door was finally opened by a woman who worked with Liz named Ethel Ormsby. I remember thinking to myself, Why didn't Liz answer? She was probably expecting me. Ethel told me Liz was downstairs, so I went down to the basement, only to find her sitting alone, reading a book, looking distant and aloof. Her mood was completely at odds with how happy she'd been when I'd dropped by to see her at Kidbrooke just twenty-four hours ago. She'd been smiling and laughing then and she'd kissed me very tenderly. I then walked into the group home's living room and Liz even sat on my knee on the couch. One of the clients who lived there, a developmentally delayed man in his forties named William, asked Liz if she loved me, and I remember that Liz didn't even have to think about. She just said, "Yes, William, I do."*

That same night, I told Liz that I had plans to see a movie with the guys and that I couldn't stay too long. She said that was okay, and that she was glad I spent time with the guys, because she didn't want to keep me from them. Liz then said to me, "I have something for you," and went upstairs. When she came back down, she produced a white envelope with my name printed on it. "I was cleaning up my room and I found this," she said. "It's from a while ago, from my diary. I don't write much in it any more." She looked at me very strangely and smiled. I didn't—and still don't—know what to make of it. In any case, I went out to my car, dropped the envelope in the back seat, and went to get my friend Al Heys.

I grabbed Al and told him that I was just over visiting Liz. We got in the car and picked up Tony Fuchs, another friend of mine. Tony jumped in the back seat of my old Cordoba and noticed the envelope. He started to joke around and said, "Ah, what have we here?" I told him it was something Liz had written a long time ago and that she'd been smiling when she'd given it to me. Tony said, "Oh, one of those letters."

After the movie ended at about 11:00 PM, I dropped Al and Tony off and went home. I read the letter. It was a "Dear Meg" letter written in September 1988, just about a year after Liz and I first met (although we wouldn't begin dating until the following spring). It began: "I saw Rob Baltovich today . . ." She had just seen me in a social psychology class and, from what I can remember of it, the diary entry expressed her regret that she had turned me down when I had asked her out one day towards the beginning of the previous school year. It was really me she'd wanted to be with, she'd written, not her boyfriend at the time, Dean Orlando, whom I've never met.

I now recall that when I read this old diary entry, it occurred to me that I had seen Liz's diary once before—I just hadn't known what it was. I'd found it strange that Liz was writing to this friend named Meg, and she'd never mentioned the existence of such a person to me. I saw the Dear Meg letter while Liz and I were at her house alone one day, and I was looking for a scrap piece of paper in her bedroom to write down a telephone message because she was in the shower. The letter kept going on about how beautiful she wanted to be and how important it was to eat "raw" and look gorgeous. One sentence began with the words "Christ, woman . . ." which was totally out of character for Liz. It hadn't crossed my mind at the time that it was a diary entry. In fact, the idea that she had written such things to anyone, including herself, briefly made me cringe.

Anyway, when I found her looking so sullen in the basement at Kidbrooke that Sunday, my first words were, "I brought a movie." She said "great" but without much feeling. So I gathered the residents and set up the VCR to watch the movie and then sat down on one of the chesterfields. Liz chose a seat on the other side of the room. I could tell it was going to be one of those days.

Mid-way through the picture, I started thinking about my mother, who hadn't been feeling well when I'd left home. Without saying anything, I left the room to call her on the phone upstairs. After speaking to my mother, I returned to the movie, and Liz wanted to know who I'd called, so I told her. Right away, she got up and walked over to the chesterfield where I was sitting and lowered herself onto the floor near my legs. She then turned to me and whispered, "Are you disappointed with me?"

I said, "No, but I get the impression you'd rather I not be here."

"Don't be silly," she said. "There's no one I'd rather want here than you." That quickly, she became as warm and affectionate as she'd been the night before.

After the movie, we walked hand in hand outside into the backyard. It was almost eleven o'clock and Liz's shift was over. I remarked what a warm and starry night it was and asked her if she was interested in going for a late walk. She flashed me a devilish smile because she knew what I had in mind. She laughed and said, "I'd love to." I suggested the valley at Colonel Danforth Park because it was close to her house, and she thought that was fine. But first, she said, she had to give one of her co-workers, Sonia Austin, a ride home. "Well, how about this," I said. "I'll drop Ethel off at her house, and you take Sonia home, and we'll meet in the parking lot at the Recreation Centre at school." Liz just smiled and said she'd see me there.

I can still remember how Ethel, who was in her late forties, struck up a conversation with me as I drove her home. "Elizabeth is quite a girl, isn't she?" Ethel asked. "One of the best," I said. A few minutes later I turned onto Ethel's street, and she asked if Liz and I were meeting again that night. When I said we were, she wondered why we would want to be going out at such a late hour. I explained that Liz's father had been away in Florida since Tuesday, and Liz didn't get very many opportunities to stay out late like this, so we were going to make the most of it.

Liz drove into the parking lot at the Recreation Centre about ten minutes after me and pulled her car up next to mine. She had stopped at a variety store on the way to buy us a couple of diet 7-Ups, which she was carrying in a paper bag as she got out of her car. Together we went to the back of her car and opened up the trunk, and we each grabbed a blanket and a pop and started walking along the south side of the school towards what was called the H-Wing, as I scoped for an area where no one would be able to see us. In the end, I decided we would follow the trail that went down towards the tennis courts. Liz seemed a little timid, but I told her not to worry and took her hand. She kept looking back as we made our way down.

As we reached and crossed the bridge over Highland Creek, we turned right, went behind the Principal's Residence, and walked south-west along the ravine. Amid a flat, wide stretch of open grass there are two islands of trees and bush.

We laid our blankets down behind the farthest island from the Principal's Residence, closer to the Morningside Bridge. We spread out the blankets and undressed and made love. We laughed and talked about insignificant things. We stayed for about two hours. We knew it was getting late. I said it was about time for her to be getting home, but she didn't seem too concerned. Her mother wasn't as strict when it came to staying out late, and because her father was still away, doing some repairs on an investment property he owned in Florida, there was no rush.

It was almost two o'clock in the morning by the time we eventually got dressed, picked up the blankets and headed back to our cars. As we crossed the bridge, we heard a loud rustle in the bushes. Liz stopped and grabbed my hand very firmly, looking terrified. She didn't move, and I recall thinking that I had never seen her so scared, for usually she was fearless. Finally, we noticed it was a raccoon up in the tree. My own fears allayed, we began walking, with Liz holding my hand like she couldn't let go. She kept looking behind her.

When we got back to our cars, Liz turned to me and said, "I don't mean to make you sound like a ninny, but if someone had been out there, we wouldn't have stood a chance." I didn't know what she was alluding to, so we just continued chatting about something else. Liz was saying what a lousy summer she was having between work and school but she was glad that I'd seemed so much happier lately. I just laughed. It was about 2:15 AM.

Liz didn't seem to want me to go. She was working the next day, and we weren't going to see each other. She told me that she was planning to have dinner with her friend Arlene Coventry on Tuesday. Arlene had been away at university in Ottawa all year but was now home for the summer. I told her that I would be home all day Tuesday and to call and let me know if things were still on with Arlene. She then turned to me and said, "You have no idea how much I love you." We kissed. Then she got into her car and left. She went north on Military Trail to Ellesmere, turned left and drove out of sight. And, as I said, I never saw her again.

—◇—

Like most people from Scarborough, Robert Baltovich took a lot of ribbing from those he knew who lived in other parts of Toronto. For as long as he could remember, outsiders had taken pleasure in calling his suburb "Scarberia"—the cultural wasteland to Toronto's east. Someone once said Scarborough was what Toronto had instead of Jersey City. Everybody pointed to the strawberry-box bungalows built for working-class families after the Second World War and immediately conjured images of polyester and living rooms decorated with velvet paintings.

Local politicians attempted to combat Scarborough's lacklustre reputation by insisting that it be formally recognized as a city. Despite their efforts, the never-ending stream of Scarborough jokes continued. Perhaps the most prominent of these was a parody of Dylan Thomas's "A Child's Christmas in Wales," written for CBC Radio in 1969 by Toronto author Howard Engel. "A Child's Christmas in Scarborough" has become a radio classic and has been broadcast every holiday season for over two decades. It begins: "Whenever I remember Christmas as a child in Scarborough, I can never remember whether the slush was new or old, or whether we lived on the sixth street north of the shopping plaza stoplights and I was seven years old, or whether it was the seventh street and I was six. . . ."

As far as Rob was concerned, "Scarberia" was a myth. He'd lived in Scarborough for all twenty-five years of his life and, from what he'd seen of Toronto, he had no intentions of leaving. It was a short drive to more than a dozen parks and beaches along the shore of Lake Ontario, including the Scarborough Bluffs, from which the area got its name in 1793 when Elizabeth Simcoe, the wife of the lieutenant-governor, observed that the grey cliffs were similar to those of Scarborough in England.

North of the lake, three massive parks follow the progress of the Rouge River and Highland Creek for at least fifteen kilometres. Salmon and trout still spawn in their waters, and white-tailed deer live in the dense surrounding woods, where one could walk for hours completely oblivious to any visible trace of the city. Affixed to the Glen Rouge Park in the north-east end of Scarborough is the sprawling Metro Toronto Zoo, above which there are Mennonite farms. And, if you were looking for culture, you could go to The Guild Inn and see the most eccentric sculpture park in Canada, or the Dragon Centre mall, where Scarborough's populous Chinese community barters for authentic Asian wares in its native dialects.

Rob's father, James Baltovich, took over a variety store on Kingston Road in lower Scarborough in November of 1952, just a few months away from his thirtieth birthday. The previous owner had sold it to him for a real bargain, and he renamed it Jimmy's Smoke Shop. It was the perfect place to start a new business—Scarborough would multiply in size about five times over the next decade. Although most of the 300,000 people living in Scarborough in the late 1960s were of British origin, Jim and his mother had come to Canada from Macedonia in 1935 when he was a boy, joining his father, who was, for young Jim, a shadowy figure he'd longed for on countless occasions. He'd been only three years old when his father had crossed the Atlantic en route to a farm in Alberta, where he and his brothers endured a hard year as immigrant labourers for the eventual privilege of settling in Toronto for a life of promise. His father rented a little house on Shuter Street, where a Macedonian community had been flourishing on the city's east side since the turn of the century. A modest hat-cleaning and shoe-shine store in the downtown business district became the family business, and Jim, the only child, spent many of his Saturdays at his father's side, making up for lost time.

Roughly three years after he'd opened Jimmy's Smoke Shop, Jim met his future wife, Adele. Adele, whose maiden name was White, had been born into one of those old-stock Scarborough families of British extraction. She worked at a competing smoke shop across the street from Jimmy's and would drop in for visits (that seemed to get longer and longer as time went by) on her way home. Adele's friends warned her about getting involved with a "foreigner"—the kind of man who would expect her to assume the role of the overworked, subservient housewife—but she didn't think Jim was that kind of man. And it didn't seem to bother him that she'd already been married and was the mother of four children. The youngest child, a son, Terry (whose surname, Chadwick, was never changed), was the product of a short-lived relationship she'd had after separating from her first husband, whom she'd married when she was just eighteen. Adele had maintained custody of the other three children, but, a few years later, they went to live with their father. She had little contact with them after that.

She did, however, continue to raise six-year-old Terry after she married Jim back in Regent Park at the Macedonian Bulgarian Orthodox Cathedral in 1962, a few blocks from his parents' old house on Shuter Street, as well as the one they bought in 1941 at 18 Regent Street. Jim was thirty-eight; Adele was thirty-three. Four months after the wedding, Adele discovered she was expecting their first child, who would be named Paul. Next came Robert, Paul's junior by two and a half years, on July 17, 1965.

Watching Paul and Rob grow up, Terry always felt they shared the kind of healthy sibling rivalry one might expect from two brothers so close in age. Whenever they fought over a toy or the last cookie, Terry would just smile, content with the knowledge that the boys had some life in them. They were both still pretty young when Terry left home at seventeen (he was married at twenty), but he remained in close contact with his half-brothers. Rob always looked forward to seeing Terry and his young wife, who quite often took Rob along for little trips around town, or brought him over to the house to work on things together.

Terry realized early on that Rob's childhood was paralleling his own much more than it was Paul's. This had a lot to do with their father's store. All three boys had been involved with the shop at one time or another, but Paul hadn't stayed as long or immersed himself in the day-to-day responsibilities the way Terry and Rob had. And perhaps this is what made their bond more tangible, along with the fact that when Terry started a family of his own, Rob was the one who remembered the kids' birthdays with some sort of trinket or candy. Rob had always possessed a gift with children, Terry thought, even when he was one himself.

Terry, Paul and Rob were raised in a modest two-storey, semi-detached brick home on Midland Avenue, which was just around the corner from Jimmy's Smoke Shop. Jim's parents had bought the house in 1956, four years after Jim had bought the store. Before then, he had been commuting to the shop from Regent Park, where he still lived with his parents. So when they moved, Jim went along with them. Suddenly, getting to work became as easy as a stroll down the road.

For Jim's father, however, the move represented the end of his life, for he was struck and killed by a drunk driver at the intersection of Midland and Kingston Road four years later. Instead of leaving his mother alone when he married Adele, Jim had his bride and her son Terry move into the house with him and his mother, whose English, even after thirty years in Toronto, remained poor. Then, not long after Rob was born, Jim's mother collapsed on the sidewalk one sweltering day, surrounded by the heavy fruits and vegetables she had been carrying home from the market.

After her mother-in-law passed away, Adele decided to redecorate. No more Persian rugs and rickety old love seats. Anything with that melancholy eastern

European style went out. She picked out some colourful wallpaper, shiny fixtures and fluffy carpets, gave the place a facelift. Put her own stamp on it.

Yet, in spite of her bright new abode, Adele suffered a nervous breakdown when Rob was still small, maybe two years old. She continued to be afflicted by bouts of depression for most of her life; when Rob was a young boy, he occasionally had to spend several days with relatives or friends of the family while his mother was being treated in the hospital. Once, when Rob was about ten, he stayed with the family of two brothers, Ian and Bruce Lindsay, who were his best friends in those days. They lived a few houses up the street, right next to the Pentecostal church where their father, Doug, was the pastor. Through his kinship with the Lindsay brothers, Rob became very involved with the church, as did Paul, but when Rob was thirteen, Doug Lindsay and his family were relocated and Rob began to drift away from religion. Instead, he became interested in sports. Paul, on the other hand, remained devoted to a life with the church and was cultivating a knack for the less athletic sport of fishing. This was about the time that Rob became a regular at his father's store, stocking shelves and sweeping the floor at the age of eleven, and he continued to help out until he was halfway through university.

By that time, he'd already formed a distinct clique of friends from his years at R.H. King High School. Although Rob was the only one in the group to continue his studies at the University of Toronto's Scarborough campus, his closest friends—Tony Fuchs and Al Heys—ended up hanging around with Rob and his new college pals. Rob was a little unusual in that he didn't drink, smoke or mess around with drugs. His parents didn't own a car until Rob was almost a teenager. (Adele went out one day and bought a used '72 Chevelle without telling Jim, who, like Adele, didn't even have a driver's licence. But even once Jim did obtain one, the car was used very little. The day the rusted-out vehicle was towed out of the driveway for good many years later, it had seen a mere 22,000 miles of road.) Rob's stay-at-home parents had a lot to do with the fact that he didn't travel outside of Scarborough until the age of sixteen, when he made a day-long excursion into downtown Toronto with a group of friends. And when you considered that he was an honour student, sang in the choir and worked dutifully at his father's corner store, it wasn't difficult to understand why even his closest friends saw him as a bit of a square and kidded him about being like the Richie Cunningham character that the actor Ron Howard played on the television show "Happy Days."

—◦—

When Rob began his university studies in September 1985, Scarborough College had grown considerably since the first day its doors had opened to just two hundred full-time students twenty years earlier. The idea to establish two new satellite campuses in Scarborough and Mississauga (at that time still known as Toronto Township), a suburb to the west of Toronto, was first proposed in 1956 when the University of Toronto decided that it would soon outgrow the Queen's Park campus downtown. The university selected an Australian-born, Harvard-educated architect named John Andrews to design the new campus in Scarborough.

Andrews had 202 acres of land to work with. The property, purchased from an elderly local farmer in 1963, straddled a road known as Military Trail, originally laid out in 1799 to connect Toronto to Kingston, Ontario. It also included a vast section of the lush valley surrounding Highland Creek. Since the valley was a combination of flood plain and steep forested slopes, Andrews selected the plateau to the north of the valley as the site for the new college.

Although Andrews later wrote that "the formulative concept was Scarborough College as a small Canadian town," its buildings have about as much in common with rural Canadian hamlets as the Pentagon. The two main wings of the college rise above the treetops at the rim of the valley like an ancient Aztec monument constructed from concrete and glass. Scarborough College has been hailed by architectural historians from all over the globe as one of the world's finest examples of what is known as a "Neo-Brutalist megastructure." The "megastructure" was a popular built form for a short period in the 1950s and 1960s, and Andrews's contribution to the style made the college one of a handful of buildings in Toronto of international architectural significance. However, despite the lofty praise, there is no getting around the fact that, from certain angles, Andrews's megastructure looks like a massive spaceship that fell from the sky in another era, its solid, dark exterior marked with white vertical lines carved by centuries of rainwater.

While Andrews's architectural ambitions were being realized, the university was planning to make Scarborough College a laboratory for the largest experiment in educational television ever conducted. About six thousand square feet of space and $1.25 million were allocated to build a number of cutting-edge television studios and to equip the college's lecture theatres with monitors. As much as fifty per cent of the college's classes were to be taught using carefully prepared videotapes, cutting about thirty per cent from the cost of conventional lecturing. But when the college's new faculty caught wind of this ground-breaking "experiment," it fought against it. As indignant as its professors were at the prospect of being replaced by talking heads, the students were equally dismayed about staring at television screens for hours at a time, and the entire program was scrapped. Ironically, the only large-scale video projects to subsequently grace the campus were a variety of science fiction films and television programs whose directors declared that the alien backdrop of Andrews's architectural masterpiece was exactly what they were looking for.

The college's layout wasn't something Rob cared much about. He knew that its main buildings were pretty bizarre-looking, but on the inside the place was like a giant high school. The enormous buildings of Scarborough campus were joined by a complex web of hallways lined with never-ending rows of multicoloured lockers. To protect the students from the harsh Canadian winters, everything was connected by covered walkways and underground passages: the classrooms, the cafeteria, the college's modest library and the gymnasium complex. Compared to the overwhelming size of the downtown campus, which had an enrolment of approximately fifty thousand, Rob much preferred the community atmosphere of the college, with its thirty-five hundred full-time students. The most attractive feature of all, though, was the fact that he could roll out of bed in his basement room and get to the campus in half an hour—provided he caught both buses on time.

In his second year of university, Rob decided to become a history major. This interest in history could be traced back to his boyhood, when he watched an incredible number of historical documentaries on television with his father. Just about every course Rob took that second year was a study in one historical period or another. One of the few exceptions was a psychology course he signed up for as an elective. Rob had always had a general curiosity about people and how they behaved and what motivated them, but he was aware that, on a subconscious level, his interest might have had something to do with his mother's emotional difficulties. He hadn't anticipated how fascinated he would become with what he was learning in his psychology course and that, in turn, his enthusiasm for history would wane slightly. It wasn't that he didn't enjoy history any more—he certainly didn't want to abandon it—so he decided to embark on a double major in psychology *and* history.

Rob also began to work less and less at his father's store. The summer before he began university, he got a job as a counsellor at the Greenwood Day Camp, which was run by the Scarborough YMCA. Rob had enjoyed working with children so much that he returned to the camp the following year, which was 1986, in a more senior position. This time he was a coordinator for Greenwood's organized overnight hiking and biking trips, known as the Voyageur Program. Rob's co-counsellor, a girl named Debbie King, also became his girlfriend. (Before Debbie, with whom he lost his virginity that summer, there were only two girls Rob had gone out with in high school beyond the first date.) According to the camp's rules, Debbie was too young to be a Voyageur counsellor, but she'd lied about her age on her job application. Rob hadn't thought much of it until a few weeks later when he began to wonder more and more about whether Debbie was truly mature enough to be responsible for the care of a group of young kids.

During one of their bike trips, they'd set up their tents at a well-used campground, and Rob cycled into the nearby town to get some supplies, leaving Debbie to look after their campers. While Rob was gone, the commissioner for the Scarborough YMCA made a surprise visit to the site and found Debbie wearing a bikini—not considered proper attire for a counsellor—and teaching a group of girls how to apply make-up. One boy was off in a corner wildly swinging an axe and three others were wandering in an adjacent field—which was being constructed into a golf course—swimming in one of the water traps. Not long after Rob returned from town, his supervisor showed up with two other counsellors to announce that he and Debbie had been fired. As it turned out, Rob managed to keep his job; Debbie didn't. Needless to say, the firing put a bit of a strain on the relationship, and their union did not outlast the summer.

Six months or so later at a campus party, he met Caitlin Fleury, a plump, friendly girl. Rob spoke with her most of the night, and Caitlin revealed that she'd been adopted by a Scarborough family when she was very young. They continued talking for hours, the vibes of their mutual flirtation working like a giant magnet until, finally, she surprised him by letting it be known that she had no problem sleeping with him that very night. For Rob, the next few months with Caitlin were an extension of that first encounter, and then, as summer began, she said she needed a bit of a break to straighten out some personal problems. Caitlin came back to him before long, but it was too late. Rob was happy being single.

He couldn't have been more thankful for his unattached state than on the day in September 1987 when, sitting through one of his first lectures of the semester, a class in developmental psychology, he was unable to take his eyes off a raven-haired girl across the room. What he didn't know, however, was that this same girl had also been secretly admiring him. Rob also had dark hair, which he kept short, sweeping the bangs upward off his forehead with the aid of hair gel. She liked the fact that he had a muscular physique. A strong jaw, a long, fine nose, round hazel eyes, thin well-shaped lips. His face definitely had character.

Rob kept his eye on her as everyone filed out of the room after the lecture. Her diminutive body was curvaceous but toned. What really gave him butterflies, though, were her exotic features, especially the striking dark eyes, almost Polynesian in their angularity. He was so taken by her that he did something he'd never done before in his life—he just walked right up to her, introduced himself and struck up a conversation.

She said her name was Elizabeth Bain, but that most people called her Liz or Lisa. It was her second year of university but her first year at Scarborough College. She'd taken some physical education courses at the downtown campus the year before, but she hadn't done that well, nor had she found it very enjoyable. She'd grown up in Scarborough, so it made sense to make a fresh start at the local campus. Like Rob, Liz had also selected to major in psychology as well as another field of study, sociology. As she spoke, Rob started to get the feeling that he'd seen her somewhere before but he couldn't quite remember where. She'd gone to a different high school, Cardinal Newman, which wasn't very far from R.H. King, and he was pretty sure he'd never seen her during his high school days. Neither of them could figure out where they might have met. It wasn't until Liz said that she did a lot of jogging that it finally came back to him.

Just a few months earlier, he'd been driving around Scarborough in a van with the words "The Weed Man" plastered across the side panels—it was the name of the landscaping outfit he'd worked for that summer—when he'd cranked his head to the side to catch a glimpse of a beautiful girl who was jogging along the sidewalk. He now realized that it had been her, but he thought it best for the moment not to mention it. Instead, he asked her if she'd like to have lunch with him. "Maybe another time," she said. She was very polite about it, maybe even a little coy, and they were both smiling as they parted ways.

It was only a matter of days before they had lunch at the Scarborough campus cafeteria. Pretty soon there were more lunches together and, as time went on, they began taking long walks and keeping each other company to and from their various classes. There was something really different about talking with Liz—she listened so intently, focusing on you as if there was no one else in the world she would rather be with.

He showed her around the school, introduced her to his friends, few of whom had any difficulty picking up on the fact that he was smitten with her. And it looked as though she was pretty interested in him, too. Rob had never felt this way around any of his old girlfriends and he had yet to even kiss her. Liz made him dizzy with infatuation.

It wasn't until November, two months into the school year, that Rob finally asked her out on a date, a real date—away from the campus. That's when she dropped the bomb. She told him that she was seeing someone else, a guy named Dean Orlando. Rob was stunned. The look of despair on his face made her feel sick with guilt. She didn't know what else to say but that she was sorry. She just turned and walked away, and, although she didn't show it, she was almost in tears.

Rob was absolutely convinced that she had led him on, intentionally trampling on his feelings, which, as he saw it, couldn't have been misinterpreted. Never before in his life had he been so hurt and angry. Walking the halls in a dark cloud, he ran into one of his best friends, Jim Isaacs, and told him what had just happened. Jim was incredulous. He had no idea that she was seeing someone. No one did.

Rob didn't see her again for another week. He was no longer infuriated by her rejection as much as he was baffled by it. He said hi to her and forced a half-hearted smile. Liz was a little surprised that he said anything at all—she didn't think he would ever want to speak to her again. He asked why she had taken so long to tell him about having a boyfriend. She tried to explain herself by saying that she'd had no idea that he was interested in her romantically. Scarborough College was a new place for her, and Rob was literally the first person she'd met there. She was just looking for a friend in a strange place, and he was, in her mind, playing the role of the perfect host.

Still, Rob wished that things had gone differently, but this talk with Liz eased the blow somewhat. They bumped into each other one more time before Christmas and then fell out of contact for almost a year. This happened for two reasons. One, the developmental psychology class they had taken together had ended, and two, Liz wasn't one to spend much of her free time on campus. In the meantime, he began dating a girl named Ann Kristiansen the following spring. Rob always thought of Ann as the quintessential nice girl next door and they got along very well, even after they stopped dating at the end of the summer.

He ran into Liz again at school in the fall, during the University of Toronto's homecoming day celebrations at the main campus downtown. Jim Isaacs had seen her limbering up for a jog near the Scarborough campus a week earlier and he'd told Rob that she was looking more beautiful than ever. Now that she was standing in front of him, Rob couldn't disagree. That year, Scarborough campus students were responsible for setting up an area to keep visiting alumni's children entertained for at least part of the afternoon. Jim had organized a ring-toss booth in which the targets were posters of the Seven Dwarfs. When Rob found out that Liz was going to be dressing up as Snow White, he asked the assistant director of the kids' area if he could be Prince Charming.

Despite the prince routine, it seemed as though Liz was still not interested, and Rob began seeing a girl named Margot Simmons. For quite a while, the only person through whom he heard anything about Liz was Jim. Even though Rob was taking a class with Jim and Liz that year, Rob had assumed that he and Liz were destined to be nothing more than friends. It was clear, though, that Jim had taken a liking to her, and Rob would occasionally listen to Jim's accounts of his walks in the valley with Liz, which usually included detailed descriptions of how drop-dead gorgeous she was looking that day. Rob kept urging Jim to ask her out, but he was too shy and never seemed able to summon the courage.

Then one day in March 1989, Rob came home from school and his mother told him that Elizabeth Bain had called. He had a hard time getting through to her on the phone and spoke to her for the first time when he ran into her at the class they were taking together at school a few days later. When he asked her about the phone call, he couldn't believe her response—now she was asking *him* if he'd like to go out.

Rob had ended things with Margot Simmons a few weeks earlier but he was a little unsure about Liz because, even though she'd been single for some time, she was still spending quite a bit of time with Jim. Liz assured him that she and Jim would never be more than friends, so Rob asked her out to a movie. Rob wanted to take her to a good, wholesome type of film, so he picked one that he'd already seen, not mentioning that to Liz. The movie, *Beaches*, was a bit of a tear-jerker and Rob later thought it might have been a bad choice for a first date because it was overly emotional—the actress Barbara Hershey plays a woman with terminal cancer who leaves her young daughter to be raised by a lifelong friend, portrayed by Bette Midler. The idea to take Liz to *Beaches* also backfired when Jim revealed to her that Rob had chosen a movie he'd already seen. Liz found that a little strange.

Rob started wondering what he should do. It seemed as though Jim had been hurt by the fact that Rob had taken Liz on a date; at least that's how he interpreted Jim's lack of discretion. From what Rob knew, Liz was the only girl Jim had ever been interested in and they'd done quite a few things together around Christmas time. Jim was a tall, gangly guy with short, curly blond hair, his brow as menacing as his disposition was gentle. He'd never been too smooth with the ladies and, with Liz, he was too paralyzed by her beauty to act on his feelings. Rob later felt that she might have had the impression that Jim was gay, because she was so used to guys coming on strong.

Rob was determined not to make the same mistake—after all, he might not get another chance. Two weeks later, he took her to a play. Even though they had yet to display any physical signs of affection, Rob was happy with the way things were going. Then, several days later, he found out that Jim had taken Liz to a museum the afternoon following their date. The only saving grace was that she had told Jim about being with Rob the night before and said that she'd had a really good time.

Rob wasn't sure whether Jim was trying to undermine his efforts, but he resolved to take Liz out for dinner at a restaurant on the same block as his father's store, a place called Vincent's Spot. Having passed Vincent's Spot on countless occasions as he walked to and from Jimmy's Smoke Shop, Rob had never been too impressed with its shabby exterior. The brick front was dimly lit by a well-faded yellow and green awning, and there was one small window with a glaring red neon sign—OPEN—that made it impossible to catch a glimpse of the interior unless you stuck your face right up against the glass. He'd always just assumed the place was a total dive. It wasn't until he'd been strolling by one night and had seen a friend pull up out front with his family that he gave the place a second thought. "You're going in there?" Rob asked the friend, trying to be discreet. His friend explained that despite its greasy-spoon appearance, it was a beautiful restaurant inside with impeccable service, and even though it was a well-kept secret, you could wait half an hour on a Saturday evening for a table. Rob made a mental note to check it out one day.

When he called her to confirm their dinner date, Liz said she wasn't feeling too well and might not be able to make it that night. Rob said he hoped it wasn't serious and that he would cancel the reservation. "Reservation?" Liz said, sounding surprised. "You know what, maybe I can make it." He figured that she might have thought he was taking her to McDonald's but when she found out it was going to be considerably more sophisticated, only then did she agree to go.

Liz knew right away that dinner at Vincent's Spot was going to be special. She read a glowing review from *The Toronto Star* hanging in a frame on the wall beside her as they waited to be seated. It was a tiny one-room establishment that held about thirty people, with the kitchen in the back. Rich wood panelling, a lovely oil painting, and shaded lighting created the atmosphere for a romantic evening. The smell of sage and roasted quail permeated the room. There were lovely little tea candles floating in vases of water on every table, flickering beneath the masterfully folded napkins that rose from each sparkling glass.

It was so much more than Liz had expected—it was perfect, really—and she told Rob that she was genuinely touched. After dinner they decided to go for a walk along the boardwalk at Kew Beach, which was just ten minutes away by car. Rob drove her there in the gold Camaro his father had recently bought from Rob's older brother Paul to replace the Chevelle. They both thought it was pretty funny that a man who was almost seventy would be driving around in the vehicle of choice for twenty-something males suffering from testosterone overload.

As they walked along the boardwalk that night, they had their first long talk. Liz revealed that she had very few friends and often felt quite lonely. Rob was a little taken aback by this show of vulnerability because Liz's obvious beauty had, for some reason, always led him to assume that she had countless friends. It wasn't that he now thought there was anything wrong with her; it just appeared as though there was a hole in her life, and, somewhat selfishly, he hoped that he might be the one to fill it.

It was a cool spring night and they stopped at a park bench, where Liz told him that, as far as she was concerned, every friend she'd ever had had tried to take advantage of her in one way or another. Rob thought this was her way of letting him know in her own subtle way that she was a little suspicious of his motives. He tried to reassure her by invoking the eighteenth-century German philosopher Immanuel Kant, who, as Rob remembered it, had written that the true nature of friendship and human relations was to treat people not as a means to an end but as an end unto themselves.

Rob drove her home a few hours later and, as he pulled into the driveway, he felt as though they were entering one of those moments in which life imitated a TV sit-com, both of them anxious about how the date would end. Liz put him at ease pretty quickly when she leaned over and kissed him on the cheek. "Thank you very much," she said. "I had a wonderful time."

On his way home, Rob was on cloud nine. A kiss on the cheek from Liz was worth a hundred times more than anything another woman could have done for him. If I never get to spend another night with this girl, he thought to himself, no one can take this evening away from me.

A few weeks later, Rob rode his bicycle to her house one evening after working out at the campus gym. Liz said she wanted to light a bonfire together in the pit in her backyard. Soon they were sitting alone, holding each other near the warmth of the rising flames, when Liz began to smile and laugh a little bit. "What are you giggling about?" Rob asked.

Liz said, "I was just thinking about something."

"What's that?"

"I was thinking that I wanted you to kiss me," she said, standing up. She started to run around the yard. "But you're going to have to catch me first."

Rob caught up to her under a big tree. He turned her around in his arms and kissed her deeply. Later that night, as evening faded, they sat under the tree and carved their initials into the trunk.

—◌—

July 1989

Dear Rob,

I know that your big day is not until next Monday but I really wanted to write you something before then.

About two years ago, I asked you when your birthday was, and when you said the seventeenth of this month, I remember how I felt a big spark inside because of something I had read earlier. I know this sounds insane and I don't believe in astrology, but you have turned out to be as unreal as the page of that book. You make me feel "one thousand per cent woman." When you hold me you are not only tender and passionate but you make me feel that way too. Your energy makes me feel so young and your inquiring mind, with so much optimism, keeps reminding me that you are a very mature adult. No matter how young or old I feel with you, you listen so well and, because you seem to have such an open mind, you support me even in your silence. But perhaps the greatest quality you have shown is that you never try to control me or take advantage of me or humiliate me and, because of this respect, I have kept what I describe as a candle of hope lit up for you inside of me, even long before we began to spend time alone together.

I hope that I am not writing with too much sentiment but I have never felt so compatible with anyone and, for once, I don't feel insecure, inferior, used and evaluated. I am not plagued with "the other girl." I remember we had a little talk some time ago and I told you that I never had a male friend even though I'd wanted one very much. It was you who said it would be very hard for a guy to want to just "be my friend," but the ironic part is that you are one of the extreme few who has ever told me that you would be happy to just "go out as friends."

To you, this may be irrelevant and perhaps unnecessary to bring up, but way back when you asked me out, and I told you I was seeing someone, you gave me this look that, to this very day, I can picture perfectly in my mind. I remember crying as I walked home that afternoon because you looked so let down, and you scared the shit out of me with that look. Not only that, but I had just let down the first person who made me feel like I had a place in that school. It was you who showed me around and introduced me to most of the people I knew that year.

I didn't mean to be so horrible to you and I know I should have told you I was seeing someone right away. I lied when I said that I had no idea you were interested in me. I knew damn well that you were but I needed a friend at the time. It was so hard to walk into a totally new environment with a thousand unfamiliar faces staring from every direction. I felt so lost, but you were there, and I wanted so badly for you to be the person who would keep telling me: "You'll be okay here."

I remember calling one time early last summer, and your mother answered the telephone. Before I could say who I was, she called me by another girl's name. I guess I got what I deserved.

As you can see, you have come a long way, Robert. I don't think you ever knew this but I have been attracted to you since day one, when I was sitting in class and noticed you because you were the only one not looking at the professor. I couldn't understand why you were looking my way, but you sure looked occupied. I didn't expect you to run up to me after class the way you did and say what you did but, believe me, I already knew who you were.

Thank you for standing by me and for not giving up. It is an honour for me to know someone like you, and I feel extremely fortunate that you would stick around this long for someone like me. When I think about what I once did to you, I feel that I don't deserve this. I don't deserve you, with all of your beautiful qualities. I am really going to try to be everything you ever wanted in a girl. I hope that I truly have the ability to make you happy. I love you very, very much, Rob. You are, by far, the best thing that has ever happened to me.

Liz

---⊖---

Robert Baltovich: Lazy Tuesday

The Tuesday that Liz went missing began no differently than most others. I woke up at about 9:15, got dressed and went upstairs to prepare my usual breakfast: Shredded Wheat with milk, an orange, a piece of toast, a hard-boiled egg and a glass of apple juice. My dad said good-bye and left for the store. I ate my breakfast in front of the television in the living room but didn't have a lot of time. My brother Paul was having his wisdom teeth removed that morning, and, because his wife, Dana, had to work, I offered to pick him up after the surgery. Paul and Dana were living in eastern Scarborough in the basement apartment of a house belonging to the youth pastor at their church, Malvern Christian Assembly, but Paul had planned to spend the rest of the day recuperating at our place.

I got ready to go and get Paul shortly after ten o'clock. I hadn't spoken to Liz since Sunday night, but I was expecting her to call at some point during the day. As I was going out the door, I asked my mother to take a message if she called while I was out. I was at the dentist's office in no time, only to find Paul sprawled out on a couch with a mouth full of gauze, groggy from the anaesthetic. He slept for a good twenty minutes before I helped him out to the car.

When we arrived home, my mother told me that Liz had called. She wanted me to call her back, and had said she would be home all day. At 11:15 AM, I called Liz and she answered the phone. The first thing I told her was that I'd been at the dentist's picking up Paul. Liz said, "What's wrong with your family?" It turned out that my mother had been to the hospital Sunday night for a bladder infection and had told Liz about it. I laughed and told Liz we all get our ailments at the same time. Liz then said, "Well, Rob, I'm still planning on having dinner with Arlene tonight." I said fine and that I was planning on working out. "I might drop in to see you after class," I told her, but, if not, that I would see her Thursday. Liz said okay, and then I waited for her to say I love you, but she didn't, so neither did I. I just said good-bye.

As soon as I got off the phone, I told my mom that I was going downtown to fill out some job applications. Now that my undergraduate days were behind me, I had to get started on the path to a career. Although library sciences and teachers' college were still my two top choices, both required post-graduate studies and I hadn't yet made up my mind as to which route I was going to take, so I'd decided to take a year away from school to think about it while I made some money doing something else.

Up until a few weeks ago, I had still been working part-time at Oh Yes! Toronto, a clothing store in the Queen's Quay Terminal, which is in the Harbourfront area, right on Lake Ontario. I'd had to quit because, in April, I got a second part-time job as a scorer/timekeeper for the Scarborough campus's summer basketball league and, even though my boss at the store had agreed to arrange my hours around this new job, my availability eventually became a source of conflict, and we mutually agreed to part ways.

While working at Oh Yes! Toronto, I had spent countless hours milling around in the W.H. Smith (Classic) book store during my breaks. So when I arrived at the Queen's Quay Terminal around noon, it was the first place I went for a job application. At the time, I thought working in a bookstore would have been the perfect job, and the manager said there might be an opening in the near future.

Once I was outside W.H. Smith with an application in my hands, it suddenly dawned on me that I hadn't brought a pen. I decided to head up the escalator to a store called The Signature Shop, which was owned by Oh Yes! Toronto, and borrowed one from a former co-worker. After filling out the form, I walked over to Oh Yes! Toronto and caught up with some of my old colleagues before returning the pen and handing in my application at the bookstore. I walked around the mall looking for other stores that I might like to work at. After about fifteen minutes, I went back to my car and drove home.

I made some lunch and sat down in front of the TV again, watching a talk show called "The Shirley Show." The topic that day had to do with the legalization of drugs. A journalist on the program named Victor Malarek, who was obviously against the idea, called pro-legalizers "naive intellectuals." I got a kick out of that because I couldn't have agreed more. I flicked through the channels until around 2:45 PM and then went outside to water the back and front yards, paying special attention to the flower beds.

Seeing as the hose was out and the water on, I thought it would also be a good day to wash my car. That took me to about 5:00 PM. Next I went back in the house and saw that Paul was now up and around, so I asked him if he wanted a ride home on my way to the gym. Paul wanted to know what time I was leaving, and I said 6:30. He said that he wanted to be on his way before then.

Paul and his wife had first met during a church youth retreat—Dana's father, who was a minister, had assisted with their wedding ceremony—and were now tithing members, which meant they contributed ten per cent of their income to support the church. Paul also played on his church's slow-pitch baseball team. Even though he didn't plan on playing that night because of his surgery, the game started at 6:45 in the nearby town of Ajax and he wanted to cheer the team on.

Paul ended up calling Dana and asking her to come and pick him up, and I got the impression she wasn't too pleased. She had a nine-to-five job as a marketing services co-ordinator with an electronic components company called AMP of Canada. AMP's offices were at least a thirty-minute drive north of my house in Scarborough and then they would have another twenty-minute drive home from there. It was going to mean more than an hour of driving in heavy traffic. She thought maybe Paul could give her a break and just take the bus home. She knew that he hated the bus, but wasn't that how he got to the dentist's in the first place? Public transit sure hadn't killed him that morning. But she must have figured there was no point in getting into it with Paul when he'd just had his wisdom teeth yanked out, so it looked like she'd soon be making the trek to pick him up.

Paul waited for Dana in a lawn chair on the back porch. I joined him and we talked for a while before I began reading the book I was into, Destructive Generation, *which was about the lasting but negative impact of the flower-power generation of the 1960s on American society. Around 5:30, I went inside to cook up some yams and rice for dinner. I had been in the kitchen for just a few minutes when I heard Dana come in the front door. Dana, Paul and my mom had a short visit in the narrow landing by the door, and once I had dinner under control, I walked to the top of the stairs off the kitchen and said hello to Dana. She stayed for about fifteen minutes and then she and Paul left. I then ate my third meal of the day in front of the television, this time watching the evening news. I wanted to change my clothes before going to the gym, so after cleaning up my mess from dinner, I went downstairs, took off my shorts and T-shirt and put on a pair of jeans, along with my favourite blue-and-white-striped sweater and my Sperry topsiders. Soon I was back up the stairs again, saying good-bye to Mom on the way out. It was 6:30.*

—◯—

For Rob, that first summer with Liz was shaping up to be one of the best ever. For the second year in a row, he was making good money working as a warehouse technician with Molson Breweries in downtown Toronto. He and Liz were spending more and more time together and, for the first time in his life, he thought he might be falling in love. Liz had introduced him to her family, and he quickly discovered that her background was almost as complicated as his.

Her father, Rick Bain, was an engineer with Ontario Hydro. Rick had been born and raised in Argentina; he'd anglicized his name from Ricardo when he came to the North America to study mechanical engineering in the early 1960s. It was at a University of Toronto dance that he met his future wife, a young nursing student from the Philippines. After obtaining a nursing degree in her native country in 1957, Julita, the second eldest of ten siblings, had left Manila for New Jersey, where she was an exchange student. She moved from one city to another in the United States for a few years before landing at the U of T, where she was accepted into the hospital nursing service in 1964. And that's where Rick came into the picture. By the time he got a job with Ontario Hydro in 1965, you might say that things were getting pretty serious. They were married the following summer and moved into a Scarborough bungalow, where the young couple spent a few years starting a family—their first child, Elizabeth, was born on July 11, 1967—before moving to a two-storey home at 59 Scarboro Avenue. This is where the Bains would live for many years to come. In the summer, with the big deck at the back of the house and the lush surrounding gardens, shaded by clusters of small, wiry trees, it had the feel of a suburban hacienda.

While Liz laid claim to her father's South American roots, she inherited her exotic features from her mother. A year after Liz was born, they had their first son, Mark, and almost three years later, a second daughter, Catherine, was born on March 17, 1971. Their youngest child, Paul, born on August 27, 1973, was adopted.

Rob thought that Liz's parents were wonderful people, especially Mrs. Bain, who worked as a registered nurse at the Scarborough General Hospital. She was such a tiny, friendly woman and, right away, Rob could tell that she and Liz were very close. Mr. Bain, on the other hand, could be somewhat intimidating. The night of Rob's first date with Liz—when he took her to see the movie *Beaches*—Mr. Bain had answered the door when he came to pick her up. Rob introduced himself, and Mr. Bain, a trim, bespectacled man with distinguished looks, politely invited him inside. It happened to be Easter weekend and, while waiting for Liz to come downstairs, Mr. Bain, a devout Catholic, asked Rob if his parents celebrated Easter. "Well, my parents aren't particularly religious people," Rob explained. "We do get together with family but we don't celebrate it in any religious sense."

"Still lost in the forest, eh?" Mr. Bain said.

Trying to be diplomatic, Rob said, "I guess that could be debated."

Their conversation didn't go much beyond that but Liz later told him that her father had been impressed. "He thinks you're very serious," Liz said.

Not knowing whether that was good or bad, Rob asked, "Is that right?"

"Yes," she said, "he thinks you're a very serious person."

Rob held the same opinion of Liz's brother Mark, so he deduced that Mr. Bain was paying him a backhanded compliment. During his third year at university, Rob had been in the same biology class as Mark, who was then a first-year student. Mark was one of those people who always had his textbook open, flipping through its pages whenever the professor made a specific reference to something. He was also an imposing figure physically, having been on the wrestling team in high school and a regular at the gym ever since. Rob found him to be somewhat aloof, even with his own family. And while his older sister, Liz, was still required to adhere to their father's curfew, Mark was free to come and go as he pleased.

Before Rob met Liz's younger sister, Cathy, Liz forewarned him that she was a bit of a "wild child." As he got to know her, he was surprised by how sophisticated she was for an eighteen-year-old and that, in certain ways, she seemed more mature than Liz, who was almost four years her senior. From Rob's perspective, they were opposites in just about every conceivable way. Cathy was bigger and taller and possessed a harder look. One might say she was a little rough around the edges.

While Liz was quite open about the importance of her chastity, Cathy didn't appear to be nearly as concerned about maintaining the same image. Liz had spoken of an incident that had occurred before she and Rob began dating, which involved Cathy, in the middle of the night, sneaking her boyfriend, Steve Annett, in through her second-floor bedroom window with the aid of a ladder. Hearing the sound of a strange male's voice in her sister's room, Liz scurried down the hall to alert her sleeping father. Rob could barely imagine Mr. Bain's contained fury as he burst into Cathy's room in his dressing gown to discover his youngest daughter fooling around with her motorcycle-riding boyfriend.

Liz confided to Rob that, of her three siblings, she was closest to her brother Paul, whom she often called "Paulie." The irony, of course, was that Paul had been adopted and, at sixteen, he and Liz were the bookends of the children. Liz and Rob hadn't really discussed what had motivated her parents to adopt a child after having three of their own, but from what Liz had told him, Paul's birth father was of Polish heritage, and that he and his wife were in dire financial straits when Paul was born.

Aside from Liz, Rob found Paul to be the most agreeable of the Bain children. He'd always seen Paul as the perfect illustration for the genetic theory of human behaviour because he was so unlike the Bains' biological children. Paul seemed much more at ease with himself than the others, a far more poised individual who was kind, articulate, sensitive and bright. His two favourite pastimes were somewhat typical for a Scarborough teenager—fixing up old cars and hanging around with his friends. Paul's thirst for knowledge about anything mechanical meant that he and his father, who often supplied him with books about how things worked, shared a mutual interest. Paul wanted to be an engineer, just like his father, and Rob quickly got the impression that Paul had formed a closer bond with Mr. Bain than Mark had. Liz and Paul got along well enough to harmoniously share her car, a well-used 1981 Toyota Tercel. Rob couldn't count the number of times he'd seen Paul under the hood of the tiny silver car, trying to resuscitate one dying part or another.

—◦—

That first summer they were together, Rob and Liz drove up to Wasaga Beach in his car. They couldn't believe how the place was swarming with young people. A totally half-naked zoo. They staked out a spot on the beach and alternated between talking and reading in the sun next to the ice-cold waters of Georgian Bay. Liz had an incredible shape but she had this thing about being "evaluated" so she usually wore a pair of jean shorts over her bikini bottoms. Yet, as shy as Liz was about showing off her own body, her favourite beach activity was checking out other girls' figures. It reminded Rob of the time they'd gone to Kew Beach in Toronto and seen Andrea Beitinger, who'd been a good friend of Rob's since his days at Greenwood Day Camp, where Andrea had also been a counsellor. Andrea was wearing a sexy bikini that day and she filled it out perfectly, a real knockout. Every thirty seconds you could hear the sound of squealing bicycle brakes as guys slowed down to prolong their view, cruising by on the boardwalk. Rob could tell by the way Liz was looking at her that she was in awe of Andrea's body and was probably thinking to herself, This is the friend he keeps talking about? It didn't take much for her to feel inadequate or threatened that way.

After grabbing a bite to eat at one of the countless burger joints that faced the Wasaga strip, Rob and Liz returned to the beach to watch the sunset. They were just lying on the cool sand, practically the last people there. The sun had made Rob so drowsy that, on the drive back to Scarborough, he began to feel himself nodding off behind the wheel and thought it best to pull over to a secluded spot at the side of the highway. Liz tried to soothe him by caressing the back of his neck and then she leaned across to give him a hug. The next thing they knew, they were all over each other, tangled up like pretzels, hands roaming wildly. "Do you want me to take my top off?" Liz asked.

"If you want to, sure," Rob said.

"Whenever I'm with you, I feel like such a slut," she said, pulling her top off. "I just want you to molest me."

Rob watched as she unclasped her bra. "You've certainly got a way with words, Liz," he said, shaking his head in amusement. And just then, their bodies were washed by the light of a passing car, and Rob reached out and cradled her breasts gently in his hands.

—○—

When, towards the end of the summer, Mr. Bain announced to the family that he was planning a three-week trip to visit his relatives in Argentina in September and early October, no one jumped at the opportunity to accompany him. Mrs. Bain had never travelled to Argentina as a result of the lukewarm reception she'd received from her in-laws over the years, presumably due to the fact that their son had wed a Filipino woman, and she wasn't about to travel halfway across the world to subject herself to their unwavering disapproval. It was clear that Mr. Bain didn't want to go alone, which meant that the spotlight was suddenly on the children. Liz was the obvious choice for a number of reasons, including the fact that she was the only one who could speak Spanish. But when it came right down to it, Liz told Rob, she agreed to go to Argentina—disrupting the beginning of her school year—because none of her siblings were enthusiastic about the trip and, to a certain degree, this made her feel pity for her father.

By that time, Liz's parents had taken Rob in as if he were a member of the family. He was coming to the house with some regularity to visit and had been extended an open invitation to join the family for its sit-down brunch after church each Sunday. By no means, though, was Rob seeing Liz on a daily basis. In fact, if there was one thing he'd learned about Liz, it was that she was quite a solitary person who easily felt crowded. It was as though she compartmentalized her life, keeping home separate from school and school separate from her friends. Liz was often quite content to let a day or two pass without communicating with Rob at all, which he found a little unusual, especially since she was always so happy to see him when she did. And, with Liz, surprise visits were completely out of the question. They just got her flustered.

The day Liz returned from her trip, she called Rob and invited him over. She'd brought him a beautiful Argentine wool jacket and couldn't wait to give it to him. But then he didn't see her again until a few days later when he ran into her at the campus. He was walking up a set of stairs on his way to class when, at the top, he saw Liz out of the corner of his eye, making her way down the hallway. She didn't see him until he walked up to her to say hello. Liz stopped and gave him a very strange look, as if she'd seen a ghost. "What's wrong?" Rob asked.

"Oh, nothing," Liz said, snapping out of her trance-like state. "It's just that I had kind of a weird feeling when I saw you."

"Why is that?"

"I've never really dated anyone that I went to school with before."

Rob knew that Liz wasn't one to spend a lot of time at the school, socializing. She spent far less time there than he. In large part, this was due to the fact that she was taking a much lighter course load. After transferring to Scarborough College, Liz had been a full-time student for just a year, long enough to get herself off academic probation, a status that had come as a result of her lacklustre performance at the downtown campus. But redeeming herself at a new school had been quite an exhausting effort, and she'd often found it difficult to cope with the pressure. The following year, she decided to enrol on a part-time basis, which turned out to be much more manageable.

While Liz had been overwhelmed by university, Rob had been underachieving. Deep down, he knew that he had yet to truly apply himself and that his grades had been merely acceptable. But now that things with Liz were starting to get more serious, he felt as though he wasn't just going to school for himself any more and he began to think about his future and a career. He was somewhat interested in the field of library sciences and the thought of applying to teachers' college had also crossed his mind. With his grades the way they were, though, the latter seemed like a long shot. If he had any hope at all, there was no choice but to put his nose to the grindstone.

Despite their conflicting schedules, Rob and Liz managed to meet on campus once in a while, usually in the library. Sometimes, if the weather cooperated, they would go for walks. But as fall turned to winter, they began to spend more time in the basement at Liz's house, watching TV or cuddled together in front of the fireplace, which was their favourite pastime of all. It was during one of those evenings that Liz told Rob she was contemplating going on the birth control pill. They had never discussed anything like this before and he was a little astonished that she'd even brought it up. He'd always thought he would be the one to broach the subject of sex, but he hadn't foreseen that happening for some time.

Liz said she'd already spoken with her family doctor about birth control, and her doctor had given her a three-month prescription for the Pill. But first she had to regulate her menstrual cycle, which, for her, had always been a bit of a problem. (It was Rob's understanding that the irregularity of her periods had been caused by her intense jogging.) While Rob wasn't about to try to talk her out of wanting to make love to him, he and Liz both expressed reservations about the various side effects of the birth control pill, and, weighing its risks, they agreed to wait.

But waiting wasn't as easy as it sounded. Making out in front of the fire had now progressed to the point that they were taking off enough clothing to necessitate a discreet relocation to the shed in the backyard, which they could get to unnoticed through the basement door. On one cold fall night in the musty darkness of the shed, Liz said she was reconsidering the Pill. Then, a few weeks later, when they were in a similar state of undress, things got so hot and heavy in the shed that Rob expectantly asked if she'd started taking it. She said she hadn't.

"When is this going to begin?" he asked.

She said, "It's not."

"But I thought you said you were," Rob said, disappointed.

"Well, no," she said. "I'm a bit scared because I hear it makes you gain weight."

Rob told her that they might have to cut back a little because he didn't want them to do anything they weren't ready for. The girlfriends with whom he'd had his previous sexual experiences had all been taking the Pill, and Rob had never used a condom. He was willing to begin using condoms now, but Liz just didn't trust them.

The result was that, for a while, they became less affectionate. This was frustrating for both of them and, eventually, Liz suggested they use the rhythm method as a means of birth control. Her doctor had explained how it worked and she was going to start charting her menstrual cycle. Rob told her that he didn't have much faith in the rhythm method, but Liz said that her doctor had insisted it was safe.

Skeptical, he later went so far as to call a hospital in Toronto, St. Michael's, to see what they thought of it, and a doctor there reassured him that, if it was used properly, it was quite reliable.

When they finally did it for the first time, it was outside, under the stars on a chilly autumn night. The Bains had an exceptionally long backyard, the end of which could not be seen from the house after dark. Liz put down a couple of blankets on a flat square of grass obstructed by a scattered wall of trees and bush. They were both nervous and awkward, and, after months of anticipation, it was over in an instant.

One evening a few weeks later, when the cold, biting air of winter had finally arrived, Rob invited Liz over to his house; they watched television for a little while in the living room with his parents. Rob quickly got the impression that Liz was becoming restless, and when his parents left the room at one point, he asked her if she wanted to head out to a movie or for something to eat. "I kind of had something else in mind," Liz said, with a bashful smile. "But I don't know if you would be into it or not."

"Well," he said, "what is it?"

"I can't tell you. It's a surprise."

Rob told his parents they were going out for a while. Outside the house, Rob began to open the passenger door of his new car—a brown 1981 Chrysler Cordoba he'd just bought for peanuts from his good friend Al Heys. "We have to go in separate cars," she said, walking towards her little Toyota. "Just follow me."

They started driving east on Kingston Road towards her house. Beyond that, Rob hadn't a clue where they were going. Eventually, Liz turned off into the lot of a plaza and parked her car. Rob pulled his car up next to hers as she was walking into the lobby of the Roycroft Motel. Two minutes later she reappeared dangling a set of room keys.

The Roycroft was no five-star establishment. He wasn't even sure if it qualified as a one-star. It was your typical fleabag motel, but they didn't care. They opened up the curtains of their shabby little room and undressed each other in the faint light of the busy street. After they'd made love, Liz cuddled up next to him and they watched an endless stream of snowflakes falling outside the window. "This sure beats the shed," Rob said, and they both started to laugh.

—◯—

Robert Baltovich: Down in the Valley

A *t exactly 6:45 PM, I was driving east along Old Kingston Road. That's when I saw Liz's car, parked by itself in the rectangular lot that cuts into the valley area on the north side of the street. I pulled up alongside it and got out of my car. Noticing at once that the windows had been left down, I bent down and looked around inside. It was pretty much empty. No books. No purse. There was just a little piece of yellow paper on the floor behind the passenger seat.*

The feeling I had was one of complete puzzlement. There was also, I admit, a certain degree of suspicion. I just could not understand why she would have been in the valley so close to her 7:00 PM night class. Initially, I thought she might have gone for a jog on one of the park trails or maybe had wanted to get some exercise by parking in the valley and walking to the campus on the same uphill path we'd taken into the park on Sunday night.

I got back in my car and by this time it was about 6:50. I drove to the tennis courts, got out of my car, walked down the stairs and casually glanced around to see if I could see her, but I could only see a few people playing tennis. I walked back up to my car and returned to where Liz's car was.

That's when I began to wonder if Liz had come down to the park to meet with another guy. My mind went back a week to the previous Tuesday. I had picked Liz up at about 1:00 PM to go and play tennis at the very courts I'd just been to. We had played for almost two hours before heading back to her house. No one was home—her father had left for Florida that day and her mother was at work—so we went up to Liz's room and made love.

Afterwards, while Liz was in the washroom taking a shower, I was milling around her room and saw a letter from a guy named Mark Fielden on top of her dresser. I had no idea who Mark Fielden was but he'd sent her a formal graduation announcement from the University of California. The postmark was only a week or so old. There was a little note on the inside of the card that said something like: Well, I'm graduating (cum laude, no less). I hope this doesn't mean that I have to act like a grown-up now! *And then the guy had written about how he was coming home for a few weeks soon—I can no longer remember the precise dates—and that he hoped to see her while he was in town. I didn't say anything to Liz about the letter after I'd read it, but the present circumstances had me thinking about the* hope to see you then *part once again.*

And then there was the strange phone call she'd received later that same day. Around 4:00, we went to pick up William at Kidbrooke. Liz was specially insured to drive clients from the group home, so we took her car. Although I usually liked to drive, I hadn't yet learned how to use a standard transmission, so in her car being a passenger was the only option available.

With William on board, we grabbed a bucket of Kentucky Fried Chicken and drove to Bluffers Park. We ate at a picnic table and fed the seagulls and then walked inland, where some hungry Canada geese had congregated on the grass. We were having such a pleasant afternoon that Liz announced she was going to skip her class that evening. She wanted to rent some movies and watch them back at her house with William and me.

The first movie we watched was Uncle Buck, *a family comedy starring John Candy. And not only was William with us, Liz had invited the two children who lived next door, Cathy and Robert, to come over as well. Around 8:30, the phone rang and little Cathy answered it. She handed it to Liz and said, "It's for you." Liz put the receiver to her ear and said, "Hello . . . yes . . . bye-bye." And then she hung up. I remember thinking that she had a weird look on her face. "Who was that?" I asked. "Eric," she said, almost defiantly.*

I knew that Eric was her old boyfriend Eric Genuis. Liz had mentioned that he still called once in a while, and it didn't sound as though she was that crazy about it. I couldn't say that Eric's call really bothered me—after all, I was still in frequent contact with a number of ex-girlfriends, including Caitlin Fleury. The calls from Eric were obviously more of an irritant for her. She said that no matter how many subtle hints she dropped, he wouldn't stop calling.

We watched movies for a little while longer and then Liz got ready to take William back to Kidbrooke. Little Cathy wanted to go along for the ride, but Liz didn't seem to want to take her. Facetiously, I said, "What should I say if Eric calls back?"

"He won't," Liz said abruptly. And then she left.

The kids from next door went home, and I returned to the basement to watch the end of the movie we had interrupted so Liz could take William home. Liz was gone longer than I expected the trip would take—it seemed like almost an hour had passed before she returned. She was acting very quiet, and I assumed she was feeling uncomfortable about Eric calling. "Don't worry about what happened tonight," I said.

"What do you mean?" she asked.

I smiled and said, "You know." And that was all that was said about it before I left for the night.

Now, as I stumbled around looking for her, the phone call from Eric and memories of the week before fresh in my mind, I couldn't help but wonder if the reason Liz had taken so long driving William home was that she'd met Eric as a result of something he'd said during the phone call. So, with my car alongside hers again, I sat in my Cordoba and wrote her a little note. If, in fact, she was there meeting with some other guy, I wanted her to know that I'd seen her car.

I grabbed a parking receipt and wrote a note on the back that said something like "Don't leave your car windows open. Have a good time tonight." But I'm not positive. I put the note right on the driver's seat so she wouldn't miss it. And then I got back in my car and continued on my way to the campus, driving up the hill at the east end of the valley. When I came to Military Trail, the intersection at which I would normally turn left, I suddenly changed my mind and pulled into the parking lot of the Marquis Tavern on the right-hand side of the road. There, I turned around and got back onto Old Kingston Road, driving into the valley towards Liz's car again.

I was going back to take the note out of Liz's car. The whole thing was just too weird. If she was with someone else in the valley, I now decided that I didn't want her to know that I'd seen her car, thus giving her time to come up with a story. This was the third time in the last twenty minutes that I was up close to her car. I removed the note, went back to my car, threw it in the back seat and headed west through the valley, away from the Marquis Tavern and the campus. Coming out of the park area, I turned left onto the first side street, Manse Road. Next

I U-turned and got back onto Old Kingston Road so that I was moving east towards her car again and I pulled in behind a big beige car that was parked against the south shoulder, about a sixty-second walk from her car. I sat there for ten minutes, waiting for her to appear, but she never did. She'd either gone to her class via the scenic route or she'd been up to no good and had seen me near her car and was hiding in the trees or bushes, where she would probably stay until I left. Either way, it was 7:15, and I started the ignition and once again drove through the valley to my original destination—the gym. I had already made up my mind to go to her class when it ended at 9:00. Even if she was in a rush to get to Arlene's, there would be enough time for her to explain why she'd left her car out in the valley with the windows down.

—◦—

On Christmas Eve, the Bains held quite a large gathering. It was mostly family, but Mr. and Mrs. Bain had invited a number of friends, as did their children. Liz had asked Rob to bring his parents along but, as he'd expected, they declined. His parents were getting older—his father was sixty-six and his mother was sixty-one—and had never been particularly social people. They had nothing against their son's girlfriend—on the contrary, they quite adored her—but they hadn't yet met Liz's parents, and it didn't surprise Rob in the least that they were going to stay at home instead of spending the evening with a group of strangers.

Some people at the party were openly intrigued when Liz introduced Rob as her boyfriend. One woman pulled her aside within earshot of him and began whispering: *You have a boyfriend now? Is it serious?* Another woman, one of Liz's aunts, later approached Rob and said, "It's always a big step when two young people want to get married." Rob wondered what had given her the idea that he wanted to get married. "My husband and I got married when we were going to school, and it was tough for the first couple of years, but, in the end, things worked out really well." Had Liz implied they were getting married? It was either that, Rob thought, or these people just assumed wedlock was the proper thing for two young people in love, regardless of their circumstances. Or maybe it was both.

Later on, Rob was with a group of people standing around telling jokes. Mr. Bain was there, along with Liz and some relatives. It was non-stop laughter—even the lame jokes seemed funny that night. When it was Rob's turn, he got on a real roll, churning out the punchlines. And then he told an old standard: "Why did they close the Cyclops school?" He paused a beat. "Because they only had one pupil." For some reason, no one laughed. He couldn't figure it out, but it had been such a dud that it pretty much killed the comedy segment, and everyone began to disperse into different parts of the house.

Soon, everyone gathered around the piano in the living room to sing Christmas carols. Rob had been anxiously awaiting this moment because Liz was going to be the one providing the musical accompaniment. Liz had begun studying piano at the Royal Conservatory of Music in Toronto when she was a little girl, and Rob had seen at least a decade's worth of framed certificates lining the walls in her basement, but in the nine months they'd been dating, he had yet to hear her play. It wasn't because he hadn't asked. Rob loved music and had spent years singing in the choir at high school. He always thought it would be fun if they could sit down at the piano together. He thought Liz might be able to teach him a few things, but she never seemed too anxious to take him up on the suggestion.

Liz had said that, as a young girl, she'd been pushed to play the piano by her father and had no intrinsic love for the instrument. Like a lot of other kids, she really wanted to play the guitar. Rob had no difficulty envisioning Mr. Bain driving little Elizabeth through sleet and snow to her piano lessons at the conservatory. Mr. Bain was also a music aficionado. On numerous occasions, Rob had seen him sitting at the piano, messing around with chords. He didn't know how to play the instrument, but his sounds were actually quite musical, although not in a disciplined sense. He would just rock back and forth on the little bench like a human metronome.

As Liz got ready to play, Rob didn't know what to expect. She said she hadn't played very much since high school. But as soon as she began tickling the keys, Rob went bug-eyed. He knew she was good but he didn't know she was that good. He was in awe of her musical virtuosity. It was like listening to a professional—she didn't even have sheet music in front of her. In a crowd of people, Liz tended to be on the shy side and was usually quite tentative. But as everyone belted out the carols, there was Liz, at the centre of attention, in complete control, supremely self-confident. Rob couldn't help but notice that, across the room, her parents were beaming.

After the musical interlude, people began exchanging Christmas gifts. Mr. and

Mrs. Bain gave Rob a thick grey winter overcoat stitched with a smart, rectangular pattern of black, white and red. And from Liz, he received two sweaters and a pair of casual pants. Rob had decided that, instead of getting Liz one big present, he would buy her a bunch of little things: a watch decorated with pretty imitation jewels, a porcelain music box, a crystal atomizer and two tickets to *The Nutcracker* at the O'Keefe Centre downtown. He'd picked up a cardboard box and covered the inside with a red velvet-like blanket and filled it with fake snow. Once the presents were wrapped, he buried them under the "snow" so that she'd have to feel around for them. He thought she would love it.

Just before he left the party, Rob told Liz that he'd secretly put a box in her room and that he didn't want her to open it until he'd left. He wanted it to be a surprise, and she could tell him all about it the next day. But Liz insisted that he show it to her before going out the door, so they went up to her room. When she saw her present sitting there, the first thing she said was: "Why is the box so big?" Rob thought she was worried that he'd gone out and bought her something terribly expensive. "You'll see," he said.

Driving home, Rob was thinking about the Cyclops joke that had bombed. *Oh, my god.* It came to him suddenly in a flash. Mr. Bain had a glass eye. He remembered Liz telling him about the childhood accident, that his brother, Hugo, had been playing with him when it had happened. Rob couldn't believe he'd forgotten all about it. He slapped his forehead in embarrassment.

———◇———

Rob spent the following day celebrating Christmas with his parents and their extended family at his aunt's house in Stouffville, a town just north of Toronto. In the afternoon he phoned Liz's house to find out if she liked his presents. Immediately, Rob could tell that something was wrong. Her voice sounded flat and she responded to his questions in lifeless spurts: "It's okay . . . yeah . . . I really like them . . . yeah . . . uh-huh . . . see you later . . . bye."

Rob didn't have an opportunity to call her again until he was at school a couple of days later, but she wasn't home. He tried calling three or four more times over the next few hours, but different members of her family kept telling him she was out. This was odd—Liz had said she'd be home all day. Considering how strange she'd sounded on the phone on Christmas Day, he decided to drive to her house to see if she'd returned.

Liz's brother Mark answered the front door. When Rob asked if it was all right for him to wait for Liz, Mark invited him down to the basement, where they watched some television. A few minutes later, Liz came walking down the basement steps. Mark started to chuckle, then he stood up and went upstairs. Liz was standing there looking at Rob like some kind of a zombie. "Have you been here the whole time I've been calling you?" he asked.

"Yes," she said meekly.

"What's going on?"

"I just want you to leave now."

"What? Why do you want me to leave?"

"I don't want to talk to you right now," she said. "I'll talk to you later when I can speak rationally."

Bewildered, Rob said, "I'm not leaving until you tell me what's going on."

"You can stay here, then. I'm going to my room."

Rob followed her until they were standing in the doorway of her bedroom. She closed the door in his face. He banged on the door and said, "Liz, you have to tell me what is happening here. I don't understand what the problem is. What did I do wrong?" Waiting for Liz to respond, he heard Cathy in her room down the hall, calling to Mark. "Is that Rob?" she asked. "Yeah," Mark answered back. Cathy said, "Why doesn't he just get the hell out of here?" At that point, Liz opened the door and let him in.

As Rob sat on her bed, Liz explained why she was so upset. When Rob hadn't invited her to spend Christmas with him and his family in Stouffville, she became convinced that he'd taken some other girl with him. As far as she was concerned, he was cheating on her and their relationship was a farce.

For quite some time, Rob was nonplussed, struggling to understand how she could conjure up such a far-fetched scenario. Eventually, he said, "How could you possibly think I would do something like that? If I didn't want to see you, I'd just say, 'I don't want to see you any more.' You've known me long enough to know that I would never hurt you."

Liz told him about an old boyfriend named Jeff she'd dated towards the end of high school. Jeff had been going to university outside of Toronto and when Liz went to visit him one weekend as a surprise, she found out that he was seeing some other girl. Since then, she'd been convinced that all men were low-lifes and, at heart, cheaters.

Once and for all, he tried to set her straight. "I love you," Rob said. "And I want to spend my life with you. Do you understand? The rest is ridiculous."

Liz turned her glance downward and she became flushed with embarrassment. Suddenly, Rob noticed that all of the little trinkets he'd bought her over the last nine months—miniature porcelain figurines, along with some of the cards, letters and poems he'd given her—weren't in their usual places. Breaking the silence, Rob asked, "Where are all the things I got you?"

"I threw them in the closet," she said. "I didn't want to look at them."

He didn't say anything but Rob felt as though he'd been hit by a Mack truck. On previous occasions, she'd exhibited some behaviour that he'd considered out of the norm, but he had no idea that she was capable of anything this extreme. On the way home, Rob kept asking himself the same question: "Is this the kind of person I want to spend the rest of my life with?"

Despite her insecurities, he still thought Liz was a wonderful person who, in many other ways, had her life very much together. But there was no denying that her behaviour had scared him. She couldn't see how beautiful she was, or how talented. There was definitely something making her miserable, but he couldn't put his finger on what that might be. He began to think about his mother's breakdowns and he took solace in the fact that she'd managed to get through her most profound episodes of unhappiness. On the other hand, dealing with his mother's depression when he was a child had been anything but pleasant, and he really wasn't sure if he wanted to go through something like that again.

When Rob talked to his friends about the incident, they thought it was a big joke. The whole notion that Rob would cheat on one of the most gorgeous girls at Scarborough College was a little much for them to stomach. They figured that, if anything, she would be the one to look elsewhere. Rob was lucky to have her in the first place.

—◦—

January 4, 1990

Dear Meg,

Today is day twenty-seven of my cycle. Noticeable signs? Severe depression. Last night I had drastic mood changes with Rob. First I was so weary that I had to sleep after our long walk. I resented myself a little for not inviting him to stay. Instead, guilt soared. I wanted to study. I didn't really want to be with him. After dinner, I deliberately stayed upstairs with Mark & Nan while he was in the basement. When I came down I felt myself growing tired. I didn't want affection, but he kept touching me. I closed my eyes. By the fireplace I was still weary. Then, I told him how beat I felt from all the walking. Told him how before my period I feel weak, depressed, sore on the bust. But he started to turn me on—passion soared—strength came. Then on Bad Dreams, *the movie we were watching, the image of the woman cutting into her body. For Rob, this brought memories of* Fatal Attraction—*Glenn Close slitting her wrists. He mentioned how sick it had made him feel in the theatre.*

I, as always, remembered what happened to me. For some reason, I could always brush the thought out of my mind but last night I couldn't. It was almost as if I wanted him to know. I took my arms off him and stared at the screen. Why? I questioned his repulsion to it. I didn't even listen to what he said but I know I wanted him to figure out in his own way that it had happened to me. I sat back and put my hand over my mouth and nose. I could feel myself breathing deeply and saying to Rob, "I tried it once"—and showing him the evidence. But I continued to think no—I can't—he doesn't need to know that. Then I thought, if he's going to marry me, he must know. But I couldn't tell him. Hopefully, from my reaction, my behaviour, he can figure it out on his own and be silent about it. I almost felt that, when he asked those questions, kind of elaborating on it, and then said, "You look like you've seen a ghost," that he knew something already and was trying to fish something out of me, to trick me, trap me, test me, tease me into spelling it out.

Okay, so it happened twice—yes, okay, so I tried it maybe three times. And okay, maybe I tried alternative ways before that. So what? He doesn't need to know and then baby me for it. I don't need his gentleness & sympathy. I think it is becoming a reinforcement for my depressive state. Furthermore, Rob is creating a build-up of resentment. One day, he's going to say, "Fuck you, lady, I'm sick of your miserable moods and hearing you complain—I have enough problems of my own." He does not use harshness, strength, authority. He just puts up with me. I know those qualities are there—I've seen him on the courts. I know how angry he was, telling Mark how pissed off he was. He didn't even raise an eyebrow that Wednesday when I so rudely ignored his call.

I couldn't tell him about my own wrists because I've fed so much from him. I am draining his energy. He is going to hate me for it one day but he can't see it right now. He thinks he's doing me a favour by seeking out every anxiety I have and trying to heal it. He's going to wear himself out. On top of this, he hides his anger from me and pretends it was never there. He is harming himself.

The only way I will heal my anxiety is by knowing that, if I don't, I am not going to live any more. That is plenty of motivation. His tender consoling is good, yes, but he puts no limits on it. It is becoming useless now because it only reinforces my anxiety.

I am getting fed up. I don't just need someone to hold me like a mother and tell me comforting lies continuously. I also need someone to whip me into shape sometimes—to justly yell, scream, dictate, drill some sense into me. I need a disciplinarian . . .

I am very lost and depressed and my bowels are totally dependent on artificial means, which isn't helping at all. Neither is my lack of motivation to study. Rob sucks up to me so much. I get away with murder with him. It's ridiculous. I can't have a man who will let himself be walked upon. I need someone who will give me direction. He's such a panzee sometimes. I can't believe it. God. I need some animal, some tough guy, some masculine traits. Me, being so conditioned to be feminine, I am fed up with being brushed aside as an airhead, sweet, innocent, little, kind, gentle. I need to be strong. I need to learn leadership. I need to have charisma.

Liza

P.S. Why do I keep thinking about breaking up with this guy?

I don't want to be with him for the rest of my life, or do I?

My senses tell me I'm very confused. I need time alone to make myself a better person.

I am not happy. My hormones are satisfied but I am not happy. Or am I? Why do I keep thinking I need time alone—and should I tell Rob about it?

It's fucken lonely without a boyfriend. Very, very lonely.

My youth is dying on me. Soon I will be weary. I will have no spark within me. As I age, I will have less and less and less to offer a man.

But what about Rob? It isn't fair that I stick around here when I'm so doubtful. He treats me like gold, and all I can think of are negative things. He really, really loves me. I know he does but I don't think I love him as much. I get fed up too easily. Things he puts up with from me I could never put up with. But I am getting very, very tired of this relationship. I don't want him any more. I'm fed up.

—◯—

After the ordeal at Christmas, Rob began to pay more attention to Liz's behaviour. It was almost as if he was putting things through a finer filter, searching for the source of her inexplicable mood swings. For example, about a month before Christmas, Liz told him that she was suffering from various food allergies that caused her skin to blotch in places, along with general discomfort. So far, she said, her doctor had been unable to help. After discussing it with Tia (Liz had been raised to use the Spanish word for "aunt") Diana, Mr. Bain's younger sister, she decided to try something new.

Diana Bain, who was also Liz's godmother, worked as a "body and mind" therapist who offered "body/mind counselling" and massage treatments at her private practice on Bloor Street West in downtown Toronto. She arranged for Liz to see a naturopathic practitioner named Arthur Dilama, who worked from his home on Dupont Street. When Liz showed Rob the various over-the-counter homeopathic remedies she'd been sold, he couldn't believe how expensive they were. Rob marvelled at the fact that she'd bought hundreds of dollars worth of exotic pills with indecipherable foreign labels. It was a senseless waste of time and money as far as he was concerned, but Liz was so buoyant and hopeful at the prospect of returning to perfect health that he didn't want to dampen her enthusiasm.

The more Liz became convinced that holistic medicine would make her better, the more Rob began to link her health problems to a particular cause—her diet. For some time, Liz had been restricting herself to a diet of raw vegetables. She rarely ate with Rob or her family, and she tended to prepare her own salads or vegetables separately—her brother Mark would teasingly call this "rabbit food." And while Rob hardly ever saw her eat, every so often she could polish off a tremendous amount of food in one sitting. One night they were watching a movie on television in the basement, and Liz brought down a big bowl of popcorn. She kept the bowl in her lap and wolfed down nearly the entire batch on her own. Next thing he knew, she was upstairs making another one and it was happening all over again.

Rob had studied various models of what triggered eating disorders such as anorexia and bulimia in his psychology courses, and he couldn't help noticing that some of these patterns reflected Liz's behaviour perfectly. One day, he set out to ask her a series of questions to see if he was on the right path. He asked, "Have you ever made yourself throw up?" Liz admitted that she had once, back when she was a teenager, but she hadn't tried it again. "How did you make yourself sick?" he asked.

Liz said, "You don't want to know." And the truth was, he didn't.

Rob decided to drop the subject, but he knew that Liz had a number of characteristics indicative of someone afflicted with an eating disorder. In addition to her erratic eating habits, she'd been very particular about her appearance since the beginning of their relationship. She wore a thick layer of a cosmetic tanning lotion with her make-up, along with the false eyelashes she'd found a long time ago in her mother's old make-up case. Lately, she'd also been talking about saving up enough money for surgery to reduce the size of her breasts. Rob couldn't understand why she wanted smaller breasts—they were ample but by no means oversized. Liz said that, for her, the ideal female body was that of an Olympic gymnast. Compact, muscular, adolescent in proportion. When she hit puberty and her breasts began to bud, Liz was so fearful about what was happening, she said, that she'd tried flattening them with a frying pan. Her obsession with this unattainable physique reminded him of something she'd said to him the summer before—that, if she ever lost what looks she had, she would feel worthless. Now he was thinking back to that comment and how it had bothered him so much that he'd written her a short letter about what her beauty meant to him:

> Many times I have told you how beautiful you are, both on the outside and the inside, and I will continue to do so. But what is appreciated is not what is valued most in a person. A house is but a house if not a home. How it hurts me to see this pain you feel. Who are these people who make you feel this way? Tell me. Must you feel this way? Please tell me. I want to know.

Liz, I love you so much. More than anyone could love another. I realize I can't change the way you feel just like that. I wish my love was enough to make you see the futility of your private journey. I wish my love was what mattered most to you but I know it is not. But without love, there is nothing. All pales in comparison. Please take it, secure in the knowledge that it asks nothing in return, but seeks to conquer all the demons within you.

Love always, Rob xxxooo

——◯——

As Valentine's Day approached, Rob set out on a specific mission. It had been fairly obvious that Liz had been disappointed with his Christmas gifts, and because this had left him somewhat confused, he had called his friend Andrea Beitinger. Whenever Rob needed advice about the opposite sex, he would call Andrea. From what Rob had told her, Andrea got the impression that Liz might have been expecting him to buy her a ring for Christmas. Not an engagement ring, more like a promise ring, something to indicate the seriousness of his intentions.

For weeks, Rob scoured jewellery stores in Scarborough and at the Queen's Quay Terminal. Finally, he settled on a small diamond ring with a delicate gold band and tiny rubies around the larger stone. His mother helped him pick it out. It cost about $250.

He arrived at Liz's house early in the afternoon on Valentine's Day. They sat alone in the living room for a while before Rob asked her if she would mind getting him a glass of water. Liz got up and went into the kitchen and when she returned there was a small, beautifully wrapped box resting on the stool where she'd been sitting. "Is that for me?" she asked, with a big smile.

"Happy Valentine's Day," Rob said. "Go ahead and open it."

Liz carefully opened the box and admired the ring. She tried it on; it was a perfect fit. "It's beautiful," she said. She was giving him a big hug when the doorbell rang. Mrs. Bain called from the kitchen to tell Liz that someone had sent her flowers. As Liz left the room again, Rob was wondering who would have sent her flowers—it certainly hadn't been him. Maybe it was Eric Genuis. Or maybe it was someone he'd never heard of. The way he looked at it, Liz was a stunning young woman and men were probably approaching her all the time—the exact same way he had. Whoever it was, he wasn't going to let it bother him, apart from the timing. The timing couldn't have been much worse, that was for sure.

When Rob told her the flowers weren't from him, other possibilities rushed through her mind before she opened the small envelope taped to the box. The first person that came to mind was Mark Fielden. She'd met Mark back in June during a night out with her cousin Mary Lou at an Oshawa dance club called Illusions. Mark had enlisted the help of a friend to get a conversation started with Liz, whom he found extremely attractive. She was obviously quite shy but, apparently, interested. Mark was a tall blond with a good tan and an even better smile. Before the night was over they'd exchanged phone numbers and agreed to have dinner the following Monday. She'd already been on a few dates with Rob at this stage, but they had not yet kissed in her backyard next to the fire, an evening that had marked the genesis of something more serious and, therefore, more exclusive.

Mark had taken her to a Mexican restaurant and afterwards for a romantic stroll in Morningside Park. Their second date lasted an entire day, beginning with a picnic at Rouge Beach and continuing downtown in the evening at the Harbourfront area, where they caught a ferry over to Centre Island. Looking out at the bright lights of the city's skyline—the flickering CN Tower standing guard over the clustered, toy-like skyscrapers and the old Royal York Hotel off to the left, its weathered stone aglow from a legion of floodlights—they confessed to having strong feelings for each other. Hours later, they were back at Harbourfront, listening to some jazz on an outdoor patio. Liz didn't get home until 1:30 in the morning.

She got together with Mark a handful of times before mid-July, when, to his shock, she told him that there was another man in her life, someone she'd known prior to meeting him. Liz said she wasn't the kind of girl to date two guys at the same time, and that, from now on, she would only be going out with this other person she had feelings for. She said his name was Rob, but Mark was so disappointed he didn't really care what his name was—all he knew was that it wasn't him.

Since then, they'd spoken on the phone a few times and had exchanged the odd letter. Even if she didn't want to be his girlfriend, Mark wasn't about to forget about her. There was no way of knowing whether things with this Rob fellow would last that long. Mark was off to university in California in the fall and it wouldn't hurt to keep in touch. Liz received a postcard from him at Christmas and sent him a short letter in early January. Fortunately, she'd managed to keep Mark Fielden's existence a secret from Rob. He would have been just as floored as Mark had been to learn that she had been out with someone else during their short courtship.

Mark Fielden was not the only person on her mind when she wrote about the drama of her Valentine's Day for Meg:

Last Wednesday was Valentine's. Rob gave me a ring, but I got flowers from another guy. Who? John—I couldn't believe it. At first I thought Mark Fielden sent them from California but I opened the box and read the card. I thought it was a man I spoke to at Tia Diana's party. When I said goodbye to him, he took my hand and kissed it. A tall, lean, Yugoslavian man with glasses. Very harmless looking, very funny, very pleasant & warm. He was sitting by these women who looked like prostitutes. He could barely speak English and I hardly spoke to him.

Rob didn't look at all jealous. He just looked hurt. I didn't know what to do. Some florist phoned beforehand to get our address straight. I was very embarrassed. I smiled and then left the room. I didn't know who it was but I felt so much that Rob thought I did. When the flowers came my heart was ripping through the seams. Mom said to open the box so Rob wouldn't think I was hiding anything. I told him I was sorry—I didn't know who it was from. It was true. I didn't know any John. I felt bad for him. I felt that Rob was going to say, "Forget this—I'm going to find someone who gives me the attention I need, someone who I don't have to doubt." I felt like I was going to lose him. It would have hurt me if the roles had been reversed—I sympathized completely.

I didn't think it bothered him at all, but he asked me about it Saturday & yesterday.

Sometimes Rob puts himself down & when he gets into a situation where he can be walked on, he allows it to happen. On Thursday, he was calling himself a loser. I couldn't believe what humility he had. And he thinks he's proud. That's what kills me. Yesterday at lunch, my brother Mark was describing how Rob had been waiting at our door at 1:00 & nobody was home. Mark was calling him a loser while Rob was sitting there, allowing it to continue. I had to use all my strength to say very firmly: "Watch your mouth." "My life is an open book," Rob said so gently.

I've seen so much more of the delicate side of him. He is rarely firm. In the gym during second and third year, I remember countless times when he was very authoritative, yelling "Shut up!" to the guys. Forceful, commanding, in total control of his voice. Now, more & more, I see someone who is vulnerable, a "don't hurt me" man. It's like he makes no effort to defend himself once he's been put down. "It's true, what you say" is almost what he was making me believe when Mark was cutting him up.

On Thursday he broke out in tears when he started to talk about drugs. I can't understand it, but he hates himself for using his "innocence" as a way of putting himself above (and enabling him to judge) people on drugs. Why does the issue bother him so much? Even the issue of sex never made me cry like that in front of him and that was way more severe, because I was changing my whole outlook, engaging in something I hated and feared right before my very eyes.

*Rob is a very
delicate person.*

Liz

—◦—

While Liz adored her sparkling new ring and hardly ever took it off her finger, the gift ushered in a particularly difficult period of their young relationship. For it was around this time that Rob found he could no longer refrain from commenting on Liz's prolonged experiment with holistic medicine. After spending a few hours in the library researching the history of naturopathy, Rob wrote a long letter spelling out the lunacy of abandoning traditional medicine for false promises. From his point of view, "natural" treatments were the equivalent of modern-day snake oil.

Once he'd presented his argument, Liz put up little resistance. She promised to stop seeing Arthur Dilama and Rob was content to have steered clear of what was, in his mind, a considerable problem. But just a month later, he caught her speaking on the phone with another naturopath, Sat Dharam Kaur, who had been referred to her by her aunt Diana. So they got into it again, a discussion that concluded with Rob walking stone-faced out of her house, full of disappointment. Liz wrote him a letter the next day telling him that he should give her a little credit. "Holistic medicine may be a way to live my life to the fullest," she wrote. "I used to want to die but now I want to live forever. Shouldn't that reason alone tell you I'm going in the right direction?"

In the end, Rob decided he wouldn't bother harping on holistic medicine any more. She would have to learn these lessons on her own. Just three short weeks later, however, they had their first real argument about something that wasn't related to holistic medicine. It happened while they were at Rob's house, on a rare evening when both of his parents had gone out. They used the opportunity to have sex in Rob's bedroom, and it was afterwards, while both of them were sitting up on the bed propped against some pillows, that Liz began giggling even though neither of them had said anything. "What's so funny?" Rob asked. Liz shifted onto her side, now facing him, and began telling a funny story she'd just heard from her sister Cathy. It was about Cathy's boyfriend, Steve Annett. Steve worked at the Scarborough Town Centre as a security guard and, from what Cathy had said, Steve and his partner had beaten up some kid at the mall. Soon enough, someone called the police, and Steve had ended up on the receiving end of an assault charge and had been forced to spend a night in jail.

Rob didn't find the story amusing, mostly because he didn't like Steve. He'd always found him to be a bit of a shady character. If it had been about anyone else, he probably would have just gone with the flow and laughed. But this was Steve, and Rob didn't think it was funny. Within seconds, Liz's mood turned sour. She tried to defend Steve by pointing out that the kid he'd beaten up was a known troublemaker. "So what?" Rob asked. "Well," she said, tears welling up in her eyes, "so he deserved it." Rob wasn't feeling sympathetic. "Come on, Liz," he said. "Don't cry. I want you to tell me why you think this is funny. Two minutes ago you were laughing because Steve beat someone up and spent the night in jail."

Liz didn't answer. She just continued to sob. He knew that once Liz was crying, it was impossible to talk to her. It was getting to the point where any expression of anger or disappointment on his part would cause her to break down. But now he wanted her to be stronger. He couldn't handle this kind of melodrama every time they had a little dispute—it just wasn't healthy. For that reason alone, he wasn't going to back down and comfort her this time. Instead, he told her that he didn't feel like arguing and suggested it might be best if she went home. They could get together and discuss it later.

April 15, 1990

Dear Meg,

Leave Rob. You can do so much better. You deserve better. I know you slept with him but forgive yourself. He will condemn you to death. There was nothing you said yesterday that was wrong. How dare he call you an idiot for having a laugh with your sister over something she considers a joke. Even if it wasn't, I can react any way I want. I never judged him when I was a virgin, nor did I ever judge him because he's an atheist. I let him insult me to tears in my own home about something I rest my health upon and the second time I go to his house, he calls me an idiot and sends me to the door after making love. After I sewed his pants. After I bought him flowers and a bear. I let myself pay for almost every outing because he wasn't working and invited him over to the house for free meals all the time. Free entertainment. It was me who got those cold, heartbreaking notes—the one in the summer he wrote about my beauty and the paper about holistic health. If you cannot see by now what a cold, ugly streak he has inside of him, Liza, it is because you don't want to. He has already called you an idiot and a suck. I am going to make him pay for all of the pain he has cast upon anyone. I am going to dump him the next time he phones me. I will say—as I said to Jeff four years ago—"I do not want this relationship any more" and that is that. It's bad enough that he never once invited me to his house to dine with his parents. He hides me from his friends and family. He brings me over to his house like I am some kind of whore. Oh God, the sadness within me is so great. I feel so much hatred for him. Today I went to the beach all day, crying, telling myself how much I loved him, telling God I would die for him. What is really happening right now is that he is at his aunt's house in Stouffville for Easter, laughing, socializing, just as he was at Christmas while I stayed at home, weeping. Down at the beach alone I was telling myself to forgive and to love but I went too far and began eating away at my self-esteem. I can no longer survive like this. I have honestly suffered for this man so much. I have given my whole self—so much so now that I have drained myself to a state of anxiety where I cannot return or forgive. God only knows how much I willingly suffered for this love.

I want to believe that he is going to lose out on a great thing by leaving him but it's not true. In a way, this year was as much my fault for not standing up to my opinions, my right to be me. Look at me now. I feel the exact same way I did with Jeff and Eric. I gave so much and got so hurt. God, when will I ever learn?

Forgive me, Father, for staying with this cruel person and submitting my thoughts and values to him only because I wanted so much to please him. Today I am his idiot, his suck, his whore, his convenience. Please, I beg of you, give me the strength I need to get rid of him. I don't want to hate him. I will learn to forgive him and myself. But deep in my heart, that man would judge and criticize my children, deprive them of things he never had. Make enemies with anyone who didn't agree with his judgments, thus making enemies in my family.

How many times have I told you I would leave him and I didn't? God, forgive me. Let him remember that the last day we ever spent together was in his own room. All the tears and words of sorry I had were in that room. Let him remember that our whole relationship ended because of what happened in his room, right on top of the bed he lies upon every night. Goodbye Rob.

This time do it. Had you done it three weeks ago, you wouldn't be in this rut right now. Had you done it when he wrote you that letter annihilating holistic health, you wouldn't have gone through the latest insult. Had you done it when you should have—in the summer—you could have saved yourself all the misery on earth. I know. Since that holistic health quarrel, I should have left & never returned.

DON'T BE AFRAID TO BE ALONE. DON'T BE AFRAID TO STAND UP FOR WHAT YOU BELIEVE IN. DON'T LET ANYONE WALK OVER YOU. DON'T SURRENDER YOUSELF. HOW MANY MORE TIMES DO I HAVE TO TELL YOU TO LEAVE HIM? HE HAS DESTROYED YOU. HE HAS NOT MADE YOU INTO A BETTER PERSON. HE RUINED YOU.

GET OUT WHILE YOU HAVE SOMETHING LEFT.

PLEASE GOD—

Give me Courage

Liza

———◇———

Robert Baltovich: Rear Exit

I was out of the weight room at the Recreation Centre by quarter to nine. On
my way to the locker room, I ran into my friend Neil Winton near the stairs.
Neil had been playing volleyball and was taking a water break. That is when I
am certain I told him about seeing Liz's car in the valley and that I was going to
her class to find out what was up. Neil then went back upstairs to his game and
I hit the showers, intending to go straight to Liz's lecture.

The first thing I noticed as I approached Liz's classroom was that a dark-
haired, Italian-looking guy was standing in the hallway near the door. Still somewhat suspicious about what Liz was up to, I thought this guy might be there
waiting for her. It even entered my mind that he could be Eric Genuis, whom Liz
had described as having a Maltese background with dark, Mediterranean features. There was a landing overlooking the hallway from the floor above, so I
climbed the nearby stairs thinking that if this guy was waiting for Liz, she would-
n't know that I was up there.

As it turned out, the first girl out of the class was the person whom the guy
was waiting for. Although that relieved me somewhat, I decided to stay up on
my perch in the balcony. I didn't want to get halfway down the stairs and have
Liz catch me spying on her. And if she did walk out of her class, wondering if I'd
come to meet her, I would pop out of nowhere and surprise her for a laugh,
which provided me with an explanation for hiding.

But then several minutes passed, and students had stopped filing out into the
hallway. So far, Liz hadn't been among them. I figured it was time to go down
to the classroom for a look. I was now thinking that she might have stayed
behind to have a discussion with her professor about a project she was working
on, but, as I peered in, I saw that the professor was the only one left in the room.
He was seated at one of the student desks near the front, possibly marking
papers. That's when I noticed there was a second exit on the other side of the
room and I wondered if Liz had gone out that way, taking the path down into
the valley to her car.

It was at that point that my suspicion turned to worry. Attendance was
mandatory for this course, and it had cost Liz five per cent of her overall grade
to skip the class last week to watch movies with William and the kids next door.

I was having a hard time believing that she would miss another one, even to spend time with her friend Arlene. But, on the other hand, Liz's behaviour hadn't been all that predictable lately and, the way I saw it, anything was possible.

In case Liz had used the alternate exit out of her class, I ran to my car and drove to the little lot in the valley. There was a silver car there but it wasn't Liz's, so I kept driving and then turned around on Manse Road, as I had done earlier, doubling back along Old Kingston Road. I drove up and out of the valley until I hit Deep Dene Drive and went north to Ellesmere Road, which I crossed to get to the Bains' house on Scarboro Avenue.

What first struck me at the Bains' was that Mark's car was parked in the driveway, but not Liz's. I was on my way to the front door when Mrs. Bain walked out of the garage holding a rake. There was a big stack of patio stones piled up on the front drive near the area where she was in the process of making a new parking space. She was working so late into the night, she said, because she wanted to get this project of hers completed before Mr. Bain came home from Florida the following afternoon. While she was smoothing out the gravel, I asked if she knew where Liz was. "I thought she was with you," Mrs. Bain said.

I said, "No, she wasn't with me. And I think she missed her class."

"Well, she left around four o'clock," said Mrs. Bain. "She said she was going to check the tennis schedule." That struck me as odd because there was no tennis schedule—the courts worked on a first-come-first-serve basis at thirty-minute intervals. And who would she be playing with? Tennis was not one of Liz's regular activities. Even though we had played as recently as a week ago, Liz had said it was the first time she'd been on a tennis court in a couple of years. I immediately assumed Liz had come up with this fabricated tennis schedule story as a spur-of-the-moment way of placating her mother. Mrs. Bain said, "Liz told me that she would be back around six-thirty." Now that was even more bizarre. It meant that Liz had been planning to come home before her class at 7:00 and hadn't done so.

I was shaking my head and saying, "That's strange, that's strange," struggling to make sense of it all. I then asked, "Did Liz tell you that she was having dinner at Arlene Coventry's?"

Mrs. Bain said no, so I asked if she knew Arlene's address. "I know she lives in the Brandywine area." I then asked if she had Arlene's phone number, and she

said no. Mrs. Bain asked if I wanted to stay and wait for Liz, but I declined. Mrs.
Bain also told me that she didn't know Liz had a class. "When Liz gets home," I
said. "Please tell her that I'll see her on Thursday." And I turned and began
walking back to my car.

—◦—

The quarrel over Steve Annett's alleged fisticuffs didn't last for long. Rob and Liz
resolved matters during a long walk on the boardwalk in the Beaches. Liz wondered aloud if she was strong enough for him. Of course, Rob was now wondering the same thing, but he knew the best thing for now was to offer her reassurance,
not constructive criticism. It obviously worked. A few days later, Rob opened up
his locker at school and found a dozen red roses inside, along with a note from Liz.

The next thing Rob knew, Liz started talking about wanting to go away on a little
trip. Just the two of them. She'd just learned that her parents were going away to
New Orleans for the second week of May, a trip paid for by Ontario Hydro, as part
of her father's job. Liz decided this was their chance to get away without her parents knowing about it.

Before Christmas, Rob had wanted to take her down to Niagara-on-the-Lake for
a weekend. He was going to get them a room at the historic Oban Inn. But first he
had to get permission from her parents. Rob had asked Liz's brother Mark for his
opinion on which parent he had better chances with. In the end, he spoke to Mrs.
Bain, and she told him that she didn't think it was a good idea, so he dropped it.

But now the opportunity had presented itself once more under more promising
circumstances. There was just one problem: Rob was short on cash. Liz told him
not to worry about it. She had enough money from her two part-time jobs, the one
on weekends at Kidbrooke, and the other on week nights at a place called Family
Day Care Services, where she helped look after the children of working parents.
Money was the least of her concerns. Things had been tense at home lately and she
really wanted to get away.

The latest bout of turmoil began on May 1, when Cathy had come home after her
curfew one night and had woken up her father while making a sandwich in the
kitchen. He came downstairs and began yelling at her for being so noisy. Cathy proceeded to get a little too mouthy for his liking, and Mr. Bain slapped her across the

face. For Cathy, whose relationship with her father was already strained, this was the last straw. She went up to her room, packed her bags and moved out. Her mother helped her find a basement apartment at a house in which one of Julita's younger sisters, also named Elizabeth, was renting a flat. Cathy continued to keep in touch with everyone in the family except Mr. Bain, whom she refused to speak to.

Despite the problems with Cathy, Mr. and Mrs. Bain were off to New Orleans a few weeks later, and Rob and Liz put a few things together and drove to Niagara Falls in his Cordoba. They booked themselves into a decent hotel room at the Oakes Inn. Worlds away from the Roycroft, their room had a clear view of the Falls. Rob had seen the rotating Skylon Tower during a trip to Niagara Falls the summer before with a group of buddies and he really wanted to take Liz there for a fancy dinner.

The restaurant was filled with candles and there was a guy playing a baby grand in the corner—he was no Harry Connick, Jr., but he was all right—and the Falls were alight with the colours of the rainbow. When they ordered their meal, Rob wasn't too surprised that Liz just wanted a small salad. But once she finished that, she asked for another appetizer, and then a little dessert. After a couple of hours, Rob asked if she wanted to get going, but Liz said, "I still have to order something."

"I don't want you to take this the wrong way," Rob said, sensing that she didn't really want all of this food. "But why do you keep ordering all these small dishes?"

"Because my bill isn't fifteen dollars yet." She was referring to the minimum charge listed on the menu.

"Does that make any difference?" he asked.

"Well, of course. It says right here that you have to order at least fifteen dollars' worth of food."

"No, Liz, what it means is that, regardless of what you order, you have to pay a minimum of fifteen dollars."

At times, it was hard to believe how naive she could be, and that was one of the things that endeared her to him, but it also occasionally made him wonder.

The next morning Rob was terribly sick, throwing up in their hotel bathroom. Liz searched in her purse for something that might settle his stomach but all she found were her laxatives. She had told him in the past about her problems having regular bowel movements, so he didn't think twice about her carrying around laxatives in her purse. She suggested that he take one, so he did, but that just made him even more ill. He was back in the bathroom again, and Liz decided to walk to the nearest drugstore, which was about ten minutes away.

Rob had vomited for the third or fourth time no more than five minutes after she'd gone. Suddenly, he felt a lot better. He felt so good, in fact, that he cleaned himself up and left the hotel to find her. He finally caught up to her not too far from the drugstore. Liz said it was best to buy some medication anyway—just to be on the safe side.

It turned out to be a gorgeous day and Liz had brought an enormous basket of food for a picnic on a patch of grass overlooking the Falls. They spent the rest of the afternoon walking around holding hands, seeing the sights. That night, they went to a cheap, corny horror flick about druids who turned people into trees. On the way to the film, they had been driving along a suburban street and had passed a group of kids playing street hockey. In accordance with longstanding tradition, the boys lifted their goal nets and moved off to the sides of the road. As Rob drove by, he waved out the window and asked how everyone was doing. They said great. A few seconds later, Liz looked at him and asked, "You know them?" He couldn't believe it—she wasn't kidding. His mind went back to the $15 minimum charge at the Skylon. "No, no," he said, not wanting to say anything that would hurt her feelings. "Just being friendly."

The following morning, it was Liz's turn to feel a little under the weather. But, like Rob's bouts in the washroom, hers didn't last too long, and they eventually drove to Lake Ontario and sat at the water's edge, having another picnic. They were really having a wonderful weekend—perhaps the best time they'd ever spent together—and Rob was convinced that her steady mood had something to do with the fact that she was away from her family. He had come to the conclusion that although Liz loved her parents, her self-confidence (and, therefore, a good degree of her happiness) had been sapped over the years, mostly by her father, who could be very hard on her. And it wasn't as though Mr. Bain was unaware of this. Rob remembered that back around Christmas time, he and Mr. Bain had been having one of their philosophical chats when Mr. Bain had confided that his rigidity was intentional. "I know that Liz has suffered a great deal," was how Rob recalled him putting it. "And I may have had a part in that. But I think pain and suffering are necessary parts of life."

This child-rearing method, sound or not, had certainly not been the right choice for Liz. By no means, though, did Rob believe Mr. Bain was entirely hard-hearted. Liz had once shown him a home-made videotape of a party her parents had thrown to celebrate her eighteenth birthday. It had been a perfect July day, with the sun reflecting brightly off the white linen covering the dozen or so small rented tables set out in their spacious backyard. There was a long buffet area on the left, shaded beneath the canopy of a tent-trailer that had been raised for the occasion. Julio Iglesias and Willie Nelson could be heard crooning "To All the Girls I've Loved Before" over the sound system. At least fifty friends and relatives, many of them Filipino families from her mother's side, milled around or sat at the tables eating off paper plates, drinking cans of Coca-Cola or (the older men) bottles of beer. Clusters of children scrambled around with badminton racquets on either side of the drooping net at the rear of the yard. The women were wearing pastel sundresses and the men conservative short-sleeved dress shirts, a few with neckties. The first glimpse of Liz was a shot of her ferrying cartons of food from the house to the buffet tables. She was wearing tiny pink jogging shorts with matching summer flats and a check-patterned shirt. Beyond this opening moment, Rob had retained bits and pieces of subsequent footage, but there was one scene in particular that had stayed with him for months.

It begins with a close-up of a large, rectangular chocolate cake, which the camera pulls back from as Mrs. Bain lights the candles and everyone gathers near the buffet tables to sing "Happy Birthday." Liz is captured in profile, staring blankly at the flickering candles as she waits for the song to end so she can blow them out. With the candles extinguished, her parents join her and pose for a photograph as the guests cheer the occasion. Liz begins cutting the cake, and her father gently rests his chin on her left shoulder and says a few quiet words into her ear before smiling and walking away. With the camera concentrating on her face again, Liz looks up and smiles at someone and thanks them for wishing her a happy birthday.

Moments later, Liz turns to her mother and suggests that it might be easier for everyone to serve themselves because otherwise dishing out the cake piece by piece on her own might "take forever." The camera doesn't pick up her mother's response, but Liz hands out a few platefuls, offering a brief smile each time before her eyes shoot right back to the cake, almost as if she is consciously warding off conversation. After handing out maybe the fourth piece, Liz takes a quick glance to her right and, seeing that the next people in line are distracted by another offering at the table, she quickly spins and darts off towards the house, running by the time she disappears from view around a tree. When the camera returns to the cake several minutes later, Liz's mother has taken her place.

The next time you see Liz on the tape, she is sitting on the rear deck with her sister and another teenage girl roughly their age. She has changed out of her pink shorts and is now wearing a pair of dark blue jeans. Liz turns to Cathy and says, "Everybody is so dressed up, and I'm wearing jeans." (If that was the case, Rob thought, why didn't she replace the shorts with a skirt or a pair of dress pants?) When Liz reappears minutes later, she has got rid of her checked top in favour of a pink sweater.

If he didn't know Liz, Rob probably wouldn't have picked up on her wardrobe changes. You could chalk up her actions to the simple possibility that she was getting cold—except that no one else seemed to be. Or maybe she was self-conscious about what she had on, no more self-conscious than any eighteen-year-old girl would be at her own birthday party. It was tough to say. The problem for Rob was that he saw this behaviour as being somehow connected to the same Liz who was never without her fake eyelashes and the Liz who had claimed to have pressed frying pans against her breasts. Here were her parents treating her so lovingly, having gone to considerable effort to throw her a party she would always remember, but Liz seemed more often than not ill at ease.

If people weren't born shy and insecure, Rob wondered, were these traits nurtured throughout one's childhood by the kind of "pain and suffering" Mr. Bain deemed necessary? It probably wasn't an answer to this question, but Liz had once told Rob that, for her, an ideal relationship was one that involved no criticism whatsoever. So, regardless of the origins of Liz's inner demons, the fact that she was coming out of her shell there in Niagara Falls was a sign, Rob felt, that represented what Liz had to do before she could be truly happy—move out on her own.

On the way back to the car from their picnic lunch by the Falls, Rob picked a pink-and-white flower the size of his hand from a bush when she wasn't looking. He handed it to her once they were in the Cordoba and said, "This is for you."

She said, "Oh, my god, it's beautiful," and leaned over to kiss him.

By the time they drove into the little town of Niagara-on-the-Lake, most of the tourist-oriented stores had already closed for the day. But Rob found a bookstore that was still open. He was really excited about it, and Liz was a little surprised that he was so passionate about bookstores. Scanning the shelves, he spotted a book one of his professors had written. "He won the Trillium Award for this one," he said. Liz didn't look very impressed, and Rob said, "I can tell this is boring you. Maybe we should go."

"No, no," she said, smiling. "I think it's great that you're so interested in books." So they stayed awhile longer.

They stopped at a nearby gas station before getting on the highway back to Scarborough. Rob pulled the car up in front of a self-serve gas pump, and they both got out of the car. As he was unscrewing the gas cap, Rob noticed that the gas attendant, a boy no more than nineteen years old, was giving Liz a long, lustful look as she passed him to buy a drink inside the canteen. She offered the boy a polite smile and, bashfully, he smiled back. Perhaps realizing that her boyfriend might have noticed his shameless gaze, the boy glanced at Rob, who'd seen the whole thing. Grinning, Rob said, "So, what do you think?" The boy, red-faced, offered a shy but approving look and turned away.

When Liz got back in the car, Rob turned to her and said, "From the way that kid was looking at you, Liz, I don't think he's seen anyone so gorgeous in his entire life." Liz blushed and pecked him on the cheek. "That's so sweet," she said.

May 15, 1990

Dear Meg,

I spent three days at Niagara Falls with Rob. It turned out to be really nice. I can't believe we didn't argue once. I know he tried hard to get along with me and I with him. It was really romantic, and even though we both got sick, I felt happy to be there.

I started summer school yesterday. I am bingeing again. Eating absolute trash food—hamburgers, chips, cookies, pancakes and syrup, roasted peanuts, lemonade, pasta. On my eleventh day of the flu. I ran one time in the last two weeks. I need to fast so much but I can't. God only knows why. I need to get my self-control back. I haven't let go like this since August of last year.

Last night, I was so worried about school, work and my future. I want this summer to be educational and next year to be my last year of school. I want to graduate next June. I want to move out of the house and live on my own next summer. I hope I can get surgery this summer. I hope I can get my two credits and graduate with a B.A. in psychology next spring. I want to live with Rob but I don't think either of us are ready for that. He's going to be 25 and me 23—can you believe it? I do want to get married and live with him but not in Toronto. It's too expensive. I've got so much self-correcting to do it's unbelievable.

I think I know what I want in life finally. Oh God, thank you for him. I'll never be happier with anyone else. I just hope to God that his intentions are as sincere as mine. Dear God, please help us cope with the future—and don't let him leave me. Last night, I was looking around my psychology class—at Linda Phillips, Kim Partridge—girls Rob knows. I was trying to figure out why he put me above all of them. I drove home and I began to think about how many people I know because of Rob and I started to feel water rise in my eyes. So often I wonder what he sees in me and if I'm ever going to change. Or if I will last with him or if he really really loves me or what our future looks like—if there is one at all. It's all so real, so scary. But I could never stop loving Rob after all I've gone through with him. I think I am so blessed. I don't know why sometimes I think I should leave Rob when I really, truly love him.

Liza

About a week after their trip, Liz stepped on a rusty nail while walking around in the basement of her parents' house. It wasn't too serious but it had definitely punctured the skin and she was limping a little. She told Rob about it when he came over early that evening on his way to the gym for a workout. He looked at the wound and wanted to know if she'd been to see a doctor. Liz said that, yes, she'd gone to her doctor and had been given some pills to stop the infection, if indeed there was one, but she was reluctant to take the medication. Rob was about to say that she was making absolutely no sense when the phone rang. It was Sat, Liz's latest holistic adviser, a woman who claimed to specialize in such areas as homeopathy, nutrition, acupuncture, herbal medicine and kundalini yoga. Liz really wished that she'd taken this call in another room, away from Rob, but it was too late now. She just bit the bullet and asked Sat if she had any herbs to prescribe for her foot. Rob hit the roof when he heard that. He turned in disgust and walked right out the door, just as he'd done when he'd found Liz on the phone with Sat back in March.

But this time it was much worse. A few months earlier, Rob had been inclined to let Liz learn for herself just how ineffectual holistic medicine truly was, but now he felt he had to take a stand. And if there was one main reason for his change of heart, it had to do with a story he'd been following lately in the news.

The Toronto media had been giving extensive coverage to the three-week-old trial of Khachadour Atikian and his wife, Sonia, middle-aged Lebanese immigrants who'd been charged with failing to provide the necessities of life for their seventeen-month-old daughter, Lorie, who died of malnutrition and bronchial pneumonia on September 25, 1987. The Atikians' defence lawyers were pointing the finger at a herbalist from Scarborough named Gerhard Hanswille. The charismatic Hanswille had been in business for at least sixteen years and now owned five retail outlets in Ontario called House of Herbs. Sonia Atikian had been consulting Hanswille for five years by the time she became pregnant with Lorie in 1985.

When Hanswille learned Sonia was expecting, he persuaded her to keep the baby "pure" by refusing a number of standard medical procedures, including ultrasound and, after the baby was born, vaccinations. In their place, little Lorie was treated with Hanswille's "biochemical tissue salts," a solution called "royal jelly" and a herbal concoction known as Formula 12. Her diet consisted of brown rice, raw vegetables, puréed fruits and fruit juices. Hanswille had advised Sonia not to give her infant daughter milk. Even though the Atikians' two teenage children, who had been raised using modern medicine, were models of health, Hanswille promised the Atikians a "superbaby" if they followed his direction.

The result was that, one and a half years into her life, Lorie weighed eleven pounds—the average weight of a two-month-old baby—and was on the verge of death. Her jaundiced skin was covered in rashes, especially her buttocks and upper thighs, which appeared as though they'd been dipped in some kind of acid. Her half-bald head was covered with lesions. A mixture of blood and pus was draining from her ears.

That's how Lorie appeared when Sonia Atikian took her child, who hadn't been seen by a medical doctor for more than eight months, to Hanswille's flagship store, which was sandwiched between a coin-operated laundromat and a pet grooming salon called Shear Purrfection at a strip mall in Markham. According to Sonia's testimony, Hanswille told her not to worry about Lorie's falling weight and that the blood coming from her ears was a very good sign because it meant that the "poisons" in her system were being expelled. Hanswille took the infant into the basement of his store to treat her with an "electromagnetic machine" that would "vitalize the blood." Once that procedure had been completed, he told Sonia to wrap Lorie in the leaves of a Savoy cabbage when they got home. He said that would continue to draw out the poisons infecting her system. Lorie died the next day.

During his testimony, Gerhard Hanswille insisted that he told Sonia Atikian to "seek medical advice." But the herbalist's credibility was repeatedly undermined. He had received his "doctoral" degree from Bernadean University, a Las Vegas correspondence school that accepted its students the moment their cheques cleared. Of Bernadean's four faculty members, the most qualified had a high school diploma. Through two defence witnesses, the jury learned that Hanswille promised sight to a legally blind diabetic and the dissolution of a tumour to a man with rectal cancer. The cancer patient, who, having gone off radiation and chemotherapy treatments, paid for Hainsville to travel to Cuba and Mexico—no doubt in search of rare tropical herbs—died after losing more than eighty pounds. The much lighter diabetic lost forty pounds by the time she was rushed to the hospital. A doctor told her that, had she not been treated, she would have died from malnutrition within days.

For Rob, this story hit a little too close to home. He simply couldn't be with someone who would treat herself with such careless disregard. So the night after Liz had called Sat about the rusty nail, Rob dropped by Liz's house with the express purpose of delivering a stern ultimatum. He told her that she was going to have to choose between holistic medicine and him.

She just couldn't understand why he kept making such a big deal about this. "Why do you find this so threatening?" she asked.

"It's not threatening to me," he said. "It's threatening to you. I can't go along with you on this when I feel that it's bad for you. This is always going to be a bone of contention so you're just going to have to pick one or the other. Whichever route you choose, I'll respect your decision."

Perhaps sensing that she was about to lose him, Liz went to put her arms around his neck, but Rob stepped away and said, "No, I am sorry. Call me within the next three days and let me know what your decision is."

Three days later, she called him with her decision. She was through with holistic medicine.

That night, they went to Morningside Park down in the valley behind Scarborough College and lit a bonfire. They started kissing, and Rob was lying back on the grass with Liz on top of him when a police car hit them with a spotlight from the road and, through the car megaphone, an ominous, crackling voice told them to put out the fire.

—◦—

On the last Sunday in May, Rob brought a movie over to the Kidbrooke Home, as he usually did as part of his weekly routine. It wasn't very busy at Kidbrooke on Sunday evenings and it was the perfect chance for him to spend time with Liz as well as some of the residents. Rob was now considered part of the Kidbrooke family—he'd even been approached about applying for volunteer status—and he'd come to enjoy their company. But this night looked as though it might not be so enjoyable. Liz was unresponsive from the moment she answered the door, a dour greeting that he was, much to his chagrin, getting increasingly accustomed to. Rob didn't say anything for a while, but he could take her brooding only for so long before he asked her for a word outside. But, out on the front veranda, it was Liz who spoke first. "I have to tell you something," she said, her eyes darting everywhere but in his direction.

Rob asked, "What is it?"

"I don't know how to tell you."

"Well, is it bad?"

"Yes," she said, now staring at the ground.

"Why don't you just tell me what it is?" Rob had no idea what she was getting at. "Did you get drunk? Stoned? Is there another guy? Help me out, Liz. I'm lost."

Liz kept shaking her head. And then—wham!—it hit him. He thought back to the time that Liz had told him about a suicide attempt during her senior year of high school. She'd wanted to cut her wrists but she hadn't been able to go through with it and she'd ended up with some bad-looking scratches. She'd said she had wanted to tell him about this many times before but hadn't had the courage.

Rob looked down at her wrists. He could see white gauze bandages sticking out of the long sleeves of her black shirt. The gauze was wrapped loosely around both wrists. Liz burst into tears and said, "I did it again." She threw her arms around him and sobbed hysterically.

Rob kept saying, "Why? Why? Why did this happen?" She didn't answer. He said, "I want to see them. Please. I have to see them." But she wouldn't show him and she kept holding her hands behind her back. He continued begging but to no avail. He reached out and grabbed one of her arms and, for an instant, the bandage pulled away and he could see that there was a prominent scab. It wasn't too deep, but there was no mistaking the fact that she'd wounded herself. Rob grabbed her by the shoulders and locked his eyes with hers. "Liz," he said. "You have to get the hell out of that house."

In some ways, this scene took him back to his childhood and to those years when his mother was in a constant state of depression. It seemed as though his mother had threatened to kill herself just about every other day during his early adolescence. And now that Liz was talking about ending her life, his reaction was somewhat tempered by the fact that his mother was still alive. He didn't really believe that his mother wanted to die. And it didn't seem as though Liz was any different. Nevertheless, he made Liz promise to get some psychiatric help. "I'm not crazy," she said. "All I need is you."

Rob was sure that this crisis had been brought on not by their rift over holistic medicine, but by her home life. But Liz denied that her family had been the cause of it. She said that if anyone was to blame, it was her. Though, having said that, she described how her father, shortly after he'd returned from New Orleans, had informed her that he wasn't going to pay her tuition for the upcoming school year.

Liz surmised that this announcement was directly related to an incident that had occurred just before her parents' trip. An unopened package of birth control pills her doctor had given her back in the fall had disappeared from her dresser while her mother was at work putting a fresh coat of paint on the walls of Liz's bedroom. Liz feared that, at some point during their trip to New Orleans, her mother had disclosed this find to her father.

Rob and Liz agreed that that was quite likely what had happened. There was no other logical explanation. Liz was trying to convince herself that her father's intentions weren't all bad—maybe he was imparting a valuable lesson. Paying for her own schooling might make her more independent. Rob didn't buy it. He was overcome with resentment for Mr. Bain. What went on in that man's head was a mystery to him.

Later that night, they returned to the Bains' house. Liz still had the same shirt on but she was no longer making a conscious effort to cover up the bandages on her wrists. It was almost as if she forgot they were there. Rob and Liz were sitting in the kitchen when Mark walked in and began preparing himself something to eat. He sat down at the table finally, and Rob watched as Liz reached across the table, her bandaged wrist right under Mark's nose, and it made no impression on him whatsoever. Rob couldn't believe it. Once Mark had left the kitchen, Rob said, "Are you going to tell me that Mark didn't see those bandages on your wrists?"

"Rob, I went to mass this morning with these on, and no one in the family said a word."

He had no difficulty believing that. He'd once found a roach clip on the back of the television set in the basement. When he showed it to Liz, she didn't even know what it was. "It's what you use to hold on to the end of a joint," he said.

"That figures," Liz said. "It's probably my sister's. She and Steve were in the basement when I came home."

Being the anti-drug advocate that he was, Rob thought that Liz's parents should be informed right away. The situation called for immediate parental intervention. Rob wasn't too fond of Steve but he liked Cathy, and getting her into trouble was the only possible consequence that gave him pause. In the end he decided that whatever the fallout, telling Mrs. Bain was the right thing to do.

He found Liz's mother upstairs. "I found this in your basement," he said, handing her the clip. "It may be of concern to you." She wasn't quite sure what it was, so he told her. Instead of expressing the appropriate degree of shock, Mrs. Bain was so skeptical about the whole thing that she started to giggle. Trying to emphasize the severity of this find, Rob grabbed a piece of tissue paper and rolled it up like a joint to illustrate how the clip worked. He put the clip close to his lips and sucked air as if he was toking on a joint. "Really?" she said, giggling even louder now. Rob, mystified by her reaction, left it with her and went back downstairs.

---⊖---

Robert Baltovich: A Brief Spiking Session

*L*eaving the Bains' house, I was now thinking that Liz must have exited her class from the rear door of her classroom, thus beating me to her car in the valley before taking off straight for Arlene's. I returned to the Recreation Centre and made one final attempt to find out for certain if Liz had missed her class. One of the people I had seen walk out of Liz's class was a fellow student named Linda Phillips, with her friend Kim Partridge alongside her. Linda was also well acquainted with Liz, and I thought that, once I got to the Recreation Centre, I would try calling her on the phone to see if Liz had been at class.

I walked into the gymnasium and saw Neil Winton again sitting on the bleachers near the volleyball courts with a group of guys I knew from the campus, including Rob Cortina, Tony Scarpino and Jack Caruso. I asked Neil if Linda Phillips's boyfriend, Brent, still lived in one of the campus's residence buildings. Neil said that Brent was now living north of the city, managing his parents' restaurant or something like that. If that was the case, I thought, Linda had probably gone straight home after her class.

To make sure that Linda had plenty of time to get home, I waited another ten minutes before going downstairs to call her on the free phone near the athletic desk, where I asked for a telephone book to look up her number. Luckily, Linda was home when I called. She said Liz hadn't been in class that night. "Are you sure?" I asked.

"Yes," she said. "Liz always sits in front of me, but tonight she wasn't there."

I thanked her and hung up. As I walked back to the gym, I was starting to feel a little bit more worried. The only logical explanation I could now think of was that Liz had met with Arlene, possibly for a walk in the valley, and that, at some point, Liz had decided to skip her class in order to spend the evening with her friend. And Arlene wasn't just any friend. Arlene was perhaps the only close female friend Liz had—it was just too bad that she'd gone to university as far away as Ottawa.

I joined the guys on the bleachers in the gym. They talked sports for a while, baseball in particular, and then Jack Caruso began telling this story about a girl *who'd approached him in a bar on Sunday. Apparently, she had rather forwardly demanded that he buy her a drink. No one was too impressed with this style of approach, and, according to Tony Scarpino's testimony at my trial, I responded by saying, "Don't worry, Jack, girls aren't really worth the trouble." I might have said that, although I must say I have no memory of it.*

I do, though, remember that we discussed girls for a short while longer and then Jack, Tony and Rob Cortina were on their way. Neil and I stayed behind, talking on the bleachers. At about 10:00, we were joined by Rick Gostick, who was managing some of the Recreation Centre's athletic programs that summer. Rick knew me pretty well but he'd been friends with Neil for years, and the three of us were feeling pretty laid back, shooting the breeze. After a few minutes, we went out onto one of the volleyball courts to hit a ball around. We chose the court that had the net adjusted to the regulation height for women, which was a lot easier to spike the ball over. For about twenty minutes, we set each other up with easy balls to hammer into the opposite side of the court.

Everybody had to be out of the gym by 10:30, so Neil and I helped Rick take down the net and then we went with him to the main foyer as he locked up the front doors to the gym. Neil and Rick were planning on going to a local restaurant called Kelsey's once Rick had finished locking up the entire facility and they invited me to join them. Every so often I would go along, but on this occasion, I told them maybe next time.

On my way home, I drove through the valley one last time. The silver car I'd seen earlier was still in the little parking area adjacent to the park, but Liz's car was nowhere in sight. To me, it meant she must have spent the evening at Arlene's.

—◇—

Rob's graduation ceremony was scheduled to take place on Friday, June 8, 1990, at the University of Toronto's Convocation Hall on the main campus downtown. Academically, it had been his best year at Scarborough College. He'd received two A's in the Applied Psychology of Learning and Introduction to Sociology; a B minus for a history course, British Imperialism in India; and a C in Current Topical Social Psychology. His grade point average that year, 3.23 (the equivalent of eighty-one per cent), had pulled up his mediocre cumulative G.P.A. to 2.54 (sixty-four per cent).

Two days before the convocation ceremony, Liz told Rob that she might not be able to attend because she was scheduled to work. He asked if she could get someone to switch shifts with her, and she said she'd been trying and hadn't had much luck. She didn't sound too upset about it, and that really nagged at him. After all, he was only going to graduate once. He thought being there should have meant more to her.

There was a graduation ball at the Scarborough campus the night before convocation. Again, Liz couldn't make it, this time because of her summer night course. Rob ended up going to the ball with two friends who were also graduating, Neil Winton and Steve Doucette. He'd arranged to meet Liz outside of her class when it ended at 9:00 PM, but when he got there, she was nowhere to be seen, so he went back to the ball and found Neil and Steve. They decided to go to Kelsey's to celebrate with a couple of Fudge Fantasy desserts. They walked out to their cars in the parking lot and much to Rob's surprise, there was Liz leaning against his Cordoba. Rob told the guys to go ahead without him—he would meet them there.

Liz had a look on her face as if she were disappointed with him. "What are you doing *here*?" Rob asked.

She said, "I'm waiting for you."

"But I thought we were going to meet after your class at our regular spot."

"Well," she said, "we got out early."

"So why didn't you just stay at the meeting place?"

Liz didn't know, and Rob didn't feel like getting into an argument about it. He chalked it up to crossed wires. The evening had been going well so far and, despite the mix-up, he was happy to see her. He told her how great she looked and gave her a hug and they began to kiss. He invited Liz to Kelsey's, but she declined, promising to see him the next night, after his graduation.

Rob and his parents drove downtown for the ceremony the next day. Jim and Adele were perched up high in their balcony seats, watching intently as Rob made his way down the red carpet, his black gown flowing behind him, eventually kneeling before the president of the university. Up above, his father snapped a photo with his camera. Jim's presence was a testament to the magnitude of the occasion. It was the first time he'd taken time off work to attend a function for his son. As Rob knelt on the soft cushions before the president, he was overcome with emotion, and it was as though his entire life flashed before his eyes, in what he imagined was the closest he might come to a moment of epiphany.

Later that night, after driving his parents back to Scarborough, he went over to Liz's house. Rob was now at the point where he could deduce her mood within the first few seconds of seeing her. And despite the fact that it was a joyous day for him, he immediately observed that the same could not be said for her. Here she was giving him these wonderful graduation gifts—a watch, flowers and a card with a funny little poem inside—acting as if she'd rather be anywhere but with him. It was the old zombie routine. He'd learned that he had little control over her emotions in situations like this, so he just made the best of it, trying without success to bring her back with endless gratitude for her thoughtful presents. He was beginning to pick up on a pattern. The happier he was about the way things were going in his life, the more sullen Liz seemed to get.

Thankfully, she'd snapped out of it by the next night and they made a little trip to the Lido Motel, another dive on the north side of Kingston Road. They'd started going to the Lido with some regularity around Christmas because the rooms were a lot nicer than the ones at the Roycroft. Usually they would pick up some pizza or Chinese food and sit on the bed watching movies or turn out the lights and get under the covers—or a little of both.

But that night, Liz seemed on edge, almost skittish. They were in the middle of making love when, all of a sudden, she jumped right off the bed and ran to the window. She was convinced that someone was out there, watching them.

—◦—

Robert Baltovich: Busy Signal

*A*s soon as my mother saw me walk into the kitchen, she could tell that something was wrong. "What's the matter?" she asked. I told her about how Liz's car had been in the valley with the windows open, and that she'd missed her class. My mom suggested I try calling the Bains', which I did. I called three times during the next twenty minutes, but kept getting a busy signal. My mom didn't want me to go to bed until I got through to them, so I tried Mark's private line and got his answering machine. I left a message for him to ask Liz to call me or, if she wasn't home, for him to call—I was worried about her and wanted either one of them to call at any hour of the night. Mom urged me to keep trying the Bains' main line but it was 11:00 PM, and I was ready to go to bed.

Before heading down to my bedroom, I wrote a little note that I left with my mom in case Liz called after I'd gone to sleep. In addition to the fact that my mother is a bit of an insomniac, I didn't have a telephone in my room, so if someone called in the middle of the night, my mom would be the first to answer the one in the kitchen. If, by chance, the phone didn't wake me, Mom was to read the following message if Liz happened to call and everything was all right: Wanted to know if you were okay. For some reason I was a little worried. Explain everything on Thursday. Thanks. *I also knew that if Mrs. Bain or Mark called to say that Liz didn't come home, my mom would be intelligent enough to wake me up.*

---—⊝—---

Once Rob had gone to bed, Adele was having an especially difficult time getting to sleep. Jim had just nodded off upstairs in the bedroom, but she rarely slept up there. She was too restless, tossing and turning and getting out of bed all the time, and it just kept poor Jim from a decent night's rest. As a result, most of her nights were spent on the daybed in the living room, trapped in the hazy world between dreams and reality, her body framed by the flickering glare of the television.

She was fretting about Liz, as she often did. The girl was always driving around alone in her car at night. Adele couldn't understand it—she didn't venture beyond her front door after dark. Whenever Liz visited their home late at night, Adele would ask her to call when she got back to her house. She was to let the phone ring once so that Adele could sleep properly, knowing that Liz was safe and sound. She didn't know how Robert could go to bed when he didn't know where Liz was, and she'd told him as much on his way to his room. By now, he was probably sleeping like a baby down there. She wouldn't mind drifting off herself, if only Liz would call.

Part 2

—○—

Through the Valley
of the Shadow

The sharp ring of the old telephone up in the kitchen shot through the stillness of the somnolent household. Rob opened his eyes in the basement darkness and listened to his mother shuffle across the linoleum floor to answer it. He looked at his clock radio. It was 6:30. His mother was speaking with someone, but he couldn't make out any specific words. Then came a brief moment of silence before his mother's loud, anxious voice called out from the top of the stairs. "Robert, come here, hurry up," she said. "Liz didn't come home last night!"

At once, he was wide awake, bounding up the stairs to the kitchen. When Rob picked up the phone, Mrs. Bain asked if Liz was there. "No," he replied. "Why?"

"She didn't come home last night."

"Oh, no," Rob said. "Something is definitely wrong." He knew that Liz wouldn't stay out all night without calling her mother. "Why did you wait so long to call?" Rob asked.

"I didn't want to disturb you in the middle of the night."

"Did you get in touch with Arlene?"

"No," she answered.

"Okay," he said, "I'll be right over."

Mrs. Bain was waiting in the foyer when he parked his car and came running into the house about half an hour later. Without exchanging any words, Rob went straight upstairs to Liz's room, Mrs. Bain trailing behind him. She watched as he began rummaging through the papers on her desk. "What are you looking for?" she asked. He said that he was trying to find Liz's address book so that he could figure out where Arlene lived. The project that Liz had been working on for her abnormal child psychology course was laid out on her desk, as if she'd just stepped out of the room for a minute.

At that very moment the phone rang. Mrs. Bain answered it just outside of Liz's room. Rob quickly realized that she was speaking to Mark and he asked Mrs. Bain if he could have a word with him, and she handed him the receiver. Mark had a summer job with a landscaping company and was already at a work site up in Markham. He asked Mark how to get to Arlene's house, and Mark gave him some rough directions. Without wasting any time, Rob hung up the phone and told Mrs. Bain he was on his way.

Rob had actually been to Arlene's once before, back in December when he and Liz had picked her up on the way to the Bains' Christmas party, but his sense of direction was notoriously bad and he had no clear memory of the route they'd taken. He did, however, have a vague recollection of what the house looked like, so, using Mark's instructions, he drove to her street, Leameadow Way, and knocked on the front door of a house that resembled Arlene's. A man, still half-asleep in his dressing gown, informed him that he had the wrong house, so Rob got back in his car and drove to the next block, where he hit the jackpot—a house with a wooden sign out front that read "The Coventrys'" (beneath was the word "Kilami," which was the Afrikaans word for "Welcome," a nod to their South African roots).

Arlene was getting ready to go to work at her summer job when she heard the knock at her front door. It was no later than 7:30 and she was the only person in her family who was up, so she came downstairs to peer through the blinds onto the front porch. At first, she didn't recognize the young man standing there. She'd only met Rob once, on the night of the Christmas party, but he looked different somehow in his summer clothes, his skin not as pale as it had been then. However, it wasn't until she opened the door, and he explained that he was "Liz's Rob" that it all began to click. He hurriedly asked if Liz had made it over the night before, and Arlene said that, no, she hadn't. "You and Liz didn't have plans to get together for dinner last night?" he asked.

"No," Arlene said. "We talked about setting a time to get together this week, but we had no plans last night."

Arlene could tell that this news had made him seriously distressed. She asked him to wait while she finished getting ready for work. She intended to go back to the Bains' with Rob and make sure everything was all right before heading off to her job.

On the way to Liz's house in Rob's messy Cordoba—he'd had to clear a bunch of papers off the passenger seat as he opened the door for her—Arlene was thinking about the last time she'd seen Liz. They'd spoken over the telephone three or four times after the Christmas break, but Arlene hadn't seen her until she'd returned home from university in Ottawa in early May. They'd gotten together one night while Liz's parents were on their trip to New Orleans, renting a movie to take back to Arlene's, where they sat and talked and watched the film. Liz had brought up her disagreements with Rob over holistic medicine and had described how Rob had asked her to leave his house as a result of a harmless anecdote she'd told about Cathy's boyfriend, Steve Annett. Liz had seemed quite upset by it all, and Arlene suggested that, if things weren't working out, maybe the two of them should break up. In fact, she made the suggestion more than once, but, on each occasion, Liz had been adamant about her desire to work things out. The entire conversation that night was slightly unusual because, as a general rule, they didn't talk about Rob all that much, and during their calls throughout the spring Liz had been relatively happy.

When Rob and Arlene pulled into the Bains' driveway, a uniformed officer was ahead of them, getting out of his police cruiser. The gravity of the situation was starting to sink in. The officer introduced himself as Constable Victor Stinson, and they followed him into the house. He was responding to Mrs. Bain's missing-person call, which she'd made before Rob had first arrived. Mrs. Bain and her teenage niece, Kim, who'd just arrived for a visit from Boston, met the officer and led him to the dining-room table, where the small group now gathered.

Constable Stinson began asking Mrs. Bain, who was notably upset, the standard questions to ascertain basic information: height, weight, general description, what she'd been wearing. While this was going on, Rob and Arlene decided to go and check the area in the valley where Rob had last seen her car.

Liz's car was nowhere in sight, so Rob drove to the lot next to the tennis courts.

He and Arlene got out of his Cordoba and walked down the stairs to the courts. David Phillips, who was working as a tennis instructor for the summer, was giving an early-morning lesson on court 1. David (who was no relation to Linda Phillips) was slightly annoyed when Rob came through the fence gate and walked right onto the court, interrupting his lesson. But Rob explained that Liz had gone missing and wanted to know if David had seen her any time last night or this morning. David said that he was sorry but he hadn't.

Rob and Arlene walked around in the valley for about twenty minutes, following the progress of Highland Creek towards the Morningside Bridge, passing the island of trees behind which he and Liz had made love on Sunday night. As they walked through the fields, wet with morning dew, they talked about Liz. "Has Liz been saying anything about me lately?" Arlene asked.

"Yes," Rob said. "She was a little worried that the two of you were going to grow apart because of you being in Ottawa for so long." And then he told her about seeing the letter from Mark Fielden and that, the night before, Rob thought she'd been down in the valley to meet someone. "Do you think she was seeing anyone else?" he asked. Arlene just couldn't imagine Liz behaving that way and she said no.

Back at the Bains', Mrs. Bain and Constable Stinson were still talking at the dining-room table, now joined by Cathy, who'd come over after her mother had called in a panic at 7:00 AM. Stinson was now asking questions about whether Liz might be missing as a result of problems at school, or depression, or anything like that. Mrs. Bain said she wasn't aware of any such reason. Then, seeing that Rob and Arlene were in the room, Stinson asked Rob what Liz had said about getting together with Arlene and then elicited a rundown of what Rob had been doing the night before.

Stinson called in his missing-person report from inside the house and, hanging up the phone, announced that, for now, he'd done all he could. He would be in touch as soon as they heard something. As he neared the door, Rob approached the officer and quietly asked if they could have a word alone outside. Stinson said, "Fine," and they went out to the driveway. Away from Liz's family, Rob told the officer about her aborted attempt at cutting her wrists a month ago. "Is the family aware of this?" Stinson inquired. Rob said that he didn't think so, but that Liz had been depressed recently.

He told Stinson about an incident that had taken place as recently as the previous

Thursday evening. They'd been down in the basement watching television. Liz had been the perfect picture of glumness since he'd met her after her class, and relaxing on the couch wasn't helping. So Rob turned the television down and asked what was bothering her. Liz said it was something that had happened at the day care. A baby girl she'd been looking after had escaped from her crib and fallen down some stairs while Liz had taken a quick trip to the ladies' room. Liz had panicked, she said, and instead of calling the emergency 911 number, she'd tried contacting the baby's father. Unfortunately, neither of the baby's parents got home for some time, and when the little girl's mother found out what had happened, she became hysterical and started screaming at Liz, threatening to sue for negligence. Eventually, the woman settled down and everyone went home, but Liz was shattered. She was saying things like "I might just go away." Of course, Rob had asked her where, but she wouldn't say.

Stinson asked if Rob knew of any places where Liz might go if she was feeling depressed and wanted to be alone. Rob told him about her favourite spot down in the Rouge Beach Park, which was in the south-eastern corner of Scarborough, bordering Pickering. When Rob had first met Liz, she was fond of hiking to these secluded, hard-to-get-to areas of the park. Rouge Beach was much closer to her house than Kew Beach, which was more of a hang-out for Rob. Stinson got in his cruiser and sent a message to his sergeant over the radio—they needed to meet in order to discuss the latest circumstances involving the missing girl. After signing off, Stinson got out of the car and walked over to Rob and said, "I don't want to alarm you, but I'm going to be blunt."

Rob said, "Okay."

"If we find her dead, will you be surprised?"

The officer noted the look of shock on Rob's face as he paused before responding, "No, I wouldn't."

Stinson asked Rob if he would go down to Rouge Beach and check the spot he'd just spoken of. If he happened to find Liz's car, Stinson told him not to go anywhere near it but to immediately notify the police.

By the time Rob went back inside the house, Paul Bain was out of bed and Rob suggested they go down to Rouge Beach together. Paul drove them there in the used car he'd bought for himself a few months back and, once they'd parked, they began walking to the spot where Rob and Liz had spent a pleasant evening just a few weeks earlier. They weren't too far along when Rob realized that it was going to be a long walk there and back, so he asked Paul to bring the car to another parking area closer to the desired location. Rob started to jog down the path and stopped along the way to ask a woman walking with a young child and a dog if she'd seen a girl matching Liz's description the night before. The woman said she hadn't. So he kept going until he reached a little cove where he saw an Asian couple seated at a picnic table under a tree. This time he didn't stop. He kept going to the end of the road and walked in a daze along the edge of the bluffs, realizing that he wasn't even sure what he was looking for as he waited for Paul to come around with the car.

While Rob and Paul were at Rouge Beach, Cathy and Arlene—who by now had written off the idea of going to work—had gone up to Liz's room to read her diary, hoping that it might indicate where Liz had gone. Although Liz was completely unaware of it, Cathy had been sneaking into her older sister's room for years to read her diary. Even during several visits home since Cathy had moved out, she'd gone into Liz's room when she was out and flipped through the loose-leaf pages of her latest diary book—an orange three-ring binder.

Cathy opened the binder and went straight to the last three pages, which she read quickly but with care. The page at the very back of the binder had not yet been inserted on the metal rings but it had writing on both sides. The first side contained a diary entry dated May 15, 1990, and, on the back, the final entry, dated June 16, 1990, which began in green ink and finished in blue. Cathy was so moved by what Liz had written that she took the piece of paper and handed it to Arlene. Once she'd finished reading it, Cathy told her to hold on to it but not to show it to Rob.

Rob and Paul had returned from Rouge Beach by the time Arlene numbly followed Cathy downstairs. As soon as Cathy saw Rob, she asked, "Have you and Liz been fighting?"

Rob said, "No." Cathy asked him the same question again, and Rob repeated his initial response. After she'd put the query to him for the third time, Rob said, "Why are you asking me this?" And then Arlene jumped in and said, "Because of this." Defying Cathy's request, she handed him the page with the two final diary entries.

Seeing "Dear Meg" written at the top, Rob immediately knew it was from Liz's diary. Arlene was perplexed by what she'd read and was hoping that Rob might be able explain it, even though it was going to upset him, as it had her. She told him he should read it alone outside, which he did.

June 16, 1990

Dear Meg,

Life sucks—and it's getting worse by the day. Every morning when I rise I try to find a reason why I shouldn't kill myself. Last night I wanted to put a bullet through Rob's head and everybody that was bothering me. My temper is swarming. I am going to murder someone if I don't get a hold of myself. I hate my job. I hate school and Rob is becoming a pest. I have to break free and be alone. Bingeing—crying—I feel like a pig from hell. Last night while Rob was waiting by the chair, I told him to hold on to my bag. I went upstairs and bawled my eyes out. He drains me so much. When I saw him follow me home yesterday, I felt like killing myself. I was an emotional & physical wreck, and there he was, all pepped up. He didn't even tell me he was coming. I hate surprises.

I don't wanna go on—boyfriend or not I am just as unhappy. I am never going to want to be part of a family. I hate this life. I want to get up and kill somebody. Everyone in this world can go fuck themselves—I hate it here. I am always so burned out and I know I don't have to be. Life really sucks with this fucken summer school course & 2 jobs—eating 15% RAW & running 1x weekly. I want to kill someone I tell you.

I WANT DEATH TO COME
AND END THIS ALL THIS
PATHETIC LIFE THAT IS
GETTING WORSE BY THE DAY
AND DEATH TO THOSE
FUCKEN PEOPLE WHO
TOIL ON ME DAY AFTER DAY
MAY THEY ROT IN HELL

Liza

The entry definitely threw him for a loop, but it wasn't as much a blow to him as Arlene had perhaps expected it to be. While Arlene had never seen this side of Liz—in fact, it was difficult for her to even conceive that her childhood friend had held the pen that had scripted these harsh words—Rob had at least caught a glimpse of it. In this instance, Liz's private rage seemed to have been uncorked by the incident after the baby had fallen at work. That was what she was alluding to when she wrote about handing him her school bag after class and running off to the ladies' room to cry. As for the part about following her, it hadn't quite happened that way. Rob had been driving home from his friend Milton Tjin-a-Tjie's place—Milton had just restrung Rob's tennis racquet for him—when he saw Liz's car in front of him as she came off the exit ramp from Highway 401. He hadn't planned on going to Liz's, but now that her car was right in front of him, Rob followed her for a few blocks until they were in her driveway.

As a result of Liz writing about both incidents as though they'd happened the night before, Rob assumed she'd written the entry on Friday. If that was the case, Liz had the incorrect date at the top of the page. June 16 had been Saturday. Rob thought it was quite obvious that she'd actually written the final entry on June 15, the Friday.

When he went back inside, Cathy tried in vain to put him at ease, saying, "Rob, I know she didn't mean it. She writes stuff like that all the time."

"It's not the things she wrote about me that I'm worried about," he said. "It's the part about wanting death to come to her." Rob and Arlene looked at each other, their faces revealing their disquiet. "Would you guys calm down," Cathy said, watching them. "She just took off, that's all. Rob, are you sure there wasn't anything wrong between you two?"

"Well," he said, pensively, "there's only one thing that comes to mind."

"What's that?" Cathy asked.

"A few weeks ago, I told her to stop using holistic medicine or, basically, I would end the relationship."

There was a brief pause as Rob waited for Cathy to say something, but she didn't, and their minds drifted off in different directions as they stood, still facing one another.

—◦—

Throughout the morning, Rob made a number of phone calls hoping to find that Liz was staying with someone she knew. One of the people he contacted was Mark Bain's girlfriend, Nancy Sicchia. A slender brunette with a troublesome adolescent complexion, Nancy had started dating Mark about a year and a half earlier, when she was sixteen and he was twenty. It hadn't been the smoothest of relationships, which may have been a result of their sizable age gap. But Nancy and Liz had become friends despite an even greater number of years between them. Liz had confided in Nancy about her feelings about her family. What bothered her most, Liz had said, was that each person in her family was introverted, which had led to a lack of communications between them. As for Liz's father, both Liz and Nancy agreed that he was a male chauvinist—for example, they had both observed that Mark was allowed to do things Liz would never be permitted to do.

A couple of weeks ago, Nancy and Mark had got into a terrible screaming match at the Bains', and Nancy, in tears, demanded to be taken home. With Mark storming around in a fury, Paul and Liz began their own verbal jousting over who was going to drive her. Nancy said she didn't care who it was, she just wanted to get the hell out of there.

Paul ended up winning the job, and he returned to Nancy's the following day to deliver a two-page letter from Liz. It began: *I know I don't have my life all together. But being imperfect is not going to stop me from trying to help a friend I love so much and one of the very few people I feel so close to.* Liz explained that abuse isn't just physical, it's also verbal, which can just as easily lead to mental and emotional distress, especially when you're left out in the cold during the times you need someone the most. Liz was sure that her brother loved Nancy as much as she loved him, but he just didn't know how to show it. *I don't want to tell you how to run your life,* Liz wrote at the end, *but please, Nancy, make sure you are getting back what you are giving because, if you aren't, you will suffer in the end more than anyone else. Don't let him treat you this way. Find a way to make him stop or he will keep ripping up your self-esteem until you have none left for your own well-being. P.S. Don't get used to abuse. You'll never know anything else. Love, Liz xoxoxo.*

Nancy and Mark had made up since then, and she never did tell him about Liz's letter. Now, Nancy was a little surprised to be getting a phone call from Rob and, barely awake, she spoke with him long enough to say that Liz wasn't with her and then she went back to sleep. Later, when she got up, she immediately thought back to Rob's phone call and asked her sister if she could give her a lift over to the Bains'.

Nancy was dropped off at about 1:00 PM and saw Arlene, whom she'd never met but knew of, standing beside Rob in the front yard. They said Cathy was in the house with her cousin from Boston and that Mrs. Bain had already left to pick up her husband at the airport. Nancy was quite startled to hear Rob talking about the possibility that Liz had committed suicide. He was uncharacteristically agitated, calling Mrs. Bain a moron for having gone grocery shopping that morning when her daughter was nowhere to be found. Nancy thought he was jumping the gun.

They started listing the places where Liz might have gone. Arlene suggested they go down to Kew Beach because, like Rouge Beach, it might be a place where Liz would go if she wanted to just sit and think. All three piled into Rob's Cordoba.

On the way, Arlene gave Nancy the page containing Liz's two final diary entries. When she saw "Dear Meg" at the top, she asked who Meg was. Arlene explained it was the "person" Liz wrote to in her journal. "This is from her journal?" Nancy asked. She said she didn't like looking into people's private things, but Arlene convinced her to read it.

Like everyone else, Nancy was shocked. She couldn't believe the intensity of the letter. That just wasn't like Liz. Speechless, she handed it back to Arlene.

Walking along the same boardwalk where Rob and Liz had strolled after their first dinner together at Vincent's Spot, they tried to make sense of Liz's final diary entry. In the twelve or so years Arlene had known her, Liz had never mentioned suicide. However, the same could not be said for Nancy. Liz had told her about scratching her wrists when she was in high school. She'd wanted to slit them but couldn't go through with it. Before Arlene had the chance to absorb this startling detail, Rob continued with the story of how she'd done the same thing just a month ago.

One part of the last entry that Arlene was still trying to make sense of was the reference to Rob following her. What was that all about? Rob told her about seeing Liz's car coming off the highway on his way back from picking up his tennis racquet and how she hadn't found his little joke quite as funny as he had. "What about last night?" said Arlene. "Is it possible that Liz saw you when you pulled your car up next to hers in the valley?"

"Yes," he said. "It's possible that she might have been hiding on me."

They followed the boardwalk west until it ended near the Olympic-sized outdoor pool at the foot of Woodbine Avenue. It was a warm summer day down by the beach, and they felt as though they were just about the only people not wearing bathing suits. Before making their way back to the car, they lingered near a rocky cove at the end of the boardwalk where Liz and Arlene had gone a few times in the past.

Driving into Scarborough, Rob was still sounding pessimistic. "You know, Arlene," he said, "maybe Liz did commit suicide. I'll bet that if we find her car, we'll probably find her." Rob decided to take Old Kingston Road back to the Bains' and he turned north onto the little road that led to the tennis courts. He parked the car and, as he opened his door, told them to stay put—he was going to be just a few minutes. Through the trees, Arlene and Nancy could see Rob walk onto the courts below and strike up a conversation with three guys who were playing tennis.

Rob hadn't expected to run into Neil Winton, Steve Doucette and Rick Gostick. But now that he had, he informed them that Liz hadn't come home the night before and that in her final diary entry she'd written about wanting to put a bullet in his head and death to come to her. He seemed concerned but, true to the Rob they knew, not frantic. Rob was always so calm and rational. Even with his girlfriend missing, he remembered that he was supposed to work that night and he asked Neil if he would cover for him. Neil said it was no problem and Rob left the group.

Nancy and Arlene witnessed the entire scene from inside the car, parked on the bank above. Nancy was becoming impatient with Rob. She had no idea why he would be canvassing people at the tennis courts, but Arlene seemed at ease with what he was doing. When Rob got back into the car, Nancy was very quiet.

Ten minutes later, everyone was sitting in the Bains' living room with the curtains drawn and no lights on, completely silent. Mrs. Bain had not yet returned from picking up Mr. Bain at the airport. Nancy suddenly remembered that she had her graduation formal that night. Not surprisingly, she wasn't sure if she was in the mood for it. But she didn't have much time to decide. She'd made an appointment at the hairdresser's for 3:00 PM. When Rob offered to give her a ride, that pretty much settled it—she was going to her party.

—◦—

Mrs. Bain had waited until they'd loaded her husband's luggage into the car at the airport parking lot before she told him about Liz not coming home. As one might expect, he was full of questions, and Mrs. Bain did her best to recount everything that had happened.

Mrs. Bain had lent her car to Cathy that Monday morning and therefore had no choice but to take Liz's Toyota on her shopping run. She was on her way to a local nursery to order some limestone for the driveway but stopped on the way at a service station to fill up the car with gas; she took the attendant's advice and had him add two litres of oil while he was at it.

Around three o'clock that afternoon, the three Bain women were off to work, Liz at the day-care service, and Mrs. Bain and Cathy at Scarborough General Hospital (where her mother had helped her get a job in the kitchen). Mrs. Bain didn't get home from her shift until a few minutes before midnight. When she went up to Liz's room, the door was partly open and all her lights were off. Mrs. Bain pushed the door open and could see from the light spilling into the room from the hallway that Liz was lying on her bed. She was partly covered with a sheet, but Mrs. Bain could see that she hadn't bothered to change into her pyjamas—she was wearing a blue skirt and a white blouse. Still asleep, Liz turned over onto her side, away from the light, and her mother tiptoed over to kiss her goodnight before turning in.

Mrs. Bain had asked Cathy to stay over that night and, because her father wasn't home, she said she would. Cathy also went up to her sister's room on the way to bed and saw Liz. Liz, still in her clothes, remained fast asleep but was now turned so that she was facing the door, and Cathy noticed that she was clutching a single red rose across her chest. And there were dark, thin streaks of mascara lining her cheeks, marking the paths her tears had likely taken as she'd cried herself to sleep.

As well, Cathy said she'd gone into Liz's room at about 10:00 the next morning and had seen her sitting on the floor reading some books, still wearing the clothes she'd had on in bed the night before. Liz had seemed preoccupied with what she was reading and wasn't too interested in talking, which Cathy found somewhat unusual, considering that they hadn't seen each other for a while.

Mrs. Bain saw her that morning as well, around the same time as Cathy, she figured. She had been working with the limestone in the front yard when Liz had popped her head out of a window and said, "What are you doing, Mom? You look like a lumberjack!"

Liz was in good spirits. She was asking about her cousin flying in from Boston the next day. "Is it true that Kim broke up with her boyfriend?"

"That's what her mother told me," said Mrs. Bain.

"Why are the girls in that family always coming here when they break up with their boyfriends?" Liz was shaking her head and laughing.

A little later Liz came outside and said she was going to Scarborough College to "check some papers." Her mother asked her to pick up a jug of milk on her way home. She pulled in the driveway with the milk half an hour later.

She left again in the early afternoon, possibly between 1:00 and 2:00. She was wearing shorts and said she was going for a jog, but left in her car. Mrs. Bain assumed she was going to park at the campus and go from there. This time, she returned within an hour.

Before Liz's third and final trip of the day, she said she was leaving to check the tennis schedule. Mrs. Bain thought this might have taken place between 4:00 and 4:30 PM. Liz was wearing black cotton pants, a white blouse decorated with a bright floral pattern and black leather flats with no socks. Her hair was pinned at the back with a hair clip and she wasn't carrying any books or tennis equipment. On her way to her car, Liz told her mother that she'd be back in a couple of hours. And that, Mrs. Bain told her anxious husband, was the last time she'd seen her.

When Mr. and Mrs. Bain drove up in their cream-coloured Volvo station wagon, Rob had already returned from taking Nancy to the hairdresser's and was standing in the driveway. As soon as Mr. Bain got out of the car, he began drilling him with questions. Rob spelled out everything that had happened since he'd seen Liz's car in the valley. Mr. Bain listened carefully, thinking there had to be an explanation for all of this, one that, for whatever reason, had eluded everyone thus far. But from the look on his face, Rob could tell he was struggling for an answer and coming up empty. "Mr. Bain," he said, "there's something quite horrible that no one wants to tell you about, but I think you should see it."

Rob retrieved the final diary entry from Arlene and presented it to Mr. Bain. As he quickly read what his daughter had written less than a week before, he felt his heart sink and was completely stunned by it. He'd never read anything like it in his entire life and he could scarcely believe that his daughter could have written such things.

Rob felt that he had no choice but to tell him about Liz's attempt at cutting her wrists a month ago, and how surprised he'd been that no one in her family had noticed her bandages. Mr. Bain was incredulous—if one of his children had bandages on her wrists, he would have seen it. "Have you ever known Liz to want to commit suicide?" Rob asked.

Mr. Bain admitted that there had been an incident years ago, when Liz was in Grade 13. He'd gone up to her room to ask her to join the rest of the family for dinner, but Liz didn't want to. This response hadn't come as a surprise, given her unusual eating habits, but he sensed that something was wrong and he sat down to have a talk with her. It was during the course of that conversation that Liz told her father she'd once tried to cut her wrists.

Astonished, he tried to get her to explain why she would want to attempt such an act, but she didn't really open up very much. "Do you mind showing me your wrists?" he asked.

"This happened a year ago, Dad," she said. "There's nothing to see." And sure enough, with her dainty wrists in the palms of his hands, he could see no scars.

"Do you think you're likely to ever try this again, Elizabeth?"

She assured him that she wouldn't and they continued talking about it for some time. Despite what Liz had told him that night, Mr. Bain was never convinced that Liz had really tried to cut her wrists. To him, it was conceivable that she'd contrived the outrageous story to get attention. Kids were like that sometimes.

But now, after he'd read his daughter's disturbing final diary entry and having listened to Rob talk of this most recent attempt to harm herself, his mind was working at a fevered pitch, trying to decide whether his daughter was truly capable of this most desperate act. "Rob, why didn't you tell me about this incident before now?" asked Mr. Bain.

Although Rob didn't say it, he hadn't told Mr. Bain because he thought Liz's suicidal episode was the direct result of her father's refusal to pay her tuition for the upcoming school year. And then there was the issue of trust: surely Liz had chosen to confide in him and not her parents for her own reasons. Instead, Rob told Mr. Bain that relations between Mr. Bain and him had been strained for some time, and Rob didn't feel he could talk to him. Mr. Bain said, "I know I've been cold lately, but there are a number of innuendos surrounding your relationship with my daughter that I have difficulties with."

"Look, Mr. Bain, this is hardly the time for us to be arguing. The important thing is to find Liz."

With those words, the two men found themselves walking towards the front door, aware that their lives would never again be the same.

—◇—

Pretty soon, a small group was assembled in Liz's bedroom, looking through her present diary as well as an old book-style journal. Mr. and Mrs. Bain were there, along with Rob and Arlene Coventry. Liz's parents had known about her keeping a diary—she'd even let her father in on the fact that she addressed it to "Meg"—but, unlike her younger sister, neither of them had ever violated her privacy by sneaking into her room and reading it. In fact, Mrs. Bain was uncomfortable with people reading it even now. "This is Lisa's private diary," she said. "We shouldn't be looking at it."

Arlene and Mrs. Bain left the room, but Mr. Bain and Rob remained where they were. Mr. Bain felt that his wife's remark had not been directed at him because she was as aware as anyone that the diary, especially the last few entries, might contain valuable clues regarding their daughter's whereabouts. And Rob's presence was, in many ways, more crucial than his own. There was no disputing that, for the past year, no one had been more in tune with the intimate details of Liz's life than Rob. And so Mr. Bain removed the loose-leaf pages from the orange binder and spread them out on her bed. They each grabbed a section of pages and knelt on the floor, back to back, in different corners of the room, confronting the private obsessions, hopes and fears of a young woman they both loved and about whom, they were quickly realizing, they knew so little.

One of the first things Rob noticed was that Liz didn't keep a daily diary. On average, she wrote four or five entries a month and almost always used both sides of the pages. As he scanned section after section for anything of importance, it became apparent that the entries had somehow been mixed up so that, in places, they were no longer in chronological order.

What Rob found most troubling were entries such as the one Liz had written on May 3, 1990:

Dear Meg,

Today I went to see Betsy Watanabe, the holistic woman Dad referred me to a few years ago. Stress—such a high stress level. Why? She said I have too many repressed emotions. Don't worry about Rob—just praise him & love but don't try to change him. Just love him. All you have to do is make him feel good about himself and he will love you genuinely. Change yourself. Improve yourself. Set a loving example.

Talk about stress? I've just written my last exam—walking into the course with a 52% average. Tia Diana is out of my life because I have been cheated by her friends Sat & Arthur, who have given me nothing but a letdown. It's been murder this last week. I have poison ivy. Cathy left home after she scratched Dad's face. André, John and Eric have been calling. I am beginning to spend a lot of time with Eric. I am also beginning to fear a loss of interest in Rob.

I binged 3800 calories yesterday—Popsicles, hamburgers, cookies—and, today, fried chicken. I haven't eaten so abhorrently in years and I can't ever remember having so much gas. I took off my fake eyelashes today and can't believe how ordinary I look without them. All the ridicule in the world wouldn't stop me from wearing them. They bring out my eyes so much. I asked myself yesterday—Why? Why are you eating like this? It's some kind of emotional need. I want to break down, cry and reveal my every cell to someone but can't. I can't do it with Eric or with Rob because they suit different needs. I don't want to reveal my whole self to Eric because I'm afraid that, if I get too close to him, I'll lose my love for Rob. And Rob is so physically attractive to me, so romantic, so sensuous, so masculine—I need that. And Eric doesn't have it. But Eric makes excellent sense and I have this affinity with Eric that I've never had with anyone.

Reading about Liz's unsurpassed bond with this complete stranger, Eric, was difficult for Rob. But at least Eric was a name he'd heard Liz mention before. Who the hell were André and John? And in January she wrote about some other mystery guy named Archie. Archie? When did she meet him? Rob asked Mr. Bain if these names meant anything to him, but, apart from Eric, he was just as stumped.

Meanwhile, Mr. Bain was finding the diary no less perplexing and hurtful, especially passages such as the one towards the end of her entry for February 2, 1990:

I don't want to have any part of Dad's life after I'm married. Mom, yes. I remember all the times she saved me from the anxieties he put me through. I always thought I was the selfish, cruel, conniving, helpless, stubborn idiot he always made me out to be. I will never forget it. Nobody else has ever insulted me. Everyone except him tells me I'm kind or loving in some way. That's o.k., I don't need it. In a way it's good because it taught me to hate men, to be strong, to fend for myself, to not let anyone have enough power over me so that they can walk all over me like he does.

As disturbing and riveting as the diary was, it offered no immediate explanation for Liz's disappearance. Late in the afternoon, at about 5:30, Mr. Bain and Rob decided to drive to the valley and take a look around. They drove together in Mr. Bain's Volvo and parked in the little lot where Rob had seen Liz's car the night before. They set out to ask people in the park if they'd seen Liz or her car the previous evening; Mr. Bain began walking north towards a family having a picnic in the park, while Rob went in the opposite direction. He had also spotted a middle-aged couple at a picnic table in an opening on the other side of Old Kingston Road, directly across from where Liz's car had been.

Roger Herriott was watching the young man meandering in his direction, unsure as to whether he was going to approach him and his wife, Mary. For the most part, Rob's eyes were cast downward but when he spied a wire garbage basket off to the left, he changed course slightly and went straight for it. He looked in and then around the basket before taking a circuitous route back to Roger and his wife at the picnic table. "Excuse me," Rob said, his dishevelled hair and five-o'clock shadow giving him the appearance of someone who had just rolled out of bed. "Do you come here every day? I believe that I've seen your car parked here before."

As a matter of fact, Rob was right. Roger Herriott drove a ready-mix concrete truck from 6:00 AM to 2:00 PM and would spend the remaining hours of just about every warm afternoon he could at the same picnic table in Colonel Danforth Park, reading or relaxing, almost always listening to some music. He would park his car, a distinctive AMC Concord with a shiny two-tone paint job of brown and beige, and wait for his wife to meet him on her way home from work at IBM, so they could enjoy an hour's respite before relieving their two-year-old daughter's nanny at six. In fact, Mary had pulled up behind her husband's car at the very moment Rob and Mr. Bain were getting out of the Volvo.

Rob asked if they had seen anything out of the ordinary the day before. He told them how his girlfriend, whom he described, had gone missing and that her car had last been seen just across the road. When Mary asked, Rob assured her that the police had been contacted and that no one yet suspected foul play. They were more concerned about suicide. Rob said that he and his girlfriend's father, the older gentleman on the other side of the road, had read her diary. "She is upset about some personal things that really shouldn't be bothering her," he said.

"Did your girlfriend ever wear barrettes in her hair?" Roger asked.

Rob said, "Sometimes. Why?"

" I found a blue barrette in the grass walking here from the car a couple of hours ago and I saved it, thinking I might clean it up and give it to my little girl."

"Could I see it?" Rob asked.

"Sure." Roger reached for his gym bag. He brought out a barrette shaped like a bow tie, about two inches in length. Rob didn't think it was the type of thing Liz would wear, but he asked the man if he could keep it in order to check with Liz's mother. Roger said that was fine, and Rob put the barrette in his pocket. Then, in case the Herriotts heard or saw anything that might help, Rob gave them Mr. Bain's name and telephone number, which Roger wrote down on the back of an envelope.

Mr. Bain was still wandering around in the park on the north side of the road when Rob met up with him. Rob handed him the barrette, and Mr. Bain said, "I don't think it's important." Neither did Rob, and they walked back to the car.

At Rob's suggestion, they drove to Morningside Park, which borders Colonel Danforth Park at its widest point beneath the Morningside Bridge, just a short distance west of the Scarborough campus. Morningside Park was yet another place he and Liz liked to go. As they pulled into the westernmost lot in the park, they saw a police car sitting there, and Mr. Bain got out to ask the officer if he'd seen any sign of his missing daughter. Once the constable realized who he was speaking to, he told Mr. Bain that there was a sergeant en route to his house to follow up on the missing-person report.

Sergeant Paul Martin was sitting in his police car, which he'd parked on Scarboro Avenue in front of the Bain home, talking to Cathy Bain and her young cousin, Kim, when Mr. Bain turned into his driveway. Mr. Bain quickly got out of his car and led Sergeant Martin into the house where, once again, everyone gathered around the living-room table. Rob reiterated everything that had happened the night before, and then Mr. Bain presented Martin with the final diary entry. Mrs. Bain also mentioned that she'd just spoken to one of Liz's friends, Laura Pallone, who, earlier that day, had received a letter Liz had mailed on Monday. After Martin had read the entry, Rob pointed out that Liz had dated it incorrectly and that it had been written on June 15—not June 16. Mr. Bain said that the kinds of emotions Liz had expressed on that page were so foreign to him that he couldn't be entirely sure that she had, in fact, written it—a painful truth that everyone else had already accepted.

Just as Stinson had done that morning, Martin asked Rob to name some locations where Liz might have gone on her own. Rob named the same set of beaches but, this time, added the Oakes Inn, where he and Liz had stayed during their trip to Niagara Falls, as well as Wasaga Beach. Mr. Bain mentioned a couple of provincial parks where he had taken his kids camping years ago, but Rob didn't think she would go to a wooded area because, lately, she'd been acting a bit frightened during their walks in the local parks after dark—even with him at her side.

After asking Mr. Bain if it was all right, Rob told Martin about the two times— at least the two that they knew about—that Liz had attempted to slit her wrists. Mr. and Mrs. Bain couldn't believe that they wouldn't have noticed the bandages on Liz's wrists after the most recent incident a month ago. Mrs. Bain was becoming visibly distraught. "Why didn't you tell us about this?" she asked Rob. "We could have helped her. I'm a registered nurse."

"I thought that, if I did, it might make things worse," Rob said. "For the last ten years, my mother has been saying she was going to kill herself and she never has, so I guess I thought it was all talk. My mother is actually a very functional human being."

Martin altered the course of the conversation by asking if Liz had taken any identification with her when she'd last left home. To the family's surprise, they'd found Liz's wallet in her room earlier in the day. Normally, she wouldn't leave home without it, especially if she was driving. In addition to the wallet, Martin was also shown the bank book for Liz's account with the Canadian Imperial Bank of Commerce, as well as a withdrawal slip issued from an automated banking machine at the CIBC's branch at the nearby Morningside Mall. According to the slip, Liz had withdrawn $80 at exactly 3:45 PM. This would turn out to be an interesting find for a number of reasons, the first of which was that it contradicted the times Mrs. Bain had given regarding Liz's comings and goings that afternoon (presuming the bank machine's clock was accurate). She'd said that Liz had been home from 3:00 PM to 4:00 PM and had driven off to check the tennis schedules some time before 4:30 PM.

Martin asked for an accurate description of Liz's car. As he jotted down the particulars, Liz's brothers, Paul and Mark, arrived home one after the other. Martin thought that young Paul looked astonished to see a uniformed police officer in his house, and the boy, quiet and subdued, said very little. Mark was the polar opposite, storming into the room in a state of animated distress, asking one question after another in rapid-fire succession without giving Martin a chance to reply.

About two hours after he'd arrived, Martin felt that he'd gathered just about all of the information he could and he was off to notify various police forces from Wasaga Beach to Niagara Falls to check the locations that had been mentioned to him by Rob. As he was leaving, Mr. Bain asked Martin if he suspected foul play. "Based on everything I've heard and know," said the eighteen-year police-force veteran, "there is no indication of foul play at this time." Although he didn't say it, what Martin was really thinking was that this case had all the markings of one profoundly tragic outcome: suicide.

—◦—

As darkness reluctantly blanketed the city on one of the longest days of the year, Rob drove home, engrossed in deep thought. Was Liz really the type of person who would commit suicide? If she hadn't been able to carry it through before, did it seem likely that she could do so now? Even after Sergeant Martin had left, Mr. and Mrs. Bain continued to grill Rob about his reasons for not telling them about Liz's latest attempt at hurting herself. Rob had responded by reminding Mrs. Bain of the night he'd shown her the roach clip he'd found in the basement, and that, even after telling her that it belonged to Cathy, all she'd done was laugh at him. In her own defence, Mrs. Bain said she'd thought that he'd just been kidding around (the same way Mr. Bain had long ago concluded that Liz had been fibbing about cutting her wrists in high school, Rob was tempted to say). Liz's problems were obviously more serious than anyone had imagined. Now that Rob and Mr. Bain had read about Liz's penchant for daily enemas, laxatives and food binges, it was quite obvious that Liz had managed to conceal a chronic eating disorder from everyone who loved her for quite a long time, perhaps even years. Again, Mr. Bain wasn't convinced that this behaviour was abnormal: "I thought all girls were like that," Rob had heard him say.

Before leaving the Bains', Rob had asked Mr. Bain if he could take the pages from Liz's diary home to read. From Rob's perspective, Liz's parents hadn't yet placed much importance on the diary, nor had they come close to accepting the possibility that she might have had plans to do away with herself. Not only did Rob feel that he knew Liz better than anyone else, he believed that, with his background in psychology, he was likely the best candidate to pick up on any indication, direct or implied, that might exist in her diary as to her whereabouts. When he went up to Liz's room to retrieve the diary, its loose-leaf pages, which had been strewn across her bed rather haphazardly, were now tucked neatly into a file folder.

At home, Rob sat down at the kitchen table and began leafing through the diary pages. The first thing he looked for were the most recent entries. What he discovered, however, was that, apart from the final entry, there weren't any. The closest entries to it were from early May. Even though it was unusual for Liz to go an entire month without writing in her diary, the gap made perfect sense. The entry on the flip side of what was really a June 15 entry had been written exactly a month earlier, on May 15.

Rob started with May and began skimming back in time. If Liz's mood swings had caused him inexplicable heartbreak over the past year, the experience of taking in the secret torments of her darkest days, laid out in the most uninhibited, soulbearing way imaginable, was infinitely more hurtful. It seemed that one-half of the diary was about bingeing, enemas, laxatives, suicide and Liz trying to muster enough courage to break up with him, and the other half was about how wonderful he was, such a catch that she wanted to marry him and bear two children with his name. And she alternated between the two extremes with mind-boggling regularity. Her last entry in April ended with her writing about how "phenomenal" it felt to be imagining the two of them raising a family together. *Experiencing this with Rob,* she wrote, *is the reason for life itself. I was born to love this guy.*

And then, just a couple of weeks later, on May 10, she concluded with this:

Break up with Rob because he will never be able to give you the things you need. You will always be giving, surrendering, the one enduring the anxiety, feeling ripped off, feeling like what you have to say is irrelevant. The little voice inside of me says leave him because he doesn't deserve your sacrifices and will never truly appreciate you. The voice within me says the root of your anxiety is linked to Rob. He isn't someone you will grow, enrich yourself or be fulfilled with. He is taking but he is not giving anything back.

If you could just accept that you're no longer a virgin and that you made a mistake sleeping with him, if you could forgive yourself, you'd leave him. But as long as you can't, you're trapped.

In a nutshell, it was the same set of incongruous feelings she'd displayed in the two final diary entries that Arlene had handed him early that morning. On one side of the page, she'd written about how great their trip to Niagara Falls had been, begging God not to let him leave her, and, on the other side, she wanted to put a bullet through his head. And then there were the guys she was secretly meeting with, corresponding with—pining over—proclaiming love for him all the while. Riding the emotional roller coaster of these unbridled confessions was like having your heart ripped out of your chest and placed on the table in front of you.

Rob called when I walked with Eric yesterday. I lied to him later, saying that I went to see Laura. I couldn't leave Eric in the sadness he was in. He needed a friend to listen to his worries and anxieties. But Rob would never understand that in such a way that he wouldn't be hurt by it. Would he? He sounded so upset on the phone as it was; I couldn't add to it. Sometimes I feel like leaving Rob for Eric because Eric needs me more. He's so funny and always cheers me up. Eric is also much more open-minded. Rob is so judgmental. I hate that.

*   *   *

I got a postcard from Mark Fielden again. He said if I don't write him soon he will lock himself in his room & cry his eyes out. He said that he is trying to pick up the pieces of his pathetic life & go on aimlessly. That stupid card made me cry and binge and write him and take laxatives, something I haven't done in ages.

*   *   *

Archie. Archie. Archie. Why can't I stop thinking about Archie?

*   *   *

I thought you were going to be strong and single all your life. What about Archie? What about that independence? You can do better. Why restrict yourself? Don't do it—then I think "I can't leave him, I've slept with him, he knows everything about me." So what? We all make mistakes.

*   *   *

I wrote Mark Fielden a little letter in reply to his. I don't feel obligated to him, it's just that I remember him calling himself a jerk. He's great, a great man, but I am in love. As usual, Eric Genuis calls out of the blue and doesn't return my call when he says he will. That guy may have the bucks but he will never get anyone who respects him.

*   *   *

Poor Eric. He came over to Kidbrooke, and I knew he wanted me back. I thought very briefly about leaving Rob for him. Then I said to myself, "Are you out of your mind?" No way. I really love Rob but I can't understand why. It's totally unexplainable. I just know that I have to really start preparing myself for a life with him.

Liz had led him to believe that her platonic relationship with Eric involved nothing more than the occasional chat over the phone. She hadn't mentioned anything about the guy dropping in on her at work to woo her back into his life! Rob picked up the phone and dialled Eric Genuis's number, which he'd copied from Liz's address book that afternoon. Originally, Rob had simply wanted to ask Eric if he'd had any contact with Liz during the past few days. But now he had additional motives to call—anger and, to a lesser degree, a nagging suspicion that Eric might have something to do with all of this.

When Rob got Eric on the line, he was in no mood for small talk. He got straight to the point. "Hello, Eric," he said. "My name is Robert Baltovich, Elizabeth Bain's boyfriend. I'm calling for several reasons, the first being that I know you've been seeing Liz, so don't deny it."

It took Eric a few seconds to respond. The only thing that had in any way prepared him for this blunt accusation was his telephone conversation with Liz's father earlier that day. Mr. Bain had called to inquire if Eric had seen his daughter last night because she hadn't come home. Eric was sorry to say that he hadn't seen her for about a month. They had a fairly long conversation, and Eric had been wondering about Liz ever since, but he never could have predicted that her boyfriend would be calling him at home to ask such a preposterous question.

"There is nothing to deny," Eric told him. "I wasn't trying to hide anything. Liz always told me that you were aware of our friendship."

"I knew that the two of you would speak on the phone once in a while," Rob said. "But I had no idea you were visiting with her, trying to win her back."

"Well, yes, I would get together with her but I wasn't trying to get her back. We were just good friends. That's all. She always made it clear that you had no problem with that. I didn't want her keeping it a secret from you."

"Eric, let me read to you what Liz wrote in her diary on January fourteenth—"

"You have her diary?"

"I borrowed it to see if she'd written anything that might help us find her."

Rob read Eric the passage about him visiting her at Kidbrooke and wanting her back. "So, Eric, what's she talking about there?" His tone was snide.

"Well, okay," Eric said. He was going to have to back-pedal a little. "When I broached the subject of dating again that day, I had no idea that she was seeing anyone. The second she said she had a boyfriend, it was completely out of the question."

As their conversation continued, Rob became convinced that Eric was telling the truth and he apologized for the misunderstanding. Yet while Eric claimed that Liz had purported to be open with Rob about the nature of their friendship, he must have had some doubt about whether she had informed her boyfriend of their sporadic get-togethers. After all, Eric knew that Liz wasn't crazy about talking to him over the phone when Rob was within earshot. Even as recently as a week ago, Eric had called her one evening, and Liz's greeting was abnormally curt. Eric sensed what was wrong. "Is Rob there?"

"Yes," she had said.

"Okay, I'll hang up and talk to you later."

Liz returned his call soon afterwards. Rob was still there, she said, but he was down in the basement watching a movie. She'd come upstairs to call him back in private. The conversation lasted for no more than a minute—she just wanted to explain why she'd been so short earlier.

Liz and Eric had now known each other for almost four years, having first met at the University of Toronto's downtown campus in the fall of 1986. It was her first year at university—his second—and she'd just enrolled in the physical education program. They became friends that year and remained so even when Liz transferred to the Scarborough campus the following September. Like Liz, Eric lived in Scarborough and was a member of the Catholic Church. In fact, he'd been the choir director and organist at the St. Thomas More Church on Ellesmere Road for about as long as he'd known her.

Then, in the fall of 1988, after two years, their friendship suddenly blossomed into something a little more serious. But before they could grow comfortable with their new feelings, Liz broke things off after just a month. Eric hadn't seen it coming. He would never forget his consternation as she attempted to explain why she no longer wished to be his girlfriend. "You treat me too well," she said. *You treat me too well?* What did that mean? How else was he supposed to treat her? Like he couldn't care less? Liz could tell from his reaction that she'd upset him terribly, and now she was in tears. "You don't deserve this," she sobbed. "I'm sorry, really sorry." In an instant, the tables had turned, and Eric was now comforting the girl who'd just drawn the curtain on him.

These memories had flooded back to him when he spoke to Mr. Bain during his lunch break at the Lever Brothers soap factory on Lakeshore Boulevard East, where Toronto's Don Valley Parkway ends at the southern edge of the city. By chance, Eric had phoned home only to have his father urge him to call Mr. Bain right away. As he answered Mr. Bain's queries, Eric was pondering a moral dilemma. During his last visit with Liz, she had made a harrowing confession, something so personal that, surely, she wouldn't want him discussing it with her father. But Eric perceived that he *must* tell him—this was no time to worry about betraying the confidence of a friend.

Mr. Bain listened intently as Eric related the details of that Sunday in May—it was either May 19 or May 26—when he and Liz had arranged to go for a walk after church. They met at the Scarborough campus, near the tennis courts. Their conversation got off to a rocky start when Liz turned to him and lifted her wrists, exposing thin, horizontal scabs. They were comparable to a series of paper cuts because, as far as he could tell, she hadn't really broken the skin. They looked like the same type of wounds Liz had once described inflicting on herself back in high school, before they'd met. "Look, Eric," she said, breaking out in tears. "I've tried it again."

As soon as he was able to calm her down, they began their walk through Colonel Danforth Park. Liz vented a litany of problems. She went on about where she was going with school. What was she going to do with a degree in psychology? In addition to that, her family hadn't been providing her with much solace lately—tensions had reached the boiling point, especially since Cathy had moved out. And, finally, things hadn't been going very well with Rob. She claimed that he had friends spying on her in class. Things had degenerated to the point that she'd stopped having sex with the man she'd given her virginity to. She said she was contemplating putting an end to the whole relationship, once and for all. (This confession is at odds with her trip with Rob to the Lido Motel ten days before she disappeared; a receipt in Rob's name is on file.)

Eric also told Mr. Bain that he'd talked to Liz just two days earlier, on Monday, but over the phone. He'd called her during the day from the soap factory to ask if she'd do him a favour. Eric was breaking into the teaching profession and had been offered a job teaching a summer course at a Scarborough high school called Bendale. Until then, though, he was loading bars of soap into boxes every weekday from 6:30 AM until 7:00 PM. He asked Liz if she would mind going to the school to pick up the textbook he needed to prepare his lessons.

Liz said she would do it for him, but didn't have time to go that day. She asked where the school was, but Eric didn't know. He said he would find out and call her back, which he finally got around to doing the following night, Tuesday. Eric imagined that, being the thoughtful person she was, Liz might well have taken the time to locate Bendale on her own and had already picked up his book by now. He called her at home shortly after 8:00 PM—when, unbeknownst to him, she was supposed to be at her night class—but the phone was busy. Eric went down to the beach to play some volleyball, and when it got dark he returned home and tried the Bains' number again, but he was still getting the busy signal. By now, it was 10:00 PM and Eric wasn't going to call her house much later than that. He would just have to try her again tomorrow.

What he hadn't been able to figure out was why he kept getting a busy signal at Liz's house. The Bains had "call waiting," a service that picks up incoming phone calls even when someone is already on the line. Eric asked Mr. Bain if he still had call waiting.

"As a matter of fact, we do," said Mr. Bain. "But it's funny you say that because I heard the same thing happened to someone else. You see, I just learned that my son Paul bought a cordless phone for his bedroom and, apparently, if you have more than one cordless phone connected to a phone line, the intermittent waves can knock out your line altogether. Anyone who called would have got a busy signal. I'm almost positive that's what happened."

And now, hours after his conversation with Mr. Bain, Eric could hear Rob Baltovich on the other end of the phone flipping through the loose pages of Liz's diary. "Do you know who Archie is?" Rob asked.

"No," said Eric. "Liz never mentioned anyone named Archie. What does it say about him?"

Rob read the Archie passages to him. "Geez," Eric said. He didn't know what else to say.

"What about John and André? Do those names ring a bell?"

"John and André?" Eric hadn't heard of them either. Rob read a few more excerpts from the diary. "Is there anything else?" Eric asked. He sounded quite interested in hearing more from the diary, but Rob wanted to get off the phone. "Would you mind if I called you tomorrow night?" Eric asked. No problem, Rob said.

Rob was exhausted. It had been one of those adrenaline-charged days that would shoot across his memory like a red-hot comet for the rest of his life. As he reflected on it, he was overcome by the sad irony that, on a day Liz was nowhere to be found, he'd discovered there was a whole side of her that she'd kept bottled up, secret from him. He sat up late with his mother, trying to make sense of it all. Did Liz really have it within her to take her own life? Rob and his mother both knew that this question was, for now, unanswerable, and, watching Rob stagger off wearily to bed, Adele had an anxious feeling that she was in for her second sleepless night in a row.

The next day, Mrs. Bain and Rob drove across Scarborough together to talk to Archie. Mr. and Mrs. Bain had no idea who John and André were, but Archie was a different story. His full name was Archie Allison and he was a young man, about Rob's age, who worked as a physical education instructor at Variety Village, a sports complex that had integrated facilities for disabled youth. Liz was a member at Variety Village, but it had been a couple of years earlier that she used to work out there several times a week. That was when Mrs. Bain had first heard her mention Archie's name.

Liz had quite a crush on Archie. In 1988, she'd sent him several letters and poems at work and had a bouquet of flowers delivered at Christmas. Archie sat her down for a nice little talk after that and explained that, while he was flattered by the attention, he was already involved with someone else. He'd always found Liz to be extremely shy, and he was trying to let her down as easily as he could. They could still be friends, he said, and Liz nervously said she would like that. Archie received his last letter from her on July 26, 1989, a couple of weeks after Liz had told Mark Fielden that she could no longer see him because of her feelings for Rob.

Mrs. Bain could tell by the way Rob was talking in the car that he'd been hurt by some of the things Liz had written in her diary. He just came right out and said that things between him and Liz wouldn't be the same when she came back. As far as he was concerned, the relationship was over. "Why do you say that?" asked Mrs. Bain.

"All along," Rob said, "I thought that Elizabeth and I shared the same feelings for each other. But according to her diary, that wasn't the case."

Mrs. Bain was perturbed by this talk of breaking up with Liz. Wasn't it a little premature? They needed to find her first. Nevertheless, she sympathized with his pain. "I know she didn't mean those things, Rob. We all have our other selves," she said. "I've wanted to leave Mr. Bain many times, but I'm still here. In the same way, Liz told me she loved you, and I'm sure she does."

When they got to Variety Village, they were told Archie wasn't in that day.

On the way home, Rob asked Mrs. Bain if she would like to meet his mother. Although Rob and Liz had been dating for a year, the two women had yet to be introduced, so Mrs. Bain agreed. Anything to take her mind off Liz.

Adele was a little surprised by the unexpected visit. She invited Mrs. Bain to sit at the kitchen table for a quick snack and expressed her sincerest hope that Liz would come home soon, very soon. Out of the corner of her eye, Mrs. Bain saw one of Liz's diary entries lying on the surface of the table. "What's this doing here?" she asked Rob.

With a puzzled look, Rob said he wasn't sure. Earlier in the day, he'd returned the folder he'd borrowed the night before to Cathy, containing what he'd thought were all the diary entries. Before going to bed, he'd been thumbing through different sections of the diary in different parts of the house, and he assumed that his mother had moved some of the pages without telling him. "My mother has this habit of moving things and not putting them back," Rob said. His mother offered an apologetic smile.

They talked about the diary for a little while, but the topic just got Mrs. Bain agitated. "If I couldn't find something better to do than write such garbage," she said, "I'd feel pretty bad about myself."

Mrs. Bain didn't stay for more than a few minutes before she and Rob were on their way again. As they were getting out of the car in the Bains' driveway, she said, "When Liz comes back, I don't think we should tell her that we looked in her diary."

Mr. Bain had already taken him to task for telling people that Liz was suicidal. He had also emphasized how important it was to keep things quiet. Rob disagreed. He had the distinct impression that this was about protecting the family more than anything else and it just made him angry. "Mrs. Bain, it's about time we all realized that Liz needs help. If we tell her that we've read her diary, then she won't be able to deny it any more."

"You're right, Rob," she said. "I'm convinced." He hadn't thought it would be that easy.

—◦—

That same afternoon, a group of people went back down into the valley to look around. Rob and Mr. Bain were joined by Paul and Cathy and her boyfriend, Steve Annett, along with Cathy's good friend Tina and her boyfriend, Peter. Walking towards the tennis courts, Rob found an ivory-coloured hair comb, which he handed to Cathy. "Liz wouldn't wear something like this, would she?" he asked.

"No," Cathy said. "She wouldn't."

"I didn't think so."

Rob and Paul branched off alone, going beyond the tennis courts to the trail that led to the campus. Rob showed Paul where he and Liz had carved their initials into the banister of the bridge east of the tennis courts. As they hooked up with everyone else, Rob overheard Cathy telling her father about how Liz had met a guy named André while jogging in the valley one day. Apparently, this André often rode his bicycle there and, for some reason, Cathy thought Liz had said he might be into drugs. Rob asked if Cathy had heard anything else about him, but apparently that was all Liz had said.

Once again, they left the valley as mystified as they'd been when they arrived, and the search party returned home. It seemed as though there was nothing to do but wait; everyone sat around the house talking. Kim, the cousin visiting from Boston, started in on the story of the boy she'd just broken up with back home. Rob could handle only so much of this idle chit-chat—he had to get up off his ass and do something.

Having already inquired about Liz at the Oakes Inn in Niagara Falls earlier that day, he drove by himself to the Lido Motel. Rob asked the desk manager if he recognized him, and the man said he did. Rob asked if he remembered what his girl-friend looked like. The man nodded. "Do you remember seeing her here any time on Tuesday night?" The manager said he was pretty sure he hadn't. Rob was hoping that he'd offer to check his records, but he didn't, so Rob thanked him and left.

From there, Rob went to the Recreation Centre and spoke to Rick Gostick. Rick had an idea. There were at least four hundred people coming in to play volleyball that night and Rick thought it couldn't hurt to type up a brief description of Liz and her car on the computer. He would make enough printouts to go around. Rob helped him with the particulars, then went to the campus police station and filled them in on Liz's disappearance.

He left in time to make it to Liz's abnormal child psychology class before it started. Standing in the doorway of classroom H-214, Rob saw Kristine Kangas in the front row; she'd been in a few of his classes in the past. "Kris, can I speak to you?" She nodded her head and followed him out into the hallway. "Hey, Rob," she said. "What's going on?"

"I was wondering if you've seen Liz at all lately."

"Why?"

"Because she's missing." Rob paused and, thinking back to what Mr. Bain had said about keeping things quiet, added, "But don't tell anybody because her parents don't want anyone to know."

Kris didn't say anything, but she couldn't figure out why someone would want to keep quiet about someone who was missing. "I'm pretty sure I saw her in the library before our class on Tuesday," she said.

"What time?" Rob asked.

"Around 5:00, maybe 5:30."

"Yeah? What was she wearing?"

"Black pants and a purple T-shirt."

"That's strange," he said. "Liz's mother said she was wearing a floral blouse on Tuesday. Did you happen to go to the library on Monday too?"

"Yes. I've been working like mad to get this project done for tonight."

"Maybe you're confusing Tuesday with Monday."

"I don't know, Rob. I've been under so much pressure to get this project done. I thought it was Tuesday that I saw her but maybe it wasn't. I'm not sure."

"Well, if you remember later on, please give me a call at home by 11:30 and let me know."

"Okay."

"I was just wondering," he said. "If Liz hands her project in a week late, do you think she can still pass the course?"

"I'm not sure."

"How did Liz seem when you saw her in the library?"

"Fine," Kris said.

He thanked her and headed straight for the library. On the way, it occurred to him that, if Liz had been in the library on Tuesday, she more than likely hadn't had her student cards with her because, as he now knew, she'd left her wallet in her room. And without her student card, she wouldn't have been able to sign out any books. He remembered that he'd once shown her how to use the library's CD-ROMS to access material directly related to psychology or sociology or any other subject she was interested in. And he knew that some librarians would let you use the CD-ROMS without a card. Maybe that's what Liz was doing in the library, he thought.

Rob asked one of the librarians, a woman in her mid-fifties, if the library would still have a list of those people who had signed up to use the CD-ROMS on Tuesday afternoon. She asked why he needed that information, and Rob told her that his girlfriend had gone missing. "We don't release this kind of information as a rule," the librarian said.

"Would it help if I asked one of the campus police to request the information?"

"Yes, that would be all right. You should probably speak to the librarian who was on duty that afternoon." She gave Rob her colleague's work number.

Rob decided not to bother going to the campus police right away. Instead, he headed back to the Bains', where he found Cathy wearing, of all things, a purple T-shirt. He couldn't believe it. He told her about Kris Kangas and then asked Cathy if the shirt belonged to her or Liz. Cathy said it was Liz's—she'd just borrowed it from her room. Rob was now positive that Kris Kangas had seen Liz in the library wearing her purple T-shirt but not on Tuesday.

It wasn't too long before Mrs. Bain gathered everyone around and announced that it was a good time for them to help her finish off the job of moving the patio stones. Rob didn't show it, but his frustration had hit a new peak. He was unable to comprehend how Mrs. Bain could be worried about the patio stones when her daughter was God knew where. But there was no point in getting into it, so he just helped finish the job. When the stones were finally all in place, everyone went inside and Mrs. Bain disappeared out back to light the barbecue for dinner. That's when Rob got the message that a Detective McKennitt had called, wondering if Rob could come down to 42 Division as soon as possible. Rob told the Bains he would be on his way once he'd had something to eat.

—◯—

Not long after Detective Richard McKennitt and his partner, Detective Austin May, had shown up for the afternoon shift at 42 Division, word filtered down that they would be working a detail on a missing-person case. They were to interview a missing girl's boyfriend, Robert Baltovich. The detectives knew next to nothing about the case, but it was pretty straightforward police work. When it came to missing women, the husband or boyfriend was usually the best place to start.

McKennitt left messages with Baltovich's mother as well as with the missing girl's family, but Baltovich hadn't called back. He just showed up unannounced at the front counter of the station a few minutes before 10:00 PM. The detectives walked him to one of the small interview rooms just off the main hallway. Rob's hands were still dirty from moving the patio stones, as were his running shoes. The detectives also noticed that he had a day or two's worth of stubble. Rob didn't bother explaining that shaving hadn't been one of his top priorities for the past forty-eight hours.

They started off with the basics: name, date of birth, address, occupation and so on. Then they moved on to how he and Liz had met. Calmly, Rob just started talking, sometimes looking a bit restless as he moved around in his chair or tightened his arms, and he just kept going. May and McKennitt had to slow him down once in a while so they could write everything down. They took turns transcribing so their hands wouldn't cramp.

Rob narrated the history of their relationship in two hours and fifty minutes. The detectives asked just a handful of questions the entire time. Towards the end of the interview, though, Rob began to fade. A few times, he began to doze off mid-sentence, suddenly jolting himself awake before carrying on. At the very end, Rob said that, in the last two days, he'd found out that Liz had been corresponding with and seeing other guys. He mentioned his conversation with Eric Genuis and suggested that, because Eric had known Liz longer than he had, he might be able to provide them with more information about her long-term mental state. When it came to her psychological make-up, Rob said he wasn't sure any more. So much had been kept from him. While reading bits of her diary in her room, he'd taken a look at the calendar tacked to her wall. Liz had written the word "FAST" on each day for that week, as if she'd been engaged in some self-imposed hunger strike. "She is quite capable of spending days in one place without moving," Rob said. "She could very well be hidden."

Those were the last words the detectives wrote down. Twice, they asked Rob if he would like to read over his statement, but it was almost one o'clock in the morning and he said he was too tired. It seemed as though they'd been carefully writing everything down and Rob was content to sign the last page, as instructed, and call it a night.

—◯—

While Rob was with McKennitt and May at 42 Division on Thursday night, Cathy Bain went up to her sister's room to take another look at the diary. The first thing she noticed as she laid eyes on the orange binder was that it was nowhere near as full as she remembered when she'd found it the day before. Then, it had been so stuffed with paper that the front and back covers of the binder were parallel. Now it was sloped shut on a definite angle.

Cathy asked her father if he'd removed sections from the diary since Rob had returned it that morning, but he said he hadn't. Perhaps Rob had kept some of it, said Mr. Bain. He decided to call Rob at home and ask, but his mother said that he was out, so he just left a message for Rob to call about some pages missing from Liz's diary.

Having not gone to bed until close to 2:00 AM, Rob woke up a little later than usual the next morning. By the time he stumbled upstairs to rustle up some break-fast, it was mid-morning. He was cleaning up after his usual morning meal when the phone rang. It was a police officer calling on behalf of Detective Sergeant Tony Warr. The message was this: the detective sergeant wanted to know if Rob could meet him back at 42 Division at 1:30 in the afternoon. Okay, Rob said.

Down at the station, Warr laid eyes on Robert Baltovich for the first time. It was the third consecutive morning that Rob hadn't bothered to shave, and Warr thought the kid looked like he was in pretty rough shape. He was wearing a loose-fitting, horizontally striped sweater and a pair of jeans.

Warr had racked up about as many years as you could on the police force. He'd been a cop for twenty-two years, the last nine of which had been spent on the Homicide Squad before he retired in 1987. Dealing with the darkest aspects of human existence got to just about all cops at one point or another, and it was Warr's time for a change of scene so he had landed a job with the Fire Marshal's office. But it didn't take long for him to start missing police work, and he returned to the force via 42 Division in February of 1990. After four months at 42 Division, this was the first day of his new assignment with its Criminal Investigation Bureau office, and he'd come into work early, at 6:40 AM, almost an hour and a half before his shift started. Detective Sergeant Mike Boyd, who was in charge of the CIB office, turned the Elizabeth Bain file over to him.

Despite a careful reading of the reports filed by Constable Stinson, as well as Detectives McKennitt and May, Warr still had no clear idea about what might have happened to this girl. Could be suicide. Could be foul play. Too close to call. All he knew was that three days had gone by since her disappearance, and, according to the force's procedures regarding missing persons, it was time to step up the inves-tigation to Phase Three. This phase involved an all-out search, including full police search teams, canine tracking units and, with the help of a media blitz, a good num-ber of civilian volunteers.

But first he wanted to speak to Baltovich, the boyfriend. Accompanied in the interview room by a detective constable named Ken Norton, Warr said that he wanted Rob to tell him everything he'd done from the moment he'd woken up on the Tuesday of Elizabeth's disappearance to the time he went to bed. And he meant everything. Warr even wanted to know what he'd had for breakfast. As requested, Rob started at the beginning: *On Tuesday, June 19, 1990, I awoke at 9:20 AM. I get up at the same time every morning. I always get up when my dad is putting his coat on, getting ready for work. I know then that the kitchen is clear. I threw on a pair of pants and a loose T-shirt. I probably put it on inside out too. Walked upstairs and began to prepare breakfast—Shredded Wheat and a piece of toast, apple juice and an egg and an orange. Went into the living room and watched "The Brady Bunch"....*

Without interruption, Rob described the rest of the day in fifty minutes. Like McKennitt and May, Warr also found Rob a touch restless, not that he was bouncing around in his seat or anything; it just appeared as though it disturbed him to talk about it. Warr had Rob read over his statement and sign each page before he asked if Rob still had the note he'd left in Liz's car on Tuesday evening, only to return and remove it. Rob said that, as far as he could remember, he'd thrown it in the back seat and that's where it stayed. Warr asked if he would mind taking Detective Constable Norton out to his car so that they could take a look at it.

Norton followed Rob out to his car in the parking lot. Rob was yakking away and Norton would later note that he'd said something about not being able to drive Liz's car because he'd never learned how to operate a standard transmission. He also said something to the effect that, if Liz had been contemplating suicide, she likely would have changed her mind. When they finally got to Rob's Cordoba, Norton saw that the back seat was cluttered with all kinds of stuff: a yellow raincoat, a pair of rubber boots (his mother had insisted he take his cousin's boots and a raincoat if he was going to be searching in the park), a tennis racquet, a can of balls, a screwdriver, transaction records and all kinds of scrap paper. Norton watched as Rob rummaged through it all until, finally, he emerged with a blank parking receipt, saying that the note had been written on the back of a receipt just like it. After a few more minutes of watching Rob tear his back seat apart, Norton told him not to worry about it and, while Rob carried on his search for the elusive note, he went back into the station.

—◯—

Paul Bain hadn't been able to cure the ills that had visited his old jalopy lately—she'd been running a little rough. In spite of the fact that the entire family, including himself, was consumed with worry over Liz, he decided to take the old beast over to his mechanic. It was a little before 2:00 PM as he drove south towards Old Kingston Road, where he turned right and then, a few seconds later, took a short cut south to the intersection at which Kingston Road meets Military Trail and Morrish Road, a less-used thoroughfare shooting straight north between the two. As he neared the intersection, his brother's girlfriend, Nancy Sicchia, came into his view, jogging straight for him on Kingston Road. He waved her down and pulled up close to the curb and asked where she was headed. "To your place," she said, catching her breath.

"There's not much farther to go," Paul said. "Do you want a ride?"

Nancy said that would be great and hopped in. Paul put the car into gear and turned north onto Morrish Road. Then, just a few yards later, as he was beginning to pick up speed, he slammed on the brakes. "No way," he said, cranking his head to the left. "That can't be." He shifted into reverse and backed up so that Nancy could see what he was talking about. It was Liz's little Tercel, with its rear bumper up against a dilapidated snow fence about fifteen feet off the road. With a vacant parcel of land behind it, the tiny silver car was sandwiched in a row of banged-up vehicles, which made sense considering that the Three R Auto Body Shop was directly across the street.

Nancy bolted out of the car and ran to the Tercel. There was no one inside and all the windows were completely shut. She tried lifting the driver's door handle but it was locked. The passenger door was locked too. Peering in through the windows, Nancy could see that the passenger seat was fully reclined, almost touching the back seat. There were dry, crumpled leaves in the back seat along with a yellow parking ticket. "Nancy!" Paul said, still in the car. "Stay back!"

As much as she wanted to, Nancy couldn't pull herself away. Then, she noticed the parking ticket had her address on it (she couldn't think of why this would be). All of a sudden, she felt like running. Sprinting all the way to the Bains'. Paul watched as she turned and shot up the road like a frightened deer. He could hear the sand and stones crunching under her feet as her arms and legs pumped furiously. He stepped on the gas and caught up to her. "Get in the car!" Paul was screaming at her through his open window. "I'll take you there." Nancy finally came to and ran around to the other side of the car and got in. Screeching to a halt in front of the house, Nancy told Paul to stay put—she would get his mom and dad.

Inside, she found Mr. and Mrs. Bain sitting in the dining room with their priest, Father Gerry Scott. "Mr. Bain," she said, bursting into the room. "Come quickly. We found the car." Everyone leapt out of their seats, and Mr. Bain almost fell as he tripped on a chair racing out of the room. Nancy followed him out to the driveway, and Father Scott was right behind her. When Mr. Bain got to the car, he turned to Nancy and asked her to stay behind with Mrs. Bain, who didn't want to leave the house in case Liz called—someone had to mind the telephone. "She's probably pretty worried," said Mr. Bain. "I'd really appreciate it." Nancy agreed to stay. Her only concern was how she would get home later. "That's no problem," said Father Scott. "I'll give you a lift." And within seconds, the young girl and the priest were standing alone in front of the house, listening to the fading pitch of the engine as the car accelerated down Scarboro Avenue.

—◦—

As Ken Norton made his way back into 42 Division from the parking lot, Tony Warr walked up to him and said, "They found the car. Let's go." Warr grabbed another detective and the three of them drove down to the scene in a pair of cruisers, roof lights blazing. Whipping onto Morrish Road, they could see that a small group had already gathered near the car. Warr was thinking that he needed to rope off the scene before any potential evidence was contaminated. And then a call came in for Detective Constable Norton from one of the officers working the front desk back at the station. A Mr. Robert Baltovich had just turned in a note written on the back of a parking receipt. It read: *Have a nice day. You shouldn't leave your windows open. Love, you know who.*

Warr got out of his cruiser and started talking to Mr. Bain. Liz's car was eerily quiet. Warr could see that the windows were shut, and Mr. Bain said the doors were also locked. Mr. Bain advised Warr that he'd kept everyone away from the car but had taken a look inside only to discover it was empty. Mark Bain, who'd just rushed over—having heard about the car from his mother at home—overheard Warr ask his father if anyone had a spare set of keys. "I do," Mark interjected. "Do you want me to go and get them?"

"Yes, please," Warr said. He had a hunch. "But do me a favour. If you see Robert, don't say anything to him about the car being found."

But by the time Mark got home, it was too late. Cathy and Steve Annett had come over from her basement apartment as soon as Mrs. Bain had called to tell them about Paul finding Liz's car. They had been in the middle of packing up Cathy's belongings. Liz's disappearance had overshadowed the squabble between Cathy and her father and so, when her mother asked her to move back home, Cathy did it without a second thought.

Rob, having just left 42 Division, pulled in the driveway just behind them. Looking slightly panicked, Steve walked up to him and said, "They found the car."

"Yeah?" Rob was so shocked that he didn't know what else to say; he just waited for Steve to go on.

"Do you want to go and see it?"

"Where is it?"

"Across from the Three R Auto Body Shop on Morrish Road," Steve said. "You know where that is?"

"No, you better come and show me."

As Mark was coming downstairs from his room with the spare keys, he looked out the window and saw Steve and Rob get into Rob's Cordoba and back out of the driveway. "Where are they going?" he asked his mother. She said that they were probably going to see Liz's car. So much for Rob not knowing, he thought.

As Rob swung his car onto Morrish Road, he immediately saw the police cruisers and Mr. Bain, who was walking across the street. Rob pulled over to the side of the road, jumped out from behind the wheel and started running towards Liz's car. He could feel himself starting to cry but he held back. "Stay away from that car!" Warr barked. Rob stopped in his tracks but something was compelling him to get a closer look at it. He took one step closer. Warr yelled again.

Rob walked back to where Steve was standing and asked if he noticed anything different about Liz's car. "Not really," Steve said. "Just the dirt around the tires. Looks like it's been through the mud." Scanning the car for any other oddities, Rob focused on the door guards affixed to the driver's side door. The door guards were a novelty item that Paul had bought as a gag gift for his sister. They were plastic, flesh-coloured fingertips designed to look as though the car door had been slammed shut on someone's hand. What caught Rob's attention was the fact that both sets of fingers were on the driver's door. Didn't it make sense that one door guard would go on each door? Steve said he didn't know—he'd never really noticed much about the fingers before.

Mark Bain, who'd just delivered the spare set of keys to Warr, was watching Rob and Steve from inside his car. He'd been told there was nothing else for him to do, and he was overcome with a feeling of helplessness. They'd been looking for Liz's car for three days, and, now, here it was, surrounded by onlookers like a meteorite that had just fallen to earth. He was too scared to get any closer to it. Steve Annett was leaning against the hood of Rob's big Cordoba with his hands in his pockets, staring at the car. Rob also had his hands in his pockets but he was pacing up and down the side of Mark's car, back and forth from the hood to the door. It was bothering the hell out of Mark. He just wanted to be alone. He was about to start the car and leave when Rob stopped beside his door and put his hands up to cover his face. Mark thought he looked pretty intense. His hands were shaking. Slowly, Rob lowered his arms, burying his hands in his pockets again. In an anguished voice, he said, "Mark, what's going on?"

"I don't know, Rob," he said. "I don't feel like talking to anybody right now." Mark was filled with a dark cloud of anger. He called out to his father down the road, asking if there was anything else he could do. There wasn't. He thought of his mother's agony as she waited at home, and he turned the key in the ignition and left to join her.

Rob was thinking of his mother as well. He went across the street to call her from the phone at Three R Auto Body. As he told her about Liz's car, Adele could hear the distress in his voice and she tried to comfort him, assuring him that everything would be all right.

Five minutes later, he was back at the car, telling Steve that he had to go. Rob was scheduled to work the campus basketball league in a few hours and he was going to have to let one of his bosses know that he wouldn't be coming in. They got into the Cordoba and drove back to the Bains'. Rob asked Steve if he thought foul play was involved. "Unfortunately, I do," Steve said. "It's not a good sign that we found the car and not Liz."

"Do you think Liz was seeing someone behind my back?" Rob asked.

"I don't know," Steve said.

"Maybe Liz was down in the valley meeting someone."

"Who?" Steve asked.

"I'm not sure," Rob said. "Over these past few days I've discovered there was a lot about Liz I didn't know. I know our relationship is over now. I just want to find her. And then I want to find the guy who did this and when I find the guy I want to kill him."

Mr. Bain had just arrived home from the scene and saw Rob's car pull up out front. He'd seen Rob down on Morrish Road but, in the excitement of the moment, it hadn't crossed his mind to ask him about the missing diary pages or why Rob hadn't bothered to return his call the previous night. Mr. Bain just walked right up to him and got to the point. "Rob," he said, "Cathy informed me last night that a number of diary pages are still missing. It's a bit of a mystery to us and I just assumed you have them. Do you?"

Rob had a look of incredulity on his face, as though he was tracing his movements in his mind, unsure of just where along the way he could have lost part of the diary. "Maybe some of them fell on the way from my car to the house," he postulated.

That wasn't the kind of sure-footed answer Mr. Bain had hoped for. "Rob, we are talking about my daughter's diary," he said sternly. "This is a very private matter, and I'm sure that if something like that fell on the road you wouldn't let it lie there for everyone to read. You were given the privilege of taking something out of our house."

Still dazed by the discovery of Liz's car, Rob appeared to be lost in thought. Mr. Bain wasn't even sure if he'd been listening. For the longest moment, the boy didn't say a word. And then, finally, Rob remembered Mrs. Bain seeing something from the diary on the kitchen table during her visit the day before. Mr. Bain watched Rob's face slowly transform into a look of recognition. "Oh, yeah, yeah, maybe, yeah, yeah," Rob said. He was realizing that his mother must have moved a stack of pages before he returned the folder. "You're right. Yeah, you're right. My mother moved them from the table. They were on the table. She wouldn't have read them though, Mr. Bain. Don't worry, she wouldn't have read them. Do you want me to go and get them?"

"No, you don't have to get them now," said Mr. Bain. "But I want you to bring them back today. Every one of them. Please."

"All right," Rob said. "I will."

—◯—

Jaan Laaniste was working behind the athletic desk when Rob walked into the Recreation Centre. Twenty years ago, Jaan had been a three-time basketball scoring champion in the Ontario University Athletic Association league and Rob saw him as one of those life-long jocks settling uncomfortably into middle age. He was now the Recreation Centre's associate athletic director, an extremely social character around the gym who had befriended both Rob and Liz well before they began dating. Rob had been the one to introduce her to Jaan and, for the longest time, Jaan had teased her, always making it a point to ask her if she'd started dating Rob yet. And Liz would kiddingly say, "No, and we never will." Jaan had bugged her about it so many times that, when they finally did begin dating, Liz said, with a laugh, that Jaan must have been right all along.

Although he probably didn't know it, Jaan had given Liz a real lift one day back in the winter. They'd been alone that day, and Jaan had told her Rob had always been a little too serious-minded for his own good. But since he'd started seeing Liz, Jaan said Rob had been so much happier. Rob is one lucky guy to have a girl like you, Liz, he'd said. Rob was certainly getting the better end of the deal, no doubt about that, but he was a young man with admirable qualities, someone worth holding on to. Liz felt proud when Jaan said that and she told him she wasn't about to let him go.

Seeing Jaan now behind the counter made Rob think about those first beautiful few weeks when he'd got to know Liz and how he'd introduced her to all his friends on campus, including Jaan. Overwhelmed by these memories—now so distant—Rob was trying to explain to Jaan that he couldn't work that night because Liz's car had just been found and, for obvious reasons, he just didn't think he was in the proper frame of mind. Jaan, who was well aware of Liz's disappearance, was unsure of how to respond, other than to say that, of course, he could take the night off. He noticed that Rob was fighting back tears and glanced toward Taimo Pallandi, who, as the athletic director, was their boss (and fellow Estonian). Together, they stepped out from behind the counter and escorted Rob into the nearby equipment room, where they could console him without an audience.

Just because Liz's car was found without her, they said, it didn't mean that she wasn't okay. But Rob wasn't so sure. Everything was really starting to sink in. Liz could very well be gone forever.

He tried to pull himself together. Jaan said not to worry about tonight. He would make sure Rob was covered.

Rob had no idea that his old friend Jim Isaacs would be waiting for him at home with his mother when he got there. Earlier that afternoon, Jim had called Rob from work to see how he was holding up, and Mrs. Baltovich had told him that Liz's car had just been found. She'd said that Rob was more than likely at the Bains', so Jim cut out of work early and went to Liz's house.

Mrs. Bain had answered the front door. He'd just missed Rob, she said. She thought he might have gone back to Liz's car. Jim decided to take a spin down to Morrish Road, but the scene had been roped off and police cars were blocking the road, so he turned around and headed towards Rob's.

Jim was sitting in the kitchen with Mrs. Baltovich when Rob got home from the Recreation Centre. Once Rob had filled Jim in on what was happening, he asked his mother if she'd seen any pages from Liz's diary lying around. That reminded her— she'd forgotten to tell him that Mr. Bain had called the night before asking about diary pages. "That's what he wants to know, Mom," he said. "Have you seen any?"

"Well," she said, "I took a stack of papers downstairs and put them on the freezer. But I wasn't wearing my glasses, so I don't know whether they were diary pages or not."

Rob went downstairs and returned seconds later with the pages. They were diary entries, he said. He would have to return them to the Bains right away, but his mother wanted him to sit down and have a quick meal before he left.

Rob and Jim drove off to the Bains' in their separate cars. They went inside, and Rob returned the missing batch of diary pages before they met up with Cathy in the living room. She told them about an interesting phone call Mark had just received from an old high school friend named Lou Torrone. Torrone remembered Liz well from the halls of Cardinal Newman and as soon as he had heard about her disappearance, he called Mark with some important information.

Torrone said that he'd been driving east on Kingston Road when, at about 3:30 PM on the Tuesday of Liz's disappearance, he'd spotted her in her car as he stopped at a red light at Lawrence Avenue. He'd been in the lane just to her left and his car hadn't quite been parallel with hers so his vantage point had been at a slight angle from behind. But he'd had a good enough look at her profile to be sure that it was Liz. His memory of the woman in the passenger seat was just as good, considering he hadn't recognized her. She was an older, attractive-looking lady in her mid-fifties, with streaks of grey in her loosely curled, neatly brushed hair. She'd been wearing a light-coloured raincoat, which sounded right—it had rained that afternoon. And, like Liz, the woman had been looking straight ahead, as though they were in the middle of running a common chore. Torrone thought the older woman might have been wearing earrings and light make-up.

"Do we have any idea who this lady is?" Rob asked.

Cathy said no. Rob was racking his brain, trying to remember if Liz had mentioned any older women in her diary. "What about this 'Betsy' woman she wrote about seeing?" Rob said. "Who is that?"

"Betsy Watanabe?" Cathy said.

"Could be," he answered.

"She's one of Liz's holistic people."

"Liz never told me about her," he said. "What does she look like?"

"I don't know," Cathy said. "But she's probably older. Actually, Liz has one of her pamphlets upstairs. I'll go get it."

Cathy returned moments later with the pamphlet in her hand. Betsy Watanabe specialized in herbal treatments and also practised iridology, nutrition and reflexology. There was an address listed and Rob said he was thinking about taking a drive over to this Betsy's place to see if she'd been in Liz's car on Tuesday. The only problem was that Rob had no idea where to find her street. "Problem solved," Jim said. "I've got a Perly's map of Toronto in my car."

When they arrived at the address, they were told that Betsy had moved. At a nearby shopping plaza, they looked her up in a telephone book at a pay phone. According to Jim's map, her new address, on Dalmation Crescent, was half a kilometre east of where Liz's car had been found. That made them even more eager to find this woman.

Dalmation Crescent looked as though it was part of a new subdivision and the road was covered with mud. Rob mentioned the mud Steve Annett had pointed out on the tires of Liz's car. Maybe Liz had gone to Betsy looking for a place to stay so she could get away from everything. Jim thought it certainly seemed possible.

Betsy's door was answered by a man who appeared to be Japanese and who said he was Betsy's husband. Rob explained that he was looking for his girlfriend, who was one of Betsy's clients. Betsy's husband said she was at work, so Rob asked if he would mind writing down that address for him. The husband invited Rob and Jim into the foyer while he went to find a piece of paper in a room towards the rear of the house. The instant the man was out of their sight, Jim watched Rob as he darted into the rooms adjoining the foyer, looking for a pair of Liz's shoes or any other sign she might be there. Rob shook his head. Nothing.

Jim and Rob drove to Betsy's store, Health With Herbs on Markham Road, only to discover that it had already closed for the day.

When they returned to the Bains', the first thing Mr. Bain said was "Where were you guys?" Rob explained where they'd been. "You guys were off on a wild-goose chase," Mr. Bain said. He didn't sound very appreciative of their efforts. "I just spoke to Betsy, and she said she didn't see Liz on Tuesday."

"You know this Betsy?" Rob asked.

"Sure I know Betsy," Mr. Bain said reproachfully. "I'm the one who introduced Liz to her ages ago. Do me a favour, Rob, and let me know before you take off on another one of these excursions by yourself." Mr. Bain turned to leave the room, then stopped and turned. "By the way, Rob," he said, "did you bring the rest of those diary pages like I asked?" Rob said that he had.

When Mr. Bain was gone, Rob broke down again. Jim just sat beside him silently on the couch until Rob regained his composure. "Let's go back to your house," Jim said. Rob dabbed at his runny nose with the sleeve of his sweater and said, "Good idea."

—◦—

Fifteen minutes after arriving at the scene on Morrish Road, Detective Sergeant Tony Warr called the Homicide Squad. From his nine years with Homicide, he knew there would be a team on call for the weekend, but it was getting close to that time on a Friday afternoon when all the detectives would be running for the office door, and Warr wanted to make contact with someone in case he needed to call them down to the scene. Warr's foresight paid off—forty-five minutes after his initial call to Homicide, Detective Constable Norton informed him that a large quantity of blood had been found on the floor behind the front seats of the young woman's car.

Without delay, Warr called Homicide again and asked for Detective Sergeant Steven Reesor. Warr told Reesor about the blood. Warr didn't even have to say the word "murder"—they both knew the score. Reesor wanted to know if he had any suspects. Nothing solid, Warr said, but he had a gut feeling there was something fishy about the boyfriend. He'd been acting strange at the scene (although he was later unable to describe exactly how). Reesor suggested they put him under surveillance right away, and Warr agreed, giving him a cursory description of one twenty-four-year-old Robert Baltovich: male, white, five feet eight inches tall, athletic build, dark brown hair, straight, combed back, wet look. "Great," Reesor said. "Let me take care of a few things, and my partner and I will get down there as soon as we can."

—◦—

At about nine o'clock that evening, Eric Genuis called Rob Baltovich to get an update on Liz. Eric had called three times the night before between eleven and one in the morning, but Rob had been down at the police station. Mrs. Baltovich had simply told Eric that Rob was out, but to try back as late as he wanted—she would be up. Rob now apologized for not getting back to him but explained how hectic things had been, especially since Liz's car had been found. Startled by the news, Eric started asking a lot of questions about the car and still seemed quite interested in hearing what Liz had written about him in her diary. Eric came up with the idea that they get together somewhere to discuss everything. Rob suggested meeting at Lick's Burgers on Queen Street in the Beaches; he would be bringing his friend Jim. Eric said he would see them there.

Eric showed up at Lick's with a friend named Arnold, a short Filipino whom Rob recognized from Scarborough campus. Rob couldn't believe how wimpy Eric looked. Liz had always made him out to be a physically robust, almost imposing figure, but he was a little smaller than Rob and his voice was quite soft, almost effeminate. They grabbed some food and a couple of soft drinks and went to the upper level of the restaurant. Eric was feeling the weight of a sizable tragedy. A girl he had cared about a great deal for almost five years had disappeared off the face of the earth, and now he was sitting face to face with her tormented boyfriend, his weary eyes round and sad.

Eric talked about how depressed Liz was all the time. How they would go for long strolls on the boardwalk, holding hands—all while her relationship with Rob was going full steam. Although she occasionally gave him the cold-shoulder treatment when they got together (that sounded like the Liz he knew, Rob thought), Liz would also say things like "I want to be with you, Eric" and "If I love Rob, then why am I here with you?" Eric told Rob that, in response to sentiments such as these, he would tell her, "No, no. You're with Rob and that's the way things are."

"Well, Eric," Rob said, "that's not exactly how Liz described her relationship with you. Not to offend you or anything, but Liz often referred to you as a pest who wouldn't stop calling her. Someone who couldn't take the hint that she was no longer interested."

Emphatically, Eric professed that it was the exact opposite—Liz was the one calling him! As he listened, Rob was in such utter disbelief that he didn't bother to question what Eric was saying. He was pretty sure that Eric was feeding him a line, but he also quickly realized that any challenge to Eric's point of view was a waste of energy.

It was getting late, and Eric suggested they continue the discussion back at his house. Jim and Arnold had contributed next to nothing to the conversation but they tagged along anyway. By 3:00 AM the discussion was winding down, and when Eric mused aloud about how beautiful Liz was, that she was the kind of woman who could stop traffic, Rob thought it was time to call it quits. On the way home, Rob didn't even bother to ask Jim what his impressions were. For the most part, Eric had simply confirmed his feelings about Liz's diary, that Rob's relationship with her had been one big lie. So many guys had been spending time with her that he didn't know what to think. Eric certainly wasn't the kind of person Liz had made him out to be—a hot-headed, arrogant, self-righteous guy who had no respect for their relationship. It was just more lies.

Jim spent the rest of the night on the couch at Rob's. They were both exhausted and went straight to sleep. They would need their rest for the big search at the campus the police had organized for the morning..

After breakfast, Rob and Jim drove down to the main entrance of Scarborough campus, next to the campus security station. The couldn't believe how many people had showed up to search the valley. At least two hundred had gathered, possibly even three hundred. And that didn't include the police force's mounted horseback officers or its canine unit.

It wasn't long before Rob and Jim bumped into Paul Bain. Rob could see Mark and Cathy Bain, along with Arlene Coventry, walking towards them from a short distance away. That's when Paul mentioned how his brother had told him that whoever had been driving Liz's car had left it parked in reverse.

"That *was* strange," Rob said, "the way it was backed in like that. I don't recall seeing Liz reverse her car into a spot before."

"No," Paul said. "I mean it was in reverse gear."

The police were dividing the crowd into groups of ten or so, each of which proceeded into the valley, near the lot where Rob had last seen Liz's car on Tuesday evening. It was there that Rob ran into Ethel Ormsby, the woman he'd driven home from Kidbrooke before he and Liz had met at the campus after her shift on Sunday night. And then he saw Liz's uncle, Hugo Bain, who'd always been so nice to him, so friendly. Rob was pleased to see him, but Hugo was distant and aloof and barely spoke to him. Rob wondered if his dour mood was due to Liz's disappearance or to Mr. Bain bad-mouthing him to the relatives.

And then, practically out of nowhere, as if in answer to his own suspicions, Rob saw Mr. Bain barrelling towards him with an angry look on his face. Mr. Bain grabbed him by the arm and wheeled him around, away from Jim and the others, saying he wanted to have a word alone with him. Once they were a few feet away from everyone else, Mr. Bain started to really let him have it. "What do you think you're doing telling everyone that Liz committed suicide?" Mr. Bain asked.

"I haven't said anything like that since you asked me to keep it quiet," Rob said.

"Rob, that information is to be confined to the police. In a time like this we must maintain Elizabeth's dignity and integrity and you must learn to be discreet—because you have a big mouth." He added that, when all else failed, Liz still had her faith, and that was worth something.

Rob could see where Mr. Bain was coming from—he didn't want the world to know that his daughter harboured suicidal thoughts. Fair enough. But, in Rob's mind, sullying her reputation was nothing more than the unfortunate consequence of his efforts to find out what had happened to her. Regardless, Rob was getting the distinct impression that Mr. Bain would rather he not be there at all. As Liz's father, he was taking command. Rob couldn't help but feel that he was getting in the man's way.

—◌—

Detective Norman Rowntree had his work cut out for him when he showed up for work on Saturday morning at the Centre for Forensic Sciences, an unspectacular five-storey government building in downtown Toronto. As a crime scene examiner with the Metropolitan Toronto Police Force's Forensic Identification Services branch, Rowntree had been dispatched to Morrish Road in Scarborough the previous evening to preserve and gather any evidence related to a missing girl's 1981 silver-grey Toyota Tercel, licence plate number 397 CNB.

When Rowntree had arrived at the scene, he made a note of the fact that it was exactly 6:15 PM. The Tercel had been cordoned off with yellow police tape, and an officer had placed a plastic sheet over it to protect it from the rain that had just begun to fall. Rowntree was immediately ushered to the car, and he examined the surrounding area for things like footprints (in this case, too many people had already walked around the vehicle), tire tracks or blood but found nothing useful. The car was then opened and he was shown the bloodstains on the floor mat behind the driver's seat. He could detect no odour related to human decomposition. He took a cursory look at the rest of the interior and saw that the hand brake was on and that the gearshift had been left in reverse.

After three years as a crime scene examiner, Rowntree knew blood when he saw it, and the dried red stains on the blue carpet definitely looked like blood. It was enough for him to place a call to the Ontario Provincial Police, which possessed a truck specially designed for transporting vehicles of possible evidential value in criminal cases. The OPP truck ferried such cars within an enclosed space (to guard against exposure to the elements) and loaded and unloaded them with minimal agitation (to preserve the original state of the vehicle and its contents).

With the truck on its way, Rowntree went back to the car and, using a pair of scissors, cut a square inch out of the bloodstained floor mat so that the lab could confirm it to be human blood as quickly as possible. Yet, as he lifted the square from the mat, drops of red liquid fell from its lowest corner, and he could see that, underneath the carpeting, the blood had not yet congealed. It was still wet, pooled in a thin layer against the body of the car.

At the CFS garage the following morning, Rowntree photographed the exterior of the Tercel from every angle before he cut through the police seal he'd taped to its doors and trunk at the scene on Morrish Road. And then he went through a couple of rolls of film meticulously photographing just about every square inch of the car's interior. Having established a visual record of how the car had been found, Rowntree began to document its present state using every scientific method at his disposal. He measured the driver's seat and found that it was twelve centimetres back from its full-forward position. Rowntree, who stood just half an inch short of six feet, sat in the seat and figured that, to operate the clutch comfortably, he would move it back just a touch more.

At exactly 10:41 PM, the moment Rowntree was informed by the lab that the liquid in Elizabeth Bain's vehicle was confirmed as human blood, he called Detective Sergeant Steve Reesor to let him know.

In addition to the blood on the carpet behind the driver and passenger seats, there were blood smears along the front edge of the rear bench seat; on the passenger-side rocker panel; the front edge of the passenger-side door frame; the seat-belt floor restraint near the passenger door; and on the two seat-belt anchor points on the floor between the front seats. There were also a number of items on the floor behind the front seats that had been smeared by blood: several small twigs and leaves; a piece of yellow tissue paper that had been affixed to a crushed Sprite pop can by dried blood; two pieces of crumpled paper that, unfolded, contained a job description for Elizabeth's position at Kidbrooke dated January 31, 1990, and the instruction page of a Provincial Offences ticket (issued for either speeding or parking); and a dark-coloured plastic hair barrette about two or three inches long. On the floor behind the passenger seat, Rowntree also discovered two unused matches. After placing all these items in separate evidence bags, Rowntree took swabs of blood from various stains in the interior and removed the entire carpet for further forensic testing.

In the front area of the car, the glove box was closed and the slot designed to hold an ashtray was empty. The fuel gauge showed the tank was three-quarters full. The tape deck contained a cassette labelled "Techniques," the title of an album by a British techno band called New Order. The radio was tuned to 102.1 FM, known in Toronto as CFNY, a station that played "alternative" music by bands such as New Order, the Smiths, R.E.M., Echo & the Bunnymen, and the Waterboys.

Rowntree next fingerprinted the entire vehicle, inside and out. He was unable to pick anything up in the usual places—steering wheel, stick shift, door handles. But with the passenger-door window he hit the jackpot. In total, there were eight fingerprints on both sides of the window. On the exterior panel of the driver's door, the fingerprint powder traced the outline of a partial shoe print, as though someone had back-kicked the door shut after walking in mud or dirt.

Rowntree collected the twigs and vegetation from the driver's seat cover for testing. Dead bugs were plucked from the headlights and the grille and packaged to be sent for identification by an insect expert at the Royal Ontario Museum.

Resting on top of other items in the glove box was a small-sized package of du Maurier Light cigarettes. Lying beside the open pack was a single cigarette, the tobacco end of which had been lit but not really smoked. What was unique about this cigarette was that part of its filter had been snipped off, most likely by the scissors that were also in the glove box. The missing filter was nowhere inside the car. Rowntree, himself a smoker, was thinking about how he would cut the filters off his wife's mild cigarettes when he had a craving but no smokes around the house. He had no use for light cigarettes and getting rid of their filters was the only way to get a really good draw on a mild dart.

Beside the cigarette package were three books of matches. The first two were the generic fold-out kind and contained matches that looked like the two unused matches on the floor behind the passenger seat. One book had "15 Ways to Success" on its cover and the other had "Family Inns of America, Knoxville, Tennessee. North I-75, Merchant Drive, exit 108." The third set of matches were made of wood and packaged in a small push-out box. They were from a restaurant in Toronto called Mr. Greenjeans. Beneath the cigarettes and matches was a miscellany of typical glove-box paraphernalia: a black vinyl change purse with loose change, a Scarborough General Hospital intake sheet, a month-old parking tag, a Bell telephone bill, gas receipts and so on.

The last part of the car Rowntree inspected was the trunk, which he quickly determined had not been soiled by blood. He listed its contents: blankets, one pair of women's boots and a fly wheel.

Finally, Rowntree called a mechanic from the police garage and had him bring a big tank of gasoline over to the CFS. Using a one-litre jug, he filled the car's gas tank up to its neck. They counted a little over 12.5 litres (an amount, it was later determined, that, taking into account the small trips the car made within Scarborough after Mrs. Bain filled the tank on June 18, would allow it to travel approximately eighty kilometres away from Colonel Danforth Park before returning).

———◇———

By noon, the search at Colonel Danforth Park north of Old Kingston Road had turned up nothing, and Rob suggested to Tony Warr that they get a small group together and check out a couple of other nearby areas Liz was fond of. So Rob, Jim and Eric Genuis, along with Warr and another detective, drove to Morningside Park, south of Ellesmere Road. Rob led the group through some fairly thick bush up an embankment, and they ended up in the parking lot of the Centenary Hospital, just west of the campus. At the other end of the parking lot was a steep ravine, and, using his walkie-talkie, Warr contacted the command post and requested that an additional group of searchers be sent up to comb through the ravine. But, again, their efforts were for naught, and Rob and Jim drove back to the Bains' no further ahead than they'd been when they rolled out of bed that morning.

As Jim angled his car onto the shoulder of the road in front of the Bains', they could see that a small cluster of reporters was gathered on the road at the top of the driveway. A car from a local television station was parked at the next house over, and a small crew was on the neighbours' veranda, interviewing the parents of little Cathy and Robert, who, just a week and a half earlier had been over watching *Uncle Buck* with Rob and Liz and William from the group home. One of the reporters walked briskly towards Jim's car, notebook in hand, saying, "One of you wouldn't happen to be Elizabeth Bain's boyfriend, would you?"

Instinctively, Jim pointed at Rob, but before the reporter could spit out the next question, Mrs. Bain came flying across the front lawn, right up to the fence that ran parallel with the road. Fluttering in her hand was a "MISSING" poster with Liz's picture on it. "Come inside, Rob," she panted. "Come on inside. Don't talk to the press." After Mr. Bain's tirade before the search that morning, Rob presumed that Mrs. Bain was concerned he would spread more suicide "rumours." Although he didn't agree with such secrecy, he could appreciate that this wasn't the kind of thing Liz's parents wanted people reading about, especially if Liz were still alive.

Regardless, he obeyed Mrs. Bain and, with Jim in tow, they followed her into the house without speaking to the reporter. Some of Liz's relatives were there, as was Liz's friend from school, Laura Pallone, who was helping with the posters. Rob didn't stay long; he was too exhausted to be in the midst of such activity. He grabbed a few posters, and he and Jim went back to his house.

Together, they sat in Rob's living room and began reading the information printed on the posters. Rob choked up when he reached the part about the ring Liz wore on her finger, the one with the pretty sparkling rubies dancing around the little diamond he'd bought her for Valentine's Day. Seeing tears rolling down her grown son's face was almost too much for Adele to bear, but, calling on the strength that often surfaces in highly emotional moments, she took her son by the hand and led him into the kitchen. She sat him down at the table and guided his head into her chest with her arms, the way she remembered doing when he was a young boy.

Just when he thought the searches were turning out to be nothing more than an exercise in futility, Detective Sergeant Tony Warr got his first big break. It came in the form of a young, sun-kissed brunette named Marianne Perz. Perz, whose father, John, was a physics professor at Scarborough College, was teaching children's tennis clinics at the campus courts for the summer. Saturday was a full work day for her but, having heard about the searches for Elizabeth Bain, whom she had known from high school, Perz walked up to the campus security centre during her lunch break to see what was going on. Perz saw Mr. Bain and told him how strange it was that Liz had disappeared on Tuesday evening because she was sure that she'd seen Liz down by the tennis courts that afternoon. Next thing she knew, Mr. Bain was driving her down into the valley and introducing her to Tony Warr. After a few words with Warr, Perz found herself getting into his police cruiser for a lift down to 42 Division to give a statement, her lunch break extending unexpectedly into the mid-afternoon.

Perz told Warr what she remembered of her brief encounter with Liz Bain on Tuesday. Between 5:30 and 6:15 PM, Perz had taken the group of kids she was teaching for a drink at the water fountain. Perz led them through the fence door at the end of the courts and veered right to the fountain, which was on the grass against the fence. No more than a few steps from the fountain, she glanced to her left and saw Elizabeth Bain seated at the farthest of two picnic tables. Having spent most of the past year at the University of Western Ontario, two hours by car outside of Toronto, Perz hadn't seen Liz for quite some time, but she was positive that it had been she.

Liz was sitting on the near side of the table facing east. A woman, about the same age as Liz, was on the bench to her right. A third female was on the other side of the table. Cryptically, Perz told Warr that the person to Liz's left "could have been the man." "He had dark hair," she said. "I believe he was white. I don't remember what he was wearing." Perz got the impression that the four of them were together, even though they weren't saying much, just hanging around watching tennis.

The female at the end of the bench to Liz's right was white, with a dark complexion and straight brown hair to her shoulders, and was wearing dark clothing. Perz couldn't recall anything about the woman on the other side of the table, other than that "the two females didn't seem to be overly attractive, they were very plain-looking people." Except for Liz, Perz didn't recognize any of them.

As far as she could remember, it didn't appear as though anyone at the table had been dressed for tennis. Liz had been wearing pants. "She had dark colours on," Perz told Warr. "Nothing bright. Her hair was back, off her face. I said hello and she said hello back." Once Perz and the kids had got a drink of water from the fountain, they returned to their court. When they came back for a second water break an hour or so later, Liz and her group were gone.

That was about the extent of her memory. She thought there might have been another group of people at the picnic table closer to the fountain. Warr asked if she would be able to recognize the man sitting next to Elizabeth Bain if she saw him in a photograph. Perz said she wasn't sure.

Later that afternoon, after Perz had been given a lift back from the station, Warr decided to call Rob. Before his interview with Perz, Warr had wanted to ask him to suggest other areas where they might conduct further searches for Elizabeth, but now the old Homicide investigator in him was looking to see what Rob's reaction would be to the Perz sighting by the tennis courts. If Baltovich was responsible, Warr was experienced enough to pick up on the kind of fear guilty people have difficulty hiding when confronted with the fact that the cops are on to them—you could get stunned silence (followed by mad scrambling for an explanation), loud protestations that someone has given the police bad information or a disheartened "I don't know what to say about that." Warr jotted down rough notes of their conversation and later transcribed them into his notebook in greater detail. According to Warr's notes, Rob's response to the news about Perz was as follows:

BALTOVICH: It sounds great to me. Though I can't imagine Liz going to the tennis courts.

WARR: She was watching the tennis.

BALTOVICH: She often does that.

WARR: What do you feel happened to her?

BALTOVICH: Gut feeling? There was no foul play. She was confused about her relationship with Eric and me. Taking a summer course, had two jobs, not happy at home. She either hurt herself or disappeared.

WARR: What about her car?

BALTOVICH: That was strange. She never parked the car by reversing it or leaving it in reverse gear.

WARR: How do you know it was in reverse?

BALTOVICH: The brother told me.

It sounds great to me was hardly the incriminating reply of a murderer stung by the existence of a witness who could place him at or near the scene of the crime. But Warr might have scored big with the admission that Rob knew the car had been left in reverse gear. Warr didn't think Rob had been close enough to the vehicle to see what gear it was in. He would have to verify Rob's stories with Liz's brothers.

At this stage of their conversation, Warr, instead of asking Rob to clarify which brother had imparted this information to him, decided to change the subject. He asked if Rob thought there was any connection to "the Scarborough rapist," an unapprehended serial rapist who had terrorized at least a dozen young women in the eastern suburb since 1987. His latest victim, a young brunette, had been attacked on May 26, three weeks before Elizabeth Bain disappeared. Well after midnight, the nineteen-year-old victim had stepped off a bus and was walking a few blocks north of Rob's house on Midland Avenue when a tall, preppy-looking blond fellow, not more than a few years older than she, came right up to her and whipped out a knife. Once he'd cut her face, he took her to a secluded area of a nearby high school and raped her.

The violence of the Scarborough rapist's attacks seemed to be escalating with each victim. In addition to being slashed, the latest victim had her arm broken while her hands and feet were being bound with twine. He'd also bitten one of her breasts and had pulled out a tuft of her pubic hair, sadistic acts that, as far as the police were aware, were new additions to the serial rapist's twisted repertoire.

After being treated at a hospital in Scarborough, the shattered young woman agreed to give a description of her attacker to a police artist with the forensic identification bureau downtown. For some reason, the Scarborough rapist wasn't very careful about concealing his face from his victims, and the police already had a good idea of what he looked like. The latest victim, however, was able to recall his features in unprecedented detail. Three days after the rape had occurred, the police issued a computer-generated composite sketch of the man they believed to be the Scarborough rapist. The drawing, featured prominently in Toronto newspapers and plastered on city bus shelters—where the rapist was fond of spotting his victims—was accompanied by a description of the suspect: "Male, white, 18 to 22 years old, light coloured eyes—possibly blue, medium to heavy build—muscular, blonde hair—parted and feathered back to the sides, hair to the ears & to collar at back, clean shaven, smooth tanned complexion, no accent, wearing baby blue coloured top and tan knee length shorts, running shoes."

"So," Warr was asking, "do you think the Scarborough rapist might have had something to do with this?" He was curious to find out whether Rob would jump at the chance to ascribe blame to such an easy target. Warr anxiously scribbled down Rob's answer: "No, too much of a coincidence." If the kid had killed his girlfriend, Warr thought, he was too smart to take the bait.

Warr was at home two hours later when his pager went off. He called 42 Division, and a detective passed on a message to call Robert Baltovich at home. Once he'd grabbed a pen and a pad of foolscap, Warr called him back, again making rough notes of what Rob had to say, augmenting them later in his notebook:

I am starting to more or less come over to your thinking that there is foul play involved. Thinking it over, at least two times in deserted areas Liz seemed terrified of being attacked or injured.

The fact that her sister wasn't concerned about the last diary entry—it was normal for Liz. I think Liz has been just as low at other times in her life. She told me a month ago she wouldn't kill herself. She doesn't have the guts. Why contemplate hurting yourself if you're afraid of dying?

If she just disappeared, she would have left a note. The last thing she would ever want is that type of attention.

If she were to return—which she would eventually—it wouldn't be the same. Her relationship with me would end. Her relationship with Eric, even though just a friend, would change.

I have been giving the last diary entry too much weight. I can see how, in a depressed state, she may have made a bad decision.

If someone was to attempt to rape or assault her, she would fight to the death.

When she jogged, she carried a small knife—I just found that out a few weeks ago. At the time it surprised me, but it didn't seem to be a fib.

I am not saying foul play is a certainty, but, more and more, it's a possibility if the car had been driven by someone else.

It's a very good idea to do a more intense search, especially in the Principal's Residence area. We last made love there on Sunday night, twenty-five to thirty feet south of the river.

Rob said he was going over to his friend Al Heys's house for the evening, and he gave Warr Al's phone number in case he needed to get in touch with him. Otherwise, Rob said, he would see him at the park at 10:00 AM for another day of searching.

—◦—

Standing next to Warr in the parking lot where he'd last seen Liz's car in the valley on Tuesday night, Rob looked on as Warr briefed the officers designated as team leaders, each of whom would be responsible for a group of civilian searchers. A uniformed sergeant was to divide Colonel Danforth Park into grids and assign each search team to a specific section of the park. While Warr was delivering his last-minute instructions, Rob caught a glimpse of a black man with tinted glasses standing a few feet away, and, suddenly, he was thinking back to the Sunday night tryst behind the Principal's Residence and just how scared Liz had been by the raccoon up in the tree as they were walking back to their cars. She'd held on to him for dear life after that and, as they continued on, she told him about a recent incident that had really frightened her. She'd been jogging one day and had seen a black man wearing sunglasses blocking her way. He hadn't allowed her to pass until the last possible second. But the oddest thing of all, Liz had said, was that it was dark—initially, she'd only noticed him because the end of his cigarette was lit—and this guy was walking around with sunglasses on. What for, she'd wondered.

By now, Warr had finished rallying the troops, and Rob thought it best to fill him in on what Liz had told him about the black man who'd blocked her way. Warr wrote about it in his notebook. "Liz said she kept thinking she was going to meet up with him again one day," Rob said. "She didn't want me to think she was a ninny but she'd thought he was going to accost her that night."

Warr decided it was a good time to ask Rob another one of his test questions. The same way he'd thrown Marianne Perz at him the day before, he now informed Rob of a new "witness"—whom Warr intentionally left unnamed—and said this person might have seen Liz in the library on Tuesday afternoon. "Is this Kris Kangas?" Rob asked. Warr nodded. "Yes, I already spoke with her, but I don't think she saw Liz on Tuesday because Kris said Liz was wearing a purple T-shirt, not a blouse."

What was it going to take to catch this guy off guard? Warr still didn't know what to make of him. Flipping his notebook closed, he went back to organizing the searchers.

—◦—

Tony Warr didn't speak with Rob Baltovich again until that day's uneventful search had come to an end and he'd returned to his desk at 42 Division. At 5:20 PM he called Rob at home and asked him to come down to the station. Warr didn't say why. Nonetheless, Rob, without inquiring, said he'd be there shortly.

What Rob didn't know was that two detective sergeants from the Homicide Squad, Steve Reesor and his partner, Brian Raybould, had been at 42 Division since 8:00 AM, reviewing all statements and reports filed regarding the Bain case. Just after noon, Reesor had called Arlene Coventry to confirm that she and Elizabeth Bain hadn't made dinner plans on the night of the disappearance. Later, when Warr was back at the station following the search, he filled them in on his conversations with Rob the day before, and how, to Warr's surprise, Rob had known about the car being left in reverse gear.

Reesor and Raybould said they wanted to meet Baltovich, ask him a few questions.

No time like the present, Warr thought. As a matter of fact, he had a question of his own, and getting Rob to come directly to the station would allow him to kill two birds with one stone.

Warr's query stemmed from a discussion he'd had with Mr. Bain during the course of that day's search in the valley. Mr. Bain had expressed his concern about the present state of Liz's diary. According to his other daughter, Cathy, Liz's diary binder wasn't nearly as full as it had been when she'd first opened it on the morning after the disappearance. Mr. Bain had said that, even after Rob had returned the second, misplaced batch of pages, Cathy still felt that a number of pages were missing. But when asked about it, Rob was adamant—everything had been returned.

A few minutes before six o'clock, Warr greeted Rob at 42 Division's front desk and escorted him to the same room in which he and Rob had spoken on Friday, just prior to the car being found. Inside the bland ten-by-ten-foot space known as the Resource Room, Rob seemed a little more relaxed than he had on Friday. With the door closed behind them, Warr wasted no time asking Rob if he still had any pages from Liz's diary. "No," Rob said. "I gave them all back."

Apparently satisfied with his answer, Warr informed Rob that the investigation was being transferred from 42 Division to the Homicide Squad and that a couple of Homicide detectives happened to be in the building. "Would you have any objection to speaking with them now?" Warr asked.

"No," Rob said. "I'll stay here all night if it will help out."

Warr buzzed Reesor and Raybould on the internal phone and within thirty seconds there was a knock on the door.

Warr handled the introductions. Brian Raybould was six feet two inches tall, and thin. His height, along with his tweed jacket and receding hairline, gave Rob the mistaken impression that he was the senior partner. Although Raybould had, as recently as a week ago, been promoted from detective to detective sergeant—a rank equal to his partner, Steve Reesor—Raybould was still considered the junior of the pair. In fact, when they had taken the Bain call on Friday, it was one of their last days of working together, as a batch of new detectives were arriving on Monday, and both men would be taking a new partner under their wing. But now that they'd done some preliminary investigating into the matter, they decided to take the Bain case on as a kind of swansong, one last homicide for old times' sake.

Rob quickly picked up on the fact that Reesor, a stocky man about four inches shorter than Raybould, was the one who would be doing most, if not all, of the talking. Reesor, who, at thirty-seven, was a rising young star on the force, sported a well-tailored dark suit. Clothes aside, though, Rob found Reesor to be an exceptionally unattractive man, maybe even ugly. His blondish hair was thinning on top, and a terrible scar ran off the right corner of his mouth and curled up towards his eye, remnants of an old injury, which, Rob later learned, was the souvenir of a nasty snowmobile accident.

Once Warr had left the room, Reesor explained that as Homicide investigators, they had been called in because a quantity of blood had been found in Elizabeth Bain's car. Raybould, who was keeping notes of their conversation, wrote down Rob's response to the news that there was blood in his girlfriend's car: *Was that in the trunk or the back seat?* Adroitly, Reesor said that he was not at liberty to disclose that information.

Their job now was to interview witnesses, Reesor said, and that before he could go any further, he would have to read Rob his rights to counsel. "Do you understand?" Reesor asked.

"I am fully aware," Rob replied. "If I was in your position, I would be the first one I would come to."

"Do you wish to call a lawyer now?"

Rob said, "No, I do not."

"Is it okay with you if we tape-record this conversation, as opposed to writing the whole thing down?"

"I don't mind at all."

Reesor opened up his attaché case and pulled out his trusty old Radio Shack tape recorder, along with a couple of empty tapes. He ran a couple of tests to make sure it was working before he placed it on the table and indicated that he was ready to begin. For the record, Reesor identified everyone present, got the correct spelling of Baltovich and stated the date, time and location of the interview (Raybould even drew a little diagram to show where everyone was sitting).

"Okay," Reesor said. "The first thing is that you are not under arrest, nor are you charged with any criminal offence in relation to Elizabeth Bain's disappearance. As a result of further investigations, you could be charged with an offence sometime in the future. Do you wish to say anything to us about her disappearance? You are not obliged to say anything, unless you wish to do so, but whatever you say may be given in evidence. Do you understand?"

Rob said he did. For the benefit of the tape, Reesor went over his rights to a lawyer, but Rob said he didn't feel it was necessary. Just as Tony Warr had done on Friday, Reesor asked Rob to tell them everything he'd done on the Tuesday of Liz's disappearance right from the moment he'd woken up. And, again, Rob began by chronicling his usual breakfast routine (. . . *I grabbed two Shredded Wheat, poured water on them before I put milk in the bowl and I took them into the living room where I turned on the television to watch "The Brady Bunch," which I do every morning at 9:30 . . .*)

It took him an hour to get to the point in his narrative at which Arlene Coventry handed him Liz's final diary entry the morning after the disappearance. Reesor decided to take a ten-minute break so that he and Raybould could leave the room to discuss their impressions in private. When Reesor turned the tape back on at 7:16 PM, he was ready to ask some questions. By the time they took their next break two hours later, Reesor was convinced that Robert Baltovich was deceiving the authorities about his culpability in what Reesor believed to be the death of Elizabeth Bain. Reesor had his reasons—ten of them:

1. Reesor had a hard time believing that Liz would plan to meet her friend Arlene Coventry for dinner after 9:00 PM, when her night class ended. When Rob cited Liz's "erratic eating habits" and explained that, in addition to sharing a meal, "dinner" might have also meant getting together to see each other, Reesor didn't buy it.

2. After Rob had attempted to describe the awkward conclusion to his phone call with Liz on Tuesday morning, Reesor tried to suggest that there "might have been a little bit of a strain" between them. On the contrary, Rob said, she seemed to be in very good spirits.

3. Reesor wanted to know why Rob had been up in Liz's room the afternoon he'd seen the letter from Mark Fielden on her dresser. Reluctant to disclose to a complete stranger that he and Liz had been making love in her room on a rare occasion when nobody else was home, Rob lied and said that he'd gone to her room

because he thought he'd left his wallet there. When Rob backtracked a few moments later, telling him the true version, Reesor said, "Okay, but what about the wallet?" "That's . . . " Rob began. "That was a fabrication."

4. Rob could remember what he'd been wearing at home while watering the plants and washing his car, as well as the workout clothes he kept in his locker at the gym, but he had no recall of what street clothes he'd changed into before heading off to the Recreation Centre.

5. Reesor found it suspicious that Rob had entertained the notion that the man waiting in the hall outside of Liz's class might be Eric Genuis based solely on Liz's description of him as looking "Maltese."

6. Reesor couldn't understand why Rob wouldn't have asked Liz's professor, who was sitting alone in the class when he peered in, if he'd seen her that night. Rob's explanation—that he didn't think the professor knew Liz personally and that he was in a hurry to get down to the valley—didn't hold water, as far as Reesor was concerned.

7. In response to Rob's claim that during his brief visit to the Bains' on Tuesday night, he'd asked Mrs. Bain if Liz had mentioned any plans with Arlene Coventry, Reesor informed Rob that he'd spoken with Mrs. Bain, and she'd said that Rob hadn't mentioned anything about Arlene until the following morning. "Oh, that doesn't surprise me," Rob said. "Mrs. Bain often forgets things."

"She often forgets things?" Reesor scoffed.

"Yes, that's true."

If Mrs. Bain had really told him that Arlene lived in the Brandywine area, Reesor wondered why Rob hadn't just gone to the neighbourhood and cruised around on the lookout for Liz's car.

8. The way Rob remembered it, he'd told Neil Winton about seeing Liz's car in the valley when they'd bumped into each other at the Recreation Centre Tuesday night. But when Reesor said he'd spoken to Neil, and Neil had no recollection of Rob saying this, Rob said, "Um, it's possible, and perhaps that I'm, I mean I recall something that didn't eff ... ah, in effect, take place."

"That you what?" Reesor said. "You recall something that didn't take place?"

"In essence that I'm . . . I remember telling Neil something but, in fact, I didn't tell him that. That, ah, my memory is mistaken."

"You're mistaken?"

"That's right."

"Well, how much of what you've been telling me here tonight are you mistaken about?"

"Ah," Rob said, sighing. "Very little."

9. If Rob had been so concerned about Liz's whereabouts Tuesday evening, why hadn't he called Liz's classmate Linda Phillips from the Bains' house instead of waiting until he'd returned to the Recreation Centre? "I could have," Rob said. "But, at that point, I wasn't concerned enough to feel that the call was urgent. And, as well, the fact that I felt I had to give Linda a few minutes' grace to get home, because I knew that her house is at least a ten- or fifteen-minute drive from the school." Reesor found that reply "evasive."

10. Contrary to what Rob had said, Mr. Bain told Reesor earlier in the day that Rob had never mentioned his discussion with Kris Kangas to him. "Like, what's the explanation for that?" Reesor asked.

"He doesn't remember," Rob said.

Reesor couldn't believe it—now the kid was blaming both of the girl's parents for having faulty memories. "So," Reesor said, his tone growing more belligerent, "now what you're telling us is that you're aware of a person who thinks she saw Liz at 5:30 on Tuesday over at the school. It seems to me that this would be of crucial importance to our investigation, and you've been aware of this since last Wednesday and you didn't disclose this to Detective McKennitt or Detective Warr or myself, until after I start asking all kinds of questions on this stuff. Now what's going on here, Rob? I am getting the feeling that you're not being perfectly frank with me."

Once again, Rob attempted to put Kris's sighting in perspective. If Kris saw Liz wearing a purple T-shirt—and not a blouse—then she had more than likely seen Liz on a day other than Tuesday. Rob then told Reesor about having seen Cathy wear a purple T-shirt after his talk with Kris. "How do you know that Liz had only one purple T-shirt?" Reesor asked. "And how do you know that her sister doesn't have exactly the same one?"

"Well, first of all," Rob said, "when I got to the Bains' house, I asked Cathy if that was Liz's shirt, and she said, 'Yes, are you kidding? Of course.' She borrowed Liz's clothes all the time."

"So you thought enough about what Kris had told you about seeing Liz on Tuesday and wearing a purple T-shirt that you would question Cathy about the shirt she was wearing?"

"Uh-huh."

"But you didn't think enough of it to mention anything to Detective McKennitt a couple of hours later?"

"Okay," Rob said. "This is the reason why. I felt that what Kris had disclosed was very important but, at the same time, we were looking at so many leads that I thought it was just as likely a non-lead. As well, I made it perfectly clear to Kris that this was a very serious undertaking and that she was to phone me at my home at 11:30 Thursday evening. And I thought to myself, well, if Kris phones me on Thursday at 11:30, she's gonna make damn sure that she knows whether she saw Liz on Tuesday or Monday—"

"Well, if you could just hold on a minute," Reesor said, interrupting him. "You told Mr. Bain about this conversation with Kris last Wednesday night?"

"No, last Thursday night."

Even though Reesor was wrong, he insisted that Rob had claimed to have mentioned Kris Kangas to Mr. Bain on Wednesday night. Rob said Reesor was mistaken. "I didn't speak to Kris until Thursday night," he said. There was a long pause. It was the moment at which Reesor had to either make his move or back off.

"Well, Rob," he said, "I've come into this interview trying to keep a very open mind about things. But, quite truthfully, I've found you to be very evasive. As soon as I challenge you on something, you become evasive or change your position or qualify your position. Now, with my experience as a police officer and a Homicide detective, this is the type of behaviour you get from someone who's trying to hide something. There is no doubt in my mind whatsoever, and I'm sure my partner feels the exact same way—because this isn't something that isn't totally obvious to both of us—that you are hiding something about all of this. Now, Liz is and was a beautiful girl and there are a lot of people right now in a lot of grief about what's happened to her, and where she is and about ensuring that she is put to rest in a proper way. And I truthfully believe that you're withholding crucial information from us, and that, if, in fact, you've not killed her by yourself, you know what's happened to her and where she is. You must be aware that we're going to continue this investigation and we are going to be treating it from this point on as a homicide. We are very thorough. We don't close cases. We work on them as long as it takes to come to a resolution. This case is not going to be going away. If this is the situation and you can provide us with information right now, then this thing can be resolved one way or another, because it's going to be resolved eventually anyhow."

Numb with fear, all Rob could say was "Oh."

"Now frankly, I think that she's been murdered. From the forensic information we have about the car, all indications point in that direction. If, in fact, she was not murdered in the car, her body was certainly transported inside of it. At this point, I've spoken with you and various other people, and, frankly, everybody has been very straightforward—except for you. You're the only person who has been evasive in any way, shape or form."

"I, oh, I'm sorry," Rob sputtered. "I must say that I see absolutely no reason to believe that I've been evasive. Perhaps 'inaccurate' is the word."

"No, that's not the case. You were really sure about certain things, and, then, when I start to question you about them, you begin weaving your way around my challenges. I mean, we've got a lengthy interview here, and these things can be charted out to show every point where you've been dishonest with us. In particular, this bit about finding out from Cindy about—"

"Kris," Rob said, correcting him. Here Reesor was expecting Rob to have perfect recall of events that occurred several days ago, and now he'd forgotten a name he'd referred to repeatedly just two minutes earlier. Vexed, Reesor went on to list some of the areas in Rob's story that gave him pause and he explained that, at some later date, these contradictory statements could be used as circumstantial evidence against him.

"We do not require direct evidence to lay a murder charge," Reesor said. "As a matter of fact, we laid a first-degree murder charge as recently as this past June 1989, where there was no body." Reesor was possibly too modest to admit that it had been his investigation into the disappearance of forty-seven-year-old Susan O'Neal that had resulted in the charge against her common-law husband, Robert Adamson. "We did subsequently recover the body," Reesor said. "But we deal with circumstantial evidence quite often with murder cases."

Reesor said that he was going to give Rob an opportunity to be truthful about the night of Liz's disappearance before he left. But Rob was adamant he'd been telling them the truth—"without a shadow of a doubt." Reesor then turned his attention to the diary pages Rob had taken home with him. "Where are those papers now?" he asked.

Rob answered, "At the Bain house."

"All the papers?"

"That is correct."

"How many papers have you taken?"

"I really don't know. I didn't count them."

"Did you read them?"

While, of course, Rob had skimmed through all the entries he'd borrowed, stopping to read passages here and there, he remembered reading only a couple of entries that pertained to Liz's relationship with Eric Genuis; these he'd read carefully from beginning to end. That's what he was thinking when he answered, "I read two."

"Out of how many?"

"Thirty pages."

"So you've returned all thirty papers?"

"That's right."

The next thing Reesor wanted to talk about was Rob's assertion that he'd never learned to drive a car with a standard transmission. Reesor found this hard to believe. "You've never ever driven a standard?" His tone was doubtful.

"I have never ever driven a standard vehicle in my entire life, and that is a skill lacking in me that everyone close to me is aware of."

"You've never even tried it?"

"Yes," Rob said. "I tried it once with my friend Phil in his Suzuki Samurai."

"Phil who?"

"Phil Dach." Rob spelled out Phil's surname.

"And how long ago was that?" Reesor asked.

"Oh, at least two years ago. I was quite unsuccessful."

"What do you mean by that?"

"I stalled it every time. At one point, Phil said, 'Rob, you're gonna wreck my car.' And he didn't want to teach me any more. I've never tried it again since."

On the subject of standard transmissions, Reesor was anxious to find out how Rob knew about Liz's car being left in reverse when he'd never been close enough to the car to see the position of the gearshift. Rob's answer was the same one he'd given over the phone to Tony Warr: "Her brother told me."

"This is Paul or Mark?" Reesor asked.

"Paul."

"Now we checked with Paul on that, and Paul said he never mentioned anything to you about what gear the car was in."

"Um, hmm."

"And that you never got close enough to the car—"

"Well—"

"To see the position of the gearshift."

"That's right," Rob said. "I also remember that Mark had said that the car had been backed in. It didn't occur to me that the car being backed in was pertinent information—"

"I'm not talking about the car being backed in. I'm talking about the gearshift. To park your car in backwards with a standard transmission, you've got to change the position of the gearshift."

"That's right," Rob said. "But the word used was 'reversed,' okay?"

"But I'm just asking you about the gearshift. First you said it was Paul who told you this, and now you're saying it was Mark."

"No, what I'm saying is that I was told Mark had reasoned that Liz probably wasn't the one who'd driven her car or had left it there, because it was parked in reverse. Now, when I heard 'in reverse,' I thought to myself, what he meant by 'in reverse' was that someone had backed it in. But later I got the impression that what they meant by 'in reverse' was in reverse gear."

"And when did Mark make these comments?"

"Well," Rob said, "Mark never made the comments to me."

"When did you hear these comments, then?"

"I guess that would be when we were congregating in front of the main entrance to Scarborough campus yesterday."

"But you were quite succinct, for instance, with Detective Warr. You told him that Liz wouldn't have put the car there because the gearshift was in reverse, and she never used the car when the gearshift was in reverse."

She never used the car when the gearshift was in reverse? Even for someone familiar with the use of a standard transmission, this was a nonsensical pronouncement.

How did Liz make her car go backwards if she never used reverse gear? Not only was this an indecipherable suggestion, Rob had never said such a thing. Unsure of what exactly Reesor was trying to say, Rob decided to reiterate what he'd said to Detective Warr. "I told him that she never reverses into a parking spot," Rob said. "But, you see, at that point, I was mixed up because I had been led to believe that—"

Reesor cut him off. He didn't want to hear another word. Every time he figured he had Rob backed into a corner, Reesor thought, the kid would bob and weave his way back into the centre of the ring, flipping little jabs at him on the way, as if it was Rob's way of letting him know that he was going to get toyed with all night long. "You know," Reesor said. "I ask you something, and you say 'That's right,' and then when I challenge you on how you knew that, you just go on and on, trying to make up excuses. What you're doing right now is telling us that everybody else is lying and that you're the only one telling the truth. And you're lying because you know the gearshift was in reverse because, more than likely, that's where you left it."

"Hardly likely," Rob said.

"I think it's very likely."

"Well, I mean, obviously that's your position."

They went back and forth for another minute or two until Reesor said he'd like to take another short break. "I know you don't mind being here," Reesor said. "We're going to try and get you out of here as soon as we can, but I would like to ask you more questions."

"Certainly," Rob said. "I'm in no hurry." There was a brief silence. Rob looked down at the floor and said, "I'm very frightened."

"Yeah, well, I appreciate that. I mean, as I told you before, you're not under arrest and you're not facing any charges—not to say that there might not be any in the future. You're only here as a witness at this time. I want to make sure that's clear to you."

"That is, ah, yes, very clear."

Reesor asked Rob if he would like anything to drink. "Another drink of water would be fine," Rob said. For the record, Reesor gave the time: 9:17 PM. And then he reached for his tape recorder and, with a flick of his thumb, stopped the tape.

—◇—

When Reesor and Raybould rejoined Rob, who'd been waiting alone in the Resource Room for over twenty minutes, Raybould had the package of cigarettes in Elizabeth Bain's glove box on his mind, and, without tipping his hand, he mused aloud about the possibility of Liz being a smoker. Reesor, who was handing Rob his glass of water, had not yet started the tape. "She didn't smoke," Rob said, his perplexity now transformed into indignation by such a fantastic suggestion.

"Oh, we thought she might have been a social smoker or something like that," Raybould said. Reesor reached for the tape recorder and turned it back on. "The time is now 9:40 PM," Reesor said into the machine. "And Detective Raybould and myself—"

"I'm sorry," Rob interjected. "I'm sorry."

"You want to stop," Reesor guessed.

"I'd like to stop *that*," Rob said, pointing to the tape recorder.

"Okay, it's 9:40 and Rob has asked that we stop the tape for a second."

Completely mystified as to who would suggest that Liz smoked, socially or otherwise, Rob wasn't quite ready to begin the interview (or was it an interrogation?—he wasn't sure any more) until the smoking issue had been clarified. "Liz told me that she'd only taken one puff of a cigarette in her life," Rob said. "And that was years ago. She told me it happened when she was visiting her cousins in Florida and that she felt so guilty about it the next day that she jogged five miles in the blazing heat."

When Reesor realized that Rob had asked him to turn off the tape for no obvious reason, he simply switched it back on a few seconds later, picking up where he'd left off before the break. Reesor spent the better part of the next hour leading Rob through the sequence of events that had occurred between the time he'd arrived home from the gym on Tuesday night to the moment he'd been handed Liz's last diary entry by Arlene Coventry the following morning. Again, he confronted Rob about the fact that he was unable to recall what he'd worn to the gym that night, which, presumably, were the same clothes he'd changed out of before going to bed.

"It would make sense to me," Reesor posited, "that, if a person had, for instance, got some blood on their clothing or something, they may not be forthright in declaring what they'd been wearing in case there was a possibility of blood being on that clothing. They wouldn't want someone to know exactly what they'd been wearing."

"Yeah," said Rob. "I think that's a logical assumption."

"Right. That's why I'm wondering what's so difficult about remembering what you were wearing that night."

Rob exhaled deeply enough for the tape to pick it up.

"Well, Rob, you know our position, so—"

"Yes, I do."

"We feel you're being evasive and withholding information," Reesor said. He stumbled awkwardly into the query that he'd been itching to ask for several hours now. "Ah, um, I mean, the question is . . . I mean, the question I'm going to put to you, right, is, ah, did you kill Liz?"

Rob was emphatic. "Absolutely not. I never would. I loved Liz and I wanted to spend the rest of my life with her."

"Okay," Reesor said. "But what if she didn't want to spend the rest of her life with you and she made you aware of that? That's frequently a motive for, ah, murder. You know, 'Well, I can't have her, so nobody else will.'"

"That's a feeling that I can understand you guys having when it came to Liz," Rob said. "But, in the past, there were times that I had come face to face with the idea of perhaps never seeing Liz again and that never really aroused in me any anger or violent feelings, though certainly disappointment. If Liz had wanted to be on her own, I'm quite certain, positive in fact, that I would have let her be free. Of course I would have been very disappointed and, at times, distraught, because I loved Liz and I felt in my heart that she was the only girl that I ever loved."

"What do you think happened to her?" Reesor asked.

"I think Liz was murdered."

"And how do you think that happened?"

There was a long pause. "Well, at this point, anything could have happened," Rob said. He said that she could have been attacked.

"Where do you think this attack might have taken place, and when?"

"I believe the attack took place in the valley on Tuesday night between seven-fifteen and nine."

"Why do you say seven-fifteen?"

"Because that's the last time I saw her car in the valley."

"Why don't you think it could have happened before then?"

"Because, at that time, the tennis courts would have had a better chance of being populated by people who might have seen her assailant."

"Assuming she was at the tennis courts," Reesor added.

"Assuming she was at the tennis courts," Rob repeated. He then reiterated his doubt regarding the veracity of what Liz had told her mother before leaving home the final time on Tuesday, which was that she was going to check the tennis schedule. Considering there was no way to book a court more than half an hour in advance, Rob concluded this claim was dubious at best.

"I'm not that familiar with the area," Reesor said. "But I would assume there are many places between the tennis courts and where her car was parked. She could have been attacked and dragged into the bushes."

"Sure, but there are many well-used paths around there. It's just not a place where you would attack someone when there was still sufficient light."

If Liz was killed in the valley, Reesor wanted to know how and where Rob thought it might have happened.

"It's beyond me," Rob said. "I don't know. There's always the possibility that she met up with someone she might have known. Someone that she would have had cause to trust and who may have asked her for a ride somewhere. Either that or perhaps she was accosted in the valley—but not killed—maybe threatened and taken to her car against her will. Not necessarily a struggle, but if a weapon were produced, Liz might be convinced that this person was going to hurt her and, if she didn't go along with what he was saying, then he could have walked with her to her car, forced her to drive somewhere isolated and then killed her."

"Or killed her in the car," Reesor offered. He told Rob that the amount of blood found in the car was so great that the chance of Liz still being alive was minute.

Rob was surprised to hear that. "Is that right?" he asked, not quite ready to accept she might be dead. "At the same time, though, I'm quite sure it's possible that the blood in the car doesn't necessarily point to a murder."

"Well, what could it point to?"

"For one thing, Liz often had unexpected, ah, bleeding."

"What do you mean?"

"Ah, her menstrual cycle, you know."

"But the blood isn't on the seat, so . . . " Reesor shrugged. He then asked why someone would have transported her to another location in her car.

"To try and hide her," Rob said.

"And what's the advantage of hiding her?"

"Well, the delay would give a greater opportunity for an alibi, for escape. In a way, that's why I was so surprised to find her car so close to the potential scene of the crime. It didn't seem very logical to me."

"But a stranger doesn't really need an alibi or to get away," Reesor argued. "A stranger could just leave her body lying somewhere and walk away. Nobody would know the difference. So, from what you know about the case, you feel this has to be a person she knows?"

"Yes," Rob said. "I do believe that, if Liz was killed, it was by someone she knows."

Rob was being so cooperative that Reesor decided to push the envelope of their hypothetical conversation, knowing that, if Rob took the bait, his responses, no matter how speculative, would carry dark, confessional overtones if Reesor ever got the chance to play his tapes for a jury. "If you were going to kill Liz—and I'm not saying that you did," Reesor said, treading carefully, "but in a hypothetical situation—"

"I can't answer that."

"You can't think of how it might happen?"

"No, I couldn't."

Reesor tried a more oblique approach. "Well, you probably wouldn't use a gun because you probably don't have a gun."

"I would never use a gun," Rob said.

"Isn't it possible that, during an argument, in the heat of the moment, you may be capable of losing control and—"

"We didn't argue."

"No, I know," Reesor assured him. "I'm just saying, if you could conceive yourself in a position where you might, you know, lose control, I'm just wondering what you might do?"

"Basically, what you're asking me is if I was going to kill someone, how would I do it?"

No question about it, Reesor said to himself, this kid could really read between the lines. Even though this was precisely what Reesor was asking, he never would have been foolish enough to state it so baldly. "No," Reesor promised. "I'm not. Really. I'm just saying that, if you could hypothesize at all about you and Liz in a situation—"

Having come to the realization that Reesor wasn't going to give up, Rob opted to get it over with by answering his hypothetical question. "Choking," he said, wearily. "I would never mutilate her."

Finally! It had taken four hours, but now Reesor was getting somewhere. "Yeah," he said, meaning that he wanted Rob to continue.

"I would never want to do damage to her body. I'd never shoot her."

"Yeah."

"I would never stab her."

"Yeah."

"It would be something like choking. But I mean . . . "

"And that would be perhaps as a result of an argument or a fight? Like in a rage or something, maybe?"

"Well, perhaps, but I mean . . . "

Reesor jumped right in. "See, something like that happens when you're in a rage, you know, during an argument, for instance, when the person loses control. That isn't necessarily murder, you know."

"Yeah," Rob said. "I know."

"It could be considered manslaughter."

"Yeah," Rob said flatly. "But, as far as rage goes, I have been angry with Liz before, quite angry, in fact. Angry enough to ask her to leave my house and to do it in quite a cold fashion. But my way of dealing with Liz in a state of rage was to ask her to go away. I couldn't bear to feel angry towards her, so it was easier to just not see her when I felt that way."

"Do you have any feeling right now for where her body might be?"

"No. But Detective Warr mentioned that it was conceivable that the car was driven some distance away either after the assault or while the assault was taking place and perhaps brought back."

"You think that likely?" Reesor inquired.

"Yes, I do."

"So then it wasn't just moved from point A in the valley to point B up on top of the hill."

"You see, Liz wasn't a big girl, and it did occur to me that she could have easily been carried. I wouldn't suspect that because by nine o'clock it's probably beginning to get dark in some places, but it's still pretty conspicuous. That's one of the reasons I wanted to go to the area in the valley we searched today. I thought there was a chance that her assailant might have taken her body up to the junction at Manse and Old Kingston Road, just west of the road to the tennis courts. Once he left her there, he could then go down, get in her car, drive up, put her in the car and take her somewhere."

"How would you get from the valley to Manse and Old Kingston Road? You mean, like, through the bush?"

Rob suggested it would be easier for him to draw them a map. "Would that help?"

"Okay," said Reesor. "Sure."

Rob drew a rough map of the valley and pointed out a clearing where Liz's assailant could have easily dragged her or carried her into a thick expanse of bush. There was a spot Rob had seen in the west end of the valley where the bush came right up to the edge of Old Kingston Road on the north side, and Rob thought it might be the right kind of place for her attacker to leave the body while he retrieved her car. Then, all he would have to do was pull up close to the bushes at the side of the road and drag the body into the car. From there, Rob theorized, the man could come around Manse, pass West Hill and hit Kingston Road, where he'd be free to go either east or west.

If that was the case, Reesor said, the attacker was either someone who knew Liz (and, therefore, knew that the silver Tercel was hers) or he saw her get out of the car. "Now," Reesor said, "if this person had backed out of the parking lot and gone westbound on Old Kingston Road and stopped here on the north side where you said, then I guess he would have had to bring her in through the passenger side of the car because that side would be right up next to the bushes." Reesor was leading Rob into a nifty little trap. From the bloodstains around the frame of the passenger door, Reesor knew that, if a body had been dragged in or out of the car, it had happened on that side.

"I don't know," Rob said. "But it's possible."

Reesor would have to do better than that. "Does that mean you're in agreement that if, as you pointed out here, the way the car's facing west on the north side of the road, there's no way someone would bring it around to the driver's side to put it in?"

"No, I can't see that happening because he'd be more open to exposure."

"Did you ride in Liz's car very often?"

"Well, I rode in the car but not that often."

"When was the last time you were in the car?"

"The last time was, um, a week ago Tuesday. And the only reason I rode in her car then was because we were with a client of hers from the group home and she informed me that my liability was not high enough to insure me against any potential damage to William. But I'm quite certain that, had that not been the case, I would have driven. In the last four months, I've been in her car maybe three times."

Next, Reesor decided to pump Rob for his theories on why Liz's car had been left across the street from Three R Auto Body. For once, Rob was truly stumped—he had no idea. So Reesor, looking to show Rob up with a little investigative razzle-dazzle of his own, laid out his own theory of how and why the murder had occurred.

This is how it went. Rob sees Liz's car in the valley on his way to the gym. He drives over to the tennis courts, meets her and suggests they go for a walk towards the area of bush that Rob was kind enough to point out on his little map. He and Liz get into an argument and he chokes her—maybe not on purpose—but she ends up dying. Rob panics, hides her corpse in the bushes and goes to his car on the south side of Old Kingston Road, where he said he'd parked for a few minutes to spy on Liz's car. Rob drives up to the gym at 7:15 PM and gets changed for his workout. Before going to the Bains' shortly after nine o'clock, Rob would have had enough time to either walk or drive back down into the valley where he gets into Liz's car and pulls up onto the shoulder of the road against the bushes in which he'd left her body. Then he hoists her corpse into the car on the passenger side, the precise way he himself had just suggested, and gets behind the wheel, taking her somewhere to dump the body. After that chore has been completed, he returns, parking her car on Morrish Road because it's close enough to the university for him to walk to his car, which he'd likely parked at the Recreation Centre or in the valley—leaving himself plenty of time to get to the Bains' around nine.

Instead of wilting at Reesor's genius—the way bad guys do on television when an effusive Columbo, waving his soggy, unlit cigar around for effect, confronts the murderer with the true details of what was supposed to be the perfect crime—Rob conceded that Reesor's theory was "quite conceivable." "So what you're saying," Reesor suggested, "is that it's a logical scenario."

"I wouldn't use the word 'logical,' " Rob said. "I would say quite possible."

"It's a possible scenario."

"Yes."

Reesor wondered how, without an alibi, Rob was going to be able to disprove his version of the crime. Rob said, "I believe that, over the course of your investigation in the next day or two, you will find that I was indeed working out between the time of twenty after seven and twenty to nine."

"We might," Reesor said, his tone doubtful. "I'm just saying . . . "

Apparently unsatisfied with Rob's response to his first theory, Reesor sprang a second one on him. In this one, the murder happens the same way as before, but, instead of moving the body that evening, there is nothing stopping Rob from going home to hit the sack, leaving Liz safely hidden in the bushes. Then, he sneaks out of the house in the middle of the night and loads her body into the car under the cover of darkness.

Rob said it could never happen. His mom tended to sleep during the day, and she spent her nights on the daybed in the living room, less than twenty feet from the front door. "But let's face it," Reesor said. "There's probably more than one way to get out of your house besides going through the front door." That was true, Rob said, but Reesor just didn't understand how jittery his mother was—she could hear a mouse run across the kitchen floor.

"I find it very difficult to exclude you as a suspect at this point, I really do," Reesor said, wearing his grimmest expression. "As a matter of fact, some of the stuff you've told me raises my suspicions for you quite higher. What do you think of coming down to police headquarters tomorrow morning to take a polygraph test to see if maybe we can resolve some of this? If you have no objections, perhaps the test will—"

"Excuse me, I'm sorry. A polygraph test? A lie detector?"

"Yeah."

"I have an objection."

"You do? What's that?"

"Well, for one thing, I don't trust polygraph tests."

Reesor tried to alleviate his concerns by pointing out that polygraph tests can't be used as evidence in a court of law. It was nothing more than an "investigative tool" that helped the police come to important decisions regarding their potential suspects. "If the person fails it, it doesn't mean they're guilty," he explained. "But if they pass with flying colours, then we say, 'Forget him, let's go on to the next guy.' And it really makes our job a lot easier."

"Does it?" Rob said. "Okay. In that event, yes, I will come down then."

While he was in such an accommodating mood, Reesor thought he'd see what Rob thought of driving down to another police station in the Birchmount and Eglinton area to give some forensic samples—fingerprints, hair and blood. They could get going in a couple of minutes. Over the years, Reesor had learned that it was best to do these things sooner rather than later. Once a suspect got in touch with a lawyer, polygraphs and blood samples were much more difficult to come by. With nothing to hide, Rob agreed to give them whatever they wanted, even though it was now 10:30 on a Sunday evening.

"We'll leave it at that," Reesor said. "And then we'll do a polygraph tomorrow and, hopefully, you'll pass with flying colours and we can discount you altogether as a suspect."

Rob wasn't so sure. "To be honest with you, I don't think passing a polygraph test is grounds to discount me, would you not agree?"

"Well, it's a pretty good indicator."

"I don't know," Rob said. "I don't know if I believe that. I know a little bit about polygraph tests. A lot of people who have committed crimes have passed them, and the reverse is true for innocent people who have failed them."

Rob had him there. "I'm not saying it hasn't happened," Reesor confessed. "I'm trying to be objective about this investigation. We're not just going to be looking at you, but, by the same token, if we can get rid of you as a suspect, it certainly helps us focus on somebody else, right?"

Rob somehow managed to be sympathetic. "I realize that this isn't exactly enjoyable for you and I realize you're just doing your job. That's why I related to you my feeling that I was going to be seen as a suspect. It didn't really surprise me because that's part of your job, and I wouldn't have it any other way."

Reesor said that Rob had been most patient with them. Before he brought the interview to a close, he asked Rob if there was anything else he'd like to say for the record. "Yeah," he said. "I'd just like to say that, because in many ways I was the closest to Liz, it's very logical that I'm seen as someone who would potentially harm her. She was a source of love for me, and we do hurt or are more likely to hurt the ones we love. Ours was a very passionate relationship and that passion often did involve anger, but never the potential for physical harm. I don't feel I've been mistreated. I've provided as much information as I can recall. Right now, I'm very upset because a person I felt that I was going to spend the rest of my life with is perhaps gone. Consequently, I don't even think I could tell you what my actions were yesterday. I'm very distraught but, as I sit here, I know that what's important is not to be distraught, but truthful. Not only am I endeavouring to clear my own name— which I think, in the end, obviously will be—but I want to find whoever did this, because I don't want it to happen again. And I don't want them to go free."

"That's fine," said Reesor. "Is there anything else?"

"I did not kill Elizabeth Bain."

—◦—

"Don't you guys have to wear your seat belts?" Rob asked, sitting alone in the back seat of Reesor's sedan. "I thought that was the new law."

You had to hand it to him, Reesor thought, the kid had balls. "No, Rob," Reesor said. "We're exempt from the law. What if we have to get out of the car in a hurry to chase a suspect or defend our lives? Get it?"

Reesor just shook his head. He was too busy mulling over the last five hours to engage in any more meaningless banter about seat belts. The problem was that, by just about any standard, the "interview" had been a bust. Sure, Reesor had slyly engaged Rob in a hypothetical conversation about how Liz's murder might have occurred, a bit of dialogue that could prove to be valuable at a later date, but overall Rob's response to their endless stream of terse questions and to their suggestion that he might have killed his girlfriend did not follow any pattern.

It is well documented that murderers have two fundamental reactions to an interrogation or an arrest. Overwhelmed by guilt, one out of four breaks down and confesses, usually without too much prodding. Typically, those who confess are people who have just killed a loved one, be it a spouse or a family member. The other seventy-five per cent, possessing a basic grasp of their constitutional rights, clam up and demand to speak to a lawyer. There was the incredibly slight chance that Rob Baltovich was a psychopath, and that his long-windedness was simply a twisted game he'd knowingly engaged them in, confident that his innate guile would provide his pursuers with nothing but torment. However, Baltovich displayed none of the classic characteristics of a psychopath, neither the hollow voice nor the slightly detached air of someone completely devoid of a conscience.

Having worked at 41 Division for a stretch, Brian Raybould knew what room they had to go to for Rob to get fingerprinted. They'd been told on the way in that the print man would be joining them in a few minutes, so Rob took a seat at a small desk while Reesor and Raybould stood leaning against the wall on either side of the door, as though they'd been posted sentry. They were all talked out, each man left with his own thoughts. And then, looking up from the desk, Rob broke the tense silence. "I hope this will prove it wasn't me who touched the gearshift," he said.

Reesor and Raybould gave each other one of those looks that said, *Is this guy trying to write himself a one-way ticket to the slammer, or what?* Raybould opened up a file folder and wrote down the entire utterance on a piece of foolscap.

It was almost midnight by the time they got around to recording his fingerprints and drawing his blood. Rob was then handed a pair of tweezers and directed to pluck hairs from various places on his body, including his pubic area, while Reesor and Raybould looked on—an appropriate end to the most surreal evening of Rob's life.

Once he was alone again in the back of the sedan on the return trip to 42 Division, where he'd left his car, Rob's mind drifted back to the only time he'd ever been inside a police station prior to Liz's disappearance. It had happened about a year and a half earlier. A seventeen-year-old named Wade Lawson had been shot at by a pair of Toronto police officers who'd been staking out a stolen car that Lawson and his friend had attempted to drive past the cops when they stepped in front of Lawson's vehicle, guns drawn. One of the six shots fired by the officers had hit Lawson in the back of the head, killing him. Lawson was black, the officers were white. The incident immediately set off a massive controversy regarding the issue of systemic racism within the Metropolitan Toronto Police Force. Even though one of the officers had claimed to have been hit in the leg by Lawson's car as he sped away, the officer whose bullet had fatally wounded Lawson was charged with second-degree murder (mostly due to the fact that the shot had been fired from behind), and his partner faced charges of shooting with intent to wound and with endangering life.

Rob had always thought Toronto police were top-notch and he was one of their big supporters. So when he learned that people were going to various police stations around the city to sign petitions of support for a beleaguered force, Rob felt that it was his civic duty to drive to a police building a few miles north of his house where he walked into the lobby, signed the petition and left.

His reverie was cut short by the sound of Reesor taking a loud, deep breath of the warm summer air that was blowing in through his open window. Reesor turned his head to look at the passing trees and said, "It's a beautiful night to smell the flowers—too bad Liz won't be smelling the flowers any more." Rob shuddered with a combination of fear and disgust. He had no idea that police officers could treat people in such a cavalier and hurtful manner, especially innocent people. And so, over the course of just one evening, the memory of signing the petition had become a distasteful one, little more than a painful reminder of a sheltered and naive young man who once saw himself as anything but that.

—◯—

The first thing Rob did as he walked through the front door at home was call upstairs, where his father was asleep in bed. "You better come down to the kitchen, Dad," he said. "I've got to talk to you. It's important." Adele, who was up in a flash, sat with Jim at the kitchen table while Rob paced the floor and recounted how Reesor had methodically placed his cards on the table, fingering him as Liz's killer.

Jim and Adele were completely bewildered—"Why would they think such a thing?" No one knew what to do. Rob decided to call his brother, Paul, even though it was now one o'clock in the morning. The situation had suddenly become extremely grave. Rob knew that his parents weren't the most worldly people, especially when it came to the law. He felt that Paul, now out and working in the real world, would be the most likely candidate within their immediate family to come up with a plan.

Paul and his wife, Dana, had been asleep for several hours by the time the phone on their bedside table rang. He'd heard from his mother, once at 11:00 PM and again at midnight, who'd been calling to ask if he'd heard from Rob. She'd been ringing the police station to see if her son was still there but kept getting the same line— that he wasn't in the building. But Paul hadn't heard from Rob until now. They spoke for only a couple of minutes before Paul nudged Dana awake to tell her what had happened. He said he'd be home as soon as he could.

Early into the morning, the family sat around the kitchen table, analyzing everything that had happened since Tuesday. By the end of their discussion, everyone
agreed that it wouldn't be wise for Rob to do anything more with the police until
he'd spoken to a lawyer. Paul suggested that they get in touch with Gordon McIntyre, whose daughter, Karen, was engaged to marry a cousin of theirs named Gregg
Anderson. McIntyre was a detective sergeant at Toronto's 51 Division. Paul figured
that, of all the people they knew, he would be in the best position to know the
names of a few good criminal defence lawyers. Everyone agreed.

Paul didn't leave until three o'clock in the morning, not noticing the unmarked
cruiser parked on the other side of the street two houses down from his parents' as
he backed out of the driveway and drove south on Midland Avenue. Sitting inside
was Constable Donald Keeley from the Metropolitan Toronto Police Force's Intelligence Services unit, which specialized in physical and electronic surveillance; Keeley recorded the car's licence plate number and the exact time of departure for the
report he would file at the end of his shift.

Keeley waited exactly six minutes before starting his car and circling the block
for any sign of the Toyota (he thought it was either light blue or grey). No luck.
Using his cellular phone, he called the office and had them search the registration
for the plate. The vehicle was registered to Dana Baltovich, obviously a relative of
the suspect, who lived in a basement apartment on Holmcrest Trail. Keeley reached
for his map of the city. He thought he'd take a little drive.

While Keeley was trying to locate the house in the index of his map book, Paul
was taking a slight detour through the valley on Old Kingston Road on his way
home. He'd just spent the better part of two hours listening to Rob describe what
he'd seen on the night Liz had vanished into thin air and now he thought he'd refa-
miliarize himself with the area. Slowing slightly as he neared the small, rectangular
lot in which Rob had said he'd last seen Liz's car, Paul saw that there was a muddy
four-by-four pick-up truck with a cab on the back parked all by itself. And then he
noticed a man walking along the path adjacent to the lot, not far from the pick-up.
What was this guy doing down here at three o'clock in the morning? It was
definitely eerie, especially in light of what Rob had said about the police finding
blood in Liz's car.

As soon as he got back to the apartment, he woke up Dana and told her about
the pick-up in the valley. He wanted to call the police so they could send down an

officer to check it out. But he didn't want to call on their home phone, as he was under the impression that the police routinely traced the numbers of those who called in tips, and, from what he now knew, it seemed highly unlikely that the police would follow up a tip regarding the Elizabeth Bain disappearance given to them by Robert Baltovich's brother.

Paul grabbed a quarter out of the change bottle on the dresser and said he was going to call it in from a pay phone. He drove north onto Cherry Hill Avenue and didn't bother coming to a complete stop before turning right at Lawrence Avenue. There was another car coming straight at him as he made his blind turn. If the man behind the wheel of the oncoming car hadn't been paying attention, they would have side-swiped each other. Keeley couldn't believe it. That was the fucking car he was looking for that almost killed him!

Once he'd gathered himself together, Keeley turned his car around and headed east on Lawrence, overtaking Paul in the left-hand lane. Quickly, Keeley switched back into the right lane, keeping an eye on Paul in the rear-view mirror. Not sure if the subject had recognized his car from back on Midland Avenue, Keeley decided to play it safe and pulled into the parking lot of the Centennial Plaza where Lawrence meets Port Union Road. Wouldn't you know it, the Toyota pulled in right behind him. Surveillance work could get pretty fucked up like this sometimes, and you had to play it cool.

Keeley spotted a pizza joint up ahead and came up with a little plan. He would pretend to be the hungry guy with a craving for pepperoni and anchovies at 3:30 AM. Casually, he got out of his car and walked up to the front of the pizza parlour and shook the front doors for effect, just to make sure that "CLOSED" sign and the lack of one illuminated light bulb weren't some kind of cruel hoax on the character he was portraying.

On the way back to his car, he watched Paul step into a phone booth near the Sears store at the west end of the mall. Keeley made notes of the subject's next few movements. *Picks up receiver. Drops coin into phone. Dials number.* Suddenly, Keeley realized that their two cars were the only ones in the entire lot and he thought it would be a wise move to drive across the street and park there instead. Safely ensconced in his new location, he had enough cover to leave his vehicle and walk towards the plaza for a better vantage point.

Paul dialled the operator and asked to be connected to 42 Division. He told a male constable about the pick-up in the valley and suggested that there might be a connection to the Bain disappearance. Unfortunately, he hadn't taken notice of the truck's licence plate number. The officer thanked him for the anonymous tip and said they would look into it.

Keeley scurried back to his car as Paul's Toyota lurched out of the plaza parking lot. He trailed him as far as Cherry Hill and watched as Paul turned south off Lawrence. Although he was tempted to follow, Keeley just kept moving west. It was high time he got back to his stake-out on Midland Avenue.

Part 3

—o—

Closing in on the Heart

Having caught about five hours of sleep, Steve Reesor showed up for work at 42 Division before eight o'clock on Monday so he could make arrangements for Rob to take a polygraph at Metro Police Headquarters downtown. Now that he had confronted Rob with the fact that he was their only suspect, they couldn't be sure how much longer he would remain a willing participant in the investigation. Reesor wanted to get the kid strapped up to lie-detector equipment before he changed his mind or, even worse, got in touch with a lawyer.

Around half-past nine, he called Rob at home and said he'd made an appointment for him to take the test at eleven. "I could come down and pick you up, if you like," Reesor offered.

"My willingness has changed," Rob said. "I've made plans to consult a lawyer."

This was exactly what Reesor didn't want to hear. All he could think to say was "Who's the lawyer?"

Rob said, "I'm not sure—it's being arranged by my family. I'll have to call you later today if you want to know who it is."

"Okay," said Reesor. "I'll expect your call."

Rob didn't bother disclosing that his family had already been in touch with Gregg Anderson, and that Anderson was going to call his future father-in-law,

Gordon McIntyre, and get the name of a decent lawyer. McIntyre worked at 51 Division, also known as Fort Apache, where two hundred cops assigned to keep the peace in the notorious Regent Park area, a haven for crack dealers and prostitutes, waged a daily street war otherwise known as "community patrol." (Among Toronto cops, it was well known that one year on the job at Fort Apache was worth ten years of experience at just about any other division in the city.) Adele hoped that he would be able to help—her faith in police officers had reached an all-time low—and she was anxious throughout the morning waiting to hear what McIntyre had to say. She must have chain-smoked an entire pack of cigarettes before noon.

When Gregg finally got through to him, McIntyre gave him the name and number of a young Crown attorney he'd worked closely with over the years named Bill Gatward. Gatward had gone into private practice about a year and a half ago, and McIntyre had just spoken to him at his new firm, Kirby, Lyon and Gatward. McIntyre had always liked Gatward, not only because he was a good lawyer and family man, but he was also a straight shooter with a great sense of humour. He rarely turned down the opportunity to share a few pints of draft beer with the guys at the end of the day. Over the phone, McIntyre had asked Gatward if he'd read any articles about Elizabeth Bain. Gatward said that he hadn't, so McIntyre filled him in on what little he knew about Rob's situation and wanted to know if he'd be willing to speak with him. Gatward said he'd be happy to.

Around noon, Rob got through to Gatward at his office and, although Gatward didn't yet think it was necessary to meet in person, he listened patiently to Rob's story before clearly and forcefully spelling out his advice. Gatward explained that the French word for lawyer was *avocat*, which meant someone who speaks on your behalf. From now on, Gatward asserted, Rob would communicate with the police and media only through him and under no circumstances was he to participate in a polygraph test.

Although Rob promised to go along with everything Gatward had just said, moments after hanging up the phone, Rob did the very thing he'd just agreed not to do—he called Reesor's pager number, as he'd promised earlier that morning. Reesor returned his call within minutes. "I'm calling to let you know that I just spoke with a lawyer named Bill Gatward," Rob said. "And as a result of our discussion, I also wanted you to know that I'm not going to be providing you with any more statements and I won't be taking a polygraph test."

"Is that your decision or are you doing what your lawyer told you to?" asked Reesor.

"It's my decision based on what my lawyer told me," Rob said.

"Which member of your family knows this lawyer, Gatward?"

"My cousin's father-in-law just happens to be a police officer with Metro," Rob said. "We got Mr. Gatward's name through him."

"Who's that?"

"A man named Gordon McIntyre."

"At 51 Division?"

"That's right," Rob said.

Not long after Reesor got off the phone with Rob, Brian Raybould rang McIntyre at Fort Apache and asked if he knew anything about the Baltovich situation. McIntyre told him that he knew next to nothing about the whole thing. "Look, Brian," said McIntyre. "My daughter's engaged to marry Robert Baltovich's cousin, so this is a little too close to home for me. I don't want to know anything about the case and I'm staying right out of it." McIntyre figured that Raybould and Reesor were not likely to be pleased about his referring the Baltoviches to a lawyer—which, over the course of his career, he'd done for all kinds of people—and there was an outside chance Raybould might throw a few snide remarks his way for interfering. Were that to happen, McIntyre was prepared to tell Raybould, also a detective sergeant, to sweetly fuck right off. Raybould, however, was smart enough to keep his thoughts to himself, and McIntyre never heard from him again.

—◦—

On his way to work at the Recreation Centre that morning, Rick Gostick stopped at the campus security desk and phoned the police from the hot line number set up for anyone who had information about Elizabeth Bain's disappearance. It was pretty much the same spot where he'd spoken to Detective Sergeant Tony Warr during the search on Saturday. He was now calling the police because later that weekend it had occurred to Rick that he'd forgotten to tell Warr about hitting the volleyball around with Rob and Neil Winton on Tuesday night.

He explained all of this to Detective Sergeant Steve Reesor over the hot line. The first thing Reesor said to him when he was finished was "Did Rob Baltovich ask you to tell us about this?"

"No," Rick said.

"Are you sure about that?"

Rick couldn't understand why they would suggest such a thing and he was startled by Reesor's hostile tone. Rick wasn't about to lie to protect Rob Baltovich, who was, at best, an acquaintance. "Positive," Rick answered. "If you don't believe me over the phone, then come out here and I'll swear on a stack of Bibles."

Reesor didn't come but, later in the day, Rob did. He was scheduled to work the basketball league starting at six-thirty but he decided to come in an hour ahead of time to see if anyone in the gym could remember seeing him there last Tuesday. When Rob saw Rick, he explained that the police were looking at him as a suspect and that he needed to find people who remembered seeing him in the weight room that night. Rick said that, he'd told the police about playing volleyball together but he didn't recall seeing him working out.

When Rob went down to the weight room to ask around, Rick decided to tag along. Rick knew that, because it was the middle of June and school had been out for some time, most of the people who used the weight room were "community" members, not students. He didn't think too many summer people would know Rob.

Together, they approached a fellow named Kaedmon Nancoo, who had been a member at the Recreation Centre since graduating from Scarborough College a year back. Kaedmon was working out with a friend of his, Lance Hettarachichi, when Rob asked if either of them remembered seeing him in the gym on Tuesday. Rob explained that he was a suspect in the disappearance of Elizabeth Bain, whom Kaedmon had recognized when he saw her picture on the news. "Yeah," Kaedmon said. "I think I remember seeing you in here."

"Great," Rob said.

"Yeah, I think it was around four-thirty."

"It couldn't have been," Rob said. "I wasn't in here until after seven."

"Maybe it was Monday then," Kaedmon said.

Rick knew that Rob worked the basketball league on Mondays, Wednesdays and Fridays and he tended to work out earlier on those days because the games began at 6:30 PM. He figured that Kaedmon had simply got the days mixed up. Rob was thinking the same thing and said, "It must have been Monday."

"Well," Kaedmon said, "I think it was Monday but I'm not sure."

"Can you remember what day it was for sure?" Rick asked.

"No," Kaedmon replied.

Rob said, "The police are probably going to come around at some point and ask questions. If you're positive you saw me, then say so. But if you're not sure, don't say you are. I know you're only trying to help, but what would really help most is for you not to guess."

"Okay," Kaedmon said. "But I'm pretty sure now that it was Monday."

Rob and Rick canvassed a few more people, but no one remembered seeing Rob on Tuesday. It was starting to look like it might not be that easy finding anyone else who saw him lifting weights. There was an anxious feeling in the pit of Rob's stomach as he went to the basketball courts for work.

—◦—

Reesor had no intention of letting Rob shake him off his tail, especially in light of the media coverage the story was getting. Tuesday morning's edition of *The Toronto Star* carried a decent-sized story, "Blood found in car of missing student, 22," on page two. The city's tabloid daily, *The Toronto Sun*, carried a blow-up photo of Liz on the front page, with the headline "Student feared dead." "There's no reason for this," Mrs. Bain told the *Sun*. "Liz said she's going to be engaged. She said she loved her boyfriend Rob."

Reesor called Rob at eleven o'clock that morning. When Adele answered the phone, Reesor asked her if Rob was home. "He is," she said, "but he's not feeling well." The truth was that Rob wasn't really sick, she was just trying to abide by Gatward's caution not to speak to the police.

"Is he well enough to come to the phone?" Reesor asked.

Adele said, "Let me go downstairs and check."

Rob picked up the phone moments later and Reesor asked how he was feeling. "Not too well," Rob said.

"I was a little surprised to hear from Detective Warr that you weren't out helping with the search down at Rouge Beach today," said Reesor. "I thought you'd be out there."

"My lawyer told me not to go on the searches any more," Rob said.

"Why not?"

"He said it wouldn't look too good if I happened to be with the team that found Liz's body."

"I see," Reesor said. "Would you mind going down to the Command Post and pointing out for Detective Warr where it was that you told us Liz used to go?"

As the conversation inched along, it became quite obvious that Reesor wasn't going to take no for an answer. Rob explained several times that he was waiting for his friend Jim Isaacs to come over, and that he might be able to go if Jim was willing to give him a drive. "Then I'll call Detective Warr and tell him you're on your way," Reesor said. Rob hung up the phone in silent agreement, knowing it was easier to simply not show up than to reiterate once again that he was heeding his lawyer's advice and would no longer be helping out with the searches.

When Rob didn't show up at the searches, Reesor and Raybould decided to take a little drive over to his house to see if he would talk to them. Adele could feel her heart start to pump when she opened her door and saw the two men who were accusing Robert of killing young Elizabeth. Part of her wanted to run and part of her wanted to order them off the property. They said they wanted to speak with Rob. She said he wasn't in and, even if he was, he had nothing more to say to either of them. The one named Raybould kept putting his big goofy hands up in the air and pleading, "But Mrs. Baltovich, we just want to talk with him for a minute."

Rob's mother was a lot older than they'd expected. She looked to be close in age to their own mothers. They didn't think it would take much to achieve Plan B— getting inside the house to have a cursory look around. They told her they needed to take a statement from her. She could either do that in the comfort of her own home or down at the station.

They sat down at the kitchen table and wrote out what she could remember about the night Liz disappeared. How Dana had come to pick up Paul because Rob had said he wasn't leaving for the gym until 6:30 PM. Reesor asked if she still had the note Rob had left for her to read in case Liz called after he'd gone to bed. Adele sifted through the shelves by the phone, saying she was pretty sure she'd put it somewhere. And then sure enough, there it was: *Wanted to know if you were okay. For some reason I was a little worried. Explain everything on Thursday. Thanks.*

They wanted to know if Rob could have sneaked out a window in the basement in the middle of the night without her knowing. No way, she said. All of the windows had an extra layer of storm glass on the outside except for one. And if he tried crawling out that window she would have heard him. It wasn't like they lived in some kind of palace or something. Besides, Rob was a grown man and free to come and go as he pleased. Why would he go crawling out a basement window when he could just walk out the front door?

"I don't really think you knew what was going on that day," Reesor said.

"Do you think I'm some kind of dummy or something?" Adele said. "Of course I knew what was going on."

"We know your son killed Elizabeth Bain, Mrs. Baltovich," Reesor said. "And we're going to prove it."

"Robert has never been in trouble in his entire life," she said. "He would never lay a hand on her. And if I knew otherwise, I wouldn't hesitate to call."

But they just kept saying those same terrible words over and over. *We know he killed her.* Said it like it was a fact she just couldn't grasp because she was too daft. Said it shrugging their shoulders as if to say, What can we do? Said it right up until they walked out the front door.

—⊖—

That same afternoon the police received a phone call from a man named Walter Brech, who was the supervisor of the Scarborough campus tennis courts. Brech was calling to report that a man had come by the courts around 1:30 PM asking a lot of questions about Elizabeth Bain. It wasn't that Brech thought that this man had anything to do with her disappearance, it was just that he knew the Bains and found it odd that this stranger was asking questions that he would know the answers to were he close to the family. There was just something not quite right about the whole encounter and Brech couldn't help but notice that the young man—who left his name, John Camunias, and his phone number—had a large, bandaged wound on one of his hands.

An officer with the Homicide Squad finally made contact with Camunias over the phone at 9:45 the next morning. Camunias was twenty-six years old and lived in the city of Brampton, north-west of Toronto, where he worked at a local restaurant called Kelsey's. He said that he'd met Lisa Bain at a party at her house in February 1988. Months went by and he just couldn't get her off his mind but it wasn't until the entire year had practically expired that he decided to call and ask her out on a date. She said yes, and he took her to a Christmas party at the Constellation Hotel out by the airport.

Camunias said he didn't have any contact with her for the next fourteen months when, out of the blue, he decided to send her flowers for Valentine's Day. That was just a few months ago now, he said. He'd written his phone number at the bottom of the card attached to the flowers, which he'd signed "John," giving no last name. She'd rung him up at home several days later, but Camunias wasn't in. Instead she spoke to his roommate for a while, asking questions about the John who'd sent her flowers, as though she were trying to place him in her mind. When Camunias got the message that Lisa Bain had called, he was so embarrassed about the whole thing that he couldn't muster the courage to pick up the phone. But exactly one week after her first call, she called again and, this time, caught him at home. She thanked him for the flowers and they continued speaking for a good hour and a half.

Camunias said that he'd tried calling her a number of times over the next few months but she either wasn't home or her parents answered and weren't giving her the messages for some reason. It wasn't until the middle of May that Lisa herself answered the phone, and Camunias sheepishly inquired about the possibility of a second date. As he now explained it to the officer, Lisa agreed to go for dinner sometime but told him to call her again when her exams were over on June the fourth. Of course he never spoke to her again and he told the officer that he now felt as though part of his life had been ripped from him, stolen. Camunias sounded a little melodramatic—what, in police terminology, is referred to as "out there"—and it didn't come as a surprise that the cut on his hand was self-inflicted or that he offered to assist the police with their investigation—he was sure that his modest psychic abilities could help lead them in the right direction.

That was all they needed—some nutcase going around conducting his own "psychic" investigation. Someone was going to have to put a stop to that little project. And although it wasn't a priority, a Homicide dick was eventually going to have to drive out to Brampton and verify that Camunias was working the evening Bain went missing. As far as Reesor and Raybould were concerned, the only good thing about John Camunias was that he solved one half of the "John and André" mystery from Liz's diary.

Nevertheless, Camunias felt compelled to outline in greater detail everything that had happened since his May phone call with Liz in a letter to the police:

I recall that she answered the phone in an energetic fashion (I somewhat got the impression she was high). I told her that I was glad to get a hold of her and she responded likewise. We talked for over an hour about our lives. She mentioned that she was as healthy as a horse but had picked up poison ivy while jogging. She also discussed some deep issues (i.e. her father being too strict with her).

Listening to her, I became worried because my sixth sense indicated she was in danger and I told her to be careful, for what I saw in my vision was that she was suspended between life & death. She seemed to believe me but assured me that she would never go with strangers or pick up anyone in her car she didn't know. We then discussed her boyfriend. She said, "It's over between me and Rob." I then asked if she would have dinner with me in the near future, and she said yes.

I tried to get in touch with her during the first week of June, but to no avail. Then, on June 19, between 8:00 and 8:15 PM, I saw something in my mind that would devastate me for the rest of my life. I was preparing salads at Kelsey's and my mind went blank & was suddenly transported into a psychic transmission, which made me frightened and overwhelmed with a feeling of uselessness. For what I saw in this transmission was Lisa getting into her car and two men jumping in behind her. I heard her call out my name to help her, and then she mentioned a name in the car (it could have been Rob). She said, "I should have listened to you, John."

Next I saw the two men doing something to her. One was injecting a sedative drug and the other was taking blood out of her arm at the same time. She then collapsed into unconsciousness and mumbled something I couldn't hear. I cried out to her—"No!" At that instant, the workers around me were shouting. "John, John, what's wrong?" I snapped out of my trance and the kitchen manager wanted to know what was the matter. "I'm okay now," I said, and eventually forgot about this experience.

The next day I phoned her at home. Her father told me that she hadn't come home yet and he even asked if she was with me! A few weeks later, my landlord asked me if I'd read about Elizabeth Bain in the newspaper. I said no, so he showed it to me. I couldn't believe it so I phoned, and Mrs. Bain answered the phone and told me it was true. I had a hard time sleeping that night and I called Mrs. Bain back in the morning and asked if I could drive down for a visit. She said yes.

With my roommate and a friend named Cathy, we arrived at the Bains' around 9:30 AM. In private, I told Mr. Bain about the phone call I had with Lisa, and he thanked me for mentioning it. Later I was talking to Lisa's best friend, her sister and then her aunt, who brought me back to the piano that Lisa played. There was a book of sheet music opened up to a song written by Bryan Adams called "Cuts like a Knife," which Lisa apparently played quite often. Suddenly, it occurred to me that this was one of the songs on the tape I played in my car when I drove her home from our date. I remembered her taking an interest in the song while we were driving but didn't say anything.

Anyhow, going back to the aunt, I asked her where Lisa liked to jog. She told me the name and location of the park, and I made plans to go there by myself. I didn't join my friends, who went with a search party, because I wanted to do some investigating on my own. I headed towards the campus tennis courts and interviewed a young man who was in charge of the area. He told me that he didn't know much about her, but I didn't believe him. I told him I was a friend of hers and wanted to get to the bottom of this. Tears ran down his eyes as he told me she often came to check on the schedule board and to talk to him. I asked again if he knew her, and he said yes. I almost cried, too. I gave him my phone number and told him that if someone came up with anything to call me directly.

I spoke to a few other people in the area before my roommate picked me up at 2:00 PM. As we drove back to the Bains' house, my friends scolded me for going off alone. They'd been worried about me. Later, at home in Brampton, I sat in our apartment, exhausted.

The next day I went to work as usual but quit a little early so I could catch the late news on TV at eleven o'clock. But around 11:15 the phone rang and my friend said it was for me and handed me the phone. "Is this John Camunias?" It was a male voice. I said, "Yes." "I have some information about Lisa Bain," said the voice. And then there was a pause before the voice said, "Fuck you!" And then the line went dead.

I was confused. Scared. Obviously, the message was for me to stay away from the case and not to interfere. I stopped investigating after that but continued to watch the news and read the papers for fear of my life.

—◦—

The same Wednesday morning that John Camunias heard from the Homicide squad, Andrea Beitinger gave Rob a quick call to see how her old friend was holding up. They spoke for a while and then Rob offered to give her a lift to her night class that evening. She'd first heard about Liz's disappearance on Saturday's news and she'd phoned Rob right away to see if it was really his girlfriend that everyone was talking about. It had been around dinnertime and Rob was home, having spent most of the day in the valley searching. Andrea just couldn't believe that it was the same Liz whose face was all over the television and newspapers. Sad but true, said Rob. Naturally, Andrea said she'd join everyone else in the valley the following morning for the Sunday search.

After hours of slogging through some pretty remote terrain in Colonel Danforth Park, Andrea invited Rob and some of his friends—Jim Isaacs, Al Heys, Tony Fuchs, Steve Doucette, Neil Winton and Sheila Banks, the lone female in their pack of friends—back to her place to watch a movie. Andrea had never seen Rob in such rough shape before. He was unshaven and his eyes were swollen. A real mess.

For a while, they sat around in the basement trying to figure out what had happened to Liz. Andrea and a few others were of the belief that Liz had killed herself. Someone else theorized that she might have just taken off. And still there were others who wondered if someone had followed her from the tennis courts to her car. At this point, Rob just buried his head in his hands. He might have been weeping. "If I'd just stayed and watched her car a little while longer," he said, "Liz might still be here."

Needless to say, Andrea was worried about him and decided to ring him up the next night when she got home from work. This was the day after Reesor had interrogated him and he told her what had happened. Rob's story was especially striking to Andrea because, for the third year in a row, she had a summer job with the

Metropolitan Toronto Police Force. And it wasn't just your average clerical position—Andrea was with the Intelligence department, which had its own building at the end of a remote industrial cul-de-sac called Dyas Road, a short distance from where Toronto's two major highways, the Don Valley Parkway and Highway 401, intersect. She'd started off at the reception desk, answering the phones, but by the following summer, she'd progressed to working on the computers, entering backlog information about cases that had been closed. It was pretty mundane work, but the material she was dealing with was considered highly sensitive and Andrea had been required to take an oath of confidentiality.

It was now two nights later, and Rob arrived to pick her up for her class on his way to work at the Recreation Centre. He was a little early, and Andrea lived only a block away from the campus, so they sat around in her backyard for twenty minutes, talking in more detail about why the police considered him the primary suspect. As she listened to his story, Andrea had this feeling that the police were making a terrible mistake. She was trying to keep things straight in her mind so that when they came to her—and, surely, they eventually would—she would be able to try to convince them that Rob was an innocent man.

"Have you heard anything about me at work?" Rob asked.

"No," Andrea said. "But this isn't really the kind of thing I deal with."

"Do you think they might be following me or listening in on the phone?"

"It's possible," she said.

"Geez," said Rob. "That's really spooky." He looked down at his watch. "Wow, check out the time. We better get going." So Andrea grabbed her books and they walked around front to the car.

—◇—

Shortly after reporting for duty at 8:00 AM, Friday, June 29, Reesor walked into the Homicide Squad's Team Room at 42 Division, where Brian Raybould was waiting for him. "Did you see this morning's *Star*?" Raybould asked.

"Not yet," Reesor said.

"Well then, you better take a look at this."

Raybould laid the newspaper on the conference table and opened it up to the second page. Reesor was well aware that Raybould had held a press conference the previous afternoon at the Centre of Forensic Sciences, and that a group of photographers had been taken into the garage to take pictures of Liz's car. They wanted photos of her vehicle splashed across newspapers and television screens all across southern Ontario, hoping to trigger the memories of any potential witnesses. They also wanted people to be on the lookout for Liz's blue-and-white sponge key chain, which had still not been found; in fact, Reesor immediately saw Liz's picture and the short article below the headline "Missing Key Chain May Be Murder Clue" near the bottom of the page. Raybould placed his finger on it, directing Reesor's attention to a section about halfway through the article:

> Rob Baltovich, Bain's 24-year-old boyfriend, was on his way to a fitness workout when he spotted her car parked in the lot off Old Kingston Road west of Military Trail about 6:45 that night.
>
> "But that's where the trail goes cold," said Detective Sergeant Brian Raybould, one of the homicide investigators probing the disappearance.
>
> Baltovich was not at home yesterday afternoon, but his mother said he was not talking to the media.
>
> "Rob spoke to a lawyer after the police asked him to take a polygraph test."
>
> She said her son did not take the test.

Without saying another word, Reesor dialled Rob's number. When Rob answered, Reesor identified himself and asked him if he'd seen *The Toronto Star* yet that morning. Rob said that he hadn't.

"By the looks of things," Reesor said, "your mother spoke to one of their reporters yesterday."

"I'm aware of that," Rob said.

"Are you aware that your mother told the reporter that you'd been interviewed by the police and refused to take the polygraph test?"

"She did?" Rob said. He sounded surprised. "She didn't mention anything about that."

"Rob, you're perceptive enough to know that this article is going to create a cloud of suspicion over your head as far as the general public is concerned."

Rob didn't buy that. "I don't think that's the case," he said.

"Just so you know," said Reesor, "I'm still extending you the invitation to take a polygraph test. And, if you pass the test, not only will you be cleared as a suspect, I'd be willing to release the results to the media, thereby clearing up any suspicions people might have right now."

"I'll have to think about it," Rob said. "I would like to see the article and then consult with my lawyer. I'll call you back."

Although Reesor was hopeful, five days went by and he didn't hear from Rob. As promised, the media's interest in Rob increased sharply after his mother had gone on record about his refusal to take the polygraph. Over the Canada Day long weekend several local television reporters showed up on his doorstep unannounced, but no one answered. He'd already made that mistake once and he wasn't about to make it again. He'd opened the door to find a young woman waiting for him on the front stoop with a reporter's notebook in her hand. She said her name was Kathleen Griffin and that she was with *The Toronto Sun*. She wondered if he might answer a couple of questions about the missing diary pages and other rumours. Rob began telling her that he'd been instructed not to speak with the press when, all of a sudden, he detected some movement out of the corner of his eye near the white car Griffin had apparently parked in the driveway. He took a half step forward so that he could see what was going on when, suddenly, a guy jumped up from behind the car to take his photograph with a fat telephoto lens. Rob quickly moved back inside again and said, "You guys really don't have a lot of ethics, do you?" And he shut the door.

In the next morning's *Toronto Sun*, which was the Canada Day Sunday edition, a picture of Rob standing in his front doorway, looking timid, appeared on page two beside a short article:

> The boyfriend of missing student Elizabeth Bain is upset at "innuendos" in news reports about their relationship.
>
> Metro Police have been quoted as saying friends told them Bain, a 22-year-old University of Toronto student, was having trouble with her love life.

And they said several pages from her diary may have been ripped out.

U of T graduate Rob Baltovich, 24, said "there are a lot of in-nuendos" about those pages and their year-old romance.

At his home on Midland Avenue, Scarborough, yesterday Bal-tovich said his lawyer told him not to talk to the media, although "I'd like to."

Ricardo Bain said Baltovich and his daughter were "romanti-cally involved."

He was "perturbed" at Baltovich's lack of involvement in recent searches. But Bain said he can understand that Baltovich "perhaps wants to keep a low profile."

—◦—

With the extensive coverage the story had garnered in the local media, the police were getting dozens of calls from people all over southern Ontario who claimed to have seen either Elizabeth Bain or her car around the time of her disappearance. One of these tips came in to 42 Division at 11:45 AM on Sunday, July 1, from a man named David Dibben. Dibben told the detective who took his call, John Reynolds, that he lived in Cavan, a rural hamlet eighty kilometres north-east of Scarborough, a short drive from where the Trent River runs south out of Peterborough (in fact, Dibben had first contacted the Ontario Provincial Police detachment in Peterbor-ough before being directed to call the Metro force in Toronto).

The reason for his call to the police was that, a week ago Saturday, he'd seen Eliz-abeth Bain's car on a television newscast during his lunch break at the Maple Stamping plant, where he worked as a press operator. He told the officer that as soon as he saw the pink plastic fingers sticking out from the door, he was sure that it was the same car he'd seen on his way to work the day before, Friday, June 22. From what he'd heard on the news, it was later that afternoon that Elizabeth Bain's car had been found on Morrish Road in Scarborough.

Dibben usually carpooled to work with a buddy named Mike Turcotte, who, like him, was in his early thirties and also worked at Maple Stamping. The community of Maple, north-west of Toronto, was a good hour-and-a-half's drive from Cavan.

The way Dibben remembered it, Turcotte, who lived in the part of Cavan known as "the hill," had picked him up at his house on Highway 7A, which ran through the centre of town, around 5:15 AM.

By Dibben's best estimate, the co-workers, in Turcotte's twenty-year-old Cutlass Supreme, had reached the intersection of Highway 7A and Highway 12, not far from the south shores of a swampy, doughnut-shaped body of water called Lake Scugog, some time around 6:00 AM. (They were now almost fifty kilometres northeast of Colonel Danforth Park in Scarborough.) Turcotte eased his old clunker to a stop as they approached the red light. They'd driven through this familiar area countless times.

Ahead of them, Highway 7A turned into Durham Road Number 21, which would take them west across the top of Toronto, and on either side of the road were rolling fields watched over by imposing wooden barns and a handful of modest homes. A big white sign on the north-west corner indicated that a gas bar would soon be erected where the tall, wet grass was motionless in the early morning calm. Presumably, the gas bar would benefit from the patrons who stopped for something to eat at Baba's Burgers—which sat dark and empty to their right. In the opposite direction, to the south, you could see the big orange sign with "Haugen's Chicken & Ribs Barbeque" in big white letters on the east side of Highway 12. Just in case the sign didn't catch your eye, the long sloping roof was an even brighter shade of orange. Haugen's was such a local landmark that the sign for the town of Manchester was situated right out front.

Looking to his left out Turcotte's window, Dibben noticed that there was a small silver import braking beside them in the left-turn lane. The only reason for taking more than a passing glance at the car, he was now explaining to the detective, was that he saw those weird-looking plastic fingers sticking out of the door and he wanted to have a look at the driver. It was like pulling up beside somebody with a "Honk if You Love Jesus" bumper sticker or the ass end of a Garfield the cat doll hanging from the trunk—it was hard to resist the urge to size up the kind of person who would want to draw that kind of attention to themselves out on the road.

So Dibben peered across Turcotte and through the passenger window of the silver car, which was a foot or so closer to the intersection than theirs. Reynolds wrote down what Dibben recalled about the man he saw behind the wheel: *Lone occupant, described as male, white, 24-25, blond hair, semi-receding, wearing white fluorescent*

T-shirt; also driver had blond moustache and was thin faced. Dibben remembered that, for a brief instant, their eyes met before the guy quickly glanced away and began fiddling around inside—down between the seats, up in the dash and then back down below the seats again—as though he was looking for something. It sort of struck him that the guy didn't look like he belonged in the car.

It also appeared as though he'd been on a real bender the night before. Besides the five o'clock shadow on his face, his longish hair, which came halfway down his ear and just below the collar at the back, was all over the place. Turcotte hadn't really seen any of this, Dibben said, as he'd been watching the lights, a bit anxious that they might be late for work. After no more than a minute, the light turned green and they were off, and Dibben's gaze was back on the road in front of them, not bothering to watch the other car make its turn south.

That was pretty much all he could remember. When asked why he'd waited more than a week before contacting the police, Dibben didn't really have a solid answer; he just said that he'd wanted to talk it over with his wife. Reynolds could hear a couple of young kids horsing around in the background.

As Reynold's typed report on Dibben's observations filtered through the Homicide Squad, it was met with little fanfare. Neither Steve Reesor nor Brian Raybould bothered visiting or even calling Dibben—that job was left up to another, more junior detective. Their lack of enthusiasm was the result of disbelief—their standing theory was that Elizabeth Bain's car had never left Scarborough. They had come to this conclusion because of what the receptionist at the Three R Auto Body had told them about Bain's car. The receptionist had been adamant that she'd seen the silver Tercel across the road when she'd arrived for work the Wednesday morning after Bain's disappearance and that it had remained in the exact same position during regular working hours until the police arrived on Friday afternoon. With the receptionist's version of events already accepted, Dibben's sighting was, for the time being, officially deemed "impossible."

The first day back on the job after the Canada Day long weekend, Reesor decided to take another shot at getting Rob to take the lie-detector test. Reesor called him a few minutes before ten o'clock that Tuesday evening and asked if he'd given any more thought to taking the polygraph. Rob said that he just didn't think it was in his best interests. "Why do you say that?" Reesor asked.

Rob said, "Remember, Detective Reesor, I was a psychology major. I studied polygraph tests and I know for a fact that they're unreliable."

"But they're not admissible in a court of law," pressed Reesor. "As I said before, they're used as an investigative tool and I've got enough confidence in them that, if you passed one, I'd be able to clear you as a suspect."

Rob once again told him that he didn't think it was in his best interests.

"What could be the downside to taking the test?" Reesor asked.

"That I might fail it and then you would treat me as a suspect."

"We're already treating you as a suspect," Reesor said. "I don't think a person who had anything to hide would refuse the test. The results can't be admitted as evidence in court, so you've got nothing to lose. If you fail, we'll just continue treating you as a suspect. And if you pass, we'll clear you. I'm even prepared to issue a press release stating just that."

Rob didn't respond.

"From what I've heard, Rob, your brother Paul wants you to take the test."

"That's probably true," Rob said.

"And I'm sure your father would want you to take it."

"How do you know that?" asked Rob.

"Well, I haven't discussed it with him," Reesor explained. "But I'm certain that, if I explained the polygraph to him, he would want you to take it so that you could clear your name and assist with the investigation. Liz deserves the best investigation we can give her, and by refusing to take the test, we're forced to continue considering you as a suspect. Look, if you *didn't* do it, Rob, then we're wasting a lot of precious time that we could be using to find the real killer."

"I'm sorry," Rob said, "but I still don't think it's in my best interests."

"Is that your opinion or are you just regurgitating what your lawyer told you?"

"It's my opinion," Rob said, pausing momentarily. "If I fail the test, what assurances do I have that the public won't find out?"

"We can't release things like that," said Reesor. "We'd get our asses sued off." Reesor didn't think he was going to get Rob to change his mind over the phone so he told him to sleep on it. Rob said he would call Reesor the next day. "That's what you told me last time," said Reesor. "And I never heard from you."

"Well," said Rob, "this time you have my word."

Rob was already reeling from the intense pressure he was under, but this conversation made it even worse. Reesor wasn't the only one all over him; the media were still hounding him on a daily basis, publishing and broadcasting dozens of stories that made him look like someone with something to hide. Even Mrs. Bain had called, trying to figure out why on earth he'd refused to take the polygraph, not to mention why he wasn't coming around the house any more to help out with the searches. He tried to explain, but she didn't care what his lawyers had advised him. After all, she was talking about someone he loved, and love was the supreme consideration, not lawyers.

A few minutes after speaking with Reesor, Rob decided to call Paul. Rob told his brother that Reesor had offered to issue a press release clearing his name if he passed a lie-detector test and that he was seriously contemplating taking him up on it. Rob and Paul agreed that the investigation was taking its toll on their elderly parents, both of whom were used to leading quiet, solitary lives. Paul had already been interviewed by Raybould about his contact with Rob on the day Liz had disappeared and he got the impression that the police were trying to be fair. In accordance with his strong Christian beliefs, Paul thought it was Rob's duty to be completely honest and to assist the police to the best of his ability. Once Reesor and Raybould recognized the error of their ways, everything would return to normal.

But what if I fail the test, Rob asked. The answer was that Paul didn't think it was possible and, if by some remote chance he did fail, it would be the result of some technical glitch that could likely be worked out so that, eventually, the machine would show the proper findings. What it all boils down to, Paul said, is that right now this is your only chance to bring all of this to an end—for everyone.

The possibility of failure was so minute that it was barely worth considering. They finally agreed that Rob should take the test and that neither of them would discuss their decision with Bill Gatward, who was away on vacation with his family that week, or their parents. Rob said he would call Reesor in the morning to make the arrangements but then he suddenly realized that he was going to be out all day at job interviews. Paul said that he would call Reesor on Rob's behalf and tell him to set up an appointment for Thursday.

Paul got in touch with Reesor around ten in the morning from work and told him Rob was willing to take the polygraph the following day. He also told Reesor not to try calling Rob at home because they didn't want Bill Gatward or their parents to know about Rob's decision. Reesor said that he would contact the polygraph unit to set up an appointment and would call Paul at home in the evening to give him the time.

At 2:00 that afternoon, Reesor drove downtown to meet with Detective Frank Wozniak, a twenty-five-year veteran with the Metropolitan Toronto Police who became a polygraph examiner with Investigative Support Services in 1987. Joining the Polygraph Unit hadn't necessarily been a good career move—they locked you in for at least three years—but then he wasn't exactly vying for the chief's position. The truth was that the Polygraph Unit was an easy job as far as police duties went. Hardly any paperwork.

Reesor briefed him on the status of their investigation to date, emphasizing that the case against Rob was completely circumstantial and that, although Liz's body was yet to be found, the amount of gas left in her car suggested that it could have travelled no more than eighty kilometres outside of Scarborough. This gave Wozniak an idea. He suggested that, once Rob had completed his standard polygraph test, he be presented with a grid map of southern Ontario. Wozniak would have him concentrate on each area and, if he'd stashed the corpse in one of those sections, the needles would start shooting up and down the chart like a seismograph during an earthquake.

Reesor had pushed so hard for Rob to take the polygraph test because he knew it was much more than an investigative tool used to determine whether someone was telling the truth. Of course, in the event that Rob failed the polygraph, Reesor's suspicions would be confirmed—that much he'd been open about with Rob. However, there was much more at stake that Reesor hadn't been up-front about. For example, if Rob did fail the polygraph, Reesor hadn't told him that the results could be used to establish what Homicide investigators called R.P.G.—reasonable and probable grounds. Placed in front of a judge, the results of a failed polygraph were often just enough for the police to obtain search warrants and wire-tap authorizations in cases where incriminating evidence was scant.

For police investigators, the polygraph examination is structured in three parts, all of which are extremely valuable. During the first part, the examiner gets the subject to tell his side of the story—even if he's already told it a dozen times to a handful of investigators. The more versions of a suspect's story the police can elicit, the easier it will be to find inconsistencies. And while the test results aren't admissible in a court of law, what the subject says to the examiner is.

The second part is the test itself, when the instrument is attached to the subject, monitoring his physiological reactions while he responds to the examiner's questions. Once the test has been completed, the examiner leaves the subject alone in the polygraph room and retires to a separate office where he studies the charts upon which the subject's involuntary reactions have been recorded. If the examiner finds the subject to be truthful, then he returns to the polygraph room, advises the subject that he has passed and sends him on his way. However, if the subject is found to be deceitful, examiners are trained to conduct what is known as the post-test, the polygraph's third and final component. At this stage, the examiner, who may have spent hours developing the trust and confidence of his subject, informs the person that he has failed and, reverting to his true role as a police investigator, exerts pressure on an emotionally frail suspect to procure a confession. This aspect of the polygraph test has been condemned in Canadian courts as a "psychological sledgehammer" that is a "shock to the community" in the way that some suspects can be reduced to look like "a penitent offering his confession" when, in reality, the person has no concept of what he is confessing to or the consequences of his confession.

However, more than anything else, this is what Reesor was hoping for—a confession. So far, Rob had repeatedly and adamantly proclaimed his innocence, and, without a body or any direct evidence linking Rob to Liz's disappearance, their case against him would remain completely circumstantial, perhaps forever.

—◯—

Paul and Rob walked into the bustling, spacious lobby on the main floor of the new Metro Police Headquarters on College Street downtown, about ten minutes before 11:00 AM on Thursday. Even though the building was only two years old, it was a lot more modern than they'd expected. There weren't many people there and, if it hadn't been for the handful of uniformed police officers behind the Duty Desk, they might have been in the lobby of a bank tower.

Within minutes, Reesor came down to escort them up the giant, curving staircase overlooking the lobby, a passageway constructed from giant slabs of brown stone, to the second floor, where the Polygraph Unit was located. Reesor asked them to wait in the unit's outer office while he went inside to speak with Detective Woz-niak. He came back out just a few moments later and told Paul that he would have to wait for his brother in the main lobby downstairs. Reesor led Paul down the same massive staircase. Back in the lobby, Reesor gave Paul his pager number and said to call at any time during the test if he had any questions.

Rob was still waiting in the outer offices of the Polygraph Unit when Reesor got back upstairs. While Reesor had been taking Paul down to the lobby, Wozniak had come out to tell Rob that he was busy setting up the equipment and would return in a few minutes. However, that wasn't really true; Wozniak had been ready for some time. It was just that Reesor didn't want Wozniak to begin the test until he was in a nearby office that was equipped with a television monitor wired to a video camera and microphone, which had been expertly camouflaged above the ceiling tile of the polygraph room. When Reesor was in place, his eyes glued to the screen as Wozniak and Rob walked into a room just a few feet down the hall, he pulled up an uncomfortable office chair in front of the TV and sat down, leaning forward to push record on the VCR.

Wozniak led Rob into the unadorned polygraph room, its walls of concrete blocks painted an industrial beige. As he introduced himself, Rob couldn't help thinking that he reminded him of a pockmarked Charles Grodin, the actor who'd played the messed-up father in the popular Disney movie *Beethoven*, about a family that falls in love with an enormous Saint Bernard. But Wozniak's slow, almost hypnotic tone of voice was strictly professional, more family doctor than comedian. He indicated that Rob's seat was the big black comfortable one next to the wooden desk upon which the briefcase-sized polygraph machine rested. Pulling up a chair so that he was a foot or two right in front Rob, Wozniak asked him if he'd ever taken a polygraph test before. Rob said that he hadn't. "No?" said Wozniak. "Well, do you know anything about them?"

"A little," Rob said. "I know about control questions and galvanic skin response and conductivity and things like that."

"It seems as though you know a bit more than the average person."

"Yeah," said Rob, with a chuckle. "I was talking to my brother this morning about how I used to watch the polygraph show on television with F. Lee Bailey."

Before the conversation went any further, Wozniak gave Rob a rough outline of what was going to take place in the examination's first two parts and then asked Rob if he would want to know how he did on the test before leaving. "I'm pretty confident that I'll do a good job," Rob said. "But, yeah, I'd very much like to know."

"Okay," said Wozniak, "then we'll talk about your results at the end of the day. Do you know anything else about the polygraph?"

"Well, I studied it very superficially," Rob said. "I know there are four physiological components to it. As I said, I know about galvanic skin response and that, physiologically, it's a manifestation of whether you're lying or not. When the skin sweats, it has to conduct electricity a little more efficiently than if it were dry— things like that. I think heart rate may be another component. Perhaps body temperature as well."

Of the more than three hundred subjects Wozniak had tested in his career, none of them had known this much about the polygraph. He didn't think it was a good idea to get into a technical discussion about it, because, ultimately, that could only lead to a debate about its reliability, so he moved on. "Do you have any questions about what might take place?" he asked. "I'm going to have to get started."

"Ah, no questions," Rob said. "It looks like this may be a learning experience as well."

"Well, perhaps you can tell me why you're here today to have this done."

"Basically," said Rob, "to assist with the investigation. Obviously, I was a little hesitant in the beginning. My reluctance to take the polygraph was more or less a result of the feeling that it wasn't very wise to second-guess my lawyer's advice. But I've made the decision to be here because a lot of suspicion has been directed towards me. I can see from the police point of view that they're drawing a blank on this case, and so am I. So I think it's time to try and get it moving a little more and, if eliminating me as a suspect is going to help them, then I'm game because, more than anyone else, I want to find out what happened to Liz."

Wozniak nodded and prompted Rob to continue.

"And the other reason I'm here has to do with the waiting. All of the waiting I've been doing is really bothering me."

"Well, that's exactly what we're going to do here today," said Wozniak. "This polygraph examination is going to determine whether or not you were involved in any way whatsoever with the disappearance of Elizabeth Bain, okay? Now I'm told that you claim to have had nothing to do with her disappearance, is that correct?"

"Yes," Rob said.

"Well, after I conduct this examination on you today, there will be no doubt in my mind as to whether or not you're telling me the truth. If you are, then that's what I'm going to tell you when we're done. But if you're not, you can't very well expect me to lie for you."

"No," said Rob, "certainly not."

"And just so we're clear," said Wozniak. "You understand that this is a homicide investigation and that you're here to determine whether or not you were involved in Elizabeth's disappearance. Is that your understanding?"

Rob thought about it for a moment and said, "You should include the fact that I'm under a degree of pressure from certain parties and, as I just said, there is this waiting factor. Knowing that polygraph tests aren't really one hundred per cent accurate has been a dissuading factor from the beginning but, frankly, I have nothing to hide."

"What do you mean when you say it's not a hundred per cent accurate?"

"The statistic given to me is that it's only eighty per cent accurate."

"Let me give you something to ponder before we start," Wozniak said, getting very serious. "This machine that you see here beside you is going to record your physiological reactions and what it records is going to be one hundred per cent accurate, okay? It doesn't make a mistake. There are different opinions about how these charts are interpreted but, by the time we're done, there will be no doubt in my mind as to whether or not you're telling the truth."

With that established, Wozniak went on to inform Rob of his rights as a citizen of Canada. He asked Rob if he'd spoken to a lawyer, and Rob told him about Bill Gatward. "Have you phoned or talked to him today?" asked Wozniak.

"No, I haven't," said Rob.

"One of the rights you have, Rob, is the right to speak to a lawyer before you speak to me, obviously. Do you want to speak to him before we start the test?"

"No."

Wozniak made it clear that Rob could call his lawyer any time and that the door wasn't locked; he was free to leave whenever he wanted to. Wozniak then presented Rob with a Polygraph Consent Form and asked him to read it out loud, which he did:

I, Robert Baltovich, do hereby voluntarily, without threats, promises of immunity or reward and without duress, coercion or force, agree to take a polygraph (lie detector) examination, to be given to me by a member of the Metropolitan Police Force. I fully realize that I am not obliged to say anything and that anything I say may be given in evidence.

Rob continued to read the section that Wozniak had added beneath in his own writing:

That I choose to be here, but that by choosing I realize that what I say can still be used as evidence, regardless of my choice to be here or not.

Wozniak had drawn an X where he wanted Rob to sign his name, and once he'd done so, the detective asked him who was aware that he was taking the test. "My brother and myself and Detective Reesor," Rob said. "I believe that is all."

Wozniak led him through the preliminary questioning—address, height, weight, education, medical history and family background. He congratulated him on his recent graduation, and Rob told Wozniak about his plans to attend teachers' college after working for a year so that he could teach at a primary school, preferably Grade 7 or 8. Rob was candid about his mother's nervous breakdowns, and his father's long hours at the smoke shop. He spoke of his disdain for drug and alcohol abuse as well as smoking and lack of exercise—he preferred to be around people who wanted to be healthy. "What other types of qualities do you dislike or disrespect?" asked Wozniak.

"Dishonesty. Thieves. Ignorance."

"Is there someone who has those qualities who you disrespect more than anyone?"

"No, I can't say there's any one person I could single out."

"How about generally speaking?"

"I would have to say people who are excessively religious."

"Like a religious fanatic?"

"Yeah."

"Are you religious?"

"No, not at all."

"What's the worst physical hurt you've ever suffered?"

"Probably spraining my ankle."

"What about an emotional hurt? What would be the worst emotional hurt you've ever had?"

"Probably being turned down as a romantic partner by Liz."

"Conversely, what's the best thing that's ever happened to you?"

"Being accepted as a romantic partner by Liz." Rob reflected on that for a moment and said, "Yeah, that is, by far, the happiest moment."

"If you could change one thing in your life, what would it be?"

"I would want to be less inclined to follow the wishes of others."

"Have you ever been arrested before? How about as a child, were you ever taken home by the police as a juvenile?"

"Well, there are two incidents that stand out in my mind. One was hitting a golf ball in the school yard—the police were afraid I was going to break a window. And another time, farther down the street from my house, I was coming home with some friends and we started kicking a bunch of empty boxes in a parking lot and the police came to tell us that we were making too much noise. But, apart from that, no."

"Have you ever been treated unfairly by the police?"

"Never."

"What's your greatest ambition?"

"Just to have a family. A healthy, happy family."

"What do you think of yourself as an individual?"

"I think I'm a very caring and intelligent person. However, on the downside, I would say that certain people have perhaps been put out by me and my moralizing."

"What do you mean?"

"Well, if I see a wrong I try to right it. I'm not what most people would consider a liberal. If I feel that people aren't living their lives in a way that I find acceptable, well, I'm not quite as tolerant as a lot of other people. So people are sometimes put out because they feel I like to tell others how to live their lives."

"Are you an honest person?"

"Yeah, I would think so."

"If you were to rate your honesty on a scale of one to a hundred, a hundred being the highest, where would you fit?"

"Maybe ninety-five."

"Yeah? Are you a violent person?"

"No, definitely not."

"Again, using the same scale, where would you be?"

"Fifteen."

"Yeah? Fifteen per cent?"

"Well, when you say violent, do you mean causing another physical harm?"

"Yes."

"Oh, then maybe even lower than fifteen per cent. I do get angry and I do have a temper. But my anger is usually manifested in words, not actions."

"Well," said Wozniak, "I can't see any problems with administering a polygraph test on you today. It looks pretty good. No problems at all. Do you have any questions?"

"No," Rob said. "I don't think I've ever had to answer so many questions about myself as I have in the last two weeks. I wish I was being asked all of these under better circumstances."

At this point, Wozniak asked Rob to tell him about his contact with Liz in the days leading up to her disappearance. He soon discovered that Rob could be a real chatterbox, often speaking for fifteen or twenty minutes without a pause. Over the next two hours Wozniak was able to squeeze in only a handful of questions as Rob related pretty much the same story that he'd given Reesor and Raybould two weeks earlier. After a while, Wozniak figured that, without interruption, Rob could go on all day, so he moved on to the next section of the examination, which was a lesson on how the polygraph machine worked.

Wozniak explained that he wasn't interested in monitoring Rob's voluntary nervous system but would be keeping a close eye on his involuntary or autonomic nervous system, which is connected to the heart. He showed Rob the cuff that he would be wrapping tightly around his upper arm to record any rise or fall in his blood pressure. "You can't control your heartbeat in a sitting position," said Wozniak. "Do you agree with that?"

Rob said, "Well, I don't know. What about these Indian yogis I've heard of?"

"But that's taken years and years and years to perfect," said Wozniak. "These monks in the Himalaya Mountains devote their entire lives to just one physiological change—manipulating their blood flow."

"Yeah, I know," said Rob. "I agree with you. I wish I could control that, but, obviously, I can't."

Wozniak pulled out the two long tubes and pointed to the spots just above and below Rob's heart where they would be attached, monitoring activity in his rib cage. He also lifted up two small silver plates and slipped one on Rob's index finger and the other on his ring finger to illustrate how they would fit. One was going to monitor his galvanic skin response and the other was going to keep track of how much blood was reaching Rob's extremities.

"The reason I'm concentrating on the heart," said Wozniak, "is that when a person *knowingly* tells a lie, and I have to stress that word, knowingly, their heart is going to fight it. This is called the fight or flight syndrome, which is brought on by a chemical process in our bodies that either fights danger or prompts us to run away from it. On the surface, some of us can maintain a poker face when we lie, but most of us can't stop our hearts from racing on the inside."

"You say you're interested in my heart rate, which I understand," Rob said. "But, obviously, I'm a little nervous right now, given the surroundings, and my heart must be beating a little faster."

"That has no bearing on the test," explained Wozniak. "We're not testing that system in our body, I'm just testing the fight or flight syndrome. You might be slightly nervous because of your fear of the unknown. The majority of the people I see are afraid of being caught lying. If that's the case with you today, Rob, I can't help that because, if you're not telling the truth, I'll be able to detect that. But, if you're afraid of the unknown, I'll do my best to answer any of your questions at any time. Do you have any questions?"

"No, no questions," Rob said. "I'm actually looking forward to it."

"Well, I think I may have some questions for you. You know, I like to play armchair detective now and then. And I'm always trying to figure things out. Now I'm sure you've given a lot of thought to Liz's disappearance, and I was just curious to hear if you have any theories about what happened."

"To be honest, I fluctuate between thinking of foul play and suicide or just simply voluntary disappearance. I can see her reasons for everything. But I'm not sure that Liz Bain has been murdered."

"Why do you say that?"

"I believe that she may have taken her own life," Rob said. "But at the same time I think she may have just wanted to get away somewhere until she was ready to come back."

"Now, don't get me wrong, Rob, I'm not suggesting that you're the type of guy who would do something like this, okay, but have you ever thought about maybe harming Liz in any way?"

This question, coming almost three hours into the interview, perhaps epitomized the moment at which, as one appeal court judge in Quebec described it, "The relationship of confidence established between the polygraph technician and the subject led the latter, during the course of the test, to co-operate entirely and to admit things that he would not otherwise have admitted." The question Wozniak had asked was a simple one but the atmosphere in which it was delivered was rife with psychological pressures. While Rob had never contemplated actually harming Liz, he thought that, being totally honest with himself—after all, he was there to take a lie-detector test—he might have wished harm upon her once, but only briefly. It was when he thought she'd intentionally strung him along back in the fall of 1987, telling him she had a boyfriend when she damn well knew that he'd been falling for her for months. Wasn't it a natural human reaction to want to hurt someone who had caused you to suffer?

As a result of his studies in the field of psychology, Rob believed that, in general, people were dishonest when they denied having ever had thoughts of harming someone, or even imagined killing them. If we were truthful, most of us would admit to having had some pretty strange thoughts at different times in our lives. But, as his professors had pointed out ad nauseam, the human conscience is the buffer between immoral thoughts and responsible actions. As long as someone is equipped with a functioning conscience, the thoughts themselves are not reprehensible.

For close to two weeks now, since Reesor had laid bare his unshakable belief that Rob was Elizabeth Bain's murderer, Rob had been engaged in this kind of deep philosophical and moral examination of himself. *Who am I? Why is this happening to me? Why do they think I would have done something like this?* After a while, the human mind can play tricks on itself and even the most rational, grounded people are capable of convincing themselves to accept things that are untrue. *Can all of these people in authority be wrong? Should I say something that isn't true—just in case they're right? Yet, even if they're wrong, and I tell them what they want to hear, will they be satisfied? Conversely, if I tell them the truth, will they condemn me for being insincere?*

Without the energy or presence of mind to articulate any of this, Rob simply said, "Yes. Yes, I have."

This was the break Wozniak was waiting for, but he couldn't let on that he thought Rob's answer was anything out of the ordinary. "Is that right?" he said, playing it cool. "Again, Rob, I'm not suggesting you're the kind of guy who would do something like this, but have you ever thought about killing her?"

Again, Rob replied with a yes.

Wozniak knew that he was on to something big. In fact, he suspected that Rob was on the verge of confessing—and he hadn't even put him through the rigours of the polygraph yet. "Oh, yeah?" he said. "When was that?"

"That was in the fall of '87," Rob said.

"If you thought about it, then how would you have planned it out?"

"Oh, well, no, I had absolutely no thoughts of planning it out. The only way I can really describe the situation is that, when I first met Liz and got to know her for a while, I became convinced in my heart that there was no one more right for her than me, and no one more right for me than her. It was an inner feeling that we just belonged together. And this depression that I felt after being rejected by her initially plunged me very deep into despair. Detective Reesor used the phrase 'Liz was a beautiful girl, and we might have it figured that if you couldn't have her, no one would.' That is a very accurate assessment of what my feelings were in the fall of 1987. But that quickly faded and there has been no time during the course of my relationship with Liz in the last year where I've ever thought of harming her—ever. I loved her and never wanted to harm her. And I couldn't bear the thought of someone else doing the same."

"Okay, Rob. And, again, don't get me wrong or think I'm suggesting anything, but if you were to plan harming her, how would you have planned it?"

"I can't really answer that because, I believe that—I mean, this is going to sound very corny to you—if you do something wrong, somewhere along the line you're going to get caught. So I never really conceived of planning it. All I can say is that, if I was to ever kill Liz, it would never involve any pain or blood or suffering. That's about the extent of it."

"What type of person do you think would have killed Liz Bain?"

"A jealous person. Someone who would perhaps benefit by her loss."

Wozniak asked Rob who he could eliminate as Liz's murderer, and Rob eliminated just about everyone involved, including himself. But he said that he couldn't exclude Liz's sister, her brother Mark or her aunt Diana. "I don't know if you've been made aware of it or not," he said, "but Elizabeth's involved in something called holistic medicine. Have you heard of the Atikian case?" Wozniak nodded. "Well,"

Rob said, "she was dealing with several doctors of that persuasion and we got into some interesting discussions about it. I didn't really support her in that because I felt that a lot of the people she was dealing with were somewhat strange. And that's why I feel that one of those holistic doctors may be responsible for her harm."

One of the last things Wozniak was required to ask before starting the test was if there was anything Rob had done before his last birthday that he would be embarrassed or ashamed to talk about. Rob could only think of two incidents. The first one was the time he swore and mooned his brother when Paul had been bugging him during a game of pick-up basketball one night at a local playground. Rob was seventeen. The other incident was when he and Liz got into their first serious argument over holistic medicine. That was just two months ago, when Rob had asked Liz to leave his house after an argument.

Wozniak asked if Rob had ever committed any crimes for which he'd never been caught. Rob told him about the time he saw a restricted movie when he was sixteen. He admitted to drinking beer on a few occasions while he was under age. Wozniak didn't think that Rob properly understood what he meant by a crime, which was an offence like vandalism, theft or fraud. Rob hadn't ever done anything along those lines, so Wozniak excused himself and left the room.

Wozniak went down the hall to speak with Reesor, who'd been watching the entire interview on his monitor. He wanted Reesor to go over the test questions before he got started. Once they were done, and Wozniak was on his way back to the polygraph room, Reesor noticed on the screen that Rob was twisting around in his chair, checking everything out. And then, as soon as he heard Wozniak opening the door, he quickly bowed his head and looked down at his feet.

Wozniak reviewed the final questions with Rob one last time. One of the questions, which Wozniak had decided to include as a control, was "Do you now remember doing anything before your last birthday—besides what you've told me—that you would be ashamed or embarrassed to talk about?" Rob said that he now remembered one other incident. It happened at a neighbourhood party three years ago, during his second year at university. He said that he'd slept with a girl named Caitlin Fleury even though they'd met for the first time that night. He liked Caitlin and dated her for about five months but he was still uneasy with the fact that he'd slept with someone that he didn't really know. Rob just didn't see himself as that kind of person.

With that out of the way, Wozniak began attaching the various cuffs, tubes and plates to Rob's body. Rob told him that his heart was pounding. It was okay, Wozniak said, they were going to do the test about four times. Wozniak handed Rob a small deck of about twenty numbered cards and instructed him to pick one and memorize it before shuffling it back into the deck. He was going to go through the numbers, asking Rob if it was the one he'd picked. When I get to the one you chose, Wozniak said, I want you to lie and just say no. After going through eight numbers, Wozniak asked Rob if he'd picked number seven. Rob said that he had. "That's excellent," said Wozniak excitedly. "Your chart tells me a couple of things, Rob. It tells me that you're a sensitive individual, even though from talking to you I knew that. More importantly, it tells me that you're not a very good liar."

"At least physiologically, I'm not," Rob said, smiling. "That's really wild."

Wozniak told Rob that he was now ready to move on to the real test. "Okay, Rob," he said, "remain perfectly still, look straight ahead, keep your eyes open and your feet on the floor at all times." Wozniak paused for a few seconds and then asked, "Do you live in Canada?"

"Yes," Rob said.

"Are you afraid I'll ask you a question that we did not review?"

"No."

"Do you intend to answer truthfully to each of the questions on this test?"

"Yes."

"Besides what you've told me, do you now remember doing anything else before your last birthday you would be ashamed or embarrassed to talk about?"

"No."

"On Tuesday, June the nineteenth, did you do anything to cause the death of Elizabeth Bain?"

"No."

"Besides what you've told me, do you now remember ever committing any other crimes before your last birthday for which you were not caught?"

"No."

"On Tuesday, June the nineteenth, did you commit the assault on Liz which resulted in her disappearance?"

"No." He was a little more insistent, shaking his head.

"Are you presently living in Ontario?"

"Yes."

"Do you now remember, even once, cheating someone before your last birthday?"

"No."

"Right now, do you know where Liz can be found?"

"No."

That was the end of the test. Wozniak asked Rob if any of the questions had given him trouble. "The crime one didn't and the cheating one didn't but the one about being ashamed and embarrassed did a little because it's almost as if I remember something in my past that would embarrass me, but I just can't put my finger on what it is." Wozniak said it would only affect the test if it was something Rob could remember. Rob agreed that he would only change his answer if he could recall what it was, and Wozniak then repeated the same set of questions one more time. By the time Wozniak asked again about whether Rob would be embarrassed or ashamed to discuss anything that had happened prior to his birthday, Rob had suddenly remembered something else and this time around responded "Yes."

A few seconds after Rob had answered the last question, Wozniak asked him why he'd changed his answer from the one he gave during the first set of questions. Rob said, "When I was in first year university, I had to write an essay on a play called *Waiting for Godot* for an English course I was taking. Anyway, I bought the Cole's Notes on the play and committed what was considered unconscious plagiarism. Apparently, I incorporated the notes into my essay without being aware of it. I found out later from my teaching assistant that quite a number of people in the class had done the same thing."

"You were caught doing that?" asked Wozniak.

"Oh, yes. I was."

"You were ashamed about being caught, I suppose?"

"No," said Rob, "I was ashamed of actually doing it."

Once Wozniak had established that Rob hadn't committed the act of "unconscious plagiarism" on more than one occasion, he told Rob that he was going to ask him the same set of questions one last time, but that he wanted Rob to respond to each question in his mind only, without spoken words. When they were finished, Wozniak told Rob that he was going to confer with the investigators in another room and that he would return in a few minutes. He was leaving Rob hooked up to the polygraph, he said, because he thought Reesor might want to run him through another test. As Wozniak stood in the open doorway, he turned and asked, "What do you think these charts are going to tell me, Rob?"

"I think they'll tell you that I didn't really have anything to do with the disappearance of Liz," Rob said. Wozniak just nodded and closed the door behind him.

Wozniak soon returned and told Rob that he was, in fact, going to conduct one more test. This was the grid test he'd explained to Reesor the day before, where Rob would be shown a map of southern Ontario divided into seven sections. Wozniak was going to ask him if he knew whether Liz could be found in each of the seven areas. Rob, who was obviously going to answer no to each query, went along with the idea but, just before the test started, he said, "I guess my ride has gone by now, eh?"

"No," said Wozniak, "I think Paul is still downstairs in the lobby."

"Wow," said Rob, "I didn't think he would stick around this long."

Wozniak began to question him using the grid, and Rob consistently denied knowing where Liz's body could be found. *Can Liz be found in section A? No. In section F? No* . . . Once again, Wozniak left the room to analyze Rob's physiological reactions. But this time, he had a considerably more stern look about him when he re-entered the room. Rob, who was still attached to the polygraph, was slightly nervous but still in an upbeat mood. "I figured I've been here this long," he said, "I might as well stay." He let out a hearty but nervous laugh. Wozniak remained stone-faced as he removed the instruments from Rob's body.

Once he was back in his chair, he informed Rob of what the polygraph had revealed. "I've looked over your charts, Rob," he said, "and, as a result of my investigation here today, there's no doubt in my mind that you are responsible for Elizabeth's death. No doubt at all. And while I'm certain of your involvement, the polygraph can't tell me why things happen. Now, I've been studying you for the last couple of hours and I find you to be a warm, caring individual. What I've been wondering about, though, is that, if you're responsible, would you have planned this thing out or would it have been a spur of the moment type of thing? To be honest, I just don't think you're capable of planning something like this out."

"No, certainly not," Rob said.

"No," agreed Wozniak. "So it would only lead me to believe that something happened spur of the moment. As a sensitive person, you must be carrying a great weight on your shoulders."

Thinking Wozniak was referring to the pressure of being a murder suspect and the pressure of having your girlfriend vanish off the face of the planet, Rob said, "Very much so."

"And I look at you and I say, you're not a planner. You're a guy who's in love. There's no doubt in my mind that you had a lot of respect for your girlfriend, and I've got a lot of respect for you. But you know what? There's a time when each one of us has to sit back and reflect. I understand human feelings and I know you've probably studied Abraham Maslow and the hierarchy of human needs. You know that love is right up there with food and shelter. Sometimes, when a person rejects that love, the other person can't be held accountable for what happens next. That's why I say 'spur of the moment,' because you're not the type of person who would go out and plan to hurt someone like that, are you?"

"No," Rob said. "Nor am I the person."

"Rob, look—"

"Can I just interrupt you for a second?" Rob asked. "What I don't understand in this case is where the idea came about that, if Liz were to decide to leave me, I would react so violently."

For the better part of the next hour, Wozniak employed a number of tactics to persuade Rob to confess. The "spur of the moment" theory wasn't working. "What I can't understand," Rob said, "is how anyone can possibly feel that I would want to put Liz through this pain. I'm responsible enough to live by my mistakes and, were I to ever commit such a horrendous crime, I would certainly not deny it. I would stand up to it like a man. I would never put the Bains through such pain."

Later, Wozniak suggested that maybe Rob had murdered Liz out of love, and that maybe that was okay. "I'll tell you what you're not innocent of," Wozniak said, feeling inspired. "You're not innocent of loving that young woman very much. And is that a crime? Is it a crime to love someone? Is it a crime to want to spend the rest of your life with an individual? Is that a crime? Is it a crime to want to have a family with an individual? It's not a crime. If you're guilty of loving someone, so be it. But don't think for a moment that it's going to go away."

"It's never going to go away," Rob said. "I came here today to clear myself. I really don't have anything else to say."

"Well," continued Wozniak, "I've got lots to say because I like talking to people."

Rob could no longer take Wozniak's routine with a straight face. He couldn't believe that the guy thought he was so gullible. "If you want to snicker and sneer," Wozniak said, "then I'll leave."

"I'm not snickering. But what I want to know right now is this: Am I being charged in the death of Elizabeth Bain?" Wozniak told him that it was up to Reesor and Raybould to make that decision.

For a while, they argued about the reliability of the polygraph. "I'm sorry," Rob said, "but if this machine indicates that I murdered Elizabeth Bain, then forget it."

"Forget what?"

"It's absolutely, unequivocally unreliable and not an accurate indicator."

"Remember," said Wozniak, "the machine doesn't make mistakes."

"But I wasn't with Liz that night."

"No mistake has been made here today, Rob. The only mistake being made right now is the way you're giving me these unequivocal denials."

"I can't admit to something I'm not guilty of, can I? I was not responsible for Elizabeth Bain's death. And I will maintain that position until the end of time."

Wozniak suggested that Rob might have killed Liz out of self-defence. Rob was exasperated. "Self-defence?" he said. "This is ludicrous."

"Why do you find that so ludicrous?"

"Why would I need to defend myself against Liz? She was a tiny person who never wanted to hurt me, or anyone for that matter."

"Look, I'm not saying that you're some kind of homicidal maniac like Ted Bundy."

"Frankly, that doesn't comfort me," Rob said. "Whether I was a homicidal maniac or just killed Liz spur of the moment, it wouldn't matter because I'd still feel just as guilty."

"But you're never going to feel good about what's happened to Liz."

"Certainly not. I feel worse now."

"And I hope that you never do feel good about what happened to her because, if you did, that would show that you have absolutely no remorse."

"You know what?" Rob said. "It's one thing to lose someone, but it's another to be held responsible for the pain that that loss causes. From the very beginning, I've been forced to defend myself and my innocence. Basically, I've been denied the right to mourn and grieve."

In total, Rob proclaimed his innocence no less than thirty times, but Wozniak kept at him like a wily attack dog. Finally, Rob said, "Oh, man. Are you guys ever missing the boat." He asked to speak to Reesor or Raybould and, with no confession in sight, Wozniak obliged. In fact, when Wozniak walked out of the polygraph room, he saw that Reesor was already waiting for him in the hallway.

With Reesor now joining them, Wozniak pretended that his colleague had no idea about what had been going on for the last five hours and explained that, in his opinion, Rob hadn't been truthful in his answers to the three questions pertaining to Liz's disappearance. Before leaving, Wozniak thanked Rob for being so cooperative and said that nothing would have made him happier than to tell Reesor that things had worked out differently. Rob said that he realized he couldn't do that.

Alone with Rob, Reesor said that he wasn't surprised by the results. "I would have been awfully shocked if you'd passed it, to tell you the truth, Rob. Nothing has happened here today to change my opinion that you are the person who, eventually, is going to be charged with murdering Liz. We're not waiting for a confession from you to lay a charge. We'll just have to build a case against you without one. It's my job now to prove you're guilty."

"So my status hasn't changed," Rob said.

"Right."

"Well, that makes me feel better."

Reesor didn't want him to feel better—he wanted to see him squirm, sweat— something. This kid was definitely getting under his skin. "Why would that make you feel better?" he asked.

"Because the gentleman who administered the test seemed so convinced of my guilt that I thought you might charge me today."

"No," said Reesor. "It's just confirmed my feelings."

Rob asked if the police had located the woman seen in Liz's car on the afternoon of the day she disappeared. Reesor said that they hadn't. "But we don't know for sure that Liz didn't see that lady later on that night," Rob said.

"We don't know for sure that she didn't see anybody else later on that night either," Reesor said, "including you. The only reason we went looking for this woman is because she may have had a conversation with Liz as to what her plans were that night, such as 'I'm going to meet Rob tonight' or whatever."

"My greatest fear," Rob said, "is that this mystery woman has had two weeks to deduce that you are pointing the finger at me so that when you do find her, she's just going to say exactly what you want her to—that Liz planned on seeing me that night."

"Maybe this woman hasn't come forward because she's on holidays," Reesor said. "And, as you know, Liz worked with handicapped adults. What if she was just giving one of those handicapped adults a ride somewhere? They might not have the ability to realize what's going on or that we're even looking for them. To be honest, Rob, my desire to find this woman was more to develop evidence against you."

Reesor was willing to admit that, at this stage, he had a weak circumstantial case against Rob and needed to gather more evidence. But he made it clear to Rob that he didn't have any information that implicated anyone but him. "Yeah," Rob said dejectedly. "I'm well aware of that." He looked at his watch. "You wouldn't happen to be driving out to Scarborough, would you?"

"No," Reesor said. "Paul's still here."

"You're kidding."

"Yeah, he's downstairs." They both stood up and got ready to go. "As I've said before, Rob, this isn't personal."

"I know, but frankly—"

"I'm trying to do a professional job."

"I know that," Rob said. "All I can say is that I hope it means as much to you to find out who really did it."

"That's what I mean by a professional job. I don't just grab the person I have the most evidence against and say, 'Okay, this is the person we're going to charge.' "

"Look, Steve—"

"We're objective. We don't lay charges based on suspicion and conjecture. It would give me no satisfaction whatsoever to charge someone if I didn't feel a hundred per cent in my own heart that they were guilty and was able to prove it."

"That's music to my ears," Rob said. "I hope you find out what happened."

"I don't know if we'll find out what happened unless you tell us," Reesor said. "But, okay, Rob, let's go down."

—◦—

POLICE PROBE STUDENT'S DIARY
Final entries may give tip to missing woman's fate,
police say

July 6, 1990—Homicide detectives are poring over what may be the last entries Elizabeth Bain recorded in her diary in the hope it will reveal her killer.

But several pages of the looseleaf notebook where she wrote about her life and jotted down intimate thoughts may be missing, friends say.

The missing pages may reveal a souring love relationship, or her state of mind the day the 22-year-old psychology and sociology student disappeared, police said yesterday.

Although friends suspect some of her diary entries are missing, police say the notes were loose, so they can't be positive some are missing.

"We haven't confirmed that ourselves," said Detective Steve Reesor of the homicide squad. "But there might be (some missing)."

It wouldn't be "inaccurate" to say she was having problems with her love life, as friends have alleged, Reesor said.

There are also rumours the diary may have been removed and then returned to the family. "They (the papers) could well have been removed and returned by someone else," Reesor said.

Family, friends and police have been searching almost daily for signs of Bain near the Scarborough campus of the University of Toronto where she was last seen 16 days ago.

Last Sunday night, investigators in a Royal Canadian Mounted Police Bell Jet Ranger helicopter equipped with the infra-red system scanned the ground around Colonel Danforth Park and Morningside Park for her.

The largest search yet for Bain didn't turn up any clues yesterday.

About 500 people, including more than 300 Ontario Hydro

employees and 100 police officers, walked in the rain through mud and heavy brush for six hours in Morningside Park.

Hydro, where Bain's father, Rick, is an engineer, let employees take the day off yesterday to join the search after many had asked earlier in the week.

"I was very impressed with how many people from Hydro came out to help," said Bain, who joined the search team for the morning.

Bain said he hopes an unidentified woman who was seen travelling with his daughter in her car about 3:30 PM the day she disappeared will come forward and talk to police. The woman is described as in her 50s with graying, black hair.

Bain said his daughter's car had bright pink door guards in the shape of fingers that may jog someone's memory.

Rob Baltovich, Bain's boyfriend of about a year, was the last person to see her car the day she disappeared. He would not comment yesterday, saying his lawyer advised him not to talk to anyone about the missing student.

"I'm not at liberty to say anything," said Baltovich. "The best way for me to help is to stay silent."

TORONTO STAR

—◦—

Tina McEwan had been closely following the news stories about Elizabeth Bain. And why not—she'd been Cathy Bain's good friend for at least six years. Just two days after Liz went missing, Tina and her boyfriend, Peter Magnusan, searched down in the valley one afternoon with Cathy and Steve Annett. Mr. Bain and Rob Baltovich, whom she'd occasionally run into at Cathy's house, were also there.

Tina hadn't seen Rob since that first weekend of searches in the valley but she'd heard plenty about how he was now staying away from the Bains and the searches. You couldn't help but get a funny feeling about him consulting lawyers and refusing to speak to reporters. Cathy wasn't making much of an effort to hide her opinion that the police were convinced Rob was Liz's murderer.

That was how things stood on July 7, a Friday, when Tina went to see a movie, *Die Hard II*, with three friends (her boyfriend, Peter, had returned to his native country, Norway, before his student visa expired at the end of June). After the movie, Tina and her friends went to a restaurant called Tapp's. It was shortly past midnight when she walked through the front door and saw Rob Baltovich on the other side of the inner doors. He was wearing the same clothes as always—the sweater with the broad blue and white horizontal stripes and faded jeans with the cuffs rolled up.

Rob had seen her as soon as she passed through the second set of doors—she was sure of it. She was trying to sneak by, but wouldn't you know, he turned around and said, "Hi, Tina, how are you?" Trapped between the cake tray and the maître d's station, she tried to signal to her friend Selina that she wanted her to stay at her side, but Selina didn't catch on and headed towards the back of the restaurant, sitting down at a table with the rest of the group. "Hey, Rob," she said, seeing no escape. "What are you doing here?"

"I'm here with some friends," he said, pointing to Jim Isaacs behind him. Jim was wearing shorts and a white sweat top with a hood. Tina thought he looked a bit out of shape and sunburned. He seemed to be leering at her while she spoke to Rob.

Tina said, "It's funny finding you here at Tapp's" and added that she'd just come from the movies. Rob asked, "Did you come here by yourself?" "No," she said, looking back at her friends and seeing that they'd ordered her a wine cooler. "I'm with them," she said, pointing. She wanted to say something about Liz but wasn't sure quite how to put it, so she said, "I wouldn't want to be alone either, after what happened to Liz."

He just said, "Yeah," as though he knew what she meant. His face was expressionless. "You must find it strange that I'm in here having a good time."

"I didn't say that," she said.

"Then you probably hate me because I haven't been going on the searches."

"I didn't say that, either."

"I'm sure the Bains hate me for not going on the searches."

"I wouldn't know. I haven't spoken to them," she lied.

"Well, you must have been talking to Cathy?"

"No, not in about a week."

Rob told her how his life had been turned upside down—the police accusing him of murder, reporters hounding him, Mrs. Bain leaning into him for heeding his lawyer's advice, which, more than anything else, was just making him look guilty. There was a bit of a pause before Rob said, "It's been three weeks, Tina."

"No way," she said. "It can't be." Rob could tell that she was nervous, and in fact, he commented on the way she was twirling her hair with her finger, biting her fingernails and constantly looking over her shoulder. He told her not to sweat it. Eager to change the subject, Tina asked what he thought had happened to Liz. "It looks like she's dead," said Rob.

"But we don't know that for sure. She could be anywhere. She could be held hostage."

"That's true."

"Do you think she's here in Scarborough?"

"I doubt it," he said. Just then Rick Gostick came up to them from the dance floor. "These guys have been taking me out every night, trying to help me keep my mind off things," Rob explained. Rick said he was ready to go, and Rob said he'd meet him outside in a minute. He turned back to Tina. "So how's Peter? I heard he left in a hurry."

"No, he bought his ticket a month in advance."

"Do you miss him?" She thought he was being sarcastic.

"What do you think? Does Batman miss Robin?"

Good one, Rob thought. He suggested that she should join her waiting friends, and they said good-bye. Tina began to turn away and then felt him grab her left shoulder. "Take care of yourself," he said. "And say hi to Cathy for me. I'll see you around." As she walked towards her friends' table again, turning her head to glance at him as he left, she could still feel the impression of his fingers on her collarbone like a clamp.

—◦—

Three days after the polygraph test, Detective Sergeant Tony Warr asked Marianne Perz, the young tennis instructor who had seen Elizabeth Bain at a picnic table the afternoon she disappeared, to drive down to the Scarborough campus courts with him. He was hoping that she might be able to show him around the area—the route she'd taken to the water fountain, where the picnic table was situated and so on. After taking Warr on a quick tour, she gave him a second, lengthier statement, which he transcribed as they sat in his police cruiser. Three weeks had gone by since Bain had vanished, and Perz was still the only witness they had who'd seen her in the company of a young man that day. The problem was that, beyond recalling that he had dark hair and was Caucasian, she was still unable to give them anything more specific.

The next day Warr called to ask whether she'd be willing to undergo hypnosis because, as he explained, it might be able to enhance her memory of what exactly she'd seen that day. It was their best shot at identifying the man who might very well be the killer. Perz agreed to do it, even though she said she was a little bit sceptical of hypnosis. Deep down inside, though, she knew she didn't have much of a choice.

Apart from her desire to help the police solve the case of a missing girl she'd known from her childhood, Perz's parents had, like her, become quite involved in the searches and had formed a bond with Liz's parents. In fact, the Perz family's home phone number had been added to the list of contacts at the bottom of the more recent sets of Missing posters distributed around the city. Perz had spent a considerable amount of time discussing the disappearance with the Bains, forever trying to make sense of what might have happened to Liz.

When Perz had seen the article in *The Toronto Sun* on Canada Day—the one in which the picture taken by the hidden photographer appeared—it only confirmed what she already knew through the Bains—that Rob Baltovich was a suspect the police had under surveillance. At first, the Bains had seemed hesitant to point the finger at anyone but, after a while, they stopped discussing what might have happened to Liz. Perz got the impression that this silence reflected their belief that Rob was the person who'd killed their daughter. At the same time, there were all kinds of people talking about the Scarborough rapist, an unknown monster lurking out there in the shadows.

Tony Warr was able to get an appointment for Perz with Dr. George Matheson, a psychologist at the Etobicoke General Hospital in west Toronto, for 3:00 PM the next day. Matheson specialized in clinical hypnosis and had been using the technique on victims and witnesses at the request of the police for close to thirteen years. Gradually, it had reached a point that detectives were now bringing him someone at least once or twice a week.

Warr accompanied Perz to the hospital and led her up to Matheson's office, where on numerous occasions he'd taken witnesses whose memories might contain crucial details buried in their unconscious minds. As was the usual practice, Warr asked her to wait in the lobby while he went inside to brief the doctor. Matheson fit the stereotype of a psychologist—trim beard, thinning dark hair, square wire-rimmed glasses on a roundish face, grey jacket, conservative tie, probably from the men's department at Eaton's. When Warr walked into his office, the doctor was fiddling with his new video equipment, which was used to record all police-related hypnosis sessions. He knew from experience that lawyers made his life a lot easier when they could watch a tape instead of picking apart his notes, which was the only recording method he'd used when he'd started out.

Warr explained to the doctor how Marianne Perz was a key link in the Bain case. They needed a better identification of the people sitting at the picnic table that day, especially the male. And they wanted a more precise description of what Bain was wearing—they weren't sure how accurate the memory of the missing girl's mother was on that point. "Between you and me," Warr said, "we suspect Lisa's boyfriend." Matheson nodded. "He's been acting weird all the way along, but there's no real evidence to arrest him. I should also mention that Perz doesn't know him to see him. But the only problem is that she saw him on the way down here. And his picture was in the newspaper, so an identification might not be that good anyway."

Matheson, not bothering to ask Warr what he meant when he said Perz had seen the boyfriend "on the way down here," said, "Well, we'll see. We'll do what we can."

They chatted for another minute and then, together, they retrieved Perz from the waiting room. The video camera caught Matheson and Perz as they entered the room and he directed her to take a seat in a big brown chair, which was in direct view of the camera lens. Matheson told her that the first thing he wanted to do was get to know her better. He had a soft, gentle voice. He told her how it was that he'd come to be involved with the police.

Next they went over her medical history, and Matheson found no impediments to a successful hypnotic state. Perz said she was going into her third year at university, majoring in English literature. She said she wanted to go to graduate school and get her Ph.D. so that she could teach. Matheson next asked her to go over what she remembered about seeing Lisa Bain on June 19, which took Perz about five minutes to do.

Before he hypnotized her, he wanted to dispel some myths about hypnosis. Matheson had given this speech a thousand times and it was almost as if he was reading from a script. "If you watch hypnosis on TV, it looks like you can make people rob banks, kill people, things like that," he said. "They are trying to make you believe that, under hypnosis, you can make people do things against their will. And that would be really exciting, but it is all wrong. Hypnosis is not a state where I can make you do things against your will. I wouldn't even try but I assure you I can't do it. You will remember everything. You will hear my voice. You will know what is going on around you. And yet it is almost like you can drift off. I don't know if you ever daydream, but that's what hypnosis is like."

"I'm just curious," said Perz. "About what percentage of people can be hypnotized?"

"Almost everybody." Matheson said it was a very relaxing experience. "Some people can go so deeply into hypnosis that you could do general surgery and they wouldn't even feel it. But we don't have to do any of that today. Okay?"

"The detective didn't mention anything about that," she said, laughing.

Matheson laughed too. "No, no, that's extra. Surgery costs more."

The doctor was ready to begin hypnotizing her. He instructed Perz to turn her chair sideways so that he could pull his up closer. He guided her right arm above her head, bending the elbow until the back of her hand was facing her brow. "As long as your eyes are open I want you to find a spot, maybe a freckle or a hair and look at it on the back of your hand. Just continue looking at that one spot and as you do I'm going to let go of your hand and it will stay right there and as it does your fingers will begin to spread apart. First you will notice them twitching and then they will begin to drift apart. That's right. Your little finger is starting to glide out. Your first finger has already moved and it's moving more. Gradually your fingers will just begin to spread apart like spokes on a wheel. As you continue looking at that spot on the back of your hand, you are going to begin to notice some other movement. And that's the movement of your hand towards your face. Feel your elbow bend as your hand gradually moves in, almost as if something was pushing it or pulling it. . . ."

Matheson kept directing her in these soft, flowing, soothing phrases until her eyes shut and her hand gently fell onto her forehead. Matheson placed it in her lap. "Just allow yourself to relax more and more. Just drift. Just relaxing. Just noticing that feeling and enjoying it. In a moment I want you to imagine yourself at the top of a set of stairs. I'm going to count from one to ten and each number I count you can imagine going down one step. See yourself going down. Feel yourself going down. Going down one step. So that the larger the number, the further down the stairs you are, the more comfortable you will be. You're just getting ready. One. One step. Down the staircase. Just allowing yourself to get ready. Two. Two steps. Down the staircase. . . ."

It took some patient coaxing to get her to the bottom of the stairs. *Perhaps you notice your eyelids twitch occasionally. Stay relaxed and just notice that soft loose feeling in your cheeks. Gradually begin to notice a space starting to develop between the tops of your teeth.* And then he was getting her to drift back to that Tuesday evening in June. Standing on the tennis court, hugging her new racquet in her arms. "You can let your eyes stay closed. And perhaps you can find your voice. Without disturbing your memory in any way, you can talk to me. Just tell me what it is that your memory sees as you stand right there in the courts. Perhaps even noticing how warm it is as you stand there."

"It's really hot," said Perz. "William is absolutely making jokes. I'm with Paul and Paul is laughing."

"Are you laughing?"

"I'm laughing so hard I'm worried people are going to think I'm not doing my job."

Perz described how she got the kids to line up before they headed off to the water fountain. "What do you notice as you go down to the water fountain?" Matheson asked.

"There are these people I don't know. I didn't look at them. They're at the picnic table. And I see Lisa sitting there."

"Where is the picnic table?"

"It's under a tree."

"What do you see?"

"The people with her, they belong with her. They look like they . . ." There was a pause. "One person belongs with her."

"One person?"

"It looks like there are some people. Somebody is sitting on the grass near the picnic table. She is smiling. I look at her. She looks different. She's got her hair up in a barrette. She's not wearing as much make-up as usual and she's got pants on."

"What kind of pants?"

"Black pants. I noticed her shirt was something pretty but I couldn't think of what it was. I don't have a shirt like that myself. It looks really nice."

"Can you tell me what her shirt looks like?"

"It's kind of yellow-beige with a black print of flowers. And she's got her arms in front of her wrapped around the picnic table. She's looking straight ahead."

"What's she doing?"

"She's just looking at me. It looks like she doesn't want to be with the other people. Or she doesn't look at them. Her attention was obviously focused ahead of her on the other courts, at me. She was happy to see me."

"Can you see the people she's with? Who's on the grass?"

"Somebody with short hair."

"Is that person facing you?"

"No. That person is sort of facing another person behind someone on the picnic table."

"Is it male or female?"

"It's hard to tell. I think they look Oriental. I think it might be female."

"What do you notice about that person?"

"Dark hair. She's just sitting there. Her attention isn't on Lisa. There are three people behind her and they're all together. None of them are dressed in tennis clothes. They all look like they're going to class. But there's someone else."

"Who's this someone else?"

"On her left. That's what tells me she's not alone. Because he's right with her."

"What's he look like?"

"He has dark hair. Short and straight. He's just plain. He's not fabulous. Neither are the people behind her. They are all students. He looks like a student as well. He's sitting farther back than Lisa. His hands aren't forward or up on the table."

"What's he doing?"

"He's looking at her. He's got something funny with his eyes. There's something about his eyes. They're just . . . small. I can't . . . There's something strange about them. The same eyes as Lisa. About the same. They're sitting. He's a little bit taller maybe."

"What else do you notice about his face? Does it look friendly or unfriendly?"

"Unfriendly. He doesn't have the same look that she does. She's looking happy and ahead. He's looking more impatient. Not really angry. He doesn't want to be there and she does. She just wants to sit there. She doesn't want to leave. She looks really happy and content. He's pale, very white."

"Does he have any hair on his face?"

"No."

"Do you notice anything he's wearing? Is he dressed for class or dressed for tennis?"

"Not for tennis. Just regular running shoes. He's wearing shorts. That's why he sticks out in my mind because she was wearing pants."

"What does she do when she sees you?"

"Her eyes just look right into mine. I know her but she's never been like that. Like really really happy friendly, looking at me. Right in my eyes."

"What do the others do when they see you?"

"The people behind her aren't doing anything. There even might be two on the ground. But they are way on her right side in that corner of the picnic table, sitting down. His attention is not on the court like Lisa's. His is on her. No. Wait. Now he starts turning his head. He was looking at her but now he's looking at tennis on court 5. He's small. Not thin, not huge. Just sort of average."

"Does he look Canadian?"

"I think so. But he's got straight dark hair. Some of it is coming forward. The way it was reminded me of the way an Oriental person would have their hair."

"How do you know he's with her?"

"Because he was looking at her. He's so close. It's just this feeling. I know she's not alone."

"Are the others with her?"

"I don't know. They're kind of towards the back of her, all in their own group. They look out of place. There are about five sitting on the grass. Yes. No. Sorry. Four on the grass. Two more on the picnic table behind her."

"Who are the two on the picnic table?"

"They are females but they aren't very pretty. It's almost as if she was framed with people. And she's not in the group. They're just there."

Matheson tried to get her to tell him more about the man Lisa was with, but all she could add was that he "might be a little bit stocky in the legs." And she couldn't remember much more about Lisa either. Matheson got her to walk back to the courts after her drink at the fountain. "Do you look back to see if she's still there?"

"Yes, she's still there. And then I go back to the court and I teach my next lesson."

"Do you see her again?"

"I haven't looked yet. I don't look until six because that's when Paul and Chris were playing on court 1."

"What do you see when you look? Is she gone?"

"She's gone."

"Is anybody else still there?"

"There are still some people around. She's gone and he's gone. And there are still some people left in that group. That's why it stuck in my mind that they weren't together."

"Marianne, I just want you to relax. In a couple of moments I am going to count from five to one. As I do, you can gradually get ready so that at the count of one, you can open your eyes. But even when your eyes are open and even when we are through, later on, if you want to remember what he looked like and what she looked like, all you have to do is close your eyes and look carefully and you'll be able to remember seeing both of them."

"Okay."

Matheson slowly counted from five to one, and Perz opened her eyes. "Without looking at your watch, how long does it feel that you and I have been here since you put your hand up?"

"Ten minutes."

"Ten minutes?" He was removing his microphone. "It might surprise you. It's been fifty minutes. How are you? Okay?"

"Yeah, I'm okay."

"Good, I'm going to ask you to head out to the waiting room for a couple of minutes. I expect the detective will want to talk to you. I'm just going to speak to him briefly and then you and he can chat."

Perz, lifting herself slowly from the chair, said, "Okay."

—◯—

Marianne Perz sat in the waiting room for about five minutes while Dr. Matheson briefed Tony Warr about the session and gave him the videotape of it. The hypnosis had been relaxing, just as the doctor had promised. It was as though you had not a care in the world and suddenly your mind cleared and you could remember things that were previously blocked from your mind's vision. If she could compare it to anything, it would be driving on a highway and finding yourself in a trance, momentarily mesmerized by the road, thinking about nothing and then—out of nowhere—the thing you'd been racking your brain to remember half an hour ago comes to you in a flash of clarity.

When Warr emerged from the doctor's office, he took Perz into an adjacent anteroom and asked if she might be able to identify a photograph of the man she saw with Elizabeth while under hypnosis. Perz said, "I think so." Warr then pulled out a file folder with twelve wallet-sized photographs stapled to it and presented it to Perz, saying, "Rob's photo is in the group."

Warr's reasons for making this remark are open to interpretation. Was he telling her—without saying so directly—whose picture he wanted her to choose? Or, as Warr later asserted, did he say it so Perz would pick the person she envisioned in her mind at the picnic table and not the man who best resembled the photo of Rob she'd seen in the newspaper. In any case, Perz looked at the line-up for a minute or two and then pointed to photographs number one and number six, saying, "These are the eyes." She concentrated intently awhile longer before announcing that number six was the closest—but she didn't want to say for sure. It's the eyes, she said, there was definitely something familiar about those eyes. Warr was writing down her words as she spoke. Without looking, he knew that number six was Robert Baltovich.

—◦—

While Marianne Perz was being hypnotized in Etobicoke, the Bains held a press conference in their backyard. Their purpose for assembling the local media was revealed on the cover of the following morning's *Toronto Sun*. The banner headline for July 11, 1990, read "DAD PLEADS WITH KILLER," below which a photograph of Rick and Julita Bain appeared, both of them seated behind a cluster of microphones, he looking downward, as though reading from a prepared document, she wiping a tear from her eye with a tissue.

Inside, on page five, the *Sun*'s well-known and occasionally controversial columnist Christie Blatchford wrote a piece titled "A Plea for Lisa":

Today is Lisa Bain's 23rd birthday. Her parents are hoping for a gift, a special gift, the gift of peace. Rick and Julie Bain are hoping today, on the very day their beautiful daughter was born, they will find her body.

"If our daughter is . . . at rest, we want her to have a proper Christian burial," says Rick. "We are a Christian family, we believe in prayer . . . even if she is at rest, we want to *know*."

He thanks the thousands who have searched for Lisa since June 19, when she disappeared from the Scarboro campus of U of T.

He thanks the friends, the nurses who work with Julie Bain at Scarboro General and who come to the house every day with food and wet eyes. He asks all Torontonians to search *their* backyards (especially if they edge onto ravines); he asks people who might know something, anything, to phone the hotline.

And then he talks directly to *him*, the dark one.

Rick Bain is 50, and he is an engineer by trade, and he describes himself as a practical man. But as he looks into the TV cameras he has assembled here, at his lovely, leafy West Hill home, he talks softly, and like a poet.

"To the person involved in hurting our daughter, I don't know who you are . . . but you're a member of the human race. You must have experienced some love, some disappointment. Now you are suffering with a horrible burden. You have done a terrible thing. You have hurt a caring person, a loving person, a *shy* person . . .

"Whoever you are, come out of your dark place. Lighten your burden. Tell us where she is. Take that load off your back and help us find our daughter. We plead with you."

Julie, beside him at the picnic table in Lisa's huge backyard (as a child, it was here Lisa learned to love running, jogged in the greenness while, from the second floor of the house, her daddy watched, his heart bursting with happiness as much as it is now, with grief) is blinking hard.

She is strong, as brave as she is pretty (Lisa has—had—her mother's shine of dark hair), ruthlessly honest. "I can't afford to lie in my room with a blindfold, sedated. There are things to be done. I cry, but I cry alone."

Rick is as tough. He turns his hard intelligence on himself. He believes he's resigned to finding Lisa dead, but wonders if he isn't saying it aloud to get *used* to the terrible sound of it.

This is a good family. You can feel it everywhere, in the hand-lettered sign (*The Bain's*) at the gate, in the way Julie's friends, the nurses, prepared food and coffee for the reporters, in the exquisite manner of Julie and Rick.

One of the nurses, Mary Heitzner, puts to words the question that haunts her. "Why the best of them? Why do they always go for the best of them?" Her question is repeated, later, to Rick. He is asked if his faith is being tested. No, he says, and quotes Milton about good coming out of evil.

But he talks about "walking by your daughter's room every night, and wanting to open the door. But you don't." Julie talks about living in a twilight zone, where there is only emptiness. And Rick senses their first-born child "is not very far away."

In another part of *Paradise Lost*, Milton wrote: "And princely counsel in his face yet shone, Majestic, though in ruin." And that is Rick and Julie Bain—majestic, though in ruin.

Check your backyard. If you're going out of town, take a poster. And if you can help, can ease their anguish, *call* the hotline at 324-0854.

—◇—

The Bains' appeal for help was a tremendous success. "There's been a lot of activity around here," Brian Raybould told the press the next day. "We've had a couple of calls that are definitely investigative leads." In total, the police received over six hundred calls that were turned into reports. About a dozen investigators were working "long and hard" on this case alone, the press was told. They were all crammed into an office now dubbed the Team Room, where the walls were covered with posters and charts, standard visual aids to help them piece the case together in their minds.

As was the case with any high-profile investigation in which the public's assistance is actively sought, the police were getting all kinds of calls from people who believed they might have seen something important—that being a petite, attractive brunette resembling Elizabeth Bain around the time she went missing. One caller saw her sandwiched between two men, one blond, the other dark-haired, in a beige Ford pick-up late at night. Another was nearby when a red sports car came shooting out onto Morningside Avenue just south of Ellesmere Road causing oncoming traffic to squeal to a halt. Neither the blond male driver, nor the female passenger whom he was holding on to—a carbon copy of a drugged or inebriated Elizabeth Bain—in order to keep her upright, bothered to look behind them at the cacophonous havoc they had caused. While stopped at a red light on Kingston Road a few blocks away from Colonel Danforth Park at 10:10 PM on Tuesday, June 19, a black man was seen dragging a crying girl across the road in front of him. The woman, who looked part Asian, was screaming, "Don't do that! Let me go!"

Six days after she vanished, Elizabeth Bain was seen walking up the ramp to the SkyDome stadium. She was thought to be living in a hotel in Trenton, Ontario, disguising herself with a blond wig. The day after the Bains' plea for help, she and a tall blond man walked into the Scott Mission downtown looking for a free warm meal. Even later than that, she and a man were seen walking in front of a Howard Johnson hotel in St. Catharines, just a few miles from Niagara Falls; they both looked hung over. She'd also been suffering from a late night and a few too many at a gas station way up in Sudbury, where she was seen in a Volkswagen with two men. She was also observed sleeping in the woods at Applewood Hills Park in Mississauga, hitchhiking on Highway 401 both in Toronto and east near Cambridge, getting on the subway at Yonge and Bloor, and sitting by the front doors of the Hospital for Sick Children on University Avenue.

On the night that Liz disappeared, a twenty-eight-year-old woman named Anita Ledingham was in a cab heading west on Danforth Road in Scarborough when she was almost struck by a small blue car driving erratically. The driver, who looked just like the missing girl, was yelling "Call the police!" An old, white-haired woman was in the passenger seat, but the car took off before Ledingham could get a better look. In their report, the police dutifully wrote down that Ms. Ledingham claimed to have psychic abilities, read tarot cards and meditated in a monastery. She was quite willing to share what the cards had told her: someone was spying on Elizabeth Bain; the murder was planned in advance; Bain had two men in her life; she was killed by a jealous boyfriend; the family would be ruined by this affair; and that someone was paid to kill her.

Not every report, however, was tossed in the No Need to Follow Up file. There was a core group of witnesses that enabled Reesor and Raybould to patch together a rough chronology of what might have taken place on the evening of June 19. So far, this was what they knew:

3:30-3:45 PM: Lou Torrone sees Liz in her car at a stop light on Kingston Road. There is an attractive older woman in the passenger seat. (No such woman has yet come forward.)

3:45 PM: Liz withdraws $80 from a bank machine just a few blocks away.

4:15 PM: A young man named Chris Decastro, who knew Liz from the neighbourhood, sees her driving in her car alone near Watson Road and Ellesmere, about a hundred metres from where her car was found three days later on Morrish Road.

5:30 PM: Dana Baltovich picks up her husband Paul at his parents' house. She stays and speaks with Adele in the foyer for fifteen minutes. Rob, who is in the middle of preparing dinner, comes to the top of the stairs to say a quick hello.

5:45 PM: Marianne Perz sees Liz at the picnic table by the tennis courts. Two days after she was hypnotized the police located three Asian girls—Jenny Lo, Cecelia Chan and Gigi Pang—all of whom claimed to have been sitting at a picnic table near the tennis courts between 5:45 and 7:30 PM. Under hypnosis, Perz said there were three "Oriental" females together behind Liz. While this lent credibility to Perz's sighting, none of the girls remembered seeing anyone fitting the description of Elizabeth Bain or Robert Baltovich, both of whom were, according to Perz, sitting just a few feet away. In addition to the Asian girls, there were at least six other witnesses in the vicinity of the courts between 5:00 and 7:20 PM, including three other tennis instructors, David Phillips, Chris Monday and Paul Keller (whom Perz mentioned under hypnosis—"I'm with Paul, and Paul is laughing"). Not one of these people could recall seeing anyone resembling Rob or Liz.

6:20 PM: A twenty-three-year-old woman named Marilyn Vasconcelos gets home from work around six o'clock—she still lives with her parents—changes clothes and drives to Colonel Danforth Park with her mother and her dog. They park in the rectangular lot next to a small grey car. As Vasconcelos steps out of her car, she notices some pink plastic fingers on the driver's side door. Curious, she moves closer and touches them. The window is open and she sees an orange and blue striped cloth on the driver's seat and a red package of du Maurier cigarettes on the passenger seat before heading off into the park for her walk.

6:30 PM: Adele says good-bye to Rob as he leaves the house on his way to the gym.

6:45 PM: As Rob spots Liz's car on his way through the valley, a Scarborough man named Rein Raud is walking on a path with his five-year-old son and his German short-haired pointer in the heavily wooded area east of the tennis courts, closer to Morrish Road. About to cross a bridge on his way back towards the courts, he sees a white female with dark hair, approximately five feet four inches tall, wearing a bright-coloured long-sleeved blouse, black pants and black, flat-heeled shoes walking towards him at a quick pace. The woman veers off the path in order to walk around them in a wide arc. She has a nervous look about her and Raud deliberately avoids making eye contact as she passes so she will have no further cause for fear. He doesn't notice anyone following her. (Although Raud's description of the woman's clothes were a perfect match with those of Elizabeth Bain, he didn't look at her face long enough to make a solid identification.)

7:15 PM: While getting out of his car, twenty-five-year-old Marc Singleton sees Rob—whose brother Paul he is familiar with—step-
ping out of his Cordoba in the Recreation Centre parking lot.
As Singleton locks his car, Rob casually jogs past him to the
front doors of the Rec Centre and goes inside. (When later
asked what Rob was wearing, Singleton says a blue and white
striped sweater, multi-coloured dress shorts with a check
pattern and casual shoes.) Inside, Singleton sees Rob in the
basement locker room changing into his usual workout gear.
They then head upstairs, where Singleton approaches Rob as
he's hoisting the bench press and asks if he can work out with
him. Rob says sure and they spot the bar for each other and
then continue on with their separate routines. Singleton sees
Rob in the weight room until 8:30 PM.

7:30–8:30 PM: Hoping to get home in time to catch her favourite television
show, "In the Heat of the Night," starting at nine, Ruth Collins
closes up her health-food store and catches the bus heading
along Kingston Road. The forty-nine-year-old gets off at her
usual stop on Morrish Road. She crosses Kingston Road and
walks north along the right edge of Morrish; it has no side-
walks. On the paved drive in front of Three R Auto Body
(directly across the road from where the car will be found in
two and a half days) she sees a small silver car facing the building. Through the window of the passenger door is a beautiful
young woman whom Collins later identifies as Elizabeth Bain.
Twice, Collins sees her door open, and Bain begins to step out
before a large, tanned male arm seems to reach across her from
the driver's side and shut it. There is a thumping noise, along
with the man's voice, which is quite loud, almost shouting.
Bain's head and shoulders snap forward and back a couple of
times during all of this. She turns her head and looks right at
Collins, who is starting to cross over to the other side of the
street. Collins thinks she looks startled to see her, but not
terrified. Just a couple of kids fooling around. Once their eyes

meet, all of the activity in the car stops. Apart from the impression that the man is Caucasian and that his hair goes over his ears, she notices nothing more about him. The light is falling in such a way that his face is darkened by the shadows. (Whoever it is, Marc Singleton has confidently asserted that Robert Baltovich is, at this moment, pumping iron just a few feet away from him in the gym.)

9:00 PM: His hair still wet from the shower, Rob hides atop a set of stairs waiting for Liz to emerge from her class. She doesn't, and he drives to the Bains' house, speaking briefly to Liz's mother in the driveway.

9:30 PM: Rob walks into the gym and joins Neil Winton, Rob Cortina, Tony Scarpino and Jack Caruso on the bleachers. He is wearing Sperry topsiders, jeans and his ever-present blue-and-white-striped sweater. Moments later he goes downstairs to call Linda Phillips to find out if Liz was in class that night. He then goes back up to the gym and spikes volleyballs with Neil and Rick Gostick for twenty minutes.

10:15 PM: Mark Bain gets home and checks his answering machine. No message from Rob—he picks that up in the morning. Mark heads over to Nancy's for the night.

10:30-11:00 PM: Rob arrives home, talks to his mother. He tries calling Liz at home three times, but keeps getting a busy signal. Giving up, he leaves a message on Mark's machine, writes out a note for his mother to read to Liz (if she calls late and everything is okay) and goes to bed.

—⊖—

What were Reesor and Raybould to make of all this? How could Baltovich be the person Marianne Perz sees with Liz at 5:45 PM near the tennis courts if he didn't leave home until 6:30? And if he did kill his girlfriend, when exactly did the crime take place? Perhaps the most difficult question of all was one of motive—what reason did he have to kill the woman he loved?

Reesor and Raybould thought that the answers to these and other questions hovering over this case were relatively straightforward. First of all, they had no reason to doubt that Marianne Perz had seen Robert Baltovich by the tennis courts at 5:45 even though Perz herself wasn't entirely sure it had been him. The Asian girls, along with the handful of other people who couldn't remember seeing Baltovich or Bain in the area, could be easily discounted—Perz knew Bain, and they didn't. (The undoing of this argument? Tennis instructor David Phillips was well acquainted with both Baltovich and Bain.) As for Rob being at home until six-thirty, Reesor and Raybould were convinced that Rob's family had lied about the time of his departure to protect him. In fact, the night Paul Baltovich was observed by the undercover surveillance officer pulling into his parents' driveway at one in the morning was an important piece of the puzzle. The two hours that Paul spent inside the home that night were surely spent coordinating the stories each member of the Baltovich family was going to spoon-feed the police, establishing 6:30 PM as the time Rob left the house. That would hardly give him enough time to commit murder before he was seen at the Recreation Centre forty-five minutes later.

They also seized upon the fact that Marc Singleton said he'd seen Rob Baltovich wearing shorts on his way into the gym—Rob's friends at the volleyball courts said he was wearing jeans just a few hours later. What happened to these pink-and-blue checked dress shorts Singleton saw? And why was he wearing something different after his workout? Was Baltovich's inability to remember what he'd worn to the gym that day a coincidence or a convenient lapse? The logical explanation, of course, was that Baltovich, having committed the murder in the valley on his way to the gym, had spatters of blood on his shorts. He changed into jeans after his workout so that he could dispose of the shorts. Maybe that was the reason he'd jogged past Singleton instead of walking—he didn't want him to get a good look at the bloodstains. (Then again, why didn't Baltovich just wait for Singleton to go inside ahead of him or, better yet, change into his jeans in his car?)

But, if the detectives clung to the notion that Rob was with Liz at the tennis courts at 5:45 and had killed her before Singleton saw him at 7:15, how were they going to explain the statements given by Rein Raud and Ruth Collins? Raud saw a woman wearing the same outfit as Bain just half an hour before Baltovich showed up at the Recreation Centre—and she was walking alone in the park a good distance east of the tennis courts. Collins represented an even greater blow to their theory. If Bain was dead by 7:15, then how could Collins see her alive and in the company of a man between 7:30 and 8:30 when Baltovich was known to be somewhere else? Perhaps as tips continued to pour into the Team Room, these questions would be answered and their theory would gradually alter over the course of time. But the way it stood now, with the equivocal Marianne Perz as the only eyewitness backing up their shaky version of an unknown crime, the investigation was a long way from over.

If, eventually, Reesor and Raybould were somehow able to prove that Baltovich had the opportunity to kill his girlfriend, they were going to have to back up Reesor's hunch that he'd taken her life because she'd tried cutting him out of hers. And what evidence was there to suggest that? Well, originally, when Reesor sprang the idea on his suspect, there really wasn't any. But as the investigation rolled along, Reesor was gathering witnesses who, together, might turn his gut instinct on this one into self-fulfilled prophecy.

He and his partner had read Liz's diary and knew that, for many months, she'd repeatedly expressed her desire to break up with Rob. If she'd finally managed to go through with it, was he likely to kill her for it? One problem with this theory was that Baltovich had also threatened to break up with her—the ultimatum over holistic medicine being one example—and hadn't seemed too concerned about the ramifications of asking her to leave his house after a disagreement just a few months previously. The other difficulty with establishing a bona fide intention to give Rob his walking papers was that her feelings were constantly fluctuating. For every contemptuous entry about him, there was another that professed undying and everlasting love. Similarly, in the spring, when she'd actually gone as far as telling people—Jim Isaacs and John Camunias, to name two—that things were over between her and Rob, the police couldn't deny that they'd continued their relationship.

And then there was the issue of the missing diary pages. Cathy Bain contended that when Rob borrowed a stack of Liz's entries, only a fifth of what she'd originally seen in the orange binder remained. And even when he said he'd returned the last of what he'd taken home, Cathy estimated that nearly half of the diary was still missing. Reesor and Raybould didn't think it was a coincidence that no entries existed from May 15 until the bleak final entry, written a month later. Surely Baltovich had destroyed them in a frenzied effort to eliminate any mention of her intention to part ways, an event that, ultimately, pushed him to the brink of losing self-control. He'd killed her in a rage. They'd come across it all before.

With each successive interview, Cathy's role in the case against Rob became more significant. It was during her second formal interview that Reesor and Raybould were able to satisfactorily resolve the issue of the du Maurier cigarettes found in her sister's glove compartment. Cathy was the only person in the family to whom Liz had confided that she smoked when under a lot of stress. But that was a couple of years ago, and Cathy hadn't seen Liz with a cigarette since, hadn't even heard her talk about having one. Reesor and Raybould thought that hardly mattered when they wrote down her answer to their next question, which was: "Do you know what brand she smoked?" Cathy said du Maurier was the only one she knew of.

Her third interview was the result of an incident that she'd forgotten until weeks after Liz had gone missing (which is why, apparently, she never mentioned it to Rob after reading Liz's final diary entry, when Cathy had asked if he and Liz had been arguing). It had taken place on the Thursday evening previous to that strange, terrible night. Cathy was staying at home that week because her father, to whom she was still not speaking, was away in Florida. She got home from her kitchen job at Centenary Hospital around eight-thirty, and by the time she changed clothes and went downstairs to make something to eat it was probably nine o'clock. That's when Liz and Rob walked in the front door, and everyone said hello.

A few minutes later, Cathy realized that she'd forgotten to give Liz a telephone message from one of her managers at the day-care centre—they wanted to know if she could work a shift the next day. By that time, Liz and Rob had gone down into the basement, and from the top of the basement steps, Cathy couldn't hear any sound from the TV. Not wanting to walk in on anything, she called out the message to Liz from where she stood. When Liz didn't respond, Cathy called out again. Still, silence. After the third yell, Liz finally uttered a meek-sounding "Okay."

Cathy knelt down to peek through the bars on the railing, but couldn't see either one of them anywhere in the recreation room. It sounded as if the voice had come instead from the direction of the laundry room, but she couldn't tell for sure because the door was shut.

Liz came upstairs ten minutes later, alone. Cathy thought she noticed tears that had dried beneath her eyes. Liz was shaking her head in disdain as she picked up the phone. "Rob is such an asshole," she said, dialling her manager's number. After the phone call, Liz went up to her room—to fix her face, Cathy presumed. An hour later, when Cathy was heading out the door, she could hear Liz in the kitchen doing the dishes. The only person she could see was Rob, and he was by himself in the living room, pacing.

The next hint that something was amiss came, somewhat surprisingly, from one of Rob's best friends, Al Heys. When Al got a phone call requesting an interview from a detective named Brody Smollet, his first inclination was to put it off until the weekend. He was working the midnight shift at the Molson Brewery and, nine times out of ten, he was asleep in the early afternoon, but when Smollet called, he was awake. By delaying the interview, Al thought he might give the police the impression he had something to hide, which he didn't, so he said it was all right for Smollet to come over.

Within the hour, Smollet and his partner arrived, and Al was telling them about his friendship with Rob and what he knew about Liz's disappearance, which he figured wasn't anything very helpful to them. Soon enough, they got on the subject of the last time he saw Rob before June 19, which was the Saturday night Rob had picked him and Tony Fuchs up to go and see a movie. He remembered that Tony had found an envelope in the back seat. Tony hadn't opened it, but he had a fuzzy recollection that it was an excerpt from Liz's diary. It was a "Dear something" letter, but he couldn't remember the exact term. Was it a Dear John letter maybe, Smollet asked. Yeah, Al thought out loud, Dear John might have been what it was, but he made it clear that those weren't the words Rob had used to describe it. The only thing about the note he was certain of, though, was that it was something she'd written a long time ago and, for whatever reason, had given to him earlier that evening. Smollet didn't really care when it had been written; what was important was that Heys had referred to it as a Dear John letter in his statement. Regardless of what Heys would say later on, they now had one of Baltovich's closest friends suggesting on the record that Liz had initiated a break-up three days before she vanished.

A day or two later, when Al told Rob that he'd referred to the old diary entry as a Dear John letter during his interview with the police, Rob was concerned. "Oh my god, Al," he said. "You know what a Dear John letter is, don't you?"

"Yeah," Al said. "It's like a love letter, isn't it?"

Rob was thinking that only a guy like Al, who as far as he knew had never had a girlfriend, would make a mistake like this. "Al," Rob said, "a Dear John letter is what someone sends you when they want to end the relationship."

"Oh," Al said. "Sorry." What else could he say?

Rob told him not to worry about it. Tony was also in the car that night and, hopefully, he wouldn't fall victim to the same misunderstanding as Al. It wouldn't really matter, except that, besides Tony, there was no other dependable way to prove that it hadn't been a Dear John letter in the back of his car. He'd given the old diary entry (from September 1988) back to Mr. Bain within days of Liz's disappearance, along with a few other pieces of correspondence that Rob figured the police would want to take a look at.

Although Rob and his friends had no way of knowing it, the truth was that the Dear Meg entry (now believed to be a Dear John letter) was a drop in the bucket compared to what the police thought they had on Rob for the following night. This was the Sunday night Rob brought the rented movie over to Kidbrooke and then met Liz for their late-night tryst in the valley at the end of her shift. Rob had told Reesor and everyone else that he and Liz had been lying on some blankets next to the river until at least two in the morning. To Reesor and Raybould, this story was starting to look like another elaborate lie.

The same day that Rob had been taking his polygraph test, the police had received a call from a woman named Susanne Nadon on the tips hotline. Nadon was thirty-two and had been living at her mother's house on the north side of Kingston Road roughly two kilometres east of Colonel Danforth Park since separating from her husband in September. She told the police that she'd been getting into bed about half an hour past midnight—she had to be downtown for work in the morning at CN Rail, where she'd been an office assistant for almost thirteen years—when she heard some people arguing outside. Nadon put her glasses on and walked across the room to have a look through her third-floor window. There were some pretty big trees in front of her mother's old house and plenty of thick bushes too, and she couldn't see where the sound was coming from. For about ten seconds all she could hear were two voices—one male, one female. She heard the female say no a few times but couldn't pick up any other bits of dialogue.

Next a car door slammed, and a silver car pulled out from behind the bushes, moving west on Kingston Road in front of the house. The car accelerated at a fairly normal speed but, because of the trees, it was visible for only a brief instant and, although Nadon made out the black stripe that ran along the side of the car between the wheels, she couldn't see the driver or make out the plate number. Then, a few seconds later, the woman appeared, walking along the sidewalk in a clearing between the trees in the same direction as the car. She looked young, in her early twenties, petite, about five feet three inches with thick, wavy, brown hair down to her shoulder blades. She was wearing a dark mini skirt or loose shorts and a "summer-style" top that might have been a summer pastel like yellow or blue. Her shoes were dark with a flat heel.

When the police eagerly presented Nadon with a photo of Elizabeth Bain, their hopes were quickly dashed as she declared that she couldn't really say for certain that it had been her. But all was not lost. Ethel Ormsby, the Kidbrooke employee Rob had driven home before meeting Liz, told the police she remembered Liz wearing a black short skirt, a sleeveless top (she couldn't remember the colour) and black flat shoes to work that day—practically the same outfit Nadon had described. Reesor and Raybould didn't really buy Rob's making-love-in-the-park story anyway, since Eric Genuis had told them about how, back in May, Liz had confided to him that she was no longer sexually intimate with Rob.

The obvious conclusion was that they'd spent half the night fighting, more than likely because she was trying to get rid of him and he wasn't taking it too well. So he kicked her out of the car and drove away in a snit. It made such perfect sense that Reesor and Raybould didn't seem bothered by a series of incongruous facts bedevilling this scenario. For example, why was Rob driving her car? No one had seen him drive it before, so why would he try now? And, if they'd spent the night fighting, possibly even breaking up, why didn't Liz look at all upset when her mother saw her come home at 2:00 AM? Liz had been reduced to tears as a result of experiences that were infinitely less traumatic.

Regardless, Reesor and Raybould were going to have to make sense of Tuesday, in conjunction with Sunday night. If Rob killed her in the valley on Tuesday, was it something he plotted after being dumped on Sunday? Or maybe the bad news wasn't delivered until an arranged meeting in the park on Tuesday, and killing her was his violent, spontaneous reaction. And then there was Liz's phone call Tuesday morning, which was returned once Rob had picked up his brother at the oral surgeon's office. If Liz had already broken up with him, why would she call? Perhaps they hadn't, and she was calling to set up a time and place to meet before her class, intending to sever their ties then. If that was the case, why wouldn't Liz tell her mother she was getting together with Rob in the park, rather than saying she was going to check the tennis schedule? And, if Rob had no idea that the purpose of their rendezvous was to effect an end to their relationship, he was in a similar position. What harm would there be in letting his mother or his brother and Dana know he was seeing Liz on his way to the Recreation Centre?

A couple of people Reesor and Raybould had interviewed had them thinking they might be on their way to answering some of these questions. Cathy Bain's boyfriend, Steve Annett, was now claiming that, when he and Rob were on their way to Three R Auto Body, where Liz's car had just been found, Rob said he'd seen Liz ducking behind her car when she'd spotted him driving through the valley on Tuesday. Nancy Sicchia recalled him making a similar comment—that he'd seen Liz hiding from him—to her and Arlene Coventry when they were driving to Kew Beach to look for Liz. While Reesor and Raybould were ecstatic to see Rob's story contradicted in such a dramatic manner, it just saddled them with more perplexing questions. The most obvious was: why would Liz be hiding from Rob if they were supposed to be meeting? Conversely, if Liz was trying to avoid him, why had she chosen to park her car in such a conspicuous spot, where there was a reasonable chance Rob would see it on the way to his workout? Was she hiding because they'd broken up over the phone in the morning and she didn't want to see him? When he saw she was trying to hide from him, did he jealously stalk and kill her in a remote area of the park? Or did he stalk and kill her after she'd dumped him at the picnic table by the tennis courts?

Who knew? Reesor and Raybould were discovering that you could talk about this case until you were blue in the face and end up no further ahead than you were when you started. In the end, even the story about Rob claiming to have seen Liz ducking down behind her car had fault lines. Arlene Coventry, who'd been in the car with Nancy when Rob was supposed to have made the comment, told the police she remembered asking Rob if it was possible that Liz had seen his car when he pulled up next to hers on his way to the gym. "It's possible," she recalled him saying. "And she might have hid." Nothing about ducking or actually seeing her.

Did Reesor and Raybould have enough to convince a jury that Elizabeth Bain had tried to break off with Robert Baltovich on June 19, 1990, thus giving him a motive to kill her? As it stood, they were going to have to rely on Susanne Nadon and Vanessa Sherman to make the case that, at the very least, their relationship was on the rocks and that Rob possessed a quick temper. The most glaring weakness, though—one that any competent defence lawyer would surely point out—was that the police had been unable to find one living soul whom Liz had informed of her plans to end things with Rob either on Sunday or Tuesday, or that she was even thinking about doing so. What would a jury make of that? Reesor and Raybould had been around long enough to know that, with a circumstantial case like this, you had to take some chances. It was a big crap shoot when it came to juries. But they knew one thing for certain—they still needed more evidence before they could arrest Baltovich.

———○———

Andrea Beitinger's interview with the police didn't go quite as she expected it would. First of all, the Homicide Squad investigators didn't get around to her until almost a month after the disappearance. This was a bit of a surprise, considering she'd made no secret of her friendship with Robert Baltovich. After that first weekend of searching for Liz Bain in the valley, Andrea had shown up for work at the Intelligence Services building on Monday morning, telling her co-workers about the unusual events of her weekend.

One of Andrea's favourites at Intelligence was a cop named Miro Pristupa. Pristupa had his detractors on the force, but he was a colourful veteran, and no one could deny he had a knack for his job. Pristupa was known as an "analyst." It was one of those behind-the-scenes positions that didn't garner much in the way of public attention, despite its potentially important role in the resolution of complex investigations. Pristupa would act as a resource to detectives like Steve Reesor and Brian Raybould, correlating the hundreds of reports they were receiving, establishing patterns between witness statements and suspects, running background checks, often drawing up lovely, huge flowcharts (which most cops, at the end of the day, felt didn't amount to anything). He'd worked as an analyst on some intricate undercover biker operations in the late seventies and early eighties and was currently embroiled in the Scarborough rapist investigation, which, as far as he was concerned, was going nowhere fast.

With Andrea speaking freely to Pristupa about her connections to Elizabeth Bain's boyfriend, it wasn't difficult to imagine Pristupa setting himself up as a direct pipeline back to Steve Reesor's Team Room. He'd be on the phone before she could take more than a few steps out of his office. Even Andrea was getting the distinct impression that her employers were taking some time to check her out more thoroughly and that this might have been the reason it took the Homicide investigators so long to request a formal interview.

Andrea was well aware that Brody Smollet and Jake Poranganel, the men who eventually came to meet with her at Intelligence, escorting her into a vacant office, were among the detectives pursuing Rob. She'd been anxiously awaiting this moment since the day she'd spoken with Rob in her backyard about the way they'd interrogated him, unable to bridge the gulf in her mind that existed between the Rob she knew and the Rob they were depicting, a Rob they claimed had taken his girlfriend's life. She was fully prepared to speak at length about just how preposterous a notion this was.

It didn't take long, however, for that intention to evaporate in a whirlwind of confusion and doubt. Years later, when Andrea better understood these things, she realized that Poranganel and Smollet had used the classic good-cop bad-cop routine—which she had seen played out on television countless times since—to make her question everything she believed about one of her closest, most trusted friends. She felt that Smollet was being incredibly mean, twisting her words time and time again. They told her Rob had failed a polygraph test. What did she think about that? They kept throwing out one incriminating revelation after another until her resolve began to vanish.

Andrea didn't know what they wanted her to say. It wasn't so much that there was anything in particular they wanted her to say, Poranganel explained, it was more along the lines of something she could do. And that was for her to allow them to attach a recording device to her home telephone. As expected, Andrea was clearly reluctant to participate in a scheme that, no matter how you looked at it, was an act of betrayal. Getting the feeling that she was definitely starting to crack, Smollet and Poranganel turned up the heat.

And in doing so, Andrea began to see just how much these officers despised Rob—it seemed quite personal. His beloved girlfriend goes missing, and not one cop sees him shed a tear in grief. And, like the worst kind of murderer, they said, Baltovich was equipped with remarkable cunning; he was a highly intelligent young man familiar with the intricacies of human psychology through his university studies. He'd turned the entire investigation into his own sick little game. The cocky little bastard thought he was going to run circles around a couple of stupid coppers and continue on with his life as if nothing had happened. Well, Mister Smartypants wasn't so brilliant after all. Throwing him behind bars was going to be the most satisfying day of their careers. Make no mistake, Andrea, they were saying, this nice, sweet-talkin' friend of yours is a cold-blooded killer.

Reduced to tears, Andrea eventually broke, and after four hours caved in to their wishes. Now she was being sensible, they said, unencumbered by her clouded vision. The good cop, Poranganel, consoled her, located some fresh tissue. The bad cop spelled out the game plan: arrangements would be made to affix the recorder to her phone as soon as possible. And then they said, "We'll be in touch." Andrea wasn't sure if she was in any kind of state to be driving home, but by the time it occurred to her that she should ask for a lift, Poranganel and Smollet were long gone.

—◦—

Norm Rowntree, the Forensic Identification Services detective who'd examined Elizabeth Bain's car, was slowly gathering reports from various scientific experts around the city. An insect specialist at the Royal Ontario Museum told him that the dead bugs taken from the head lamp of Elizabeth Bain's car were not moths, as originally suspected, but were in fact caddis-flies from the Hydropsychisdae family. Caddis-flies, Raybould was advised, were aquatic insects found near running water such as Highland Creek (or a thousand other rivers in southern Ontario), nocturnal flying creatures that spin pupa cases and webs.

As for the plant samples sent to Dr. John MacAndrews, another scientist at the Royal Ontario Museum, there was not much that stood out—all were common to just about every region of the province. There was only one exception, a blood-stained leaf found on the floor behind the driver's seat. It belonged to a vine known as the Dog Strangling Vine, which grew abundantly among the thick bush of the Highland Creek area, as well as the dense foliage of other river valleys in southern Ontario. Samples had been collected primarily from Toronto, but also from Kingston, Cobourg, Milton, Rice Lake and Scugog Township (where the disregarded David Dibben was sure he'd seen Bain's Tercel early on June 22).

And then there was the blood. The Centre for Forensic Sciences, using samples taken from Elizabeth Bain's parents, had determined that it was from a female offspring of the couple. The Centre's DNA expert, Pam Newall, had come to this conclusion using a reverse-paternity DNA test, in which the DNA (otherwise known as the "genetic fingerprint") of a child can be matched to its parents through genetic coding. This finding narrowed the source of the blood to two—Liz and Cathy Bain—but Cathy was quickly eliminated when she told the police that she'd never bled in her sister's car.

All of this simply backed up what Reesor and Raybould already suspected—that Elizabeth was killed in the valley, possibly hidden in the dense bushes among the Dog Strangling Vine, before her dead body was dragged into the back of her car and driven, after nightfall, to some remote location to be disposed of. What they needed now, more than anything else, was something concrete that tied Baltovich to this scenario.

—◯—

It was a good day for a visit to Jimmy's Smoke Shop. Reesor and Raybould strolled beneath the white awning out front and through the glass door, their nostrils invaded at once by the sweet smell of cigars. Jim moved slowly behind the counter in a short-sleeved dress shirt that he had buttoned up to his neck. He looked especially frail and elderly (he was, after all, in his sixty-eighth year) in comparison with the enormous man with long red hair and a scruffy beard who set two cans of V8 juice on the counter and then inserted a few fat fingers of one hand into the narrow pocket of his leather vest and searched for change in his blue jeans with the other. His arms were covered in a maze of tattoos; Jim's eyes darted to the spider web that circled outward from the ball of his elbow. "You guys are getting addicted to this stuff over there," said Jim, ringing up the V8s. The man simply nodded his head and grunted. He worked at a neighbouring tattoo parlour.

Once Big Red had clomped across the worn tile floor in his motorcycle boots, Reesor flipped his badge open and introduced himself. He said he and his partner wanted to ask a few questions. "All right," said Jim. He had a soft voice, gentle old eyes and a head of thin grey hair that looked as if it had been combed neatly into place with a little Brylcreem. "We don't really want to talk here in the store," said

Reesor. "It would be a lot more private if you were to join us in the cruiser. We're parked right out front."

"I guess I'll have to lock up for a while then," Jim said. He had creamy, youthful skin and a heart-shaped mouth. Raybould took a quick look around the store while Jim searched beneath the register for his keys. The greeting-card racks behind him had maybe half a dozen dusty cards left in them, most curling at the corners from the humidity. Jim was making his way around the old freezers with the sliding glass covers, a rainbow of Popsicles and shiny ice-cream bars nice and frosty inside. The shelves on the wall behind him, which many years ago had been filled with canned goods, loaves of bread and other necessities of life, now provided storage for bundles of blank lottery tickets—his main source of revenue, as attested by the Certificate of Appreciation from the Ontario Lottery Corporation tacked to the wall. There was even an old rack for small glass jars of coloured paints for model cars, boats or planes. Was there one child in the entire country since the advent of video games who'd glued together a B-52 bomber?

Jim rounded the corner of the antique Coca-Cola freezer and passed between the men near the magazine shelf. One of Rob's old university textbooks on postmodern literature (was it for sale?) sat tantalizingly in front of the latest issue of *Playboy*. A metal paperback stand stood a few feet from the door. There was no telling how old those sun-faded covers might be—hopefully they weren't as ancient as the typewriter sitting in the window.

Reesor and Raybould stepped out onto the sidewalk while Jim locked the front door. As he turned the key, they couldn't help but notice his unusually long, delicate fingers. Jim followed them to the cruiser about three parking spots east of the store front and slowly eased his way into the back seat as Raybould held the door open for him. Reesor started the car and turned up the air-conditioning a notch. Twisting around, Reesor rested his arm on the back of his seat and set the tone of the discussion: "I'm going to be straight with you, Mr. Baltovich. We know your son killed Liz. . . ." And it just got worse from there. Jim kept trying to tell them that his son wasn't capable of such a thing and, besides, did he really have enough time to commit a murder between the time he left home at 6:30 PM and his arrival at the Recreation Centre forty-five minutes later? Reesor said, "I think he left the house a lot earlier than 6:30, Mr. Baltovich."

"He couldn't have," Jim protested. "My wife looked up at the kitchen clock as Robert was going out the door. The clock read six-thirty—I'm telling you."

It was no use. They refused to listen. "Please speak to your son, Mr. Baltovich. Appeal to his sense of decency. We know he's got a conscience. You raised him so. He'll feel so much better with this weight lifted from his shoulders." After a while, Jim decided to appease them and, getting out of the car, said he would do what he could. He was about to shut the door when Reesor asked Jim where he parked his car. Jim pointed to the outdoor mall on the other side of Kingston Road, where at least two hundred cars were parked in front of the stores, which included a supermarket, a Woolworth and a Blockbuster video. "Can you point it out?" Reesor asked.

"Not from here," said Jim. He couldn't imagine their reason for wanting to look at his car.

"Well," Reesor began, "why don't we give you a lift over there and you can show it to us?"

Jim didn't really want to go to his car just yet—he had to turn out the lights in the store and empty the cash first—but he went along with it anyway. They let him out right behind the gold Camaro he'd bought from Paul. "That's it?" Reesor asked. "You drive this Camaro?" Jim carefully shut the back door of the cruiser. "That's my car," he said. He thought he detected a pair of wry smiles before they took off, and Reesor reminded him one last time to have that talk with Rob. Jim waited until the cruiser was out of sight down Kingston Road before beginning to make his way to the crosswalk up at the traffic lights. He was thinking he'd better call Adele to let her know why he hadn't made it home yet. As sure as the sun would soon set, she was pacing around the house right now with dinner keeping warm in the oven, a little bundle of nerves.

—◦—

Rob arrived early to work the Wednesday night basketball league at the Recreation Centre on July 25 only to discover that one of the teams he was scheduled to score hadn't shown up. With some unexpected free time on his hands, he was trying to decide whether to head home or stay for a workout. Weighing his options, he picked up a *Toronto Star* lying next to him on the bleachers in the gymnasium and looked over the front page. Above the fold was a photograph of little doe-eyed Lorie

Atikian, who'd died in her parents' attempt to produce "superbaby." The headline indicated that Lorie's parents, Khachadour and Sonia, had been sentenced to two years in prison for failing to provide her with the necessities of life.

Just then, Andrea Beitinger plopped herself down on the bleacher beside him. "Aren't you working?" she asked.

"I got the night off," said Rob. "So how was class?"

"Oh, I don't know." She was trying to affect a casual air that belied how she truly felt. She'd gone home in such a horrible state after her interview with Poranganel and Smollet that her mother, afraid for her daughter's safety, had gone down to speak with the staff inspector of the Intelligence Division. Ultimately, Andrea and her mother agreed to have a tape recorder hooked up to their home telephone, but Andrea still had hard feelings for Brody Smollet because of the way he'd treated her and said she wouldn't help them if it meant she had to deal with him. She never saw Smollet again.

The problem was that, after a dozen or so secretly recorded telephone conversations, Baltovich hadn't deviated from his story. Reesor and Raybould were contemplating an added dimension to their approach. They wanted her to hide a tiny microcassette recorder in a handbag and secretly record all of her face-to-face encounters with Rob, sometimes asking him "set-up" questions, which she would be briefed on ahead of time.

Once again she agreed—the device was whirring away in her bag as they now spoke—despite her protests that the whole charade was becoming one of the most distressing episodes of her life. How was she going to explain this to her friends if it ever came to that? The entire thing had spun out of control with the detectives in the Team Room, whom she felt had lost their perspective in the glory of it all. Desperate for an opinion about Rob's culpability from someone who wasn't quite so blinded by the limelight of the hunt, Andrea turned to Miro Pristupa. She looked him straight in the eye and asked whether he believed Rob had comitted murder. Pristupa was firm in his reply—his gut instinct was that this was truly the case and he assured her that she was doing the right and proper thing.

"So, how's everything with you?" she asked Rob.

Sounding slightly tired, he said, "Oh, okay."

"I take it things have really quieted down."

"Yeah, it feels eerie," he said. "I'm starting to think that maybe they'll just forget the whole thing, but I doubt they ever will."

He was certainly right about that, she thought. "Well, you have to wonder what their rationalization was."

"It's just so scary," Rob said. "What little they have."

As advised, Andrea steered him onto the subject of the blood found in Liz's car. "The only thing I can imagine," Rob said, "is that they probably found blood in the trunk."

"In the trunk? Why do you think that?"

"When Nancy first ran up to the car and looked in, she didn't see any blood. At least that's what she told me. So, if there was some blood, it must not have been any place too conspicuous."

All Andrea could say to that was "Wow."

"I know," Rob said, appreciating her surprise. "I know. And if the blood was in the trunk, then there goes a lot of hope out the window. That would mean she is dead for sure." Out on the basketball court, someone slamdunked the ball through the hoop. "Nice dunk," Rob said.

He began by telling her about his recent conversations with Nancy Sicchia, whom he'd run into after a movie one night a week or so before. They'd spent a lot of time discussing Eric Genuis. Rob was really starting to wonder if Liz had led Eric to believe that they were going to be together again, and when Eric found out they weren't, he'd reacted in the manner the police had ascribed to Rob. Hadn't Liz and Eric met on several occasions for walks in the valley—the very scene of the crime? And Rob was quite sure he'd seen a silver sedan like Eric's in the small parking area near Liz's Tercel that night. He'd asked Nancy to give Eric a call, primarily so that she could inquire about the possibility of his having pursued Liz as more than just a "friend." Nancy said she thought Eric was harmless, but agreed to the plan. Instead of calling Eric, though, she called Detective Sergeant Tony Warr, who promptly came over to write down what she could remember of her conversation. And when Rob dropped by late in the afternoon two days later, Nancy made detailed notes for Warr, who was back the following morning, this time equipped with a tape recorder for Nancy to read into.

"Nancy said that the police have probably checked Eric out already," Rob said.

"Yeah," Andrea agreed, "they would have."

"So, you haven't heard anything?"

"Nothing at all."

"Has anybody been around to talk to you about it?" he asked.

"No," she lied. "Have they approached anyone else?"

"I'm not aware of them speaking to anyone since my dad, and that was a week ago Tuesday. I don't know if that means they're off my case or not."

They spoke for a while about the possibility that Liz had been leading someone on—the same way he felt she'd strung him along in the fall of 1987, never once dropping a hint that she had a boyfriend, Dean Orlando. After a while, they got on the subject of Mr. Bain telling Liz shortly after his return from New Orleans he would no longer be paying her tuition. Rob said he thought this had something to do with Liz trying to cut her wrists. "But how was Liz's relationship with her parents after that?" Andrea wanted to know. "Because Mr. Bain seems . . . "

"Bad," Rob offered.

"Yeah?"

"Well, whatever you read in the paper about it being an Ozzie and Harriet scene is total garbage."

"I don't believe that either," she said.

"Once Mrs. Bain found the birth control pills in May," Rob said, "both of Liz's parents began treating me like shit. Mr. Bain's job wasn't going too well and apparently down in New Orleans his wife didn't want to have anything to do with him. She said it was the worst trip she'd ever had in her life."

"Really," said Andrea.

The reverberating echo of voices, buzzers, squeeking high-tops and bouncing basketballs was getting so loud that their conversation was being drowned out on the tape in Andrea's bag. It faintly picked up Rob talking about the Atikian case, how upset his mother was and something about "bizarre coincidences." The last complete recorded question she asked was "Have you come to grips with the fact that this might go on for a long time?"

As later transcribed, his answer was:

BALTOVICH: No . . . no. What do you do? It's not something you can prepare for . . . [inaudible] . . . I mean, I haven't had to deal with very much tragedy, very little. It's one thing to break up with someone but another . . . [inaudible] . . . to never see them again or not to know if they're dead or alive . . . [inaudible] . . .

—◌—

At exactly 6:47 PM, while Rob was being kept occupied at the campus by Andrea Beitinger, Adele Baltovich heard a loud knock on her front door. It was Steven Reesor and Brian Raybould, along with a handful of other officers. Reesor said he had a warrant to search the house. Adele was petrified, not quite sure of what to say or do. But they obviously weren't prepared to wait for a response. Instead, they brushed right by her, spreading out into her narrow abode like a gang of siblings on an Easter egg hunt.

Once Reesor had sat Adele down at the kitchen table to read the warrant, he asked if she might give him a tour of the second floor, indicating which rooms were used for what purpose. Under the circumstances, she seemed content enough to oblige, but they were delayed slightly when the phone rang. It was Jim. He was calling to let her know that he might be home a little later than usual. He'd closed up the store at seven and walked across the road to his Camaro only to discover that it had a flat tire. Someone had punctured the damn thing. There was an obvious slit right near the rim. Could you believe that? He'd been parking his car in the same spot for fifteen years without incident and now there was this random vandalism. He walked back to the store and called the CAA automobile club for a tow truck. Next he called Adele to let her know he'd be late for dinner. "Don't worry," said Adele. "Dinner is going to be late anyway."

"Oh?" Jim sensed something was wrong. "Why's that?"

"The police are here searching the house."

"They're what?" He was now thinking back to Reesor driving him across the road to get a look at his car. "I'll be home as soon as the tow truck gets here." He locked up the store and returned to the parking lot, where he found a note tucked under one of his windshield wipers. He must have missed it when he first saw the flat. It was written with a black felt marker on the inside of a torn box of decongestant capsules:

dark Blue Truck (RV9 262)
Did something
to your front
Driver's
side
wheel

(Months later, Jim's son Paul asked a private investigator to run a computer search on the plate number with the Ontario Ministry of Transportation. When the investigator discovered that the plate number was "not in the system," he inquired further, only to learn that undercover police vehicles are routinely removed from the ministry's records to avoid detection by those groups the officers are trying to infiltrate.)

Jim waited an hour and a half for the tow truck to come. Every few minutes he'd been tempted to call up the auto club from the store to cancel it. Then he could just take a taxi home to Adele. But he wasn't sure what would happen if the tow truck arrived and he wasn't there. The confusion was paralyzing. It was like one of those bad dreams where you've got to be at the train station for 9:00 AM and there is one thing after another keeping you trapped in the house.

Reesor kept Adele up on the second floor for almost half an hour—giving an officer down in the kitchen plenty of time to insert a listening probe into the telephone—asking dozens of seemingly pointless questions about items that had nothing to do with Robert while a police photographer snapped dozens of shots, covering every square inch of each room. Adele was wishing they'd called ahead—she could have tidied up a little. Jim tended to perspire in his sleep and he'd left his damp pyjamas hanging from the dresser to dry.

Next she took them into the basement to show them Robert's room. His favourite pair of blue jeans was lying in a clump underneath his blue-and-white-striped sweater on the sofa against the wall. Adele pointed them out and said, "I'm sure that's one thing you're looking for." Detective Norm Rowntree gathered up several items of clothing from the closet, including the canvas Sperry topsider shoes Rob was wearing the night Liz disappeared. They even seized the rubber boots up in the foyer that belonged to Rob's cousin, Gregg Anderson, who often went on fishing trips with Paul. But what they were really hoping for, the pair of multi-coloured shorts and the dress sandals (footwear Rob later declared he'd never worn in his life) Marc Singleton said he'd seen Rob wearing, was nowhere to be found.

They also rifled through a stack of magazines and found a rough draft of an old letter from Rob to Liz folded within the pages of an *Esquire* magazine. It was the letter he'd written during their first summer together, when he discovered that she was tremendously insecure about the way she looked (*Many times I have told you how beautiful you are, both on the outside and the inside, and I will continue to do so. . . .*) They also found a letter from Liz on the shelf of a hutch in the kitchen. Like Rob's letter to Liz, there was no date at the top, but it began "Rob, Last night I felt like an animal being kicked in the head. . . ." A promising first line. Apparently, that was how she felt after Rob had attacked her use of holistic medicine. From his desk drawers they snatched up most of his personal writings—poems, exercises in creative writing, memoirs. And then, when it finally looked like there was no more fun to be had, somebody lifted up the mattress on Rob's bed and found a journal called *Variations* hidden underneath. There was an attractive woman in expensive lingerie on the cover, which made sense considering that it was a book of erotica, mostly in prose form, published by *Penthouse* magazine. This was, without question, a keeper.

When the search team left the Baltovich house—almost two hours after they'd arrived—most of the guys were talking about how freaky the place was. The father upstairs, the mother camping out in the living room, Rob in the basement. As most of them were seeing the inside of the house for the first time, it gave them the willies, especially knowing what they did about Rob.

Brian Raybould then drove to the Scarborough campus and met up with Detective Jake Poranganel and his partner, Constable Peter Harmsen, at the Recreation Centre. At the main counter, they informed two staff members, Rose Needham and Randy Thomas, that they had a warrant to search Rob Baltovich's locker. Two minutes later, Thomas had the combination lock off the door and another detective with the Forensic Identification Services named Mike Maloney was spraying luminol—a liquid that, upon contact with traces of human blood, takes on a fluorescent hue—on various pieces of clothing, but with negative results.

While Maloney was photographing the contents of the locker, Thomas retrieved Rob from the gymnasium, where he was still on duty with the basketball league. Seeing Rob approaching down the hallway, Raybould informed him that he'd just executed the search warrant on his locker and they now wanted to take a look inside his car. Rob couldn't understand why, but he wasn't too concerned. "No problem," he said, snapping his fingers. That really drove Raybould bananas.

With the other officers now converged around the Cordoba in the parking lot, Raybould said, "Rob, we're taking your car."

"You're taking my car?" Rob asked plaintively. "How am I supposed to get home?"

Raybould was in no mood for whining. "Rob," he bellowed. "We're taking your car!"

"Fine," he said.

"Do you want to see the warrant?" Raybould asked. Poranganel pulled it out of his pocket, but Rob just shook his head and said no.

Then Poranganel piped up. "I'll give you a ride home if you want, Rob."

"That sounds like a good idea. I'll be off at about ten-thirty." Rob handed Raybould the keys and said, "Good luck."

"Rob," said Raybould, "we don't need luck."

"Well, in this case you just might." Rob made his way back to the main entrance of the Recreation Centre.

The car had been towed away to the Centre for Forensic Sciences by the time Raybould and Poranganel walked into the gymnasium at ten-thirty, taking a seat on the bleachers while Rob put away the electronic scoreboards. Once he'd completed his various tasks, Rob said to them, "Okay guys, I'm ready to roll."

Rob rode alone in the back seat. Raybould, apparently trying to strike up a conversation that would, under any other set of circumstances, be considered perfectly normal, asked Rob what he planned on doing with his future. The fact that Raybould wanted to take the kind of future he was referring to away from Rob gave the query a nasty edge to it. It was hard not to pick up on that, but Rob decided to give him a straight answer anyway. He told them that, after working full-time for a year, he was hoping to enrol in teachers' college. "I'm just going to take it day by day," he said.

"Oh, that's interesting," said Raybould, almost as though he genuinely found it so.

Rob called up his lawyer, Bill Gatward, the following morning to tell him about the search warrant. Gatward said it might be a good idea for Rob to come down to his office the next day for a little chat. By that time, Gatward had put a call in to Reesor to discuss the grounds upon which they'd obtained the warrant. Reesor was somewhat vague about the evidence he had against Rob but he did inform Gatward that his client had failed a polygraph test. (Actually, as Detective Wozniak would later testify, Baltovich's physiological reactions to the three "relevant" questions—"Did you do anything to cause the death of Elizabeth Bain?" and "Did you commit the assault on Liz which resulted in her disappearance?" and "Right now, do you know where Liz can be found?"—indicated, from Wozniak's experience, deception. When it came to the grid map, however, Baltovich's reactions were more muted and Wozniak would tell the court that he was unable to render an opinion.)

This was the first Gatward had heard about Rob taking a lie-detector test—it was a month ago now that he'd instructed Rob not to. The way Reesor dropped it into the conversation was part of the game, letting the lawyer know that he'd been out-foxed. Gatward was going to have to make sure it didn't happen again.

Once he had Rob sitting across from him in his office, Gatward, who was young-looking despite his premature balding, discussed the possibility that Rob could be arrested somewhere down the line. Rob agreed that, should the unthinkable happen, he would surrender himself to the authorities. "My biggest fear," Rob said, "is that someone is going to come forward and lie."

"Let's hope not," said Gatward. He still had no clear handle on whether this kid had iced his girlfriend, not that it really mattered—he would defend him either way.

Gatward then moved on to the subject of the polygraph. Rob was quite surprised that he'd found out about it—he'd been hoping he wouldn't. "The next time I give you some advice," said Gatward, sternly, "take it."

"Okay," Rob said. He felt like a little kid.

Gatward looked straight into his eyes. "No more fuck-ups," he said.

Steve Reesor paid a visit to Andrea Beitinger at Intelligence the following Monday. Much to her chagrin, he wanted her to visit Rob while he worked the basketball league that night and tape another conversation. She could pop in on him when her class was over. Just act naturally, he reminded her. Be yourself. He was sure Rob would slip up sooner or later.

That evening, Andrea ran into Rick Gostick near the bleachers. "Hey, how's it going?" she said. "Where's Rob?"

"He's on the other side," he said. "Scoring the game."

Andrea peeked around the corner and saw Rob sitting courtside at the scorer's table. "Hey good-looking," she said beaming. Her smile was a real knockout.

"Hey," said Rob. "How are ya?"

"Fine."

"You got some sun this weekend."

"Yeah," she said. "Finally."

Rob said, "I've got good news."

"What?" she asked.

"I get my car back."

"When?"

"Tomorrow morning," he said.

"Where?"

"Police headquarters," he said. "So how was class?"

"All right," she said.

"Just all right?"

"Hard." She didn't want to get into it. "So, nothing new?"

"Nothing new." Some girls had walked up the side of the court and stood right in front of Rob's desk, blocking his view of the game. "Steve sounded really depressed about the—"

Andrea cut in. "Steve sounded depressed?"

"Yeah."

"Why?"

"Because they didn't find any evidence in the car."

"Oh."

Rob said, "I feel sorry for him."

"Why in the world would you feel sorry for him?"

"Well, they're trying to solve the case. I mean, they're not just trying to put me away. Right? They're searching for the truth. And I want to help but I can't." He paused before changing the subject. "How's your essay going?"

"Well, it's there."

The referee called out to Rob from the other side of the court. "Stop the clock!"

"Oh," Rob said, flicking the switch. "I'm sorry."

"Anyways," said Andrea. Now was not a good time. "I guess I'll waddle."

"You're waddling already?" Rob was punching a few more seconds into the clock to make up for the ones he let elapse. "That team in black likes me."

"They like you?" she said.

"I like them."

"You like them?"

"Yeah, I'll show you the one I like. She's on the bench. She's gonna be hot in five years. Oh well. Do I get a good-bye hug?"

"Sure," said Andrea, wrapping her arms around him for a quick squeeze. "See you later."

"See ya."

"Take care."

"Good luck on your essay. Bye."

As promised, Steve Reesor was waiting in front of the Centre for Forensic Science's garage at eleven the next morning when Rob and Neil Winton, who'd given him a ride downtown, pulled up nearby. Reesor asked Rob for the spare keys to his car. He was going to retrieve it while they waited outside. But wouldn't you know it, Reesor stuck the key in the ignition and the damn thing wouldn't turn over. The battery was dead as a doornail. Maybe the guys in the garage left the interior lights on after they'd finished installing the listening probe behind the dashboard.

Once Reesor made arrangements for someone to come into the garage and recharge Rob's battery, he went back out for a talk with Rob and his friend. "You remember that first-degree murder case I told you about before, Rob," Reesor said. "The one where we laid the charge despite the fact that it wasn't until later that we found the woman's body?"

"Somewhat," Rob said.

"Well, the accused, whose name also happens to be Robert—Adamson—has confessed to the crime but is now claiming that it was manslaughter. But he'll have to tell it to the jury and see if they believe him. I bet they won't."

"I probably wouldn't either," said Rob.

"You know, Rob, I feel sorry for all the stress your parents are enduring, but, as far as I'm concerned, you're the one responsible for it."

"Don't worry about my parents, Steve. They know you guys are just doing your job."

"One more thing, Rob," Reesor said. "I was wondering if you happen to own a pair of multi-coloured shorts. We were looking for them during the search but couldn't find any."

Rob was scratching his head, thinking about multi-coloured shorts. "Actually, I do have a pair," he said. "But they're not at my place. They're at my friend Phil's house."

"Is this Phil Dach? The one Detective Warr interviewed about trying to teach you how to drive standard in his Suzuki Samurai?"

"Yes," Rob said. "But he wasn't able to teach me."

"I know," said Reesor scornfully. "Why are these shorts at his house?"

"Because Phil's parents have a swimming pool and I just leave them there for when I feel like having a dip. You can go and get them if you want."

"I just might do that, Rob," said Reesor. He turned and looked at the garage. "Your battery should be juiced up by now," he said. "I'll go get it."

Rob called his mother when he got back to Neil's house. "Did the car go okay?" she asked. Rob told her about the battery dying. She figured they might have left the lights on. "Did they say anything about your clothes?" she asked. He'd forgotten to ask when they might be giving him clothes back, but Rob told her about Reesor looking for a pair of multi-coloured shorts and how he'd sent him over to Phil Dach's place.

And then he heard his brother Paul, who was over that afternoon to cut the grass for Adele, come on the line from another phone. "Rob," he said, "are those the linen shorts you wear all the time? The ones I bought during my trip to Georgia? The ones with the multi-coloured stripes?"

"No, no, no. These are the West Beach brand shorts. They're very tight. Light green and aqua blue."

"Have I ever seen them?" Paul asked.

"Yeah, you've worn them. They're like canvas."

"Yes, I've worn them, that's right. They're the same one's I took down south and then brought back to you."

Rob said, "Right."

"Didn't you have them on that Tuesday when Liz went missing?"

"I don't know."

"Dana told me that when we left the house that day you were in a T-shirt and multi-coloured shorts."

"Maybe I was," Rob said. "I was watering the lawn, so it's possible."

"But, you know, Dana hasn't spoken to the police yet, and I didn't tell them you were wearing shorts. I didn't remember."

"Yeah, well, they're welcome to look at whatever shorts they want to."

"They sure are," Paul agreed. "So, the car's running okay?"

"I don't know. It needs to get charged up but I guess so." Adele wanted to know when he was going to be home for dinner. "The regular time," he said.

"Just take her out for a good boot on the highway," Paul said. "That'll do it. Talk to you later."

Back at Intelligence Services, monitoring officer Brenda Goss (number M34) noted that this conversation, call number 39, was recorded on Master Tape 19 between 241 and 265 on the counter. Once the investigators had determined the footage was of potential value to their case, it was copied onto Relevant Tape 13.

—◦—

Reesor had the multi-coloured shorts from Phil Dach's house in his hands by Thursday. They were blue and pink in front with some green on the back. Reesor couldn't believe his luck. There were tiny reddish spots on the front of the shorts and a stain on the seat that appeared to be a bloody hand print. Carefully placing them back in a plastic evidence bag, Reesor grabbed Brody Smollet (Raybould had gone on vacation for two weeks) and together they drove down to the CFS to submit them for testing.

In the Team Room later that afternoon, Reesor took a call from Rob. He wanted to know when he was getting his clothes back, saying he had a limited wardrobe. Reesor told him there wasn't much he could do. The stuff was still being tested. "About the shorts, though, Rob," said Reesor. "Is it possible that you might have had an accident of some kind where you cut your hand and then wiped the blood off on your shorts?"

"No," said Rob. "But you might find a little blood on the top left corner of my blue-and-white sweater and possibly on the khaki walking shorts you took as well."

"A couple of spots on khaki shorts did look like blood," said Reesor. "Where did that come from?"

"I cut myself opening a tin of tennis balls."

"Well, we'll find out soon enough if the blood is yours," Reesor said. "We thought there might be blood on the rubber boots but the tests came back negative so we'll be returning those."

Rob reiterated that the boots belonged to his cousin.

Reesor said, "I take it you made it home all right when you picked up your car."

"I did," Rob said. "Look, I guess I'll call next week about my clothes."

"Sounds like a plan," said Reesor.

A few minutes after hanging up with Rob, Reesor got a call from someone at Intelligence. They'd picked up Baltovich on the phone telling someone that he was coming down to the station to speak with him. Reesor stayed at 42 Division until 8:00 PM, but the kid never showed.

About noon the next day, Reesor and Brody Smollet went to AMP of Canada to interview Paul's wife, Dana. If she'd seen Rob while speaking to Adele inside the front door between 5:30 and 5:45 PM on June 19, as she insisted she did, Reesor wanted to know what Rob had been wearing. "He came to the top of the stairs and we both said a quick hello," she said. "That's usually all we say to each other. But I think he was wearing a white T-shirt and shorts."

"Do you remember what colour the shorts were?" asked Reesor.

"Not very well," she answered. "They were either his navy blue ones or the ones he swims in, the multi-coloured ones that, from what I've heard, you guys have."

Before leaving, Reesor asked if she knew of Rob ever driving a standard-transmission car. "I don't know," said Dana. "We have a standard transmission in our car, and he's never driven it."

Rob called his buddy Neil Winton on the weekend and asked if he wanted to go downtown to the Holt Renfrew Centre to check out a bookstore called Science City. Neil said great, and they made an afternoon of it. They wandered around inside Science City for almost an hour, and Rob picked out a couple of books, which he was now taking to the front counter to pay for. Waiting for the girl working the cash register to ring them up, he turned to look at the racks of posters set up near the entrance. "No way," he said, turning back to Neil at the counter. "That can't be."

"What?" asked Neil.

"Take a look over at the posters." Together, they turned around. "Is that Steve Reesor?" Rob asked. The man, whose back was to them, was wearing a T-shirt and shorts, flipping through the posters. He looked pretty heavy around the middle. When he shifted slightly to the side, they could make out his profile. "Holy shit," said Neil. "It's him." Reesor kept his eyes on the racks.

The girl at the cash announced the total for the books, and they turned back to the counter and paid. Rob thought about walking up to Reesor and saying something. He doubted that he frequented Science City in his spare time. Instead, he just took the bag of books from the girl and walked out of the store, fairly sure that his pursuer would soon follow. "Creepy," said Neil.

—⊖—

Five days had gone by since Reesor and Smollet had taken the multi-coloured shorts down to the CFS for testing and Reesor was anxiously awaiting the results. It could be the break they were looking for. He called up Ray Higaki, a biologist at the CFS who specialized in blood and body fluids (as well as hair, fibres and bloodstain patterns), to see if they'd figured out what was on the shorts. Not yet, said Higaki. So Reesor called back the next morning. "Bad news," said Higaki. "It's not blood. Sorry."

While the hand print on the shorts turned out to be yet another red herring, there were a few interviews that gave Reesor and the rest of the Team Room hope. They'd tracked down most of Rob's old girlfriends (just as they had spoken to Liz's former boyfriends, all of whom, including John Camunias, the police had determined were not involved). From Reesor's perspective, the two most useful of the ex-girlfriends were Anne Kristiansen and Debbie King. Anne, who'd dated Rob two summers earlier, said he was her first "major relationship," although she hadn't been in love with him. "He's very intellectual," said Anne. "And that was part of the attraction. Looking back, I think he wanted to be more serious about the relationship than I did, more of a commitment. My impression was that Rob was jealous of some of the guys I would speak to and when I told him that we should see other people, he was very hurt." It felt good to see the word "jealous" down on the page in black and white, but they were still a few good miles from homicidal rage.

There was one admission from Anne, though, that stood in stark contrast to the relationship Debbie King described having had with Rob, and that was the fact that Anne and Rob had never been sexually intimate. Debbie, who was now twenty-one, said that she and Rob had engaged in sexual intercourse two or three times during the summer they worked together as counsellors at the Greenwood Day Camp in 1986. During her interview with the police, Debbie said that Rob was "very weird sexually, rough and demanding, with no thought to my needs." He wanted to have anal sex. And not only that: one time when they were really going at it, he held her down and wouldn't let her get up. The cops asked if he had any other kinky habits. Debbie said that he once poured orange juice all over her body and licked it off. She repeated that he was demanding.

When Debbie's statement was later disclosed to Rob, it left him visibly shaken. Debbie was the first girl he'd had a sexual encounter with. Is anyone bold enough, he asked, to demand anal sex and an orange-juice bath during their first few nerve-racking rolls in the hay? And wasn't pinning her down against her will not a rape for which he should be charged? In any case, none of these questions would ever be answered, as Debbie King's involvement in the case against Robert Baltovich would go no further than her statement.

And then there was the confounding statement given by Marie Anderson, who'd separated from Rob's cousin Gregg last summer after just a year of marriage. There were still a lot of hard feelings between them, which was understandable, considering that Marie had pretty much left him to move in with another guy. Now she was telling the cops that Rob had always spoken of his girlfriends with insecure overtones, as though he were constantly worried they might be cheating on him, seeing other guys on the sly. He was reluctant to give them any space. After one girl had dumped him, said Marie, he tried to commit suicide.

Teresa Javier, a friend of Liz's from the campus, told the police that she thought Rob had behaved strangely on the morning of the first mass search in the valley. She maintained that Rob had appeared dishevelled that day but perhaps not as dishevelled as a person whose loved one had gone missing should. He was a touch too composed for her liking as well. And cynical. "I don't think we're going to find her here," she'd heard him say. That just didn't seem like a feeling one would have in that situation.

Yet, for every interview like this, dropped like manna from heaven, there was at least one other that didn't quite go the way Reesor and Raybould had hoped:

GREGG ANDERSON
Yeah, Reesor and another detective named Smollet came to see me at work, which is a landscaping outfit called the Weed Man. Rob worked here a few summers ago, back when it was owned by Gordon McIntyre, whom I'm sure you've heard

of. Gordon, who, by the way, has retired from the police force since all of this, is the father of my present wife, Karen. Anyway, he hasn't been involved in the business since I bought it from him along with some partners a few years back.

Reesor asked me all kinds of questions about Rob. Was I closer to Robert than to Paul, that kind of thing. They wanted to know about the rubber boots, and I explained that I'd lent them to Paul—he also worked for the Weed Man for a time—and never bothered to ask for them back. And then they started asking more pointed questions, like "Would you lie for Rob?" That's when some of their tactics started to become kind of childish, if I can put it that way.

It all began when they asked if I'd ever taught Rob how to drive a standard vehicle. I said we weren't that close that I'd teach him how to drive my car. So then they wondered, wouldn't Rob have been taught to drive standard so that he could operate the company vehicles? No, I said, all our vehicles are automatic. Reesor quite boldly said to me: "I think you're lying—there's a standard vehicle right out front." I said, "No, you asked me about the trucks that Robert drove. The one you're referring to is an owner's vehicle. The technicians' trucks are in the back, all automatics."

Reesor then asked me if I thought Robert had "done it." I said, quite firmly, "No, I don't think he did. My lifelong experience with Robert is that he's not that kind of person." Reesor said, "We have a pretty good idea of what we're looking at. You really don't know anyone in your family well enough to know if they could or could not kill, so you can't really make that assumption."

Quite often, when I gave Reesor an answer, he would attempt to reword it to see if I'd be willing to change something. Towards the end, I challenged him on that. I said, if you're going to ask the questions, fine, but don't keep re-asking them in a different fashion, hoping that I'm going to change my statement, because I'm being as honest as I can.

Before leaving, he asked me if I was married, and I explained that I was divorced but that I was presently dating Karen—now my wife—whose father they might have heard of at 51 Division. They said they hadn't. But, from what I understand, they did track down my former wife, Marie. The things she said about Rob are one hundred per cent garbage. Although I did catch her in a situation that I didn't appreciate a few weeks after she'd moved out, there wasn't too much animosity between us during the separation. It had a kind of inevitability to it. All of this talk about Rob being jealous of his girlfriends and trying to kill himself over one of them is total nonsense. The truth is that Rob and I never discussed his girlfriends; we just weren't that close. I was far more likely to spend time with Paul, fishing up at the cottage. I don't know where she came up with this stuff. It's a load of crap.

HEATHER GROVES

I suppose that the police came to speak to me because I had worked with Rob at the Greenwood Day Camp and we've remained friends ever since. Actually, I think they got my name from Rob's little address book, which they'd photocopied somehow. Anyway, I remember it was a crazy week when I spoke with them— my father had just lost his job, and my cat had died [laughter]. *That cat was like my brother—don't you dare write that* [more laughter].

It was Detective Reesor who came to see me at my school. It was my first year of teaching classes in Grades 1 and 2. I remember that I was also being evaluated at the time. He just came into my classroom during a break and asked if he could have a few moments of my time. He wanted to know how I knew Rob and I told him about our camp days and so on.

And then he asked, "Do you ever remember Rob being violent?"

I said, "Absolutely not. He's one of the most easy-going people I've ever known."

Then he went on to say, "Well, that has nothing to do with Rob being a potential murderer, because people who aren't wife abusers, for example, don't know the limits of their anger, whereas an abuser would. Perhaps he wasn't familiar with having to cope with his own rage and, therefore, didn't know how to control it. Did you ever see him act violently with children at the camp?"

I said, "No, Rob was extremely fair with children. In fact, he never lost his cool. He always dealt with them in a very adult, caring way."

He obviously felt I wasn't on the right wavelength, so he started in about the fact that, according to statistics, ninety-nine per cent of the time people are murdered by a jilted lover or spouse. Reesor was convinced that Rob was basically a cold, calculating murderer. He again asked me if I could remember a time when

Rob had lost his cool and, once more, I said no. With that, he handed me his card and said, "Well, it doesn't really matter because, if he wasn't used to controlling his temper, he could have struck her and killed her before he knew what he was doing. But, if you can think of a time, any time, that Rob maybe did flare up a little, please give me a call."

STEVE TRAENKMAN

I think they got my name out of Rob's address book or something like that. Rob and I were friends. So they called, and I went down to the station. I spoke to Raybould. He was pretty good, actually. I guess the two do the good-cop bad-cop routine. Reesor gets to play the prick.

TERRY CHADWICK

I knew that Reesor was coming and, because I suspected his motives, I had the lady of the house sit in on the interview. I remember him saying to me at one point, "So Rob's a big fisherman, eh?" I said, "Rob? I don't think we're talking about the right guy here. Now, if you're referring to Paul, one hundred per cent. Paul is without question a fishing addict."

"Well," Reesor said, "you know there's a boat in their driveway. We think that Rob might have taken it up to some lake in the middle of the night to get rid of her body."

I said, "Okay. Sure. Right." You should have seen this boat. This was a big boat. Huge. Rob was going to get up in the dead of night, put the hitch on the boat and drive off? This was the kind of nonsense they were up to.

Seeing that I was sceptical, Reesor decided to drop a bomb: "We have Rob's shorts," he said. "And they've got blood on them so, basically, he's done." Of course, I later learned this wasn't the case, but that statement hit me as if I'd driven a car into a wall. Seeing me sitting there with my jaw on the ground, Reesor said that, as Rob's oldest brother, someone he looks up to, I should go and talk to him and tell him to give in (or at the very least convince him to somehow provide the police with an anonymous tip about the location of Liz's body).

And that's exactly what I did. I called Rob at home to make sure he was there and then drove down to the house. So as not to alarm our mother, I took him outside and said, "Look Rob, they've got the evidence." I was being deadly serious.

And he just looked at me like I was crazy and said, "They don't have any evidence—because I didn't do it." And that was pretty much it. I knew he was telling me the truth.

ERIC GENUIS

I met with Detective Reesor only once, on August 21 of that summer. I gave a long statement and then he asked me to call Rob and ask him three questions. He wrote them out on the back of his business card.

The first question was: Did Rob think that Liz had been sleeping around on him? The second was: Was Rob going around telling people that I had Tuesdays off work and, therefore, had no alibi? The final one was: Did Rob and Liz stop having sex at some point prior to her disappearance?

I said to Reesor: "Would you like me to phone him in front of you right now?" He said, "No, just phone him and call me back."

ALANNA MCKEOWN

I don't remember the names of the officers who came to meet with me. They just knew that I'd been Rob's supervisor at the YMCA camp and thought that I might be able to assist them. They picked me up in an unmarked car and drove me north of the city, to some places where Rob might have taken his campers on some bicycle trips. Their idea, I suppose, was that Rob had disposed of her body in a place he was familiar with from those days.

The first thing one of the officers asked me was: "Do you think he did it?" I said, "No, no. Not at all." He said to me: "Well, I'm going to tell you some things that are going to change your mind." So, he basically changed my mind, gave me reasons to doubt everything I thought [mild laughing]. They were very persuasive people, that's for sure. That said, I should make it clear that he didn't convert me entirely—I've always doubted Rob had anything to do with it.

They asked me to put myself in Rob's mind. You're in a bit of a panic and you have to get rid of a body. Where do you go? There was a specific type of sand found in Elizabeth Bain's car and they wanted me to focus on beach areas. As you know, we didn't find a thing.

Yes, I knew Debbie King and Andrea Beitinger very well—they both worked *under me, as did Rob. What did I think of Debbie King? She was a wild, wild girl. I recognized that from the beginning. She was nowhere near my first choice for the job, but our hands were tied—we didn't have many people volunteering for the program back then. Andrea, on the other hand, was tremendously responsible, an amazing girl. All Debbie ever wanted to be was a movie star. (Years later, I heard she was spotted as an extra in a Tom Cruise movie shot in Toronto called* Cocktail.*) I was there the entire time they were dating and Debbie was the one always draping herself over him. He was the more calm, let's-not-do-this-in-front-of-the-kids person. If anything, she was the most sexual being I had met in all of my camp experience. She wore little tiny bikini tops on purpose and her shorts right up her rear end. She even flirted with the little kids, twelve- or thirteen-year-old boys. That's why, when it came to the question of who was going to be fired—her or Rob—there was never any doubt about the choice on my part. So, even today, if it came down to a contest of reliability between Robert Baltovich and Debbie King, I wouldn't have much difficulty making a decision.*

SHEILA BANKS

I went away to university and returned to Scarborough in 1990 when I graduated. That's when I hooked up again with Rob and Tony Fuchs, Jim Isaacs, Neil Winton, Steve Doucette, and that group of guys I'd known for a while. They were my boys. I was another friend the police learned about through Rob's Day-Timer. They might also have heard me in Rob's car. Later, once we'd found out about them putting a bug in there, we used to get in his Cordoba and say, "Hi, officer." It was a big joke, so bizarre, the strangest thing that ever happened to me. Imagine these cops sitting in a room somewhere having to listen to Rob singing to himself in his car, because that's what he did—he didn't have a working radio! You couldn't pay me enough to do that job [laughter].

Anyway, the detectives phoned my mother at home, and she passed the message on to me at the office. I had a new job, and the officer wanted to come down and pick me up at work for an interview. I really didn't want these guys showing up at reception, so I told them I'd meet them out on the corner at lunch. I immediately got the impression that these guys didn't care about how any of this was affecting us—not that it's their job to care, but I think they took it over the top. *All of the doubts I had about Rob being involved were used against me while I was being questioned. They were manipulating my emotions, trying to get me so upset that I might say, "Maybe you're right." Or remember something that never happened. They kept coming back to the possibility of Rob being violent, which is pretty laughable, really.*

They asked me to give them a longer, second statement down at the police station. There, they kept concentrating on the fact that none of the guys had ever hit on me, which they found weird, considering that we all used to hang out together every weekend. "You're a good-looking girl," they would say. "Why do you think these guys wouldn't make a move on you?" I said, "Because they're like my brothers." "Did it ever occur to you," one of the detectives said, "that all of those guys, Rob included, might be gay?" I said, "What?" [laughter] I thought to myself, That's right, Liz found out they were all gay so they had to kill her. It was so stupid. "Who cares?" I said. "What difference does it make?"

They said, "Don't you think it's odd that a bunch of twenty-year-old guys would rather go out together on a Saturday night than be with their girlfriends?"

"Nooo," I said. "They're twenty. We're not talking about men in their forties." I immediately realized that these two officers were definitely in their forties.

"And they wouldn't hit on you, ever?" they asked.

"No, we're just friends. Why is that so hard to comprehend? None of these guys had ever met any of my boyfriends, so there you go." They weren't too interested in exploring that point. I guess it didn't matter to them if I was a lesbian.

Their whole theory regarding Rob's supposed homosexuality had to do with the fact that, when homosexuals kill people of the opposite sex, they said it tended to be more violent than heterosexual murders. I asked them how they could assess the violence of the crime considering they didn't have a body or a weapon. And they said, "We have this kind of evidence." It was very assuring. They said to me: "We know Rob killed her, and you've gotta help us. By saying you don't know anything, you're not helping the process."

"But I don't know anything."

They said, "You're helping him get away with murder. How do you feel about that? Can you live with yourself? We know he's responsible."

"If you know," I said, "then why do you need me?" That probably sounds

disrespectful, but, if someone asks me a stupid question, I'm going to throw it right back at them. That's just the way I am.

KARA MCCARTNEY

It was Reesor and Raybould, I believe, who came to my house to speak with me. I found that they would say things to make you answer the way they wanted you to. For example, they told my father that they thought Rob was a serial killer, and because I had brown curly hair and a nice smile, I was probably going to be his next victim. They said, "All serial killers have to start somewhere." My father was advised not to let me near Rob any more. So I said to them: "But that doesn't fit the motive you just gave to me—that he killed Liz because he couldn't have her. Now you're telling us he's a serial killer."

They asked me what my relationship was with Rob when we first met. I said we were friends and had a class together. "Did you ever go out with him?" they asked. I explained that we were just friends, not really interested in each other that way. "Well, why not?" they asked. "For one thing," I said. "I had a boyfriend at the time. And to be honest, I don't think Rob ever asked me out."

"What was it about him that you didn't like?" they asked. They kept asking that question over and over.

"Nothing," I said. "I don't know what you want me to say. I didn't fancy him? He wore too much gel in his hair? I don't know."

Then they told me they'd found a dirty magazine in his room that contained a couple of homoerotic passages and that somehow this implied Rob was gay. "Now you're saying he's gay?" I said. "I thought he was supposed to be madly in love with his girlfriend." This was sheer madness.

Rob came over to play tennis one afternoon late that summer and this car that seemed to be following him parked around the corner from our house. When we left the house we went in my car and the car around the corner pulled up behind us and trailed us all the way to the courts. It parked nearby for an hour while we hit the ball back and forth. It was behind us again on the way back home when, suddenly, I suggested we rent a video. Rob agreed, and so I turned the car around and went to the video store.

As soon as we walked in the store, I said, "Oh shit, I forgot my rental card." So we went back to my house, the car following us the entire time. Once I had the card, we were on our way to the video store again. By now I'm panicking a bit with this car behind me, saying, "Jesus, they're really following us." I almost went through a red light [laughter], *but they didn't pull us over. Not traffic cops, I guess.*

———◯———

Before the summer came to an end, and Andrea Beitinger's employment with Intelligence Services concluded, the guys in the Team Room decided to put their young agent into action one last time. So on August 22, a Wednesday, they hatched a plan for her to go up to Rob and tip him off that the police might have found Liz's body. That way, his reaction would be permanently recorded on tape. If Rob said, "Where? Up near the town of X?" and they subsequently found her corpse anywhere near X, he was cooked. It would also give them a solid location to begin searching.

Andrea was told to call Rob at home and say that she needed to see him right away. To make it sound urgent. But Adele answered the phone and said that Rob was over at the gym. Andrea went straight there and found Rob playing badminton with Neil Winton and Steve Doucette. She walked right up to the net and said, "Rob, I have to talk with you. Do you have a minute? I'm sorry. Hi, Neil. Hi, Steve." Rob could tell that she wanted to speak in private. "Do those doors go outside?" she asked.

"I don't think we need to go outside," said Rob. "We can stay right here."

"No, let's go outside."

Rob followed her. He was squinting from the brightness of the sun. "Looks more like good news than bad news," he said.

"I don't know, Rob. You have to promise me you won't tell anybody. I could be fired or even face criminal charges, but you already know that."

"You don't have to tell me," he assured her.

"Well, Rob, I was walking past this guy's office who does the charts," said Andrea, using Miro Pristupa, the Intelligence analyst, as part of her ruse. "He was on the phone. I didn't get all of the conversation but he said, 'You think it was Liz?' After that, all I got was 'out of town' and then 'I'll see you in twenty minutes' and he just left the building."

"They found her," he guessed. He wished she would just finish the story, but she apparently already had. "I don't know," she said.

"Didn't they find a body in Hamilton?" he asked.

"That was a hooker."

"Was it? But I don't understand. You think this one is Liz."

"Well—"

"It sounds more like she's alive than dead, I guess," he said, looking pensive. "You just don't know."

She couldn't help wondering what Reesor and Raybould were going to make of that comment. "I needed," she said, "I needed to tell you."

"What are you smiling about?" asked Rob. "Is that a nervous smile?"

"That's . . . um . . . yeah." She tried moving on. "You can interpret all of this any way you want, but whether or not this will clear you, I don't know."

"The way I look at it," said Rob, "even with a body there is still no evidence that I killed her. In fact, you may have heard on the weekend about how they found a body in the Don River. We were going crazy because, first of all, it was said to be a woman. Then I heard she was in her early twenties, then that she was five feet tall. So the more we kept learning, the more nervous we were getting."

"I saw that," Andrea said. "But this girl was wearing brown clothes, not a colourful top and black pants."

"Yeah, but we didn't know that at the time. So on the one hand, there was a good chance it would clear me, but on the other hand, we heard that Reesor was the first one on the scene."

"Oh, really?"

"He wants this bad," Rob said. "Where did they say they might have found Liz— out of town?"

"That's all I got. I couldn't very well stand there and listen."

"Do you know who he was talking to?"

"I have no idea."

"That's okay," he said. "This goes no further than me. If it's Liz, I'm going to find out anyway. Actually, it's funny you showed up because I got a call last night from Liz's friend, Eric Genuis."

"And?"

"He started chewing me out because he says I've been spreading rumours about her—that she was sleeping around, which is totally crazy. I figured that he'd been talking to Reesor, and that Reesor had told him I was saying things about Liz when I wasn't. That really bothered me. I thought to myself, How could Eric be so stupid not to see that they're just using him as a stooge. They have to get as many people against me as they can."

Possibly worried that he might start suspecting her, Andrea interrupted his rant. "I'm sorry. I'm sorry. Maybe I shouldn't have told you."

"It's okay," Rob said. "So that's all you've heard?"

"I haven't seen anything as far as surveillance reports, or wire-tapping or anything like that, and those things have to go through Intelligence."

"Really."

"The only thing I saw was a chart that had something to do with your case. It was done by an analyst. He does charts on the computer for everybody."

"Is that right?" he said. "Anyway, let's face it. At this point, we've got to expect the worst."

Andrea was hopeful. "But you could be cleared," she said.

"Maybe," he said. "Maybe not. Let me put it this way. Obviously, because I didn't have anything to do with it, they're not going to find anything on her body or in that area to suggest I've been there."

"Then they can't really talk their way out of it."

"That's right," he said. "Well, let's hope for the best."

"Take care of yourself, okay?"

"I will. You interrupted a nice badminton game."

Andrea said she was sorry but that she felt better having told him the news. As she turned to leave, Rob told her to keep her head up. "You," she insisted. "You keep your head up."

"Ah," he said. "They're not going to break me."

Somewhat unexpectedly, Rob showed up at her front door the next day at about six o'clock in the evening. Andrea quickly set up the microcassette recorder before letting him in. Her hair was still wet from the shower. "I've got a date tonight," she said.

"Oh, is that right? With who?"

"This guy John."

"John," he said. "Kind of plain." Andrea directed him into the living room. "So what happened yesterday? Still no word on what they found?"

"I have no idea," she said. "You want something to drink?"

"No, that's okay. I've got to boot soon but I want to tell you a story about something that happened to me today."

"What's your story? You've got a big smile on your face."

"I witnessed a jewellery store robbery today," Rob said.

"Get out. Where? What jewellery store?"

"It's called Grenadier Jewellers, on Kingston Road. I was in Steve Doucette's car. We were driving down to the beach, waiting for the red light to change at Victoria Park. Suddenly, I heard this *crash*. I looked to my left and saw some kid reaching in the store window he'd just smashed. He's just grabbing all these rings and stuff and then he runs to this car that's waiting for him and climbs in. It all happened so quickly, but I got a good look at the kid and then I turned around and got the licence plate number of the car. Steve didn't get the plate number but he got a good look at the car. So Steve pulls over and I run into a dry cleaning store. I tell them about the robbery across the street and ask if I can use their phone. They said fine, so I dialled 911 and said, 'Yeah, I'd like to report a robbery.' I gave them all the information and then the woman asks, 'What's your name?' I said, 'Robert Baltovich.' I can hear her typing it up, right, and then, all of a sudden, she says, 'Can you hold on a second?' So her screen must have lit up like a Christmas tree, you see. She came back on and asked me to stay on the scene until the police arrived. For a second, I was going to say, 'No, I don't want all this crap because these guys hassle me enough.' But then I thought, Yeah, all right, I'll stay. So they showed up and I told them the whole story."

"And then?"

"It was just kind of funny. Steve and I were laughing all the way to the beach. We were thinking about the look on Reesor's face when he finds out."

"Murder suspect foils robbery," she said.

"Yeah, right. Like I said to Steve, the only thing that would have been better is if he'd turned the car around and we'd caught them ourselves. Reesor will probably wonder if I staged the whole thing to make me look good. It's like I've lived for almost twenty-five years without anything happening to me and now . . ." He didn't have to finish that thought. "What's next?"

A little while later he was telling Andrea that she had to be careful. "The police might be testing you," he said.

"You think so?"

"It's possible," he said. "If they are tapping my phone line, which a source close to my dad in the police force said they are, then they've probably identified you by now."

"Yeah, I don't know." She was running her fingers through her still-damp hair.

"Basically, you could get into a lot more trouble telling me these things than I could. I'm just listening, but you're telling. So how much longer do you have to go with this job?"

"About a week."

"Well, I don't know. I know you're just trying to do what's best for me." His gaze was locked on some distant object out the window. Maybe a cloud. Or a bird. "I was nervous last night."

"Yeah? Why?"

He looked back to Andrea on the couch. "I'm just wondering if it's possible that they found her but have, for some reason, decided not to say anything."

"I have no idea," said Andrea.

"From what I've heard," Rob said, "the police were monitoring Liz's car for at least a full day before her brother found it. They were waiting to see if anyone was going to come back and try to move it in the middle of the night."

—◯—

ERIC GOSTICK

The police came to the Recreation Centre to search the weight room on the second Tuesday after Elizabeth Bain disappeared. I asked what had taken them so long, and they said there were other priorities. I accompanied them to the weight room, where they approached all seven of the community members working out that night. They pulled out a picture of Liz and showed it to everyone, but no one had seen her. They never displayed a picture of Rob or asked any questions about him, which, I had assumed, was their whole reason for being there—to see if anyone had seen him in the gym that night. They came back again within a week and did the same thing. At most, they spent twenty minutes canvassing people in the weight room. They never bothered to obtain the records of all the people who had a weight club membership—I checked into that—and I found it very odd that they'd made what seemed to be a conscious decision not to make any inquiries about Rob being there.

About two or three weeks after Rob and I had spoken to Kaedmon Nancoo in the weight room, I decided to give him a call. Kaedmon hadn't been too sure about when he'd seen Rob, other than it might have been four-thirty in the afternoon. He wasn't even sure if it had been the Tuesday. It seemed more likely to me, knowing Rob's work schedule with the basketball league, that Kaedmon had been confusing this with Monday, and he'd pretty much agreed that was the case.

So I called Kaedmon to see if his memory had cleared up at all as to what day he'd seen Rob. I should make it clear that Rob never asked me to do this—I just thought it was important. But Kaedmon said, "No, I'm still not sure." I ended the conversation saying, "Well, if you're not sure, you're not sure. Thanks anyways." And that was it.

Then, on a Friday morning towards the end of August, Jake Poranganel and another officer came to my house at nine o'clock in the morning. I worked until eleven every night, so I was still sleeping and my mother came upstairs to wake me up. So I got dressed and went downstairs, and they were in my face right off the bat. "Why was I lying?" they wanted to know. "Why was I trying to cover up evidence?" Jake Poranganel said, "It would be a shame to have to charge you with being an accessory to murder after the fact." My mother was in the room and she was quite shocked by this. We both were. It was after this incident that I told Rob we shouldn't talk about the case any more. It was getting out of hand.

I think the reason the police were so upset with me was because Poranganel said it took them a week to find Kaedmon, and they couldn't understand why I would go to all that trouble. "But it was no trouble," I told them. "It only took me two minutes."

Let's face it, Kaedmon must have told them something, and the police weren't too eager to seek out people who would contradict him. What's disturbing about all of this is that these people are supposed to be finding the truth and, after dealing with them, I was one hundred per cent positive in my heart that they weren't really interested in finding the truth. They were only interested in building a case against Rob Baltovich.

—◯—

Reesor decided it was time to send a few more witnesses down to Dr. Matheson in Etobicoke. It had really paid off with Marianne Perz—one day she remembers Liz being at the picnic table with a dark-haired man and after a few minutes in the doctor's dream chair, the man goes from being faceless to possibly having the face of Robert Baltovich. He could truly use another break like that. After compiling hundreds of hours' worth of wire-taps, not only did they have no confession, they had not a single utterance that could fairly be classified as inculpatory, or even suspicious. The main reason for this, Reesor had effortlessly concluded, was that Baltovich knew his phone was being tapped and, therefore, was watching his words. His medium for working around this dilemma, Andrea Beitinger, had been almost as futile as the wire-taps. The only useful piece of information the Beitinger tapes had given them was that Rob had an inkling his phone was bugged—and you weren't going to swing a murder trial jury with that, at least not without something substantial to back it up.

So, on August 30, Constable Jim Shadgett was dispatched from the Team Room to shuttle Susanne Nadon—the woman who'd heard a couple arguing in front of her home at a time when Rob and Liz were supposed to be naked on some blankets alongside Highland Creek—to Etobicoke General Hospital. As Tony Warr had done prior to Perz's hypnosis session, Shadgett went into Matheson's office for a quick briefing. "I watched the tape of the previous witness back at the station," said Shadgett. "Geez, I almost went to sleep." He and the doctor shared a good laugh. Then Shadgett outlined what Nadon had seen and heard according to her statement. If, under hypnosis, she could remember anything more about Bain's car— the licence plate number or the Canadian Automobile Association sticker on the right side of the trunk—that would really help them determine that it wasn't some other similar-looking vehicle. Shadgett said there were dozens of silver Tercels around town.

"Does she know about the CAA sticker?" Matheson asked.

"She has seen pictures of the car since," said Shadgett. "She knows about it now."

"Well, it might be that she recalls the picture rather than what she actually saw."

"Yeah," said Shadgett. What could you do? "We're also wondering if we can get out of her somehow whether she saw the guy driving the car. Can she describe him?"

"Okay."

"Hopefully, it's our boy. You see, by his own admission the suspect was with the victim until two in the morning. This witness is talking about 12:35 AM, so it had to be him."

"The only potential problem here," said Matheson, "is that any descriptions involving the car may be a little complicated because she has now seen photographs. So we're getting a mixture."

Flipping through his notes, Shadgett abruptly cut in. "Oh, one other thing. If we can pick up on any of the conversation. For example, if she heard the girl say, 'No, Rob! No, Rob!'—if she actually said his name, that would be very helpful. She says she heard 'No!' a couple of times, but there's no specific name given."

Matheson said he would see what he could do, and together they went out to get Susanne Nadon in the waiting room. The first thing she told him was that she'd been hypnotized just last May in an attempt to wean herself off cigarette smoking. It had worked for a while but she'd gone back to the cancer sticks before long. And there was another time, years ago, when she'd signed up for a program to lose weight through hypnosis. You went into a dark room with a bunch of other women and listened to hypnotic tapes that were supposed to set your subconscious mind on the path to a slimmer figure.

Matheson had an easy time transferring her into a hypnotic state. If anything, Nadon was overly motivated to submit to hypnosis. In no time she was back to the early morning hours of June 18, lying down in her room, hearing the steady buzz from Highway 401 just beyond her mother's backyard, and even the wind blowing through the trees out front. And then, like a shotgun blast come the voices.

Nadon can tell that the woman hidden off behind the trees near the road is naturally soft-spoken, but sounds upset. "She says, 'I don't want to.' Then the male voice says, 'Why?' So she says the same thing again, 'No, I don't want to.' I don't know what they're talking about, but it doesn't seem like a sex thing." That's when she hears the car door slam shut a few seconds before she can see it drive by. It isn't going all that fast. There is a black stripe between the wheels. "I'm looking for people in the car," Nadon said. "But there's no one in the passenger seat or in the back. I can't even see the outline of the driver."

Matheson asked, "Is the car quiet or noisy?"

"A little noisy. It's an older car. I think I heard a grind. Could be a gear. When you don't have the clutch pushed in. Now I'm looking at the licence plate. It's white. I see the licence plate sticker and the blue lettering. I'm mad because I can't make out the licence plate. I try but . . . There's something on the back of the car, too. I can make it out. It's brown and oval."

And then the woman appears from behind the trees walking down the gravel part of the road. "I see the street light shining down on her head," Nadon said. "I can't see her that well from the side. She's got a little nose, nice features, small chin."

"Is she big busted?"

"She isn't big busted, or anything like that, no."

"What do you notice about her as she walks away?"

"She doesn't seem really concerned to me. I'd be scared. I'm scared of the dark. She's going west. I don't understand why she's going down there . . . maybe she lives around here because the road is closed off . . . for the construction of the new sewer pipes. I'm thinking the guy's gonna be down there waiting for her. He can't go any farther than Meadowvale. I think she's gonna get back in the car because she's not walking like she's concerned about running into him, you know? I'm losing sight of her so I put my ear up to where the window would be if it was closed."

Matheson instructed her to relax. Soon he was going to count to five and wake her up. Before he did, though, he wondered if there was anything she hadn't mentioned. "Oh, the sewers!" Nadon was flailing around in the chair. "She's there. I know it. I can . . . she's there. Down there. They're putting them in . . . " She suddenly calmed herself. "I'm sorry about that," she said.

Matheson said, "You're worried about her, aren't you?"

"I'm really worried about her. Just a funny feeling I have. I'm really worried. She didn't do anything wrong. I just don't trust him."

"What is it about him you don't trust?"

"Sometimes guys try to humour you. They go along with what you're saying. Not loud, but sarcastic. I just know that sound in a voice."

Matheson snapped her out of it and asked her how long she thought they'd been talking. "Fifteen minutes," she answered.

"So that would make it what? Ten-thirty?"

Nadon looked at her watch. It was much later than that. "No way," she said. "Look at the time already. This is scary."

Matheson's next appointment, Kaedmon Nancoo, was escorted across the city by

Jake Poranganel. The detective informed Matheson that Nancoo's recollection of seeing the suspect in the weight room was "quite clear" and, therefore, needed no special probing by the doctor. In truth, his memory was anything but lucid. During his interview with the police, Nancoo had said that he'd definitely left the gym before 6:30 PM—however, when the investigators later asked if he could be more specific, he moved the time back closer to five-thirty. It was about fifteen minutes prior to his departure, Nancoo said, that he'd said hello to Rob, who was stretching on the floor in his workout clothes. In the end, Nancoo wasn't all that sure about leaving at five-thirty either—he admitted that it could have been as much as twenty minutes earlier or later than that (which was still at odds with the four-thirty sighting of Rob that Rick Gostick remembered Nancoo giving back in late June).

In addition to the problem of pinpointing the precise time he'd seen Rob, Nancoo expressed a degree of uncertainty that it had been the Tuesday. He just knew that his friend Lance had taken the day off work that afternoon, which would be an essential piece of information had Lance not also taken the previous day off. Could he be positive that it had happened on Tuesday? Or could it have been Monday? When confronted by Rob and Rick Gostick, Nancoo had been willing to go with Monday, but when the police homed in on Tuesday, he swung like a weathervane in a crosswind. Tuesday it was, then. So, having established that Nancoo had seen Rob in the weight room approximately half an hour before Marianne Perz claimed to have seen a man who might be Rob sitting beside Liz at a picnic table in the valley, the boys back in the Team Room didn't want a videotaped hypnosis session possibly mucking it all up.

The only thing they were interested in having the doctor help Nancoo recall from the depths of his subconscious was his faint memory of having once seen Rob driving Liz's Tercel. He thought he might have seen this back in March or April. The guys in the Team Room were now celebrating the fact that Susanne Nadon had told Matheson she'd heard the sound of gears grinding as the car began to accelerate in front of her house—wasn't that a sure sign of a standard-transmission novice like Baltovich? If Nancoo now remembered Rob behind the wheel of Liz's car, they might be home free, as that would be catching him in one big, fat, juicy lie.

With this objective in mind, Matheson made Nancoo bend his elbow like a creaky hinge, his hand drifting, floating, moving around, up and down, until he saw her in the car on that day:

MATHESON: What do you think when you see her go by?

NANCOO: I just notice her. She's a pretty young thing.

MATHESON: What about the type of car?

NANCOO: A silver Tercel. Pretty girls usually like to drive nicer cars. She should be going out with somebody who has a nicer car.

MATHESON: Is she driving it?

NANCOO: Mmm, I don't picture her driving. Just a passenger.

MATHESON: Just for a moment, notice whether it's a man or woman driving it. [*Long pause*]

NANCOO: Nothing. [*Long pause*]

MATHESON: Just notice whether you have an impression of her being with a girlfriend or a boyfriend.

NANCOO: I know she's with a guy.

MATHESON: How do you know she's with a guy?

NANCOO: 'Cause I said to myself, you know, "Her boyfriend could at least drive a nicer car."

MATHESON: And that's her boyfriend Rob in the car? [*Long pause*]

NANCOO: Yeah, it is Rob. But I can't see him driving. It's funny. I remember. I know, I remember. I can see Liz sitting in the passenger seat. But it doesn't stick in my mind that Rob is driving.

—◦—

On the first Saturday morning after the Labour Day holiday, Steve Reesor got the idea to call Rob at home. He wanted to ask a few questions about the Herriotts, the couple who'd given Rob the blue barrette they'd found in Colonel Danforth Park. "That's right," said Rob. "I remember that."

"Do you still have it?" asked Reesor.

"No," said Rob. "I gave it to Mr. Bain minutes after they handed it to me. He said it wasn't important because there was no way it belonged to Liz."

"Well, Rob, I have to tell you that I've spoken to Mr. Bain about this, and he says that you never showed him a barrette. And when I repeated for him the description of the barrette I got from the Herriotts, he said that it might have been Liz's."

"That's not what he said when he looked at it," Rob insisted. "He knew as well as I did that it wasn't the kind of thing Liz would put in her hair."

"How would Mr. Bain know that?"

"He is her father, isn't he?" Rob was exasperated. "Okay, I'll look around to see if I have it but I suggest you call Mr. Bain again and go over it one more time. I find it hard to believe that moment is completely erased from his memory."

Reesor wasn't sure if he'd bother. The lies were starting to rack up just the way he'd hoped they would.

On Monday Reesor's next task was to get Ruth Collins, the only witness who'd seen Liz Bain in her car with a man on the day of her disappearance, to Dr. Matheson's office. It had taken a while to convince her to undergo hypnosis, as she was frightened of reliving that moment so vividly in her mind, but Reesor had given her one of Dr. Matheson's preparatory videotapes and that seemed to have made her more amenable to the request. Reesor explained to Matheson that he was interested in Collins's description of the car (which she'd observed parked in front of Three R Auto Body) and its occupants, especially that of the guy in the driver's seat. Under normal circumstances, said Reesor, it wouldn't really prove anything if she now said it was Bain's boyfriend, but, in this case, the boyfriend says he never saw her that day. Reesor even went as far as telling Matheson that, during the period of time Collins had purported to have witnessed the scene in front of Three R Auto Body, his "suspect," Baltovich, was "unaccounted for." "He does not have an alibi for that time frame," Reesor continued, knowing full well that another key witness, Marc Singleton, had already told Homicide detectives that Baltovich had been in the weight room for every minute of the Collins "time frame."

Collins was quite nervous as she took her place in the big brown chair. Finding out that the girl she'd seen that night was Elizabeth Bain had been a cause for upset the entire summer. "It's just that I always kind of feel guilty," said Collins. "If it was her and she was looking for help, and I didn't help her, how can I not feel that way? Because I did see her little face turn around and look at me, you know."

Once transported back in time through her memory, Collins is walking up Morrish Road on her way home to watch "In the Heat of the Night" on television. A cool breeze blows as dusk approaches. There's a couple scuffling in the car. A lot of hands moving around. She's closest to me. On the passenger side. Her head goes back. Her head goes forward, then back again. There is a thumping sound and it looks like he hit her. It looks like he grabs her by the neck. His hand goes out and pulls her head back. Maybe by her hair. There is a man's voice. Can't hear what he's saying. The door opens. I can see her foot come out. She's wearing a black shoe. It may be patent leather. With a slight heel. Her foot does not quite touch the ground. She has slacks on. Black slacks. The door closes now. I see a man's bare arm reach across her towards the door. The door goes bang shut. Now the same thing happens again. Head forward. Thumping. Head back. I can't see the man. I can't see his face. His arm was quite tanned. Maybe some kind of shiny object on him. I can't tell if it's a watch or a bracelet. Mostly he's just a form. It's the way the sun is hitting them. The way the shadow is on him. He's just a form.

As I get up to the car, she turns and looks at me. Her eyes are kind of fearful looking. She looks at me again over her left shoulder as I cross the road. Eyes flash. A very pretty girl. Dark, dark, straight hair behind her ears. Neat. Bangs over her forehead. Very dark complexion or a really deep tan. Dark brown eyes. Beautiful, expressive eyes. I hear loud voices. Could be the radio. Wait a minute. It's a loud, deep voice. What's he saying? The wind is kind of carrying the sound away. It sounds like they're yelling. I don't know why her head keeps going down towards her knees. Maybe they're just fooling around. I don't know. Her window is down a wee bit. The car is shiny grey with black trim along the bottom. Black lines. A small two-door. The form beside her is like a shadow. A little taller than her. Maybe he's hiding behind her. Every once in a while an arm goes up and her head goes down. Then as I cross, the two of them seem to sit up and the commotion stops as they see me leave. I'm still thinking about her face. She looked familiar. But the look. The look was either startled or fearful. Maybe I startled her when I came up the hill. Maybe she didn't see me. Maybe he saw me. I don't know. But her eyes flashed. Fearful or startled. Nobody parks there. Just nobody. There was nothing else around. Just this one little car, so shiny in the sun.

—◇—

Rob was racking his brain to figure out where in the world Reesor and Raybould had come up with this idea that he was homosexual. The only thing he could think of was an incident that had occurred a week or two after Liz's disappearance. A group of guys—Neil, Steve, Al and Jim—had taken him out to see a movie as part of their scheme to keep his mind from dwelling on Liz. Yet, despite their noble intentions, they hadn't been able to foresee how the whole evening would eventually go awry. The movie, *Robocop II*, was incredibly violent, and there was one scene in particular that involved the vicious murder of a young woman. Rob couldn't stop thinking, Is that what happened to Liz?

As they left the theatre, Rob noticed the young couples strolling along around them, holding hands on that warm summer night and, thinking of similar evenings with Liz, his eyes filled with tears. By the time they reached Neil's car on the other side of the street, he was really crying. The ride seemed to soothe him, and when Neil dropped Rob off in front of his house, he apologized to the guys for "losing it." That's when Al put his arms around him and said, "That's okay, Rob."

Now, Rob wondered if some cop—or even Reesor himself—had witnessed this brief, sympathetic embrace and interpreted it as something else. It had been Rob's understanding for some time that, on the subject of homosexuality, male police officers tended to be a little touchy, spending so much of their time alone with a partner as they did.

If there was a silver lining to this slanderous rumour, it was that, for the first time since Liz had gone missing, entire weeks passed by without any word of the investigation filtering down through the grapevine to Rob. No more news of bizarre interviews with family and friends or police theories from left field. And, best of all, there were no intimidating phone calls from Reesor. The refreshing breezes of September that autumn seemed to signal more than just a change of seasons. It was quite apparent that Reesor and Raybould had shifted their efforts in some other direction (otherwise they surely would have come to take him away by now), and that he was free to resume his life as it might have been had he never laid eyes on Elizabeth Bain. The summer basketball league had come to an end, and Rob got started on the task of landing himself a full-time job that would hold him until he made up his mind about attending teachers' college in a year.

He began perusing the employment sections of the newspapers and applying to all kinds of jobs that he thought might be interesting. There were a few nibbles to start with, but it wasn't until he picked up a *Buy & Sell* magazine and put his résumé in for a research assistant position advertised by a company called Mediastats, that he got his first formal interview. Mediastats was a media consulting firm located in nearby Markham.

Rob was impressed with the well-designed modern office space, and with the way Kerry Wicks, the young woman conducting the interview, put him at ease by promising not to hold it against him that he was the last of twenty candidates to be spoken to about the job. (It was obvious that she didn't recognize his name or face from the news, and he thought it best, for now, not to bring it up.) Kerry explained that Mediastats monitored the habits of the Canadian television audience the way A.C. Neilsen did in the United States, although on a much smaller scale. The research assistant position was going to involve compiling data for the Canadian cable and broadcast industries. Kerry also talked about the various surveys the company conducted and how the job would occasionally require him to drive to the offices of Canadian networks like CITYTV and TSN (The Sports Network) to pick up or drop off important documents. Kind of like a "man Friday." It was an entry-level job, there was no hiding that, but if he proved that he was able to handle the position, this would all change.

Kerry called him up a few days later with good news—the research assistant job was his if he was still interested. Rob didn't have to think about it for very long; he said he'd take it. He couldn't have been happier, really. A new job with a slick young media company and still not a peep from Reesor and Raybould.

He was waking up good and early for the first few weeks, determined to make a positive impression on his new employer. Then, one morning, walking down the front stoop to his car, he saw a folded piece of white paper wedged into a crack along the edge of the concrete steps beneath the iron railing. He bent down and lifted it out. Unfolded, the page revealed four swirling, computer-generated words, the kind of thing Rob had seen printed out on the machines at school, or by friends lucky enough to have their own equipment at home. But this one read: I LOVED ELIZA-BETH BAIN. What? Who loved Elizabeth Bain? And what kind of love? Romantic? Familial? Platonic? Could this be a clue? And yet, what bothered him more than anything else was that the person who'd left it had been so close to him while he slept, approaching in the darkness no more than ten feet from his bedroom window. He laid the page out flat on the passenger seat and sneaked glances at it as he navigated his way through swelling traffic to Markham. In his head, he could hear the printer labouring back and forth across the page, zapping it with a thousand minuscule dots of black ink as it created the shading necessary to give the letters in Elizabeth Bain a raised, three-dimensional look.

This anonymous, cryptic message brought him to an important realization—that, regardless of what he now attempted to do with his life, none of this was going to go away. Liz was gone, and the police weren't about to stop trying to solve the case. The Bains weren't about to stop looking for her. And as long as people spoke about Liz, they would also speak of him. That would never change.

And so when he got to Mediastats, Rob walked into Kerry's office and said there were some things he felt that, for the sake of honesty, he should share with her. "You've probably heard about the disappearance of Elizabeth Bain," he said. Kerry said she was vaguely aware of it. "Well, she was my girlfriend, and you may not know it, but the police have targeted me as a suspect. For quite a while, they were bothering me a lot, but, as of late, that's all stopped. And I don't anticipate any of this will arise again."

Kerry wasted little time letting Rob know how she felt. She told him it was her understanding that, in Canada, accused people were innocent until proven guilty. (When Kerry expressed this to the Homicide detectives who eventually came to speak with her, they tried to change her mind. "If Rob is a murderer," she asked them, "then why are you letting him come to my office every day? Why don't you arrest him and get him off the streets?" To which the detectives responded by assuring Kerry that they didn't consider him a threat to society, and, therefore, were in no rush to do anything until the time was right.) What Rob had told her hadn't really fazed her, Kerry said. "In addition to that, Rob," she continued, " I like to think that I'm a pretty good judge of character, and even from the short amount of time I've known you, I doubt you would be involved in something like that."

A sense of overwhelming relief flushed through his body and he said, "I just thought you should know." Then, out of nowhere, Kerry's mouth widened in an amused smile. "What's so funny?" he asked.

"It's just that here I am telling you how I'm such a great judge of character and the truth is that, when you walked into my office just now and said you wanted to speak to me, the first thing that sprang into my head was that you were going to tell me you were gay."

Part 4

—◦—

Private Investigations

Tired and dirty after a long hard day, John Secord soaked in the bathtub and sifted through his mail. He was in the middle of a big excavation job for a new shopping centre in Markham. Secord had moved to the Markham community of Unionville in 1976 from an old village slightly south and west, called Thornhill, where he'd been born and raised. He'd spent a couple of years at York University out in the west end, studying for a general sciences degree, but it hadn't held his interest and he'd dropped out, bought himself a pick-up truck and gone into the construction business.

At first, a lot of the work came from residential subdivisions sprouting up in the Unionville area, and so he grabbed himself a little townhouse there when he was twenty-seven and got married. Although the marriage didn't last long, the next thirteen years had been a boom period in new housing, with plenty of lucrative contracts to keep hard hats like him off the welfare line. Secord started his own company, Secord Construction Limited, and bought himself a big old backhoe, along with a few other good rigs, all of which helped him put a down payment on a brand-new $400,000 home in 1988.

Secord had already scrubbed the leathery, weather-beaten skin on his forehead as well as his sun-reddened neck. He was of average size, but for a man at the gate of middle age, noticeably muscular, especially in his forearms, which were hard as rock from decades of working a shovel. His short, thick, permanently soiled fingers thumbed through the moderate stack of envelopes, most of which were bills, and he was in no mood for that. The only item he felt like taking a look at right then was a single-page flyer—the rest he tossed on the bathroom floor. At the top was the word MISSING and beneath that a grainy black-and-white photograph of a girl named Elizabeth (Liz) Marie Bain (DID YOU SEE LIZ OR HER 1981 2-DR SILVER TOYOTA BETWEEN 4:00 PM TUESDAY, JUNE 19 AND 6:00 AM WEDNESDAY JUNE 20, 1990?). You could easily make out the fantastic whiteness of her teeth and her alluring eyes, which reminded him of Cleopatra or some other ancient Egyptian goddess.

He didn't know exactly what it was, but there was something about that flyer that got to him. He ended up putting it on his kitchen table, where he would sit down to look at it for a few minutes every night after work. That went on for a couple of weeks. Then, one Sunday afternoon, he drove down to Morrish Road in Scarborough (where the map indicated the girl's car had been found) and walked around in front of Three R Auto Body, checking things out, seeing if he could catch some kind of vibe. In the end, it just left him wanting to know more, so the next night he looked up Rick Bain in the telephone book and called him up. Luckily, Mr. Bain was in and seemed comfortable sharing a few words with him about his daughter's disappearance. He suggested Secord come out for the weekend search in the Ganaraska Forest, a good drive east on Highway 401. "I'll be there," Secord said, and they left it at that.

But the very next day, on his way home from the mall job in Markham, Secord stopped in at St. Joseph's Church at the corner of Morrish Road and Old Kingston Road. Mr. Bain had said that this was his family's place of worship, and as such, it had become a kind of meeting place for volunteers involved in the searches, as well as other efforts organized by what was now known as "Friends In Search For Elizabeth Bain"—poster distribution, canvassing, vigils, catering for volunteers and so on.

Secord parked his pick-up and was making his way across the church parking lot when a white Volvo station wagon came burning around a bend straight for him. He leapt out of the way and the Volvo kept going, stopping to back into a space farther down the lot. The driver quickly sprang out of his vehicle to apologize. Secord couldn't believe it, but it turned out to be Mr. Bain, who then invited him inside St.

Joseph's for a quick tour. They spent quite a while in front of the announcement board, filled with posters and sheets of information about the searches for Liz.

Two nights later, Secord figured he'd just drive over to the Bains' house on his way home. That was how Secord first met Mrs. Bain; he and Mr. Bain stood in the driveway for a while, talking. Secord noticed that Liz's Tercel was parked just a few feet away; in fact, the presence of the car was making it next to impossible to concentrate on what Mr. Bain was saying to him. So he just cut him off and asked if he could sit in Liz's car for a minute. Although caught off guard, Mr. Bain obliged, opening the door, and Secord got in behind the wheel. He took a good long look at the dash and then twisted around towards the back seats. He even looked up and noticed some long slashes in the vinyl lining of the roof. Mr. Bain explained that the police had torn it in the process of taking the seats out of the car. Secord just nodded but he found that explanation lacking—he was thinking something more along the lines of fingernail marks—but he kept it to himself.

On Saturday, Secord went out to the Ganaraska Forest with the rest of the search team. He met Dave Madder, Mr. Bain's search co-ordinator, who was, like Secord, a hard-working man who'd just hit forty. Madder had read about Liz's disappearance in June during a hospital stay for a stomach ulcer. Some years ago, Madder had lived in the West Hill area of Scarborough, and although he didn't know the Bains, he'd read about them in the papers, which is how he recognized Julita Bain at the Cedarbrae Mall one afternoon, standing behind the counter of a volunteer recruiting booth. He'd spoken to her for fifteen minutes and ended up helping out at the following weekend's searches. Before long, he was working between twenty and twenty-five hours a week on the search efforts, as well as the two days in the field every weekend. Even beyond that, his part-time job as a courier enabled him to distribute a large quantity of missing-person flyers on his various travels around the city.

Madder had taken over the search coordinator position from Maria Laszko, who'd lasted just three weeks on the job. After she'd quit, Madder had asked her what the problem was, and she'd just said she and Mr. Bain hadn't been seeing eye to eye on things. That was it. The job was his.

Only a few hours into the first morning of searching in Ganaraska, Secord began to grasp how Mr. Bain might frustrate someone whose primary responsibility was tracking down items that might provide some answers. For instance, that very morning, someone had found a blouse with a floral pattern on it lying in a crumpled pile on the ground. Without touching it, the person had marked its location with a stake, as well as on the map, and then hightailed it back to the base camp. As soon as Madder was told about the blouse, he went straight to Mr. Bain, but for some reason Mr. Bain didn't seem all that anxious to go and look at it. Secord mentioned it to him a couple more times that day, but Mr. Bain just kept saying he'd go when he had a few spare minutes. It wasn't until the afternoon of the following day, however, that Mr. Bain finally relented and a crew of them, including Madder and Secord, drove out to the blouse.

When they found it beneath the shade of some overhanging tree branches, Mr. Bain picked it up. It was definitely a woman's blouse with a floral motif in various shades of light blue. Unlike Secord, who was trembling like an ice-cold kitten, Mr. Bain was unmoved by their find, which, a few seconds later, he tossed to the ground—"That was not the blouse she was wearing"—and turned on his heel, not giving it another thought. Secord just couldn't understand that. What if that was Liz's floral blouse? He was tempted to go and retrieve it but didn't.

Back home in Unionville later that afternoon, Secord stretched out on his couch. He was holding the month-old Missing flyer in his hands, studying it for the hundredth time, until he began to fade and, drifting off, lowered the page down on top of his face and fell asleep. It was right there on the couch that he had his first dream about Liz. She was standing there, fully visible, her legs together, arms hanging straight against her body. He didn't know why, but she kept shaking her head from side to side. She wouldn't stop doing that. To her left was an object that looked like a triangle with something hovering inside of it, but he couldn't make it out. What made the whole dream even stranger was the fact that everything was in black and white—normally, he dreamt in colour.

Secord was soaking wet from perspiration when he woke up but he didn't move. Just lay still. He'd had only one other vision like this before in his life. That was fifteen years earlier, back in the days when he used to drink. He and two women friends had been fooling around with a Ouija board one night. When it was Secord's turn, he placed his fingers on the empty wine glass they were using as a guide and closed his eyes, feeling the glass move freely around the board. Big, circular motions around and around. And then, out of nowhere, he felt a massive explosion and in his mind saw two cars collide in the dark and then disappear off the road, leaving him with the image of two yellow lines running parallel up an empty, star-lit road in the countryside.

When he came to, the women were kneeling down on either side of him. He'd jolted himself back from the table so hard, they said, that he'd gone over backwards in his chair and smashed his head against the floor. He had one hell of a headache the next day.

Not long after that, Secord got some bad news. His best friend's brother, Les, had died in a car crash. Once the funeral was over, Secord let some time pass and then he asked his friend to take him up to the spot where Les's accident had occurred, which was a stretch of rural highway between Keswick and Sutton. Secord was prac-tically in a trance as he got out of his truck at the side of the road. Without ques-tion it was the very scene that had appeared in his mind that night at the Ouija board. The only difference was the dividing lines on the surface of the highway—they were white instead of yellow.

When he finally told the two women about Les's fatal accident and about how it had been the identical piece of landscape he'd seen in his head that night, they both turned pale and stared at each other. "What?" Secord said. "Why are you looking at each other like that? Tell me!"

"We don't know how to tell you this, John," said one of the women. "I guess nei-ther of us mentioned it before because we didn't think it meant anything. But when your head hit the floor, it was real quiet for a second. And then you kind of moaned."

"What did I say?" Secord asked.

"Well . . . " She almost didn't want to utter it. "What you said was 'Oh, Les.' "

Rob piled into a car with Tony, Jim, Neil and Steve and they cruised down to Har-bourfront for an outdoor Latin festival. Quite a crowd had congregated down there, and the guys were taking turns goofing around, doing their lame inter-pretation of the samba, now and then letting loose with a high-pitched "*Arriba!*" Rob stopped at one venue to try his hand at a Mexican hat dance, and the guys stood back and laughed as he spun around in circles with his hand on his stom-ach like some anguished flamenco dancer who'd just sat through *Saturday Night*

Fever. At the end of the song, Rob stomped his feet in a real flourish and screamed, "*Buon' giorno!*"

Then, out of nowhere, came a soft, female voice: "It's *ola*, not *buon' giorno.*" Rob looked up and saw a sultry brunette standing right next to the guys. She said her name was Sandra Avelino and it turned out she was of Colombian descent. It didn't appear as though she was with anyone so Rob introduced her to the guys, and from that moment on, she just hung around with them for the rest of the evening.

Before long, she had her arm hooked around Rob's, really snuggling up close to his side, even dropping her hand into his with such ease that he hardly noticed. He couldn't believe how assertive she was being (for a second, he wondered if Reesor was up to something, but didn't think even he was *that* devious). It was like she'd come there that night on a mission to find a guy. Tony, especially, was pretty impressed. He took Rob aside at one point to say just how much of a babe this Sandra girl was and how he wouldn't mind seeing her in a bikini one bit.

When it was time for the guys to head back to Scarborough, Sandra made a point of writing down her phone number for Rob on a little scrap of paper, and he did the same for her. It didn't take long for Sandra to call. Rob listened as she gave him the quick rundown on her life. She was going to the University of Toronto and had no boyfriend. That was the good part. The flip side was that, generally speaking, she was going through a rough patch these days, mostly because of her parents, with whom she didn't get along very well. Her younger brother was in the same boat as her parents. Gave her nothing but grief.

Rob kept thinking to himself, Gee, this sounds like a familiar tune. It was a good time to bolt. And Sandra's problems made him think about Liz in that all-consuming way he'd just begun to break free of. Liz had been gone for four months. Man, it seemed a lot longer than that. Still, he was not ready to begin another relationship, even if Sandra had been the most well-adjusted young woman in the universe. So, without mentioning Liz, he just said there were some things going on his life that made it a bad idea for them to have a romantic liaison at any point in the near future. He was sorry, he said, but that was the way it had to be.

Sandra called him back an hour later. "I'm sitting here in my bathtub," she said. "And I was just thinking to myself, What did I say or do that turned you off so much?"

"Sandra," he said, "please understand, it's not that you did anything wrong, it's just that I don't think us getting together right now is a good idea. As I said, I'm very sorry. I didn't mean to hurt your feelings."

Having let Sandra down as gently as he could, he called up Steve Doucette and told him about his conversations with Sandra. He could hear Steve chuckling on the other end of the phone as he played them out. "What's wrong with you, Rob?" Steve said. "You always pick the nuts."

—— ⊖ ——

Jake Poranganel called Rob at Mediastats in the middle of the afternoon to say he needed to deliver some documents to him. Rob said fine and told him where the company was located. But roughly half an hour later, Poranganel was back on the line from a payphone somewhere. "We're lost," he said. "We can't find the friggin' place." Rob gave him the most basic directions imaginable and that seemed to do it.

Poranganel and a younger cop whom Rob hadn't seen before walked into the lobby a short while later. Rob escorted them to his office, which was just inside and to the right. "Geez, Rob," said Poranganel. "This is a *niiice* office." Rob savoured the stunned look on his face. "Thank you," he replied. Rob surmised that, for Poranganel anyway, it was really starting to sink in that he was face to face with a guy who was determined to get on with his life. Someone who wasn't going to buckle under their endless harassment. Instead of being the guilt-ridden guy wasting away in his lonely basement room, they were now confronted with an educated young man wearing a jacket and tie, working on some sophisticated hardware in an office that was far more plush than anything the Homicide squad could provide. "Well, Rob," said Poranganel. "You want to come outside for a talk?"

"Actually, no," he said. "We can talk right here."

"No, no, no. We'd like you to come outside." So there was no choice—they went outside, all three leaning against the railing at the top of the front steps. Poranganel handed him a folded sheaf of papers and indicated that the police were bound by law to inform him in writing that they were listening in on his home phone line. "Oh, this is interesting," Rob said. "You're going to start listening to my phone calls now, after all these months?"

Poranganel didn't bother straightening him out by explaining that, according to the law, police must inform their wire-tap targets of their electronic eavesdropping three months after receiving judicial authorization. (The meaning of the documents would be clarified by his mother when he got home. She told him that Jake Poranganel had dropped by earlier that day with identical papers. Unlike Rob, Adele had picked up on the fact that the phone had *already* been tapped—they weren't starting now. Once Poranganel had given her the news, he just kept standing in her front doorway, staring at her, waiting for some kind of response. But Adele had simply said, "Is there anything else?" And Poranganel had replied no, so she'd closed the door in his face.)

The thing about Rob that really got to Poranganel was his apparent indifference to the wire tap. "Rob," said Poranganel, "I've got to tip my hat to you. You are one cool customer." Rob just looked at him and then at his partner, who was half smiling and half trying to get a good read on him. Obviously, Rob gathered, these two had him pegged as some sort of case study in the psychopathic criminal mind—the master of emotional control. Rob said, "When you're innocent, you can't help the fact that you're acting normal."

Rob played along for a few more minutes, subjecting himself to their childish probing, before looking at his watch and announcing that he had to get going. "Guys," he said, "I just have to go inside and get my coat. I'll be back in a second." So he went back to the office for his coat and his briefcase and then went back outside, going to his car, where Poranganel and his partner were waiting. What more did they want to know? Rob unlocked his doors and put his things in the back seat. "You guys have a good day, all right," he said. He didn't know what else to say or why they were still hanging around. He just hopped in behind the wheel, turned the key in the ignition and drove away, looking in the rear-view mirror as he pulled out of the parking lot. He couldn't believe it—they were *still* standing there, like the two characters he'd studied in *Waiting for Godot*, pacing around aimlessly in a barren, one-treed lot after closing time, in search of god only knew what.

—◇—

Just as suburbia braced itself for Devil's Night, the prank-filled eve preceding Hallowe'en—when your front windows might get pelted with raw eggs or balls of wet toilet paper, if not something worse, like a couple of bricks—John Secord pulled up in front of the Bains' in his pick-up. Over the last month, he'd become quite close with the family, especially Julita. She quickly discovered that he was incredibly handy around the house. Could fix just about anything from furniture to the sewing machine. That very morning he'd dropped off a load of topsoil for her garden. But now that it was getting dark, he told her it was too late to start doing any wheel-barrelling. Instead, he joined her inside at the kitchen table. She said Rick was in another room having a long conversation over the phone with Brian Raybould. Secord and Julita were alone for at least half an hour before Rick walked into the kitchen with a big smile on his face, looking like he was on cloud nine. "I've got something to tell you, Lita," he said. "But it's crucial that you not tell anybody."

Secord offered to leave the room, but Rick said, "No, I want you to hear this too. Besides, Lita will just end up telling you anyway. Brian Raybould just told me that Rob Baltovich failed a lie-detector test back in July."

Secord let that sink in for a moment—Julita looked startled—and then assured Rick that he would keep it quiet. "That's good," said Rick, his big grin widening. "Because if you tell anyone, I'll cut off your left hand." Secord offered a little laugh to match Rick's but couldn't see what was so amusing about threatening to do someone bodily harm.

This kind of thing had been happening a lot lately. Why, just last Saturday night, as Secord had been leaving the Bains' with Dave Madder, Rick had reached into a pocket on his denim jacket for a piece of paper and in the process a latex surgical glove (which had been found on a search) had fallen out and landed on the floor. Secord thought Rick had looked embarrassed about this, almost panicky. Rick had quickly bent down to pick it up, saying, "That wasn't supposed to happen." Ever since Rick had disregarded that blouse in the Ganaraska forest, Secord had been unable to make head or tail of the man and, unquestionably, there was something about him that Secord found deeply disturbing.

None of this, however, prevented Secord from returning the following morning at ten o'clock to move the mound of topsoil to Julita's vegetable garden at the back of the house, while she tended the flower beds out front. A few hours later, she made him a salad for lunch, which they ate in the kitchen. Then, instead of return-ing to the yard work, Julita gave him a tour of the second floor, and they ended up spending the better part of an hour in Liz's room. There was a photograph of Liz and her father taken during their trip to Argentina that caught Secord's eye. He said that Rick looked different without his beard. "He started growing the beard when Liz went missing," she said. Secord raised his eyebrows and nodded. What did that mean? he thought to himself. Was she trying to tell him something?

Secord looked at the small wastebasket on the floor beside Liz's desk and noticed that there were some items at the bottom of it. He asked Julita if he could dump them out. She said it had been empty the last time she'd checked, but go ahead and dump it, so he picked up the container and turned it upside down over Liz's bed. Out came three items: Liz's social insurance card, her Scarborough Centenary Hospital card and her immunization record. "How did these end up in here?" Secord asked. Julita said she had no idea—she cleaned out all the wastebaskets every week, including that one. He asked her if she had any plastic bags he could put them in—he didn't want to touch them in case they were important somehow.

While Julita went to get some Baggies, Secord opened the doors to Liz's closet and took a quick peek. Before long, he was standing right inside the closet, his face brushing against her soft shirt sleeves, turning himself in a slow circle among Liz's clothing, opening his eyes as he faced her room through the closet door. And almost because he knew something would be there, he looked up. Sure enough, two pieces of paper had been tacked a few inches apart on the wall above the door. One was a drawing of a man and a much shorter, younger woman standing in a few feet of water next to an island (Liz and her father?). The other was a poem written in green calligraphic letters on half a page of lined paper:

THE SEA OF LOVE

Love is like the sea
that sustains those
who want it.
It's tender, delicate
and always generous.
It quenches the thirsty
and bathes those
with yesterday's dirt.
The heart that has no reason

but always giving
and never receiving.

The waves are soothing
Like tender words.
It senses your presence
and all your thoughts
It relaxes & alleviates you
Listens and accepts you
and without repayment
it sends you off enriched
and if ever in your life
you need it again
it's there. Just the same

Secord reached up and carefully removed both the drawing and the poem from the wall. Jesus, he thought, how could the police miss this stuff? Just then, Julita returned with some bags and he showed her what he'd found in the closet. He placed everything in separate bags and told her that it might be best if he took them home for safekeeping. Things seem to end up in the garbage around here, he said. Julita didn't seem to mind him taking them, so that's exactly what he did.

—◯—

The way things were going, Secord thought it would be a good idea to keep detailed notes, which he would file in yellow folders. He had one called History of Bain Family, one for the mileage tests he'd done on Liz's Tercel, and another that contained a copy of Environment Canada's Monthly Meteorological Summary for the city of Toronto during the month of June 1990. There were dozens of these yellow file folders in his big leather briefcase: Cards in Garbage, Elizabeth Bain—Psychological Profile, Possibilities & Questions, Plastic Fingers, General Reference, Rob Baltovich, Blood in Car, Motels. One contained nothing but in-depth accounts of his dreams, which he would climb out of bed to make sense of at all hours of the night.

On November 4, he wrote: *I talked to Paul and Lita for 2 hours after my drive. I gave Lita some flowers for her table. I made notes about June 17-20 and then I drove her to a church at Ellesmere & Markham Road. Paul will pick her up later. She asked me if I had any idea yet as to where her daughter is. I said I had a much better idea of what could have happened than about where she is.*

A week later Secord drew a diagram that contained the precise measurements of the two massive dents he'd noticed on the oil pan guard of Liz's Tercel when he inspected the underbelly for clues. Three days after that he chartered a flight with a company called Skycraft in Oshawa. A pilot named Steve flew them over the nuclear energy plant in Pickering in his two-seater, and Secord realized that there were all kinds of ponds visible from the sky that would be hard to locate driving around in his truck.

Nov. 14/90

Real early. 12-2 AM. I did some excavating in the dark. Home to bed. Tired!

After I finished Ed's concrete, I dropped in at the Bains. Rick was home but had taken a taxi because he was too sick to drive. Bad headache, dizzy and sick to his stomach. He was sitting in the den by the table with the phone. He said he liked the work bench I brought him. Then he went to bed. Lita & I talked for at least two and a half hours. Paul joined in a few times. Lita made me some supper. I had whitefish, rice & squash & some tea. It was good! We discussed some scenarios & facts & possibilities & shared some feelings about what was happening & how people deal with this kind of situation.

Lita had been at Ganaraska all day with some friends searching. She said she felt as if she had wasted the day.

———◯———

As winter approached, marking the second full season to pass since Liz's disappearance, the atmosphere in the Team Room was becoming progressively more anxious and grim. For the most part, the wire-taps had been a bust. Over two hundred "relevant" conversations involving Rob, his family and a vast array of friends had been recorded, transcribed and proofed during the last four months. The much-anticipated confession—or even something one might refer to as "condemning"—didn't appear to be forthcoming. The tapes contained little more than months and months' worth of speculation by Rob and everyone around him. Liz's disappearance had been interpreted by some as an intentional attempt to frame Rob, by others as a suicide and there were a few who saw it as a cold-blooded murder committed by someone Liz (and quite possibly Rob) knew. And of course, the police had picked up endless bantering about the investigation: *What do they want with a pair of multi-coloured shorts? Why on earth do they think I would want to hurt Liz if she wanted to break up with me?* While the guys in the Team Room saw this as one long, masterful act played out for their benefit by a family of conniving crazies, in reality the Baltoviches were as desperate for answers as the police were.

Since early September, when Ruth Collins had been unable to identify the man behind the wheel of Liz's Tercel during her hypnosis session with Dr. Matheson, the investigation had pretty much hit a wall. If Collins had been able to identify the driver as Baltovich, that probably would have been it. As it stood, Marianne Perz remained the only witness connecting Baltovich to Bain on June 19, and even then, she hadn't been able to swear he was the one she'd seen at the picnic table.

While the Homicide detectives had also assembled a supporting cast of witnesses to suggest that Baltovich and Bain had fought in the days leading up to her disappearance, there were at least half a dozen people who pointed to an entirely different set of possibilities. For example, there was still no explanation for the older woman Lou Torrone had seen in Liz's car that Tuesday. Nor was there any way to explain David Singh, if you believed him at all—because the police sure didn't. Singh, a Scarborough dental assistant who knew Elizabeth Bain from high school and later Scarborough College, claimed to have seen her the day after she'd disappeared (he'd ruled out June 19 after consulting his employment records). She'd been standing by a mailbox in front of the Guardian Drug Store on the north-east corner of the intersection at which Morrish Road connected with Old Kingston Road as it rose out of the valley. Singh had been driving by in his car when Liz caught his eye as she gestured to a tall white man standing a few feet away, as though offering him directions. Although he hadn't noticed anything out of the ordinary about her mood and was unable to recall what she'd been wearing, there was no doubt in his mind that it had been her.

A woman named Tasmin Sheikh, who was acquainted with Liz from her days at Cardinal Newman High School as well as St. Joseph's Church, told the police that she had seen her one Tuesday evening in the weeks prior to her disappearance. Sheikh saw her sitting in the passenger seat of a red Jeep parked in front of a plaza close to the Scarborough campus. She didn't get a good look at the driver but saw that he was in his early twenties with collar-length blond hair sticking out from under a baseball hat. He was yelling while Liz pouted, with her arms folded across her chest, as though they were in the middle of an argument.

Even more troubling to the Team Room detectives was that Sheikh wasn't the only person who had seen Liz with a similar unidentified blond man. George Chau told the police that late one afternoon in May 1990, he'd seen Liz Bain walk into his Chinese restaurant in Scarborough, the Silver Dragon, where she and Rob were fairly regular take-out customers. She'd been accompanied that day by a young man whom Chau described as being in his early twenties, with sandy blond hair, a fair complexion and a slim build. It was definitely not Rob. Chau asked him if he was being looked after, and he nodded at Liz and said, "I'm with her." The Team Room staff had yet to determine who this might have been.

Similarly, on July 3, the police received a call from a woman who identified herself as Julie Smith. Apparently a student at the Scarborough campus, Smith said she'd seen Liz on June 19 between 5:25 and 6:35 PM walking out of the library with a young man, approximately twenty-four years of age with sandy brown hair, a dark complexion and white shorts. Smith, who was speaking in rushed phrases, said the couple had been strolling towards a set of stairs near the campus pub. When the officer taking the call asked for her address, Smith panicked and hung up the phone. Fortunately, the officer had taken down the phone number Smith had given her earlier, which had a Bowmanville exchange from far out in the Oshawa area. When the police called the number back, they got Bowmanville all right, but Wallace Auto Supply, not Julie Smith. Subsequent checks of the University of Toronto records, as well as the Ministry of Transportation, came up empty and the entire Julie Smith episode was thrown on the back burner.

Being the good friend of a staff inspector with Metro's Internal Affairs Unit, Bert Dawson was far more cooperative. Dawson told investigators that, at about four o'clock one afternoon close to June 19, he'd been driving his Bell Canada telephone truck on Morningside Avenue, just around the corner from Scarborough College, when traffic came to an abrupt stop and he had to slam on the brakes. What he'd found strange was that the couple in the reddish two-door sports car in front of him hadn't turned around to glance at the source of the squealing tires, which was in Dawson's experience the natural reaction. The driver was a strikingly attractive young man in his early to mid twenties, with short blond hair. But what really stood out in Dawson's mind was that the driver had his arm around the young woman as though he'd been holding her upright in her seat. The dark-haired beauty could answer the description of Elizabeth Bain.

And, as recently as November 1, Detective Jake Poranganel interviewed a Scarborough woman named Marie Irene Decosimo, who seemed quite certain that she'd seen someone very similar to Elizabeth Bain walking with a man in Colonel Danforth Park, early in the afternoon of Monday, June 18. The man, described as five feet eight inches and 160 pounds, had salt-and-pepper hair. Decosimo hadn't got a good look at his face and, therefore, wasn't sure about his age, but he'd been wearing tan pants and a light-coloured shirt. If Decosimo had seen Bain, there was a chance she could resolve the mystery of who had given Liz the red rose her sister Cathy had seen her clutching to her chest later that night. Either way, no one would ever know. Reesor and Raybould deemed her unworthy of hypnosis, or even a follow-up interview.

Instead, the lead detectives held a Team Room meeting not long after the Decosimo interview. With winter about to put a serious damper on the Bain family's search efforts, their only hope for a forensic breakthrough—the discovery of Liz's body—was looking bleak. The investigation was on the verge of its five-month mark and new leads on Baltovich had all but dried up, so everyone agreed that the only thing left for them to do was check out some old ones.

Thus, on Thursday, November 15, Detective Brody Smollet, the man with whom Andrea Beitinger refused to have contact after he'd "broken" her, was alone in a cruiser, driving north to the Maple Stamping Plant for an impromptu interview with David Dibben, the previously disregarded Lake Scugog witness. After conferring with Dibben's employers, Smollet met with him in a vacant office, where he took a formal statement in writing and had Dibben read it over and initial each page. Although Smollet didn't realize it right away, there were a number of glaring differences between the statement Dibben gave that day and what he'd told the police four and a half months earlier. On July 1, Dibben had said he'd seen Bain's car at 6:30 AM, waiting for a traffic light to turn green at an intersection near the somnolent blip known as Manchester. Now he was saying this had happened at

6:00 AM or as much as ten minutes before that. He'd also told the police in early summer that the car's lone male occupant was twenty-four to twenty-five years of age, with blond semi-receding hair and a blond moustache, wearing a white fluorescent T-shirt. With Smollet, the driver was twenty-four to twenty-eight, with "dirty blond" hair, wearing a grey T-shirt with something colourful on the front.

Once the statement was completed, Smollet presented Dibben with the same twelve-man photographic line-up that Tony Warr had placed in front of Marianne Perz months ago. Dibben looked at it for about a minute, maybe a little more, before picking out number six, Robert Baltovich. Admittedly, number six's dark hair didn't look much like the blond, or even the dirty-blond-haired man he'd just described, yet there was something about the eyes (the precise remark Perz had made to Dr. Matheson) that had him quite convinced this was the driver of the silver Tercel with the pink plastic fingers.

Smollet couldn't get back to 42 Division fast enough. And when he delivered the news, there was a collective sense of relief, followed by congratulations and back-slaps all around. With Dibben, they had two less-than-ideal eyewitnesses to prop up their circumstantial case. But two identification witnesses, no matter how shaky, were better than one. Reesor concluded that it was time to move forward with the first-degree murder charge. No one stopped to ponder how Dibben could fairly reconcile Baltovich's dark hair with "dirty blond." No one gave much consideration to the fact that Tasmin Sheikh and George Chau (and possibly others) had seen Elizabeth Bain in the company of a mysterious young blond man they had yet to identify. No one seriously contemplated taking David Dibben to Dr. Matheson's office for hypnosis, just to make sure it really was Baltovich he'd seen behind the wheel. Why would they want to do that when he'd already picked their suspect out of the line-up? Why risk having Dibben tell the doctor on videotape that he was wrong—that he hadn't seen number six? What was to be gained from that?

Reesor decided they would wait four days before making the arrest. The temptation to have this dramatic announcement occur in conjunction with the five-month anniversary of lovely young Elizabeth's tragic exit from this unforgiving world—November 19—outweighed their concerns that this potential "serial killer" might strike again in the meantime. And then it was suggested that someone get on the horn to Mr. Bain and inform him of this blessed turn of events.

—◯—

PLEA TO A KILLER

November 16, 1990—The father of a murdered Scarborough woman has appealed to the murderer he "trusted" to help police find the body.

Rick Bain said he knows who killed his daughter but so far the person has acted "like a robot" and covered his tracks well.

He said the man has lied to the police, withheld evidence and ignored public appeals by the family to anonymously report the location of the body.

Bain said he's frustrated because the killer knows where she is and won't even make an anonymous call to the Crime Stoppers number.

"Today would be appropriate to ask him to use the last vestige of humanity left in him and let us know where she's been left," Bain said.

"He knows that I know who he is and he knows that all he has to do is call [Crime Stoppers]. Is that too much to ask?"

Bain said the killer "forfeited any trust we put in him.

"I'm in turn tempted by the desire to give him the same treatment he's given my daughter," Bain said. "But I'm tempered with the thought—if only he would tell me where my daughter has been put to rest."

Homicide officers have received a psychological profile of the killer from an FBI expert but have not released the details.

THE TORONTO SUN

Rob, Neil and Tony were talking about the *Toronto Sun* article on the way to the movies that night. "The killer he trusted," said Rob, in a deep, news anchor voice. "Oh, yes, we know who he is but he's acting like a robot blah blah blah." Mr. Bain had finally gone too far. Rob said that, after the weekend, it was his intention to contact a lawyer and look into filing a lawsuit. Tony wasn't quite so civil about the whole thing. Said he'd like to have a crack at Mr. Bain—that's how pissed off he was.

The next morning Rob drove up to Barrie for the weekend with Al Heys, and he didn't get home until Sunday evening. The moment he walked into the kitchen, Adele told him that Steve Reesor had called while he was gone. "What did he have to say?" Rob asked.

"He said, 'We have a witness!' He said it really quickly, like he was saying 'Happy Birthday!' "

"Is that all he said?"

"When he said that, I said, 'That's fine. If you have a witness, then call the lawyer.' And then I hung up."

—◯—

Having just turned off his alarm clock, Rob was in that fugue state between sleep and wakefulness, still warm under the covers, conscious only of the fact that he had to get up for work. As this flickering reality was slowly dragging him into the waiting day, he heard a car door being shut just outside his window. It was a few minutes after seven and he had no idea who could be pulling up at that time of the morning. He slid out from beneath the covers and stood up on the bed, pushing aside the dusty, rust-orange curtains covering his small ground-level window. All he could see was a plain blue sedan parked on the street just past his driveway. Whoever had left it there was now out of his line of vision.

And then, with his face still pressed against the window, he heard someone knocking on the front door upstairs. This was followed by the sound of his mother, asleep in her usual spot on the daybed in the living room, shuffling across the kitchen and down the stairs to the front landing. Rob, who was now lying down again, wondering who could be at the front door, heard her say, "He's downstairs." And then there were muffled voices. "Hold on, please," Adele said. "I'm not dressed." Seconds later, heavy footsteps thundered down the stairs into the basement.

Rob was sitting up now, his eyes glued to the doorway, where, in the grainy light of a basement room at dawn, the unmistakable, bulky silhouette of Steve Reesor appeared in its frame. The first thing that shot through Rob's mind was that the police wanted to search the house again. So he just looked at Reesor and said, "Yes?"

"Robert Baltovich," said Reesor, "you're under arrest for the first-degree murder of Elizabeth Bain."

There was a momentary pause as the words continued to permeate the silence. Rob offered another one-word query: "Why?"

Reesor said, "Because you did it." Rob just shook his foggy head. "You are allowed one phone call," Reesor added. "I gather you'll want to call your lawyer."

"Yeah," Rob said. "You want to give me a couple minutes to get dressed?"

By the time he'd put some clothes on and gone upstairs, his father had heard the commotion and come down to the kitchen, where he and Adele were anxiously pacing around in their dressing gowns. "I don't understand this," said Jim. "There's no evidence. *No evidence.*"

"Mr. Baltovich," said Reesor, "you have no idea what evidence we have."

Rob was at the phone with Bill Gatward's business card in his hand, dialling the home number that Gatward had written in pen on the back. When Rob got him on the line, Gatward said, "Rob, what's going on?" His tone was one of joviality rather than concern.

Rob said, "They're here."

"Who's there?"

"Reesor and Raybould."

Gatward said, "You'll have to let them look around. What can you do?"

"No, they're not outside, *they're here.* I'm under arrest!"

"Okay," said Gatward. He told Rob not to say anything and that he'd see him in a couple of hours. They'd get everything straightened out. Gatward spoke with great authority—to Rob, it was like the voice of God.

Rob hung up the phone and grabbed the overcoat Mr. and Mrs. Bain had given him for Christmas. Putting his arms through the sleeves, he told his mother to call Mediastats and tell them that he wouldn't be coming in. Seeing tears on his mother's cheeks as Reesor secured the handcuffs around his wrists, Rob said, "Don't worry, Mom. Everything will be okay."

Reesor and Raybould led him out onto the front steps, where he could see two detectives at the back of his car, one of them actually sitting on the edge of his open trunk, gathering what looked to be several feet of thin wire and other items that were definitely foreign to him. He was still too stunned to recognize that they were removing a listening device from his car—that understanding would come to him a few days later.

Once again riding alone in the back seat of a cruiser with Reesor and Raybould up front, he felt deep within him, believe it or not, a faint sense of relief beginning to rise like a small bubble in a great lake of fear. And this came from the realization that, finally, all of this would be resolved and he wouldn't have to deal with these two sorely misguided individuals for the rest of his life. The one and only thing he knew for sure as they travelled up Midland Avenue was that come hell or high water, he was not saying one single word to these guys.

So they drove in silence to 41 Division at Birchmount and Eglinton—where they'd taken him to provide forensic samples after their interrogation in June—and pulled into its immense parking lot, which at this early hour of the morning was practically empty. Close to the station, about fifty metres away, he could see a gaggle of people huddled together like sheep. And then, as though someone had fired off a starter's pistol, the entire pack of them, all cameramen and photographers, came sprinting towards the cruiser. "Oh, boy," said Raybould. "Here come the vultures." Raybould's distaste was somewhat at odds with the fact that it was 7:30 AM and there was no way the media could have known about Robert Baltovich's early-morning arrest unless the police had tipped them off in advance. Any cameraman in the city worth his salt knew how to find out (if they hadn't already been told) when and where events such as this were going to occur.

They were buzzing around the car, flashbulbs sparkling from all angles, like a swarm of fireflies at dawn. Rob decided that he wasn't going to hide, just keep looking straight ahead with an expressionless face, trying to maintain whatever dignity he could muster considering that he was handcuffed in the back of a police cruiser, charged with murder, being photographed from just about every conceivable angle. And then they came to a full stop as Raybould waited for the painfully arthritic garage door to open, allowing everyone to get plenty of good footage for the evening news, or maybe a photograph worthy of the front page.

Inside the station, he was fingerprinted and then left alone, seated in a small room. The door had been left open a crack and at one point Jake Poranganel walked by in the hallway and looked right into Rob's eyes but didn't say anything, as Rob expected he would. No different than if Poranganel had been glancing at the guy who cleans out the wastepaper baskets. Very weird.

A few minutes later, Reesor came to pick him up and announced that they were on their way to the Scarborough courthouse for his arraignment. Reesor led Rob out to the foyer, where they waited for Raybould, who was supposed to be meeting them. But Raybould was nowhere in sight and, with each passing minute, Reesor became increasingly agitated, so that when his partner did finally show up, he really let him have it. "Where the fuck were you?" Reesor said. "Let's go! We're in a hurry! C'mon, we can't fool around here." He was chastising Raybould as though he were late for the school bus. Raybould, rebuked, said, "I'm sorry. I'm coming, I'm coming." Rob was about to say, "He likes to bully you too, eh?" but he decided it wasn't worth breaking his vow of silence.

During the ride to court, Reesor made one final pitch. "Well, Rob," he began, "at this point I should inform you that we have a witness." Rob had already heard this much from his mother. "And this person saw you driving Elizabeth's car in the Lake Scugog area."

Lake Scugog? he thought. What the hell is he talking about?

Reesor continued, "I guess I'm going to appeal to whatever self-respect you have left, and ask you to tell us where Elizabeth's body is, so that her family can have the dignity of a Christian burial."

Rob, steadfastly observing his private pact, remained silent, his gaze frozen on the grey industrial streets in the belly of Scarborough.

"Rob, I'm going to give you some free advice," said Reesor, as the car pulled into the bay of the courthouse garage. "You might want to request that you be placed in protective custody. If you don't, the odds are pretty good that you'll get beat up." Rob just kept staring quietly ahead, noticing the large, rippled shape of Reesor's cranium.

—◯—

Rob was in the prisoner's dock, still handcuffed, a few minutes before noon. The arraignment was over in a flash—no one even mentioned what the charges were. No one mentioned Elizabeth Bain. And then they were off to the Metro East Detention Centre, an enormous characterless brick structure (it could well have been another factory or warehouse) situated about three major streets north-west of the Baltovich house on Midland Avenue. At first, Rob recognized it only as the place he'd been taken during the parallel parking segment of his driving test when he was twenty. He hadn't known then—nor did he now—that there was a massive jail smack-dab in the middle of town.

Once inside the building, they went immediately into the basement, and Rob was placed in a small holding cell by himself. Dingy blue cinder-block walls and a cold, dirty white floor replete with urine stains and shoe scuffs. He sat down on a small wooden bench and waited. He had no idea what time it was. Just felt dazed.

Eventually, there was the clicking sound of a key unlocking the door of his cell. "Baltovich," said the guard. "It's time for your photo shoot." So they walked through some corridors to yet another room, where he was directed to sit on yet another wooden bench. Three white-shirted guards were giving him puzzled looks from the other side of the room. "Why did they arrest you?" asked the one working the camera. He sounded sincere. Rob shrugged his shoulders and answered, "I have no idea."

"Let me give you a piece of advice," said the one in the corner. "You know a guy named Babinski?" Raymond Babinski was on trial for the first-degree murder of a woman named Eva Mead, who had disappeared three days after Babinski broke into her apartment to speak with her.

He was already serving a three-year sentence for the break-in and, at the murder trial, a jailhouse informant testified that Babinski had boasted to him about having committed "the perfect crime." "Don't worry," the informant also recalled him saying. "They'll never find her." But, eventually, she was located—bound and strangled to death.

Rob said he'd never heard of Babinski. So the guard said, "Keep your mouth shut." Rob wasn't sure if he meant don't talk to *anyone* or just not to talk about his case. Whatever it was, he didn't bother to ask for clarification.

After the mug shots had been taken, he was told to take his clothes off behind a small barrier not far from the camera. There he was strip-searched and commanded to fold his street clothes into a neat stack, which he handed to the guard in exchange for his institutional clothing—an ugly light blue shirt, a pair of dark blue pants, a cheap pair of socks, an incredibly cheap pair of running shoes, with a toothbrush and small tube of toothpaste resting on top. Sporting his new outfit, he was fingerprinted again and then led back to the dirty little holding cell with the wooden bench.

Maybe half an hour later, another guard came and led him up one flight of stairs after another and through countless heavy metal doors until they arrived at a wide-open range of cells. (It was a while before Rob learned he was being housed in a "Super" Protective Custody range reserved primarily for informers and sexual offenders.) Walking along, Rob was unable to stop everything around him from swirling like a mirage. It was all he could do to keep his eyes focused on the smooth cement floor in front of him. "Okay, Baltovich," came the voice of the guard. "Here's your cell."

The door was open. The cell was about twelve feet by six feet with a single bed against one wall and a thin, stained mattress on the floor against the other. There was a short, older guy with a beard already sitting on the bed, so Rob lay down on the mattress. The guard shut the door, which was wood this time instead of bars, and the little guy on the bed said his name was Gord. Rob introduced himself in turn, and Gord quickly picked up on his young new cellmate's extreme exhaustion, which he knew might also be the result of some kind of shock. So Gord didn't say another word, just let the kid put his head down on his pillow and sleep.

When Rob woke up, Gord was sitting cross-legged on the table against the back of the cell staring out the lone, face-sized window. He continued to sit there, absolutely motionless and silent, for at least an hour, maybe longer. And even then, when he did move, it was only because dinner arrived through a slot in the middle of the door. Talking in between mouthfuls of soupy mashed potatoes, Gord revealed that he was a Wiccan by faith (and therefore believed himself to be a witch) and was most distressed, it seemed, not by his incarceration—he never did reveal why he was there—but by the fact that the institution would not allow him to practise his religion. Apparently, the Wiccan high priest had been denied entry by the warden. Gord hadn't given up hope entirely, though. He'd filed a formal request that he be allowed access to his full Wicca regalia so that he could perform a proper Wicca ceremony some time soon. Gord also said he was writing a textbook on Greek mythology but didn't seem to have anything to write with, so he just sat on the table well into the night, lost in some mysterious Wiccan trance, staring out the tiny window at the institution parking lot below.

The next morning Rob was moved out of the cell with Gord, and into an empty cell three doors down. But now that he was, quite happily, on his own, a new phenomenon began to develop that was considerably more disquieting than being confined with Gord. Throughout the day, groups of two or three guards would congregate outside his cell, cramming their faces together to peer in through the square of Plexiglas three-quarters of the way up his cell door. "Is that him?" one would ask.

"Yep." Like they were sizing up some new panda at the zoo.

What Rob didn't yet know was that his picture—taken during the prolonged photo opportunity more than twenty-four hours earlier as the cruiser idled in front of the garage at 41 Division—had been plastered on the front pages of both *The Toronto Star* and *The Toronto Sun* ("BOYFRIEND CHARGED IN BAIN MURDER"). In a place like Metro East, he had unknowingly entered the realm of celebrity without knowing it. The guards, along with a good portion of the entire city, had already read or heard Reesor's solemn declaration to the press—that the investigation had been "tough," dropping suggestive tidbits of information along the way about DNA and forensic tests. ("Arrest follows new test results," was the sub-headline on the cover of the *Sun*. The story inside reported that "Baltovich was arrested about a week after the detectives received the results of DNA testing on blood found in Bain's Toyota Tercel," which implied that the blood was Baltovich's. In truth, the blood was determined to have come from a female offspring of Rick and Julita Bain.) When asked about their previously disclosed "psychological profile" from an expert with the FBI, the police said they were unable to release any details (most likely, as later became clear, because it did not exist). But investigators did reveal that they were still looking for witnesses, including a cab driver named Spinner.

Julita Bain admitted to the press that, when told of the arrest, the first thing that had entered her mind was the fact that it was exactly five months ago that her daughter had disappeared. "I kept thinking to myself this is so coincidental," she said. One reporter asked her if she felt happy about the arrest. "'Happy' isn't a word I would use. There's nothing happy about a murder." Equally dour, Mr. Bain declared that he would not be going to court to see Baltovich. "I don't want to sit there and stare into his face." Both parents promised not to rest until they found their daughter's body.

By the afternoon, Rob was so used to the pitter-patter of ogling guards that he didn't even bother looking up at the window on his door when he heard another set of approaching shoes clicking sharply on the concrete floor. But this time, there was a light knocking on the door and the sound of an older woman's voice. "Would you like some books?" He jumped to his feet and went straight for the door. "Books?" he said. "We're allowed to have books?" At the woman's side was an entire cart full of paperbacks and assorted magazines. "Sure," she said. Rob selected a few science periodicals, as well as *A Prayer for Owen Meany* by John Irving. He was into the thick Irving novel in no time, thoroughly enjoying the opportunity to read, but thought the story was a bit of a rip-off of Robertson Davies's *Fifth Business*.

The next thing offered to him was the use of a phone. Books and the telephone. Rob had no idea that people behind bars were allowed such amenities. The guard handed him the phone, which Rob plugged into the jack in his cell. He called Bill Gatward to find out when he could get out. Gatward said the bail hearing was scheduled for Friday but the Crown attorneys had the option of carrying it over to Monday. Rob hung up thinking that bail was inevitable. After all, they had no evidence. He started rehearsing what he was going to say to the press after being released, proclaiming his innocence loud and clear from the courthouse steps.

On Thursday, the walls started closing in on him. He didn't know what he was going to do if he didn't get home before the weekend. Panic attacks came in waves. He was really flipping out. A couple of times his lungs just wouldn't open themselves for air. He began screaming at himself, WHOA!, get hold of yourself, it's going to be over soon. Bail tomorrow. He called his buddy Phil Dach when he got the telephone, and Phil told him to stay strong—everything was going to work out.

That afternoon, a guard opened the door and said that he had a visitor. He hadn't a notion of who it might be but he followed the guard down into a long room divided by stations with glass partitions, just like in the movies, and sat down in the appointed chair. A few seconds later, in walked Kara McCartney through the door on the other side of the room. What a surprise! Kara was a good friend, but he wouldn't have guessed in a million years that she would be the first person to come and see him. She looked beautiful, smiling as though she'd just whacked a cheeky forehand winner down the line during one of their casual games of tennis. He was flattered and thankful to the point that he just wanted to break into tears, but he didn't.

As they talked, they tried to figure out exactly why he'd been arrested so long after the fact, and Rob recounted what Reesor had said about the witness up in Lake Scugog. "Give me a break," said Kara. "This guy doesn't even know you, so how in the world can he say he saw you, especially after so many months?" Kara mentioned how the Babinski guy she'd been reading about in the papers had been acquitted the same day Rob had been arrested, this despite the fact that Babinski had broken into the dead woman's apartment days earlier, that her decomposed body had been found in a farmer's field near the furniture factory where Babinski worked six months after her disappearance, her limbs bound with a unique type of wire that couldn't be bought in Canada, but was used in one of the machines at Babisnki's workplace. If Babinski could get off facing that kind of evidence, Kara was saying, Rob wouldn't have any problems.

Later that day, Rob got his second visitor, which turned out to be an even bigger shock than the first. It was Dana's father, Bill Rowe. As a retired Pentecostal minister, Rowe had been able to procure a "chaplaincy visit" with Rob in an open room, without the glass barrier. "So, Rob, what do you think about all of this?" he asked.

Rob said, "I'm just looking forward to the bail hearing and getting out of here."

"Rob, I think you should understand that you probably won't get bail." He watched Rob's face turn the colour of his wife's pie-crust.

"Why? Why?"

"They don't usually give bail on a charge of first-degree murder."

"Yeah, but I didn't do this!"

"I understand that, but it's a serious charge."

Rowe had really rained on Rob's parade. He asked for the phone as soon as he got back to his cell so he could call his mother. What's this about no bail, he wanted to know. Adele said she'd spoken to Bill Gatward and that he was very confident about getting bail. "Don't you worry, he's going to look after things," Adele said. He said good-bye and sat cradling the phone in his lap, struck by the role reversal that had just transpired, his mother now taking over as the pillar of strength as he slid into a pit of helpless vulnerability.

The next morning, a guard rapped on his door at 5:30 and said it was time to get up for court. Rob decided to forgo the Styrofoam bowl of soggy Corn Flakes the guard had placed on the edge of his slot and went straight down to Admissions & Discharge, where he was handed a suit that his parents had, a few days earlier, delivered for him to wear to court. The suit was noticeably wrinkled, but the pressed shirt felt nice and smooth against his shoulder blades, then he knotted his favourite tie. The guards working Admissions & Discharge gave him a series of does-that-guy-ever-look-respectable looks (several inmates later inquired if he was a lawyer) on the way to his own waiting cell, where he sat for more than three hours, staring at the walls.

Having always been susceptible to car sickness, he was on the verge of throwing up by the time the paddy wagon got all the way downtown to the courthouse on University Avenue. Two guards escorted him upstairs to the bail hearing. With his hands still cuffed behind his back and marched into a cathedral-sized courtroom through a side door, Rob was startled to be facing a gallery that was absolutely packed. He estimated three-quarters of the people were friends and family there to support him. But he did catch a quick glimpse of a small contingent surrounding the Bains, including Mr. Bain (who had obviously changed his mind about attending since speaking to reporters a week ago). Bill Gatward, who was wearing a black gown, smiled at him from behind a long table on the way in.

No sooner were his wrists freed by the court officer than the Crown prosecutor, Mary Hall, walked into the room and requested that the entire proceeding be delayed until Monday. Without reservation, the judge conceded. Next matter on the docket, please, he said. The entire ordeal had been for nothing.

Rob didn't know how he was going to survive the weekend. He shrugged his shoulders and turned to his parents and mouthed an "Oh, well," trying not to look as crushed as he truly felt.

—◦—

Sitting behind the wheel of his pick-up truck, John Secord wrote out the day's events while they were still fresh in his mind:

Saturday, November 24

> *Flurries & cold & cloudy.*
>
> *I went to Uxbridge fire hall for the search. Rick & Lita wanted me to look with them but I declined & told them I must keep working independently.*
>
> *So I went to Jim Baltovich's store and bought an ice tea & a bag of peanuts & then I introduced myself & asked him if he was Mr. Baltovich. He said yes & I voiced my condolences about Rob.*
>
> *He looked me square in the eyes & he told me that he knows his son is innocent & that Rob has an alibi for every minute of June 19th—all day and all night. He told me that his son is being framed. I asked by who & he said, "By the police . . . " Oh, and by Liz's father. "Did you hear the things he said last week on the news?" I said that I had.*

I told him that I have my own idea of what happened & that it does not include his son but that I was hoping Rob could possibly shed some light on events for me. He said that, considering the way the police feel, neither he nor his son could talk to me because they cannot see why I would be so interested. But, if I could somehow help to prove Rob's innocence, he (Jim) would be the happiest man on earth. (He really looked excited.)

Jim told me that their lawyer's name is William Gatward. I asked him why he felt his son had stopped searching after five days. He just said to talk to the lawyer, if possible. I said okay & good-bye for now Jim, see you later & I left.

He had a very steady flow of customers and about 90% of them knew him by name. They all seemed to care about him very much. He appears to be a very clean, honest, quiet man.

Monday began as a replay of Friday. Up at 5:30 AM and then, wearing the same suit, Rob waited for hours to be taken downtown in the paddy wagon. In the courtroom, Rob noticed that his platoon of supporters had dwindled noticeably—it was hard for most people to get two days in a row off work, he assumed.

Right away, Mary Hall called Brian Raybould to the witness stand and pronounced her intention to lead him through the twenty-five-page synopsis of the case he and his partner, Detective Sergeant Reesor, had prepared over the weekend. Raybould told the judge how intensive their investigation had been, that seventy-five witnesses had been interviewed, that 120 days' worth of judicially authorized interceptions of private communications had been monitored, and, of course, there were the searches. He then gave a cursory outline of Elizabeth Bain's disappearance before reading the text of their case, an admittedly circumstantial one, against Robert Baltovich.

Raybould's synopsis of the "evidence" was recounted in no particular order, but could be broken down into three distinct categories: incriminating behaviour, opportunity to commit the crime and motive. By far, most of the items belonged in the first grouping, beginning with the assertions made by both Nancy Sicchia and Steve Annett, that in the frantic days following the disappearance, Rob had claimed he'd seen Liz ducking behind her car in the valley on June 19. Raybould also referred to the shorts Marc Singleton thought Rob had been wearing on his way into the Recreation Centre and connected this to the fact that Rob hadn't been able to remember what he'd worn that night during his initial interviews with the police. The most convincing evidence of out-and-out deception was the part of Rob's narrative in which he'd declared to have tried calling Liz at home before 11:00 PM, only to get a busy signal. This was "not possible," according to Raybould, because the Bains' phone line had the call-waiting service.

As Rob listened to all of this, rapt with attention, he shuddered at each of these false statements, which, to Rob, amounted to lies, delivered with the authority of a police officer. What Rob and his lawyer didn't know was that Eric Genuis and Mr. Bain, both of whom had already been interviewed at length by the police, would subsequently confirm that the Bains' phone line had been dead that evening, which explained how Genuis, like Rob, had also heard a busy signal.

Raybould also portrayed Rob as having tried to influence witnesses to stay silent or alter their statements to investigators. For example, Rob had told Kris Kangas, who thought she might have seen Liz coming out of the library on Tuesday in a purple T-shirt, to keep the disappearance quiet because her parents didn't want people to know. While talking to Kaedmon Nancoo in the weight room with Rick Gostick, Rob had suggested Nancoo not say anything to the police about what day he'd seen him in the gym if he wasn't sure. And then there was a tape-recorded telephone conversation between Rob and Tony Fuchs in mid-August, during which they had discussed the old diary entry of Liz's that Al Heys had referred to as a Dear John letter to the police. Towards the end of their discussion, Rob told Tony that he didn't want to delve into the incident any further because it might come across as rehearsed when Tony was eventually questioned.

Every suspicious comment Rob had made to the police—from "I hope this will prove it wasn't me who touched the gearshift" to Liz's car having been left in "reverse gear"—was chronicled. Raybould revealed that the polygraph interview had been secretly taped (the amount of surreptitious taping that had gone on left Rob completely stupefied) and, thus, the Crown possessed video of the accused admitting he had thought of killing Liz in 1987 when she had rejected him. For a few seconds, Rob couldn't remember saying any such thing, but eventually it came to him: *I did say something stupid like that, didn't I.*

While Raybould conceded that Adele Baltovich had adamantly stated her son had not left the house that Tuesday until about 6:30 PM, Raybould told the court that Kaedmon Nancoo would testify to seeing Baltovich in the Recreation Centre at 5:20. Which made it possible for Marianne Perz to have seen Elizabeth Bain (and possibly, subsequent to hypnosis, Robert Baltovich as well) sitting at a picnic table near the tennis courts at 5:45, although she "did not want to say it was definitely" Baltovich. As a result of profound negligence or something far more insidious, Raybould, under oath, assured Mary Hall that Perz (referred to only as "a witness" in order to keep her identity secret from Baltovich until he'd been denied bail and was safely behind bars, where he would not be a threat to her) was "the last known sighting of Elizabeth Bain, other than that of her murderer." Not once did he refer to what Ruth Collins had seen in front of Three R Auto Body, at a time when Rob was known to be in the campus weight room. Raybould not only failed to mention Collins by name, he never once even alluded to the existence of this crucial piece of the puzzle.

Finally, Raybould got around to the part that Rob was most anxious to hear—the story behind the new witness, David Dibben. Raybould's theory was that Liz's car had been moved late Thursday night—to back this up, they had a witness who hadn't seen the Tercel while walking her dog along that stretch of Morrish Road at 11:30 PM that night and again at 5:30 the next morning—and then parked in its identical spot before the receptionist at Three R Auto Body arrived for work at 8:30 AM. From the amount of gas left in the Tercel, the police had calculated that a return trip to the Lake Scugog area was "well within its range." In addition, Lake Scugog was a "shallow and muddy" lake, ideal for disposing of a body. Raybould pointed out that, several years ago, Baltovich had taken YMCA campers on hiking and biking trips "in the area south and east of Lake Scugog." Again, what he did not bother mentioning was that Rob had been in a police interview on Thursday night from ten until one in the morning, barely able to keep himself awake near the end. This meant that Rob would have had to have moved Liz's car before going to his police interview. Rob thought, to what purpose? Would he really risk driving her car such a long distance when he knew that every police force in the province was on the lookout for it? What if he got stopped? What if he got in an accident? What if someone saw him parking it? Surely, they didn't think he was that stupid.

Lastly, there was motive, the weakest part of the case. Cathy Bain was certain that diary pages had gone missing, and Raybould left little doubt that he was of the belief that substantial sections had been destroyed because they contained evidence of a deteriorating relationship. If so, enough of the diary remained for Raybould to conclude that Rob had "taken to following her, pestering her and harassing her—basically, she couldn't get rid of him." Raybould gave considerable play to Susanne Nadon, bolstering the possibility that Rob and Liz might have been fighting, instead of making love, two nights before the disappearance. With Nadon, the icing on the cake was that she now recalled hearing the male driver grind the gears as he drove away, which, of course, a standard-transmission novice like Baltovich would more than likely do.

When Mary Hall indicated she had completed her questions, Bill Gatward walked over to Rob in the prisoner's box, put his mouth inches from his left ear, and said, "Well, they got fuck-all." He then turned, grabbed his binder of notes and strolled to the lectern to begin his cross-examination. First on Gatward's agenda was to get Raybould to admit the extent to which his client had cooperated with the police and conducted his own searches for his missing girlfriend. Raybould made it clear that he didn't see it that way.

Later, he pressed the detective for the number of sightings of Elizabeth Bain on June 19, with or without her car. Perhaps nervous about the Collins omission, Raybould was reluctant to answer, but Gatward eventually pinned him down. "In the area of five," Raybould said. Then, while discussing the wire taps, Raybould told Gatward that, in his opinion, the Baltovich family was "obsessed with the investigation."

"I suppose this might be understandable," Gatward shot back. "Given that this was the first dealing with the police that any of these people had ever had." Gatward then asked if, by submitting himself for fingerprints, photographs and other forensic samples, his client was not fully cooperating with the police. "Certainly," Raybould answered somewhat smugly. "He is also aware, I'm quite sure, that there is no dead body to compare those samples with."

The judge, Mr. Justice Richard Trainor, jumped into the fray. "Just a moment," he said. "I think, officer, you should refrain from giving your opinion like that and simply answer the question."

"Thank you, my lord," said Raybould sheepishly.

"Considering that my client has been living at the same address in Scarborough since he was born," Gatward said, "and has not made any attempt to depart the country throughout all of this, I take it you are not concerned that he is going to leave town should he be released on bail."

"I don't know what he might do, sir. I have no idea."

With that, Gatward called first Rob and then his mother to the stand, a pre-arranged plan to assure the court that, if granted bail, Rob would continue living at home and resume his job at Mediastats, where he had been informed by his superiors that the position was still his. Adele told the judge that she and her husband were willing to pledge their home, as well as $50,000 in bonds, to free their son on bail pending his trial.

In his submissions, Gatward argued that his client's background, in conjunction with the way he had cooperated with the police investigation, gave the court no cause for concern. As for the charge of first-degree murder, Gatward said he'd seen no evidence of the planning or deliberation that the charge indicated. There was also no forensic evidence linking his client to the missing woman, who, for all he knew, could still be alive. The Crown's assertion that someone had driven Bain's car up to Lake Scugog, only to return it to its precise spot on Morrish Road, reflected "upon a weak Crown case," which Gatward characterized as "comparisons in and out of context between a lengthy statement my client gave to the police, broken up into little pieces, compared with excerpts from telephone conversations and what different witnesses are prepared to say—and that's it."

When Mary Hall took to her feet to deliver the Crown's submissions, Judge Trainor told her to be seated, as he did not need to hear from her. This was bad news. And within seconds he expressed his satisfaction that there was, at that stage, "cogent evidence of identification and motive, the real issues, as I see them, in this charge of first-degree murder.

"There is, in addition, evidence that the accused began an investigation on his own before the disappearance of Miss Bain had been reported. This investigation has resulted in the loss to date of what might have been important evidence. In addition, he has cautioned other potential witnesses to be silent. His own statements given to the police are contradictory, and they are seriously contradicted by other evidence from other witnesses in important areas. It may be inferred from the evidence that he has misled teams involved in the search for this young victim. In the circumstances, it is not in the public interest to release this accused on bail. The application is, therefore, dismissed."

Rob turned to glance at his family's reaction. His brother Paul was shaking his head, saying, "This is crap." A couple of friends were throwing their hands up in the air. He twisted around again and put his head in his hands. "Time to pull yourself together," he said to himself.

———◇———

John Secord finally decided that he was in over his head. His two-month investigation had raised more questions than he could keep track of but no answers. It wasn't that he wanted to give up; in fact, it was just the opposite, especially now that the police had arrested Robert Baltovich—on a charge that, from everything he knew, was seriously doubtful—and he was more determined than ever to solve this perplexing mystery. But he wasn't going to be able to do it all on his own, that was for sure. It was taking him away from his excavating work far too often and he was paying great sums of money out of his own pocket for gas and other expenses, costs that were taking a big chunk out of his savings.

A couple of weeks ago, he'd been talking about all of this with an old friend, Chrissa Hayes, who had suggested that it might be worth his while to contact a private investigator if it was really bugging him that much. Chrissa had worked in the investigative business up until a few years ago, when she'd decided to put up a few thousand for some breast implants and had gone into stripping. She had someone in mind to call if he was interested in going that route. When Secord said that sounded like a great idea, Chrissa said she would contact an old colleague, Nino Calabrese, who, when she finally tracked him down, was now working at an investigative firm called King-Reed & Associates Limited. Chrissa asked Calabrese if he could do a favour for a friend of hers who was involved in the search for Elizabeth Bain. She was hoping he might be able to check some airline records to confirm that Bain's father had indeed been out of the country when she went missing. Hedging, Calabrese told her that he wasn't sure if he'd be able to do something that sensitive without his boss's permission. So he said he would put her on hold and see if it was all right.

Calabrese went down the hall to see Brian King, who, as president of the company, occupied the corner office. King was always up to his eyeballs with something or other and the trick was to spit out what you had to say in three sentences or less.

When King heard the words "the Elizabeth Bain case," he expressed his interest by picking up the phone and taking the call himself. For the second time, Chrissa recounted John Secord's involvement in the searches for Elizabeth Bain. King was somewhat familiar with the case, having read about it in the newspapers and seen news reports on television, and he'd been intrigued by the news of Baltovich's arrest two weeks earlier. He remembered wondering to himself what the police had on this kid because whatever it was, they were sure keeping it a well-guarded secret. And the other thing that stuck in his mind was that the photographs of Baltovich in the back of the police car reminded him of a guy who worked out at his gym (as it turned out, it was someone else). Chrissa said that, although Secord didn't have a lot of money, he was very interested in having someone take a look at the information he'd accumulated. King told her to have Secord call, and in no time he did.

Although King didn't say so, he wouldn't have taken the time to speak with John Secord had it not been for the fact that Chrissa Hayes knew one of his investigators. While he'd been curious enough to take her call, he didn't have the time to get involved in a big murder case. In just six years, King-Reed had become one of the largest investigative firms in the country, with forty employees handling millions of dollars' worth of insurance fraud, trademark and other corporate cases, and it wasn't as if he was desperate for the work. If anything, King had too much on his plate already. As King-Reed's president (Reed, his co-founder, was no longer with the company), King was putting in between sixty and eighty hours a week for his clients, all of whom were paying top dollar for his services. In the end, King agreed to see Secord, figuring he'd listen to what he had to say, thus appeasing Chrissa Hayes, and promptly forget about the whole thing.

When King found out that Secord lived just around the corner from him in Unionville, he arranged for a week-night meeting at his house—he was too busy at the office to get together there. Secord arrived at his front door the following night carrying two immense briefcases crammed with yellow file folders full of notes and materials he'd been amassing since September. Before heading down to King's basement office, though, King introduced him to his wife, Joanne, and his two little boys, who were racing around the kitchen in their pyjamas. Secord was impressed with the work King had done on his basement. A set of glass French doors a few steps from a workout area opened up into his office, where he had a big desk with a fax machine and a computer.

A tall, narrow bookshelf was filled with hardcover books (true-crime mysteries, autobiographies of triumphant business tycoons, drug compendiums and other manuals, which Secord figured were tools of the trade) as well as framed photographs of a much younger and leaner Brian King, in various body-building poses. "Look at that guy," said King. "That's the before picture. Before career. Before family." King was laughing, pressing his hands flat around his stomach, not fat, just really filled out, approaching soft. "And I'm the *after* shot."

Secord was amazed to find out that King was only thirty-two. It wasn't his looks that were misleading, for, a few inches shy of six feet, he still had a good dose of boyishness to him. It was just that you didn't see too many thirty-two-year-olds these days with such a nice big house, happily married, kids, sitting atop a successful six-year-old company. Secord had a positive feeling about the man.

Secord started off by telling King what he knew about the disappearance and about his involvement in the searches, which had since transformed into a role that was more along the lines of an independent investigator. He said there was some inexplicable force driving him (he wasn't ready to bring up his dream just yet) to figure out what had happened to Elizabeth Bain. As far as Baltovich went, Secord said, the police were on the wrong track altogether. The kid had nothing to do with it. In his opinion, someone needed to take a closer look at the Bain family, the father in particular.

Secord opened up one of his file folders and pulled out a stapled, multi-page document he'd titled "Reasons Why Rick Bain Appears Suspicious." There was, for example, Rick's "total lack of interest in the floral clothing found in the Ganaraska Forest." Secord also found it odd that Rick had begun growing a beard around the time his daughter went missing. He also told King about the surgical glove falling onto the floor and how someone had put Liz's cards in the garbage bin. And there was more, a lot more. For example:

Reason 7: Secord had observed that Mr. Bain habitually reversed his car into parking spots. Elizabeth Bain's Tercel had been found backed up against a snow fence.

Reason 12: Mr. Bain had gone to Port Charlotte, Florida, to repair the roof of a house he owned for the week preceding his daughter's disappearance. His return flight to Toronto had arrived just hours after his family realized Liz was missing. Was this planned, or just a bizarre coincidence? Even the idea of Mr. Bain repairing a roof was, from what Secord had observed, out of character. Rick was sure no Mr. Fixit. It seemed as though every time Julita wanted something fixed, she was calling Secord, not her husband.

Reason 21: From studying the Bains' phone records Julita had supplied for him, Secord knew that at exactly 7:52 AM on June 19, Rick Bain had called home from Florida to let his wife know that he would be in transit that night from his niece's house in Altamonte Springs (he'd left Port Charlotte for the visit on Sunday, June 17) to St. Petersburg, where he would be staying with Cameron Gates and his wife, a couple Rick and Julita had met a few years before in Toronto. Presumably, he was calling her to tell her what time his flight would be arriving in Toronto the following day. The phone records also indicated that Rick had called the National Sports Store in Toronto from his niece's at exactly 5:00 PM. Had he done this to establish an alibi for that time—in the event that someone else had been hired to do the job—or was he simply checking the price of an item to see if he could purchase it at a cheaper price in Florida? Secord said that when he'd asked Julita about it, she'd found it unusual that her husband, whom she considered a frugal man, had gone to the trouble of making a long-distance phone call to comparison shop. She had insisted that it was probably "a mistake."

Reasons 25, 26 & 27: Not only had Rick's disagreements with his original search coordinator, Maria Lazsko, caused her to quit, it was Secord's understanding that Liz's aunt and godmother, Diana Bain, had been "excommunicated" from the family just days subsequent to the disappearance. He'd also been told that Rick Bain had got into a heated argument with his brother, Hugo, during one of the searches and that Hugo hadn't been seen by any of the volunteers again. Secord had also spoken to Cathy Bain at length about the fight she'd had with her father, and her subsequent departure from the family home.

Reasons 31 and 32: While the police (and therefore the Bains) were suspicious of the fact that Rob had stopped searching for Liz after the first weekend in the valley, no one seemed to find it strange that Mark Bain had participated in just one organized search for his sister. Or that Liz's youngest brother, Paul, couldn't boast a much better attendance record.

Having listened to most of Secord's thirty-two "reasons," Brian King said he would give him his professional opinion on the matter. First, said King, this wasn't the kind of thing he was prepared to get involved with half-heartedly. And because Secord hadn't derived much satisfaction from his previous conversations with the police, King suggested he contact Baltovich's defence lawyer. Secord didn't seem to jump at the idea, and King sensed that his reluctance had something to do with his personality, which was obviously a bit introverted. So King offered to call the lawyer on his behalf, and Secord seemed to be a lot more comfortable with that.

King had never heard of Bill Gatward before but he phoned him from the office the following day and gave him the rundown on John Secord. Gatward said he'd be happy to meet with him. He even asked King if he'd like to join them, and King said he would do his best to be there. King figured that he would introduce the two parties and wash his hands of the entire affair. Beyond that, he had no intentions of taking his involvement any further.

Fulfilling his final obligation, King accompanied Secord to the downtown law firm of Kirby, Lyon & Gatward. Gatward met them in the lobby and led them to his office, where King immediately recognized a stocky, dark-haired lawyer who was watching the crowd skating around the outdoor ice rink in Nathan Phillips Square, ten storeys below. It was Mike Engel, with whom King had worked twelve years earlier, when Engel was an articling student for the late Arthur Maloney, one of Canada's most revered criminal lawyers, and King was apprenticing for another investigative outfit. Engel turned around and smiled at King, and the two men shook hands. "Good to see you, Mike," said King. "I didn't know you were handling this case."

"Just came on board," said Engel. "Bill and I ran into each other a little while ago at a wake for a colleague of ours. I'd already seen quite a bit about the case on television and it looked to me to be absolutely fascinating. So I told Bill that, if he needed any sort of help with it, to give me a call. Here I am."

Gatward and Engel listened with great interest as Secord summarized his list chronicling the Bain family's suspicious behaviour. When Secord was finished, Engel asked King point-blank if he'd go to Florida and check out Mr. Bain's alibi. "Two things," said King. "One, I'll need a $5,000 retainer. And two, which is much more important, I want to meet with Baltovich and hear from his own mouth that he isn't responsible for this crime."

Being the son of a small-town cop from Woodstock, Ontario, King had no interest in bolstering the defence of someone who could very well be guilty of murder, especially when he didn't need the money. Private investigators weren't like lawyers, who were taught to abide by the philosophy that every person accused of a crime is entitled to the fullest possible defence. King's standard practice was that he had to feel comfortable with a case before he took it on. His conscience wouldn't allow him to work for anyone who was clearly guilty of a horrendous crime. Gatward and Engel said they understood his position and that they would arrange for him to meet Baltovich at Metro East as soon as possible.

On November 29, three days after Rob had been refused bail, the police interviewed a woman, Vanessa Sherman, who had worked part-time with Liz at the Kidbrooke Home. Sherman had been scheduled to work the same Sunday shift as Liz a couple of weeks before she went missing. She told the detectives that she'd arrived at Kidbrooke a little before 11:00 AM that day and was sitting in the big blue chair by the front window as Liz pulled up in her car. While Liz left her car, Sherman saw a man drive up and park across the street. (She'd never met Rob but, having seen his picture in the paper a few times since the disappearance, she now believed that it might have been him.) Liz crossed the road and spoke to him through his car door window. For a couple of minutes, they seemed caught up in an intense conversation; then she stepped back and threw her arms in the air. He was still speaking, moving his hands a lot. But Liz had heard enough and she dismissed him with a wave of her hand and began marching back across the road towards Kidbrooke. A few feet from the front steps, she turned around to face him again, and the man stuck his hand out the window and gave her the finger while he slammed the accelerator, his tires letting out a good squeal as he blasted off down the road.

The day that Sherman was telling her story to the police, Rob's cell door opened to reveal a pale, tattooed, unkempt inmate accompanied by a guard. "Hello, Robert," he chirped, as he took the blue-striped mattress from underneath his arm and laid it on the floor. "Looks like it's you and me." He said his name was Bill Mackinlay.

Mackinlay was unlike anyone Rob had ever met. He was a slight man—"one hundred and ten pounds soaking wet," as Rob would say—with teardrop tattoos on each cheek and a glazed look in his eyes. Initially, Rob didn't like the feeling of being trapped with him in such a confined space. Mackinlay said he was from Regent Park, which had become a crime-ridden neighbourhood since the days Rob's father had grown up there, and Rob could only imagine what kind of trouble his new cellmate had stirred up to land himself in Metro East.

Yet, as intimidating as Mackinlay seemed, he became less and less menacing as time went on. At night, he would remove his false teeth and take on what Rob considered a new persona. Mackinlay gave him a crash course on jail slang and regaled him with tales of criminal and penal exploits. Every once in a while a guard would engage Mackinlay in small talk in front of Rob, whereupon Mackinlay would jokingly say, "This is my bitch" or "Here's my bitch," as if he was asserting his dominion over his naive cellmate. Rob laughed in response most of the time, which Mackinlay found strange. He couldn't understand why Rob didn't take offence.

One of the bonuses of having Mackinlay as a cellmate was that he worked as a cleaner, usually in other parts of the institution, during the day. Which meant that Rob would have the cell to himself. Then, one afternoon while Rob was alone, about a week after Mackinlay had moved in, he heard his former cellmate, Gord, the Wiccan, call out to him from a few cells down the block. "Hey, Baltovich!"

"What?" answered Rob.

"Don't tell that guy anything about your case. He's already spoken to the police twice."

"Okay," Rob said.

Seconds later, the guard's footsteps came thundering down the corridor towards them. Rob went back to his bunk from the door and sat down. "What did you just say?" The guard was berating Gord. "Keep your fuckin' mouth shut!"

The guard started walking towards Rob's cell. Rob grabbed a book and pretended to read. Stopping in front of his cell, the guard peered inside, but Rob, feeling the man's eyes on him, didn't look up, and after a few seconds, the guard left.

The next day, Gord was removed from his cell. Rob never saw him again.

—◦—

As planned, the following Sunday, John Secord drove into North York and pulled up in front of the three-storey building that housed King-Reed & Associates. King-Reed's suite of offices was on the top floor and, if one were to look from the east windows at the rear of the building, the Metro Police Force's Intelligence Services headquarters was in plain view on the far side of the railway tracks that ran between the two squat grey structures. It was the police, in fact, who had inspired Secord's visit. He was concerned that someone from the Homicide Squad might come and seize his notes one day, and he thought it might be wise to make a second set with King's photocopier, just in case.

Sunday, December 9, 1990

By the time I'd photocopied all my notes at Brian King's office, it was almost dark and I drove to the Bains' house. Lita had just arrived home. I asked her if she would go to Kingston Road with me so we could have some coffee & talk. She said sure. I asked for written permission to investigate her family's financial stuff. She said I would have to ask Rick. We agreed that he would say no & she asked me why I needed it. I took a big chance & told her some of the stuff I'd been keeping from her. She seemed surprised.

She couldn't think of any reason why Rick could have anything to do with this. She said that he is a man of principles & that her family is psychologically happy & problem-free & that there has never been any incest in her family. I told her that I am quite sure that Rick is hiding something about Liz's disappearance, but I'm not sure what.

—◦—

Two days later, Rick and Julita appeared on a television program, "The Shirley Show," which was broadcast across Canada on the CTV network. That day's show was entitled "Missing Women," and the host, Shirley Solomon, a tall, unnatural blonde, got things under way by interviewing John and Pat Stanton, whose fourteen-year-old daughter, Julie, had last been seen on Easter Monday, getting into a grey Chevrolet Monte Carlo just down the street from her family's house in Pickering. The police had yet to make an arrest.

Rick and Julita, who had joined forces with the Stantons on search efforts in

September, took their place on the studio stage after the commercial break. Shirley played some videotape of the Bains' backyard plea from the summer and then cut to a long shot of Rob in the back seat of the police cruiser just after his arrest. *On Monday, November 19, a man was charged with first-degree murder in connection with Elizabeth Bain's disappearance.* Shirley said that, because the case was before the courts, they were not permitted to discuss anything but the impact Elizabeth's disappearance had had on her parents, her siblings and the people in the community.

SHIRLEY: I'd like you to meet Rick and Julita Bain. You said it has been pure hell, both of you, and I want to talk to you about how this has affected your lives. Tell me about Elizabeth, about the kind of girl she was.

JULITA: She was a perfect daughter . . . [*chokes up*].

RICK: She's a very warm, shy, timid type of person. Not the person who mixes well in a crowd, but the person who is very good on a one-to-one basis.

SHIRLEY: She's a lovely girl, huh?

RICK: She was very athletic, very musically talented—a lot of talent that she'll never be able to show. But the people that knew her closely—which a lot of people didn't because she's not the extrovert type, she's a little bit introverted. But a very warm girl in many many respects with a lot of joy to give. Um—

SHIRLEY: I want to talk to you for a moment, Julita, because you had to stop for a moment when you were talking about your daughter. You've tried to be so strong throughout all of this and now you're showing these feelings inside about Elizabeth and what her disappearance has meant to you.

JULITA: It's very hard to talk about her. We miss her so much [*crying*].

SHIRLEY: Oh, I'm sorry. You know what? We'll give you a moment to catch your breath. Okay? Um, Rick, let's talk about the day—I mean, I'm getting very upset when I just talk about it, because all of us who are parents hope that this will never, ever happen to us. May I express to you and the Stantons how terrible all of us in Canada feel, all the parents who share in your grief over the disappearance of Elizabeth. I think by now you are somewhat convinced that Elizabeth will never return. That she is dead.

JULITA: Yes.

RICK: You always have a little hope there every once in a while, but you're right, we don't expect her to come back.

SHIRLEY: The searches have been unbelievable. I think it's important for people to understand what happened, how she disappeared. Julita?

JULITA: Because there's a trial, I'm not sure if we're supposed to comment on that.

SHIRLEY: Well, not the specifics, but, Rick, I understand she left for school that day and never came back.

RICK: She never came back, that's correct. We never saw her again.

SHIRLEY: You want to find your daughter's body.

JULITA: Yes, we do. It's very important.

SHIRLEY: Can you tell us why?

JULITA: So we can close this chapter of our lives and get on with things. If we can't do that, it's like a story without an end.

SHIRLEY: What struck me are the searches you've orchestrated. June, July and August, searches were conducted daily—morning, afternoon and evening in every area. Since September, searches have been conducted on weekends, with Saturday searches still averaging between 75 and 125 volunteers. Tell me about the way the community has reached out, because you've had over ten thousand volunteers helping you to find Elizabeth. It's extraordinary. Why do you think people have reached out like that to you and Rick?

JULITA: Basically, because they are good people. They are also parents, like us. They feel it in their hearts.

SHIRLEY: You have other children.

JULITA: We have three others, yes.

SHIRLEY: The Stantons said it almost broke up their marriage. What about you? How have things been with all of the unbelievable stress?

RICK: We've been mending fences since day one [*smiles*].

JULITA: We try to be supportive to one another, you know. Everybody is under tension so we try to be more considerate.

RICK: These things tear you apart, but they also draw you together. There's no doubt about it.

SHIRLEY: So, as a family, you think you're closer together?

RICK: I think Lita will agree that in the beginning we were all extremely non-verbal and very overwhelmed by the whole thing. So that we could not communicate about it. It's only now, in the last couple of months, that they're verbalizing some of their feelings and actually engaging in conversations about different subjects. But, at first, it was an impossible task.

SHIRLEY: But they're opening up more now. That's very important.

RICK: Yes.

———○———

A few weeks after Christmas, Brian King drove downtown through a blinding snowstorm to meet Bill Gatward and Baltovich at the Metro East Detention Centre. He parked his van and jogged to the glass doors at the front of the building. Inside, he expected to see Gatward waiting for him, as the weather had put him a bit behind schedule. But the only person in the waiting area was the guard behind the visiting counter, sipping coffee from a Styrofoam cup. The guard told him that Gatward hadn't arrived yet and that King would have to wait outside until he was with a lawyer. King looked out at the storm, the wind blowing so hard that the snow was moving parallel with the ground, not even landing. He turned back and gave the guard a pleading look. The guard just shrugged. "Those are the rules," he said.

King went out to the other side of the glass doors, cursing Gatward for being late. The guards milling around in the lobby were all having a good laugh watching the big-shot private detective in the expensive suit turn into an icicle. He'd been in such a hurry to get to the jail that he hadn't bothered to bring his rubbers or a decent coat. Now he wondered if this was a message from someone up above telling him not to get involved.

When Gatward finally showed up half an hour late, King was cold and irritable, with half a mind to tell the lazy guards and the tardy lawyer to stick it and he'd be on his way. But he'd come this far and a guard was ready to take them to an interview room. It was a grungy little space, about the size of a walk-in closet, he figured, with a beat-up table and a couple of shitty chairs.

Another guard led Rob into the room moments later. King was taken aback at how terribly unhealthy he looked, so much frailer than the pictures Secord had shown him. His skin was an awful pasty colour and he was pole-thin, cheekbones protruding like a POW's beneath his cold, weary stare. And the baggy, pale blue institution outfit just made it worse. As King introduced himself, the kid barely had enough strength to give him a proper handshake.

Everyone took a seat and King cut to the chase. "As I've explained to your lawyers, Rob, I'm not prepared to take this case on until I've heard from you. So I'm just going to come out and ask you the obvious question. Did you or did you not have anything to do with Elizabeth Bain's death?"

"I can give you my word," said Rob, perking up as much as he could, "that I am completely innocent."

King acknowledged this with a nod and said, "All right." The next thing he wanted Rob to do was give him a detailed account of everything that had transpired around the time of Elizabeth's disappearance. "And I mean *everything*," he said. "Don't leave anything out." He was coming on like a steamroller, which was his style in a situation like this. For the next few hours, Rob told him as much as he could remember, in some instances revealing more than he had to the police. For instance, when it came to Rob's last few hours together with Liz in the park on Sunday night, Rob volunteered every intimate gesture he could recall about their lovemaking.

King was fascinated by Rob's cerebral nature, which, due to the circumstances, came across as rather detached. King's gut told him that he was as guileless and pure a young man as one might find these days. "Rob, I'm going to ask you to do something for me," King said. "I want you to sit down and write out everything you can remember about Elizabeth's disappearance. I want a day-by-day account for the entire month of June, if that's possible. I want your reactions to various police theories. For example, I need you to explain this whole mess regarding the multicoloured shorts. I want you to tell me everything you know about the Bain family. And finally, I want your input on possible suspects, including friends and members of Liz's family. Do you have anyone in particular in mind as we sit here?"

"Not really," said Rob. "Anybody and everybody. And no one."

"That's fine," King said. "Your lawyers and I will do what we feel is necessary. Just think about it. We'll talk this over many more times in the future."

Soon, the pudgy guard came to return Rob to his cell block, and King and Gatward were back at the front doors, bracing themselves for the whipping wind and snow. "Given the weather, I know this is going to sound bad," King said, grinning a guilty grin. "But I'm prepared to fly down to Florida on Monday."

"That's funny," said Gatward, turning up the collar on his overcoat. "I was just thinking the same thing."

—⊙—

After three days in the Sunshine State, Brian King was able to confirm Mr. Bain's alibi. His flight had departed from Lester B. Pearson International Airport in Toronto at 6:00 AM Tuesday, June 12, and had arrived later that morning in Tampa, where he'd rented a brand-new Pontiac Grand Am and driven about sixty miles south along the Gulf Coast to the house he rented out to locals in Port Charlotte. He checked into a room at the Harbour Inn Motel at the rate of $20 per night and stayed there until Sunday morning, at which point he drove north to visit his sister, Nanina, and her husband, Dr. Norberto Priu, at their daughter Anna's house in Altamonte Springs. Two days later, on the evening of his daughter's disappearance, Rick Bain drove back to Tampa and returned the Grand Am at the airport, where he boarded a shuttle bus out to his friend Cameron Gates's house in St. Petersburg, arriving shortly after 10:00 PM. Around 8:00 the next morning, Gates drove him to the St. Petersburg/Clearwater Airport, and he boarded his return flight to Toronto.

King interviewed everyone he could, including Cameron Gates and Mr. Bain's niece, Anna Priu. As well, in order to confirm that Mr. Bain had indeed been repairing the roof of his house, he knocked on a few neighbours' doors. Marie Fielder, whose house was directly left of the Bains', told King that she remembered Mr. Bain working on the roof that week. She'd got to know the Bains quite well after they'd bought the house four or five years earlier and, from time to time, had even assisted Mr. Bain with the renting of the home. In fact, the Bains had been in Port Charlotte just a few weeks earlier, around the time Fielder's husband had died, the day before Christmas. After the funeral, which the Bains had attended, Fielder told Mr. Bain she didn't want to continue helping him renting his house. He had become quite obstinate, she told King, and wouldn't allow her to quit. In her opinion, the man was "a bit of a nut case." It was hard to pinpoint a specific reason for this, but a lot of it had to do with the neurotic concern he displayed regarding his finances. Fielder suggested that King track down the tenant who'd moved out shortly after Mr. Bain had tried to repair the roof. Those two had definitely not got along, she said.

The former tenant's name was Carol Carpenter, and she agreed to be interviewed when King showed up at the offices of her employer, the United Telephone Company in Punta Gorda. Yes, she'd lived at 125 Middletown Street N.E. in Port Charlotte for thirteen months, up until August 1, 1990. She'd moved out because Mr. Bain, whom she described as "odd," had refused to spend money on necessary repairs, including the roof, which had begun leaking in the spring. Originally, Mr. Bain had indicated that he was going to hire contractors to do the job and then showed up in June to do the work himself. When he announced that he was leaving Port Charlotte on the weekend, Carpenter expressed her dissatisfaction with his work and the two had words. She gave him notice of her intention to move out in thirty days. Outraged, he said she would have to give him six months.

After Carpenter had vacated the house, Mr. Bain refused to return her deposit cheque of $100, so she took him to court. The proceedings had been postponed two or three times due to his daughter's disappearance, but the matter eventually went before a judge on January 4, just eleven days earlier. Mr. Bain and his wife had both appeared in court, Carpenter said, but all for a losing cause. The disposition had been ruled in the tenant's favour.

King hadn't been back in Toronto more than a couple of days before John Secord called to let him know that Mr. Bain had been tipped off about his trip to Florida. "Don't worry," said Secord. "I'll give you the details later. I've written everything down."

Monday, January 21, 1991

   On Sunday afternoon I went to the Bains' house & had tea & a pancake. Rick was talking to Karl in the computer room while me & Lita were in the kitchen. Then I went upstairs to carry down the sewing machine & Lita was nervous about Rick seeing me up there cause he wouldn't like that. I repaired the sewing machine & lamp. Later Rick was talking to someone else & he said he was work-

ing on his phone bills from Florida to get his whole story together so he could dis-
cuss any blanks with the police. He said he even figured out which phone call was
with Liz. I asked him when he'd talked to her & he grinned & said he wouldn't
tell me. I asked him if he talked to her the day she went missing—the 19th—&
he wouldn't tell me.

While doing up my shoelaces, I told Rick that the car being backed in still
bothered me. He changed the subject & said Mr. King was down in Florida find-
ing out if he'd been there in June. He said it must take a lot of money to send
someone there. "Wouldn't it be easier," he said, "to just check my flights over the
phone? This King must be quite a guy."

Wednesday, January 23, 1991

I called Lita at 11:00 a.m. & asked her if her car was going okay & she said
yes it starts good now. She apologized about me not coming for dinner last night
because the Stantons were coming over and that guy from Victims of Violence in
Ottawa as well. She told me she'd just been on the phone with Rick. He had called
& told her not to release any more information about the case to John Secord
because he has ulterior motives and may be working for the other side. Julita said
that Rick has been "terribly on edge the last few days." She felt it was okay if I
came over but not to ask any more questions about Elizabeth. She said she still
wants to be friends and asked if all this could be in confidence.

—○—

Initially, Rob heeded Gord's warning about Mackinlay, but as the weeks passed, he
lowered his guard further and further. Mackinlay just didn't strike Rob as the kind
of person who would deliberately lie to the police in order to implicate him in a
murder. As a result, Rob began to discuss the evidence against him, at least as far as
he understood it. Every time, Mackinlay would just shake his head and say, "There's
got to be more than that."

The more they debated it, the more Rob kept coming back to the possibility that
the police had framed him. Then, one day, Mackinlay had had enough. "There's
something you have got to understand, okay?" he began, pausing briefly. "You did
it! That's all that matters to them. Somehow, some way, you did it."

"I didn't do it!" Rob screamed back at him. "What part of what I've told you don't you understand?"

"Look, they don't just arrest anybody. And anyways, whether you did it or didn't do it doesn't mean shit. You're the one they arrested and you're the one they're prosecuting and, if you don't find a way of breaking down this guy who says he saw you driving your girlfriend's car, you're going down."

Mackinlay was a true original. He had this curious habit of affecting a Jamaican accent, whether in the middle of a serious conversation or while singing a Bob Marley song. He claimed to have developed the accent due to the amount of time he'd spent around Jamaicans in his neighbourhood. And if it wasn't Bob Marley he was imitating, it was Elvis, or Aerosmith, whose song "What It Takes" Mackinlay would break into as though it was his daily prayer, prancing around the cell. In between, Mackinlay spoke often of sexual matters, bragging regularly about his numerous conquests. Consistently, Rob avoided discussing his own experience, which caused Mackinlay to speculate that he might be a "puffer."

Mackinlay often spoke over the phone to his wife, Allison, with whom he had two daughters, currently living in Regent Park. One day, he was on the phone with his wife while Rob read a book on his bunk. As Rob picked up pieces of the conversation here and there, he realized that he was party to what was probably one of the most intimate moments in Mackinlay's life—his wife had just informed him that a man (who happened to be black) had just moved in with her. After hanging up the phone, Mackinlay went berserk. "Oh my God! How could she do this to me! Shacking up with a nigger! Why?"

Although he concealed it, Rob found the spectacle of Mackinlay pacing back and forth in the cell both amusing and slightly scary. He felt for the man but had no idea how he was going to react. Nevertheless, Rob put his two cents in. "Billy, I thought you said that you have a lot of black friends."

"I do, but this is different," wailed Mackinlay. "This guy is living in my house, for God's sake! With my kids! She's breakin' my heart!"

Suddenly, Mackinlay sat down and started to cry. Rob felt sorry for him but couldn't help thinking that Mackinlay's problems were minor by comparison. Jail was making Rob selfish and he knew it. Still, Mackinlay's pain was something he could relate to.

In the dark of night, when Mackinlay was toothless and asleep, Rob was beginning to think more and more about Liz. The arrest had shaken his sensibilities enough to make him realize that she was probably dead. While he still held on to a vestige of hope that this wasn't the case, other possibilities seemed increasingly remote. In moments of desperation and fear, he even found himself wishing he'd never met her. But whenever these feelings of self-pity began to rise up, he reminded himself that, despite his predicament, Liz was the real victim.

Rob took up the challenge issued by Brian King—he began writing about the weeks leading up to Liz's disappearance with a fury. Knowing that there was now someone out there who was trying to find out what had really happened was a tremendous inspiration. All of a sudden, reading took a back seat, as did the card games with which he and Mackinlay had passed the time. Mackinlay, sensing Rob's new mood, was resentful and admonished him for concentrating solely on the notes. Rob remained impervious, however, and wrote incessantly.

The first sheaf of notes from Robert Baltovich arrived on Brian King's desk in late January. They had been carefully written in printed block letters, filling one lined page after another. (Apart from the essays he'd cranked out for his university courses, this was the first serious bout of writing Rob had done in about three years—since before he'd begun dating Liz—when he'd tried his hand at what he called "creative writing." Rob knew, even as he was composing any one of his numerous attempts at poetry—"Someone special has awoken/an emotional slumber in my heart/it is a welcome inclusion/it is you"—that they were of minimal literary merit. But that didn't stop him from writing so many short stories and contemplative pieces about friends and girlfriends that the stack had perhaps appeared so daunting that the police hadn't taken it away during their search.)

By the time King had received all of Rob's notes, he had four hundred pages bound in two separate volumes. They contained everything King had asked Rob to expound upon, and then some. He had drawn pictures of different shorts he'd worn over the years, with arrows indicating where the material was frayed or where the junction clip was missing. He'd laid out everything he knew about Liz's former boyfriends, as well as what little he could surmise about John and André, the mystery men. Fifty pages had been devoted to an outline of what he remembered happening between June 5 and mid-July, 1990. It took another eighty-five pages to refute the theory that he'd killed Liz in a fit of jealousy:

Why would I plan to murder my girlfriend at a time when relations with her family could not have been worse! Place myself at the scene of the crime, admit that I was suspicious of her, suggest suicide when I knew she'd been murdered, tell Nancy and Steve that I saw her, then tell the police four times that I didn't, drive around with her body in the front seat of a car I can't drive with every police officer in southern Ontario looking for it. In addition to that, I would take her diary and not return it for two days, giving myself plenty of time to remove the page that says a) she wants to put a bullet through my head b) she wants to leave me, and c) I was following her, and not do it? Admit I hid outside her class and tell the police I got a busy signal when I didn't? Then give the police four separate statements, take a lie-detector test that I would fail and, throughout the entire investigation, claim that she might still be alive? It is too much to even conceive.

At King's behest, Rob had gone to great lengths to make sense of the theory that Liz might have been killed by someone in her own family, beginning with her father:

Mr. Bain, from the outset, was jealous of the time Liz and I spent together—his love was almost incestuous. Liz was afraid of him and well aware of his propensity towards violence, terrified of what he might do if he found out that we were sleeping together.

Eventually, when Rob tried to construct a scenario for Mark Bain, his notes began to resemble, in style, innumerable psychological case studies he'd pored over in university:

The psychological problems that Liz was experiencing leading up to her disappearance were presumably shared by Mark, as well as the other children. The difference, I feel, between Liz and Mark, versus Paul and Cathy, was that Paul and Cathy had access to a rich social network of friends that cushioned the emotional burden. Liz and Mark had few friends. They lacked the ability to experience deep, committed relationships because it was a difficult strain on their

identities. At the time of Liz's disappearance, the angry, violent and manipula-
tive familial milieu had worsened. Mr. Bain had been very antagonistic due to
several factors. An unhappy marriage. The pressure of maintaining a financial
empire. The growing dissatisfaction with my relationship with Liz. Mr. Bain was
finding it harder and harder to exercise control over his family. A parallel can be
drawn between Liz's desire to see harm come to herself and perhaps Mark's ten-
dency to inflict harm upon someone else. His troubles with Nancy predisposed
Mark towards violence as well. All that was needed was a reason—and Liz pro-
vided it. Mark had come to a realization that it was Liz's feminist rhetoric that
was destroying his relationship with girls, Nancy specifically. The pressures of an
angry, intimidating relationship with his family and an eroding romance with
Nancy, which Mark felt was precipitated by his sister's interference (the letter),
caused him to act out what at one time might have been only a fantasy. One that
he was angry enough to carry out. Think about it. If Liz wanted to put a bullet
through my head for merely trying to help her (read: interfering), imagine what
Mark would have felt when he realized that Liz was interfering in his life. The
opportunity was perfect. He could make it look like suicide. It was the culmina-
tion of all the above factors converging. It was a bloodletting.

In a similar vein, Rob wrote extensive "Psychological Profiles" for his friend Jim
Isaacs and for Liz's ex-boyfriend Eric Genuis, both of whom King regarded as potential suspects. Jim lived with his mother in a subsidized housing complex on Sackville
Street in Cabbagetown. Jim's father had abandoned the family for a life of vagrancy
on downtown streets when Jim was a small boy, and his mother had struggled to
make ends meet while raising four children. Over the years, Rob had listened to Jim
tell all kinds of poignant stories about his difficult childhood. How Jim got picked
on all the time at school (even though he was usually one of the biggest kids), letting himself get bullied time after time, until he would erupt in anger, pummelling
his tormentor of the day into submission. For the most part, Rob believed Jim to be
a gentle and passive friend who possessed little in the way of malice, but he began
to consider the possibility that, if triggered emotionally, Jim had the capacity for violence. But the problem was this: what would cause him to snap with Liz? Did Jim
feel that Rob had stolen her away from him, and then, after watching them together
for an agonizing year, he'd decided to steal her back by force?

Like Jim, Eric Genuis came across as being quite meek, especially for someone who was so confident, almost arrogant, about his musical talent and the degree to which he embraced the chaste, God-fearing life of Catholicism. But, from what Liz had indicated, Eric was also given to suppressing his anger. According to Liz, he hadn't taken it well when she'd broken up with him, and Eric had subjected her to a verbal tirade, yelling and swearing at her in a way she hadn't anticipated. Could Eric be yet another psychological powder keg? Had he gone to Liz and begged for a second chance only to have her turn him down? Maybe, Rob thought, that was enough for him to do something crazy.

Brian King, his curiosity raised a few notches, placed a call that very day to Jim Isaacs, and interviewed him for several hours, concluding that his version of events corroborated just about everything he'd heard from Rob. Eric Genuis, on the other hand, was a different story. His mother seemed to be screening his calls, but King finally got in touch with him later that evening. While Genuis was pleasant enough, King got the feeling he was a bit of a "momma's boy"—the kind of guy whose mother still irons his underwear. Genuis told King that he'd called Steve Reesor as soon as he'd learned that a private investigator wanted to speak with him. Apparently, Reesor didn't think it was such a great idea, and Genuis advised King that he did not wish to assist him with his investigation.

After King had talked it over with Bill Gatward, they decided to put both Genuis and Isaacs under surveillance, not because they wanted to track their movements, but to obtain some photographs of them that King could have at his disposal in case he ever wanted to put together a photo line-up of his own. Isaacs was photographed on two separate occasions getting into his car in the parking lot of the Sears Warehouse where he worked part-time. And King also knew the best place to find Genuis—coming out of St. Thomas More Church at the end of Sunday mass.

—◇—

For the next three months, Brian King immersed himself in the case. He began by interviewing each member of the Baltovich family individually and then fanned out in the obvious directions: to witnesses like Lou Torrone and the receptionist at Three R Auto Body, even the owner of the Lido Motel; to Tony Fuchs, Neil Winton, Al Heys, Phil Dach and just about every other one of Rob's friends; and to an executive with the company that distributed the "finger jams" on Liz's car, who indicated, after searching his records, that approximately 6,995 units of that product had been shipped across the country during the eighteen months preceding her disappearance. It was his duty, King felt, to also contact Elizabeth Bain's parents and inform them of his investigation, as well as express his interest in hearing their version of events. King didn't expect to be greeted with open arms but he didn't foresee finding himself on the receiving end of a restrained but contemptuous tongue-lashing from Mr. Bain, which was precisely what occurred. Mr. Bain's curt dismissal of him as someone looking to assist the man who'd murdered his daughter stung King badly. King didn't see his role that way at all—he simply wanted to seek out the truth, and if that truth implicated Robert Baltovich, then so be it.

Prior to the delivery of evidence the Crown deemed appropriate for disclosure to Rob's defence team, King had already come to the conclusion that there were potentially relevant witnesses who had, for a variety of reasons, never been in contact with the police. For example, during his interview with Al Heys, Heys mentioned a brief encounter he'd had with a fellow employee at the Molson's plant in Barrie. Although Heys didn't know the man very well, he knew that his name was Paul Curran. What made this encounter with Curran particularly memorable was that Curran told Heys he thought he might have seen Elizabeth Bain in a telephone booth the afternoon of her disappearance.

King had little difficulty locating Curran at home in Scarborough within twenty-four hours, and the two men agreed to meet at Curran's home a few days later, on a Saturday morning. When they met Curran explained how he was able to pinpoint that the incident had taken place on June 19. That was the day he'd resumed his regular jogging routine after a three-week lay-off due to a leg injury. He'd worked the day shift that Tuesday and figured he'd probably started his run between 4:30 and 5:00 PM. He ran west on Lawrence Avenue near Lake Ontario and then headed north on Port Union Road. Not long after that his leg started acting up again and he was walking by the time he decided to cross at the lights at Lawson Road. Lawson turned into Fanfare Avenue on the east side of Port Union, which was where Curran spotted a young woman in the telephone booth at the edge of the plaza parking lot on the north corner. The booth was just a few feet away from the sidewalk and he figured the girl was in her early twenties, about five feet five inches, slim, with a good complexion and dark hair that was at least to her shoulders. His attention was especially drawn to the young woman because she was crying and obviously distraught, holding the telephone to her ear with her left hand and gesturing with the other, occasionally rubbing her head. He had a vague recollection of her hair being held back with a hair band or something similar but had a much more concrete recollection about what she'd been wearing—black slacks and a lighter top that had some white on it. She looked so upset that Curran, for an instant, contemplated walking up to her to see if she was all right, but didn't. Then, just past the telephone booth, Curran noticed a dark-coloured vehicle that looked like a Toyota and could have been silver or grey. He estimated that this happened some time between 5:15 and 6:00 PM.

When he saw Elizabeth Bain's photograph in the newspapers later that month, Curran was struck by the close resemblance she bore to the woman he'd seen in the telephone booth that day. Later, he heard some of his children talking about the disappearance, as they had known some of the Bain kids growing up. King asked why he'd never come forward to the police, and Curran said that he honestly didn't believe what he'd seen was of any consequence, or he would have.

While Curran was, in King's estimation, a credible and important witness, other tips that came his way were equally intriguing but probably half-baked. An old colleague from his early days in the P.I. business named Joe Rafferty recounted for King how he'd recently been working on a case with two bounty hunters from Louisiana. Rafferty said that these two bounty hunters, who were biker types, had been in a bar in Barrie, almost one hundred kilometres north of Toronto, around the time Robert Baltovich's arrest was all over the news. Inside the bar, the bounty hunters had struck up a conversation with several members of an American motorcycle gang, as well as a few of their local affiliates, in town for some type of bikers' convention. Rafferty told King that, from what the bounty hunters had said, the local bikers had been having a good laugh over the fact that Elizabeth Bain's boyfriend had been charged with her murder. They apparently knew he was innocent and that someone else was responsible. The body, said the bikers, had been disposed of near the junction of Highway 400 and Highway 69, not too far north of Barrie. Rafferty, who had revealed to the bounty hunters his association with the private investigator working on the boyfriend's behalf, told King that the bikers had said they would provide further details for a fee of $5,000. King didn't have to mull it over for very long. Just told Rafferty he'd take a pass and that was it.

—◦—

After reading through Rob's stack of notes, King approached Betsy Watanabe, one of Liz's holistic practitioners. Getting her to sit down for an interview had taken some perseverance, as Watanabe explained that she was going through some marital problems and wanted King to contact her at her store, where they now met, on Markham Road. Watanabe, a tall woman who looked younger than her forty-plus years, told King how she first met Liz four or five years earlier through the girl's father, Rick, who'd been a patient of hers. In general, Watanabe found Liz to be in good health and the only treatments she'd ever given her were for "colostics," to help her achieve regular bowel movements, and for "minor reproduction and period problems." Watanabe had last seen Liz on May 3, 1990. According to her records, Liz's eyes showed "beautiful structure" but also revealed that stress and various emotional problems were causing trouble in her pancreas and stomach, as well as her reproductive area. Watanabe had treated these ailments with herbs.

Watanabe had nothing but fond memories of Liz. "She was very gentle and full of kindness," Watanabe said to King. "Probably the closest thing I've ever known to an angel." During Watanabe's numerous sessions with her, Liz had never said anything negative about her boyfriend. In fact, during the session on May 3, Liz had spoken of her intention to marry him. If there was anything about the young woman that had bothered Watanabe, it was that she lacked "emotional expression" and tended to keep things to herself. And she always seemed petrified that there might be something physically wrong with her.

Just as King was about to be on his way, Watanabe brought up the interesting coincidence that another one of her patients, Susanne Nadon, was a police witness who had overheard an argument on the street in front of her home late one night. Watanabe said that Nadon had told her about having "visions or dreams that Elizabeth's body was buried in some of the sewer construction taking place along her road."

The following weekend, King called Nadon at home. She was uncomfortable speaking to him about the case and said she would have to confer with the investigating police officers before agreeing to meet with him. King knew how they would advise her.

Instead, he went to see Sat Dharam Kaur, one of the naturopaths Liz had consulted through her aunt Diana. Like Watanabe, Kaur found Liz to be extremely preoccupied ("almost obsessed") with her "fairly minor skin and digestive problems." And, while Liz had confessed to Kaur that her boyfriend opposed her involvement with naturopathic medicine, Kaur had also noted that she found her parents "overbearing Catholics who wanted her to be an angel." While there were no signs indicating physical or sexual abuse, Kaur was concerned about possible psychological abuse. Kaur's initial opinion—that more than anything else, Liz was suffering from low self-esteem—was shored by her patient's admission that she was suicidal.

When a police investigator—she believed it was Steve Reesor—had come to speak with her, suicide had been the last thing on his mind. Elizabeth Bain was dead. Murdered. Soon after, Kaur had reiterated this conversation to her friend Diana Bain, who had not taken the news well. Back then, Diana had yet to be convinced that her niece was dead and had consulted several local psychics, all of whom had said Liz was still alive and living with a man. Kaur remembered the name "Mark" and "the city of Oshawa" coming up but, beyond that, could no longer recall the specifics.

King was so eager to get in touch with Diana Bain that he drove downtown and arrived unannounced at the Toronto Healing Arts Centre on Bloor Street, where she operated her own private "Body/Mind Therapy" practice. Unfortunately, the trip proved fruitless—Diana was on an extended trip to her homeland, Argentina. King persisted, however, and in mid-April he made contact with her over the phone.

"I'm just not sure," was how she responded to his request for a face-to-face meeting. To keep her on the line, King craftily slipped in a question about her belief in the psychic phenomenon. Diana couldn't resist. She confirmed that she had been to see at least two psychics, both of whom had indicated that her godchild was still among the living.

—◇—

Jailhouse Notebook (1)

We had a shakedown a couple of weeks ago. They seem to happen about once a month, always at five-thirty in the morning. As usual, we were lined up against the wall and ordered to strip naked. While our every orifice was being scrutinized, another group of guards rifled through our cells trying to find contraband. I can never quite figure out what they expect to find, seeing as we have almost nothing in the first place.

As we watched three guards turn our "house" upside down, Mackinlay turned to a supervisor: "You're not gonna find anything in there, boss." I couldn't resist adding to what he'd said, so I chimed in with "What are you guys looking for, anyway?"

"We're looking for a body," the supervisor replied, smirking. Judging by the mile-wide grin on his face, he was proud of his rather clever reply. I tried to ignore it, which he sensed. He repeated it one more time, still grinning. "Yeah, that's it—we're looking for a body!" This was par for the course and, again, I said nothing.

So then this morning, a guard asked me to step into his office. As I walked in he handed me a letter, which I immediately recognized. It was one I'd sent to a friend a few days after the shakedown. Someone had circled a portion of the letter, and he asked me to read aloud the part about the asshole guard who had made the snappy comment. I had gone on to write that I hoped to run into him some day after I was acquitted. Once I'd finished the reading exercise, the guard cautioned me that threats against staff were a serious offence. I explained that I hadn't meant it as a threat and wouldn't let it happen again. What else could I say?

—◦—

John Secord was driving north to his cottage on Georgian Bay, hoping to get the snowmobiles out one last time before spring. In the truck with him was Julita Bain's younger sister, Beth Garcia, whom Secord had begun courting a few months ago. It was a Tuesday—Beth's day off—and Secord was determined to make the most of it.

Partway to the cottage, though, Secord's cellular phone rang. He was quite a distance north of the city, almost out of range for the phone, and the line was crackling, but he could still make out that the unsettled voice was Julita's. With little preamble she said he wouldn't be able to come over to the house any more. Why not, Secord asked. Julita said that Rick was furious because he'd heard from Brian Raybould that John Secord had been going around saying that Rick had killed his daughter. Secord said he had no idea what she talking about. By now, the line was getting extremely faint, and Secord said he'd phone her back as soon as he got into town the next day.

Secord was anxious to get things cleared up when he arrived home from the cottage. He called Rick, Julita and Brian Raybould trying to ascertain where this rumour had originated but got a different story from all three. Nonetheless, Secord told Rick that he wanted to sit down and resolve things in a civilized manner. Rick agreed but suggested they meet at Secord's house—it was about time, Rick said, that they got together at his place for a change.

Given the level of Rick's wrath, Secord called Brian King and asked him to come over before the meeting. He told King that he was terrified Rick might try to do something to him. King didn't have to do anything, Secord said, just hide in basement and listen. So King came home from work a little earlier than usual and walked a few blocks over to Secord's place. No sooner did he get in the door than the phone rang. "Just a second," Secord said, leaving King by the front closet to go and answer it. Secord took the call on the living room phone. "Hello," he said into the receiver. "Hello. *Hello!*" He slammed it into the cradle. "Fuck," he said. "I hate when people hang up like that."

Twenty minutes later, the doorbell rang right on time, and King made his way down the basement stairs. "Good luck," he said offering a smile to a nervous-looking Secord. "It's been nice knowing you."

Down the hallway, Secord opened the front door and saw Rick waiting on the stoop. "Come on in, Rick," he said, holding the door open. But Rick didn't move, just put his chin down and looked at the ground. And then Jake Poranganel and Brian Raybould stepped into view from behind the brick wall at the front of the house. They walked right up to the door and stood behind Rick. "Hey, John," said Raybould. "Is it all right if we come inside for a while?"

"I don't appreciate being deceived," John said. "You guys could come over here any time. All you have to do is call."

"Sorry," said Raybould, getting that out of the way. "Can we come in?"

Steamed, Secord hesitated for a moment and then stepped back, waving his arm dramatically for the entourage to enter. Having heard the voices from his perch on the basement steps, King felt tremendously uncomfortable. The whole thing had been a set-up. An ambush. The crank call Secord got when he'd arrived had been made to ensure he was home—nothing cops hate more than a wasted trip. King thought it would look pretty bad if they came downstairs and found him standing there. What the hell would they make of that?

"So, John," King could hear Poranganel saying. "We understand you've been keeping some pretty extensive notes."

"And what if I have?" said Secord. He definitely had an agitated look to him.

"We were hoping you might let us take a look at them."

"Yeah," Secord said, clenching his jaw. "They're in the back of my dump truck. You want to go for a fuckin' ride?"

Rick dropped his head into his hands. He'd probably been afraid this might happen. On the basement steps, however, King was in stitches, trying to stifle his laughter. Stumped by Secord's response, Poranganel tried a new tack. "We understand you've been doing a lot of work for Brian King."

From the very beginning, King had been clear with Secord on this issue. At no time was Secord to represent himself as an employee of King's. In fact, he'd made Secord sign a document in January clarifying that he was investigating the Bain disappearance on his own and was supplying King with information voluntarily. Secord did not have an investigator's licence and, therefore, King believed that his licence could be jeopardized if Secord was in any way reimbursed by King-Reed for his work on the Bain case. "Everything I've done has been on my own," Secord answered.

Poranganel made a few more attempts to nail him down as an agent of Brian King's, but it was no use. Secord wouldn't deviate from his response. So Raybould wrapped things up by saying that even though Secord hadn't done anything against the law—such as impersonating a police officer—he would very much appreciate it if Secord would stop interviewing potential witnesses. Which meant that he didn't want Secord driving up and down Kingston Road, questioning every motel owner he could or popping in on Elizabeth Bain's hairdresser or into the store where she had rented videos. It was hard enough getting witnesses to testify in court, said Raybould, and the police didn't need people like him intimidating them, even if that wasn't his intention.

Secord said he understood and that he would cease his investigation. "I appreciate that," said Raybould. There wasn't much to discuss after that. And Secord was only too happy to show them the door.

—◯—

With Baltovich's preliminary hearing scheduled to begin on May 6, King had about six weeks to make sense of the various witness statements the Crown had disclosed in mid-March. He was particularly interested in getting together with the Lake Scugog witness, David Dibben, who, after speaking with King over the telephone on a Tuesday, agreed to a meeting at his home the following Friday evening. When King knocked on his door out in Cavan, however, Dibben didn't answer—another witness with cold feet.

But King's trip out to the country hadn't been a complete disappointment. Earlier that afternoon, he'd spent a few hours with a man named John Elliott, who co-owned the orange-roofed Haugen's Chicken & Ribs Barbeque in Manchester. As King had just recently learned, Elliott had been in touch with the police in late November, shortly after Baltovich's arrest, when he'd taken a close look at some of the Missing posters for Elizabeth Bain scattered around the Port Perry area. He was sure he'd seen the same car—with no one in it—parked in the lot outside his restaurant between 5:30 and 6:30 one morning around the time of Bain's disappearance. What really lent credence to Elliott's story, as far as the police were concerned, was that he'd seen a nautical-style key chain just like Bain's—without keys—in an empty dumpster behind the restaurant later that day. Elliott told King that, two weeks after giving the police an initial statement, he'd been taken to see Dr. Matheson in Etobicoke. Under hypnosis, Elliott had recalled the entire morning in vivid detail.

Looking out into the morning light through his dusty windshield, Elliott pulls his truck into the restaurant parking lot, gets out, and looks at the grey car, a small import, which reminds him of the one his old girlfriend used to own. Then, around the side of it, he sees the flesh-coloured fingers on the driver's door, and notices at the same time the weather, and that it isn't sunny or cloudy outside, but somewhere in between. He thinks a commuter has left the car in his lot and then picked up a ride to work in the city. It's the only car in the lot. He unlocks the front door of the restaurant and shuts off the security alarm, turns the coffee pot on, then the fryers and the grill. The day won't be too busy, he hopes, because he has to pick up his son Jonathan early in the afternoon so they can get fitted for tuxedos. His brother is getting married on Saturday. He's pretty sure things won't be too hectic. It is, after all, the middle of the week.

Down in the basement, he gets potatoes out of the refrigerator, bails out the French fry pails and begins bringing some chicken up to the kitchen. Now it's time to open the back door and close the screen so he's ready for the morning deliveries. Peering out through the screen, he notices the grey import is gone. Which strikes him as odd—commuters don't usually pick up their cars until the evening. His truck looks really dirty now the way the sun is hitting it. Should give it a wash, he thinks. Then back to the kitchen.

After lunch, he carries the first pail of garbage to the dumpster out back. Climbing the concrete steps and holding the pail, he looks down into the dark, empty steel basin and sees one of those floating key chains on the bottom all by itself. White foam with a bead chain—no keys. It's got a blue design on it. An anchor? A ship's wheel? Something like that. He pours the refuse on top, covering it. He doesn't want anyone jumping into the dumpster to retrieve it, especially a worker from the kitchen. Normally, he doesn't take the garbage out but today he's in a hurry. Got to get out of there and pick up Jonathan.

After the hypnosis session with Dr. Matheson, Elliott consulted his personal diary and established that his brother's wedding had taken place on Saturday, June 23, and that his son had been fitted for his tuxedo the preceding Wednesday, which just happened to be the day after Bain had gone missing. Just to be sure, King now asked Elliott if it was possible that all of this might have happened not on the Wednesday, but on the Friday (the day Dibben said he'd seen Bain's car just down the road). In response, Elliott said, "I'm sure it wasn't a Friday, no."

King saw Elliott as crucial to Baltovich's defence. It had never made sense to King that someone would risk driving Bain's car three days after she'd gone missing. At sunrise on Wednesday morning, before her family would really begin to panic—if, indeed, they were even awake—was about as late as her captor could be on the road secure in the knowledge that thousands of cops had not yet been alerted about a little grey Tercel with plastic fingers. King knew that if Elliott was right—and Dibben was either mistaken or lying—Baltovich could be proven innocent. There was no way Baltovich could have driven from Lake Scugog to Scarborough in time to answer the frantic phone call from Mrs. Bain at 6:30 Wednesday morning.

The next step was to query Dibben about how certain he was that his sighting had occurred on the Friday. The Monday evening after being stood up, King called him at home. An unsuspecting Dibben answered the phone. "Well, David, I showed up for our meeting on Friday," said King, who was recording the conversation. "And you weren't home."

"Yeah, sorry about that," Dibben replied. "I called the police before you got here, and they told me not to speak with you."

"They told you not to speak to me? They used those words?"

"Well, not exactly, I guess," Dibben said. "It was more that they preferred I not speak with you."

King decided he would do the talking for a while, turn on the charm, explain that he wasn't trying to put him on the spot, he just wanted to ask a few basic questions, the same way the police had. Right away, Dibben mellowed, and he and King were shooting the breeze about their respective families, how they worked such long hours that neither man was able to spend much time with their kids. When it looked like Dibben was willing to answer some questions, King began to secretly record their conversation with the taping device attached to his phone.

Dibben went over everything he remembered seeing that morning, and then King asked how sure he was that it had been the Friday. "I'm pretty sure it was that day," said Dibben.

A few minutes later, King asked if Dibben was aware that both sets of the plastic fingers had been on the driver's door when the car was found—Dibben had said he'd seen one set on the passenger side. "Does that make you wonder?" asked King.

"Yeah," said Dibben. "It does make me wonder. It really does. Did they get me right? Is there somebody else out there that maybe looks like him? Does the description I put together match? I don't know. It does make me wonder. It really does. Christ, I don't know. It's been eating at me for about a week. Ever since I got that subpeona. I even asked the officer about seeing the fingers on the wrong side of the car."

"What did he tell you?"

"The officer didn't know what to say about that. He thought maybe the car had been in an accident or something and the fingers had been knocked off. Something along those lines."

"Is that what he said?" King asked. " 'The fingers may have been knocked off'?"

"Yeah, that's what he said."

"Were you aware," King began, "that they arrested this man because of your testimony?"

"I didn't realize that, no. Now I do. I sort of had a funny feeling about that, though, you know."

King said, "It happened so quickly afterwards."

"I hate to put the finger on anyone."

"I was just curious," King continued, "whether that had been related to you—that he'd been arrested because of what you had told the police."

"Well, nobody ever said that."

King didn't have too many more questions. That exchange left him in a state of utter amazement. He had no idea how such a problematic witness could be relied upon as the linchpin for a first-degree murder charge. It was enough to make him feel queasy.

Subsequently, King drove out to the Maple Stamping plant to meet with Cameron Hastings, the plant's assistant general manager. When asked about David Dibben and his carpooling partner, Mike Turcotte, Hastings described them as "big kids." In the summer, it was quite common for them to play with their own miniature, radio-activated toy cars and trucks in the parking lot during their breaks. King asked Hastings to comment on Dibben's reliability. Did he have a tendency to confabulate or exaggerate? Hastings took a long time to respond and a troubled look washed over his face. When his gaze met King's again, Hastings said he didn't want to commit himself to a specific listing of Dibben's character traits.

King also met with Mike Turcotte at the Cavan General Store and Restaurant for an audiotaped interview over coffee one morning. Turcotte recounted what he could remember but, almost right off the bat, he contradicted Dibben. Turcotte said he'd been driving a red Ford Lynx that day—Dibben had been certain it was a 1972 Oldsmobile Cutlass Supreme. Their stories did, however, converge when it came to the imitation fingers on the passenger side of the car beside them. Turcotte was positive he'd seen the fingers, but less certain they'd been attached to the same car featured in the Missing photographs. He thought the car beside them, although quite similar, might have been a bit darker in colour.

Once King had turned off his tape recorder, Turcotte disclosed that, when Detective Brody Smollet had come to interview Dibben at the plant, he'd expressed little interest in taking a statement from him, mostly due to the fact that Turcotte hadn't seen the driver and had no clear recollection of what day the sighting had occurred. Turcotte also confided that Dibben had been "fascinated" by Elizabeth Bain's disappearance. And, after being interviewed by Smollet at work, Dibben had become even more excited, albeit "a little overwhelmed and scared" as well.

As far as Dibben's reliability went, Turcotte explained that, even though he and Dibben were not all that close, he had observed in the past that Dibben possessed "good attention for detail." That said, Turcotte still had a hard time believing Dibben had identified the driver five months after such a fleeting early-morning encounter. "How does this fit in with David's character?" King asked.

"I'd say it fits in with his reputation for exaggerating," said Turcotte. "He's known as a bit of a bullshitter."

—◯—

In the early spring, more than a month before the preliminary hearing was to begin, Mike Engel and Bill Gatward received word of a deal from the Crown attorney's office. If Baltovich, through his lawyers, disclosed the location of Elizabeth Bain's body, they would agree to a plea of guilty on a lesser charge of manslaughter, with Baltovich serving a suggested six-year sentence. "So what did you tell him?" Baltovich wanted to know.

"I told him to fuck off, basically," said Gatward. "I said you didn't do it, and that you had no idea where the body was."

"Good answer," said Rob, "but why would they make such an offer if they believe I did it?"

Gatward figured the Crown might be a little scared about taking the case before a jury. "Maybe so," Rob said. "But even if I was interested, I can't tell them what I don't know."

For Engel, this was a crucial point in his attitude towards Rob. Engel felt that just about any sane guilty person charged with first-degree murder would have taken the six years. During their first meeting, Engel had told Rob that he had no clear idea about his guilt or innocence and that, frankly, he didn't care—a viewpoint that troubled Rob a great deal—for Engel said it was his job to get his client off, not to formulate moral judgments. But when Rob belted the plea offer into the upper deck, Engel was undeniably moved.

—◯—

Jailhouse Notebook (2)

A number of guards have been commenting lately on how much weight I've lost, and several friends have noted that my complexion has become green. It is hard for me to monitor my appearance as we aren't allowed glass mirrors, only those of the "funhouse" variety. So, with the preliminary approaching, I have been pushing my cell workouts to a new level. I have been doing hundreds of push-ups every day. I try to jump up and touch the ceiling as many times in a row as I can. My short stature has allowed me to hang from the edge of the top bunk and do behind-the-neck chin-ups.

My voluminous collection of books and magazines are not just for reading. During the morning security promenades, someone inevitably comments that I have too many books and magazines in the cell. As such, they constitute a fire hazard and must be removed immediately. So I promise to get rid of them and then "forget." The plastic bags I hustled from the range helped me fashion a couple of makeshift dumb-bells by stuffing them full of magazines. I take one bag in each hand and use them for arm curls. The books are for shoulder raises.

Guards often pass by the cell during my workouts. Even when my back is to the door, I can hear their feet shuffle as they double back to see what I am doing. I wonder what they think. My every repetition is fuelled by my spite for Reesor and Raybould and the system that is keeping me here. Staying strong physically and mentally is my way of exacting revenge.

Intellectually, I sense a change coming over me. I have always enjoyed reading, but "literature" has, until recently, failed to invigorate me; it seemed a little boring. I was more interested in truth than fiction. But with jail taking me away from the world of physical sense, I have begun to think that I maybe put too much stock in "truth."

With the help of the librarian, I have devoured every book put on my plate. My physical senses have become sublimated to those of the mind; words that once whispered now scream out. In a sense, I feel as though I am recreating myself through men like Dostoevsky, Tolstoy, James and Hardy. The librarian is helping me immeasurably in this regard, making sure that, on the days I am away at court for my weekly remands, books are always left in my cell.

My life outside of here hadn't seemed that fast-paced while I was immersed in the joy of living it. In contrast to my present, more methodical existence, my previous life did interfere with my ability to develop an aesthetic sense and emotional depth needed to appreciate great writing. The correspondence between what I'd experienced in print and what I'd experienced in life had always seemed weak. Elizabeth's disappearance, and the turn my life has taken, read in some ways like a novel; at times I see myself as the chief protagonist in a real-life drama that is still unfolding. What makes the drama so intriguing is that it consists of both truth and fiction, yet so few know which is which.

As these revelations multiply, I am acquiring a new appreciation for the life of the mind. It is the one thing they can't take away, as it is through my thoughts that I can experience freedom.

—◯—

On May 6, Brian King was seated next to Mike Engel at the defence table as Bill Gatward addressed Mr. Justice Edward Ormston, the judge presiding over Robert Baltovich's preliminary inquiry in Scarborough. Gatward was making the usual requests for such a hearing—an order banning the publication or broadcast of any evidence until the accused was either discharged or ordered to stand trial, as well as an order excluding certain witnesses, particularly members of the Bain family, from the courtroom during certain portions of the evidence. Judge Ormston complied with these basic formalities before hearing from John McMahon, the assistant Crown attorney for Scarborough. Only thirty-four years old, McMahon could have passed for much younger—King imagined him as some flaxen-haired country boy in dirty overalls, watching his daddy's pigs at feed time with a big down-home grin, chewing on a piece of straw. But King had done some work in the past for McMahon's brother, Daniel, a Toronto lawyer, and he quickly sensed that John's looks were deceiving. McMahon already had seven years of trial experience and had established a reputation as a highly skilled prosecutor in serious criminal cases. Engel had also prosecuted several murder trials during his eight and a half years as a Crown attorney (after articling with Arthur Maloney), but, as was the case with Gatward, he had yet to defend one.

Due to the fact that preliminary inquiries are heard by judge alone—there is no jury—McMahon outlined the Crown's case against Baltovich in the briefest possible manner, sparing Judge Ormston the long-winded rhetoric often deployed for the sake of the uninitiated. Like Brian Raybould's summary at the bail hearing, it involved motive, opportunity and what McMahon referred to as conduct and statements revealing Baltovich's "consciousness of guilt." But McMahon also promised to present forensic evidence related to Elizabeth Bain's car, as well as to "her state of mind prior to her disappearance."

The Crown's first witness was Liz's best friend, Arlene Coventry, who reconstructed much of that hectic first day after the disappearance at the Bain household. McMahon also called Nancy Sicchia, who testified that Rob had admitted to having seen Liz "hiding by the car or inside the car." She was no longer sure which it had been because her memory of that conversation was now "sketchy." Regardless, Coventry, who'd also been in the car when Rob was supposed to have uttered these words, had no memory of such a statement. And then there was Al Heys, who had told the police that the envelope he'd picked up in Rob's car had been a Dear John letter. "When you used the words 'Dear John letter,'" McMahon asked, "what did you mean by that?"

"It's a letter someone writes to break off a relationship," Heys replied.

"And was that your understanding of the phrase back then?"

"When I gave my statement to the police," explained Heys, "I was not fully aware of its meaning. I believed it only indicated trouble in a relationship, not breaking off."

The following morning, the court heard from Vanessa Sherman, the Kidbrooke employee who'd seen a tiff between Liz and a man she thought might be Rob (from photographs) across the street a couple of weeks before June 19. Since providing the police with that statement, however, Sherman had come to the conclusion that this incident had taken place not a couple of weeks before the disappearance but the Saturday just prior to it—the very same day Al Heys said he'd seen the Dear John letter. Much to Rob's horror, she was now willing to, at McMahon's direction, stand up in the witness box and point him out as the man she'd seen in the car that afternoon, having words with Elizabeth Bain. When it came to identifying the man's car, though—the largest object in the entire scene—Sherman was anything but decisive. "I don't know the make of the car," she told Bill Gatward. "I don't even know the colour. I just know it was a long car, lengthwise."

"You can't tell us whether it was a North American–made car or a foreign car?" asked Gatward.

"I would have no idea."

"Whether it was silver, or grey, or green or white?"

"All I could say was that it was dark."

"Whether it appeared to be new or old?"

"No."

"Two-door or four-door?"

"I can't remember."

Sustaining the quarrelling-young-lovers theme, McMahon then presented Ethel Ormsby, primarily to establish that Liz had been wearing an outfit similar to the one Susanne Nadon had seen on an Elizabeth Bain lookalike an hour and a half later, walking beneath a lone street lamp on Kingston Road, as her male companion drove away, grinding the gears. While, in her original statement, Nadon had been reluctant to identify the woman as Elizabeth Bain, she was now, ten months later, willing to say she was "ninety-five per cent sure that it was Elizabeth Bain." In his cross-examination, Gatward attempted to elicit a concession from Nadon that she couldn't have had a clear view of the road due to the foliage on the trees in front of her house, but was met with considerable resistance. "Were these branches here in the photograph not sticking out between your window and the roadway?" he asked.

"Well, you've got to understand," replied Nadon, "I can go from window to window. The officer who took this photograph was trying to get a picture of the full view. I had full view of this large window, so I could go from side to side to see the angles."

"Isn't this picture taken from that same window?"

"Yeah, but it's not a full view of what I can see."

"All right," said Gatward, pointing to the photograph. "This is a spruce tree on the left, there is a tree trunk to the right of that and on the right-hand side what appear to be branches. It wouldn't have been much different in June than it is in this picture, which was taken in—"

Nadon didn't wait for Gatward to finish. "I had a good view," she insisted.

"Taken in early May?"

"I had a good view."

"You're agreeing with me that it would not—"

"I had a good view."

"—have been much different?"

"No, not a whole lot, no."

Before wrapping up with his questions, Gatward asked if she had any idea where Bain's body might be found. "When she first went missing," said Nadon, "I made a suggestion that the police check the sewers being put in down the road." Gatward wanted to know if she remembered telling Betsy Watanabe, the herbalist, about having a vision of the missing girl being in the sewers. "No visions," said Nadon. "Just a feeling."

"Did you see it in a dream?"

"No dreams."

The next few days of testimony concentrated on the recollections of the Bain family. In addition to assuring the judge that Liz was not the type of person to disappear, either by running away or by taking her own life, the Bains helped the Crown construct its theory that Baltovich had sneaked a substantial portion of his girlfriend's diary out of the house and then destroyed it because, presumably, it had depicted him as violent and jealous. Mr. Bain recounted how, on the evening of Wednesday, June 20, Rob had eaten a quick meal in the Bain kitchen and then left. At the front door, Rob had informed Mr. Bain that he'd "kept a couple of sheets from the diary." What Mr. Bain had found slightly strange, although he hadn't bothered to bring it up, was that Rob hadn't been holding any of the pages in his hands—Mr. Bain had, at the time, simply assumed that he'd folded the pages and tucked them in the back of his pants underneath his shirt, or something like that. But the way Rob remembered it, he'd taken the pages out to his car while everyone was eating in the kitchen before returning inside to join them. He had no memory of Mr. Bain accompanying him to the front door, although, given his distracted state, he thought it quite possible that it could have happened.

When it came to the missing diary pages part of the Crown's theory, Brian King was at a complete loss to comprehend how anyone could honestly argue that the document had been tampered with. King had looked at the original and observed that it had been Liz's usual practice to write on both sides of the looseleaf pages in her diary. On the flip side of the final June 15 entry was one dated May 15. Was it not a logical assumption that there had been no entries during that month gap? In King's mind, the bottom line was this: if Rob had destroyed diary entries because Liz had written negatively about him, why had he returned more than a dozen unflattering passages, including several in which she wrote of breaking up?

For Gatward and Engel, the preliminary hearing was the legal version of a dress rehearsal. A dry run. It was an opportunity to explore the evidential terrain of the Crown's witnesses without having to worry about a jury's reaction in the event that a defence lawyer used the wrong tactic or approach in cross-examination. In this case, Gatward and Engel believed it was the perfect time to confront the Bain family with some of the information John Secord had secretly passed on to them through Brian King. To subject the family of a missing young woman to such rough treatment would be foolhardy in front of a jury, as the accused's lawyers would risk drawing the contempt of the jurors which, of course, would be of no help to their client.

Before a judge alone, Gatward and Engel felt they could proceed. By exposing Elizabeth Bain as the unhappy product of a troubled family, they hoped to rejuvenate the possibility that suicide was not nearly as far-fetched as the Crown's case suggested. And with Liz's brother Mark, in particular, Gatward and Engel saw an opportunity to make a mockery of the evidence against their client by casting an equally hazy shadow of doubt upon a witness whose innocence they never really questioned. Seizing upon Mark's description of his relationship with his older sister as having been "very, very close," Mike Engel immediately conjured a set of circumstances with some rather dark undertones. Minutes into his cross-examination, Engel extracted the fact that Mark had taken his motorboat to Lake Scugog on two separate occasions during the summer following his sister's disappearance. Later on, Engel took Mark's proclivity for boating a step further. "Now, we've heard of the five hundred searches that your father conducted," Engel said. "How many searches did you attend in an attempt to find your sister?"

"I attended two."

"I take it you found better things to do during your summer weekends than search for your sister?"

"No," Mark said. "That's incorrect."

"Well, I guess what I'm driving at is that your whole family is out searching for your missing sister. So why would you be going to visit your friends in cottage country instead of helping your family look for Liz? What explanation do you have for that?"

Mark defended his actions by describing how he'd been working long hours with his landscaping company and had also been going to school two nights a week. At home, it had been a "media circus," especially during the first few weeks. Throughout the summer, his parents had devoted all of their energy to finding Liz. "I went to go and see these friends, who had told me I was quite welcome to come up and talk to them any time I wanted to, if I felt like I had to talk to somebody—which I did," he said. "I was under a lot of stress and I figured there were enough people going on these weekend searches that me being there wasn't going to help. It certainly wasn't going to help me, because I was under enough stress as it was."

Engel also wanted to explore the details of a physical altercation John Secord had heard about between Mark and his father. "I understand that one time you and he were on the porch, and you punched him in the face and knocked him right off the porch? Do you recall that incident?"

"No," Mark declared. "That never happened."

"Did you ever punch him at any time?"

"I've never punched my dad, no. But I pushed him once."

"When was it that that occurred?"

Mark explained that the incident had arisen as a result of an argument beween his father and his sister Cathy. From another room, Mark could hear how mouthy she was being and sensed it was only a matter of time before one of them would "break." "Then I heard something that I thought was a slap, which triggered me," Mark said. "And I came around the corner and pushed my father away from her."

"Did he fall down?"

Mark responded, "I can't remember."

Alluding to the tanned, muscular arm that Ruth Collins had seen reaching across Liz to close the passenger door of the Tercel as she attempted to step outside, Engel got Mark, who admitted to knowing how to drive a standard transmission, to agree that he was quite muscular and was probably quite tanned in mid-June from "the luxury of an outdoor job." Engel also pressed him to confirm his attendance at class the Tuesday of his sister's disappearance, as well as the following Thursday. "Do they take attendance at this class?" Engel asked.

"No, they don't," was the answer.

"And tell me, who was it you sat beside on June 19, do you recall that?"

"I don't recall that. There are no seats, just long benches."

"Do you have any recollection at all as to having seen any of your fellow classmates that night?"

"Yes, I was familiar with one person. Her name is Maria Vusnovich."

"Did you have any contact with her that night?"

"No, I can't remember that either, I'm afraid."

When Rick Bain took the witness stand, he began by confessing that when Liz began dating Rob, he found him to be a "charmer." "During the time that Elizabeth was going out with him," asked McMahon, "did you ever have any problems with Mr. Baltovich?"

"No," Rick answered. "I had absolutely no problems with him at all until this episode."

Once McMahon had led Mr. Bain through the events subsequent to June 19, Bill Gatward wasted little time delving into the explosive material provided to him through the Secord files:

GATWARD: During the first six months of 1990, the Bain household was not a happy one, is that correct?

BAIN: I think you're incorrect about that.

GATWARD: Well, let's see now. You and your wife hadn't been sleeping together for five years, is that correct?

BAIN: I think you're way out on a limb, sir.

GATWARD: Is it not also correct, sir, that you and your wife had been contemplating a separation for some time prior?

BAIN: You are absolutely way out, sir.

GATWARD: There was never any talk about a separation?

BAIN: Yes, we talk about it once a year, at least.

GATWARD: Is that an answer to my question, sir?

BAIN: Yes it is, because sometimes we talk about things like that. I don't know what kind of a marriage you contemplate, but no marriage is made in heaven. I'm not saying we have a perfect marriage but we've never seriously discussed a separation, ever. So I'm being a little bit jestful with you when I say once a year.

GATWARD: And at the time that Elizabeth went missing, I understand that your other daughter, Cathy, was not living at home, is that correct?

BAIN: That's correct, I did have a disagreement with my daughter.

GATWARD: That was a violent disagreement, was it not?

BAIN: No, I wouldn't call it a violent disagreement.

GATWARD: Didn't you actually strike your daughter?

BAIN: Yes, I did give her a slap in the face, that's correct.

GATWARD: And is it true, sir, that the slap was sufficiently hard to knock Cathy to the floor?

BAIN: My Lord, no sir. Not even close to it.

GATWARD: You're denying that?

BAIN: It never happened.

GATWARD: Was there ever any violence between you and Cathy's former boyfriend, Steve Annett? In particular, was there an incident in which you pushed him into a wall?

BAIN: No sir, I don't know where you get this information.

GATWARD: Had there been an incident, sir, where you caught your daughter in a rather embarrassing situation with Mr. Annett in your own house?

BAIN: Yes, there was a situation like that.

GATWARD: After your daughter's disappearance, sir, did you have a falling out with your sister, Diana Bain?

BAIN: I've often had arguments with my sister.

GATWARD: I mean a serious argument.

BAIN: No, not serious.

GATWARD: You've remained on relatively good terms with her since the disappearance?

BAIN: Since Elizabeth's disappearance?

GATWARD: Yes.

BAIN: Yes.

GATWARD: Are you aware, sir, that Mr. Baltovich and your daughter had gone to Niagara Falls?

BAIN: The first opportunity he had when I went away, he pressured her into that, yes. I'm aware of it, unfortunately.

GATWARD: When was that?

BAIN: When my wife and I went away on the first trip of our married life last May.

GATWARD: From your response, I take it you did not approve of this.

BAIN: No, I did not approve of it and I think it's pretty obvious why not. His principles are very different from her principles.

GATWARD: I take it you don't think people who aren't married should be spending weekends together.

BAIN: That's correct, I don't believe in it. Do you?

GATWARD: Are you aware who paid for the trip?

BAIN: I understand that my daughter took some money out, so I imagine that she probably paid for a good part of it.

GATWARD: Sir, you took your daughter to Argentina in the middle of the school year. Could I ask why you didn't take your wife?

BAIN: It wasn't in the middle of the school year, sir, it was at the beginning of it. With regards to my wife, she didn't come with me because we don't like to leave our children alone. Actually, I had asked my wife to come with me, but she didn't want to for that very reason. Therefore, I decided to take my oldest daughter, simply because she is the most conversant in Spanish of my children. She is, in fact, the only one fluent in Spanish. Plus, Liz was the eldest and had the flexibility, being in university.

GATWARD: Would it also perhaps be because your relationship with Elizabeth was a little bit closer than your relationship with your other children?

BAIN: I wouldn't say so. She was the first born, but that's about the only thing that would make her closer.

GATWARD: Your preference would be towards Elizabeth as opposed to Cathy, is that correct?

BAIN: I don't think I want to tell you what my preferences are with my kids. That's a private matter. I don't even tell my own wife that.

GATWARD: Well, I'm here to ask you questions, sir, and I'm asking you right now whether your preference was towards Elizabeth, more than, say, Cathy?

BAIN: Perhaps because she's the first born, yes.

GATWARD: Did you ever get the feeling that this closeness with Elizabeth caused her problems?

BAIN: No, on the contrary. I think a good bonding with a father is very important for a young woman.

GATWARD: And, sir, on the Tuesday, the nineteenth, do you recall making a telephone call from your niece's residence in Florida to the National Sports Store in Scarborough?

BAIN: Yes.

GATWARD: At about 5:00 PM?

BAIN: I have no idea.

GATWARD: Do you know why you would have called there from Florida?

BAIN: Yes, I bought a tennis racquet when I was with my sister and I needed to check the price at the National store to find out whether they were competitive. I don't remember how much I paid but it was a good deal.

GATWARD: Even discounting the cost of the long-distance phone call?

BAIN: Very much so. It was still a very good deal.

[Partway through his cross-examination, Gatward was forced to leave due to a pre-arranged appointment, and Engel continued in his place.]

ENGEL: I understand that, on Sunday, October twenty-eighth, your daughter's social insurance card, hospital card and immunization record were in the wastebasket of Elizabeth's room. Do you have any knowledge about that?

BAIN: No, I don't have any such knowledge.

ENGEL: You have no idea how it got there?

BAIN: John Secord was scavenging through her room and, apparently, that's where the story comes from.

ENGEL: Okay. I understand that you don't have vision in one of your eyes, is that right?

BAIN: Yes. I don't know how this is relevant, but that's correct.

ENGEL: I understand that you have an invariable practice of reversing your car into parking spots because of your lack of vision in that eye.

BAIN: That's true, but it has nothing to do with my eye. Not having vision in one eye—my God, your conclusions are amazing. I back my car into my driveway every day, sir, because it's quick to get out in the morning.

ENGEL: Now, to your knowledge, did your daughter Liz ever smoke cigarettes?

BAIN: No, it wouldn't surprise me if she'd tried it once or twice, but I don't think she smokes.

ENGEL: In the days and months preceding your daughter's disappearance, did you notice a particular dissatisfaction or friction between you and her?

BAIN: No. In fact, I think she was showing her independence by insisting she pay for her own tuition. And when I insisted this would be too hard for her, she said, "No, Dad, this is a good way for me to get more out of my schooling." And I acceded reluctantly and told her if she changed her mind to let me know.

ENGEL: Now, specifically, the passage in your daughter's diary dated February second, 1990, she writes, "I don't want to have any part of Dad's life after I'm married." Do you know what anxieties you put your daughter through, what she was making reference to in that paragraph?

BAIN: No, I couldn't tell you of any one specific thing, but I guess when it comes to discipline, I'm applying it more than my wife, so that's probably what she's talking about.

ENGEL: With respect to the last entry Liz made in her diary, I take it that you'd agree with me that your daughter's diary would appear to that of an extremely distraught young lady.

BAIN: At this particular time, I agree it's very distraught and Rob seems to be the reason for her distress.

ENGEL: Well, thank you for that observation, sir, but if you could just respond to my questions and try to refrain from other comments, I think we'd all appreciate that. We'll let His Honour draw his own conclusions. Dealing with this final entry, your daughter indicates "Life sucks—and it's getting worse by the day . . . [*reads entry*]." Now, leaving aside your conjecture, who might "everybody else" bothering her be?

BAIN: Well, I wasn't there, so you can't blame me, can you?

ENGEL: Pardon me?

BAIN: I wasn't there for that whole week, so—

ENGEL: You had an ironclad alibi, that's right.

BAIN: I don't know about the alibi, all I'm saying is that I wasn't there, so this one time you can't say it was me bothering her.

ENGEL: Let's exclude you from the formulation then. Who might be the other people, to your knowledge, other than Rob, who were bothering her?

BAIN: I honestly don't know. I wish I did.

ENGEL: Now, she says she wants to put a bullet through Rob's head, and she says, "I'm going to murder somebody." Had you ever known your daughter to express these feelings of rage and violence before?

BAIN: Never. Never. I was distraught by reading it myself.

ENGEL: Okay, throughout the course of the entry she says, "I hate this life. I hate it here." Are these feelings that she'd expressed to you before?

BAIN: Not that she hated life, no. I heard her say that she was under pressure. That she was upset with this or that or the other thing. Her school was not as good as she wanted it. I think she was taking too much on, but that's her choice.

ENGEL: Prior to your daughter's disappearance, did you become aware that she was in the habit of frequenting motels, such as the Lido Motel on Kingston Road?

BAIN: I don't think she ever did frequent the Lido Motel or any other motel. I've never been aware of that.

ENGEL: Okay, thank you, sir. Those are my questions.

—◯—

When John McMahon's co-counsel, Paul Amenta, called out the name of the first witness to follow the Bain family—Andrea Beitinger—Rob turned in his seat to watch her make her way to the front of the courtroom. He hadn't seen her for six months—Andrea was one of just a few friends who had never come to visit him at Metro East—and he was carefully scrutinizing the expression on her face, the clothes she was wearing, where she looked or chose not to look as she faced the courtroom, all in an effort to determine whether her absence was representative of her feelings. As Amenta, a man of average height who seemed to compensate for the thinning dark curls above his forehead with a thick black moustache, led her through her history with Rob at Greenwood Camp, the only emotion Rob could detect was one of extreme discomfort and nervousness.

What Rob didn't know was that Andrea's participation in this ordeal had exacted a profound toll on her life. She'd pulled herself out of Scarborough College and begun taking night classes at the downtown campus. Not knowing how her Scarborough friends would react when it eventually became known that she'd worked as an agent of the police, Andrea had, by her own choice, isolated herself from them. Essentially, she felt forced to begin life anew. As for the prospect of returning to the Metro Police Force next summer for a job, there was no chance of that—she was far too disgusted with the whole thing.

About an hour and a half into Andrea's examination by the Crown, Judge Ormston adjourned for the morning recess. Andrea, who still looked upset, perhaps on the verge of tears, walked past Rob and took a seat in the gallery. Although he didn't yet know the reasons for it, Rob could tell that she was finding this a difficult experience, so he looked over at her and, catching her eye, mouthed the words "It's okay." He really wanted to assure her that there was nothing for her to worry about. To just keep telling the truth.

When she resumed her testimony, Amenta had only a dozen or so questions left, most of them relatively innocuous. Knowing that the Beitinger tapes served little purpose to the Crown, Amenta waited until his very last question to bring up her role as an agent for the police. "Can you tell His Honour whether or not the police enlisted your assistance," said Amenta, laying it on thick with the technical jargon, "insofar as intercepting any communications between yourself and Mr. Baltovich?"

"Yes," she responded, feeling the weight of the moment. "They did." Rob blinked hard, then froze in bug-eyed stupefaction, staggered with the realization that he had been so coolly and ruthlessly deceived by someone he had considered a good friend. As Bill Gatward embarked on his cross-examination, Rob felt his earlier compassion for her dissipate.

The first thing Gatward wanted to know was how she'd become involved with the investigators. "So you thought at that point that you might have some information to provide to the police?" he asked.

"Well," said Andrea, "I felt that if they spoke to me, maybe I could tell them certain things that Rob perhaps could not get across."

"Do you mean that you wished to explain some things to the police on Mr. Baltovich's behalf?"

"Yes."

"So you wanted to act as his advocate, then?" Gatward's sarcasm was unmistakable.

"Perhaps 'advocate' is the wrong word. I wanted to tell the police what I knew."

"You mean you wanted to inform on him?" Gatward inquired. "Or did you want to tell them things for him?"

"For him," she clarified.

"So you wanted to help Mr. Baltovich, is that correct?" Gatward was perfectly aware of just how preposterous Andrea's reasoning had become. She'd secretly recorded her conversations with one of her best friends for the Homicide cops looking to put him away as a means of clearing Rob's name? Despite Gatward's incredulity, Andrea had gone too far to deviate from this stand.

"Yes, it is," she said.

"How did it come about," asked Gatward, "that you went from being a person explaining things for Mr. Baltovich to a person who was informing on him?"

"Perhaps because I worked for the police, they told me a little bit more about the case than what they would tell other people."

"Like what?"

"I knew that blood had been found in the car."

"And how did the police explain to you that this was linked to my client and his culpability?"

"Well, they did not explain it."

"How, then, did you come to the conclusion it was the right thing to start being a snitch?"

Andrea was far less flustered by this derogatory line of questioning than Rob would have guessed, especially given her earlier disquietude. If anything, her confidence seemed to be growing considerably. "They asked me if I would have conducted myself the same way if I had been in Rob's situation. If I would have stopped going on the searches for my girlfriend."

"And Mr. Baltovich had already told you there was a lot of media attention and he thought it was better to lie low, isn't that what he told you?"

"Sure, that's what he told me, but that isn't something I would do, personally." With that, Andrea revealed the truth—that she hadn't been so interested in assisting Rob after all.

"I gather he'd never been suspected of something as serious as murder, had he?"

"No, but if you're suspected of something as serious as that, and this is your girlfriend that you love, wouldn't you want to find her?"

"I don't want to debate with you, ma'am," said Gatward somewhat lamely. Instead of finding a way to explain that Rob had stopped searching at his lawyer's request, Gatward simply announced his intention to "move on."

—◦—

Dave Madder had come home late from work and had been dozing on the couch for a while when the phone rang. He looked at his watch—it was a quarter to eleven—before picking up the receiver. The voice on the other end belonged to Rick Bain. Over the last few months, Madder hadn't been in contact with Mr. Bain as frequently as he had back in the days when Madder was his search coordinator. Since mid-March, Madder had been assisting the Stanton family's search for their daughter Julie in and around the lakefront area of Pickering and had spent only one day up in Port Perry on the Bain effort. When Mr. Bain called nowadays, it had more to do with his role as Madder's landlord than with organizing searches. At the beginning of March, Madder, along with his girlfriend, Venise Young, had moved into the basement apartment of a house Mr. Bain owned on Melchior Drive in Scarborough.

At the time, Mr. Bain had said he would give them a break on putting up the last month's rent. Paying the first month would get things started sufficiently. So that's what they did and, for the first few weeks, everything went smoothly and they busied themselves getting settled.

But, on the second day of April, a Tuesday, came the first sign that life on Melchior Drive was going to be somewhat out of the ordinary. Madder came home from work that night to discover that the side door opening into the apartment had been left unlocked. Luckily, nothing had been stolen or even disturbed. When Venise got home a few hours later, he asked her about the door, and she replied that he'd probably forgotten to lock it in the morning. Madder forgot about it, until two days later he arrived home from work and the door was open again. This time he was sure he'd left it locked.

About a week later, Mr. Bain called late one night and told Madder that, if he was contacted by a private investigator named Brian King, he shouldn't speak with him. Mr. Bain said he'd been advising people, especially members of the search team, to stay away from Brian King. He also told Madder that he didn't want him attending the preliminary hearing when it began in May. He didn't offer a reason, just made it clear he didn't want him showing up. Mr. Bain also said he didn't want Madder distributing any material that had to do with the searches for his daughter. Madder said fine, he wouldn't do any of those things. For some reason, Mr. Bain called again the next morning and spoke to Venise. Madder had already left for the day. Mr. Bain asked her a lot of strange questions about Madder's whereabouts before telling her that he did not want her coming to the preliminary inquiry either.

Mr. Bain called the following week and told Madder for the second time to stay away from Brian King. Even more bothersome was that Madder found the side door unlocked again after work the next night. The only three people with keys were Venise, Mr. Bain and Madder. Venise was positive that she'd locked the door when she'd gone to work. Madder noticed that some of his materials for the Bain searches—maps and other papers—were gone.

It was an ominous sign of things to come. Three nights after that, Madder and Venise were woken up at 3:10 in the morning by a clanging sound that came from their mailbox, which was affixed to the outside wall, next to the door. Madder got out of bed and peered out the front window but couldn't see anything. He could hear a car, though, one with a standard transmission—he could tell by the shifting gears as it sped away. Outside the front door, the mailbox was empty. He went to the kitchen table and made a note of the time—he was fastidious about keeping records when it came to things like this.

Exactly ten days later—on April 30—Madder was once more jolted from his sleep, this time at 2:40 AM by noises in the backyard. He thought he might even have heard something bang against the window. He told Venise that someone might be in the yard as he tried peering out through the glass, but once again there was nothing to see. Just then he heard what sounded like the same four-speed drive away from the house. Madder was starting to wonder if Venise's ex-husband was snooping around, trying to check up on her while they were asleep. But neither was convinced it was him.

Two days later, Mr. Bain called at 7:30 AM and spoke to Venise. The message was for Madder not to show up at court.

That was the last incident before the most recent phone call from Mr. Bain, the one that had just interrupted yet another peaceful slumber. It was now May 8. Madder wasn't aware of it, but Mr. Bain had, late the previous afternoon, faced his first hour or so of Bill Gatward's alarmingly personal cross-examination and, because the Baltovich inquiry had been forced to skip a day, he was to resume that torturous affair the following morning. Mr. Bain said he had two points to make. One was not to speak to Brian King. (Presumably, King was the one digging up much of the intimate material about his family.) Madder, who was starting to lose his patience, said that this was the third time he'd agreed to comply with this request. He didn't quite grasp what the urgency was all about. The second issue, said Mr. Bain, involved Madder's rent money. A few weeks ago, Mr. Bain had called to let him know that he now wanted Madder's last month's rent, in addition to what he owed him on the first of May. They had haggled for a few weeks over the last month's rent, which Mr. Bain had originally waived, and then Madder's May rent cheque had bounced, which was the reason for the call. Mr. Bain wanted to know when he was going to get his rent money.

Madder ended up having to take the money up to Mr. Bain's house himself, which was when Mr. Bain started in on him about coming up with the last month's rent soon. "But we don't have our basic utilities," protested Madder. "No hot running water. No gas. The gas dryer isn't working. Everything is damp. Half of my stuff has been ruined because of mould damage. How about you fix the place and then I'll pay what I owe you."

"It doesn't work that way," countered Mr. Bain. "You're trying to con me."

"No, I'm not," said Madder. "All I'm asking is that you give us hot running water and what we need to live. It's cold and there's no heat down there. We've gone the last part of winter with no heat."

Mr. Bain said that was Madder's problem—he wanted the outstanding rent money. Madder said he'd pay as soon as the place got fixed. That was it, two bulls at a stand-off. A few days later, Madder decided to call an inspector with the city to come and take a look at his deplorable living conditions. The inspector came, ticked some little boxes on a form sheet and immediately contacted Mr. Bain. Now that really got him hot. He called Madder at least four or five times throughout the rest of the month, demanding his money. Madder did not reply.

That's how things went until June 6. Madder was in the middle of a long-distance telephone call when he heard a noise in the kitchen. It was 10:30 PM. Venise thought the noise was Madder speaking to her, and he thought it was someone in the kitchen with her, so he asked her who was in the kitchen. Madder interrupted his phone call and hollered, "Who is it?" A voice responded, "It's me!" It was Rick Bain. "Could you please come out here?"

"Excuse me," Madder called out. "I'm on the phone. What are you doing here?"

"Well, would you mind getting off the phone and coming out here to talk to me?"

So Madder cut off his long-distance conversation and he and Venise went into the kitchen. "Yes?" said Madder. He was downright pissed off, now. "Can I help you?" Then, before Mr. Bain could respond, Madder added, "How did you get in?"

Mr. Bain said, "I have ways to get in."

"You mean with a key?"

"Yes," said Mr. Bain. "I have a key."

"Why wouldn't you bother knocking before letting yourself in?" Madder wanted to know. Mr. Bain said that he saw a light on and just let himself in. Was real smug about it. So then they had words. Mr. Bain called Madder an idiot, a goofball and an ass-face, as well as a few other choice names. He told Madder that he was a con man and that Bain wanted nothing more to do with him. He stormed out of the apartment and got into his Volvo outside, which, as he drove away, sounded to Madder just like the car he'd heard twice before.

A week later, not long before midnight, Madder and Venise were lying in bed watching televsion, the glare from the screen the only light in the apartment, when they heard doors opening upstairs. It was windy out that night and Madder figured the wind had blown the door open, so he went upstairs to discover that both the inner door to the apartment and the outer door were swinging wide open. There was no one around, but Madder turned on the light and saw that a note had been tacked to the front of the inner door. The note, from Mr. Bain, indicated that Madder's cheque for the previous month had not been honoured—which was true—but Madder had paid Mr. Bain in person. He gathered this was all part and parcel of their dispute over the last month's rent, still. So Madder just took the note off the door and filed it along with everything else.

Mr. Bain paid yet another visit on June 20, this time accompanied by Julita, who tapped on the window above Madder's bed and said they would like to come in. Madder went up to let them into the apartment and once again they began to argue about the unpaid rent. Madder brought up the fact that he'd never been reimbursed for all the money he'd spent on long-distance phone calls related to the search effort, not to mention gas and everything else. "Forget about the search," said Julita, jumping into the conversation. "The search is garbage. What is more important is the money for rent, so give Rick the money. That's all there is to it. We're not talking search."

"Well, I'm not talking search either," insisted Madder. "The search is separate and I realize that." Julita repeated that the search was garbage. Mr. Bain ended up calling Madder a drunken bum. That was the last straw. A few days later, Madder delivered a letter of notice—he and Venise were moving out at the end of the month.

Moving day was Saturday, June 30. Madder and a friend, Ken Burnett, who was helping him out for the day, pulled up to the house to load up Madder's truck at 1:00 PM and saw Mr. Bain's car parked in front. The couple who lived upstairs were also in the process of moving. On their way to the house, Madder and Burnett had no choice but to pass Mr. Bain, who was standing near his wife. Burnett said, "Hi, Mr. Bain." Mr. Bain pointed at Madder and said, "This fellow is a con artist. He owes me money."

"I'm sorry," said Burnett. "But it's not really any of my business." Mr. Bain trailed closely behind as they made their way to the side door. Madder turned to face him and said, "Mr. Bain, look, I'm kind of busy moving. Can you wait until we finish? I'll have a word with you after."

The answer was a curt no.

"Well," said Madder. "What do you want to say?"

Mr. Bain was red and trembling, about ready to burst. "I'm gonna ram your teeth right down your throat," he said.

"Well, here I am," said Madder. They were now nose to nose. Mr. Bain repeated his threat. "I'm gonna ram your teeth right down your throat!"

"Go ahead," said Madder. "Here we are."

They just stood there for a while, Burnett a few feet off to the side, until Madder slowly turned and went down the stairs into the apartment. "He's quite upset," said Burnett, trailing behind. "Yes, he is," Madder agreed. They grabbed a couple of boxes and went back outside, where Mr. Bain was still waiting. He followed Madder to the front of the house and once again said he was going to ram Madder's teeth down his throat. Madder put the box on the ground and said, "Hold on a second, Mr. Bain. Come with me." Madder started walking towards the front door, where Jessie, the man who was moving out of the upstairs apartment, was standing. "Now, Mr. Bain," said Madder. "Would you mind telling Jessie what you just said to me?"

"I didn't say anything," said Mr. Bain. Then he whispered, so Jessie couldn't hear, "I'm gonna shove your teeth down your throat."

"I'm sorry, I don't think Jessie heard that." Madder turned slightly and Mr. Bain said, under his breath, "I'll fix you."

"What do you mean 'fix me'?" asked Madder. "How do you plan to do that?"

"That's none of your business," growled Mr. Bain. "You'll find out."

While everyone stood around and watched, Madder went back to the apartment to retrieve more of his belongings. When he returned to the laneway, Mr. Bain was all over him again. "I'm going to fix you," he declared. "Because I have the money and the means to do it."

"What do you mean by that?" Madder asked.

Mr. Bain said, "You'll see."

"Why not do it right here?"

"You've got two hours to get out of this place," said Mr. Bain. "When I come back, your stuff is on the street."

"Go ahead," Madder replied, getting in his truck. "I'd appreciate the help."

"I'll fix you."

"Fine." With that, Madder and Burnett drove away, as did the Bains.

When Madder and Burnett returned an hour or so later, Jessie and his wife quickly came up to the truck. "Come with us," said Jessie, sounding excited. "We've got to show you something. Rick was just here." Madder and Burnett followed them through the upstairs apartment and down into the basement where there was a separate entrance to Madder's flat. The door, which Madder always left locked—and for which Rick obviously had no key—had a long knife-like chisel sticking through it. "See what Rick did?" said Jessie. "He tried to get through your door."

"Are you sure?" Madder asked.

"Yeah," said Jessie. "Rick did that. He tried to force the door open to get into your apartment."

A little worried about what might happen next, Madder and Burnett went inside, gathered the rest of Madder's stuff and proceeded to get the hell away from there.

A few days later, Madder drove over to 42 Division to speak with Detective Sergeant Brian Raybould about the threats, but was told that Raybould wasn't in. Instead, Madder met with Detective Richard McKennitt and discussed his encounters with Mr. Bain for about forty-five minutes. McKennitt said he would pass everything on to Brian Raybould. Whether he ever did or not was, for Madder, a big question mark—Raybould never got back to him.

—◦—

Due to a scheduling dilemma, Rob's preliminary inquiry was forced to break for more than two months after the first week of testimony heard in early May, resuming once again in the middle of the summer, on July 22. One morning five days before that, however, there was trouble at Metro East. It was a Friday. A burly, red-headed Newfoundlander named Darren Williams was locked in Rob's cell while the guards ran off to sort out the problem. The instant they were alone, Williams set about letting Rob in on a little secret. It had to do with Billy Mackinlay, Rob's old cellmate.

Mackinlay had moved out of Rob's cell and in with Williams (who occupied the neighbouring cell) around the end of April, a short while before the preliminary hearing had commenced. For Williams, it was an opportune moment to disclose what he knew about Mackinlay—that he was a "professional informant" who had not only provided the police with a statement regarding Rob's case but was also planning on testifying against him. Williams said that Mackinlay had told the police that Rob had discussed with him many details germane to the investigation. According to what he'd told Williams, Mackinlay was going to testify that Rob had been reading a book about a fellow who murdered someone but didn't think he would be caught because the police couldn't find the victim's body. "How could he testify against me," Rob asked, "when all I've ever said from the beginning was that I was innocent?"

"I'm just telling you what he is," said Williams. "A rat. And I hate it. He says he's doing it for the money."

Rob figured that the book Mackinlay had mentioned to the police had belonged to another old cellmate, Terry Mertick. Mertick, apparently an ambulance attendant by profession, was another strange character. Mertick had a taste for pulp horror novels and true tales of sordid crimes. The bloodier the better seemed to be Mertick's rule. And Rob could only assume that Mackinlay had stumbled upon a select piece of Mertick's reading material. (Rob's reading list contained the odd thriller by someone like Stephen King but was, by and large, filled with literary classics: *The Brothers Karamazov, For Whom the Bell Tolls, Four Major Plays* by Henrik Ibsen, *The Painted Bird, Notes from Underground, All Quiet on the Western Front* and dozens more.)

Another, less incriminating find of Mackinlay's had also belonged to Mertick. Mertick had cut an advertisement out of a magazine boasting a diet product that would allow its purchasers to "lose up to sixty pounds in one month" and taped it to a photograph of a malnourished Ethiopian woman he'd cropped from the newspaper. Mackinlay, confident that evidence of Baltovich's sadistic humour would be welcomed by his prosecutors, had removed the item from the wall of his cell.

For weeks after this, Darren Williams kept after Rob, insisting that Rob have his lawyer come to speak with him. He said he would testify on his behalf, exposing Mackinlay as a liar, but that he needed to talk to Rob's lawyer first. In the beginning, Rob had been reluctant to get Williams involved but when, months later, he learned through Brian King that the police really *had* taken a statement from Mackinlay and that they had referred to him as a potential witness, Rob arranged for Gatward to meet with Williams. "Newf," as he was known in the "East," was more than happy to provide Gatward with a written statement to stand up to Mackinlay's:

The reason behind me doing all of this was because I wanted to prove to a jury that police informants ain't police informants. What they prove is that they will do anything to get their freedom, even lie in a court of law! William Edward Mackinlay, the "Rat," told me that he has a cheque from the police for $15,000 *and if he gets Robert convicted he will get another $15,000. I asked him where they get this money to pay police informants and he told me it comes straight out of a treasury fund in Ottawa.*

So when the Rat moved into my cell and told me how he is a paid police informant working on Robert Baltovich, I asked him why he moved out of Robert's cell. He told me that Robert is a sick demented person and that he killed his girlfriend. I then said, how the fuck can you come in here and tell me someone killed his girlfriend without any proof?

Now sir, that's when the Rat admitted that the police told him to say that Robert confessed that he fucked his girlfriend and then killed her in the back seat of her car with a brick or a two by four. "I guess they're banking on a blunt instrument," said the Rat. And I asked him why they would ask you to say that, and he told me, because they found some brain fragments in the back seat of the car. That's when I said, that makes sense but won't convict a person. You're going to need more than that. He said you ain't heard it all yet. Robert apparently told the Rat that he did kill his girlfriend but they won't convict him without a body. That's when he told me Robert's mind is very demented. And I said how do you plan on proving that? That's when he hauled out a picture of a black Ethiopian taped to a "lose up to sixty pounds in one month" ad. I asked the Rat where he got this and he told me that he got it out of Robert's cell when he was gone to court. I then said, don't you think he will miss it? And he said, Darren, that boy thinks he's smart but deep down inside he's stupid. The next thing he said was that Robert said he almost fucked up and it's a lucky thing that he ripped out those pages in his girlfriend's diary. Why would he rip those pages out, I asked. And the Rat said it is obvious that she wrote something down about the little weasel.

When Engel was first apprised of William Mackinlay's existence, he was more buoyed by it than dismayed. (The first thing Gatward did was get his client on the phone and tell him, yet again, to shut the fuck up about the case, to which Rob replied, "Bill, you know we get newspapers in here, don't you?") It was Engel's experience that when the Crown called evidence of a jailhouse confession, it was a red flag indicating they had no case. Once he had Williams in the bag to discount an incarcerated witness whose credibility was already in question, Engel was smacking his chops in anticipation. But, eventually, McMahon let it be known that Engel would have to get his licks in with someone else—Mackinlay was being dropped.

———◇———

Eric Genuis and Marc Singleton were the first to testify when the preliminary hearing got under way again, the most electrifying moment coming during Gatward's cross-examination of Genuis, when Genuis spoke of getting a busy signal at Liz's house on June 19. Genuis described how Mr. Bain had subsequently explained that the line had probably been knocked out by the "intermittent waves" caused by his son Paul's new cordless telephone. Rob turned to scan the courtroom for Brian Raybould, who had, at the bail hearing, suggested Rob's story about the busy signal had been nothing but a hastily invented fabrication. Rob was now beginning to wonder if he'd been denied bail for the last eight months because of Raybould's mistake.

Then came David Dibben, the elusive witness whom Rob's entire defence team, including Brian King, was seeing for the first time. King's first impression of Dibben, a thin man (what most would refer to as "skinny") with long dark hair that fell partway down his back, was that he looked like a hippie. King, who had a preference for clean-cut looks, wrote down one adjective: "scraggly." While being questioned by McMahon, Dibben confidently assured the court that Robert Baltovich, photograph number six, was the man he'd seen driving the silver car with the plastic fingers. It was this assertion, more than anything else, that Gatward, conducting the cross-examination, had to attack.

GATWARD: Was there not some uncertainty about this identification in your mind, given the passage of time?

DIBBEN: I looked at a couple of photographs and, of them all, that would be the one I would definitely say was the person driving the car.

GATWARD: That would mean that, if there was somebody in the photographic line-up who was the driver, it was definitely number six?

DIBBEN: Yes.

GATWARD: And was your answer at that point: "Out of all of them, I would say it was number six, except I thought the driver had lighter hair and a slightly heavier moustache. His hair was maybe a little bit longer. But the more I look at it, the more I say, yes, it's number six"?

DIBBEN: Yes.

GATWARD: So it was your opinion at that time that, if you had to pick one of them, it would be number six?

DIBBEN: That's correct.

GATWARD: Do I take it then that you are not a hundred per cent certain?

DIBBEN: No. I was certain that that was the person I seen driving the vehicle.

Unable to reconcile Dibben's last two responses, which appeared incongruous, Gatward pressed on.

GATWARD: How heavy did you say the driver appeared to be?

DIBBEN: Approximately, I'd say between 160 and 165 pounds. Medium weight, medium build.

GATWARD: How much would you say Mr. Baltovich weighs?

DIBBEN: I'd say about the same, in that area.

GATWARD: If I told you he weighed about 145 pounds, would that change your estimate of his weight?

DIBBEN: Well, I could be wrong on the weight, you know, but I'd say he was a medium-built person.

Dibben's testimony was then tied to that of the second Lake Scugog witness, John Elliott, next to appear before Judge Ormston. McMahon needed Elliott to corroborate the theory that hinged on Dibben's testimony—that Baltovich had dumped the body in or near Lake Scugog on the Friday morning. But during his cross-examination, Elliott told Gatward that, because of his son's tuxedo fitting, he was "eighty per cent certain" he'd seen the car and the key fob in the dumpster on Wednesday. Gatward and Engel thought it possible that this concession alone could be enough for the judge to prevent the case from going to trial. McMahon made it clear, however, that he was going to make good use of the other twenty per cent. Re-examining Elliott after Gatward had completed his cross-examination, McMahon had him elucidate how, in addition to the Wednesday tuxedo fitting, Elliott had also been in a hurry to get away from his restaurant for his brother's wedding rehearsal party on Friday. "All right," said McMahon. "So if it wasn't the Wednesday, what day during the week do you think it was?"

Elliott responded, "It would have to have been the Friday."

"Thank you, sir," said McMahon, sounding relieved. "I have no further questions."

The next major witness Rob's lawyers needed to impugn was Marianne Perz. She was one of the most unusual witnesses Gatward and Engel had ever encountered. Her original description of the man sitting at the picnic table next to Elizabeth Bain had revealed nothing beyond the fact that he was Caucasian with dark hair. Then, immediately following her session with Dr. Matheson, she selected Baltovich from a photo line-up, mostly because of the similarity of his eyes to those of the man she saw while under hypnosis, eyes that she now characterized for John McMahon as being "unusually gentle, fresh, sort of sparkling." From statements given by Detective Sergeant Tony Warr, who'd informed Perz that Baltovich's photo was in the line-up before placing it in front of her, Gatward and Engel knew that she had expressed at least a modicum of doubt about the identification, enough to delay Baltovich's arrest for four months.

When, several months earlier, Brian King had let Rob in on Perz's identity, Rob had been flabbergasted. He could still remember clearly that, one day several weeks before Liz had gone missing, he and Steve Doucette had played tennis on a court next to one where Perz had been teaching some kids. The small yellow sponge balls that the children hit with sawed-off racquets kept rolling across onto Rob and Steve's court, interrupting their game. Once, at the net gathering ball, Steve remarked on how cute Perz was.

Now, as Rob watched John McMahon question Perz, Rob was struck by her response when McMahon asked if she had seen him any time after being shown the photo line-up on July 10, 1990. She said that she remembered being on a court adjacent to Baltovich one afternoon in August of that summer. "He would not look at me in the eye," Perz told the court. "And I found that very strange because I had recognized him right away as the person I saw on the bench, and the person I had

picked out in the photographs. I found that very strange, even when I was returning tennis balls to his court, or he was returning them to mine."

The second time Perz said she'd seen Baltovich was at the bottom of the stairs
leading down to the area of the courts. When she passed by him, Baltovich asked
her if she was "still teaching the little guys." "Had Mr. Baltovich, to your knowledge,"
inquired McMahon, "been present when you were teaching children at any other
time?" Obviously unable to recall the incident when he and Steve Doucette had
played beside her and her students, Perz answered no. The implication was that Rob
knew Perz taught youngsters because he'd seen her on a water break with them the
night of Liz's disappearance.

What amazed Rob most about Perz was how much she'd seemed to have forgotten about her contact with him, especially considering her role in the case and
her family's involvement in the searches for Liz—her parents' home phone number was printed on many of the missing posters as a contact. Rob could recall playing on a court near Perz several times that summer. He'd engaged her in a number
of conversations she hadn't mentioned to McMahon. For instance, he and Neil Winton had once asked her where the closest place was to buy tennis balls. Rob had discussed with Perz the fact that she played tennis at the University of Western Ontario.
If Perz had really seen Rob sitting at the picnic table next to Liz on June 19, would
she not have recognized him at the courts throughout the summer on more occasions than the two she could remember?

For Rob, the fundamental puzzle was that if he were guilty and had been with
Liz near the tennis courts the night she disappeared, why would he return and risk
being recognized by someone like Perz? Rob had even played some tennis that
summer with Perz's fellow cousellor, Paul Keller, who'd been instructing alongside
Perz the night of the disappearance. Was that something a guilty person would do?

Although Rob had discussed all this with Engel, Engel decided to take another
route with his cross-examination. He thought the best tactic was to juxtapose the
way Perz had immediately identified Liz Bain at the picnic table with the meandering process that had led her to say that the man beside her might have been his
client. Given the uncertainty Perz had previously expressed about her identification
of Baltovich, Gatward and Engel watched in amazement as McMahon had her connect the man she'd seen during hypnosis to the photo of Baltovich, who was, as Perz
willingly pointed out for the court, the man sitting in the prisoner's dock. So, when

Engel cross-examined her, he had two major goals. The first was to suggest that Perz's enhanced memory of the man she'd seen next to Liz under hypnosis could be explained by the photograph she'd seen of Baltovich in *The Toronto Sun*, beneath an article that clearly pegged him as a suspect. (What bothered Rob was the fact that, on the videotape of Perz's hypnosis session, Detective Warr told Matheson that Perz had seen Rob "on the way down" to the hospital. To Rob, this meant that Warr had staked him out somewhere with Perz in tow so she could have a better look at him—and did not refer to the newspaper photo. This had never occurred to Engel, however, which is why he never questioned Perz or Warr about what had taken place on the way to Perz's appointment with Matheson.)

Engel was planning to argue that Perz had confabulated her memory of the original incident with the newspaper photograph—that, in lay terms, she'd pasted Baltovich's image onto what little she'd been able to recall of the man at the picnic table that day. Engel's second task was to get Perz to admit that she was still as unsure about her identification as she'd been with Warr right after her session with Dr. Matheson.

ENGEL: I take it that before you underwent hypnosis it was somehow communicated to you that, in the minds of some, Mr. Baltovich was, in fact, a suspect in this disappearance or homicide of Elizabeth, is that right?

PERZ: I was aware that he'd been questioned. But I was also under the impression, through the police and everyone else, that it had not been narrowed down to him specifically. That they were open to all kinds of other possibilities.

ENGEL: Other than Mr. Baltovich being viewed as a suspect by the police—which you knew of—who else was mentioned as a suspect?

PERZ: They thought it might have been the same person they had termed as the Scarborough rapist. They had considered it possible for it to have been him who had done something, yes.

ENGEL: Okay, it's safe to say that, at the time you picked Mr. Baltovich's picture out of the photographic line-up, you were aware of who he was, having seen his picture in the newspaper, is that right?

PERZ: No, not because of seeing his picture in the newspaper—I wish it were here because it's such an unclear picture. It does not give a very good likeness of him, it's so blurred.

ENGEL: Just to assist you in that regard, let me show you a photocopy of that clipping from *The Sunday Sun* and maybe that will help. [*Shows her the photocopy.*] Underneath here, it says, "Rob Baltovich says his lawyer advised him against talking to the media."

PERZ: This is the one.

ENGEL: Obviously, the clear inference to anyone reading this is that Mr. Baltovich was a suspect, would you agree?

PERZ: It doesn't say that he's a suspect.

ENGEL: You didn't get that impression?

PERZ: I mean, I'm sure it crossed my mind that he would be one of the suspects.

ENGEL: Well, of course it would. The title of the article is "Dated missing student, Lisa's pal riled at innuendos."

PERZ: Um-hum.

ENGEL: Would you not agree with me that this picture, even though it's a photocopy, is a relatively good likeness of Mr. Baltovich?

PERZ: I would still have to maintain that it's very blurry. For instance, it's only one side of him. It doesn't show his full body, so it's hard for me to see his build.

ENGEL: Well, you weren't really able to see his build on the date in question, either. You looked at him for thirty seconds at most, and he was sitting down, right?

PERZ: Right.

ENGEL: And you can't even recall—even after hypnosis—anything he might have been wearing or what colour it was, correct?

PERZ: Yes, I can. I told you I believe that he was wearing shorts.

ENGEL: No, what you said on the audiotape we just heard was that you thought he was wearing shorts, but couldn't be certain, isn't that right?

PERZ: Yes, this is true.

ENGEL: Being one of the last persons to see Elizabeth Bain alive, do you understand the terrible responsibility of the accuracy you must have in purporting to identify Mr. Baltovich?

PERZ: Yes, I do.

ENGEL: You know he's charged with the most serious crime known to man, that of premeditated murder?

PERZ: Yes, I do.

ENGEL: I'm going to suggest to you that, at most, you are able to recall a resemblance, albeit perhaps striking, between Mr. Baltovich, as shown in the line-up, and the person you recall seeing with Miss Bain on the night of June nineteenth.

PERZ: No, as I said before, I believe that the person sitting on her left-hand side was Mr. Baltovich.

ENGEL: Well, I'm going to suggest to you that, on at least one occasion, you have expressed a misgiving to the officers in charge of this case, with respect to your ability to positively identify Mr. Baltovich as being the person you saw seated with Liz Bain on the night in question.

PERZ: No, I'm telling you that it was Mr. Baltovich.

ENGEL: Obviously, as a student of the English language, you understand the difference between a belief and a moral certainty.

PERZ: Yes, I do.

ENGEL: Are you able to say under oath today that you have never, ever expressed any misgiving to anyone about the accuracy of your identification of Mr. Baltovich?

PERZ: No.

ENGEL: No what?

PERZ: Can you repeat the question, please?

ENGEL: Are you able to say under oath today that you have never expressed to anyone a misgiving about your ability to absolutely, positively, conclusively identify Mr. Baltovich?

PERZ: No. I'm sure I've expressed some. But only due to the fact that I'd never known Mr. Baltovich before. I cannot give the same degree of accuracy that I can with Elizabeth Bain because I knew her.

ENGEL: But, to get to the bottom line, notwithstanding your very best efforts in giving us your evidence today, I take it you agree with me that the smallest of doubts exists in your mind in terms of your ability to conclusively and absolutely identify Mr. Baltovich as having been that male you saw with Elizabeth, is that right?

PERZ: Yes, but only because I'm measuring that in terms of my identification of Lisa.

ENGEL: Ma'am, I commend you for your candour in this, but just so that we understand each other, you've admitted today that there exists some doubt in your mind about the accuracy of your identification of Mr. Baltovich being the person with Elizabeth that day, have you not?

PERZ: No, I'm admitting that there is a very slight possibility that it could have been somebody else, but I'm telling the court that I believe it was Mr. Baltovich.

(A little more than three years later, Dr. David Dunning, a psychologist at Cornell University, published the results of his research on human memory in the November 1994 issue of *The Journal of Personality and Social Psychology*. Working with photo line-up experiments, Dr. Dunning found that witnesses who said recognizing the suspect's face was "effortless" were accurate about seventy per cent of the time. However, "those who went through a careful process of elimination and comparison of faces were wrong about seventy per cent." Dr. Dunning concluded that "faces are stored in a visual pattern, not in words" and, therefore, when people fail to recognize a face at once while scanning an array of photographs, they use a process of elimination to find the most likely face, which is a separate mental process from recognition.)

—◇—

Jailhouse Notebook (3)

A few weeks ago, a bunch of my friends showed up to wish me a "happy" birthday. It was a good visit, and as it drew to a close, someone mentioned that there was going to be a surprise for me when I got up to my cell.

So when I made it back, I looked outside my window. I couldn't believe what I was seeing. One of my friends had created this huge banner, about ten feet long, that read HAPPY BIRTHDAY ROB *on it. Everybody was waving and singing "Happy Birthday" to me. Of course, from where I stood, they only appeared to be mouthing the words—the window does not open.*

Meanwhile, some of the guys on the range were yelling out to me. I figured they had never seen anything like it before. They asked me who all the people were; I yelled back that they were my friends. I'd never felt so proud about having such support. Of course, the guys also wanted to know if any of the girls were "available." "None," I answered, without having to think about it.

Then, this week, a rumour began circulating that a guy on 2A had arranged for his girlfriend to do a little striptease just outside the jail. The fact that his cell is situated close to mine made the rumour all the more pertinent—however, the prospect of seeing a woman parade around half-naked below my window struck me as being a tad unlikely.

Nevertheless, this afternoon, just after lunch, I heard Newf call out to me, asking me to look outside. Like a schoolboy, I jumped up and indulged my curiosity. With a wall shielding her from the outside entrance, a pretty blonde about twenty years of age was standing on the grass below running her hands up and down her thighs. I heard a few guys pounding on their windows, and then a couple of guards. The way some of them were acting, it seemed like they hadn't seen a woman for years. Just as I began asking myself what all the fuss was about, she took her sweater and raised it above her head, revealing a rather magnificent pair of breasts.

From that point on, it was complete bedlam. I thought that glass was going to start breaking any minute as the pounding got louder and louder. But a few seconds later, as suddenly as it began, the show was over. She waved to her boyfriend and walked towards her car. For me, it was indication that, when it comes to values, I am living with some very interesting people.

———o———

Gatward and Engel presumed that, at some point during the final third of the pre-liminary hearing, it would become clear exactly when, according to the Crown's case, Elizabeth Bain had been murdered—not to mention how. The only witness to pro-vide them with any assistance in that regard was Ruth Collins, who had suddenly surfaced as part of the Crown's case after a dubious absence during Brian Raybould's testimony at the bail hearing. Collins described for Judge Ormston what she had seen in front of Three R Auto Body, most likely sometime between 8:00 and 8:30 PM. How the young woman in the passenger seat of the silver car looked practically identical to the photographs of Elizabeth Bain and her car, although she couldn't swear for sure. Collins's testimony left Gatward and Engel more perplexed than anything. If she saw Elizabeth Bain alive in her car at a time when their client was known to be lifting weights in the Recreation Centre, then McMahon was obviously going to imply that Baltovich had killed Bain between the time he left the gym to meet her at the end of her class at 9:00 PM and the time he returned to play volleyball half an hour later. Or was McMahon going to say the murder occurred after the volleyball and that Baltovich's mother was lying about the time he got home that night? Gat-ward and Engel were starting to pick up on the notion that McMahon, as far as the murder theory went, was flying by the seat of his pants and, therefore, was unlikely to commit himself to one definitive scenario until the last possible moment.

The forensic evidence McMahon had referred to in his opening did very little to swing the case in one direction or another. Detective Norman Rowntree of the Centre for Forensic Sciences testified that Dr. Hillsdon-Smith, head of the CFS's Pathology Department, had estimated that less than half a pint of blood—which the DNA analysis had determined was from a female offspring of Rick and Julita Bain—had pooled beneath the carpet of Bain's car (Mike Engel would later point out that this was less than blood donors normally gave to the Red Cross in one sit-ting). Fingerprint dusting of the gearshift knob had revealed no marks at all, which led Rowntree to the conclusion that Bain's abductor had probably wiped it clean or worn gloves. A print found on the rear-view mirror had been matched to Paul Bain. Unfortunately, the rough texture of the steering wheel did not lend itself to preserving fingerprints, even ones detectable with the beam of a special CFS laser Rowntree had used in conjunction with glue fumes, a gas known as cyanoa latesther. In all, there were eight sets of fingerprints discovered in the car, of which the police were able to match five. None belonged to Robert Baltovich and the other three remained a mystery. It was quite possible, Rowntree conceded, that the three "uneliminated" prints were Elizabeth Bain's, yet without her actual prints to compare them to, he could never be certain.

McMahon also called upon the expert testimony of Ray Higaki, the forensic biologist with the CFS. Having analyzed photographs of the Tercel's interior, Higaki was now being asked to offer his opinions about what could be interpreted from the various blood smears. Higaki's conclusions were straightforward. A large, bulky, bloodstained object (a body) had been lowered onto the floor behind the front seats through the passenger door. The smears didn't indicate much about how the body had been removed from the vehicle, but the lack of "impact spatters"—what one would find near the victim of a gunshot or stab wound or heavy blow—had led Higaki to believe that the bleeding had begun prior to entering the vehicle. Unfortunately, according to Higaki, no tests existed to determine whether the blood had spilled from a body that was dead or alive.

There was a cluster of witnesses towards the end of the inquiry whose primary role also had to do with smearing—not of blood, but of character. Hoping to expose the accused as deceitful, McMahon had Roger Herriott describe his encounter with Baltovich in Colonel Danforth Park and how Herriott had given him the blue hair barrette he'd found in the grass (which, contradicting Baltovich's story, Mr. Bain denied receiving). And then there was Jackie Intraligi, the type of witness who, from Gatward and Engel's perspective, a Crown prosecutor called to bolster an otherwise lacklustre case. Intraligi had met Rob during her first year of studying accounting at Scarborough campus in 1986. Back then, the only place she would usually see him was in the cafeteria, gabbing around a table with a group of friends, or reading the newspaper. One time, she thought it might have been in 1987, a bunch of them were sitting around talking about an article in *The Toronto Sun* describing how a man had murdered a woman. Someone—not Rob—started saying that, if you're dumb enough to kill somebody, you should at least take the time to dispose of the body properly so that it would not be found. Another person suggested incineration, and then Rob came up with another method, but, unfortunately, Intraligi could no longer remember exactly what that had been. She just recalled being shocked by whatever it was Rob had said he would do with the body.

The final witness, whom Rob vaguely recognized as he strolled past him up to the front of the courtroom, was a young-looking man sworn in as Michael Alfred Fraser. Rob was still unsure of how he knew the man until McMahon quickly jogged his memory by having Fraser disclose that he was employed as a correctional officer at the Metro East Detention Centre. Now Rob knew who he was—Fraser looked quite different out of uniform—but what was this guy doing testifying at his preliminary hearing?

Fraser told McMahon that, on November 27, 1990, at 6:30 AM, it had been his duty to escort Baltovich from his second-floor unit to the Admitting & Discharge area, where Baltovich was to be processed before making his way to court. As they approached the elevator that would take them down to A&D, Fraser testified, he and the accused had struck up a bit of a conversation, a brief exchange that, after four days of consideration, Fraser had decided to detail in a written occurrence report. The discussion, as Fraser remembered it after the fact, was as follows:

FRASER: Do you expect to get bail on murder one?
BALTOVICH: The only good thing about this is the money I will make.
FRASER: What money?
BALTOVICH: From writing a book, not to mention the money I'll get for being here [*meaning that he intended to sue for wrongful prosecution*].
FRASER: So you think you'll get off?
BALTOVICH: Yes.
FRASER: What if they find a body?
BALTOVICH: There'd be no chance of that.
FRASER: You never know.

Rob did recall telling Fraser about his intention to sue the police and that he'd been contemplating the idea of writing a book based on this crazy episode of his life, but, in reply to Fraser's query about finding "a body," Rob knew that he hadn't said "There'd be no chance of that." What he remembered saying was "I doubt it." And, after five months of futile searching, why wouldn't he?

From Rob's perspective, Fraser was a biased witness. He'd been nothing but a colossal pain in the ass since Rob had been denied bail. "Hey, Baltovich," was the greeting Fraser had given him one day, upon returning to Metro East from a remand hearing. "Haven't they hung you yet?"

Regardless, everything Rob wanted to express about Fraser and every other witness would remain a matter for speculation for all but Brian King and Rob's lawyers. When McMahon announced that the Crown had completed its evidence, Gatward informed the judge that his client had nothing to say and no witnesses to call, and both lawyers offered their submissions.

Four days later, Judge Ormston read his decision. Citing key pieces of evidence in relation to case law, Ormston grappled at length with the issue of whether the Crown had provided enough evidence for a jury to reasonably conclude that Baltovich had not only killed Elizabeth Bain, but had done so in a manner that was both planned and deliberate, as the charge of first-degree murder required. Once he'd read his written decision, Judge Ormston asked Baltovich to stand. "I find that there is no evidence in law capable of being considered as planning or deliberation and there will not be a committal on first-degree murder," said Ormston. "However, there is sufficient evidence to be considered by a jury on second-degree murder, and I commit you for trial by judge and jury on that charge."

Part 5

—o—

No Claim to Mercy

Jailhouse Notebook (4)

A few days ago—it's been almost two weeks since the preliminary—the War-
den told me that I had been "declassified" and was being moved from Super
Protective Custody (2B) to the Protective Custody range at 4C two floors up. I
grabbed my library copy of Anna Karenina *and the plastic bags filled with mag-*
azines I was using for dumb-bells, but the guards told me to lose the magazines.
So I grabbed an old copy of The New Yorker *and my books, and with the clothes*
on my back, closed the door of my cell.

It was a weird feeling up on the new range. There were no guards in sight
and, for the first time, I felt vulnerable. Everyone was just left on their own, so
I made my way to the corner of the range and tried to make myself as unob-
trusive as possible. My attempt failed. A guy named Duguay, whom I knew
from going to court, approached me and said, "Hey man, you finally made it."
I talked to Duguay for a while and then looked around, trying to acquaint
myself with everyone and everything. I noticed another guy I knew from court
named Delroy, who was originally from Jamaica. Delroy has been charged with
first-degree murder in connection with a shooting at a Scarborough night-
club—he also maintains his innocence. He was sitting at a table all alone

watching TV with a copy of the New Testament in one hand and a toothbrush in the other.

Close to the door of the range, there is a large television set mounted inside a wall. Several guys were seated in front of it that day watching "Jenny Jones." To the right of the television is the entrance to the shower area. In the middle of the range are three picnic-style tables, all of which were occupied with inmates playing assorted games—cards, chess, Scrabble and so on. The two telephones mounted on the wall were both being used.

After sitting around for an hour and a half reading The New Yorker, *I was told that I would be sharing a cell with Rick Nichols, whom I'd also met before. Nichols is 6 feet 3 inches, three hundred pounds, with forearms thicker than my legs.*

As was the case on 2B, mid-evening on the range brought a brief respite from hunger. Unlike segregation, however, snack time on 4C was a complete free-for-all. When "jug-up" was shouted, everyone—except for one person—rushed to the door to get their juice and two cookies. I figured that I'd do the polite thing and wait until everyone had been served, but as I waited I saw a tall black guy take six cookies away. After everyone had finished, I stepped forward and realized that there were no cookies left. The guard noticed the same thing and, before I knew what was happening, he looked over at the black guy with six cookies and screamed, "Palmer!" I didn't like what was happening. Getting a guard to solve your problems was not the smartest thing to do. "Palmer, give this guy his fuckin' cookies right now."

"What the fuck are you talking about, boss?" Palmer shouted back.

To my horror, it turned into a shouting match. "Palmer, if you don't give this guy his cookies right now, you're going in the hole!"

"I don't have his fuckin' cookies! These were given to me!"

I tried to defuse the situation. "Listen, man. All I want are my cookies. That's it."

Suddenly, I was involved, and Palmer didn't appreciate it. "Listen, you fuckin' asshole, I didn't take your fuckin' cookies so get the fuck outta my face."

As pissed off as I was, I turned to the guard and told him not to worry about it. But the guard didn't want to give up and he forced Palmer to hand over the two cookies. For the remainder of the evening, I watched TV, while Palmer paced

about the range giving me the evil eye; in jail vernacular, what is known as "gun-
ning me off." I wanted to crawl under a rock.

Back in the cell, Rick said, "That was quite a first day, wasn't it?" I said it
would have been a lot more peaceful if the guy hadn't stolen my cookies. "Well,
I hate to break it to you," Rick said, "but Vince didn't steal those cookies. He won
those cookies in a card game this afternoon—that's how they pay their debts.
Someone else stole your cookies."

I knew that Rick was telling me the truth. So this morning I decided to walk
up to Palmer and apologize. He just gave me a quizzical look, as though he
wasn't exactly used to apologies, and said, "Yeah, well, I don't steal from cons,
okay? I won those cookies." Palmer asked me what I was in for, so I told him.
Then, when he found out I'd just spent nine months in the hole, Palmer started
slowly backing up, as if these two pieces of information had suddenly gotten
him concerned.

A few minutes ago, Rick told me that Palmer was afraid of me. "Why would
he be afraid of me?" I asked.

"Because Vince is here on a minor robbery beef," Rick said. "But you, pal,
you're looking at Big Time."

There was a newspaper lying open on Brian King's desk when he first entered his
office on Friday, October 25. He was staring at a small article on page sixty-four of
The Toronto Sun, where, in the upper left-hand corner, surrounded by computer
advertisements, a photograph of Elizabeth Bain appeared beneath the headline:
"Info sparks new search for her body."

> The father of missing Elizabeth Bain says he's got new informa-
> tion about the location of her remains.
> And Rick Bain is appealing for "lots" of volunteers tomorrow
> to help him in his search in Scugog Township.
> "Basically, we're zeroing in on specific areas within that area,"
> Bain said. "This is coming from the new information that wasn't
> available until about two weeks ago."

He said the information came from "a number people who
have been in that area before over the past few years."

Since the preliminary hearing, King was unaware of any information that could
be qualified as "new." Whatever Mr. Bain had been told, King knew that, by the time
the Crown eventually disclosed these latest leads, they would be "old," from his
point of view anyway. So King hatched a plan to speed up the process considerably.
He enlisted the help of one of his veteran investigators, Paul Ankcorn, a short,
stocky man with trim blond hair and large-framed glasses, a medley of unspectacular features that allowed him to blend perfectly into just about any suburban setting. Surveillance work was his specialty and Ankcorn, who had a military
background, had mastered the art of not drawing attention to himself while pursuing his quarry, usually with a long, dark telephoto lens. But what King had in
mind for Ankcorn on this assignment was slightly different. King wanted him to
join the following day's search party up in Lake Scugog—undercover, of course—
to ascertain, if possible, what the new leads were and how they had been obtained.
Ankcorn was also directed to keep a close eye on Mr. Bain and to provide a detailed
report on his actions throughout the day.

By 9:00 Saturday morning, approximately twenty-five people, including
Ankcorn, had gathered in front of the Port Perry Fire Hall, along with a reporter
from *The Oshawa Times*, as well as a television crew from Toronto's Citytv. Mr. Bain
asked all of the volunteers to come forward and sign a log book containing the
names of each person who had participated in the searches since November 1990.
Carrying a large, black, three-ring binder containing topographical maps and aer-
ial photographs of the Lake Scugog region, Mr. Bain divided the volunteers into
four groups, allotting each to a separate location. Then, just prior to their departure from the Fire Hall, Mr. Bain reiterated—for the benefit of the volunteers and
the assembled media—what he'd said in the newspaper about the new information,
adding only that it was reaffirmed by testimony given at the preliminary hearing,
which, due to the ongoing proceedings, he could not expand upon.

Ankcorn rode in the same vehicle as Mr. Bain on the way to their search location and listened as Mr. Bain remarked that the day's events were, in essence, a show
for the press designed to bring attention to his plight in the search for his daughter. Ankcorn noted that Mr. Bain "showed no signs of remorse or emotion and, in

fact, had a smile on his face at all times and was rather jovial in nature." The television reporter had also noticed this and had gone so far as to diplomatically inquire about Mr. Bain's "apparent lack of emotion." "Mr. Bain replied that, although he might not outwardly show it at this time," Ankcorn later wrote, "he does still have very intense feelings inside concerning the loss of his daughter."

Throughout what remained of the morning, Mr. Bain led Ankcorn and eleven other searchers through wooded areas adjacent to various concession lots near the crossroads community of Lotus. In Ankcorn's opinion, the searches were "disorganized and haphazard, leaving vast areas uncovered due to the presence of houses and farms—in addition, Mr. Bain did not lead searchers through extensive marshy areas or into valleys off the concession roadways." On a number of occasions Mr. Bain voiced his displeasure with how little help he had received with the searches from the police department. And then, just before noon, one of the searchers found a pair of "dark slacks" in a pile of leaves and debris. Ankcorn watched as Mr. Bain sedately dismissed the tattered trousers as immaterial and resumed the search.

They broke for lunch at half-past noon, with Mr. Bain providing the group with sandwiches and soft drinks, as well as muffins that had been baked the night before by Mrs. Bain. Thirty minutes later, they were back to searching, an exercise Ankcorn felt, as he listened to Mr. Bain expound on his knowledge of the area's foliage and wildlife, was closer in tenor to a nature walk than a search for a dead young woman. Twice that afternoon, Ankcorn was left baffled when the group came upon patches of loosened earth, both of which "went totally unnoticed and unchecked." His most memorable, and perhaps telling, moment came when Ankcorn decided to lie down behind the trunk of a fallen tree as Mr. Bain and two others approached from the opposite direction. All three of them stepped over the tree as well as the prone Ankcorn, who was "making no effort whatsoever to remain hidden." Ankcorn couldn't believe it—not one of them noticed that he was there.

—◯—

Jailhouse Notebook (5)

The telephone has become a source of many a dispute. Rick, my cell partner, seems to view the telephone as his own personal property. If he was a character in some cliché-ridden novel, he would be the stereotypical phone hog. Somehow, I don't think he appreciates the art of it all. His size erects enough of a deterrent that no one takes exception and his phone is his. The other phone, however, has become a bone of perpetual contention.

But some have a phone ritual that needs to be satisfied, which is where Delroy comes into the story. Quiet, unassuming Delroy, who spends virtually all of his time reading the Bible, has only one real desire: to call home at least once a day. It is a request that no one really interferes with.

One evening a few weeks ago, though, someone did. Like Rick Nichols, a guy named Maclean was busy fulfilling another stereotype—the range bully. This guy loves to flex his muscle. This meant that when he wanted the phone, he got it.

But that night, Delroy was leaning up against the wall carrying on a conversation when Maclean started barking at him to get off the phone. It was late and there were only a few minutes left before the phones would be turned off. As if designed to provoke a confrontation, Delroy simply repositioned himself so that he didn't have to look at Maclean's face. But Maclean wouldn't let up, and Delroy kept making like he couldn't hear him until a guard finally appeared and announced the night-time lock-up—the signal that the phones were going to be turned off.

When that happened, Delroy sat down and watched TV while Maclean circled him. Sensing that something might be brewing, Delroy started scraping his toothbrush against the edge of the table. After a few minutes, Maclean walked right up to him and said, "Delroy, who the fuck do you think you are ignoring me like that? When I tell you to get off the phone, you do it, you motherfuckin' piece of shit!"

Delroy started fingering his toothbrush in an attempt to warn Maclean he was prepared to use it; Maclean picked up on the gesture. "What? You think I'm scared of that fuckin' thing? What are you gonna do with it?"

My heart was beating like crazy. The only one who looked unfazed was Delroy. But then Maclean took a swipe at Delroy and hit him in the side of the head.

That's when all hell broke loose. Delroy jumped up and started flailing with both fists—one clenched and the other holding the freshly sharpened toothbrush. They were standing toe to toe trading punches.

Suddenly, Delroy lunged at Maclean with the toothbrush and connected in the ribs. Screaming, Maclean covered up and tried to protect himself. Delroy went crazy, jabbing the toothbrush in an uppercut motion towards Maclean's face, which Maclean tried to bury in his arms. Maclean was begging Delroy to stop and after maybe the hundredth blow, he did.

Delroy just sat down in his usual spot as Maclean uncovered himself, revealing what appeared to be an eye hanging halfway out of its socket. Blood was everywhere. "Are you fuckin' crazy?" Maclean was yelling. "You almost ripped my eye out, for Christ sake."

Maclean ran to the barrier and called out to the guards to come quick. When one arrived, he said, "What the fuck happened to you?"

Maclean's answer was bizarre, though "solid" by prison standards. "I was fooling around wrestling and slipped," he said. "You gotta get me to the hospital fast!"

It was quiet for a little while after Maclean left. Then Vince Palmer, who hated Maclean's strong-arm tactics more than anyone else, jumped to his feet and began dancing around the range, singing "Ding-dong, the witch is dead! The wicked old witch is dead, is dead!" It was like a scene out of One Flew Over the Cuckoo's Nest; *I thought that maybe I was going out of my mind because I was laughing my guts out.*

Although Maclean hasn't come back, what got me writing about all of this was that a guard just popped in to deliver a little news flash—Maclean lost his eye.

—◦—

Jailhouse Notebook (6)

A few weeks ago, a guy named Mark came on the range. Mark is a talented artist who has the ability to draw incredibly life-like faces. With every creation he never fails to elicit a generous share of oohs and aahs from everyone. I admire his talents but what I admire most is the reaction he gets from the guys on the range. In many ways, their willingness to acknowledge talent, whether athletic, intellectual, or artistic, contrasts with what I've encountered outside of prison. I've never seen so much humility.

Speaking to Mark one day, I recounted how, in my younger days, I used to spend a lot of time drawing. He didn't seem impressed, possibly resenting the suggestion that I might have a talent greater than his. Though I possessed no such thing, a few days later, while watching him working on a sketch at one of the tables, I began designing a plan to have a little fun at his expense.

I'd watched him carefully enough to familiarize myself with some of his shading techniques. A guy named Stuart was standing beside him, awe-struck, marvelling at the realism of Mark's rendering. A few minutes later, a video came on the TV and a mass exodus from the table ensued.

While everybody settled in to watch the movie, I grabbed a piece of paper and a pencil, as well as the picture Mark had left on the table. I felt confident that I would be able to reproduce Mark's drawing to a satisfactory degree so I began to work at it. As I progressed further and further, I noticed—to my own surprise—that things were turning out better than even I had expected. About an hour later, the counterfeit drawing was finished, and I was ready to have some fun.

I placed my drawing over Mark's original, on which he'd already printed his monogram in the bottom right-hand corner. So on my drawing, I scribbled a large patch over the spot where the monogram was supposed to be, as though someone had defaced his work. Then I just grabbed a book and waited.

Forty-five minutes later, when Stuart and Mark returned to the table, they immediately noticed what happened to "Mark's" drawing. "What the hell happened here?" yelled Mark. I pretended to ignore them. "Who the hell did this?" Mark demanded to know. They both looked at me for an explanation, which was when I had to play along.

"Well," I said. "I'm so sick and tired of everyone fawning over your artwork, I thought I'd teach you a lesson!"

While I struggled to keep a straight face, Stuart looked at me like I was a colossal idiot. Mark, on the other hand, looked like he wanted to punch me out. "You're a fucking asshole, Baltovich!" he screamed. I decided it was a good time to terminate the prank and reached down and slid my drawing to the side, revealing Mark's original. I started to smile.

The look on their faces was priceless. With jaws dropped, they were staring at me, then at the drawing, trying to make sense of what they'd seen. Mark continued to look right at me, only with less anger. He probably thought I was a moron, but at least I'd convinced him he wasn't the only guy who could draw.

I gave Stuart a wink, as if to say, "I gotcha," then asked him what he thought. "That was pretty good, man," was his only reply.

Even though all this happened just a few hours ago, I'm starting to think it wasn't the smartest thing to do. Given what happened to Delroy, it might not be such a bad idea to give up on being the jailhouse prankster. I have to remember that I'm not exactly around the "old gang" any more.

—◦—

Not long after the charge had been lowered to murder in the second degree at the conclusion of the preliminary hearing, Rob was putting pressure on Mike Engel to appeal his bail hearing. Engel responded with a plan for how they would proceed. If the trial date, which was soon to be scheduled, was set to begin before the new year, then they wouldn't bother appealing. Fall was already upon them, and the time consumed by preparing the appeal would be better spent getting ready for trial. If, on the other hand, the trial wasn't starting until after the new year, they would go for bail.

As it turned out, the earliest court date available was January 20, 1992, and, therefore, Engel initiated the appeal. After working on it for a month, he was granted a hearing before the Ontario Court of Appeal on November 8, 1991. Until then, Rob knew that he would be a nervous wreck around the clock. He desperately wanted bail.

In the meantime, Rob had moved out of the cell with Rick Nichols for several reasons, one of which was that he never shut up and had put a serious damper on his reading. At the same time, Stuart, the short muscular guy who'd witnessed Rob's prank with the drawing, had lost his regular cell partner and asked Rob if he wanted to make the switch. Stuart was a little rough around the edges, but they had at least one thing in common. He also lived just a few minutes away from the "East," which made him a Scarborough guy. And Stuart was also familiar with Rob's case, always going on about how crazy it was that the cops could arrest a guy without a body. He became one of Rob's staunchest supporters.

When November 8 finally came, it landed on a Friday, and Rob spent most of it pacing around on the range. His family was downtown at the appeal court with Gatward and Engel and there was no one else to call for an update. He would just have to wait. Guys kept coming up to him every once in a while, advising him to stay calm. Bail was a done deal, they would say. Delroy let it be known that God was on his side.

Pacing. *I know I'm not going to get it.* More pacing. *Maybe they will give it to me.* Still pacing. *No, man, who's kidding who? I'm stuck here.* Automatic repeat. This was his day.

There was a posse monitoring the hourly news reports on the radio all afternoon but no messenger came forth to interrupt his trance. So Rob went back to his cell and joined Stuart, who was sitting on his bunk, just in time to catch the five-thirty news. The first word of the newscast was *Bob*, which sounded so much like Rob that he closed his eyes in anticipation, but it turned out to be a story about Bob Rae, the premier of Ontario. Of course, the next person mentioned was *Robert* Bourassa, Rae's counterpart in Quebec. Then, finally, came the words of sweet salvation: "After a year behind bars, Robert Baltovich has been granted bail by the Ontario Court of Appeal...."

Rob leapt up off the bunk and started screaming. When he landed on the ground, he put his head in his hands, overcome by the most blissful feeling he'd ever experienced. White stars danced around in the darkness behind his eyes. Stuart pounced on him and gave him a big hug and then, jumping up and down, they let each other go and Rob went to the door and began pounding on it. "I got it! I got it!" he kept screaming in an unadulterated flip-out session. Delroy smiled from behind his door window across the range.

He called home a few hours later and Paul's wife said they would be down to pick him up tomorrow. Rob imagined the scene a thousand times throughout the night, lying still on his bunk, the notion of sleep not occurring to him once.

He kept an eye on the parking lot throughout the morning and, to his growing dismay, there was no sign of his parents or his lawyers. The afternoon passed, and still—nothing. It wasn't until the pre-dinner lock-up that Rob, peering out the window, saw Mike Engel and his wife get out of a car in the parking lot below and walk into the building. Right on, Rob thought, it's finally happening. Next his family wheeled in and emerged from his father's Camaro. Now he was just waiting for someone to come and open his cell door.

Much to his horror, fifteen minutes passed, and Rob watched helplessly as the entire welcoming committee walked back out to their cars and drove off. That got the panic attacks going in no time. He was sure that, somehow, bail had been cancelled. It had been too good to be true, now that he thought about it.

Half an hour after that, though, everyone showed up in their cars again. In the midst of trying to make sense of what was happening, Rob heard the gate open and the voice of a guard, the practised tone of gruff, disinterested authority—"Baltovich! Let's go!" After a quick embrace with Stuart, Rob followed the guard downstairs into a small room where everyone was waiting for him, accompanied by a justice of the peace (who'd been later than expected, which was why everyone had gone for a quick dinner rather than wait inside the institution). The JP asked Rob if he agreed to abide by the conditions of his bail, which he did, and he was off to the Admitting & Discharge room.

There to hand over his belongings was the guard who, on the day of his arrest, had advised him to keep his mouth shut. The guard handed him his things and, already turning away, said, "Well, I guess you didn't take my advice, did you?"

The second guard, a regular at A&D, led Rob to the enormous metal door that, once raised, revealed the parking lot. In the near distance, Rob could see his family waiting outside by the car and he turned for one last look at another jerk from A&D who loved to corral guys onto the paddy wagon by saying, "Okay, all you criminals, time to go to court!"

"I have to tell you," Rob said. "I'm really going to miss it here and I'm especially going to miss you. It's a real shame we'll never see each other again."

"Don't worry," the guard responded. "You'll be back." He let out a good laugh.

Rob answered, "Don't bet on it."

Out in the parking lot, Rob embraced his parents, then Paul and Dana, before they got into the Camaro. Feeling on top of the world, Jim fired up the mean-sounding engine, and switched into reverse. As they backed up, a telephone pole slowly passed within inches of Adele's window on the passenger side. "Jim!" she shrieked. Jim pumped his foot on the brake, and Adele, pointing at the pole, really let him have it. And it wasn't long before Jim, his senior-citizen's nerves already frayed as it was, returned fire.

Sandwiched in the back seat between Paul and Dana, Rob turned to his brother with a big smile and said, "Ah, it's great to be home."

SUSPECT CHARGED IN BAIN SLAYING

RELEASED ON BAIL AFTER NEARLY A YEAR

November 12, 1991—After 355 days in jail, the man accused in the slaying of missing student Elizabeth Bain has had Sunday dinner with his family.

Robert Baltovich, 25, was freed from Metro East Detention Centre late Saturday after his parents posted two sureties of $50,000 each to cover bail set by a panel of three Ontario Court of Appeal judges the day before.

"It was his first dinner at home in nearly a year and he hasn't been convicted of anything," said Brian King, the Toronto private investigator hired by the Baltovich family to run an extensive parallel investigation.

King said Baltovich would not be speaking to the media.

The private investigator refused to comment on the specifics of the case.

"Rob will be staying at home, try to enjoy a normal life and assist in preparing his defence from a normal location," King said.

THE TORONTO STAR

———◯———

About two months before Rob was released on bail, John Secord made three separate trips to Halifax, Nova Scotia, the first in late August, and the other two in September. The trips had come about as a result of his dealings with a man named Franz, who had initially contacted Brian King before King put him in touch with Secord. Franz was a retired gentleman and lived north of Toronto, not far from where Secord had grown up in Thornhill. As Secord had been informed by King, Franz specialized, although not on a professional basis, in a psychic field that tapped into something known as "pendulum energy." If, for example, Secord wanted to know whether Elizabeth Bain was dead or alive—which he did, of course—Franz would hold a long string, at the end of which was some kind of divining crystal, above a piece of paper with the two possibilities written on it and would wait to see how the invisible energy would guide the pendulum. The pendulum indicated that Elizabeth Bain was alive.

The next question was: Where was she? So they laid out a large map of North America and Franz's shiny crystal hovered, trembling, precariously close to the Atlantic Ocean, above Halifax, Nova Scotia. For Secord, there was no question about what he needed to do. He was on the phone with his travel agent the following day to purchase himself a one-way airline ticket to Halifax departing that very evening for $395.39.

That first trip lasted four days, and the next two were each a day or so shorter. Secord, who carried with him at all times a recent photograph of Elizabeth, went all over town, to video stores, to the local univerity campuses (Dalhousie and St. Mary's) and even to the local prostitutes, asking one and all if they recognized her. There were a few nibbles—one of the prostitutes was sure that a local pimp named Psycho knew something about the missing girl in the photo, although she hadn't seen him for a while—but nothing definitive.

Hard pressed for leads, Secord would occasionally drive his rental car back to the Lord Nelson Hotel and call Franz from the phone in his room. One afternoon, Franz dangled his pendulum over a map of Halifax and told Secord Elizabeth had just been moving down a street called Cogswell and was now at the Scotia Square shopping mall in the north end. Secord scrambled down to his car in the Lord Nelson parking lot and drove there in under three minutes. Jogging off the elevator that had transported him from the underground lot to the concourse, he saw a girl with dark hair leaving one of the stores; she was about the same height as Liz, although this girl's complexion seemed a few shades too light. He wanted to get a closer look at her, but the girl, who was accompanied by a well-dressed grey-haired woman (was this the woman who'd been seen in Liz's passenger seat?), hailed a taxi cab, which both women hurriedly entered, quickly directing its driver to take a U-turn east on Duke Street, towards the harbour. Gone.

In December, three months after Secord had given up on Halifax, he called Brian King with some new information, a revelation that Secord felt might provide Rob's defence team with its biggest breakthrough thus far. Secord had been with Beth Garcia when they'd gone to visit Julita and Beth's sister, Carmen Kadri, who lived with her husband, Harry, in the western suburb of Etobicoke. For the longest while, they spoke of Liz's disappearance and of Secord's tireless efforts to find her. In the midst of these sad but fascinating tales, Carmen told him of an incident that had been haunting her for the past year and a half. It had taken place at approximately eleven o'clock one morning about four or five days after the disappearance. Carmen was cooking at the time, and Harry sat nearby at the kitchen table. That's when the telephone rang. Already on her feet, Carmen answered it. There was silence for a few seconds and then she heard a hushed voice say, "Auntie Carmen, Auntie Carmen." It was almost a whisper, as if the girl didn't want to be overheard by someone not far away. Carmen hardly had a chance to respond—the line was cut off within a second or two and only the sound of the dial tone echoed loudly in her ear.

Carmen was now telling Secord how much this mysterious call had shocked her and her husband. She was sure that it had been the voice of her missing niece Elizabeth and had even called Julita's house to describe what had happened. Perhaps understandably, the Bains had reassured her that she must have been mistaken about the whole thing. Nevertheless, Carmen confided to Secord and Beth that she believed to this day that the caller had been her missing niece, Elizabeth. Brian King included a detailed report at tab 28 in his fourth and final report for Gatward and Engel prior to the trial, noting at the end that "Mr. Secord was sworn into the strictest of confidence with repect to this conversation and breached that when he advised us of it. . . . In any event, we found it far too important an issue not to be brought to your attention."

While King felt the "Auntie Carmen" call might prove to be an imposing piece of evidence, he was already preoccupied with another new development, one that would lead him to Halifax. After repeated requests, the Crown had finally—on the eve of Baltovich's trial—disclosed the background details on "Spinner," the taxi cab driver police had informed the press they were looking to speak with at the time of Baltovich's arrest. Spinner's existence had come to light as a result of a radio talk show host named John Hesselink, who hosted an after-midnight program on an FM station in Toronto known as Q107.

When interviewed, Hesselink told King that, the summer of the disappearance, he'd made a number of appeals over the air for any information that might assist with the ongoing investigation. On the first of these nights, Hesselink took a call from a man who insisted that he did not want to get involved but said that "Spinner is your man." Hesselink could hear two-way radios buzzing in the background and guessed the caller was a cab driver or dispatcher. A few weeks later, after running another piece on Elizabeth Bain, he received yet another call, possibly from the same man, who reiterated that "Spinner is the guy you want to talk to." When Hesselink inquired who Spinner was, he said, "Every cabbie knows who Spinner is."

What had King thinking about Halifax again was the fact that Hesselink had been sure that the caller had a distinct Maritime accent. Not sure of what to make of "Spinner," King talked it over with Gatward and Engel, adding what he could remember about Secord's previous trips out east. Gatward and Engel were surprisingly enthusiastic. They wanted King to fly to Halifax as soon as possible to dig around for a few days. Halifax in January was no prime vacation spot but King agreed to go anyway. And when Secord learned of King's plans, he announced that he was coming along for the ride.

King and Secord arrived in snow-covered Halifax on January 10, rented a car and immediately began consulting every taxi company in the city for drivers nicknamed Spinner. They found two. Both men, Spencer Williams and Greg Spencer, had been anointed as such because of a notoriously scrappy professional hockey player from the 1970s named Brian "Spinner" Spencer. King was able to determine to his satisfaction, however, that neither man had been driving a cab in Toronto in 1990.

It still bothered Secord that he hadn't been able to find Psycho, the pimp who might have known something about Elizabeth Bain. So he and King diverted their efforts and went to the Halifax Police Department to ask if any officers had seen any young women fitting her description on the streets. The officers were generous with their time and seemed eager to help. Among those present, the consensus was that there had been at least one young woman who shared many of Bain's physical characteristics "working the streets" over the past year or so, but that no one had seen her lately.

King and Secord approached dozens of local prostitutes, showing them Liz's photograph. Most of them simply shrugged their shoulders and said sorry. But there was one prostitute, a sixteen-year-old, who was certain she'd seen Liz once in late July or early August of last summer, standing near the corner of George and Hollis Streets with four other girls. She was dressed in black and had a nice figure. The young prostitute said she was "good with faces" and was quite certain this was the girl she remembered. King had her write out a one-page voluntary statement in which she expressed her willingness to come to Toronto to testify in court, but King had a pretty good feeling it would never come to that.

—◦—

Down at the Silver Rail, the favoured watering hole for an entire fraternity of down-town lawyers, Gatward and Engel weren't permitted to bask in the glory of their victory at the bail appeal for very long. The Baltovich trial, it had been announced, was to be presided over by Judge John O'Driscoll (the same man who had sent Khachadour and Sonia Atikian down the river, Rob would later recall), and there were few, if any, defence lawyers in Toronto who would call that good news. In fact, to many of them, O'Driscoll was known as "the hangin' judge." The irony of this reputation was that, thirty years ago, O'Driscoll had been revered as an excellent young criminal defence counsel and had earned himself a place in the annals of Canadian law for having launched an appeal of the sensational and controversial murder conviction of Steven Truscott.

Truscott had been only fourteen when Lynne Harper, a twelve-year-old class-mate, disappeared on June 9, 1959, and was found two days later. Her body, practically naked, the obvious victim of a violent rape, had been left face up in a desolate area called Lawson's Bush, not far from her Huron County home in south-western Ontario. Despite the circumstantial nature of the case against young Steven Truscott and the fact that he'd always insisted he was innocent of the murder, a jury had found him guilty as charged with a plea of mercy. Unmoved, the judge sentenced Truscott to be hanged nine weeks later.

O'Driscoll's appeal had delayed the hanging but, on January 21, 1960, the Ontario Court of Appeal turned down his arguments for a new trial, and, within the month, word came down from the Supreme Court of Canada that it declined to hear an appeal from the Ontario court's decision. Prime Minister John Diefenbaker's federal cabinet immediately commuted Truscott's sentence to life in prison. Four years later, when Truscott turned eighteen, he was transferred from the Ontario Reformatory near Guelph to the Kingston Penitentiary to do the rest of his time. Even though the Supreme Court—spurred on by the publication of a bestselling book that disputed Truscott's guilt—did eventually review the case in 1966 and early 1967, eight of the nine justices supported the original verdict, and Steven Truscott remained in prison until October 21, 1969, when he was granted parole. Under a new name, Truscott settled somewhere in Ontario, married, had two children and never entered the public spotlight again.

Not long after O'Driscoll was appointed to the bench, it became apparent he had become disenchanted by the deceptive tactics that many a defence counsel tried to employ in his courtroom. This was not an uncommon reaction for a defence lawyer turned judge, which is why most defence lawyers prefer to appear before judges who had formerly been Crown attorneys—historically, they tended to be a lot less tough. Of O'Driscoll, it has been written that he was a "harsh" man who "did not suffer fools gladly." One highly regarded criminal defence lawyer insisted that O'Driscoll will "leave you alone, provided you know what you are doing"; another described his first trial before the judge as a "baptism of fire," a "horrible" experience in which O'Driscoll had "beat the shit" out of him. After that, the same lawyer tried a long series of cases—all, confoundingly, before O'Driscoll—and regularly received words of appreciation from his colleagues for keeping O'Driscoll busy.

As much as many defence lawyers disliked O'Driscoll on the bench, he was equally admired away from it as a principled gentleman with a strict Catholic upbringing who possessed a keen sense of humour, even when it came to jokes about his own much-discussed leanings. During one renowned courtroom incident, O'Driscoll had advised two lawyers (trying to work out a mutually agreeable date to continue their proceedings) to "leave me out of it." The defence lawyer that day, well acquainted with O'Driscoll's wit, felt confident in jestfully replying, "Would you give me that in writing?"

When it came right down to it, though, lawyers on both sides of the fence usually concurred one point—that juries loved O'Driscoll. He had the kind of austere countenance most people expect of a judge. Among many senior members of the Ontario criminal defence bar, however, O'Driscoll had another, less desirable facet to his reputation. Although no statistics were kept on the matter, it was generally felt—albeit not confirmed—that O'Driscoll was one of the more successfully appealed General Division judges in Ontario, meaning that his decisions were overturned at a disproportionate rate. (The Atikians, for instance, had appealed their conviction and had been granted a new trial, which had concluded with a hung jury. When the Crown had prosecuted the couple for a third time—multiple criminal prosecutions, not an option available in American law, are permitted in Canada—the charges were stayed as a result of a witness statement that had not been properly disclosed.) "Given the wealth of legal talent we have in this province," said one prominent Toronto lawyer, "I don't think O'Driscoll should be sitting on big cases any more. Everybody knows that, if O'Driscoll's doing it, there's going to be an appeal. And that's a terrible waste of energy, not to mention the taxpayers' money."

If McMahon felt it was going to be difficult to obtain a conviction in the Baltovich case, O'Driscoll must have given him a tremendous boost after the first two weeks of the trial, which were devoted to legal arguments (known as voir dires) regarding the admissibility of specific pieces of evidence, all of which were heard and ruled upon by O'Driscoll before a jury had been assembled. Gatward and Engel argued against the jury being allowed to hear or see the following: the audiotaped interview Rob had granted to Reesor and Raybould on June 24, 1990; any part of the secretly videotaped polygraph interview with detective Wozniak; the "hypnotically enhanced" testimony of Marianne Perz; and, finally, Cathy Bain's avowal that her sister had said, "Rob is such an asshole" while in an unhappy state on the evening of June 14.

In the first voir dire, Engel attempted to deconstruct the work Reesor and Raybould had initiated on the case before their interview with Baltovich. Engel felt that, when Reesor transformed the interview into something that more closely resembled a cross-examination, his client should have been recautioned with respect to his right to counsel. In other words, his decision to waive his rights at the beginning of the session had been nullified the moment Reesor began treating him as a suspect. What got Engel riled more than anything else was the way Reesor, under cross-examination, kept denying that Baltovich had been a suspect at the outset of the interview. Then why, Engel kept wondering, had Reesor ordered surveillance on his client the afternoon Bain's car had been found? Why, well before meeting Baltovich, had he called Mrs. Bain, along with a good number of Bain's classmates (and others), to corroborate statements Baltovich had already given to other police officers? Despite these facts, Reesor repeatedly proclaimed that Baltovich had been merely a witness (albeit one he was highly suspicious of) in a missing-person investigation that he felt may have involved foul play.

With respect to the polygraph test, Engel argued that the way Reesor had hounded Baltovich to take it, offering to clear his name with the media even though the detective had been fully aware of his lawyer's advice against the test, amounted to such powerful inducement that the entire pre-test interview should be ruled involuntary and, therefore, inadmissable. The consent form Baltovich had signed prior to the test related to the test itself and in no way prepared him for the highly personal and gruelling four-hour examination of his life that was the pre-test—an exercise, Engel suggested, intended to soften up his client for the ultimate confrontation once he'd "failed" the polygraph. Furthermore, he argued, the surreptitiously recorded videotape of the interview amounted to a contravention of Baltovich's privacy, as guaranteed in the Canadian Charter of Rights and Freedoms.

For voir dire "C," related to hypnotically enhanced testimony, Engel enlisted the assistance of an expert witness, Dr. Peter Rowsell, an eminently respected and qualified psychiatrist. Rowsell testified that, while he himself used hypnosis for therapeutic purposes, the technique carried with it several inherent dangers, specifically memory hardening and confabulation (the process by which a person fills in the gaps of memory with imagined details). The only way to gauge the reliability of hypnotically induced memories, in Rowsell's opinion, was to measure the extent to which they could be corroborated by independent evidence. Usually, Rowsell explained, for every "empirically corroborated" memory, there were four or five other memories that could not be substantiated.

When it came to the hypnosis of Marianne Perz, Rowsell cited four factors that may have increased the likelihood of confabulation. First of all, seeing her friend Elizabeth Bain sitting at a picnic table was not the type of traumatic event that would become well-encoded in her memory and, thus, easier to retrieve at a later date. It wasn't until Perz discovered Bain was missing that the encounter would become fraught with emotionally charged meaning. Rowsell also contended that Dr. Matheson had questioned Perz in a suggestive or leading manner. He cited an exchange in the manuscript of the session, prior to hypnosis, in which Matheson had assured her that she would remember everything. This may have led Perz to believe that she was capable of total recall, causing her to mistakenly interpret historically inaccurate details as true. Rowsell also had difficulty reconciling the description of the male Perz had offered Matheson with his own observations of Baltovich. What concerned him even more were Perz's characterizations of the man's eyes as being unusual, with a look of impatience—in his opinion, this indicated that she had become emotional during the course of the interview, which was consistent with confabulation. Finally, there was the photograph and article she'd seen in *The Toronto Sun*, which had painted the image of Baltovich as a suspect. Perz might have subconsciously absorbed the contents of this article, in part or in full, into her memory. To determine what effect the article had on Perz, she should have been questioned about it prior to hypnosis.

To refute Rowsell, McMahon called his own expert witness to the stand—Dr. George Matheson. Matheson countered Rowsell by stating that confabulation was part of memory retrieval, whether it was done naturally or through hypnosis. He did agree, however, that memories obtained through hypnosis should be corroborated. In regard to the issue of traumatic memories being more vivid, Matheson felt that, in general, people could recall any meaningful memory (like exchanging warm glances with an old friend from high school) in detail. Matheson did not believe his questions had been leading, nor did he concur with Rowsell's position that Perz's descriptions of the man's eyes indicated an increased likelihood of confabulation. The importance of the newspaper photograph was dismissed with much professional preening. In essence, Matheson didn't think Perz's description had much in common with the shot of Baltovich in the *Sun*. When confronted with the fact that Perz had selected Baltovich out of a photo line-up moments after her session with him, Matheson pointed out that Perz had "discriminated" between her memory of the man in the valley and the photo. The differences between the two had, in fact, caused her to admit to Detective Warr that she couldn't be absolutely certain it had been Baltovich, a discrepancy that, in and of itself, Matheson felt did not constitute contamination.

On the last, "Rob is such an asshole" voir dire, Bill Gatward told O'Driscoll that the "probative value" of this alleged comment was nil. By allowing a jury to hear it, Gatward submitted, there was a risk that they would place "this utterance into some kind of chain reaction, resulting in a necessary motive on the part of Mr. Baltovich to do harm to the missing woman." O'Driscoll didn't see it that way. He found the comment "relevant to the situation," in that it was indicative of Elizabeth Bain's feelings at the time.

In keeping with his reputation, O'Driscoll ruled in favour of the Crown on each of the four voir dires. In some cases, there were binding conditions. For example, the videotape and transcript of the polygraph pre-test would have to be edited in such a way that the jury was unaware that the interview was, in fact, leading up to a lie-detector test (which was, of course, inadmissible). On the debate over hypnosis, O'Driscoll accepted the evidence of Matheson, "that hypnosis, if conducted in accordance with the accepted procedure, does not cause any more confabulation and/or contamination of one's memory than any other factor." For the time being, Gatward and Engel had no choice but to swallow this batch of bitter pills. O'Driscoll would serve them several more over the next eight weeks.

—◦—

No one could believe it when the name Philip Mascoll appeared among those selected for the Baltovich trial's jury panel. Mascoll, a reporter with *The Toronto Star*, had written a number of articles about the case, including the one about Baltovich enjoying his first Sunday dinner with his family in November after having been granted bail. It was another inconceivable coincidence, Rob thought, in a long series of inconceivable coincidences. Needless to say, when the eight-man, four-woman jury had finally been chosen, Mascoll was not on it.

As with the preliminary hearing, the Bain family was scattered among the first group of witnesses to testify. Gatward and Engel exuded far more compassion for the Bains than they had at the preliminary, but Engel still asked Mark Bain to explain why he'd attended only two searches for his sister. Engel also went out of his way to get Mark to concede that he and Rob shared a good number of physical characteristics, including tanned, muscular arms, such as the one that Ruth Collins saw reach across Liz to close her passenger door in front of Three R Auto Body. This time around, however, McMahon was prepared. As soon as Engel had completed his cross-examination, McMahon stood to ask a few short questions as part of the Crown's re-examination. "On June 19, 1990," said McMahon, "did you kill your sister?" Best to put the issue to rest, he thought, than to leave it hanging.

"No, I didn't kill my sister," Mark answered. "That's totally absurd."

Engel spared Rick Bain the debasing experience of having to relive his cross-examination at the preliminary but he still felt compelled to inquire whether Mr. Bain had ever been told about the mysterious "Auntie Carmen" phone call. O'Driscoll allowed Engel to ask Mr. Bain about it, but only as a miniature voir dire, with the jury out of the courtroom. The judge wanted to hear Mr. Bain's response before he decided that the jury should be permitted to. In the end, though, it was a moot point. Mr. Bain said repeatedly that he'd never heard such a thing from anyone.

From Gatward and Engel's perspective, the family was doing everything they could to discredit any piece of evidence that aided the defence's cause. Even Liz's mild-mannered brother, Paul, now eighteen and working full-time as a salesperson at a Canadian Tire store, had subtly altered his testimony about the location of the door guards. Paul had not appeared at the preliminary hearing, but the Crown had made arrangements for Brian King to record an interview with him on July 25, 1991. During that interview, Paul said that for the most part, both sets of fingers had been on the driver's side (a crucial fact, considering David Dibben claimed to have seen them on the other side of the car). "If we can maybe zero in on the Tuesday your sister disappeared," King had then asked. "Do you remember where the fingers were on her car?"

"If they hadn't been changed by anyone," Paul responded, "they would have been on the driver's side door."

King wanted more clarification, so he asked, "If they had been on the passenger door within the few days prior to her disappearance, would you have known?"

"Yes," said Paul, "I would have known."

Paul's response to an identical question seven months later left King shaking his head, beside himself but unable to express it. The question, posed by Bill Gatward, was: "At the time your sister disappeared, were the fingers not both on the driver's side door?"

"In all fairness," answered Paul, "I can't be sure."

Gatward did not attempt to "refresh his memory"—something lawyers are extraordinarily fond of doing for witnesses—by going over his statement with Brian King.

Even more damaging than Paul, though, was his sister Cathy. At the preliminary, she had come across as a real fireball, blazing with resentment for Rob, more as a result of Gatward's cross-examination of her father, he felt, than anything else. But now she was projecting a mood that was infinitely more demure. It was very Liz-like, Rob thought, and he wondered if she'd been coached to smooth out her rough edges while testifying, lest the jury's pangs of sympathy for Liz be diminished by association. (At the end of the day, Rob's aunt, Janet Anderson, summed up her feelings about Cathy's "act" by saying, loudly enough for the entire gallery to hear, "Well, that was quite a performance.")

Cathy retold the incident of her sister coming up from the basement and, with her mascara smudged, calling Rob an "asshole." (What Rob—who had always asserted that this entire story was a fabrication—couldn't understand was this: if this had taken place, why had Cathy not questioned him about it after he'd read Liz's final diary entry? Once he had responded in the negative to her query about whether he and Liz had been fighting, it only seemed logical that she would challenge his denial with this recent incident if it had, indeed, really happened.) Cathy then offered a sensible explanation for the du Maurier cigarettes found in Liz's car, saying that her sister had smoked that brand "years ago, when she was under stress." Cathy also happened to be the sole witness who had seen the thickness of the diary before Rob had taken some of it home and was, therefore, the Crown's main proponent of the theory that Rob had destroyed much of it.

Not very far into his cross-examination of Cathy, Gatward dealt with the topic of Liz's final diary entry, specifically the references to her desire to kill herself, as well as "those fucken people who toil on me day after day." "This appears to be a group of people, right?" Gatward asked. Cathy agreed. "Obviously you are going to say my client, but who else?"

There was a dramatic pause. "Rob's associates," said Cathy venomously. It was such a ridiculous response that, despite the circumstances, Rob was on the verge of bursting into laughter. A few minutes later, O'Driscoll halted the cross-examination for a lunch break. Rob stepped out of the prisoner's dock and turned to look at his cousin Glenn Anderson (Gregg's younger brother), who'd been attending the trial with some regularity, and even Glenn's face was beet red from holding in his intense amusement at Cathy's final remarks of the morning.

Just prior to resuming court for the afternoon, Adele asked Rob if he would accompany her out into the courtyard at the rear of the building so she could have a cigarette. Rob rode with her down the escalators to the main floor and through the heavy glass doors into the frigid winter air. "Can you believe that?" Rob said. *"Rob and his associates?"* And then he looked up, and there was Cathy right in front of him, standing next to a friend. Rob didn't say anything more, just shook his head in a show of disgust. But Cathy's cold stare remained locked as she said, "You're going down for this."

Following the lunch break, Gatward tried to deflate the missing diary pages theory by pointing out to Cathy that a number of her sister's diary entries contained lecture notes from school. "Would it be fair to say," Gatward began, "that it is quite possible that the diary, that thick binder you have described, may well have contained extraneous materials?"

"It would be fair to say," she agreed. "Because a number of people had their hands on the diary, so it could be possible other material was in the diary." (When asked if she could recall a specific entry or piece of writing that had gone missing, Cathy couldn't come up with one.)

Then, just when it looked as though Gatward couldn't be doing any better, he did. "Would you not agree with me," Gatward continued, "that, even in the parts of the diary that remain—because you say some parts are still missing—there are both complimentary and uncomplimentary remarks about Mr. Baltovich?"

"The way the diary is now?" Cathy asked.

"Yes."

"Yes," she said. "I would."

"Now," said Gatward, "on the evening that your sister looked as though she'd been crying prior to allegedly calling my client an asshole, were you aware she had a telephone conversation with Nancy Sicchia, your brother Mark's girlfriend?"

"No, I wasn't aware of that."

"Were you aware your sister had been crying during this telephone conversation with Miss Sicchia as a result of an incident at work where a girl had fallen down some stairs?"

"I had heard about the incident," said Cathy. "But I didn't know she had called Nancy."

"You told us your sister would speak to you frequently about her relationship with Mr. Baltovich?"

"Yes."

"Both the good and the bad?"

"Yes."

"I take it that, on the Tuesday your sister disappeared, she never said, 'Well, Cathy, I finally did it. After all this time of talking about it, I got up the nerve to break up with Rob.' She never said that to you, did she?"

"No."

One of the most intriguing aspects of the family's testimony was the way in which Liz's suicidal tendencies, as well as her disturbing methods of keeping her weight down, were downplayed, if not dismissed outright. The family didn't believe for a moment that Liz had taken her own life—"If she committed suicide," Julita testified, "where is her body?"—but they also knew that the slightest concession to that possibility on the witness stand would weaken the case against Rob.

GATWARD: This expression of a desire, repeated several times, to kill herself, that she wants death to come, is something you had never seen before in your daughter?

JULITA: No. If I had read the diary, I would have probably spoken to her. It is like a catharsis. Sometimes one might say, "I'm so fed up I feel like killing myself," when it doesn't mean you're going to kill yourself.

GATWARD: Are you aware of any other attempts by your daughter to kill herself?

JULITA: No, sir. The only time I heard about her attempt to commit suicide was when Rob was telling the policeman.

GATWARD: Your husband never told you of a discussion he once had with your daughter about an earlier time?

JULITA: No, sir.

GATWARD: Mr. Eric Genuis never told you that he had seen bandages on your daughter's arm prior to her disappearance?

JULITA: No, I never noticed any bandages on my daughter's arms. If I did, believe me, I would first want to question her and get to the bottom of it.

GATWARD: Doesn't this show a side of your daughter that, perhaps, you were unaware of?

JULITA: It shows that it's a low point in her life. That's what she wrote on paper, but the way I saw my daughter is a totally different thing.

GATWARD: This is not very pleasant, but the diary has repeated mentions of your daughter's use of enemas.

JULITA: That's part of her trying to control her weight.

GATWARD: That she would administer enemas to herself?

JULITA: I was aware of that.

GATWARD: On a daily basis?

JULITA: I don't know about daily, but I know she did. I used it once in a while, too.

GATWARD: You didn't see anything unusual about your daughter's use of enemas?

JULITA: No.

GATWARD: Or that she used laxatives?

JULITA: No. If she did it every day, three times a day, I would say it is abnormal. Once in a while, no.

Even more remarkably, Liz's family doctor, Dr. Janet Lewtas, testified that she didn't find her young patient's behaviour out of the ordinary. Dr. Lewtas also confirmed that, at Liz's request, she had prescribed for her three months' worth of birth control pills in October 1989. The most interesting disclosure of all, however, was that Liz had undergone a complete physical examination as recently as June 7, 1990, twelve days before her disappearance. McMahon asked the doctor if she had noticed any marks on her wrists that day, and Lewtas said she hadn't. There had been no discussion at all of suicide. But Liz had indicated that she was suffering from "bulimia" on the pre-examination form she'd filled out (along with chronic fatigue syndrome, irregular periods and nosebleeds). At Engel's request, Dr. Lewtas explained that bulimia was an eating disorder that caused people to "overstuff themselves" and then, overwhelmed by guilt about the weight they might gain, "they get rid of the food one way or another, by vomiting or taking laxatives or something like that."

Engel read Dr. Lewtas a passage in which Liz made reference to giving herself enemas for six months. The doctor had no idea about her enema use. "Is it normal for a young woman of Elizabeth's age and state of health to be giving herself enemas?" Engel asked.

"Some people do it," the doctor replied.

"Is it normal for anyone to give themselves an enema every day?"

"I think there is a much broader range of 'normal' than you are trying to pin me down to."

Engel tried again: "What about normal in the sense of it occurring with any frequency in normal, healthy people?"

"Again, I'm not sure of what you are even asking me there."

Next, Engel read Dr. Lewtas Liz's final diary entry and asked if, in her professional opinion, it was "the product of a profoundly disturbed young lady."

"Boy, no," the doctor said.

"Pardon me?" said Engel, genuinely taken aback.

"Kids sound off," Lewtas responded. Then, realizing that the patient in question was in her early twenties, the doctor corrected herself. "I mean teenagers, young adolescents, young adults, they all sound off their frustrations in many ways, and writing diaries is just one of them. Taking drugs is one. I wouldn't call them all profoundly disturbed. I would have to know more."

"Does it disturb you that she never confided any of these thoughts to you?"

"Within limits, yes. But at the same time, most adolescents have pretty wild thoughts and pretty wild fantasies and pretty wild dreams."

Knowing he wasn't going to get any further, Engel announced that he had no more questions for the witness.

—◯—

BAIN WANTED BREAKUP, MURDER TRIAL TOLD

By Wendy Darroch

Feb. 8, 1992—Just weeks before Elizabeth Bain disappeared, she told a friend she wanted to break up with her "possessive" boyfriend, a jury has heard.

Nancy Sicchia testified yesterday that Bain told her about three weeks before she went missing that she wanted to end the relationship with Robert Baltovich but didn't know how.

"The big problem with their relationship was jealousy," Sicchia, 19, testified. "She felt things were going down hill and she wanted to block him out."

She said she was dating Bain's younger brother, Mark, at the time, adding the two women would often talk together about their boyfriends.

"She told me he was quite possessive and a pretty jealous man," Sicchia said.

She said Bain told her Baltovich spied on her and suspected

he had people in her summer night classes checking up on her. "She hated it."

Meanwhile, the court heard that Baltovich told a friend he spotted Bain in the campus valley by the tennis courts at 7 p.m. on the night she vanished.

"He thought it was funny, she was hiding behind the car as if she was trying to avoid him. He didn't think she wanted to see him so he said he drove by," Stephen Annett, 21, testified. Annett was dating Bain's younger sister, Cathy, at the time.

"He asked me if I thought Liz was seeing someone behind his back," Annett said.

He said Baltovich had told him "Liz was the best thing he ever found and he wouldn't want to let her go."

THE TORONTO STAR

———◦———

The Baltovich trial was quite unusual in that all three Toronto daily newspapers each had a staff reporter covering it full time (local television stations had their people represented in force as well). After just the first week of the trial, enough had been written by the three court reporters for everyone involved on both sides of the case to get a sense of where they stood. Overall, Gatward and Engel thought the coverage was atrociously biased, and that only Thomas Claridge, a tweedy veteran with *The Globe and Mail*, was producing anything that resembled fair reporting. The worst offender, in their opinion, was *The Toronto Sun*'s Tracy Nesdoly, with Wendy Darroch of the *Star* running a close second.

The divergence of the reporting was well exemplified by the part of the trial that dealt with Elizabeth Bain's diary. As part of the Crown's evidence, John McMahon enlisted the assistance of a young female constable named Charlene Van Dyk to stand in the witness box and read the final six months' worth of the diary for the jury. In the following morning's newspapers, the headlines read: "Love affair not over, Bain diary suggests" (*The Globe and Mail*); "Bain had love-hate feelings for accused" (*The Toronto Star*); and, "Lover will condemn me: Bain" (*The Toronto Sun*).

Claridge's articles, which consistently cast doubt on the Crown's case, irritated Brian Raybould no end. Raybould, who towered over the stout, grey-haired reporter, claimed, years later, to have confronted Claridge in the hallway outside the courtroom by asking him what exactly he thought he was doing. And Claridge (who, when questioned about such inquisitions, had no recollection of them whatsoever) would usually defend himself by insisting he'd written exactly what had been said in court. "Get out of here," Raybould said at their final encounter, marching off down the corridor. "Leave me alone, you asshole. You're an idiot."

—⊖—

John McMahon called Rob's friend Al Heys to testify about the Dear John letter he'd found in the back of the Cordoba on the way to the movies. Heys appeared before the jury on the heels of Vanessa Sherman, another key fragment of the jealous-rage theory, who claimed Rob had exchanged words with Liz earlier that Saturday, causing him to drive off in a huff, squealing the tires of a car Sherman was unable to describe. The problem now, though, was that Heys had uneasy feelings about the Dear John classification. He'd simply been in tentative agreement with the detective's terminology without really thinking about what he was saying. Heys had known it was "Dear . . . " something and now believed the words he'd been trying to recall were "Dear Meg." Before testifying, Heys had even reminded Rob's lawyers to mention the "Dear Meg" connection during his cross-examination because he was sure that it was the genesis of this embarrassing misunderstanding.

So when McMahon asked Heys what Baltovich had said about the envelope in the back of the car, Heys said Rob "might have mentioned it was an entry from her diary."

"Did he say anything else about it?" asked McMahon.

"Not that I can remember," Heys answered. "Not at this time."

So McMahon placed before him a transcript of his testimony at the preliminary hearing, referring Heys to a page containing the Dear John description. McMahon couldn't "lead" the witness by saying the words "Dear John," and it didn't appear as though Heys was prepared to offer them. "I can remember being in the car," said Heys. "And I can remember the letter being mentioned but I can't remember anything with regards to its contents."

McMahon then requested that both the jury and Heys be excused from the courtroom so that he could make an application to cross-examine his own witness.

In the end, O'Driscoll complied, and McMahon succeeded in having the jury hear the words "Dear John" (although, according to Heys, this meant "problems" in a relationship, not that it was over). And because it had to be pried from such a reluctant witness, who happened to be a friend of the accused, it must have left the jury with the impression that Heys had been lying to protect Baltovich.

Gatward did his best to repair the damage. He asked, "Can you remember whether Mr. Baltovich appeared to be at all concerned about this document?"

"No," said Heys. "Not in the least, that I can remember. There was no low mood."

"Did Mr. Baltovich ever, as far as you knew, ever express jealousy about Miss Bain?"

"No."

"Did he say, 'Well, looks like this relationship is on the rocks'?"

"No."

"Never said, 'Looks like I'd better start looking for a new love in my life'?"

Again, Heys responded in the negative.

But, several days subsequent to his testimony, Heys would realize that Gatward had forgotten to ask him about "Dear Meg" and how this might have been what had prompted him to latch on to the words "Dear John" when they'd been offered by Detective Smollet.

While Heys was suffering from the blow of this oversight, McMahon was in court, questioning Steve Doucette about how he and Rob had talked to Heys about his Dear John slip. "I don't know a lot about it because I wasn't in the car," said Doucette. "But it had to do with Al thinking it was a Dear John letter and that Al had mistaken it for a letter written to a guy named John."

"And that is how he came up with Dear John?" McMahon asked.

Doucette seemed to be vaguely aware that his memory was, perhaps, not entirely accurate, as he said, "I guess so, yeah."

"And just out of curiosity, sir, were you familiar with the term 'Dear John letter'?"

"Yes, it's a break-up letter basically."

"Just what kind of guy is Alan Heys?" probed McMahon, knowing the answer. "Did he go to university and things like that?" Doucette said that he had. "Seemed like a bright guy?" McMahon asked (meaning, *Is it realistic to believe that Heys didn't know what a Dear John letter was?*).

"Yeah, yeah," Doucette affirmed.

What Rob was gradually coming to understand was that a trial had as much to do with perception as it did with truth. Was Al Heys a liar? No. Did the jury come away feeling that something fishy was going on? Probably. It was all about putting the proper spin on things.

Take Andrea Beitinger, for instance. What, apart from getting her to discuss Rob's days with the YMCA camp up near Lake Scugog, was the real purpose of putting her before the jury? It was so that Paul Amenta could elicit the fact that, despite having been Rob's friend for seven years, she agreed to "wear a body pack" anyway. Amenta didn't even bother asking her what they'd spoken about on those tapes. Didn't play them for the jury. Why? Because not one utterance from Baltovich could be fairly interpreted as displaying an iota of guilt. But by bringing it up, the Crown was saying this to the jury: Here is an attractive, bright, likeable young woman who happened to know Baltovich as well as anyone and, at the drop of a hat, she was willing to doubt him, to treat him as a suspect, betray his trust. If, the Crown was subtly proposing, this young woman was riddled with so many doubts about the integrity of one of her dearest friends, then why should you, members of the jury, feel any differently?

And then there were the numerous witnesses for whom Rob was forced to sit in the prisoner's dock, his family and friends looking on, as each one pointed to him and said, "That was the man I saw." Vanessa Sherman, who thought she had seen Rob and Liz having an argument in front of Kidbrooke, had already done this, and so had Cathy Bain with her "Rob is such an asshole" story, which, Rob was convinced, she had fabricated from beginning to end. Kaedmon Nancoo still claimed that he'd seen Rob stretching in the gym before 5:30 PM on June 19, even though his story had changed on numerous occasions and seemed highly improbable.

The most pernicious duo among these witnesses, of course, was Marianne Perz and David Dibben. Perz offered the same testimony that she had given at the preliminary, and Mike Engel meticulously documented how her memory had changed over time and concluded, as he had at the preliminary, by forcing her to concede that her identification of his client could be mistaken, as an element of doubt still existed in her mind. With Dibben, however, Engel was equally scrupulous but considerably more cynical, often disdainful.

Engel read aloud the descriptions Dibben had provided of the driver on July 1, 1990, for the police; on November 15 for Detective Brody Smollet; and, thirdly, at the preliminary inquiry. In the first statement, Dibben had said the driver was wearing "a white fluorescent T-shirt" which became, in November, "a grey T-shirt, with something colourful on the front," and, at the preliminary, was "a black or dark T-shirt with something bright in front." Engel also attacked him over the discrepancy between Dibben's original description of the driver's hair and that belonging to his client. "Sir," began Engel, "you have indicated that, in order for Mr. Baltovich to have been the driver you saw on June 22, his hair would have to be blond or dirty blond?"

"Dirty blond," replied Dibben. "Not blond."

"But Mr. Baltovich's hair that you see in the photo line-up is very dark, isn't it?"

"Not very dark, no, it is mid-brown."

"Mid-brown?"

"Yes."

"Not blond or dirty blond, is it?"

"No."

"Does that suggest to you that maybe Mr. Baltovich couldn't be the person that you saw on June 22, because his hair is completely different than the hair you recall of the driver?"

"Not necessarily."

"Does it trouble you that the hair is different?"

Contradicting the feelings Dibben had expressed to Brian King just prior to the preliminary, he answered, without apparent emotion, "No."

Engel hammered him about the placement of the fingers on Bain's car and then delved into what he was sure had been an out-and-out lie Dibben had told at the preliminary. There, Gatward had asked him if he had a criminal record. Dibben had said he didn't. Now, just hours earlier at the trial, McMahon had put the identical question to him again, and Dibben admitted to having been convicted on a narcotics charge fifteen years earlier, as well as an impaired driving charge in 1988. "Were you not sure what Mr. Gatward meant when he asked you whether you had a criminal record?" Engel asked.

Dibben answered, "I wasn't really positive what he meant, no."

"You have been in criminal court twice but you don't know what a criminal record is?"

"I wasn't sure if it still carried on or not," Dibben explained.

The next batch of witnesses was made up of the various police officers who had interviewed Rob before Reesor and Raybould. Among this group was Constable Austin May, who, with his partner, Detective Richard McKennitt, had interviewed Rob on the evening of Thursday, June 21. At McMahon's direction, May read for the jury each word that had been transcribed that night. A minute or two into the statement, Rob had been talking about his first summer together with Liz:

At that time—and still—I felt she was the most beautiful girl I had ever seen. Both on the inside and on the outside. That was probably the best summer I ever had and I got the feeling that it had been the same for her as well. I knew school was going to bring an end to a lot of the newness and innocence of our relationship. I knew it wasn't going to be the same because school does now and always did put enormous strain on her. To my surprise, we did more than just survive. We actually flourished and grew closer. And in my mind there was at that point nothing that could make our relationship less than ideal. People, both friends and relatives, commented that she had never seemed happier and that I had a new aura about me.

"Just a minute," McMahon interjected. Baltovich had just broken down in the prisoner's dock. "Counsel," McMahon said to Gatward and Engel. "Do you need time for your client? He seems very upset." Gatward agreed that now would be a good time to break for lunch.

When court reconvened, McMahon asked May to describe Baltovich's emotional state when he'd given the statement. "He was very calm, collected, normal," said May. "He wasn't upset at all."

"Did he ever break down to tears or start crying at any time when he gave the statement to you?"

"No," responded May. "Nothing like that at all."

Perception.

———◇———

Partway through the trial, Rob began to have nagging doubts about his choice of counsel. It had become apparent, to him anyway, that they lacked the proper experience to defend such a complex, intricate case. Even though they were armed with

Brian King's four thick volumes of independent reports, Rob sensed that they were concentrating on counterpunching whatever the Crown threw at them (which was a lot) and seemed reluctant to increase their workload by delving into extraneous material. At one point, Engel even enlisted Rob to read through the wire-tap transcripts and bring to his attention anything that might be construed as potentially damaging. And during a number of adjournments, Rob would listen in with great interest as Thomas Claridge approached Gatward and Engel to inquire why they hadn't attempted one approach or another. Engel would usually dismiss him haughtily as though he were some kind of crank. And this was a man who Rob figured had covered more than his share of court cases during his more than three decades as a reporter.

Rob did, however, appreciate that Engel, in particular, was pouring his heart and soul into the case. It was Gatward, on the other hand, whose efforts were, in Rob's opinion, lacklustre. At times, Rob sensed he was quite willing to feed the case to Engel and simply observe.

Brian King was silently enduring similar frustrations. As the trial progressed, it became increasingly clear to him that McMahon—aided by O'Driscoll—had turned the trial into a battle that King's side could very well lose. King liked Gatward and Engel, thought they were good guys, but had now accepted the fact that they were outclassed. And outhustled. On numerous lunch breaks, King looked on as Gatward and Engel departed for a jog, or headed off to the squash club for a quick workout, while McMahon and Amenta made their way to some cubbyhole in the Crown's office where, King imagined, the two lived for weeks on Chinese take-out, plotting their next move or poring over witness statements or case law. Throughout the trial, McMahon seemed to live at the courthouse.

If Gatward and Engel's behaviour could be explained, or better yet excused, one would have to understand that they believed the outcome of the trial to be a foregone conclusion. Rob often called Gatward in the evenings or on the weekends, fretting over one piece of evidence or another, until one day Gatward cut him off and said, "For God's sake, Rob, would you calm down. This case is a joke. There's no way in the world you'll be convicted." Which was close to Engel's mantra: "You can't be convicted. It *can't happen*."

At the preliminary hearing, Rob had come to admire Engel's combativeness, but now that he was his representative before the jury, he found him a bit of a loose cannon whose conduct often clashed with the way he wished to project himself. While cross-examining Steve Annett, for instance, Engel had asked where he'd been working in June of 1990. Annett had responded, "Cycle World," a motorcycle shop. Engel, who thought he might have said "Psycho World," asked, "Is that 'Cycle' with a 'C' as opposed to a 'psy'?" There was another incident that would always stand out in Rob's mind, this time with Ashita Masih, the woman who claimed not to have seen Liz's car across from Three R Auto Body on Thursday while walking her dog. "This little dog," Engel said to Masih. "Is he walking you or are you walking him? How powerful a little beast would he be at the time?" Moments like this left Rob sick with an anguish that he was helpless to eradicate. Mike, Rob would think to himself, the jury is going to think you're an asshole and then, because you're my lawyer, they're going to think I'm an asshole, too.

For Rob, the ultimate irony was that, of all the people involved in his case, he most identified with the technique of John McMahon, the man whose job it was to make sure that he spent a good chunk of his life in a federal correctional facility. McMahon appeared to have impeccable tact, grace, intelligence. While Engel had, in Claridge's opinion at least, turned the jury off within days, McMahon had them eating out of his hand, shooting them warm, confident glances when a ruling went in his favour or a witness's testimony forwarded the Crown's case. It was obvious that McMahon believed strongly in fair play and was not without a sense of humour. Time after time, he proved he was willing to call witnesses who went against the grain of the Crown's theory because, as McMahon repeatedly declared, the Crown's mandate was to present both sides of the evidence, both the good and the bad, and allow the jury to decide the truth.

While McMahon surely scored points with jurors for securing his footing on what appeared to be high moral ground, this was for the most part a cunning ploy. Towards the end of the Crown's evidence, McMahon announced that he would be calling David Singh, Liz's old schoolmate, who was sure he'd seen her standing next to a mailbox in front of the Guardian Drug Store the day after she'd gone missing. McMahon introduced Singh to the court by saying he was calling him as a witness "to aid the defence" and that the Crown would not be asking him any questions (which was a subtle yet patronizing way of letting the jury know that Singh was perhaps not worthy of his time). The most suspicious aspect of McMahon's apparent generosity and good will—something the jury couldn't have knowledge of at the time—was that, while he was prepared to offer up a relatively harmless witness like Singh, he was not so generous when it came to much stronger witnesses like Tasmin Sheikh, George Chau, Rein Raud and the Asian girls who'd been sitting next to Liz at the picnic table on June 19 and had no recollection of Rob, all of whom eroded the logic of what McMahon was trying to prove.

Oozing with his own sense of fairness, McMahon, having lulled his opponents to some degree, carefully selected his opportunities to pounce, casting fairness into another universe as he shaped the evidence as he saw fit. These moments were the trial's most pivotal. With Ruth Collins, for example, McMahon had a difficult decision to make. Here was a woman who, even after hypnosis, insisted she'd seen Elizabeth Bain in her car with a man whose face had been hidden in the shadows during a period of time when Rob was known to be in the gym. The fact that McMahon had called her at the preliminary hearing had left Gatward and Engel scratching their heads, if only because they had no idea when exactly McMahon was suggesting the murder had occurred.

Although McMahon had not yet revealed his murder theory, he would later ask the jury to accept that Robert Baltovich had killed Elizabeth Bain in the valley of Colonel Danforth Park before 7:00 PM on Tuesday, June 19. Which meant that, somehow, he was going to have to discredit Ruth Collins, whose sighting took place between thirty to ninety minutes later. McMahon's prayers were answered when, just before her testimony, McMahon received a letter from Collins indicating that she was suffering from a great deal of anxiety due to the prospect of testifying again, a feeling that had been exacerbated by a number of "visions" she'd had of the dead girl. As a result of the letter, Engel told O'Driscoll that he had grave misgivings about Collins's "mental wherewithal" and seemed reluctant to have her testify at all. McMahon, for reasons that would soon become apparent, was unwilling to let her go. "Ms. Collins is clearly stressed out," McMahon said, addressing O'Driscoll. "But to suggest that this lady is sort of marching to the beat of another drummer would not be fair at all."

Simply put, McMahon had set Ruth Collins up only to knock her down, to portray her as a bit of a flake. But to avoid having the jury turn against him, he had to accomplish this with delicate compassion, as though speaking to a slow child who would never guess in a million years what he was really up to. "Not to embarrass you, Ms. Collins," said McMahon, "but you are under some medication to help you through this process today?"

"Yes," said Collins meekly.

"You feel okay?"

"Not too bad so far."

Hadn't she, McMahon asked, become deeply disturbed by what she'd seen the night of June 19? Collins admitted to having had a couple of premonitions that Bain's body had been buried at a nearby construction site. McMahon asked her to describe how, on one occasion, Collins, along with a couple of friends who'd brought a shovel, had gone to one of these areas and dug around for a little while.

That was more than enough to give the jury the impression that Collins was indeed "marching to the beat of another drummer," even if McMahon himself didn't believe this was the case. Regardless, having accomplished his mission, McMahon felt weak instead of elated at his obvious victory. After six weeks and fifty-two witnesses, he was coming down with the flu.

At Engel's request, the lone cigarette found next to the open package of du Maurier Lights in Liz's glove box had been sent to the Centre of Forensic Sciences for a number of tests. Two separate experts there, one in biology and the other in toxicology, had been called as Crown witnesses to disclose their findings to the jury. The upshot of their testimony was that the cigarette, missing approximately half of its filter—which contained no traces of saliva—had not been drawn upon despite the fact that the tobacco end had been lit.

Curious to know how the cigarettes fit into the police theory, Engel asked Steven Reesor, who now held the rank of inspector, about Elizabeth Bain's "proclivity to smoke." Reesor admitted that, to the best of his knowledge, she had smoked in the past due to stress or to curb her appetite but that these occasions had been extremely rare. Engel wondered if it would be "entirely speculative" on Reesor's part to say who had been smoking in Bain's vehicle that day. "I don't believe anybody was smoking in the vehicle on that day, sir," Reesor answered.

Engel was caught off guard. "You don't believe anyone was smoking? But cigarettes were there, right? And some were missing?" Reesor agreed. "Are you able to speculate," Engel asked, "as to any imaginable reason why Ms. Bain would have cut the filter off a cigarette?"

"No, sir, I am not," said Reesor. "But I am able to speculate why another person might cut the filter off. For example, if this person wanted to make it appear that a smoker had been in the car, he might have lit the cigarette, put it up to his mouth and then, concerned that the saliva would connect him to the scene, cut the filter off after lighting it."

"This would be a person who was a smoker?" Engel asked, having already established that Baltovich detested the habit.

"It could be a nonsmoker who wanted to make it look as though a smoker had been in the car," Reesor posited. "A nonsmoker might not inhale after lighting it."

This was the most fantastic theory Engel had ever heard and he was enraged that Reesor could sit there, spelling it out with a straight face. If Rob had gone to such lengths as to think through the forensic ramifications of lighting up a butt and then cutting off the filter to destroy evidence of his saliva, presumably he would have just gone all the way and taken a drag to make it official. Who's going to worry about a little smoke when you've just killed your girlfriend? Engel was enraged. "There is no evidence of a confession, no evidence of a struggle, no weapon, you don't know when death occurred, you don't know where it happened, you don't know by what means it was accomplished and can only speculate as to the circumstances. If I was to suggest to you that the fairest interpretation of the forensic—"

O'Driscoll cut him off for "making arguments" and announced that it was time for the morning recess. Once the jury had left the courtroom, O'Driscoll told Engel that if he wished to ask Reesor about his theories, then he should expect to receive answers he might not like. "If you are playing with fire," O'Driscoll pronounced, "you are bound to be burned sooner or later. A word to the wise is sufficient."

Not buying Reesor's theory that Rob had lit the end of the cigarette as a ruse but that as a nonsmoker he hadn't wanted to inhale, Engel searched for other possible explanations for the snipped filter. While questioning Detective Sergeant Tony Warr, who had considerable experience with what Engel called "drug subcultures," Engel asked if Warr had ever heard of cigarette filters being used for the purpose "of straining amphetamines prior to injection." Warr said that he had. After the drug had been "cooked in a spoon," it was sometimes drawn through a cigarette filter to absorb any impurities before it entered the reservoir of a hypodermic needle.

Engel set out to present as many alternative theories as he could, in the hope that, by doing so, he would unhinge a tenuous case. He had already begun to develop the likelihood—in his mind, anyway—that Elizabeth Bain had been abducted and murdered by someone other than their client. The defence's number-one suspect was the still unapprehended Scarborough rapist who, for some unknown reason, had not attacked another woman in Scarborough (at least as far as the police were aware) since the rape on Midland Avenue three weeks prior to Bain's disappearance. The serial rapist's well-publicized physical description—blond male in his early twenties of above-average height with a muscular, medium build—sounded a lot like the man David Dibben had originally described to the police. He also sounded eerily similar to the man George Chau had described as being in his restaurant with Bain, as well as the man Tasmin Sheikh had seen sitting next to her in a red Jeep (Engel would later call Chau and Sheikh as defence witnesses).

The defence's Scarborough-rapist angle, as compelling as it seemed, was stopped dead in its tracks during John McMahon's examination of Brian Raybould, who was somewhat familiar with the ongoing investigation. McMahon, radiating skepticism at the mention of the Scarborough rapist during these proceedings, quickly and effortlessly dismantled Engel's legwork. "Has the Scarborough rapist ever taken anybody's vehicle or abducted them in a vehicle?" McMahon asked Raybould.

"No," said Raybould. "He has not."

"Has he ever befriended them in broad daylight at a picnic table beforehand?"

"Never, sir."

"Has he ever attacked anybody in broad daylight?"

"Never, sir."

"Ever stab anyone?"

"Threatened with a knife, sir, but never stabbed."

"Any of these ladies ever killed?"

"No, sir."

"Any of these ladies ever abducted?"

Again, Raybould answered no.

—☐—

On Wednesday, March 11, John McMahon announced that the Crown's case had come to an end. Mike Engel immediately notified the court of his intention to argue for a "directed verdict," which was a motion requesting the judge to essentially throw the case out due to lack of evidence. In other words, Engel didn't believe that his counterparts had proved that Elizabeth Bain was dead, let alone that his client had murdered her.

Having listened impatiently to Engel's arguments, Judge O'Driscoll announced on Friday morning that he would rule on the matter after the weekend. From the way O'Driscoll had grilled him throughout his submissions, Gatward and Engel had a pretty good idea that they would be expected to call witnesses for the defence on Monday. This meant that, over the weekend, a serious decision had to made—whether to put Rob on the witness stand in his own defence—and they met on Saturday to hash it out. Gatward thought Rob should testify; Engel didn't. Rob said he agreed with Gatward. If I don't take the stand, he said, I'm going to look guilty. Engel countered by pointing out that the jury had already heard Rob's version of events through about ten hours of tape-recorded interviews with the police. What more was he going to say? Gatward could understand what his partner was saying but he still didn't concur. Soon, though, Gatward began to come around to Engel's way of thinking. No matter how well Rob handled himself, Gatward was sure that McMahon would find a way to trip him up, twist things around. At best, they said to Rob, he could break even. It was an excruciating afternoon but, after several hours, Rob reluctantly yielded to their advice.

As expected, O'Driscoll got things started Monday morning by dismissing Engel's application for a directed verdict. Not long after, the jury was called into the room to listen to the defence's opening address, which Engel had opted to deliver. Engel began by telling the jury that he was going to outline the prosecution's crime theory so that they could understand how the defence's forthcoming witnesses fit into the Crown's case, which had been likened by McMahon to a jigsaw puzzle. "Consider that I am the person who bought the jigsaw puzzle," said Engel. "Consider me a dissatisfied customer who returns to the source of the purchase and angrily confronts the salesperson, Inspector Reesor in this case, and I tell him that most of the important pieces to this puzzle are missing." A few minutes later, Engel was offering a cursory outline of what Marianne Perz claimed to have seen on June 19, when O'Driscoll interrupted him and ordered the jury out of the courtroom.

Once they were gone, O'Driscoll embarked on a stiff reprimand. "Tell the jury what you are going to do as far as witnesses whom you are going to call, and what you anticipate they are going to say. You are not going to rehash the Crown's case."

Engel said, "My lord, I think I am entitled to let members of the jury understand why it is that I am calling certain witnesses. The Crown knows that my client's mother, brother and sister-in-law are going to demonstrate that Ms. Perz—"

"You tell the jury what you anticipate these witnesses are going to say," O'Driscoll pronounced, cutting him off. "Just leave Ms. Perz out of it at this point."

"My lord, if I can't make an opening address—"

"You can make a *proper* opening address," bellowed O'Driscoll.

Engel was barely maintaining his composure. "My lord, if the defence is not entitled to make its address as it sees fit, then let the trial continue without further comment from myself."

O'Driscoll was unfazed by this threat. "That is up to you," he said. The judge called for the jury and indicated to "Mr. Engel" that he was to continue his address "in a proper vein." Engel was completely deflated. His opening address, entirely ad-libbed, was in total four sentences long, the last of which was: "Without further ado, my lord, the defence would like to call the mother of Mr. Baltovich, Adele Baltovich, to the witness stand."

If the Crown had any hope at all of obtaining a conviction, McMahon had to prove that Rob's entire family was lying about his 6:30 PM departure for the gym in order for the jury to accept that it was Rob whom Marianne Perz had seen with Liz at the tennis courts at 5:45. During his cross-examination of Adele, who'd had her short reddish hair set for the occasion, McMahon implied that she was bending the time her son had left the house to keep him from being convicted of murder. "There is no way I would lie for my son if I thought he had anything to do with a murder," she protested as loudly as her soft but raspy voice would allow. "He would just have to pay his price. But I know he did not have anything to do with the disappearance."

"I take it from your answer, Mrs. Baltovich, that you wouldn't do anything to obstruct the police investigation."

"No," said Adele. "I speak the truth—always."

Intending to prove otherwise, McMahon played the jury a recording of a telephone conversation between Adele and Caitlin Fleury, one of Rob's old girlfriends. Adele liked Caitlin, who had remained friends with Rob, and the two women chatted on the phone regularly. On this day—August 26, 1990—they had been discussing the police investigation and how Rob couldn't have been the one driving Liz's car because of his inability to operate a standard. Caitlin mentioned that Rob had asked her to teach him to drive a standard the previous Christmas but that she'd never got around to giving him the lesson. When Adele heard this, she advised Caitlin to tell the truth but not to mention the request to the police unless she had to "because that Reesor will turn it around and make a lie out of it—this is what he is like." McMahon relied on this exchange to make his point.

Rob's brother, Paul, didn't fare much better. While replying to an innocuous question, he said that he hadn't been aware that a surveillance officer had seen him arrive at his parents' house at 1:00 AM the night of Rob's "interview" with Reesor and Raybould. Sensing that Paul did know and was lying in case he wasn't supposed to know, McMahon reminded Paul, the devout Christian, that he was under oath. Without delay, Paul admitted that it had been mentioned to him by his brother's lawyers at some point. "So, when you just told the jury a minute ago that you didn't know, you lied to them?" McMahon asked.

"Yes," Paul conceded. "I guess so."

McMahon's surprising advances were somewhat negated by Dana Baltovich's testimony. In his closing arguments, McMahon would ask the jury to move the Baltovich family's times back an hour, so that Dana was picking up her husband at four-thirty that day, instead of five-thirty. The problem was that Dana had a nine-to-five job with a large company and had no particular reason to head home an hour early—nor was there any evidence she'd done so. To have met Paul by 4:30, Dana would have had to leave her job in Markham at four, a scenario that Engel and Gatward felt the jury would find unlikely.

The defence also called to the stand four of Rob's friends (some of whom were more accurately described as acquaintances): Milton Tjin-a-Djie (who was used to counter the theory that Rob had followed Liz in his car when, really, he'd run into her on the night in question as he pulled off the highway, returning home from picking up a tennis racquet that Milton had strung for him at his house); David Phillips (the tennis instructor Rob had interrupted as he searched the courts, accompanied by Arlene Coventry, around 7:30 AM on June 20); Rick Gostick (who, after delivering a stinging yet eloquent attack on his treatment by police investigators, illustrated how Kaedmon Nancoo's story had changed over time); and Jim Isaacs (for a version of the relationship and disappearance from Rob's perspective).

Brian King was of the opinion that Gatward and Engel should adopt a blitz approach, wherein those potential witnesses King had interviewed and had found quite credible be called to the stand for the defence. He was thinking (although not exclusively) of people like Rein Raud (the dog walker), the Asian girls at the picnic table, Paul Curran (who thought he'd seen Elizabeth Bain crying in a Scarborough telephone booth between 4:30 and 5:00 pm on June 19), Liz's holistic practitioners, Mike Turcotte (David Dibben's carpool driver) and Lance Hettarachichi (Kaedmon Nancoo's workout partner)—all of whom the Crown had neglected to call. The most effective strategy, in King's mind, was to present the jury with so many possibilities (even if some of them conflicted) and doubts that they would be overwhelmed by confusion. Which was the most salient point—that no one had the foggiest idea about what had actually taken place on June 19. But Gatward and Engel thought they had already done plenty to turn the Crown's case on its head several times over.

Although Raybould had already thwarted the defence's effort to connect the Scarborough rapist to the disappearance, Gatward and Engel still latched onto the alternative-suspect theory and presented Tasmin Sheikh and George Chau to that end. McMahon had been expecting this, but, just prior to Chau taking the stand, Gatward announced that he planned to call a bit of a surprise witness to conclude the defence's case.

Thirty-seven-year-old Nollag Adshead had approached Gatward the day after the Crown had finished presenting evidence. Initially, she had spoken to one of Gatward's law firm partners, Dan Kirby, who had found what she had to say of enough significance that he actually summoned Gatward out of the courtroom to speak with her. Adshead explained that she was one of three complainants (along with her sister and a niece) in a sexual assault case against a fifty-six-year-old man named Patrick Mahoney, who had married her eldest sister, Yvonne, a few years after her family had emigrated from Ireland to Canada in 1957, settling ultimately in Scarborough. According to Adshead, Mahoney had sexually abused her for the first time when she was four and he had continued this incestuous behaviour for twenty years, coercing her into full intercourse at the age of fourteen. "But how does this relate to my client?" Gatward asked.

Adshead, who had been following the Baltovich case in the newspapers, had plenty of reasons. For starters, when she was a young girl, Mahoney had frequented a cottage on Shadow Lake, just north of Port Perry in the Scugog region. Mahoney had also been living in close proximity to the Scarborough campus for about twelve years and jogged regularly in both Morningside Park and Colonel Danforth Park.

And not only did she recall his attending St. Joseph's Church, Mahoney had even once advised Adshead to take her car to Three R Auto Body for repairs. All of this, in conjunction with Adshead's suspicions that Mahoney might very well be the Scarborough rapist, had brought her to Gatward. Yes, Mahoney was thirty years older than the descriptions given of this sexual predator thus far, but Adshead insisted that, because of Mahoney's athletic physique and his use of Grecian Formula to keep his hair from turning grey, he could pass for a much younger man. Gatward asked where Mahoney was currently, and Adshead explained that he had failed to show up for a scheduled preliminary hearing date in January. Having absconded, Mahoney was now believed to be in Ireland.

Gatward and Engel felt they had no alternative but to put Adshead on the stand—a decision that would backfire terribly. For, immediately following her in the witness box was Brian Raybould, whom McMahon had asked to investigate Mahoney in relation to the Bain disappearance. As he replied to the latest twist, the first thing Raybould reported was that Mahoney's fingerprints did not match any of those found in the Tercel. Raybould's second discovery, which was infinitely more damaging to the defence, was that, according to the work schedule with the company at which Mahoney had been employed as a shipper, he was supposed to have worked the 3:25 PM to 11:25 PM shift the week Liz went missing. Raybould conceded, however, that the company's personnel department had no record of whether he had taken any of those days off.

The inconclusiveness of the records hardly mattered. The jury was left with no choice but to pit Mahoney against Baltovich as the only two viable suspects. Clearly, Baltovich was the stronger of the two. In the end, Mahoney had come across as a desperate last gasp from a pair of lawyers left with no choice but to point the finger at others, when what the jurors really wanted was for Baltovich to stand before them and defend himself.

—◦—

The following morning, Bill Gatward stood to present the defence's closing address. Having conferred with his client, Gatward attempted to provide the jury with some context for a number of incidents that the Crown felt had been the gradual crescendo to a murder. For example, the evening that Cathy Bain saw her sister come upstairs from the basement, her blouse somewhat undone, apparently upset: was it not possible, Gatward suggested, that the young couple had been downstairs making love? "When Cathy interrupted them," said Gatward, "Elizabeth knew she had to go upstairs and talk to her. So when Robert Baltovich followed her, he was walking around looking impatient perhaps because he wanted to continue the session, and maybe that is why Elizabeth appeared to be so upset." Therefore, when Liz had called Rob an asshole, it was the result of his lack of understanding as opposed to some larger dilemma that spelled the end.

While Gatward outlined the inconsistencies in the Crown's case, his best moment came as he spoke of the shorts that Marc Singleton had claimed to have seen Rob wearing as he arrived in the gym parking lot at 7:20 PM. McMahon had argued that these shorts had never been produced because Rob had bloodied them killing his girlfriend. Gatward had no idea how they could rationalize this scenario when Ruth Collins, a Crown witness, had seen Elizabeth alive an hour later, while his client was in the gym. "The multi-coloured shorts," concluded Gatward, "Like so much of the rest of the Crown's case, is merely suspicion. It is a red herring."

Towards the end of his address, which lasted approximately three hours, Gatward put forth the defence's theory about what had happened on June 19, 1990. First of all, Gatward pointed out, Elizabeth Bain had not been dressed for tennis when she left home for the last time. She wasn't going to play tennis—she was on her way to meet another man. Why had she withdrawn eighty dollars from her bank account that afternoon, most of which was still unaccounted for? And what had she used the money for? No one knew. This theory was further justified by the evidence of George Chau and Tasmin Sheikh, as well as by the unexplained reference to a man named in Liz's diary.

"We know that Mrs. Bain didn't approve of Elizabeth seeing two men at the same time," Gatward explained. "Maybe Elizabeth was meeting this unidentified blond man, and she didn't want her mother knowing about it. Maybe Elizabeth was meeting this young man to tell him she couldn't see him any more, that, between juggling Mr. Baltovich, two jobs and school, she didn't have enough time. Remember Mark Fielden? He and Elizabeth took romantic walks, went out to secluded places. She accepted flowers from him and led him to believe she was really interested in him. Perhaps, like Mark Fielden, Elizabeth took this young man, this young blond fellow, to a secluded place, like she had taken Mr. Fielden, to tell him that the relationship was over. To pull the rug out from under him. Well, Mr. Fielden, he was a gentleman, and he simply dropped a card at her feet and walked away. Maybe this young man, ladies and gentlemen, didn't walk away. Maybe he got angry and hit Elizabeth. Maybe something happened in this dark, secluded place, which is the reason why he hasn't come forward."

John McMahon appeared to be personally offended by Gatward's suggestion that Liz would be meeting in the valley with someone other than her boyfriend when he took his turn behind the lectern after the lunch break. He went so far as to indignantly chastise Gatward for portraying her as a "two-timing slut." Overall, though, McMahon came across as the king of common sense. ("There is absolutely no reason for the random killer to risk detection by moving that body and burying it up north. What would be gained? Nothing. What could be lost? Everything.")

McMahon had devised explanations for every glaring weakness in the Crown's case. For instance, how did one account for the fact that Dibben had seen the plastic fingers on the passenger side of the car, when they had been on the driver's door later that day? McMahon offered this: "I have suggested all through this trial that Mr. Baltovich is exceptionally bright. Right after he has locked eyes with Dibben, Baltovich knows this guy kept looking at him in the car and he is worried about being identified. By moving the fingers off that passenger side, it is going to cast doubt on Dibben. And it almost worked."

Brian King was sure that the jurors would see right through this. If Rob was such a criminal mastermind, he wouldn't have moved the fingers from one door to the other, King thought, Rob would have thrown the things in a fucking ditch before he'd hit the highway. That was the whole problem with McMahon's vision of the crime. In one breath, he was making Rob out to be an improvisational genius who also happened to be a tremendous actor, someone who could immediately turn a new piece of information to his favour and look real slick in the process. But then, in McMahon's next breath, the homicidal prodigy was enough of a dodo to have admitted to a police officer that he'd once harboured murderous thoughts towards his girlfriend several years earlier. In essence, King thought, McMahon wanted to have his cake and eat it too.

At the end of a long day, McMahon concluded his address to the jury by appealing to their emotions. He read a passage Liz had written to Dear Meg on April 15, 1990: *Don't be afraid to be alone. Don't be afraid to stand up for what you believe in.*

Don't let anyone walk over you. Don't surrender yourself. How many more times do I have to tell you to leave him? He has destroyed you. He has not made you into a better person. He ruined you. Get out while you still have something left. Please God— give me courage.

"On June 19, 1990, Elizabeth Bain had the courage to leave Robert Baltovich," said McMahon, submitting himself to the weight of the moment. "She paid the ultimate price, ladies and gentlemen. She paid with her life. I invite you to return with the only verdict that fits with your life experience and common sense, and that is guilty of second-degree murder. Thank you very much."

Judge O'Driscoll delayed the trial for almost a week as he drafted his charge to the jury. When court resumed on the appointed morning of March 26, Engel postponed O'Driscoll's charge for another half an hour by registering a number of objections to McMahon's closing address. Engel said he found it "remarkable" that McMahon "would invite the jury to completely disregard the evidence of a witness the Crown had called—Ruth Collins." The fact that McMahon had also referred to Paul Baltovich as a "perjurer" was an "unfortunate misstatement." And his characterization of the defence's position as "desperate," "ludicrous," and an "insult to the jury's intelligence" was, Engel declared, "irresponsible." The most strenuous objection, however, related to McMahon's pious reaction to the implication that Liz might have been meeting someone else in the valley. "Never during the course of the trial or during the closing address did we question the moral character of this missing young girl," said Engel. "My friend clearly indicated to the jury that the defence position was an attempt to portray Ms. Bain as a 'two-timing slut.' That is the most inflammatory, inaccurate and irresponsible comment that could possibly have been made in this trial. On that basis, your lordship ought to consider a mistrial, unless there is some very, *very* strong remedial action that can be taken in the course of your charge to instruct the jury—that they be told that the Crown had no right to say that, and that the jury must completely disregard that astonishing comment."

"Mr. Engel," said O'Driscoll, "were you not here all of last Friday?" Engel said that he had been. "Why didn't you raise these points at the end of the addresses?"

"The more I thought about it," replied Engel, "the more enraged—"

"It didn't strike you as inflammatory as it was happening, is that it?"

"I didn't stand up and object, my lord, because I was too exhausted and stunned."

O'Driscoll then asked McMahon for his thoughts. McMahon disagreed with the defence on every point except for his use of the phrase "two-timing slut"—it had been perhaps the wrong choice of words. O'Driscoll concluded that there were no grounds for a mistrial, nor was there any reason to make "any pointed remarks to the jury with regard to the addresses of counsel." The judge then called for the jury.

O'Driscoll's charge to the jury lasted two days—twice as long as it had taken both sides to present their closing arguments. As he offered what was supposed to be an impartial outline of the facts, O'Driscoll's leanings were veiled thinly, if at all. O'Driscoll's charge consisted of twenty-four pages' worth of rhetorical questions— "Why would Robert Baltovich want to go about telling everyone that his suicidal girlfriend had gone missing?" and "Is it a big deal for a twenty-six-year-old male to drive a so-called 'four-on-the-floor'?"—all of which pointed to Baltovich's guilt. He never once asked a question as fundamental as "Had Bain told other people about her attempts at suicide?" or "Is there a single shred of forensic evidence linking Baltovich to the crime?" As for evidence led by the defence regarding Patrick Mahoney and the Scarborough rapist, O'Driscoll implored the jury not to be "sidetracked" or to "run down blind alleys."

When O'Driscoll's charge came to an end on Monday morning, March 30, ten days had passed since the jury had heard a single word from the defence. As the jury was sent away to deliberate, Engel listed his objections for the better part of an hour. Like many judges, O'Driscoll did not always take kindly to criticism. At one point, while Engel was referring to the "multi-coloured shorts," O'Driscoll interrupted him to ask, "What does this have to do with Ruth Collins?"

"Well, accepting Ruth Collins's evidence, that this girl is alive and well at eight o'clock," said Engel, "how can there possibly be blood on the shorts at seven-twenty?"

"You're playing head games," the judge pronounced. "Let's move on to the next point."

"My lord, do you not understand my point?"

"I understand exactly what you are saying," O'Driscoll shot back. Engel wasn't sure if O'Driscoll really did, or whether he was just hell-bent on ignoring the obvious (he was more inclined to believe the latter). "Let's move on," the judge instructed. And so he did.

—◦—

AN OPEN LETTER TO THE STAFF, STUDENTS AND
ADMINISTRATION OF SCARBOROUGH CAMPUS
Tuesday, March 31, 1992

On March 14 of this year, I submitted three paintings to the Annual Juried Students' Show. Two of them were chosen to be hung in the Meeting Place. Perhaps some of you had the opportunity to view both of them between March 16 and March 19. However, prior to the opening of the show on Thursday, March 19, it was deemed necessary to have one of those paintings removed.

The censored work contains images of Robert Baltovich, the man accused of second-degree murder in the disappearance of Elizabeth Bain, and excerpts taken from media and personal texts.

I have been told that the painting was removed from the show because such an "opinion" was not permitted to be displayed in a public space such as the Meeting Place, and that there was a legal issue about the painting being exhibited since the trial was in progress at the time. My understanding is that there has not been any type of publication ban in effect since the beginning of the trial.

I was also informed that my painting had been construed as containing anti-feminist sentiment, and that someone also thought that I, as the artist, condoned violence against women. In response, I would like to make my position perfectly clear: UNDER NO CORCUMSTANCES DO I CONDONE VIOLENCE AGAINST ANYONE. Nor do I intend to promote anti-feminist feelings. I am a 22-year-old woman myself. I intend no disrespect, nor do I wish to hurt anyone's feelings. The purpose of the painting is to comment upon the power that the media have in influencing public opinion against an individual accused of a crime, and to show how this affects those people associated with him. It is also intended to give those who are unfamiliar with the situation an opportunity to take media sensationalism with a grain of salt. In effect, it seems that those responsible for the removal of the painting have fallen prey to this media phenomenon, and have decided that Robert Baltovich is guilty, ahead of any decision handed down in the courtroom.

At this point in time, the painting has been re-hung in the Campus Gallery adjacent to the Meeting Place. I invite you to view it there, and to offer any comments or questions you may have.

Thank you,
Christine F. Sidlar
[19 signatures appear
below in support]

—◦—

Having deliberated for a day and a half, the jury announced at 3:00 PM on March 31 that it was prepared to render its verdict. After listening to O'Driscoll's charge, Rob thought he had a fifty-fifty chance of being convicted. ("Don't worry, Rob," Gatward had said the night before, attempting to calm his client. "You'll be sipping lemonade come tomorrow.") To break the tension, Rob and his family played a game of charades while waiting for the jury to enter the courtroom. (*Toronto Sun* reporter Tracy Nesdoly made a note of the very grim irony that Rob had been trying to act out the title of the movie *Die Hard*.)

Once the jury had filed in, the court registrar asked the foreperson to stand, as well as the accused, who was now back in the prisoner's dock. "Members of the jury," said the registrar. "Have you agreed upon a verdict?" The jurors nodded silently. "How say you all; do you find the accused at the bar guilty or not guilty?"

"We find the defendant guilty as charged," the foreperson said.

A gasp of surprise sounded throughout the courtroom. Rob bowed his head and bit his bottom lip but otherwise remained still. Adele buried her head in her hands. Jim leaned towards Bill Gatward and asked, "What happened?" Rob's aunt, Janet Anderson, turned to Steven Reesor across the room and pronounced him, for all to hear, a liar. Reesor just grinned, so then she called him a "smirking bastard."

A bailiff approached Rob, who was still standing, and told him he could be seated. The first thing Rob did was turn around and stare Reesor in the eye for a good twenty seconds. Victorious, Reesor was quite content to stare right back. Meanwhile, O'Driscoll had thanked and excused the jury, and McMahon was now requesting that the sentencing be held over for approximately a month. Gatward walked over to consult with Rob. "Let's get this over with now and get this appeal under way," said Gatward. When Rob nodded, Gatward then turned to the bench and said, "Mr. Baltovich would like to be sentenced right now if he could, my lord."

"I am inclined to grant the Crown's request to put the matter over," O'Driscoll said. Everyone quickly settled on a date. "All right," said O'Driscoll. "The indictment has been endorsed: March 31, 1992. Verdict: Guilty. Adjourned to May 1, 1992, for sentence. Bail is cancelled."

As a court officer handcuffed Rob and led him out of the prisoner's dock, he glanced at a cluster of television reporters in the gallery, many of whom had been almost genuflecting to him over the past few days, in the hopes that he would grant them post-acquittal interviews. In the following day's *Toronto Star* and *Sun*, it was reported—without context, so as to make Baltovich look as though the verdict had not fazed him—that the guilty man "winked at reporters and said, 'Take care.'" Engel, barely able to watch, was overcome with a horrific numbness that he would in years ahead find it difficult to properly describe, other than to say it was a god-damned nightmare.

Not long after O'Driscoll had disappeared through the door behind his bench, retiring to his chambers, and the spectators had begun taking the escalators down to the main floor, where television crews would be waiting outside, Engel made his way to the holding cells below to see Rob. The first thing Engel noticed was that Rob's face was very flushed. Rob was half-smiling, unnaturally happy, detached from the circumstances. He told Engel not to worry about anything—he had done his best. Engel wondered if Rob might be in some form of shock, but Rob was just doing what he'd done all along. It was almost as though he'd stepped outside him-self and was watching a movie in which he played the starring role, an ironic anti-hero trapped in an absurd fantasy-based reality. For a while, Engel just stood there, absorbing this silent image of Rob, sitting in the dirty corner of a barren cell, par-alyzed by the fear of whatever unknown fate he was to suffer—and suffer alone. This terrible picture would wound Engel forever.

—◯—

Jailhouse Notebook (7)

*T*wo hours before I was once again a passenger in the rear of a paddy wagon, I had been just another Joe walking around in the Eaton Centre mall, eating lunch with friends and relatives. Now I was on my way to the Don Jail, Toronto's version of a medieval gaol, which I had heard plenty of horror stories about during my days at the East. The Don was reputed to be crowded, its cells rat-infested and its staff the worst of the worst.

Once I'd been processed, I was taken upstairs where I quickly realized I was being thrown in the "hole." As the escorting officer closed the door, I asked why I wasn't being taken to a range with other inmates. His reply was terse: "Observation." And, with that, he shut the door.

My cell was windowless. There was no pillow and only a reasonable facsimile of a mattress, which I stretched out on, but sleep was reluctant to come. I realized that, although I wanted desperately to contact my family to let them know I was all right, I couldn't deny the fact that I wasn't. The fear that had gripped me in the first days I'd spent at the East after my arrest paled in comparison to the stark terror and loneliness that enveloped those first few hours at the Don. The cell's barrenness suppressed any emotion, as I stared into space, immobile and catatonic. I tried to cry in the hope that I might be able to conjure up some authentic emotion, but my effort was useless. I felt that, for the first time in my life, there was nothing anyone could do or say to help me.

At some point early the next morning there was a knock on my cell door. As I got up, I recognized Dave Brownlee, a high school acquaintance whom I remembered playing a series of imaginative pranks on my brother Paul years ago. I'd run into Brownlee one day in January while I was out on bail, walking down Midland Avenue en route to my dad's store. We talked about the case for a while and he said he was a guard at the Don Jail, which instantly made me wary. But he told me he was on my side. When I'd been arrested, he said, he'd told his fellow guards that the police had the wrong guy.

Now that I was a guest at his institution, Dave expressed his surprise at the verdict and asked how I was doing. I said as good as could be expected. Then he

offered to get me something to read, so I asked for a newspaper. It hadn't yet
dawned on me to wonder what the reaction of the Toronto press might be the
day after my conviction but when it did, I have to admit that I was curious.

—◦—

'IF I CAN'T HAVE HER . . .'
Elizabeth Bain's prince was a jealous monster
By Tracy Nesdoly

April 1, 1992—They were a story-book couple, or so it seemed.

Robert Baltovich and Elizabeth Bain met, through his
manoeuverings, at school, during a U of T homecoming event. It
was a children's production. She was Snow White, he was Prince
Charming. He was bright, articulate, the top of his class, sure to
rise above his working-class roots. She was exotically beautiful,
athletic, smart, gentle.

He brought her flowers and wrote her poems, comforted her
when she cried.

She wrote in her diary "he treats me like gold."

But it was fool's gold.

Yesterday, a jury found Robert Baltovich guilty of murdering
Elizabeth Bain.

Dealing with the Baltovich family in the second-last section of her long article,
Nesdoly wrote:

Room probes at the Baltovich home installed by police picked
up almost nothing but the Canadian Home Shoppers Club on TV.

"The household is . . . strange," one of the officers said. "The
mother basically lives in the living room, the father upstairs, Rob
in the basement . . . It's like a concentration camp or something."

Baltovich told police his mother has had two nervous breakdowns but she's "functional." His father is a quiet man who works
long hours in his smoke shop.

"You've crucified my son in the press," he said. "He was such a good boy, hard-working, stocking shelves and helping out since age 11, crazy about sports and the movies."

"He's just 26," said the father who would never eat with his son. "Somewhere he got unlucky."

THE TORONTO SUN

———○———

Jailhouse Notebook (8)

A fter two days at the Don, a guard cracked open my cell door and announced, "Grab your stuff, you're going to the East!" This was guard humour—I had no stuff to grab.

As I stepped out of the paddy wagon at the East a few hours later, I felt a mix-ture of relief at having reached familiar territory and sadness that I had to be there at all. I was hoping for an uneventful entrance, but fate conspired against me. "Well, well, looky here," I heard in a familiar voice. It was the same guy who'd taunted me the day I'd left on bail. "I told you you'd be back, Baltovich!"

———○———

Jailhouse Notebook (9)

W ith my sentencing hearing scheduled for May 1, I have been trying to get as comfortable as possible. I had several conversations with Mike Engel, who related his interest in having Brian Greenspan—brother of the famous criminal defence attorney Eddie Greenspan—do my appeal. In Mike's opinion, Brian Greenspan is the best appeal lawyer in Canada. Of course, Mike repeat-edly spoke of his intention to "assist."

Through conversations with my family, however, I got the impression that Mike, not Brian Greenspan, would be doing the appeal. Things were becoming confusing. I had already decided that I was not going to let my affairs fall on Mike again; he had tried valiantly, but my guys had been outgunned. So when

I found the business card of a well-known criminal lawyer named John Rosen sandwiched between a telephone and the wall to which it was fixed, I decided to give him a call.

Rosen's name is often thrown around during jailhouse conversations. Of late, his name has been in the news because he is defending Rui-Wen Pan at his second trial for the first-degree murder of Selena Shen, a former girlfriend and concert violinist. Rosen has achieved exalted status in the pantheon of lawyers that veteran convicts trust and recommend when in a jam. And my situation definitely qualifies. Rosen, I was told, did appeals, and my decision to call him was born out of desperation. I needed to know that my appeal was in good hands.

Remarkably, Rosen came to see me at 8:30 the next morning—a Saturday!— a gesture I was confident not just any lawyer would make. I held out my hand and he greeted me with a warm smile. Rosen then brought me up to speed on legal etiquette. "Rob," he said, his round Danny De Vito-like face taking on a fatherly expression. "I think I should first let you know that, as a lawyer, I felt it was my obligation to call your legal counsel this morning and inform him that I was coming to see you today." Though I had hoped our meeting might proceed incognito, I quickly resolved that my situation was too serious to worry about what Mike's reaction might be. Needless to say, I knew he'd be livid.

Rosen and I then got down to the nitty-gritty. Was he interested in doing my appeal? "Yes," he replied, smiling. Rosen ended up criticizing Mike and Bill's trial strategy, in particular the way they had suggested Elizabeth might not be dead. "They should have walked up to the jury and said, 'She's dead, it's a terrible tragedy, but our guy isn't the one who did it! Then," Rosen continued, "you create reasonable doubt with every witness they put on the stand."

Easier said than done, I thought. Rosen seemed to know a fair bit about my trial, so I asked him what he thought my sentence would be. He let me in on the fact that some lawyers he knew had started a pool based on that very question. Rosen said his money was on a minimum sentence. Great, I said to myself, my life has become a betting line.

Getting back to the chief reason for his visit, I asked him if he would handle my appeal, and he said he would. "Can you do a better job than Brian Greenspan?" I asked, probing further. As the name Brian Greenspan left my mouth, Rosen raised his eyebrows, as if I'd uttered the one name to which he

couldn't respond in the affirmative. But he recovered quickly, flashing me a con-
fident grin and replying, "As good a job as Brian Greenspan." With that out of
the way, and not having made my mind up fully, I told him I would get back to
him as soon as possible with my final decision.

That afternoon, Mike showed up and, as expected, he was none too pleased.
He began by screaming, "What the fuck are you doing calling John Rosen, Rob?
I told you I was handling the appeal!" After stopping to catch his breath, he con-
tinued, "I don't even know if Rosen does appeals!"

Though I had witnessed Mike's petty tirades before and remained impassive,
this time I wasn't in the mood. "Well, Mike," I said. "Rosen does do appeals. And
the reason I called him is because every day I talk to someone on the phone I get
a different answer. One day you're doing the appeal and Greenspan is helping,
and the next day Greenspan is doing the appeal and you're assisting. Your wife
says one thing, then Brian King says something else. My parents tell me one
thing, and the next day I hear the reverse. All I want to know is what the hell is
going on!"

Until that moment, I had never directed even a shadow of anger in Mike's
direction. For whatever reason, I could never muster the energy. But Mike knew
that I'd had it and that it was time to explain things. He was apologetic. Since the
conviction, he said, he hadn't been able to sleep, eat, or stop thinking about the
case. I reminded him that mine was the more difficult prospect. He then let out a
deep sigh and told me that Brian Greenspan was doing the appeal. Now I too was
relieved. All I really wanted to know was that my appeal was in good hands.
Breaking a moment of heavy silence, Mike expressed his desire to defend me if I
was granted a new trial. He still considered us—him, Brian King and me—a
team. I didn't bother pointing out that Bill's name was conspicuously absent.

—◯—

April 27, 1992

Dear Mr. Gatward:

Further to our telephone conversation I am requesting Mr. Baltovich to
disclose the location of Elizabeth Bain's body. As I indicated to you earlier that
if Mr. Baltovich were to turn over the remains of Elizabeth it certainly would

demonstrate his remorse. I am prepared to suggest the minimum sentence for second degree murder if your client does so.

If your client elects not to assist, the Crown will be seeking a substantial increase in the parole ineligibility for Mr. Baltovich. I have enclosed copies of the victim-impact statements which I intend to file. Would you be kind enough to review the statements and let me know whether you wish to hear viva voce evidence from the Bain family.

I also intend to call Detective Sergeant Tweedy of the Homicide Squad to give expert evidence. Tweedy, who has been a member of the Homicide Squad for ten years, will testify how the concealment of a body impairs a murder investigation and makes it more difficult to determine who is responsible.

If I can be of further assistance or you have any questions about the Crown position, please give me a call.

Yours truly,
John McMahon
Assistant Crown Attorney

—◦—

The now-familiar group of lawyers, court officers, spectators, journalists, detectives and family members packed Mr. Justice John O'Driscoll's cavernous courtroom one final time to see what punishment the judge would mete out to Robert James Baltovich. While waiting for the judge to emerge from his chambers, Rob sensed some movement in his peripheral line of vision. A few seconds later, a black-gowned figure approached. It was John Rosen, on break from the Rui-Wen Pan trial. Brian Raybould noticed him and barked out, "John, are you taking this case over now?" Rob had already contacted Rosen to let him know his services wouldn't be required.

"Just stopping in to say hi, Brian," Rosen responded diplomatically. Still, Raybould looked slightly nervous as Rosen greeted Rob near the defendant's table. The first thing Rosen noticed was that Mike Engel was absent, which Rosen found outrageous, considering the magnitude of the case. He chatted with Rob for a few minutes, and Rob asked if he should say something to the court prior to being sentenced. Rosen didn't think it was a bad idea, in contrast to Gatward, who felt it wouldn't make a difference.

As promised, John McMahon produced Detective Sergeant Neale Tweedy to offer expert testimony about the obvious—that it is extremely difficult to solve a homicide without a body. Tweedy never bothered to express, however, that a corpse could occasionally provide enough clues to guard against the wrongful conviction of an innocent person.

McMahon then indicated that he intended to read Julita Bain's two-and-a-half-page victim-impact statement, a right instituted just four years earlier, aloud to the court, which he did (. . . *Rob, if you really loved Elizabeth, you will not want her body lying and rotting away in some swamp or under some weeds . . .*). He followed this gut-wrenching plea by announcing that Robert Baltovich, after a month, had still not disclosed the location of the missing body. Then came the impact statements from Rick Bain (. . . *I wish you would stop to think clearly enough to realize your macabre undertakings can only harm you more with time—rescind your farce and choose to heal instead . . .*), as well as Mark and Cathy.

Describing "Mr. Baltovich's character subsequent to the act" as "cold, callous, calculating and manipulative," McMahon suggested that the only "just sentence" would be one that required Baltovich to serve between fifteen and twenty years of the standard twenty-five-year term before becoming eligible for parole. Gatward, describing the offence—as it was seen by the jury—as "a singular event without similar precedent," recommended the minimum period of parole ineligibility for the crime—ten years. Watching on from the gallery, Rosen was astonished by Gatward's flat performance. This wasn't some juvenile going down for shoplifting. This was Murder Two. You jump up and down, protest that an innocent man is being sent to prison. You respectfully counter McMahon's letter. You give Neale Tweedy a rough ride. You have your client read an impassioned speech. As Rosen observed and silently criticized, O'Driscoll announced he would need a mere half an hour to decide on Baltovich's sentence. Rosen shook his head in disgust.

After the break, O'Driscoll asked Baltovich if he had anything to say before being sentenced. "Yes, your honour," Rob said, standing. "I would like to say that I had absolutely nothing to do with Liz's disappearance, and I am truly innocent of the crime that I have been convicted of. That is all."

"Thank you," said O'Driscoll. "You may be seated."

After some preliminary comments, O'Driscoll launched into the body of his reasons for the sentence he would hand down:

The circumstances surrounding the offence and your character are interwoven. When the search for Elizabeth Bain started, you did everything humanly possible to deter the investigation and to hinder the police. You lied about when you had last seen her, and you pushed the theory of suicide. You tried to cultivate the theory that it might have been Eric Genuis, and other male friends of the deceased woman. Indeed, that continued through the trial.

You betrayed the trust of those who took you into their homes, namely, the Bains. You betrayed the trust of Liz's friends, both male and female.

Fortunately, for the administration of justice, your luck ran out when you encountered the members of the Metropolitan Toronto Police Force. You were a young man just out of university with a high I.Q. and a certificate giving you a Bachelor of Arts degree in psychology. I got the impression as I listened to the evidence at the trial, not only what the jury heard but two weeks before the jury got here, that you thought you would run these dumb cops around the track three or four times for a couple of weeks and then it would all be over. Well, it didn't pan out that way. You encountered some very astute officers, all of them, especially in the persons of Inspector Reesor, Detective Sergeant Raybould and Detective Sergeant Warr. At the time you didn't realize it, but they were all two or three steps ahead of you at any given moment. The pages and pages of statements that you freely gave to the police were all a stage play that you were directing—not an attempt to assist in the investigation.

At the trial and today, you have excercised your legal right to stand mute. And let there be no mistake, you are not being penalized for exercising your legal rights, and certainly not being penalized for your plea of not guilty. However, since there is a blanket denial in all those statements, which the jury didn't accept, I can only conclude that what you did was with malice and with total intent. Therefore, in cold blood, you killed your girlfriend, a young lady that you had dated, someone with whom you had been intimate, a young woman who had, on the evidence, given to you your walking papers.

Instead of accepting the pink slip and moving forward, you decided to end her life so that she could never enjoy happiness with anyone ever again. You decided to end her life, to hide her body; and you continued in this decision to cause all this grief and heartache to Elizabeth Bain's mother, father, two brothers and her sister, as well as to the members of her extended family.

You do all this with great calmness, very cool, very calculating, no emotion. You do it all as though you were moving around the figures on a chessboard.

Having chosen this route and having chosen to stay in this flight pattern, you are right to expect justice, but you have no claim to mercy.

The record shows a cold, calculating person, and that person killed a person who had loved and trusted you—in my view, a total and unrecoverable breach of trust and faith.

Your phony schemes of lying to the police, and your schemes to get relatives to participate in the alibi obviously didn't impress the jury. Your actions, from day one, have been as reprehensible as one can envisage. You have high intelligence, but you are totally devoid of heart and conscience.

You know that the mandatory sentence is life imprisonment. What I am deciding—the only matter I have to decide—is whether to increase the ineligibility period above ten years.

Considering all of the matters in the Criminal Code, the sentence which I pass is this: life imprisonment, no eligibility of parole until seventeen years have been served. [When O'Driscoll had asked the jury to briefly deliberate and then offer its recommendation on sentencing moments after delivering the verdict, seven of the twelve jurors submitted no recommendation, while the remaining five suggested Baltovich serve the minimum sentence of ten years.]

You may remove the prisoner.

—◇—

Jailhouse Notebook (10)

*I*t seems like a long time since I've written. I guess I just haven't been in the mood since my sentencing, but 1992 is about to expire and perhaps jotting down what has taken place over the last eight months might make Christmas whiz by a little more quickly.

The first notable event was the day Brian Greenspan came to see me. He told me that he'd argued a lot of appeals in his time, and he'd never before seen a case at such an early stage with so many grounds for appeal as mine. He also said he

This family photo of Elizabeth Bain appeared on the front page of The Toronto Sun *and on thousands of Missing posters across southern Ontario.*

The Toronto Sun, *June 26, 1990. Family Photo*

Julita and Rick Bain hold a press conference in their backyard three weeks after their daughter Liz disappeared. "Whoever you are," Rick pleads with her abductor, "Come out of your dark place. Tell us where she is."

The Toronto Sun, *July 11, 1990. Mike Cassese.*

Handcuffed in the back of a police cruiser, Rob tries to maintain whatever dignity he can muster as photographers buzz around him.

The Toronto Sun,
November 20, 1990.
Paul Henry.

Constructed in 1965, Scarborough College has been hailed by architectural historians from all over the globe as one of the world's finest examples of what is known as a "Neo-Brutalist megastructure." Photos by author.

Highland Creek runs below the Morningside Bridge into Colonel Danforth Park, where Rob maintains he and Liz had their last rendezvous.

*Detective Sergeants Tony Warr (left) and Brian Raybould stand next to
Elizabeth Bain's Toyota Tercel in a garage at the Centre of Forensic Sciences
while news photographers are invited to take pictures. Eight sets of fingerprints
were discovered in the car, of which the police were able to match five. None
belonged to Robert Baltovich and the other three remain a mystery.*

The Globe and Mail, *June 28, 1990. Eric Christensen.*

Bill Gatward (left) and
Mike Engel escort Rob
on a "walkabout" for
the media in order to
prevent embarrassing
ambushes during the
course of the trial.

The Toronto Sun,
February 5, 1992.
Carlo Allegri.

Paul, Cathy, Julita and Rick Bain stand outside the University Avenue courthouse after Baltovich was found guilty. In his victim-impact statement, Rick urged Rob to "rescind your farce and choose to heal instead."

The Toronto Star, *April 1, 1992. John Mahler.*

After the verdict, Adele
Baltovich is escorted
outside by her son Paul
and his wife, Dana.
"There is no way I
would lie for my son if I
thought he had
anything to do with a
murder," Rob's mother
testified. "He would just
have to pay the price."

The Toronto Sun,
April 1, 1992.
Paul Henry.

In October, 1993, eight months after Paul Bernardo's arrest, private investigator Brian King poses next to a stack of transcripts from Robert Baltovich's trial. "Convicted killer's fate hangs on new evidence" was the headline for the accompanying article in The Toronto Star.

The Toronto Star, October 14, 1993. Jeff Goode.

has argued more successful appeals against O'Driscoll than against any other judge. Though tempted, I hesitated to ask the logical question, "Why is this man a judge?" Instead, talk turned to the question of bail pending appeal, and Brian's belief that it would be very unlikely. To his knowledge only one person had ever been granted bail pending appeal on a murder conviction, in a decision that had been handed down many years before. Nevertheless, Mike had decided to try and Brian had not presented any opposition. I didn't want to come across as impatient, but I felt I had to ask him how long the appeal process might take. His ballpark figure was two years.

Brian went on to describe his style of litigation. He was averse to having his cases tried in the media and, therefore, preferred a low-key approach. His commitment, he said, was to me and only me. He knew my parents would obviously want to have my legal situation resolved as soon as possible; however, he liked to work free of any external pressures. In other words, they weren't to pester him.

The day of my sentencing, I had learned that I would be moving to the Reception unit at Millhaven Penitentiary in Kingston, Ontario, within thirty days. Until then, I shared a cell with Steve Chuvalo, son of the great Canadian boxer, George Chuvalo, who'd come out on the wrong end of two courageous bouts with Muhammad Ali. I got to know Steve quite well and really liked him. But, unfortunately, Steve was a drug addict and one day he got his hands on a "package" (read: Valium) that had been smuggled in. Steve said all he planned on doing was sleeping, which was precisely what he did for three straight days. He would wake up when supper came and ask what was for breakfast. So, you see, it was no medical mystery why Steve left the range with severe stomach pains when the Valium wore off, not returning before I left for Millhaven.

The only way to describe Millhaven is to say that it resembles a giant warehouse, both inside and out. After the long bus ride, our motley crew was marched in handcuffs and leg irons into a large building with several cage-like compartments sufficient to hold ten to twenty people. The room into which we were ushered was replete with boxes, pallets and wheel carts, leading me to privately muse that were I not there as a man wrongly convicted of murdering his girlfriend, I could have just as easily been purchasing some shelving at an IKEA furniture store.

The most immediate difference I detected between Millhaven and the East was the guards. At the East, the guards usually treated inmates with disdain and crudeness, but the Millhaven guys not only showed a great deal of respect, they often smiled and joked around with you. The flip side of that, though, was the fact that the towers at the end of each hallway were lined with panes of bullet-proof glass, out of which had been cut a small circular hole, just large enough for the snout of a rifle to fit through. Though Millhaven's mandate is to process inmates and funnel them to federal institutions throughout Ontario, the penitentiary also contains a series of population ranges known as J unit, which houses some of the most violent criminals in the country.

I was initially assigned to F1 range but wasn't there for long. Two guys who worked in the canteen had been caught stealing, and the person running the canteen, an inmate I knew from the East, offered me one of the now-vacant positions. I told him I'd start as soon as I could, and the next day I was moved to F2, the work range. A lot of guys on the waiting list for prison jobs weren't too pleased about me leapfrogging to the front of it. Prison, like many institutions, has its politics. For instance, if you come across some garbage on the floor of the range and you're not a cleaner, you're not supposed to bother cleaning it up, as other inmates might interpret this as "cutting someone else's grass."

I was getting visitors by my second week. Tony Fuchs, Sheila Banks and some others made the drive down all the way from Toronto and back, but we got to visit for as long as one stretch of the trip took—three hours. As for my job in the canteen, it was more of an adventure than I'd bargained for. Part of my job was that of delivery boy, and this included toting bags of requested items—pop, chips or foot powder—to various units, including the dreaded J unit segregation wing, where, rumour had it, the inmates were particular about their canteen and who delivered it.

The first time I went into the J unit hole, I was warned by the guard with me not to allow my hands to get close to the cell doors, most of which were terribly scratched or darkened by burn marks created when someone inside had attempted setting fire to the cell. "Why do I have to be careful with my hands?" I asked him. "Because you might lose them," he said.

No sooner had I settled into the canteen job than I was transferred to the kitchen. Within two months, I progressed from dishwasher to working the coffee window to "third" cook, which involved more cooking than I felt my talents deserved, but cooks one and two seemed interested in other things. Then one afternoon I happened to be walking down the hall as a group of guards busted into a cell and struggled with the inmate inside, who was frantically trying to flush some drugs down the toilet. Three hours later, returning from a visit, a guard called out to me from the office. "Congratulations, Baltovich! You're head cook!"

Eventually, I had a meeting with my Case Management Officer, Ted Breuer, about which institution I would be sent to. From my discussions with the guys on the range, it seemed most likely I'd be dispatched to either Joyceville or Warkworth. The low-down on Joyceville was that it was less violent and oppressive than other institutions, but I was setting my sights on medium-security Warkworth. Steve Chuvalo had called it the Shangri-la of Federal penitentiaries, a place with educational opportunities, the best recreational facilities, a huge yard, and last, but not least, a nonsmoking unit. Warkworth was also in Campbellford, halfway between Toronto and Kingston, and much easier to reach for friends and family in the Toronto area.

In my meeting with Breuer, I cited my reasons for wanting to be placed at Warkworth. "Well," said Breuer, lifting his pen. "I don't know what the situation is at Warkworth right now. From what I understand, they're pretty full up and I don't know if they're taking lifers. I'll give them a call but at this point I would say you'll probably end up going to Joyceville."

As he finished speaking, I realized that I'd left out my desire to be in a nonsmoking unit, so I decided to throw that in. "Well, that is a consideration," he said, scribbling "nonsmoker" down in red pen. Looking up, he said, "You'll be hearing something soon," and that I could go. As I walked out the door, I figured I'd be at Joyceville within a few months.

A little while later, in October, Mike's attempt at getting me bail was turned down. I had already prepared myself for that inevitability, but my mother broke down in tears at the news. By December, though, I'd had enough. I was grumpy, fielding complaints from inmates about the food, so I jumped at a new job cleaning the guards' office. Then, just three days ago, a guard told me the prison psychologist wanted to see me. Brian Greenspan had advised me against participating in meetings like this, but my curiosity got the better of me.

I waited for a few minutes in an empty classroom before a woman in her late twenties or early thirties came in to greet me. She said her name was Jean Folsom and she then walked me down a series of corridors to a small office. We agreed not to discuss the particulars of my trial, and she asked me to tell her about my childhood right up to and including my time with Elizabeth.

For once in my life, I spared someone a long dissertation in response to this request and gave Folsom a routine answer: childhood was fine; had a good relationship with my parents; went to Sunday school until I was thirteen; always did well in school; had lots of friends. I left out any references to my mother's depression, not thinking it was of any relevance. Next came questions about my lifestyle: What are your sexual habits? Do you drink? Do you smoke? What drugs have you experimented with?

This should be good, I thought. Now I get to show her what a Goody Two-Shoes I am. I quickly explained that I lost my virginity at twenty, that I didn't go out seeking sexual partners and that I didn't believe in cheating. As for smoking, I found the habit disgusting. I only had a drink on special occasions (I didn't tell her about the night I got smashed three days before my conviction—an effort to forget about O'Driscoll's brutal charge to the jury) and had never touched any illegal drugs.

"You've never tried drugs?" she blurted out. "Not even marijuana in university?" She didn't believe me. Thinking that Folsom was under the mistaken assumption that smoking weed was a prerequisite to being accepted to an institute for higher learning, I quickly added that none of my close friends had ever experimented with drugs either. Now she really thought I was full of shit. At the end of the interview, Folsom weighed in with her psychological assessment. She told me that I seemed to lack emotion and she opined that I reminded her of the android "Data" who appeared on the television program "Star Trek: The Next Generation." Looking back on it, maybe for credibility's sake I should have told her that I had smoked pot, but hadn't inhaled.

Since then, Doug Acorn, the unit clerk, has told me I've been classified. I kept naming off all of the places I could be getting sent: Kingston Pen, Joyceville, Collins Bay. He kept shaking his head. There was only one choice left. "Warkworth?" I asked. "Yup," he replied, nodding his head. I was ecstatic. The first thing I wanted to do was phone home to tell my family what I thought was good news. As I stepped out of my cell, Chris McCulloch, who was younger than me and facing a mandatory twenty-five-year sentence for first-degree, asked where I was going. "I got Warkworth," I said.

"Warkworth?" he shouted contemptuously. He'd been trying to get into Wark-worth for months, but without any success. "How the hell did you get Wark-worth? You're a lifer like me!"

ROBERT JAMES BALTOVICH
December 22, 1992
Psychological Report

PSYCHOLOGICAL WELL-BEING:

BALTOVICH was found to be of above-average intelligence. This is consistent with his educational background and with casual reports by those who have interacted with him.

On personality testing, BALTOVICH tended to present himself in a positive light. People with this response style are reluctant to admit to even minor faults in their character. However, this is not unusual in the present setting. It could result, though, in a min-imization of any emotional problems.

The scores on the clinical scales of BALTOVICH's tests were all quite low and most were below average. Therefore, they did not indicate any psychological disturbance. There is no indication of a serious mood or thinking disorder. He does not experience anger more frequently nor more intensely than normal but he does use a lot of energy to monitor and control the expression of what anger that he does feel. This could ultimately lead to emo-tional outbursts.

TREATMENT NEEDS:

At this time, BALTOVICH is not admitting to any problems and none were identified in the assessment. It is difficult to feel confident about whether what one sees of him is as he truly is or whether, instead, one sees only a carefully selected view. BAL-TOVICH is denying his conviction and he has appealed it. He indicated that he was willing to talk about the crime—as much as he knows about it—but that he was not involved.

He should briefly be re-assessed if his appeal is unsuccessful and he remains in the federal correctional system.

Jean Folsom

Psychologist

Millhaven Institution

—◦—

In September, six months after Rob's conviction, Brian King finally got his opportunity to interview Patrick Mahoney, whom Gatward and Engel had presented at trial as an alternative suspect. Mahoney was now at the Metro East Detention Centre, where he had been detained since his arrest on several sexual assault charges. Mahoney had been tracked down at a motel in Toronto about a month earlier; having just returned from Ireland, he claimed that he had planned on turning himself in the following day. Mahoney arrived on the opposite side of the glass plating in a pair of orange institutional coveralls. King recognized him easily from his photographs and thought that he indeed looked younger than he was. Speaking through the two-way telephone, Mahoney began by telling King that he'd already been interviewed by Brian Raybould and Jake Poranganel regarding the Elizabeth Bain disappearance and that, upon seeing him, they had "laughed at the idea of me being passed off for someone in their twenties." As for the charges against him, Mahoney said that he was the target of a "family conspiracy" spearheaded by his ex-wife. Mahoney conceded that he was an usher at St. Joseph's Church (although he said he was unfamiliar with the Bains), that he had once taken his car to Three R Auto Body for an estimate and had vacationed years ago on Shadow Lake, but he repeatedly denied having anything to do with the death of Elizabeth Bain. Raybould had informed Mahoney that his work schedule had him on the afternoon shift that week, and Mahoney declared that he must have worked each day, as he could recall missing no more than two days during approximately twenty-two years of employment.

Though King did not know it when he left the interview cubicle, this meeting marked the last occasion in which Mahoney would be investigated by anyone in relation to the Bain disappearance. More than a year later, Mike Engel would encounter fellow criminal defence lawyer Alan Gold, who represented Mahoney at his trial, and, according to Engel, Gold had taken "great, great pleasure in pointing out to me that his client had been acquitted."

With Rob languishing in prison and few promising leads to follow up on, King wrote a letter to Dorothy Alison, the well-known psychic from Nutley, New Jersey (who had played a prominent role in the investigation of the infamous American serial killer John Wayne Gacy, as well as the Patty Hearst case), requesting her assistance. Despite offering to cover the cost of her trip to Toronto, King never received a response. Instead, King tagged along on a few occasions with John Secord, who began consulting local psychics—more than twenty-five of them altogether—all of whom Secord paid out of his own pocket.

A good number of the psychics believed that Liz had been abducted by more than one person. A "psychic counselor" from Buffalo, New York, said she had been kidnapped by "three men into prostitution." A woman who went by Sandy envisioned a "gang rape and mutilation" carried out by "four whites" and "six blacks" involved in the human slave trade. Ruth, on the other hand, was convinced that Liz had been beheaded by a nefarious group of men who later drove "a chrome table leg through her heart, the poor thing." Just two men had been hired to kill Liz, according to a psychic named Margaret. "I could describe them," she told Secord. "But I won't allow myself to look at their faces." Ione Woodend divined Liz's body to have been "swallowed up in a large body of water." Ted Silverhand, a native soothsayer, concluded his long dissertation by advising Secord to begin using a metal detector while searching for the body: *Don't bother looking out in the open where people throw beer cans. She will be buried out among the trees. The metal detector will ring when it picks up the fillings in her cavities. I just don't see any other way. That's why I don't know if you will find her or not. It is finished. Ho!*

It was foreseen by Wendy that the man who had killed Liz was not finished, and would "do something else soon." On that point, the clairvoyant known as Annette was in agreement but picking up the details with sharper focus: *This man is abducting two more girls. He has got this obsession with young girls—he hates them with a passion and he's not getting it out of his blood. He's going to abduct two more little girls; he's going to rape and kill them. He's not through.*

Part 6

—o—

Fresh Evidence

Fall turned to winter. Another Christmas season—Rob's second behind bars—came and went.

It was now mid-February and Brian King, as usual, was burrowed away in the warmth of his office well past closing time, reading through King-Reed's stack of ongoing investigation files. He often spent a few extra hours there in the evening, when his employees had gone home and he could concentrate without distractions. But this night would be an exception. For about an hour, King's phone rang off the hook, the initial flurry of calls coming from different reporters who had covered the Bain-Baltovich story over the past few years. Each one was calling to let him know that the police were claiming to have bagged the Scarborough rapist in the St. Catharines area—an hour and a half south of Toronto by car—where, apparently, the suspect had been living with his wife in a quaint little pink house near the Welland Canal for two years. If, indeed, the police had the right man, it went a long way towards explaining the Scarborough rapist's two-and-a-half-year absence.

King was further informed that the press had been tipped off that the same man, Paul Bernardo, was also to be charged with the well-publicized murders of two teenage girls, Kristen French and Leslie Mahaffy. Fourteen-year-old Mahaffy had been abducted from her own yard in Burlington—a suburb at the western tip of

Lake Ontario, midway between Toronto and St. Catharines—on June 15, 1991. The girl had come home well after midnight, only to find the front door locked and, reluctant to wake up her parents, she had been walking around the house looking for another way in. Two weeks later, her dismembered body had been found encased in seven blocks of cement in Lake Gibson, nestled on the eastern border of St. Catharines, a few short miles from Bernardo's new home.

Almost a year later, on April 16, 1992, French, a fifteen-year-old, had been brazenly forced into a car in broad daylight on her way home from school. This time, the abduction had occurred in a church parking lot in St. Catharines, just blocks from French's house. Her naked body was also discovered about two weeks later, on April 30—the day before Baltovich was sentenced—somewhat camouflaged by the dead tree branches that filled the ditch of a rural sideroad in Burlington, only a few hundred yards from the cemetery in which Mahaffy had been laid to rest.

As Brian King watched the late-night news on television in his living room at home a few hours later, he was flipping from station to station to have a look at the various photographs each had gathered of Bernardo. The suspect was everything the Scarborough rapist composite had described: roughly six feet tall, tanned (in most pictures), with an athletic, medium build and a boyish face with blond hair that was usually short on the sides and a bit longer on top. King's mind would not stop racing. Was Bernardo the tall, blond man in his mid-twenties that Tasmin Sheikh and George Chau had seen with Bain in the weeks leading up to her disappearance? Was he the blond man David Dibben had seen driving her car? So far, King had gleaned from the news that Bernardo had graduated from the University of Toronto's Scarborough campus in 1987 and, in June 1990, was still living with his parents, just a short drive from the campus, which was too much of a coincidence to ignore.

And then another thought came to him. At Baltovich's trial, Brian Raybould had testified that the Scarborough rapist had never abducted or murdered any of his victims. Well, according to Raybould's fellow detectives, Bernardo had done so at least twice. And not only had he murdered them, he had gone to considerable lengths—especially with Leslie Mahaffy—to hide the body.

If Bernardo had killed Elizabeth Bain (and if Bain was, in fact, the first victim with whom he'd progressed from rape to rape-homicide), King was beginning to wonder what had caused his violent behaviour to suddenly escalate. The only explanation King could come up with was that, once the composite drawing had been released to the public—just three weeks before Bain had gone missing—Bernardo might have been less inclined to allow his victims to become potential eyewitnesses through survival. Also, if Bernardo had abducted and assaulted Bain, wouldn't he strangle her and dispose of her body in a remote area, as he allegedly did months later with Leslie Mahaffy and Kristen French?

Just when King thought he had things straight in his mind, arranging themselves into a plausible scenario, he heard one reporter announce that the investigation was not yet over, as detectives were "still searching for a second suspect." A second suspect? That tidbit kept King on the couch, in a state of perplexity for a long while after the television screen went black. He sat in the darkness, listening to waves of frozen rain bounce off the windows like sand.

—◯—

That same night, John Secord was lying in bed beside Elizabeth Bain's aunt, Beth Garcia, who was now his wife, a turn of events that had not gone over well with her older sister Julita and her husband. (Their concern, along with the marriage, was short-lived; not so many months later, Beth would leave Secord and move to Texas.) Like Brian King, and thousands of others, Secord had learned about the arrest of Paul Bernardo that evening. Of course, it had him thinking about Elizabeth again. The psychics had done nothing but launch him into a black hole where he hunted for ghosts in every conceivable direction, and his efforts at finding her had been stalled for months.

But now he was asleep and in the middle of a dream. A dream in which he is walking along a sidewalk and spies, standing on the porch of a nearby house, a lamb. At the front gate of the house, Secord stops to look at this strange sight. Next the lamb gingerly descends the porch steps and slowly approaches Secord at the gate. He notices as it gets closer that the animal has Paul Bernardo's eyes. Undaunted, Secord opens the gate and lets the lamb out of the yard so that he can climb on its back, as he is suddenly overcome with the feeling that it will take him where he needs to go.

—◯—

Jailhouse Notebook (11)

I *had barely settled in at Warkworth when Bernardo hit the news. Returning
from supper the day after his arrest, I was walking by the television area when
a barrage of guys started yelling out to me. "You're on the news!" they were saying. "They're talking about your case!" I took two steps inside the door and
caught a glimpse of some footage of me walking in front of the courthouse during my trial. The screen then cut quickly to an interview conducted with Brian
King that day. Brian said he wanted assurances that the police would investigate any information linking Bernardo to Elizabeth's disappearance. The
anonymity I had heretofore relished at Warkworth was, at that moment, officially terminated.*

*The next day, I got in touch with Brian King. The first thing he did was com-
plain about how much of the interview had ended up on the cutting-room floor.
Then he told me of a conversation he had had with Detective Jake Poranganel a
few hours earlier. Poranganel had disagreed with Brian's assertion that there
were a number of similarities in the French and Mahaffy murders and Elizabeth's disappearance. Brian seemed pretty miffed at whatever it was that Poranganel had to say. But I wasn't. I already knew that he was an idiot.*

*This got me thinking about the time Poranganel called Brian regarding
Patrick Mahoney during my time at Millhaven. Poranganel began by telling
Brian that he had finally become convinced I was innocent. As soon as Brian took
the bait—"Really, Jake?"—Poranganel let out a derisive laugh and confessed to
the real reason for his call. What a kidder.*

—◇—

NO LINKS TO BAIN, STANTON
By Tracy Nesdoly

February 20, 1993—Police say there is "no connection at all"
between Paul Bernardo and the disappearances of Elizabeth Bain
and Julie Stanton.

Bernardo, 28, faces 55 charges in the Scarborough rapes and
Kristen French and Leslie Mahaffy murders.

Metro Police Detective Jake Poranganel, one of the investigators in Bain's murder, said the case will not be opened.

"There is no connection at all," he said.

Her boyfriend, Robert Baltovich, has appealed his second-degree murder conviction.

Poranganel said one of the "strong dissimilarities" between the Scarborough rapist and Bain's killer is the rapist would have no reason to hide the body.

"Baltovich had every reason to hide the body. If the body were found we could link him forensically," said Poranganel.

THE TORONTO SUN

—◦—

While Jake Poranganel was unable to detect any relevant ties between Paul Bernardo and the Bain disappearance, Mike Engel saw the same alarming yet tantalizing similarities as Brian King. On February 26, Engel sent a seven-page letter to Marion Boyd, the Attorney General for Ontario, requesting that "the investigation into the death of Elizabeth Bain be reopened." Engel pointed out that, in addition to the deaths of Leslie Mahaffy and Kristen French, the media had reported that Paul Bernardo was currently being viewed as a suspect in the murders of two young women, Christine Prince and Margaret McWilliams. "As I recall the Prince case," Engel wrote, "it involved a young, dark-haired woman who disappeared mysteriously and whose remains were found in a wooded area of Scarborough's Rouge Valley [in 1982]. This, of course, is within miles of the place where Mr. Bernardo lived and the park from which Ms. Bain vanished." McWilliams, a twenty-one-year-old, was raped and murdered in the Warden Woods area five years later, also "not far from the place of Ms. Bain's disappearance."

Engel demanded that "any evidence or information supporting the possible link between Mr. Bernardo and Ms. Bain in the possession of the police presently or in the future . . . be disclosed to my office." One specific detail Engel was anxious to obtain was whether "the unidentified fingerprints in the Bain vehicle" could be "matched to Mr. Bernardo." And, finally, when it came to the speculation in the press about the chance that "an accomplice of Mr. Bernardo's" had become "an informant," Engel wanted "that person interrogated by officers independent of the Metropolitan Toronto Police Force to determine whether he or she has any knowledge of the circumstances surrounding the disappearance of Elizabeth Bain."

What Engel did not yet know, and likely never could have imagined, was that Bernardo's accomplice-turned-informant was none other than his young wife, an attractive, petite blonde named Karla Homolka. Details of their relationship— including how Homolka had participated in the spree of violent crimes that, so far, only Bernardo had been charged with—would not be fully divulged to the public for quite some time. Working under intense pressure from the press, which had whipped itself into an unprecedented frenzy over the idea of a homegrown pair of "Ken and Barbie" homicidal sexual predators (in the weeks following Bernardo's arrest, *The Toronto Sun* bought pictures of the couple's horse-and-carriage wedding in Niagara-on-the-Lake for $10,000, outbidding the *Star*), the Metro Toronto police, as well as a special task force belonging to the Niagara Regional Police, were busy putting the pieces together.

Up until the time she met Bernardo, Homolka's life had been a rather unremarkable tale of growing up as the eldest of three sisters, under the watchful eye of a blue-collar father and his devoted wife, who had been raising their girls on the same middle-class St. Catharines street since 1978. Homolka met Bernardo when she was still in high school. In Grade 12, she had opted to take just two courses so that she could work full-time at a local pet store. It was her new job, as fate would have it, that would lead her to twenty-three-year-old Paul Bernardo. In October 1987, Homolka and fellow employee Debbie Purdie, who was one of her best friends, were invited to a pet-industry convention taking place at the Howard Johnson East Hotel in Scarborough.

Homolka and Purdie were in the middle of devouring a midnight snack at the hotel restaurant when Bernardo, who had recently landed a job as an entry-level trainee at a big Toronto accounting firm, walked up to their table and asked if he and Van Smirnis, a longtime friend who had grown up across the street from the Bernardos, could join them. It was a bold move that paid off. When the meal was over, the girls invited them back to their hotel room. There, Bernardo paired off with Homolka, and Smirnis with Purdie. Purdie, however, wasn't that interested in fooling around with Smirnis, and she soon fell asleep on the pull-out couch. But just a few feet away, Homolka and Bernardo were in the bed, going at it for four solid hours. At one point, a sweat-soaked Bernardo told Homolka that he was getting really hot, so Homolka reached over to the bedside table and poured her glass of ice water on his back. Almost eight years later, at his multiple-murder trial, Bernardo reflected on that moment by telling the jury, in his own defence, that he'd thought it was "cool."

Homolka experienced the identical sensation a week later as she and Bernardo were locked in her basement bedroom at home in St. Catharines. During the week, she had invited him down for a visit on the weekend, and the two had just returned from a horror film called *Prince of Darkness*. Homolka had now pulled out a pair of handcuffs, which she asked Bernardo to clamp on her wrists behind her back before kneeling down and telling him to hike up her skirt. As this was happening, he asked her what she would think if he was a rapist. Whether or not she took him seriously, Homolka offered a response not unlike the one Bernardo would give years later when commenting on the ice-water incident.

Despite Bernardo's question to Homolka, his reign of terror as the Scarborough rapist had not yet begun. Later, there would be some evidence that, during the summer of 1987, Bernardo had approached a number of women on the streets of Scarborough late at night and, waving a knife to keep them silent, had groped them—but had gone no further than that. The police would also learn, through interviews with two young women Bernardo had dated simultaneously in the year prior to meeting Homolka, that his relationships with his girlfriends had become progressively more abusive. One of the women, who shall be known here as Leanne Santiago, had taken some courses with Bernardo at Scarborough College before they both landed accounting positions at Price Waterhouse. Santiago was, like Elizabeth Bain, of Filipino extraction, petite, dark-haired and beautiful. Confoundingly, much of her relationship with Bernardo was marred by his unwavering possessiveness. He had subjected her to some mild (by his standards) sexual role playing and had once, in a jealous rage, hit her with enough force to knock her down.

Less than a month after his first weekend visit to the Homolkas' in St. Catharines, Bernardo was accompanied to his University of Toronto convocation ceremony by his parents as well as his other girlfriend, Janine Godsoe (also a pseudonym). Bernardo had subjected Godsoe, who was a far more submissive partner than Santiago (who had actually hit Bernardo back), to much harsher treatment sexually, and now that Homolka had entered his life so promisingly, he was ready to bid

Godsoe adieu. For some reason, though, he was unable to let her go without one last show of power on the eve of his graduation. Driving her home following a humiliating scene in a downtown hotel bar, Bernardo repeatedly pulled her hair and punched her furiously all the way back to Scarborough where they finally parked, not in Godsoe's driveway, but in one of their usual spots behind a deserted factory. That's when he pulled out his knife and, running the blade flat along her throat, said he was going to kill her. Godsoe reacted by hitting his arm away and hurling herself out the passenger door as quickly as she could, escaping into the darkness of an adjacent ravine, which was actually a heavily wooded stretch of Morningside Park, where, for whatever reason, Bernardo chose not to venture in pursuit. When Godsoe was interviewed about the attack by a police officer just after New Year's, 1988, the police officer mistakenly dated his report January 5, 1987, instead of January 5, 1988, and it was misfiled.

About a month after Bernardo had threatened Godsoe, his night-time attacks escalated from inappropriate touching to full-blown rape, as he dragged a fifteen-year-old girl between two houses just a few blocks from the Bernardo family home on Sir Raymond Drive, and kept her there at knifepoint for an hour and a half. According to the police, Bernardo went on to rape fifteen more young women over the next two and a half years, the final rape occurring three weeks before Elizabeth Bain vanished.

During the week, Bernardo liked to cruise the streets of Scarborough either on foot or in his white Capri, surveying the bus stops late at night for potential victims, but he had become the Homolkas' "weekend son," visiting Karla in St. Catharines as often as he could. On January 4, 1990, he began a new job with another Toronto accounting firm, but as he was still an exam away from becoming a chartered accountant, Bernardo's annual salary was $34,000, not nearly as much as he felt he needed. Two months later, without giving notice, he simply abandoned his job, never to return. Oddly enough, he tried his hand at worm picking for a few months, but it turned out to be a bust. He was aided in his next entrepreneurial venture—cigarette smuggling—by his friend Van Smirnis and his brothers. Smirnis's parents had moved about an hour's drive north of Scarborough to the town of Sutton, nestled on the south-eastern shore of Lake Simcoe, where they had become the proprietors of a modest coffee shop. It was up in Sutton that they had met a biker who belonged to a gang known as the Para-Dice Riders, and it was through this contact that Bernardo and Smirnis were being financed in exchange for supplying the Riders with cut-rate contraband. (Of course, this had Brian King thinking of Joe Rafferty's bikers up in Barrie who had claimed to know who was responsible for Elizabeth Bain's death, as well as where her body could be found.) They would stash the cartons of cigarettes, purchased in Youngstown, New York, in various compartments hidden behind removable panels in the new 1989 gold Nissan 240 SX Bernardo had recently leased, before crossing the border into Canada. Amazingly, Bernardo was never caught.

As a result of the remarkably accurate composite drawing released to the media in late May, as well as the $150,000 reward offered by the Metropolitan Police Services Board (later augmented by $100,000 from *The Toronto Sun*, as well as the $140,000 pledged during a campaign initiated by the St. Mary's Rotary Club) for any information leading to the arrest and conviction of the Scarborough rapist, the police received two separate tips from the public about Paul Bernardo. The first, called in on June 28, was from an employee at Bernardo's bank who was struck by the obvious resemblance. The second came a few months later, in mid-September, from Tina Smirnis, who was married to Alex Smirnis, Van's brother. When the rape investigators met in person with the couple, Alex told them how, in the past, Bernardo had spoken of his bizarre sexual fantasies. And from what he'd heard from Van, Bernardo might have raped a girl during a spring-break vacation to Florida the previous year. In addition to that, it was Alex's understanding that Bernardo always kept a knife in his car.

Two detectives with the Scarborough Sexual Assualt Squad finally got around to dropping in for a talk with Bernardo at his home late in the afternoon of November 19, which just happened to be the same day that Robert Baltovich had been led away in handcuffs at the crack of dawn. To their disappointment, Bernardo wasn't home but he called them later and arrangements were made for him to meet with them at the headquarters building the following afternoon. Bernardo, who was a little nervous but otherwise playing it cool, did not strike the two investigators, who were not much older than he, as a serial rapist. But, just to be safe, they asked him if he would mind providing them with blood, hair and saliva samples (even though it was within his rights to refuse) so that, by comparing his DNA with that belonging to the semen taken from the rapist's victims, he could be eliminated as a suspect. Without hesitating, Bernardo said it wasn't a problem. Inexplicably, his samples sat, untested, in storage at the understaffed Centre of Forensic Sciences for more than two years.

While all of this was going on, Bernardo and Homolka were caught up in his growing and increasingly dangerous obsession with Homolka's youngest sister, Tammy, who was, at fifteen, a younger, more desirable version of Karla. Bernardo had made his attraction to Tammy well known to Karla, for it had become a regular topic of conversation between the couple, who were now engaged to be married. Bernardo repeatedly told Karla he wanted to be the one to deflower Tammy. Karla's reaction to this desire eventually became the most fantastic aspect of their "story," as her active role in assisting Bernardo in his pursuit of Tammy constituted a betrayal of unimaginable proportions.

On Christmas Eve, Tammy was with the rest of her family, including her future brother-in-law, watching television in the basement recreation room. Bernardo had just purchased a new Sony video camcorder and was capturing the seemingly festive scene on videotape for posterity. Earlier in the day, Bernardo and Karla had ground up half a dozen or so sleeping pills, a well-known prescription drug called Halcion, which Karla had secretly purchased as part of a drug order for the veterinary clinic where she was employed as an assistant. Bernardo had mixed between fifty and sixty milligrams' worth of crushed Halcion into two "special" drinks for Tammy—a daiquiri and a Rusty Nail—and she began showing the initial effects of the mixture before going up to her bedroom.

A short while later, once Karla's parents and her middle sister, Lori, had gone up to bed, Tammy returned to the basement to watch a movie on television with Paul and Karla. In no time at all, Tammy had passed out cold from the Halcion. This meant that it was probably safe for Bernardo to begin disrobing her. Just in case, though, Karla retrieved a bottle of halothane, an inhalant anaesthetic used at the clinic to put animals out for surgery, and poured the liquid onto a cloth before placing it over her sister's mouth and nose. Karla wanted to make sure she wouldn't wake up while Bernardo had his way with her—an offering Karla had referred to between them as her "Christmas present," an essential part of which, as she well knew, would include her own participation—his new Sony camcorder rolling the entire time.

What hadn't occurred to Karla, however, was that when halothane was administered to animals at the clinic, it was done through an oxygen tank and mask that regulated the vaporized gas with oxygen in a ratio of one or two parts to one hundred. Holding the saturated cloth over her sister's mouth and nose amounted to a lethal overdose, and the pleasure Bernardo was deriving from his "present" was abruptly disturbed when Tammy, still unconscious, began to vomit. In a panic, they dragged Tammy into Karla's bedroom and dressed her before Bernardo initiated mouth-to-mouth resuscitation and Karla dialled the 911 emergency number for an ambulance. By the time the paramedics arrived, Karla had poured the halothane down the drain and had hidden the remaining Halcion in the laundry room. Tammy was pronounced dead upon arrival at the hospital. Despite the fact that a police officer had arrived on the scene to find Karla loading the vomit-soiled blanket Tammy had been lying on into the washing machine and that Tammy had a large cherry-red burn that ran from the left side of her mouth down to her neck, the coroner ruled her death accidental (as her medical records indicated Tammy was asthmatic). She was buried the day after Boxing Day.

One month later, Bernardo and Homolka moved into their rented dream home at 57 Bayview Drive in Port Dalhousie, a suburb of St. Catharines that was, once upon a time, the original site of the Welland Canal. Undeterred by Tammy's death, the pair would continue to lure to 57 Bayview—by guile or by force—unsuspecting teenage girls, whom Karla once referred to as "our children," satisfying their mutual, pathological needs. At Bernardo's trial, his own defence lawyer referred to the house as a "Venus flytrap" to which Karla invited, on separate occasions, a pair of teenage girls—one she'd known from the pet store, the other through Tammy—both of whom were drugged and raped in the same way as Tammy but with the desired results, as both survived, unaware of what had happened.

And then there was the abducted pair who had not survived. Leslie Mahaffy's encased body parts were discovered on the same evening in late June that Bernardo and Homolka were celebrating their nuptials before one hundred guests enjoying pheasant stuffed with veal at the Queen's Landing in Niagara-on-the-Lake. Bernardo didn't bother making the same effort with the disposal of Kristen French, held captive throughout the Easter weekend of 1992 after Homolka had helped lure the girl to their car by pretending to be a lost tourist, map in hand. Once French had been killed, Homolka had also assisted with the washing of French's body, a process that involved cutting off most of her long dark hair to ensure the police would find no forensic traces linking Bernardo to the victim (forensic science being a subject both had read about extensively).

The day after French's body was found—which was also the day Baltovich was sentenced by Judge O'Driscoll—Van Smirnis called the police. Smirnis, who had been Bernardo's best man at his wedding, had been alarmed by the coincidence that the French girl had been abducted from the very town where his friend, who had been questioned as a suspect in the Scarborough rapes, now lived. In addition to his physical similarities to the Scarborough rapist, Bernardo liked petite women, and Smirnis was convinced that his friend had once raped a woman in his basement. Every time news of another Scarborough rape victim had hit the news, Smirnis now realized, Bernardo had gone into a form of temporary anti-social hiding.

But, again, nothing happened, and Bernardo's forensic samples still had not been tested. By the autumn of that year, according to Patricia Pearson, who wrote about the couple for *Saturday Night* magazine, "the Bernardo marriage was imploding from the pressure of its own moral chaos into violence, paranoia, and loathing." Two Christmas seasons after Tammy's death, Bernardo, "having smashed every boundary of human restraint and gone into crazed dissolution," the same journalist wrote, "went after Homolka like a rabid animal, pulling out her hair, hammering her head with hard objects, forcing her, once, to eat shit." Not long after Homolka's parents saw her black "raccoon" eyes a few days into the new year, they convinced her to leave the house at 57 Bayview while her husband, now an aspiring rap star, was out on a cigarette run. Somewhat reluctantly, Homolka agreed but not before searching frantically for the videotapes that had recorded her role in numerous surreal scenes with conscious and unconscious teenage girls, some of whom were now dead. More painful than the black-and-blue bruises covering much of her skull was the fact that the tapes were nowhere to be found.

A few weeks later, on February 1, 1993, while Karla was living at home with her family, a scientist with the CFS matched Paul Bernardo's DNA with semen samples taken from three victims of the Scarborough rapist. Immediately, the police initiated surveillance on Bernardo, whom they easily discovered was now living in the St. Catharines area, and the Metro police were soon in contact with the Green Ribbon Task Force, assembled in Niagara to solve the French-Mahaffy murders, as Bernardo had, for geographical reasons, automatically become their prime suspect. The main dilemma was that, although the DNA matches were compelling evidence against Bernardo for the rapes, the Green Ribbon investigators weren't guaranteed that either Bernardo or his estranged wife would offer anything helpful, or that they would now find any case-clinching evidence inside 57 Bayview to convict him of the murders.

The "second suspect" that police mentioned cryptically at the time of Bernardo's arrest two weeks later was, of course, Karla Homolka. It didn't take long for them to track her down at her aunt and uncle's house in Brampton, just outside of Toronto, where Homolka was beginning to enjoy a more active social life again. In her first face-to-face interview with investigators, the attending detectives had dropped enough hints to let her know that they had a pretty decent grasp of her involvement with the two murdered girls and, within days, she was in touch with a St. Catharines defence lawyer, whose job it soon became to negotiate a plea bargain settlement on behalf of his client with the Crown law office. The best possible deal, her lawyer felt, would be Homolka's testimony against Bernardo in exchange for blanket immunity, but her lawyer knew this might be a tough sell, given the circumstances.

As expected, Bernardo, subsequent to his arrest, denied his involvement in any sexual crimes and, with Homolka having already sought counsel, the Green Ribbon investigators were relying heavily on their search warrant for 57 Bayview, which they executed two days after Bernardo's arrest. After two months of turning the residence upside down, the police had assembled enough circumstantial evidence—a drug compendium with Halcion and halothane marked with highlighting pen being one example—to construct a strong case that French and Mahaffy had been held captive and murdered in the house. What they did not find, however, was the most incriminating evidence of all—the videotapes containing the sexual assaults of Tammy Homolka, Leslie Mahaffy and Kristen French. As a result, Homolka was still needed to deliver an open-and-shut case implicating Bernardo, whom the Green Ribbon investigators viewed as the main culprit, not his wife. At first, Homolka appeared to be nothing more than Bernardo's battered dupe. Therefore, on May 14, a deal was struck. Homolka would agree to serve two concurrent ten-year manslaughter sentences for her part in the French and Mahaffy slayings, plus two years for Tammy's death. If Karla behaved herself in prison, she would be eligible for parole in just four years.

Homolka's resolution agreement was finalized, ultimately, in a St. Catharines courtroom on July 6. Before a Crown prosecutor read into evidence a relatively brief rendition of what she and Bernardo had inflicted upon Tammy, Mahaffy and French, the judge had the public (including Brian King) removed from the courtroom and allowed accredited members of the Canadian press (American reporters were excluded) to remain but restricted them by court order from publishing any details of the proceeding except Homolka's sentence. The judge was concerned that excessive media coverage of the details of their crimes would put at risk Bernardo's right to a fair trial.

Standing before a scrum of reporters in front of the courthouse, Paul Bernardo's lawyer, Ken Murray, condemned the Crown for having made a "deal with the devil," a phrase that the media latched onto and repeated a thousand times, as though Murray might have known something the rest of the country didn't. In fact, Murray was the keeper of a terribly important secret. In early May, about a week before Homolka's twelve-year deal was agreed to, Murray and a small entourage had travelled to Port Dalhousie a short while after the police search warrant had expired for 57 Bayview. Ostensibly, Murray was there to oversee the removal of what remained of his client's personal belongings from the residence by a hired moving crew. But before that task had been initiated, Murray went upstairs to the second-floor bathroom. There, he climbed up onto the vanity and pulled a pot light that had already been dislodged during the police search even farther out of its socket. Murray reached up into the attic through the hole and felt around until his fingers finally touched something hard, as he'd been assured by his client they would. In all, Murray pulled six videotapes down from the ceiling—the same tapes Homolka had desperately wanted to take with her when she left for good.

—◦—

Jailhouse Notebook (12)

*I*n early April I was moved to a loud new range in 10 Block, a dirty, smoky building inhabited by a small army of phone hogs. Warkworth no longer seemed as great as advertised. Having to spend the day in my cell didn't thrill me either. There were a few openings in the kitchen that would have allowed me to wander around a bit, but my experiences at Millhaven caused me to balk at the opportunity. I was content to bide my time and wait for a position in the institution library, the only place I was even remotely interested in working. In the meantime, I was spending most of my days reading and the evenings working *out or playing in the basketball league. As the snow in the yard began to thaw, I really looked forward to its official opening. Especially enticing were the tennis courts I spied off in the distance.*

By the first of May, two positions had opened up in the library. I was interviewed by the librarian for the purchasing clerk position and was administered a typing test. By the time I had fumbled my way through the sample letter, I realized just how far I had let myself slip over the last few years. It came as no surprise that I was passed over. Apparently, there was no shortage of qualified people at Warkworth.

A few days later, my fortunes changed. I was informed that I was moving out of 10 Block to the Eighty-Man Unit, known as the EMU. I knew as soon as I wheeled my two cartfuls of personal effects into the new unit that I was going to enjoy my new home a lot better. For one thing, it was unimaginably clean. Sunlight cascaded through the large windows just below the ceiling, only to be reflected off the floor and cast throughout the wide expanse. Best of all, I was breathing clean air.

In the centre of the building was a control centre mounted several feet above the ground like an information booth at a shopping mall. The guards sat in chairs, supervising our every move. Branching out on either side were four ranges on the ground floor, each of which consisted of another range sitting atop. These were balconied, with staircases providing access to and from the upper ranges. Cement pillars announced each range's designation from A to H. Potted plants were spaced out on the polished floors, providing our environment with a more "civilized" ambience. My new cell was more than double the size of the one I'd just left behind, and the layout was such that the bunks sat opposite each other, instead of being stacked. A desk divided the cell in two, with shelves providing generous space for my stereo and small television set (which had been shipped up to me by my family), as well as some clothes. My new cell partner, Mike Sinclair, whom I knew from Millhaven, even offered me the side with the better TV shelf.

May turned out to be a pretty good month. I was hired as the cataloguing clerk in the library. Evidently, typing skills weren't seen as a required asset. Right away, I knew I had found a place where I could be comfortable. The guys were great to work with, the conversation was stimulating, and Tom Johnston, the librarian,

*treated us well. (And having first crack at the daily newspapers every morning
has provided me with an opportunity to follow the Bernardo case closely.)*

*A lot of people who have never seen the inside of a prison might wonder what
kind of library a place like Warkworth might have. Well, conjure up the library
you probably had in grade school and divide that in half, or maybe more. It is a
small room, about the size of three cells, with one stack of shelves devoted to nonfiction, another for fiction, and there is a rotating rack with a hodgepodge of well-
used Westerns and pulp novels. The selection is pretty limited, as we rely quite
heavily on donations. For example, you can find a book of short stories by Alice
Munro on the shelf directly above* The Canterbury Tales. *We have just about
every Shakespeare play in paperback. What we have more of than anything else
though are encyclopedias—sets that are so dated I have signed the odd one out
for a little historical perspective on countries that no longer exist. There is also a
fairly well-stocked magazine shelf, but they tend to disappear in a hurry, especially if some buxom actress or singer has posed provocatively on the cover.*

*Anyway, as May gave way to June, my life settled into its present satisfactory
pattern. I spend most of my evenings reading into the wee hours of the morning,
with staggered shifts in the library, I only work two mornings a week. In between,
I have established a regular weight routine in the yard and spend as much time
as I can playing tennis.*

*A few weeks ago, my name was announced over the P.A. system. When I
walked to control to see what they wanted, a guard gave me a two-word answer:
"Anger Management." "Excuse me," I said, trying to nip this prospect in the bud,
"but I'm not going to Anger Management. My case is under appeal."*

*With a rather cynical look on his face, the guard said, "Well, they want you
and you're on the list."*

*I asked if I could make a phone call. When, to my delight, I managed to get
hold of Brian Greenspan, I told him about my predicament. "Who's your case
management officer?" Greenspan asked me. When I replied Rob Arbuckle,
Greenspan said, "Oh, I know Rob Arbuckle. Don't worry about it. I'll take care
of it."*

*Just the other day, while picking up my mail, I was handed a letter with the
"Greenspan, Humphrey" letterhead on it. As I opened it up and read it, I realized it was the news I'd been hoping for. The letter, addressed to Rob Arbuckle,*

*stated that, in light of my appeal, Greenspan had advised me not to participate
in any programs. Thankfully, the matter of anger management seems to have
been dropped.*

———◦———

Hoping to be present at Karla Homolka's one-day trial, Brian King drove to St.
Catharines on July 6. So far, the police had been keeping the case under tight wraps
and information about Canada's most notorious couple had been difficult to come
by. By not answering or returning telephone calls from the press or speaking on the
record about even the most inconsequential details, the police, as one newspaper
reporter would later explain, were forcing the media to say, "Well, fuck you, I'll go
get the story myself." (This was a revealing comment insofar as it was a de facto
admission that members of the press were used to being spoon-fed their stories by
the police, as opposed to seeking out information independently.) And what it
meant, at least for Brian King, was that he had as many as half a dozen reporters
and journalists calling *him* instead of the police in their hunt for whatever background details on Paul Bernardo they could muster from a King-Reed credit check
or from any of the various data banks King had at his disposal.

Usually, King shared whatever information he had with a select group of journalists, many of whom went on to write books about the case (five were eventually
published), with the understanding that they were obligated to be equally forthcoming. It was the most favourable situation he could ask for—he had at least a
handful of journalists, all in pursuit of the same story, each with valuable contacts
of their own, helping him however they could. Early on, the first promising lead was
offered to him by the pair of *Toronto Sun* reporters on the Bernardo beat, Alan
Cairns and Scott Burnside, who became known among their rivals as Team Sun.

Cairns and Burnside were the first to track down Van Smirnis, who appeared
to be a font of knowledge about Bernardo and Homolka. Team Sun touted Smirnis as a major source for their book and, in an attempt to keep him loyal, put him
in contact with their Toronto literary agent, who was reportedly attempting to
drum up a movie deal in the United States. But seeing as King wasn't writing a
book, Cairns and Burnside saw no danger in helping him get in touch with their
ace-in-the-hole. King found Smirnis most accommodating. They met on three

separate occasions, each time in a different location, and spoke over the phone more often than that.

Smirnis was by no means eloquent and apparently not very educated, but King judged him to be street-smart and, more important, he believed Smirnis was being truthful. Smirnis's knowledge of the Bain case was minimal, but, just to be sure he wasn't tailoring his answers, King made it his practice to ask questions without offering any background information. (For example, when he asked whether Bernardo smoked cigarettes, King didn't mention the package of du Maurier Light found in Elizabeth Bain's glove compartment). In a subsequent letter to Brian Greenspan, King listed fourteen points (from Smirnis alone) that he felt were more than enough to justify the view that Bernardo must now be considered a serious suspect in the Bain disappearance:

1. Both of Bernardo's vehicles had standard transmissions.
2. He was known to keep a pair of gloves and a knife underneath the seat of his car.
3. Bernardo had told Smirnis that he had free-based cocaine (this having already been tabled as a possible explanation for the snipped cigarette filter).
4. Bernardo was known to smoke du Maurier Light cigarettes.
5. While Bernardo's true hair colour was brown, he was known to dye it blond.
6. Bernardo was usually well tanned in the summer (which related to the tanned arm Ruth Collins had seen reach across Bain to shut her door).
7. As a habit, Bernardo reversed his car into parking spots.
8. Bernardo had lived in the West Hill village of Guildwood and had attended Scarborough College.
9. Bernardo had continued to take night courses at the college following his graduation in 1987, the same year Bain had transferred from the downtown campus.
10. According to Smirnis, Bernardo's favourite radio station was CFNY, to which Bain's car radio had been tuned when found.
11. As Boy Scouts, Smirnis and Bernardo had canoed extensively on Lake Scugog. Smirnis's father had also taken both boys on fishing trips in the area.
12. When asked what route his father would take to the Port Perry area, Smirnis said he remembered passing a restaurant that a distant relative either part-owned or worked at called Haugen's Chicken Restaurant. King, who intentionally

neglected to disclose the relevance of Haugen's to the Baltovich case, asked if Bernardo had ever eaten there. Smirnis replied that, yes, he recalled several occasions when Bernardo had been with him and his father when they stopped at Haugen's on the way home.

13. Smirnis also indicated that, during May and June of 1990, Bernardo had visited friends in the Lindsay area just north of Lake Scugog whom he'd met during one of his spring trips to Florida. (Bernardo's annual treks to Florida also had King wondering if it had been Bernardo—not the Bain family—who had picked up the book of matches from the Family Inns of America in Knoxville, Tennessee, found next to the du Maurier Lights.)

14. King was intrigued by the fact that Bernardo had dated a young Filipino woman (Leanne Santiago), about whom King had not previously been informed.

Boosted by this avalanche of what Mike Engel would refer to in the press immediately following Homolka's court appearance as "explosive" new evidence, Brian King drove to Lindsay and interviewed three young men who confirmed that Bernardo had, indeed, visited the Lindsay area in late May and early June of 1990. King even dropped in on John Elliott at the orange-roofed Haugen's to see if he had any recollection of Paul Bernardo being in his restaurant. Elliott did not but admitted it was quite conceivable that Bernardo had been there. As it turned out, Van Smirnis hadn't been entirely accurate about having a distant relative involved with Haugen's. One of Elliott's partners, a Macedonian man, had a son who was friends with one of Smirnis's cousins in Scarborough.

Through Van Smirnis, King was able to interview another of Bernardo's friends, Mike Donald. Donald, who had dated Karla Homolka's sister Lori for a while, corroborated much of what Smirnis had said, including the fact that Bernardo had free-based cocaine and had done so by injection. This use for the missing cigarette filter was, in King's opinion, a far more plausible theory than the one the Crown had provided at Baltovich's trial.

King also went to the residence of defence witness Tasmin Sheikh and presented her with a recent photograph of Bernardo, asking if she recognized him as the man she'd seen next to Elizabeth Bain in the jeep a few weeks prior to Liz's disappearance. Sheikh hadn't seen the man from the best angle but, looking at the picture, said, "I think it could be him." But she made it clear that she was by no means certain.

Another key witness at the Baltovich trial to receive a visit from King was David Dibben. With the Scarborough rapist being a dead ringer for the blond man Dibben had originally described to the police as the driver of Bain's car (except for the moustache), King was anxious to question him. King wasn't too surprised, however, when Dibben refused to depart from his testimony at trial. The driver, he maintained, was Robert Baltovich.

The time King had invested in background checks on Bernardo and Homolka also paid dividends. Through credit card records and other "paper trails," King was hoping to determine Bernardo's whereabouts in the week of Liz's disappearance. One of the searches he conducted was with the Ontario Ministry of Transportation, through which he discovered that Bernardo had sold his worm-picking vehicle, a 1978 Chevrolet Beauville van, to a man named Michael McGouran in Richmond Hill, north of Toronto. When King interviewed McGouran, it was his recollection that the van had actually changed hands on Monday, June 18, between 4:00 and 6:00 PM, when Bernardo and a male friend had driven it from a shopping mall parking lot to McGouran's house in Richmond Hill.

And then there were those people who sought out King instead of the other way around. On July 22, for instance, King took a call that really got his heart pumping. It was from a gentle-voiced man named Ken Cuttings, who had been a member of the jury at the Baltovich trial. The barrage of news that came after Homolka's deal had been made public prompted Cuttings to call King-Reed. Cuttings confessed that, at the conclusion of the trial, he'd had serious doubts about Baltovich's guilt. During the jury's deliberations, Cuttings said, he'd been the lone "holdout."

King, realizing the importance of what he was hearing, hooked up his tape recorder before asking Cuttings what had caused him to change his mind. "It was peer pressure," said Cuttings, heaving an audible sigh. "It is hard to hold off when the others want to get back to work and are saying, 'Why are you being such a bloody fool?' I think I've been in a depression ever since the trial." His voice trailed off. "It's been quite a while."

One of the things that he'd never been able to understand, said Cuttings, was how there was no odour inside Bain's car when the police found it on the Friday afternoon. If the young woman's body had been left hidden in the bushes in Colonel Danforth Park until Thursday night when, according to the Crown's theory, it was transported to the Lake Scugog region in the rear of the vehicle, the stench of decomposition would have been so powerful that it would have lingered for days. Another intriguing (and unsolicited) revelation from Cuttings was that of all the eyewitnesses who had testified at the trial, he'd found Ruth Collins to be the most compelling. She'd had a good clear look at Bain, recalled the timing of the event in reference to her favourite television program, and had described what she'd seen that evening with equal clarity prior to and during hypnosis. Cuttings, who had emigrated from England to Canada, understood the importance of "reasonable doubt" in English law, but couldn't recall Judge O'Driscoll having stressed this concept during his charge to the jury. He told King that he had possessed "reasonable doubt" then and still did.

At this point in the conversation it occurred to King that there might be some laws governing contact between former jurors and someone like himself, who was still actively involved in the appeal. So he and Cuttings agreed that King would call Brian Greenspan to advise him on the matter, and King would call Cuttings back the following day. After talking things over with Greenspan, King told Cuttings that the law prohibited them from discussing what went on in the jury room, but that it was all right for them to have discussions about the case in general. Picking up where he'd left off the previous day, Cuttings said that he'd found the behaviour of Reesor, Raybould and the other detectives to be consistent with the "tunnel vision" exhibited during the notorious Susan Nelles affair a decade earlier. (Nelles, a nurse at Toronto's Hospital for Sick Children, had been charged in connection with a number of mysterious infant deaths, but, due to the lack of any hard evidence, the charges were dismissed following a preliminary hearing. Detective Sergeant Tony Warr, then just a sergeant new to the Homicide squad, had been one of the arresting officers.) "All evidence pointing one way, they would keep," said Cuttings. "Any other evidence, they would ignore. That was my interpretation of what was happening."

More than anything else, Cuttings seemed to want to clear his conscience by sharing his thoughts with King, hoping that he might say something that would lead King to uncover something new, something that hadn't yet occurred to him, something that would set Baltovich free. King suggested that Cuttings could help by filling out an affidavit recounting how he'd made his decision on the verdict "under the duress of insurmountable pressure, or something like that." But Cuttings said he didn't want to get into signing affidavits and so forth. Referring to King's comment about duress, Cuttings said, "I don't think that is quite fair or true. I could fill out an affidavit as to my doubt, though. But when you've got eleven people who want to get back to work, it's pretty hard."

—⊖—

Not long after the astonishing call from Cuttings, King's Bernardo leads slowly began to dry up. Even the media, locked on to one of the biggest stories in years, had been effectively curbed from providing the public with any further in-depth coverage of the case since the imposition of the publication ban. And it didn't appear as though there would be much in the way of hard news to cover until Bernardo was brought to trial.

However, just when it seemed as though the ban had cast the Bernardo-Homolka saga into hibernation, the story suddenly re-erupted. In late October and early November, Mary Garofalo, a Toronto-born reporter with Fox Television's "A Current Affair," sparked international debate by broadcasting in the United States two feature stories that contained banned details about the "Ken and Barbie of Canada" and their victims. While researching her first show, Garofalo received a tip that Glen High, an openly gay young man who claimed he had a sexual encounter with Bernardo during his stay in jail, was willing to talk—for a price. Garofalo's producers forked over $5,000 for the exclusive rights to High's story. High recalled how, on the day Homolka was sentenced to twelve years on two counts of manslaughter, Bernardo reacted to the news by saying "Can you believe that? She's the sick fucking bitch and she only gets twelve years."

In addition to High and *Toronto Star* crime reporter Nick Pron, Garofalo also talked to the parents of Kristen French and Leslie Mahaffy. Both interviews were lengthy, gut-wrenching affairs: at about the third hour of the Mahaffy session, Garofalo's sound man broke down and cried. Astoundingly, Garofalo asked for—and received—the only home videotapes both families had of their daughters, hour upon hour of figure skating, high-school formals and goofing around the house. The families agreed, at least in part, because she offered to make them long-lasting copies using broadcast-standard videotape at Fox in New York.

Shortly after her interviews with the victims' families, Garofalo received an anonymous phone call at her Toronto hotel. The caller claimed to have been in the courtroom during Karla Homolka's trial, and he divulged details about the death of Tammy Homolka that were covered by the publication ban. Garofalo had originally been more interested in reporting on the ban than the trial itself but, after checking to confirm the caller's facts, her focus began to shift.

Technically, Garofalo's Bernardo stories didn't break the ban because they weren't aired in Canada or by any of Fox's sixteen U.S. border stations (although they were readily available to Canada's 500,000 satellite-dish owners). No one Garofalo spoke to on camera provided her with banned information, but some may have felt uneasy or even betrayed when they realized they had appeared on a show that disobeyed the wishes of Canadian law. Most had agreed to be interviewed under different circumstances. This may be the reason Nick Pron, in his articles on Garofalo and her shows, decided not to mention his own appearance on "A Current Affair." The job was left to his rivals, Team Sun, who didn't forget to drop his name into their copy beneath the big, bold headline "Show Breaks Ban."

Garofalo's second show on the murders featured another $5,000 exclusive interview. This one, much to Brian King's dismay, was with Van Smirnis. Smirnis, possibly diminishing his credibility as a potential witness in support of Baltovich, nervously disclosed to Garofalo, among other things, that as a Boy Scout his childhood friend had reached the rank of Chief Scout because of his community work, and that Bernardo's favourite movie was *The Silence of the Lambs.*

Smirnis had shown up for his "Current Affair" interview with Helen Heller, Team Sun's literary agent, who had just helped them obtain their first book contract, with Warner Books in New York. Pron's story on the program in the *Star* ("Bernardo's Best Friend Selling Story") gave short shrift to Smirnis but evened the score with his literary competitors at the *Sun.* "Smirnis," wrote Pron, "along with two *Toronto Sun* reporters who are writing a book with Smirnis's aid, have hired the same publicist to market the story south of the border." Team Sun also reported on Garofalo's second program but buried the story on page twenty-seven, failing to mention their own agent's relationship with Smirnis or his role in the researching of their book. Garofalo, meanwhile, had reason to be pleased. Her Bernardo segments garnered the show's highest ratings in nine months.

Jailhouse Notebook (13)

*B*y the autumn of 1993, when Brian Greenspan first visited me at Warkworth, my biggest question was whether my appeal was going to have to wait until the Bernardo trial had been heard. By way of introduction, Greenspan stated unequivocally that Bernardo was more than just a suspect—he might very well be the suspect. But Greenspan was adamant that Bernardo would not deter our plans. "We're not waiting for Bernardo," he told me. One of the first issues I was interested in was the possibility that the uneliminated fingerprints found on Liz's car might belong to Bernardo. This would have been the coup de grâce to my imprisonment; however, Greenspan informed me that, after being compared by the police, they had found that the prints did not match Bernardo's.

As Greenspan left, I felt confident that the appeal would be heard within the next year. Christmas of 1993 passed, and my expectations grew for better things in 1994; I even began hoping that I had just lived through my final Christmas in prison. Though the spring of 1994 had emerged as our target, my suspicion that things weren't progressing as I had originally hoped were confirmed when I heard from Brian King that Greenspan had changed his mind—my appeal was now on hold until the conclusion of the Bernardo trial.

My crash course in criminal law had convinced me that there might be more to gain in waiting. I was getting used to my surroundings and, despite how anxious my family was for a resolution, I could see the advantages of holding off until the evidence against Bernardo was revealed in court. But then summer gave way to another fall, another winter and another Christmas on the block, my fourth in five years. The only good thing that happened was that I finally got my own cell, a twelve-by-ten box on the second floor of a new nonsmoking unit, with my own toilet and a sink about the size of two cupped hands. Beyond that, winter dragged, but I was helped by my most significant distraction—the Bernardo case. In one sense, I felt guilty spending so much time thinking about it. The media, in a rare bout of self-criticism, had begun to question its obsession with the case, and part of me agreed enough to want to put my interests aside, however practical they might have been.

—◦—

Defending Paul Bernardo was straining Ken Murray beyond his physical, emotional and financial resources. There was also the ethical dilemma of what to do about the tapes implicating his client (and his now-convicted wife) in a series of rapes and murders. In the end, Murray held them for fifteen months without anyone's knowledge but his client's. Towards the end of the summer of 1994, Murray approached John Rosen, the renowned murder-trial specialist Baltovich had called two years earlier, with the prospect of taking over Bernardo's defence. While, at first, Rosen was reluctant to take on a case that seemed unwinnable, he was eventually unable to resist jumping into the media vortex that was now the Bernardo-Homolka story. Not yet informed of the videotapes Murray possessed, Rosen agreed to relieve him.

Rosen didn't have to wait long to learn of the tapes, as Murray, through a lawyer of his own, presented them in court to the judge chosen to preside over Bernardo's multiple murder trial. As soon as Murray's decision to withhold the tapes for so long had become public, a debate ensued about the obligations of defence lawyers when it came to disclosing evidence that might implicate a client. The press consulted legal experts, some of whom felt that Murray was "wrong to have taken evidence that police might obtain through a legal search and put it beyond their reach." Defence lawyers were by no means required to divulge information to the Crown, but in this case, it appeared as though Murray might have "interfered with the process [or had become] an accessory after the fact." Other experts weren't so sure. Faced with the hypothetical conundrum of whether a defence lawyer should disclose evidence that assists both his client and the Crown, many declared this "a grey area that must be determined depending on the facts."

With the Bernardo tapes sealed in an envelope, about to be hand-delivered to the trial judge in open court, Rosen demanded the tapes instead be given to him so that this "defence material" could first be examined by him so he could do whatever was "legally, ethically and professionally" correct. After watching the tapes from beginning to end the following day, Rosen, who had seen a lot in his day, broke down and cried. Less than two weeks later, he turned them over to the Crown prosecutors.

Rosen was subsequently given seven months to prepare his case, as the Crown had taken the rare step of directing Bernardo straight to trial without a preliminary inquiry. The jury selected to determine his fate was assembled for the first time on the afternoon of May 1, 1995, to witness Bernardo plead not guilty to nine charges related to the deaths of Leslie Mahaffy, Kristen French and Tammy Homolka. Bernardo's denial of guilt left many Canadians bewildered. How could he claim not to have killed these girls when the videotapes implicated him? The answer was that while the tapes proved that Bernardo had abducted and raped Mahaffy and French, neither he nor Homolka had recorded their actual deaths on tape. This, of course, left Bernardo with a slight opening to blame the only other person he could—his ex-wife. And in the case of Tammy's death, Bernardo could make a strong case that the overdose that had killed her was accidental.

What made the Bernardo case the subject of such unprecedented attention from the Canadian media had less to do with him than it did with the enigma of Karla Homolka, and to what degree she had participated in these crimes. The idea of a woman going as far as she did to fulfil her husband's perverse fantasies—even in the face of physical and emotional abuse, of which Homolka had declared herself a victim—was unthinkable. During the two years between Bernardo's arrest and his trial, the entire country struggled to comprehend Homolka's role in these abductions, rapes and murders, and by extension, her role in the marriage.

Despite the handful of books written about the Bernardo-Homolka story, the most astute analysis of Homolka appeared in a feature-length magazine article by the aforementioned Patricia Pearson, who covered the trial for *Saturday Night* magazine and was in the process of writing a book about female violence. In the piece, titled "Behind Every Successful Psychopath: Why Karla Homolka Was a Perfect Match for Paul Bernardo," Pearson set out to shatter the myth that the female halves of such "destructive duets" were always the "compliant victims" of dominant, mentally superior men.

Pearson viewed the Bernardo-Homolka dynamic differently. "What Karla Homolka saw in Bernardo was a fantasy reflection of herself," wrote Pearson. "She was a narcissist. Her obsessive need for admiration and her lack of empathy for others were hallmarks of every choice she made. According to several forensic psychologists I consulted, narcissists are governed by a spectacularly wilful blindness. If Hell ran a dating service, narcissists and psychopaths would top the list as perfect pairs. Theirs is a union of grandiose, immature egos, with the narcissist artfully projecting her fantasies of success, power, and romance onto the flat, reflective surface of the psychopathic soul."

Homolka's assistance in the rape of her youngest sister was explained thus by

Pearson: "In July of 1990, Tammy ran a twenty-minute errand with Paul to a liquor store during one of his weekend visits. They did not return for six hours, and Bernardo confessed that they had been flirting, even kissing, out at the Niagara gorge. Karla was aware of Bernardo's newly expressed interest in seeing other girls, but she piously insisted on the witness stand that this episode inspired no spark of jealousy.

"Bernardo contends, on the other hand, that what happened in July sealed Tammy's fate. It was a question of what was at stake for Karla. By 1990, Bernardo was deeply embedded in her identity. He was what set her *apart* from her sisters. He was *her* fantasy, trophy, and obsession. And now he was also her fiancé.

"Her response to the threat has a distinct flavour of Homolka family values gone awry. She decided that if Paul had designs on Tammy, he was going to have to do it at Karla's home, in front of her. He was not going to be sneaking off on a clandestine rendezvous behind her back."

The most anticipated day of the Bernardo trial was when John Rosen began his cross-examination of Karla Homolka. The tapes (which, out of respect for the innocent teenage victims, the trial judge had ruled would be viewed by the jury and lawyers alone; journalists and spectators in the gallery would have to endure the haunting experience of listening to the audio portion without an accompanying image) had made Homolka's participation in the rapes all the more real. More often than not she appeared to be enjoying herself, directly contradicting what she had recounted during her early police interviews. The public now learned what those on the inside had known for many months—that the plea bargain with Homolka would go down in history as a travesty. Even the lead Crown prosecutor had conceded during his opening address that, had the Crown been in possession of the tapes by the time its search warrant had expired for 57 Bayview, a deal with Homolka never would have been struck. In fact, the tapes showed that Homolka was, by the definition of the law, party to first-degree murder. As it stood, however, it was an arrangement everyone would have to live with, especially Ken Murray— there was no way to legally retract such a binding resolution.

"So intense was public frustration with Homolka's testimony," observed Pearson, "that defence counsel John Rosen looked like a folk hero when he jumped up on July 5 for his cross-examination and said, 'Now wait just one darn minute' on behalf of us all.

" 'Ms. Homolka, let's get this straight,' he said through gritted teeth, after she gave him a haughty lecture on what battered women go through. 'You were in St. Catharines, you [lived with] your parents, you had your sister Lori . . . you had your friends. You had your co-workers. You had a doctor to confide in. And the person supposedly abusing you is in *Toronto*, an hour and a half away!'

"Homolka glared at him. 'You don't have to be physically isolated to be emotionally isolated,' she retorted, as if he were a dunce. Rosen produced a letter she had written in 1991, lecturing a friend to get a restraining order against a violent lover, saying that the situation was 'ridiculous.' He flung her own words in her face. 'You had nothing to lose but a boyfriend.'

"But Homolka *wanted* to keep her boyfriend," wrote Pearson, "come hell, high water, or murder. . . ."

After four months of surreal testimony (due to the evidentiary power of the videotapes, Van Smirnis was not called to testify) that was by turns both horrifying and banal, Rosen failed to prove his theory, that Karla Homolka had murdered both Kristen French and Leslie Mahaffy while Bernardo was either in a separate part of the house or out fetching fast food. In his own self-defence, Bernardo claimed that, with both girls, he had simply arrived back on the scene and found them dead, murdered by Karla, presumably because she didn't want to risk being caught by letting them go free. Unconvinced, the jury accepted Homolka's version of events, that Bernardo had ruthlessly strangled the life out of both girls with an electrical cord, leading them, unforgivingly, to believe right up until their last moments that they would soon be reunited with brothers and mothers and fathers.

On September 1, 1995, Paul Bernardo was found guilty as charged on all nine counts. He was sentenced to the mandatory twenty-five-year life term in prison and was later declared a dangerous offender, which meant that his chances of ever again walking outside the gates of a federal institution were zero.

—◦—

Jailhouse Notebook (14)

Whenever I read or listened to reports about the evidence being presented at the Bernardo trial, I would ask myself questions as if I were a devil's advocate trying to persuade myself that Bernardo couldn't have been involved in

Liz's disappearance. But the more questions I raised in defence of Bernardo, the less reason there was to believe he couldn't have been the perpetrator. In addition to the things Brian King had already uncovered, I pondered the viability of a number of scenarios, including the possibility that Liz and Bernardo had known each other.

Given Liz's penchant for secrecy, was it that preposterous to consider that she and Bernardo had carried on a relationship unbeknownst to all but themselves? And was this somehow connected to the fact that Liz had ceased writing in her diary for a month prior to her disappearance? Of course, the police answer would be "She didn't—Rob stole the pages." However, I knew that wasn't the case. Added to the mix was Cathy Bain's admission at trial that she had periodically perused Liz's diary, and that Liz was aware of this. Could it be that something had been taking place in Liz's life that was so taboo she couldn't bring herself to even write about it? If she was carrying on a relationship, could she have been so uncomfortable that it would have been impossible to disclose its existence, even in her diary?

For such to be the case, Bernardo would have had to be unfaithful to his beloved Karla. Was there any evidence of this? Enter Ted Brinkworth. Billed by The Globe and Mail *as "a former drinking buddy" of Bernardo's, Brinkworth recalled that having more than one girlfriend on the go had become routine for Bernardo. Brinkworth testified that Bernardo seemed to "go to elaborate lengths in deceiving Homolka, and took great pleasure in doing so."*

Every once in a while, I would read some new revelation about Bernardo that would strike a chord in my memory and really get me churning things over. For example, there was quite a bit written about his interest in self-betterment and about how Bernardo had reportedly participated in a Dale Carnegie business course in the 1980s. It seemed as though this experience was the source of the dozens of mantras—"Time is money" or "The facts don't count when you have a dream"—he'd pasted to what he called the "Wall of Words" in his room at home in Scarborough.

Right away, my mind was transported back in time to the day Liz had gone missing, when I was in Liz's room with Mr. and Mrs. Bain, as well as Arlene Coventry, looking for clues. As we wandered around the room, my gaze eventually fell on Liz's night stand. I plucked a dog-eared paperback from one of its lower shelves: it was How to Win Friends and Influence People *by Dale Carnegie. I was familiar with Carnegie, and knew that his book, published in 1936, was considered a classic in the area of self-improvement, especially for the business-minded—an Anthony Robbins of the 1940s and 1950s.*

I found it strange that Liz even knew who Dale Carnegie was. She had certainly never mentioned him to me. Given the age of the book, I felt it had been given to her. But by whom? I ruled out her aunt; she was part of the New Age set, complete with astrological readings and healing crystals. For me, the Carnegie book had a more peculiar resonance than many of the things Brian King had already discovered about Bernardo. Although it could likely never be proven, it seemed to connect Bernardo to Elizabeth's life. The book's existence was something I was certain of. I had seen it with my own eyes, touched it with my own hands.

I was quite certain I had discussed the Carnegie book during one of my police interviews, so I called Brian King, who had printed transcripts of the interviews that had been recorded, and asked him to look into it. Brian, sensing that I was pretty worked up about the whole affair, lassoed me back to reality. He said the book wasn't all that important. Still, I pressed him to find any Carnegie references. Even if my theory was wrong, I wanted to know.

DID BERNARDO CLAIM ANOTHER VICTIM?
By Jim Rankin and John Duncanson

November 8, 1995—Two days after the body of 14-year-old Terri Anderson was found floating in St. Catharines' Port Dalhousie harbor, Niagara Region police delivered their verdict to the dead girl's family.

The death was an accident.

Unlike Leslie Mahaffy and Kristen French, Anderson had not died at the hands of a killer, police said.

"There's a lot of concern in this community about a relationship between Leslie, Kristen and Terri," said Inspector Vince Bevan. "Based on what we've seen today, we don't think there is a relationship."

With those words on May 25, 1992—six months after Anderson mysteriously vanished—Bevan removed her case from the task force investigating serial-type murders in the area.

But police sources and court documents suggest the deaths may in fact have something in common: Paul Bernardo, convicted killer and rapist.

According to the sexual predator's ex-wife and accomplice Karla Homolka, Bernardo was very much aware of the tiny Grade 9 student before she disappeared in November, 1991.

Bernardo told Homolka the two once had locked eyes and that he felt a "karma" between them as their eyes met.

He said they smiled at each other. It is not clear how close Anderson's encounter with Bernardo was to her disappearance.

But the night she disappeared, Anderson walked by a doughnut shop where it has since been learned Bernardo was known to stalk women.

And in May, 1992, after the girl's partially clothed body was found floating face-down in the harbor, just a short walk from his Port Dalhousie home on Bayview Drive, Bernardo said it was "a waste" that he hadn't had sex with her.

Homolka passed these comments on to police and investigators more than a year later, after her 1993 plea bargain and double-manslaughter conviction, sources have told The Star.

And she said Bernardo was out looking for girls the night Anderson stepped out her front door and never came back.

Although police are aware of Bernardo's likely encounter with the St. Catharines girl, the Niagara force has refused to reopen the case. They won't budge from their belief she drowned accidentally after taking LSD.

But some investigators, and Anderson's stepmother, charge that the case was bungled from the beginning. It was homicide, they say.

For many, the Anderson case is another example of the cover-ups, sloppy police work and soured relations between police forces that have become hallmarks of the Bernardo case.

Anderson was last seen alive by her father around 1:30 a.m. on November 30, 1991—six months after Mahaffy's body was found, and six months before French was murdered.

Anderson's father awoke later that morning to find the front door open, his daughter gone.

The police explanation for the death was that after attending several parties that Friday night, and experimenting with LSD, Anderson wandered to a pond near her home and fell in. Eventually, police said, her body was swept over a control dam into the Port Dalhousie harbor.

Although Anderson's friends candidly told police she had taken a mild form of LSD much earlier that night, they insisted she was fine by the time she went home around midnight.

But with the LSD in mind, and a coroner's report that found no sign of vaginal penetration, no trauma to the body—or a definitive cause of death—police ruled it an accident.

Anderson's father agreed with police that an inquest was not needed. Her body was turned over to the family, and cremated.

To this day, however, there are some things police can't explain.

Why was Anderson found wearing only her shirt, bra and panties, but not her skin-tight jeans?

How did a girl who was an excellent swimmer drown in a shallow pond on a mild fall night?

A year after the investigation was closed, the startling information from Homolka surfaced.

But Bevan and other task force members apparently didn't follow up on comments made by the very person who knew Bernardo best—his former wife. Bevan refused to answer any questions when approached by Star reporters at Bernardo's dangerous offender sentencing last Friday.

According to police sources, Homolka told investigators in a 1993 interview that Bernardo had gone out early the morning of Anderson's disappearance.

When he returned home, he said nothing about any stalking exploits, Homolka told the two interviewers huddled in the interview room. (During Bernardo's trial, Homolka testified her then-husband often described his stalking activities.)

A Metro officer began asking her for more details about Bernardo's actions that night. But, police sources say, his line of questioning was quickly ended when Bevan, who was watching the interview from another room, signalled his Niagara interrogation officer to change subjects, which the officer dutifully did.

When Anderson's name came up again in February and March of 1994, in interviews with Crown attorneys Ray Houlahan and Greg Barnett, Homolka's story had apparently changed.

She said Bernardo had wanted to go out the night Anderson vanished, but didn't, contradicting what she had said earlier.

And then came several startling admissions.

According to a summary of the interview obtained by The Star, Homolka told the prosecutors Bernardo had seen Anderson sometime before her disappearance.

"He said that he had seen her sitting at the side of the road and he smiled at her," Homolka recalled in the interview. "He said something about karma between Terri and him. . . . The next day, after he learned she had disappeared, he said he should have gone out. Later, he said that it was a waste that she had died without his having had her . . . "

Homolka told the Crown attorneys she didn't think Bernardo sexually assaulted or killed the girl because he would have "bragged" about it.

Some Metro investigators see it differently. They're convinced Anderson was murdered but have been unable to sway Niagara detectives, who came up with some "interesting" explanations for what happened.

The one that irks officers—and Anderson's stepmother—the most, is the theory of how the girl's soaked jeans came off her body. Niagara police told Anderson's family that the rough currents in the harbor could have forced the jeans off or they simply "disintegrated" in the water. There was no explanation, however, for why her underwear remained on, in good condition.

At the time of her disappearance, Bernardo was roaming free, and living less than 2 kilometres from Anderson's townhouse.

When the police searched his home after his arrest, they found a half-page newspaper clipping that detailed how investigators were satisfied Anderson had simply drowned.

Donna Anderson, who has launched a letter-writing campaign urging politicians to pressure police to reopen the case, has only harsh words for the task force that dismissed her stepdaughter's death as an accident.

She remains livid over the police version of her stepdaughter's actions the night she disappeared—that she was partying all night, high on drugs.

"She didn't go to any parties," she says. "There were people who saw her all night long. They knew exactly where she was."

Donna Anderson is puzzled by the fact that her stepdaughter left the house wearing a pair of duckboots. She hated those boots.

Donna made a point of letting police know about the boots, and her stepdaughter's taste in clothing. But it seemed they didn't want to hear any of it.

When French's body was discovered, police interest faded. As far as authorities were concerned, Terri Anderson came from a broken home and she ran away.

"Terri sort of got left out in the wash," her stepmother said. "I'm not looking for a whole new trial, or the whole nine yards, I just think someone else should look at it."

THE TORONTO STAR

—◯—

A discarded newspaper on the floor of a commuter train. Pages out of order. Finger smudges. A man, faced with the half-hour ride into Toronto from Oakville, west of the city along the lake, reaches down and gathers what remains of the day's *Globe and Mail* in his hands. On the front page is a black-and-white photograph of three former prime ministers—Kim Campbell, John Turner and Pierre Trudeau—clapping appreciatively as a plaque honouring former parliamentarians is unveiled in the House of Commons. Then, below the fold, he reads the headline "Bernardo cited as suspect in murder appeal" and the subheading "Man convicted of Bain slaying tries to link 'Scarborough rapist' to disappearance." He reads on with a sense of urgency that borders on nausea.

He learns that Robert Baltovich's lawyers, Brian Greenspan and Lisa Silver, have, the week before, filed a 113-page memorandum of facts and law with the Ontario Court of Appeal. It is now Thursday, May 30, 1996. Filed along with this memorandum, also known as the appellant's factum, were "thick, sealed envelopes containing fresh evidence obtained in the more than four years since Robert Baltovich was convicted. . . ." The traveller then reads about how it is the position of the defence "that another individual, other than the appellant, committed the offence" and how, given the various witnesses who had seen a blond man with Bain or alone in her car, the Scarborough rapist could very well be that individual.

Greenspan and Silver cited twenty-five issues for the appeal court to consider, mostly related to assistant Crown attorney John McMahon's "inflammatory" closing address and Mr. Justice John O'Driscoll's charge to the jury, which "crossed the line of fairness." The article also clarified that, in order to consider the fresh evidence related to the Scarborough rapist, the appeal court will have to rule that it was unavailable at the time of the trial despite due diligence. It will also have to be judged that, had the jury known about Bernardo at Baltovich's trial, it could have affected the verdict.

The article has left the man in a haze, a state in which he is trapped until well after he has walked through the front door of his home in Willowdale, just north of Highway 401, which cuts across the top of Toronto. An avalanche of memories has come crashing down, smothering all else. For the next three weeks he plays the same six-year-old scene in his mind again and again, remembering also what followed, and he switches reels every once in a while, projecting things in a dozen or more sequences. He has known that he must get in touch with the reporter whose byline,

Thomas Claridge, appeared atop the *Globe* article, but he does not actually pick up the phone until his desk-top calendar indicates it is the nineteenth day of June.

As Claridge listened to the man on the other end of the telephone, his gut told him that this was no crank calling. He said his name was Keith Nobrega and that he was calling because he was sure he had seen Elizabeth Bain on the evening of her disappearance. Claridge had no recollection of Nobrega from the trial so he asked him if he had spoken to the police. Of course, said Nobrega. He had told them all about it the summer the girl went missing. How he'd been driving east on the 401, leaving Scarborough, and had seen her in the passenger seat of her car. He'd even had a look at the driver.

Claridge saw this as a classic conflict of interest for a reporter. Here he was listening to a man who was sure to become the centrepiece of the fresh evidence at Baltovich's appeal, yet Claridge was also aware that, by going to print with the Nobrega story, the court that would eventually be presiding over Baltovich's appeal might view it as a snub, possibly endangering Baltovich's chances of getting his conviction overturned. Claridge thought the best thing to do was to provide Nobrega with phone numbers for Brian Greenspan and Brian King, both of whom Claridge urged him to contact as soon as possible. Nobrega tried Greenspan first, but was out when his call was returned.

The next day, Claridge phoned Brian King to let him know about his conversation with Nobrega. A few hours later, Nobrega rang King himself, but King had stepped out of the office. When he returned around 10:00 PM, a message regarding Nobrega's call was waiting on his desk. King immediately dialled the number.

After exchanging pleasantries, King asked Nobrega for "a quick rundown" of his story. But Nobrega said he preferred to do that face to face. King was out of town the following day, a Friday, and Nobrega said he had a commitment to a friend on Saturday. King was so eager to speak with him that he was considering Sunday but, when Nobrega said he was currently unemployed, they made an appointment for 9:00 AM Monday morning at King's offices.

Nobrega presented himself at King's office suite at the appointed time and was greeted by King and one of his senior investigative managers, Manny Acacio. They went into the company's large but windowless boardroom. Nobrega was in his early fifties, dressed presentably but obviously not a man of tremendous means, with an air of battle-worn humility. King explained that he wanted Nobrega's permission to tape-record what might be called a voluntary statement recounting his story from beginning to end. Nobrega said that was what he wanted, so King clicked on his small recorder and placed it upright on the long black table. "Keith, just to be clear, are you here of your own free will?" asked King.

Nobrega said, "That's right."

King then asked him to give his address for the record and confirmed that Nobrega wasn't under any psychiatric care. "You've come here to talk to us about an incident that you observed in June of 1990," King announced. "I'm just going to let you explain it to us. Take as long as you would like."

"Well, on the nineteenth of June 1990, I was in Toronto," Nobrega began. "I was living and working in Oshawa at the time but that afternoon I drove into the city to do some banking. My plan was to return to the General Motors plant in Oshawa, where I used to work as a rental designer in the engineering office, for 6:00 PM that evening. I thought I would put in four hours or so and punch out around ten o'clock. On my way out of Toronto, however, the traffic was quite heavy so I stopped at a place on Eglinton near Midland in Scarborough where they have curry food. It's called Channaman's Caribbean Corner. This meant that I wasn't going to make it to work by 6:00 PM, as it was already closer to 7:00 PM. I had flexible hours at the plant so I decided to get to the plant by eight o'clock and work until midnight.

"Pretty soon I was on the 401 heading east to Oshawa again, and a few minutes later, passing through the Rouge Hill area, I noticed a car behind me. This was sometime between 7:15 and 7:40 PM. I was in the fast lane on the left-hand side when I noticed a car behind me. The traffic was still quite heavy and there were about two car lengths of space between bumpers. Nevertheless, I was doing about 110-115 clicks per hour.

"So in my rear-view mirror I saw a Toyota, a small silver Tercel, come right up to within a few inches of my back bumper and then brake heavily and recede. And then it came back up again, hit the brakes and backed off. I said to myself, What is wrong with this guy? You don't do that sort of stuff in this kind of traffic. I then looked in the rear-view mirror to see what was up with the chap and saw that the guy driving was quite big in size. He was so big that his head was right up into the roof of the car and his shoulders were quite broad. Next to him was a girl, and there was a fight going on between her and this guy. So I said to myself, What the hell is this guy doing? Fighting with a girl on the 401 at this speed. I slowed back a bit and he swung out and passed me on the right in the middle lane of the highway. As they came up alongside, I could see that he was punching at her, and she was hitting him back. And I said, Holy smoke, a big guy like that beating up a little girl. It looked as though it was getting pretty wild.

"So what I decided to do was get on the other side of them, meaning into the slowest lane, alongside the passenger side of the car in order to see more clearly what was going on. Once I'd manoeuvred myself so that my window was a few feet from the passenger window of the Tercel, I turned my head and saw the girl screaming, her mouth wide open, her hands up like this against the window. Screaming. I signalled to her to wind down her window, and then I rolled mine down all the way. I had to keep an eye on the traffic, though, because their car veered towards my car, which was a 1990 Chev Cavalier, only four months old, and I wasn't going to have it damaged for anything. When I turned my head again to see if she had wound her window down, she was out of sight, completely. It was only him there. So I said, What the heck happened? And then he accelerated and got into the fast lane, on the far left. The traffic in front of me was kind of tight, so I waited for an opening and eventually caught up to him. But when I did, I saw the girl lying on his shoulder, with his arm around her, like she was making up to him as he drove. They're having a fight on the 401, I said to myself. And now they're lovey-dovey. I'm looking at this and it's safe to say that I'm thoroughly pissed off. I really wanted to speak to this guy in a very sharp tongue. I tried to keep his car in sight so as to finally get alongside of him to tell him off. But the traffic in my lane was moving while his seemed to be slowing down and he fell behind. I was constantly checking my mirrors to see when he was going to catch up. But pretty soon we were approaching Ajax, and he didn't seem to be around at all. Like the car disappeared. I'd actually slowed down to about seventy clicks in the slow lane. I was going so slow I pulled off to the side of the highway and waited for him. But he did not appear, the car did not appear.

"The whole incident had shaken me up so badly that, when I got into Oshawa, I didn't bother going into work. Instead, I went to the O'Toole's bar at Taunton and Simcoe Street, which I frequented back then. I bought a beer and saw one of the regulars there, a big German guy named Gerhardt Hinz. He was a stonemason. Anyway, he was there and so was the bartender, a lady named Donna. She might still be working there. Now, I got in there and said, 'You wouldn't believe what I just saw on the 401.' And I told them the whole story. It was giving me a very peculiar nervous feeling.

"I didn't think about it a lot for the next few days. There were, however, a few things I had noticed about the car that kept coming back to me. For one, when the Tercel switched into the middle lane from behind me and went by, I thought it must have been either souped up or running very well for it to accelerate like that at such a speed. The second thing I noticed were the hubcaps, which were not standard Toyota issue. It was quite a bright day and these hubcaps were really reflecting the sunlight, and I said to myself, Those hubcaps look good on that car. And when the car went by I noticed the plate number. From my recollection, it was 394 CNB. I remember car numbers easily. That's something I've done since I was a kid. We used to have games about remembering car numbers back home in Guyana. I'm sure anybody in my family, brothers, cousins, will tell you that this is something I did as a hobby.

"I remember that about a week passed, and it was the time of year when the fireworks festival was going on down at the lake. And one night I went down to a German pub at Ontario Place. We were leaving in the car after the fireworks, and the traffic was moving at a crawl. One car that came by me going in the opposite direction had a picture of Ms. Bain pasted in the rear window. When I looked at that picture, my whole body jumped. Like I had a start. But, at first, I didn't know why I had that reaction to the photograph. Then I kept seeing the same picture around and I kept wondering if I'd met this girl a long time ago. I had not even thought about what happened on the 401.

"Then, on Friday, the twenty-fourth of August, 1990, I came home from work in the afternoon. I was living in an apartment at the time and I took my mail out of my postbox and found a flyer regarding Elizabeth Bain's disappearance. This flyer was a bit longer than the others I'd seen and at the bottom of it was a picture of her grey Toyota. When I got into my apartment, I put the flyer down on a table and saw the plate number and it suddenly came back to me that this was the car I'd seen on the 401. Now I knew why I'd gotten that reaction from seeing her picture previously. She was the girl I had seen screaming with her hands up against the glass and her face and eyes in real sort of horror.

"I was nervous and agitated all day Saturday at work. On Sunday, I went to Harvey's for breakfast and was reading the paper when I decided that I should call the number on the flyer and report what I had seen. So I called but there was no answer. On Monday, I told my boss that I wanted Tuesday off and briefly explained why. So I left work about 10:00 AM Tuesday morning and drove to the Military Trail area in Scarborough where the car had been found. There was a deli or a bakery nearby and I went inside to use the pay phone and dialled the number on the flyer once again. As it turned out, it was the Bains' number and Mrs. Bain answered the phone and, after listening to a bit of what I had to say, said I should come over to their house. So I drove over and she asked me to come in and sit down at the table and she got me some coffee. She'd phoned her husband, who was over at the campus speaking to some people, and he got there about ten minutes later. I explained to them just as I explained to you now exactly what I'd seen. One of the Bains' sons, he was about nineteen or twenty, was there when I was talking about how fast the car was running. The young Bain said that he had done a tune-up on the car and that it had been working very well. He also asked me if I had seen the fingers on the door. And I told them that I did remember seeing something like fingers at high speed. And then he asked me about a dent on the rear-quarter panel, and I said only that I might have but was concentrating more on the window area. At some stage, Mrs. Bain wanted to go upstairs and bring a picture of Mr. Baltovich down to ask whether he was the guy driving the car. I said to her, I think you'd better not. I don't want to be influenced by anything. So then one of them phoned the police, and they wanted to see me right away.

"I left their place and drove down to 42 Division and met with Detective Reesor. He took me upstairs to the second floor, I believe. I remember that we had to go in an elevator. We went into a big open room that was probably used for meetings. I told the whole story once again, and Reesor asked why it had taken me so long to come forward. He also asked me to describe the driver. In addition to the broad shoulders and the head up under the roof, I told him that he had a crew-cut as far as I could make out and that his hair might have been darkish blond. Why I say might have been was that I had on my sunglasses that evening and my car had tinted windows, but not heavily tinted. When he was alongside me, I saw roughly what his hair looked like, and it was not quite blond, but it was not dark black. From my point of view, it was somewhere in between.

"Mr. Reesor took a statement from me. Wrote it up in his own hand. I asked him to make a photocopy of it for me so I could have it as a record. I still have it but it's in storage. When I told him that I remembered the plate number as 394 CNB, he went to the phone to find out whether that number existed; he was informed that it had been discontinued. So, for the purposes of the statement, we decided to just say that the plate number I'd seen was the one belonging to Ms. Bain's Tercel. Oh, and this just came to me. I told Detective Reesor that I was willing to take a lie-detector test or be put under hypnosis to clarify the details of what I saw further. And he said to me, 'Oh, lots of people are going on about wanting to be hypnotized.' He said he didn't think it would be of any benefit. Afterwards, coming back downstairs with Reesor, we were talking about the traffic-control cameras on the 401. Using the film from that day, I thought he might be able to identify my car and any cars around me. Hopefully, this might provide them with exact times. Anyway, as I was leaving, Detective Reesor suggested to me that, one, he would be in touch with me and, two, he wanted me to gather as much information as I could to confirm I was on the 401 at that time.

"I believe I got back to Reesor the very next day after I'd checked my log, which showed that I had not been at work on the afternoon of the nineteenth. I'd also gone to speak with Donna and Gerhardt Hinz at O'Toole's. Donna said that, during June, she'd worked Tuesdays and Thursdays. Therefore, I knew it had to be the Tuesday. So I phoned to tell him this and that I would try to consult my bank statement. But over a month went by without Detective Reesor getting back to me, so I phoned him one day to ask how things were going. He said words to the effect that, because I couldn't pinpoint I had been on the 401 on Tuesday the nineteenth of June 1990 between 7:00 and 8:00 PM, he didn't think he could use my information. To which I said to myself, fair enough, at least I'd done my civic duty.

"Of course, later I heard about Baltovich's arrest. During his trial, out of curiosity, I went down to the courthouse twice to see what he looked like in person. The first time I saw him from the back of the courtroom. I didn't get to see his face, but he sat kind of tall on the accused's bench. His shoulders seemed wide but they sloped a bit. And he had a crew-cut. The second time I saw him he was walking towards me into court. I had not realized he isn't a very tall chap, just that his spine might be a bit longer than the rest of him. The guy I saw driving the car was quite a big guy. I also saw Mr. and Mrs. Bain at court. Mrs. Bain was trying to avoid me, I think, and didn't say anything to me. But I went up to Mr. Bain and spoke with him. He remembered that I was the guy from GM who came to them. I asked how things were going.

He said, 'Well, they're proceeding.' Or something like that. I also ran into Detective Reesor. I told him that, since speaking to him, I realized that I'd been wearing sunglasses that night and that with my tinted windows, I couldn't say for sure whether the driver had blond hair. But as far as I was concerned, he had mid-blond hair or dark blond hair. Anyway, Reesor didn't say anything. Just kind of brushed me off after a fifteen-second conversation. I left it at that. Weeks later, I read in the paper about Baltovich being found guilty, sentenced, the whole thing. I just figured the police had other information from people driving on the 401—I noticed a map of the highway to the right of the judge's bench in court—and didn't need me.

"I didn't see another thing about the case until the latest *Globe* article on the GO train. I knew right away that I had to get hold of the reporter. I had no idea whether or not the information I'd given Reesor had ever been used. It needed to be sorted out. So I called Thomas and here I am."

King knew, from the moment he'd heard Nobrega's name, that his statement had not been disclosed to Baltovich's defence at any point prior or subsequent to his trial. Had Reesor and Raybould made an honest mistake in forgetting to do so? It was highly doubtful—after all, Nobrega was only the second person to see Bain in the passenger seat of her car on the evening of her disappearance. If, on the other hand, Reesor and Raybould had failed to disclose it on purpose, it wasn't hard to figure out their motive. First of all, Nobrega claimed the incident had occurred between 7:15 and 7:40 that night—Rob had an alibi in the gym from 7:15 until 8:30. And then there was Ruth Collins. Her earliest estimate for walking past Bain's Tercel in front of Three R Auto Body had been 7:30 PM. Who was to say that Collins hadn't spooked Bain's attacker enough for him to hit the highway, where he could have been in the Rouge Hill area of the 401 within ten minutes without much difficulty? And what about Paul Curran, the man who had seen a young woman fitting Elizabeth Bain's description crying in a phone booth off Port Union Road—half a kilometre south of the 401—that same evening? King was furious that he hadn't heard about this man five years ago. Nobrega alone probably would have been enough to guarantee an acquittal under any circumstances.

Eventually, King got around to asking the question that had to be asked: Was it possible that the driver had been Paul Bernardo? "I will say this," said Nobrega. "I didn't think so until one day I saw a picture of him with a type of crew-cut. Very short on the sides. If he had a cut like that then, it could possibly be him."

Thinking of David Dibben, who had said the man driving Bain's car had the beginnings of a beard, King asked, "What about facial hair?"

"It didn't appear he had a beard or moustache as far as I could see."

King asked where his copy of the statement was being kept in storage. Nobrega explained that he'd lived in Oshawa until the summer of 1994, three years after he'd stopped working at GM. He then moved to Oakville—where the storage company was—before coming to Toronto at the end of March this year. Nobrega said he was divorced and single, and about to move again.

King turned off the tape recorder at 10:47 AM, at the conclusion of Nobrega's hour-and-a-half interview. He really wanted to get his hands on the photocopy of Nobrega's police statement so he asked if Nobrega would be willing to be taken to the storage facility by Manny Acacio in order to retrieve it. Nobrega said he'd be happy to but that he was somewhat behind on his payments and wouldn't be able to access his locker until he was up to date. Given what they were looking for, King thought getting into the locker for one document wouldn't be a problem if Acacio presented his private investigator's identification, and so he sent them on their way to Oakville.

Although Acacio kept it to himself during their drive to the storage facility, he wasn't entirely convinced Nobrega wasn't yet another crackpot. His story seemed authentic, but Acacio thought the part about the numbers game in Guyana sounded a little hokey and figured Nobrega could have just taken the licence plate number off a poster or flyer somewhere. But if he was telling the truth . . . well, he really hoped they would find the statement.

King didn't see the pair back at King-Reed for three hours. And he could tell from the grins they were wearing as they marched into his office that they had struck gold. For Nobrega, a man who seemed to move around with some frequency, Acacio explained, he had sure squirrelled away a hell of a lot of stuff—dozens upon dozens of boxes and plastic shopping bags stuffed with receipts, tax stuff, work records, personal correspondence and more. They had sifted through all of it for an hour—a facility supervisor watched on the entire time, as Nobrega's account was still in the red—until Nobrega plucked the coffee-stained photocopy from a cardboard box with an excited shriek.

Assembled back in the boardroom, Acacio and Nobrega sat in silence as King anxiously read the precious seven legal-sized pages. For all intents and purposes, it corroborated the story Nobrega had told him that morning. But there were little things that caught King's attention along the way. For example, Nobrega was off by a day when it came to the date of his meeting with Reesor—it had been a Monday, not a Tuesday. More important, though, Nobrega had been mistaken all morning about having spoken to Steve Reesor. The signature next to Nobrega's at the end of the statement belonged to Brian Raybould. Nobrega realized that it had, in fact, been Raybould he'd been talking about—he'd only clicked on to the name Reesor when King had said it aloud at the beginning of the meeting—a mistake King and Acacio found made his story even more credible because, if the whole thing was a demented ruse, he probably wouldn't have made such a simple slip.

Also, near the bottom of the first page, Raybould had written on Nobrega's behalf that the incident on the 401 had occurred only "sometime during the month of June, 1990," and not on the nineteenth. Again, Nobrega asserted that he had told Raybould he was certain it had been on the nineteenth of June, but Raybould had said that, unless Nobrega could prove it, he would write nothing more specific than "sometime during. . . ."

As for Nobrega's description of the driver, there was no mention in the original statement about hair colour. When King asked why, Nobrega said that, because he hadn't been able to "tell him exactly what colour the driver's hair was," Raybould had decided not to mention anything about it.

It was now 2:15 in the afternoon. King was out of questions, and Nobrega didn't think there was anything else to add, so they said their good-byes for now and promised to be in touch soon. Retreating to his office, King laid Nobrega's statement on his desk and lost himself in a torrent of questions, attempting to reconfigure the night of June 19, 1990, in his mind. But it was almost impossible to concentrate. The same burning thought kept interrupting him: Why hadn't Baltovich's defence been told about Keith Nobrega six years ago?

—◦—

Throughout the Canada Day weekend there was tremendous speculation in the news that a human skeleton discovered on the previous Thursday evening in a swampy area just a few miles east of Lake Scugog would turn out to be that of Elizabeth Bain or Julie Stanton. The remains were found by a local electrician who was building a fence on his farm. When later contacted by newspaper reporters, the man refused to describe what he had seen out of respect for the family of the deceased, but said that the remains had been found in a section of "very, very dense bush."

The Bains and Stantons spent much of that anguished weekend together as forensic examiners used dental records to determine the identity of the body. And then the call came from the police. It was Julie, they said.

In several front-page newspaper articles on the holiday Monday, references were made regarding how the Stantons could now have a sense of "closure." Julita Bain was quoted, saying that she was "saddened, but elated for them [the Stantons]." She also mentioned that, through burying their daughter, the Stantons would be afforded "comfort, a little bit of peace." But she wistfully added, "I wish I could say the same for myself."

Reporters had also placed calls to a prominent Toronto defence lawyer, Leo Adler, seeking his comment. Adler had represented a man named Peter Stark, who had been convicted of Stanton's first-degree murder after a seven-week trial in 1994. Although Robert Baltovich was the first man in Ontario to be convicted of second-degree murder on circumstantial evidence and without a body, *The Globe and Mail* reported that Stark's case had one-upped Baltovich because it was first-degree.

Stark, whose teenage daughter Kim had been friends with Julie Stanton, was accused by the Crown of having developed a "perverted obsession" with the girl. Evidence was presented that, nine months before she vanished, Stark had invited Julie to the boat on which he lived at the Darlington Marina, ostensibly to discuss how to resolve the serious rift that had developed between him and his daughter. While doing so, however, Stark mixed an "ice-blue cooler" drink for her, laced with enough Halcion (the same pill Bernardo and Homolka had used to sedate several young victims) to cause her to lose control of her bowels.

Under the same pretence, said the Crown, Stark called Julie on Easter Monday in 1990, suggesting another get-together. Although Stark told police he hadn't seen Julie that day, his daughter Kim would later testify that he'd admitted to picking Julie up near her house, taking her for lunch at a fast-food restaurant and then dropping her off at a nearby gas station where he said she'd wanted to meet up with a friend. In addition to a neighbour of the Stantons who had seen Julie get into a car just like Stark's that afternoon, another witness claimed Stark was alone in his car in a remote area of Scugog Township later in the day. Even Stark's own wife, Alison, corroborated the theory that he had disposed of a body in the woods. When he picked her up late from work that day, she testified that he had black soil and dried leaves matted to his clothing. As well, the jury heard that Stark had taken a hatchet and a pair of surgical gloves with him when he left his boat, which may or may not have given one of Stark's cellmates, Gerald Udall, who possessed a lengthy criminal record and had served time for sexual assault, the ammunition he needed to become the Crown's star witness.

According to Udall, after hearing Stark's private confession, he was stunned by the man's lack of remorse. "It was like staring into no eyes," Udall told an attentive jury. "He had no feelings and was very cold. He wanted to have sex with her but she wouldn't go for it. Then he got so scared she was going to run to her parents. That's when he chopped her up with an axe." When Udall asked Stark where he'd hidden the body, Stark supposedly replied, "Don't ask me that, Gerald. Without the body, there won't be a conviction."

Another aspect of Stark's case that made it wholly different from Baltovich's was his criminal and psychiatric background, which the judge had ruled the jury would not hear about for fear of bias. But once the jury had reached its verdict, the press, no longer restricted by a publication ban, was free to fit his history into the chronology. Stark had spent six months in jail and another six months in the Clarke Institute of Psychiatry after stabbing an eighteen-year-old female hitchhiker with long blond hair like Stanton's in 1970. Both a former girlfriend and his second wife, Alison, testified at Stark's preliminary hearing that he liked to play "the hitchhiker game," a fantasy of his that required the woman to wait on a country road, where he would pick her up before driving to a secluded spot and "raping" her. Stark was also the primary suspect in the 1981 disappearance and murder of another former lover, thirty-one-year-old Marie Woods, whose body was found five years later north of Toronto. Despite lacking enough evidence to lay a charge in Woods's death, the police, convinced of Stark's guilt in the Stanton case, spent two years on the investigation that led to his arrest. For a while, he was even suspected of having something to do with the murder of Leslie Mahaffy.

Then, precisely a month after Stanton's remains were found, a twenty-eight-year-old man, David West, was out for an evening stroll near an old gravel pit behind his property on Conlins Road, metres from the northern border of the

Scarborough campus, when he stumbled upon what appeared to be a blood-stained cloth and and two blackened bones about ten centimetres long. The bones seemed to have been unearthed by workers who had been digging post holes for a fence being erected around the abandoned muddy pit. What really had some reporters thinking the bones might be Elizabeth Bain's was the fact that West had also found a woman's ripped black shoe a few feet away.

When the bones were assessed as non-human by forensic scientists a few days later, the same reporters were far less enthusiastic about pursuing the story.

At the conclusion of the Bernardo trial, the Crown Law Office sent Brian Greenspan—at his request—previously undisclosed material emanating from the Bernardo investigation; in the envelope were only a few snippets and some seemed to have only the slightest connection to the Baltovich appeal. Greenspan, as always, promptly turned these items over to Brian King. From these documents King learned the particulars of Bernardo witnesses such as Karen McCartney, the employee at the bank where Bernardo was a customer; she had called the police early on to tip them off about his uncanny resemblance to the Scarborough rapist. What no one associated with Baltovich's defence knew until now was that, thirty-three pages into her police statement, McCartney had begun talking about the Elizabeth Bain disappearance. She told the Scarborough rapes investigators that, as a result of Bain's car having been found near the branch where she worked, she had received a call from Mr. Bain some time after his daughter had disappeared. He'd actually come to speak with her in person at the bank, inquiring about surveillance cameras installed in or near the automated bank machine. (Why he would do this remains a bit of a mystery. McCartney worked at a Royal Bank branch a short distance west of Scarborough campus at the corner of Ellesmere and Neilson Road, whereas Liz had withdrawn $80 on the afternoon of her disappearance from a Canadian Imperial Bank of Commerce bank machine at Morningside and Lawrence.) Mr. Bain wondered if the bank might still have the videotape from that day. McCartney said she'd told him their bank machine had no video camera. Of her encounter with Mr. Bain, McCartney also said, "At the time, it was kind of odd. It's the Bain case and then the Scarborough rapist, and they both seemed to be—"

she found herself giggling, partially in embarrassment, at the simplicity of the connection, a connection she knew the police couldn't appear to acknowledge, "concentrated in this one area."

Greenspan also forwarded King the police statement of a young man named Scott Walsh. Walsh, a graduate student in microbiology at the Scarborough campus in November 1993 (his ninth consecutive year at the college) when interviewed, had been a high-school friend of Paul Bernardo's former girlfriend Janine Godsoe, as well as an undergraduate acquaintance of Robert Baltovich's. In fact, prior to Baltovich's trial, King had interviewed Walsh at some length. But Walsh had never told King what he told the police partway through their conversation, which was that Bernardo had a regular table in the cafeteria during his Scarborough campus days, usually with "four or five pretty girls around all the time." There were approximately fifteen tables in the cafeteria, he said, with about five cliques of friends who would "hang out there regularly." Walsh said that he had belonged to the same crowd as Rob Baltovich. "Was Baltovich in the same crowd as Bernardo?" asked one of the officers.

"No," responded Walsh. "But their usual tables were right across from each other. They would have known each other at least to say hi."

Walsh struck this note again at the end of the interview when the officer asked if he had anything further to add. "Well, it would be regarding the Baltovich investigation," said Walsh. "Rob wouldn't do what he was convicted of. When they tied him to Paul, because of their proximity to each other . . . " The officer then interrupted and suggested they "discuss that afterwards," and the interview formally ended.

King had also received disclosure in the form of three statements given to the police by Janine Godsoe. From these documents, King had gleaned that, not only had Godsoe known Bernardo and Elizabeth Bain (both had attended Cardinal Newman High School as girls), but, upon hearing the news about Bain's disappearance, Godsoe had immediately linked it to the man from whom she had fled into the woods of Morningside Park three years earlier. Now that the Bernardo trial was over, and King couldn't be accused of tampering with witnesses, he was eager to speak with Godsoe, as well as the young woman whom Bernardo had, for a time, been dating on the side, Leanne Santiago.

Both women agreed to an interview with King. The session with Santiago, on

October 23, took place two weeks before Godsoe's. From King's perspective, the fact that Santiago was Filipino (having immigrated to Canada with her parents in 1971 at the age of five) was important. When he finally met Santiago, she said she didn't think she bore as much resemblance to Elizabeth Bain as others had claimed. Santiago thought her hair wasn't quite as wavy, but in 1990, her hair had been styled the same way as Bain's appeared in newspaper photographs—long with bangs. She had to admit, though, that her husband felt she shared a great number of similarities with Bain.

King had driven out to Pickering to speak with Santiago during her lunch hour. She continued to work in the accounting field—she was the financial comptroller for a window manufacturer—and had passed her Chartered Accountant exams in 1990. She married the same year and was now the mother of two sons, aged five and two.

King thought Santiago would make an excellent witness. She was cooperative, intelligent and impartial. As they discussed her year-long relationship with Bernardo, three of Santiago's divulgences stood out above the rest, leaving King with the feeling that she would almost certainly play a role in the Baltovich appeal. The first was that on at least two occasions, Bernardo had led Santiago from the main building of the campus down a walkway into Colonel Danforth Park, where they had been intimate in a secluded area near the Principal's Residence (probably a stone's throw from the spot Rob and Liz had spent their last hours together). The second had to do with smoking. Santiago didn't recall Bernardo succumbing to this habit while they were dating, but subsequent to their break-up, she had observed him smoking (she couldn't remember the brand) at a Price Waterhouse training course. And, finally, Santiago disclosed that her first date with Bernardo had taken place at a restaurant near the campus called Malibu's, where, by coincidence, Cathy Bain had once worked. The parking lot in front of Malibu's also happened to be where Tasmin Sheikh had testified seeing Elizabeth Bain in the passenger seat of a Jeep, next to a young man with blond hair sticking out the back of his baseball cap.

King was trying not to get overly worked up about Santiago. How many university-aged Scarborough couples had gone to Colonel Danforth Park to engage in some heavy petting? Or had a date at Malibu's? One had to assume the role of a Crown attorney looking to play these things down as nothing more than meaningless coincidences. King went into his meeting with Janine Godsoe with the same attitude, but was unable to maintain it. What Godsoe had to say was so powerful King felt nothing but pity for the Crown attorney stuck with the job of discrediting her.

It was apparent to King within minutes of his introduction to Godsoe that she bore more of an emotional burden from her relationship with Bernardo than Santiago, which King figured was proportional to the physical and psychological terror inflicted on them. Godsoe said she was a nurse at an old-age home in Guildwood, where Bernardo's parents still lived (as hermetically as possible). She was married now—but refused to provide King with her married name—and she and her husband lived in the house she'd grown up in, along with Godsoe's father, who was a retired officer with the Metro Police Force. Godsoe came right out and told King that she'd inquired about his credentials with the police ahead of time—she wanted to make sure she wasn't being set up by some sleazy reporter.

When Elizabeth Bain had disappeared, said Godsoe, she and the man who would become her husband had been on a two-week trip to northern Ontario. They took the bus back to Toronto from Timmins, and the first thing Godsoe remembered seeing as her feet hit the pavement was a missing poster taped to a bus stop or stapled to a hydro pole. It was hard to accept that someone she knew could just go missing like that. And Godsoe had known Liz from high school and from the church the Bains had attended before St. Joseph's. They were nothing more than casual acquaintances, but Godsoe, the younger of the two by a year, always looked up to her because of her beauty, her athletic abilities and her nice voice.

Godsoe had run into her as recently as two weeks before she disappeared. It was at a Shell gas station. Liz was filling up her car, and Godsoe recalled Mrs. Bain waiting in the passenger seat. Liz was wearing jean shorts that were really flattering, and Godsoe walked up to her and said hello. From the ring Liz had on her finger, Godsoe inquired about her being engaged, and Liz confirmed that this was true. Godsoe said something like *you must be so happy*, and then Liz said *yeah* and turned away from her. Despite Liz's (supposedly) pending marriage, Godsoe thought she looked a bit downhearted, and that her mood was somehow connected to the topic of her engagement. So Godsoe gently advised her that, if she wasn't happy now, things could get worse. But Liz didn't really respond; she just said she had to get going, and they hugged and said take care. Obviously, that was the last time she'd seen her.

The Missing poster, though, had thrown her for a loop, for the instant she'd seen it, her mind flashed back to the night Paul had put the knife to her throat and threatened to kill her, and she thought her legs were about to buckle. She couldn't stop thinking that Paul had something to do with Liz being missing. This feeling, which scared her out of her mind, had her so frightened that she thought she was going crazy. Nevertheless, two days after seeing the poster—either the end of June or early July—Godsoe, accompanied by her fiancé, drove down to 42 Division, where she spoke with an on-duty cadet. When she suggested they investigate her former boyfriend for the Bain disappearance, he merely patronized her and asked in this let's-get-right-to-the-heart-of-what-this-is-really-about way if this had been a recent break-up. Of course, that got her back up and she demanded to be taken seriously, and said he should pick up a pen and start writing some of this stuff down. (Three years later, when interviewed by police regarding the Scarborough rapes, Godsoe recounted this incident—but it couldn't be said that she was taken any more seriously.)

Given what Santiago had said about her trysts with Bernardo in Colonel Danforth Park, King began by asking Godsoe if she had also spent time there with him. Not surprisingly, Godsoe said he'd taken her to the valley where they "would make out and stuff like that." Bernardo liked to study near Highland Creek, she added, either at a picnic table or with his back up against a tree. He would usually park his white Capri in the lot near the tennis courts.

Godsoe also admitted to having a crush on Liz's brother Mark, whom she'd always considered to be a sweet, good-looking guy. For ages, she'd been carrying around an envelope in her purse with Mark's phone number on it, thinking one day she might call him up (if she could ever escape the reality of her situation at the time). Then one day when she was with Bernardo, he wanted her to write down the phone number for the pizza shop Van Smirnis and his brother were operating, so Godsoe pulled the envelope out. Paul immediately saw Mark's name and phone number and began "flipping out." *What the hell are you doing with this other guy's number?* And so on. She tried to explain that it was an old number from grade school. It better be, he said, before making her rip it to pieces right there in front of him.

A little while later, King was asking about the kinds of things Bernardo would keep in his car. Godsoe first mentioned the dagger-like knife he kept under the seat, then the handcuffs she found in the back seat (he had good excuses for both). Next, without any prompting, she told King that she'd once seen him holding a tiny plastic bag smaller than your hand filled with white powder, which, of course, had King's mind locked on to the missing cigarette filter. Not having seen drugs anywhere but on television or in the movies, Godsoe just assumed it was cocaine or heroin. At first, Bernardo's story was that it belonged to a friend, but she didn't believe him, so he tried to convince her it was a big joke, that it was a little bag of icing sugar. He dipped his finger in the bag and touched it to his tongue and said, "Now you try." She refused and said she still didn't believe it was icing sugar, and he started to get that look on his face that meant his mood was taking a turn for the worse. King asked whether this had taken place closer to the beginning or the end of the relationship. The end, said Godsoe, which was precisely what King was hoping to hear.

They continued speaking for quite a while, stopping once so that Godsoe could get a glass of water and some tissues when she momentarily lost her composure. But King eventually brought things to a close, thinking that Godsoe had provided him with much more than he'd expected. With the tape recorder off, they kept discussing things, and it occurred to King that he hadn't asked whether Godsoe was aware of Bernardo and Liz having ever met one another. As soon as she replied, he turned the tape recorder back on.

> KING: This is a continuation of the taped interview with Janine Godsoe commencing at 4:12 PM on November 5, 1996. Janine, we have just had some wrap-up conversation regarding the matter at hand and one of the questions I asked you was whether or not you were familiar with Paul Bernardo and Elizabeth Bain having ever met. Maybe you can just give me your response to that question.
>
> GODSOE: I vaguely remember a church play I was in, a Christmas play. I remember Paul came down to see it and that as we were coming out of the church, Elizabeth passed by, and I introduced them. We all said hi. That was about it. Just passing through.
>
> KING: And that would have been roughly what year?
>
> GODSOE: Uhmmm. Christmas of '85. Really early in the relationship.

The circle had closed. Paul Bernardo and Elizabeth Bain had met. Granted, it was a fleeting encounter five years prior to her disappearance, but King was overcome by the stark implication of the moment. You could just imagine it. Liz peering up at him, doe-eyed and bashful, Bernardo staring back, head bobbing as part of his goofy surfer-boy act, his empty innocent eyes sizing her up like a hawk. As Liz, seeking asylum from his gaze, perhaps not sure of how she looks in her church outfit, slinks to the door in incremental half-steps.

Thinking the interview was finished for good now, King again clicked off the tape recorder. Twenty minutes later, however, the tape was rolling once more.

KING: Janine, we were just talking about different places along Kingston Road and we had some discussion about Chinese restaurants. You mentioned to me one of your favourite places, a place you went with Paul Bernardo. What was the name of it?

GODSOE: Silver Dragon.

KING: And you were there with Paul Bernardo?

GODSOE: Yeah, a few times when we were going out.

KING: Did you ever order out there or was it always eating in?

GODSOE: Most likely eating in.

KING: And what was Paul's reaction to the place?

GODSOE: Paul liked Chinese food, especially there.

—◦—

Earlier in the year, Brian Greenspan had secured a hearing date for the Baltovich appeal on February 3, 1997. But as November neared its end, it seemed the hearing would likely be delayed. The deputy director of the Crown Law Office (Criminal), Carol Brewer, who was handling the Baltovich appeal, was quite obviously frustrated with the lack of disclosure of the fresh-evidence materials she was receiving from Greenspan's office. In a letter to Greenspan dated November 25, Brewer chided him for not abiding by his "personal undertaking" to have "the fresh evidence in this case" provided to her by September 3. Despite a three-week-old indication from Greenspan's colleague on the matter, Lisa Silver, that affidavits from Brian King and Janine Godsoe "would be forthcoming the following week,"

Brewer had not yet received them. Therefore, "notwithstanding the best efforts of everyone involved," Brewer concluded her letter, "the fresh evidence materials (including cross-examination by the parties) cannot be completed prior to the hearing date. Accordingly, the Crown will be bringing an application to have this appeal removed from the list."

(The same day that Brewer composed her letter, an interesting local story was making headlines. A twenty-three-year-old man, Jeremy Foster, had been walking his girlfriend to a bus stop at 9:00 PM on November 16, when several police cars from the York Regional force converged upon them. Within seconds, Foster was being handcuffed and told he was under arrest. The York police had been investigating a string of sexual attacks in the area and they had just received a tip from a passing motorist who had seen Foster walking along the sidewalk, insisting that he was the rapist. Once they had Foster at the station, he not only denied having raped anyone, he also offered to submit to a DNA test and consented to a search of his basement apartment. During the night of his arrest, Foster, an aspiring police officer who was one credit short of a diploma in law enforcement from a nearby community college, failed a polygraph test. By that time, it was seven the next morning, and Foster finally asked to speak to a lawyer. The police denied that request, Foster later told the press, and they wouldn't let him go to sleep either. Having purposely laced his police statement with false details that would never bear scrutiny in a court of law, Foster eventually confessed. "I just held my breath and said, 'I did it,' just once," he announced at a press conference a week later. "It was a dull, aching feeling, I kicked myself as soon as I did it. But it had to end. I had no food, no sleep and no lawyer. The only way I felt I could speak to a lawyer was if I told them what they wanted." Despite the confession and the polygraph results, Foster was released from the Metro East Detention Centre after being detained for a week, when the Centre of Forensic Sciences determined that Foster's DNA did not match samples taken from two of the rapist's victims. Foster's lawyer, Edward Sapiano, who was ultimately contacted by Foster's girlfriend, insisted that the only reason his client didn't have to spend the usual eight or nine months behind bars awaiting the test results was because of the intense media coverage surrounding his arrest, which had speeded up the process. One of the reporters at the press conference subsequent to his release asked Foster if he still wanted to be a police officer. Foster stunned the room when he responded by saying that solving problems and helping people were his real goals, and that he still felt he could achieve both wearing a police uniform.)

Carol Brewer and Brian Greenspan appeared before Chief Justice Roy McMurtry on Friday, December 7. Both lawyers agreed that there were certain difficulties with meeting the scheduled February 3 appeal date, although the request for a postponement had originated from the Crown. Lawyer Gary Trotter, representing the Crown before the Chief Justice that day, said more time was needed to properly deal with the volume and complexity of the fresh evidence. Trotter characterized the police investigation into Paul Bernardo's potential involvement in the Bain disappearance as one of the longest and most intense investigations ever conducted. McMurtry then asked Trotter how long the Crown felt it needed, and Trotter replied, vaguely, "I think a number of days."

In his article about the proceedings in the next day's *Globe and Mail*, Thomas Claridge reiterated Trotter's announcement that the court would be receiving affidavits from Reesor and Raybould "in response to allegations that they concealed the existence of a witness whose evidence, if accepted, would have exonerated Mr. Baltovich." Although he contained it to a single paragraph, Claridge finally had the opportunity to recount his own involvement in the emergence of Keith Nobrega— "The existence of the witness came to light in June when he told a Globe and Mail reporter of having seen a terrified Ms. Bain being driven in her car along Highway 401 toward Oshawa. . . ."

In the end, McMurtry had no choice but to remove the case from the list. Greenspan said he would be available in early April and that if a longer postponement was necessary he might ask the appeal court to consider releasing his client pending the appeal.

—◯—

KILLER 'GRASPS AT STRAWS'
By Michele Mandel

December 8, 1996—It is the last Christmas present she received from her daughter and it still grows in their Scarborough home.

Seven years have passed since her beloved Elizabeth (Lisa) Bain was murdered, her body never found, only memories and photos and a sole pink cyclamen that still lives on.

"Christmas was her favorite," Julita Bain recalled softly yesterday from the home where Lisa left one day in June 1990 and never returned. "*He* was here with her for a Christmas party that last Christmas. Oh yes," she adds bitterly, "he was treated like one of the family."

And now *he*, Robert Baltovich, the boyfriend now doing life for killing her daughter, reaches out from his prison cell to try and fool them once more. To try and make them and the world believe that he didn't murder Bain, that it was really schoolgirl killer Paul Bernardo who did the evil deed.

But this mother will not be deceived again.

"That's garbage," she says vehemently. "They're playing this dirty game, but it's him. I'm 100% sure he is the one. He's just grasping at straws."

She was writing Christmas cards and listening to the radio Friday when the news came and there was her daughter's name and his name, too, making her heart stop for a moment, making her pen drop. The Crown was admitting that new evidence had surfaced which may clear Baltovich and implicate Bernardo.

Since Bernardo's arrest and conviction, Baltovich's lawyers have hinted their appeal would rest on their belief that a blond man was the real killer. But Friday, Baltovich's appeal was postponed indefinitely after the Crown admitted it now needs more time to assess these new affidavits implicating Bernardo.

"This is old news," Bain's mother insists. "He's just trying to find someone to blame it on. He can deny it all his life. What we know is what we know.

"It's upsetting, but I learned to put a shield around me so it doesn't hurt. I know we'll be hearing about this time and time again throughout our lives. There's nothing we can do."

She knows that he cares not a whit about how it affects her family. "He's a psychopath. Nothing bothers him." So eloquently she speaks, so calmly. She will not allow him to disturb the peace she has fought hard to maintain. She and her husband have clung together through their tragedy, unlike other couples—such as the parents of slain Leslie Mahaffy—who have been unable to withstand their heartbreak.

"This world is full of sadness and happiness at the same time. It's up to the person to choose which you're going to keep in your life. I could go crazy with grief and end up in a psychiatric institution, but what would it serve? You go on with your life."

So she has taken early retirement from her nursing job and joined her retired husband in travelling, going often to their place in Florida.

Many have asked her why they haven't moved away from all the terrible memories and the news stories that still torture them. But they do not understand.

When Baltovich's appeal is finally heard, they must be there. "If they're talking about my daughter, I want to be there. I think that's really the reason behind our staying here, it's just me and my husband in this big house. But who's going to speak for her if we're gone, too?"

Her three other children have moved away now and she believes they are, in part, running from their pain.

Two of them now live in British Columbia, another in Michigan.

But Lisa, Lisa is always with her, she says. There is no grave to visit, but she rests in a corner of her mother's heart. At peace. And where there is no room left for the slightest doubt as to who stole her away.

"He's a very arrogant s.o.b. who, of course, wants to come out," Bain says. "But as far as I'm concerned, he should be there. And he should rot there."

There is Christmas shopping now to do. And so she leaves with a glance at the table, where a pink cyclamen still blooms.

THE TORONTO SUN

—◦—

Rob called home the day that Brian Greenspan had gone to court. It was dinner-time, and his mother was flipping from one local evening newscast to another, try-ing to find out what was going on. Then, on CFTO, Adele saw Greenspan speaking to a handful of reporters in front of the courthouse, and she cranked the volume up with the remote so Rob could listen through the receiver. She was about to ask if he could hear all right, but then Rob started blurting out little comments over the line every time the newsreader got the facts mixed up.

CFTO-TV, voice of news anchor Tom Gibney, December 8, 1996:

. . . Brian Greenspan is appealing the murder conviction of Robert Bal-tovich. The University of Toronto student [*Actually, I'd graduated*] has been in a maximum-security [*No, medium-security*] prison since he was convicted of killing his girlfriend Elizabeth Bain in March of 1992. Her body was never found but brain matter found in the back seat of her car was matched to the young woman [*Brain matter? Oh, my god, they've got Billy Mackinlay working in the research department*]. . . .

Greenspan did not want to talk about the evidence. . . . He says he's not trying to convict Bernardo, he just wants his client freed.

Baltovich was convicted on evidence that Bain wanted to end the rela-tionship and that after her death, he ripped pages from her diary in which she called him "possessive" and "crazy" [*Yeah, and so is the person who wrote this*] . . .

—◦—

In early July, when Brian Greenspan sent off a terse letter requesting full disclosure of information related to the statement of Keith Nobrega—six years after the fact—those involved in launching the Baltovich appeal had no way of predicting how the Crown Law Office was going to react. Whether it was the fault of the police, or the police and the Crown together, someone had been caught with their pants down and an interesting dance of ass-covering and buck-passing was sure to follow. It took a month for the Crown to make its first musical selection.

It came in the form of a letter to Greenspan, dated August 9, 1996, from Carol Brewer, the deputy director of the Crown Law Office, who was also one of the lawyers handling the Baltovich appeal. Brewer had not yet ascertained why the statement had not been disclosed but assured him that the matter was being looked into. For the time being, however, she was sending Greenspan a duplicate of the statement, as well as copies of the supplementary police report related to Nobrega's interview and Raybould's notes on the matter.

Brewer didn't offer anything more on Nobrega until a letter to Greenspan in mid-October, in which she wrote: "With respect to your earlier inquiry about disclosure of the statement of Keith Nobrega, I am advised that while the statement was not formally disclosed to defence counsel at trial, it was in the police investigative file, which defence counsel were invited to review." When contacted, both Bill Gatward and Mike Engel balked at Brewer's insinuation and both prepared affidavits stating that such an offer was never made. Brewer's attempt at shifting the blame was, indeed, a lame one.

Among his files, Brian King had kept a copy of a letter Engel had sent to John McMahon on December 16, 1991, in the weeks prior to Baltovich's trial. Engel listed twelve different sets of items he required "to properly prepare" for his client's defence. Item six read: "All details and particulars of any alleged sightings of Elizabeth Bain that were brought to the attention of Det. Raybould or any member of his team since the onset of this investigation." King didn't quite understand how Raybould and the others could hand over dozens of inconsequential statements by people who saw everything from Liz Bain wearing a blond wig in Trenton to savouring a handout meal at the Scott Mission, and then overlook Nobrega. Reesor and Raybould had been thorough enough to go to the press with a still undisclosed psychological profile of the killer courtesy of the FBI and had, two months before Baltovich's arrest, tried to make him sweat by announcing that they had news of a witness who saw Bain's abductor park her car on Morrish Road the morning after she'd gone missing (contradicting the theory subsequently put forward). To suggest that Nobrega had been lost in the shuffle was ludicrous.

Within days of reading Brewer's latest letter, Brian King, with the help of Manny Acacio, began the process of investigating Nobrega's story. One of the first people contacted was the assistant manager at Nobrega's Toronto bank branch. Presumably, the bank would have a record of his transactions on or around June 19, 1990. After almost two months of searching, the assistant manager, Carol Kennedy, called in mid-December to inform Acacio that she'd been able to retrieve Nobrega's records from one of their local warehouses. Specifically, Kennedy had in her hands a withdrawal slip made out for $600 by Keith Nobrega on June 19, 1990. As soon as Acacio provided the bank with a signed authorization from Mr. Nobrega, Kennedy explained, they could have a copy of it. Acacio was ecstatic. Kennedy then told him he was lucky to have inquired when he did, as it was bank policy to destroy all records after seven years.

Acacio also located Donna Lucas, the bartender whom Nobrega recalled serving him at O'Toole's on June 19. Lucas confirmed that, from 1987 until just a few months ago, she had worked at O'Toole's. What Nobrega had said about her schedule was true—her regular weekly shift was Tuesday, Friday and Saturday nights. (Unfortunately, Lucas's boss had not kept records pertaining to scheduling, only total hours worked and amounts paid, and could not confirm Lucas's presence on June 19, 1990.)

Similarly, Nobrega's former employer kept records of hours worked but not of specific shift times. Still, Acacio wanted to confirm what Nobrega had said about his flexible work hours. After some effort, he reached a man named Bruce Zavitz at the General Motors plant in Oshawa. Zavitz had been one of Nobrega's supervisors at the plant (although it was for a time prior to 1990), where Zavitz was still employed. When asked about the likelihood of Nobrega working in the evening, Zavitz explained that contract designers such as Nobrega were allowed to attend work pretty well anytime and, therefore, it wouldn't have been unusual for them to be at the plant in the late afternoon or evening hours.

It was December 23 by the time Acacio met Nobrega to have him sign the form authorizing the bank to release a copy of his withdrawal slip (to the best of his recollection, Nobrega thought the $600 was to pay his rent), which Acacio had in his possession an hour later. Back at King-Reed later that afternoon, Acacio got a call from Gerhardt Hinz, whom he'd been trying to track down for quite some time. Through Hinz's ex-wife, he'd been given the name of a motel in a part of Barrie known as "Gasoline Alley" where Hinz had apparently been living for about a year. Hinz, in his gruff German accent, said that he remembered Nobrega well from his days at O'Toole's in Oshawa. Did Hinz recall Nobrega talking about a troubling incident on the 401 back in 1990? Not only was it a long time ago, stressed Hinz, Nobrega "talked a lot," and Hinz had a tendency to block out his voice when he rambled on. So, yes, it was possible that Nobrega had told him the story—he just retained no memory of it.

—◯—

Having covered all bases on the Keith Nobrega file two days before Christmas, Brian King didn't expect to get embroiled in another investigation related to the Baltovich appeal for at least another month or two. But that presumption evaporated at precisely 10:00 on January 2, 1997, his first morning back in the office after the Christmas holidays. The receptionist buzzed King over the intercom and informed him that there was a man on the line who refused to identify himself but insisted he had important information to pass on about the Baltovich case.

Without delay, King picked up the line and found himself talking to a man with a distinguished voice who disclosed at once that he was familiar with David Dibben and his family. In a letter King would write to Brian Greenspan outlining the content of his conversation with this anonymous caller, King described him as being "somewhat cryptic" as a result of his reluctance to become "personally involved in this matter." "In any event," King wrote for Greenspan, "without coming right out and saying it, the caller indicated that David Dibben's testimony about the man driving Elizabeth Bain's car was not accurate. I was able to tell from the conversation that the information he has obtained comes from family members and friends as opposed to David Dibben himself. A 'bizarre set of circumstances' has come to light, he declared repeatedly. He implied that Dibben's testimony was not only inaccurate but probably made up entirely and that Dibben came forward due to the publicity and feeling of importance he got from being interviewed by the various people involved. The source indicated he knew of David Dibben's characteristics and that he had testified at Baltovich's trial, but the caller did not understand the importance of Dibben's testimony until he'd read the recent media coverage about the appeal. He had been unaware, for instance, that Dibben had identified Robert Baltovich as the man driving Elizabeth Bain's car subsequent to her disappearance despite his conflicting earlier statement, in which he described the man as having 'blond' hair. Various family members are now concerned about the fact that it was David Dibben's testimony that put Baltovich in jail. The caller said he has had trouble sleeping at night lately knowing that an innocent man is serving a life sentence."

King was unaware at this point that Brian Greenspan's law-firm partner, David Humphrey, had taken a similar call on December 27 from a man who, at first, was reluctant to identify himself, but when pressed, gave his name as John Wilson. Both callers, presumably the same man, were concerned about Dibben's wife and three children in the event that Dibben was eventually found guilty of perjury. Dibben's wife, Shelley, was a good person, insisted the caller, and didn't deserve such hardship. Both King and Humphrey wondered independently if Dibben had begun to question his testimony after seeing photographs of Paul Bernardo, and that perhaps Dibben had mistakenly identified Baltovich as opposed to intentionally lying. The caller insisted this wasn't the case, and that Dibben had made up his testimony, helped by the fact, King noted, "that there was undue influence by one of the police officers involved which led to the evolution of Dibben's story regarding Baltovich." At the end of his conversation with King, the caller said it was his intention to canvass a number of Dibben's family members on his own before calling King back in a few days to update him on his progress.

Instead of days, however, King didn't hear from this most intriguing but elusive caller until mid-February. (King had not yet begun investigating the anonymous Dibben allegations, as he thought it best to wait until the caller had made his own inquiries—still, King hadn't been willing to wait too much longer.) Having learned of the "John Wilson" call to David Humphrey in the interim, King now asked if this was, indeed, the man's name. He admitted it was not. This time, John Doe (as King was now referring to him) suggested that King contact Julie Battersby, David Dibben's sister-in-law, her husband, Tom, as well as two other siblings of Dibben's wife, Sally and Keith Spalton.

Ironically, the same day that John Doe was on the phone with Brian King, David Dibben called Brian Raybould to complain that his wife's uncle, a man named Ian Hood, had been calling various family members and saying that he had given false evidence at the Baltovich trial. Raybould, in response to Dibben's request for assistance with the out-of-control uncle, called him. When Raybould asked Hood why Dibben would invent such a story, Hood replied by suggesting that the entire family be investigated. But when Raybould pressed him for further details, Hood said, "I don't want to be involved." He told Raybould that he was going to change his telephone number and that was the end of the conversation.

When typing up his report on the matter, Raybould concluded with this: "Dibben advised that this was not the first time Hood had made strange statements. On a previous occasion, this uncle had tried to interject himself and/or other family members into the investigation of several sexual assaults which had occurred in a community up north. Hood had told family members at that time that there could be money made if they were to do so."

John Doe called Brian King on March 14 to find out what he had been able to accomplish since their last conversation. King said not much, which was the truth. Then King asked John Doe if he was aware of Ian Hood having been contacted by the Metropolitan Toronto Police, as King had already seen Raybould's report. Doe said he hadn't heard anything about that. He did say, though, that Hood should have known about "Dibben's lies" through his daughter, Patricia Hood, who had apparently heard Dibben admit to fabricating his evidence. The family was beginning to fracture into two camps, John Doe said, those willing to lie to protect Dibben in one corner and everyone else in the other. When it came right down to it, though, the caller didn't think even those positioning themselves in the former group would go as far as lying under oath if subpoenaed.

King decided that the best strategy was to question the various family members John Doe had named in as short a period of time as possible. Unavailable to take the assignment himself, King handed the job over to Ted Harpur, a retired detective from the Metro police force whom King had recently hired. Over the course of a week, Harpur introduced himself to four of Dibben's in-laws. Two of the relatives claimed they simply didn't know Dibben that well (and certainly hadn't heard him make any comments denouncing his testimony), and the other two were uncooperative. "It is obvious," Harpur observed in his report for Brian King, "that what has happened is that the family are all rallying around David Dibben and refusing to be interviewed."

One of the next doors Harpur knocked on was Ian Hood's, the man he and King believed to be their John Doe caller. It was, without question, the strangest encounter Harpur had had thus far on the Dibben file. A woman opened the door and told Harpur that Mr. Hood was not at home. So Harpur left a business card and started off down the front drive to his car, when an enormous man, well over two hundred pounds by Harpur's estimation, called out to him from the doorway. It was Ian Hood.

Hood was certainly acting a little strange—he refused to be taped and prohibited Harpur from even making notes. Right away, Harpur picked up on his emotional intensity, how the conviction of Robert Baltovich distressed him to the extent that some nights he didn't sleep. Despite Hood's concern for Baltovich's plight,

Harpur was not impressed with his stock as a witness of any value to the defence at Baltovich's appeal. "We now know for sure that Ian Hood is our John Doe caller," Harpur concluded in his report, "and has a history of making similar calls to the authorities on previous occasions. As a result, we can write him off as a possible witness or a useful source of information."

While this was likely a fair assessment of Hood, Harpur hadn't yet lost all hope, as Hood agreed to help arrange a meeting the following morning with his daughter, Patricia, who was a cousin to Dibben's wife, Shelley. Patricia seemed to represent King's final hope insofar as she was the last family member who might have heard Dibben's alleged recantation firsthand. Given the potential impact she could have on the appeal, it was Brian King, not Ted Harpur, who drove downtown to meet her, along with her newborn baby, at a restaurant near the intersection of Bloor and Sherbourne Streets.

Patricia Hood told King she was thirty-two years old and was finishing off her studies in "multimedia" at Seneca College. She was living in a government-subsidized apartment complex a short distance south on Sherbourne with her husband, a musician who was playing overseas for a few months. King was writing down the particulars when, suddenly, a very large man approached them from where he'd been sitting at a neighbouring table and introduced himself as Patricia's "adviser," which she responded to by rolling her eyes and saying, "Oh, Dad." It was Ian Hood again.

Patricia was full of concerns. She did not want her name released to the media and requested that she be notified by Brian Greenspan's office before details related to her statement were handed over to the Crown Attorney's office. And, like her father, she was hoping to meet Robert Baltovich in prison, just to see what kind of person he was. While this could be arranged, King assured her, he didn't think it was a wise move if she wanted to maintain full credibility as a witness.

With that settled, King finally got down to the business of what she remembered David Dibben saying about the driver of Elizabeth Bain's car. Patricia recounted how she'd been at a family gathering at the home of her aunt, Marlene Spalton (who had refused to be interviewed by Harpur), in 1990. A group was gathered in the kitchen (she refused to name anyone specifically) looking at a photograph of Elizabeth Bain's boyfriend on an inside page of *The Sunday Sun*. She told King that she could, to this day, picture the entire clipping in her "mind's eye as if it was yesterday." And that was when Dibben announced that he'd seen the car with the fingers on the door. "First, David told me that the car was coming from the opposite direction," Patricia told King, who had his tape recorder on the table between them. "Then I asked how he could have seen the fingers if it was coming from the opposite direction. He said, 'No, I mean I pulled up at the lights and the guy pulled up alongside of me and I saw the fingers.' I said, 'Did you see the guy?' He said, 'No, I couldn't.' So I said, 'Too bad, because you could have made some money from Crime Stoppers.' He said, 'How much money?' I said, 'Fifteen hundred dollars at least.'"

"What was his reaction to that?" asked King.

"His eyes kind of lit up," she answered. "I believe he was having some financial difficulties at the time."

"Do you think there are other family members who recall hearing that conversation?"

"Everybody was there," she insisted. "The table was filled with people." Still, she wouldn't identify anyone.

King asked if she'd spoken to Dibben about this incident since then. She said they had, but didn't want to discuss it while the tape recorder was on. (Afterwards, however, she told King that, a few weeks ago, Tom Battersby, a brother-in-law of Dibben's, had invited her down to his silkscreening shop to discuss some T-shirts he was printing for an upcoming family reunion. When Patricia arrived at the store, she spoke to Battersby for a few moments when, all of a sudden, David Dibben emerged from the back room and approached them. He wanted to know what she had said to the police, and he began accusing her father of all kinds of things. She was scared out of her wits and was sure that she had been lured to the store for the sole purpose of this confrontation. This, Patricia explained, is why she wanted anonymity. Dibben, in her opinion, was a "biker wannabe," and she felt it wasn't beyond him to hurt her child in retaliation for coming forward like this.)

"Has the content of David Dibben's testimony ever been brought to your attention?" asked King.

"Somebody told me that David said he'd seen the guy in the car," she answered. "But this was very recently. In the last few weeks. And it has really bothered me quite a bit."

"Okay," King said. "Is there any doubt in your mind with respect to the conversation you had several years ago where David Dibben said that he did not see the driver?"

"No, there's no doubt in my mind whatsoever. That is what he said. He said he did not see the driver. I said, too bad because you could have made some money."

"My understanding," said King, "is that this whole affair has caused some family problems."

"Oh, my God, yeah. Our family is finished. Let's just face it. If it wasn't for my conscience and the feelings inside my heart, I wouldn't be dragging my family through this murk and quagmire. But I just can't avoid saying what I know because I think it's terrible that he has put this guy in jail for life to make a few bucks."

—◦—

In early March, a month before Ted Harpur embarked on his search for David Dibben's in-laws, Brian King was fastidiously clipping articles about a high-profile court case from each of the three Toronto newspapers. Dr. George Matheson, the psychologist whom the police had used for hypnotizing Crown witnesses in the Baltovich case and many others, was now himself in the defendant's chair, facing two charges of sexual assault stemming from complaints filed with the College of Psychologists of Ontario by two former patients. The complaints had already led to Matheson, forty-eight at the time of his trial, having been stripped of his licence to practice psychology in Ontario in May 1993. Even so, his former patients, worried that he might still be able to work as an unlicensed therapist elsewhere, went to the police.

According to their testimony, both women had been suffering from acute depression when they sought therapy from Matheson. The first woman to take the witness stand said that her depression was the result of having been sexually abused as a child over an extended period of time by a family friend. It was her husband, a doctor, who had suggested that hypnotism might be more useful than psychotherapy.

About three months after her first session with Matheson in March of 1992, she was beginning to feel aroused by the way he was touching her shoulder or knee with his hands and how, later, this progressed to mutual embracing and fondling, with her often sitting on his lap. Next thing the woman knew, she said, "We stood up, took off our clothes and had sex on the floor of his office." From then on, she claimed, they alternated between therapy sessions in the office and sex at his apartment. When the woman finally came to realize that the relationship with her "therapist" was doing infinitely more harm than good, she stopped seeing him and attempted to recover almost all of the $5,000 her husband had paid Matheson for his "services." Matheson put up little resistance and granted her the near-refund but not before she had secretly taped two of their telephone conversations, during which she insisted that she "never would have done what I did if you hadn't started touching me."

"I know," responded Matheson.

"I didn't go to you for sex. I went to you for therapy."

Again, all Matheson could say was "I know."

The second former patient to testify had gone to Matheson in 1987 when she had found herself "devastated and suicidal" after she lost her job. A year and a half later, she and Matheson were having sex in her house when her husband was out of town, and subsequently in his office during therapy sessions as well. Even when the therapy sessions ended in February of 1989, their sexual relationship continued until one day in September 1993, when the witness discovered Matheson in bed with a female psychologist.

It was the contention of the Crown prosecutor, James Ramsey, that Matheson had used his authority as a psychologist to force the two women into sex. The final Crown witness was Gail Robinson, a Toronto psychologist specializing in issues surrounding patient-therapist misconduct. Robinson made it clear that "a therapist has an absolute obligation to resist advances from his patients," regardless of the feelings the patient professes, for therapists are trained to assess such emotions as the probable result of a "transference of feeling." A therapist "has a great deal of power," Robinson testified, "which he can use to obtain the illusion of consent."

Robinson's testimony proved crucial, as the judge presiding over the case (Matheson's was trial by judge alone) cited the inherent imbalance of power between therapist and patient while delivering his day-long judgment. "He [Matheson] held the power and had it by a significant degree. He had the professional status to gain and hold on to the power over the alleged victims, who were vulnerable to it," said Mr. Justice George Ferguson, eventually pronouncing Matheson guilty on both counts. Judge Ferguson sentenced Matheson to serve two years in a federal penitentiary, but Matheson was released on bail, pending an appeal.

King, along with Brian Greenspan, knew that Matheson's conviction was good news for the Baltovich appeal. In his appellant's factum, Greenspan had already argued against the admissibility of the hypnotically "enhanced" identification evidence led at Baltovich's trial. Greenspan was of the opinion that, as an investigative technique, hypnosis could not be "empirically tested" and was, furthermore, a controversial procedure "viewed by some experts as unreliable." To help Greenspan's cause, the credibility of the hypnotist in question had been diminished to microscopic proportions. If the appeal court were to grant Baltovich a new trial, the Crown would be taking a sizable risk recalling Matheson as their hypnosis expert—which the Crown would have to do if it wanted to make any use whatsoever of key witnesses like Marianne Perz and Susanne Nadon.

George Matheson was not the only member of the Crown's core group of witnesses at the Baltovich trial to experience a dose of public humiliation (although his was, by a considerable margin, the most costly). Exactly a year and a half before Matheson's trial, on December 1, 1995, *The Toronto Star* broke the story about the selection of Steve Reesor (now Staff Inspector) as the Metropolitan Toronto Police Force's newest deputy chief. Since leading "the team that sent Robert Baltovich . . . to jail for life," the *Star* noted, Reesor had spent three years as the force's internal audit director and was currently commanding 23 Division in Etobicoke. Only forty-two years of age, Reesor had spent half his life on the force and was, if the *Star*'s sources were to be relied upon, about to become the youngest deputy chief in Toronto history.

Reesor's appointment was not without controversy. Many of his colleagues across the city found him abrasive and arrogant, and it was generally expected that the vacant deputy's position would go to Wayne Oldham, the superintendent in charge of Metro's emergency task force unit and considered to be a top-notch investigator. At least one of Reesor's fellow officers was so incensed by the promotion that he launched a smear campaign, which included anonymous telephone calls and the mailing of certain police documents to various members of the media, as well as to the police services board, which had reportedly just selected Reesor from a field of eight candidates.

Rosie DiManno, a columnist for the *Star*, wrote about the campaign against Reesor almost two weeks before he was officially appointed deputy chief. Squelching any mystery as to whose side she was on, DiManno wrote, "Reesor, claim the jackals, is a wife-beater. There is, the letter [from the 'jackals'] further suggests, an internal affairs report on one particular assault, albeit no conviction." It was further disclosed by DiManno that the police services board had "also received, anonymously, a six-page occurrence report from a 1994 incident in which ambulance and police responded to a 911 call at Reesor's home."

Needless to say, the police services board, trying to avoid an embarrassing scandal, called Reesor back onto the carpet to explain himself. "In his meeting with the board," DiManno reported, "Reesor explained the 911 incident. He said he had been at home with his wife and had fainted while exercising. This was a few months after his own father had died suddenly of a heart attack. Reesor's wife, alarmed, called 911. Both ambulance and police responded. There was no indication on the occurrence report of any domestic dispute."

With no reason to disbelieve Reesor, the board stuck to its selection. While relieved, Reesor told DiManno in an interview that he was "horribly embarrassed." She wrote: "His primary concern, he told the *Star*, is that the smear campaign directed at him personally might besmirch the reputation of the force. 'It might be one or two people, out of 7,000,' he pointed out. 'This hurts me personally. But I'm proud of our police service. And I'm worried that this might bring a certain amount of discredit to police. I don't want to see any disgrace come to them.' "

The following spring, about a month before the Baltovich appeal became news, Reesor's old partner, Brian Raybould, was named executive officer of Metro's Operational Support Command—the branch responsible for field services such as the mounted and canine units, the public order unit and marine unit, as well as the communications, video, traffic, court and community services—which was now under Reesor's domain as deputy chief. For the first time since Baltovich's conviction four years ago, Raybould and Reesor were working together again, and Raybould was pleased as could be at the way things had fallen into place.

Now and again, when Elizabeth Bain or Baltovich were in the news, Raybould made it his policy to discuss the case with reporters whenever he had the opportunity, for it was his belief that, the longer the press stayed with the story, the greater the chance that a switch would suddenly click in Baltovich's conscience, causing him to come clean and confess to the authorities where he'd hidden the body. Then the Bains could finally give their daughter her long-overdue Christian burial. During one such interview over the phone with *Saturday Night* magazine in February 1996, Raybould conceded that the circumstantial evidence against Baltovich was complex. While "any one piece of evidence can be written off," Raybould said, finishing his thought with a show of antithetical logic, it "must be viewed in its totality . . . The only normal thing about Baltovich," Raybould added, "was his abnormality."

Even though the testimony Raybould had given at Baltovich's trial about the Scarborough rapist not being an abductor or a murderer turned out to be wrong—and though, as the Baltovich defence team would soon discover, Raybould's signature appeared at the end of Keith Nobrega's undisclosed police statement—Raybould remained convinced that Robert Baltovich was a cold-blooded killer. Faced with the possibility of a second trial, Raybould said to *Saturday Night*, "The next time you're talking to Rob, tell him I'm still waiting for him to give us the body back so we can work out a deal." Raybould gave a good chuckle. "If we had capital punishment," he said, suddenly getting more serious, "I'd take the guy out against a wall and shoot him and not feel bad about it."

The fact that Raybould's ill-advised venting of his true feelings was never strenuously protested—at least not publicly—could perhaps be construed as a sign of the times. When the quote appeared in print the following October, confidence in policing was at an all-time low in southern Ontario. In July, Mr. Justice Archie Campbell had released his 473-page report on the way the Metro and Niagara Regional Police forces had gone about their investigations into the crimes ultimately attributed to Paul Bernardo. In some instances, Campbell simply reiterated what many Canadians already knew—one such example being that Leslie Mahaffy and Kristen French would still be alive if Bernardo's DNA samples hadn't fallen into a "black hole" at the Centre of Forensic Sciences for more than two years. In other areas of his report, though, Campell reconstructed how Bernardo's capture was also delayed by ego clashes and petty turf possessiveness between police forces, as well as what he called "a dangerous lack of coordination."

And then there was the well-known story of Guy Paul Morin, who had been wrongly prosecuted for and convicted of the murder of his nine-year-old neighbour, Christine Jessop, who had been abducted from her home in the village of Queensville, Ontario, fifty kilometres north of Toronto, on October 3, 1984. Her partly skeletal remains were found in a remote field just west of the southern tip of Lake Scugog three months later. Similar to the Baltovich case, Morin was arrested six months later, once the police had built what they felt to be a strong circumstantial case. At Morin's first trial in 1986, he was acquitted, but the Crown successfully appealed the verdict and was granted a second crack at him in 1992. The second trial did not go as well for Morin as the first, the result of a number of complex legal factors; this time, the jury found him guilty. He subsequently spent six months in Kingston Penitentiary before being released on bail pending appeal (during his ten-year-and-counting ordeal, which began when Morin was in his early twenties, he was incarcerated for a total of sixteen months). Awaiting the appeal, several forensic experts were of the opinion that DNA testing had advanced to the point that semen samples left on Christine Jessop's underwear—which had, so far, produced inconclusive results—might now be decipherable. Tests conducted at a Boston laboratory by three scientists selected by both the defence and the Crown revealed that the semen did not belong to Morin. Within days, Morin was officially acquitted at the Ontario Court of Appeal.

Two years later, on January 24, 1997, Morin, now thirty-seven, and his elderly parents, who'd spent their life savings on their son's defence, received a full apology, in addition to a $1.25-million compensation package from the Ontario government, as well as the government-commissioned inquiry into his wrongful conviction already under way. (Morin's compensation deal was the largest ever awarded in Canada. In another well-known case, Donald Marshall, a Nova Scotia man who spent eleven years in prison for a murder he did not commit, received $700,000 under an annuity plan that will total $1 million should he live to age sixty-five. Susan Nelles, the nurse accused of killing four infants at the Hospital for Sick Children in Toronto, was awarded $60,000 in 1991—in addition to the $290,000 in legal fees the government had compensated her for previously—almost a decade after the charges against her had been dismissed.)

The Toronto news was rife with stories about "dirty" cops and bad police work. In November of 1996, a month-long trial pitted a pair of officers who'd pled guilty to planting crack cocaine on a suspect against two of their former colleagues, who claimed innocence. "The trial judge," wrote a reporter with *The Globe and Mail*, "frequently wore a troubled look as he listened to a police witness sworn to tell the truth, the whole truth and nothing but the truth give evidence that contradicted what he'd just heard from another officer." In the midst of such confusion, the jury found the officers not guilty.

"Innocent man free after 7 years in jail" was a front-page headline on the February 8, 1997, edition of *The Toronto Star*. The man, who could not be identified by court order, had gone to prison at age twenty-seven when he was convicted of multiple counts of sexual assault and uttering a threat at a 1990 jury trial. The next year he was declared a dangerous offender, which meant that, like Paul Bernardo, he faced the possibility of life-long incarceration. When the woman whom he was convicted of assaulting—the *Star* reported she suffered from "a mental disability"—later went to the police to admit she had accused the wrong man, the police responded by telling her "she could be charged with public mischief if she withdrew her complaint."

Two months later, Metro's Special Investigations Unit was called upon to probe an incident involving the stake-out of a stolen vehicle in a strip-joint parking lot in which one cop was run over and another cop was injured by a "friendly fire" bullet intended for the bad guys, all three of whom were arrested. While, initially, the SIU was called to look into the shooting, it discovered along the way that a local television cameraman had captured part of the arrest scene on tape. Once the SIU had obtained its own copy through a search warrant served to the television station, its investigators watched firsthand how one uniformed officer karate-chopped the neck of a handcuffed suspect who was offering no resistance as he was being escorted to a police cruiser. The tape also captured another suspect as he lay on the ground, face down, his hands cuffed behind his back. Two uniformed officers on either side of him seemed about to help him to his feet when into the picture stormed a plain-clothes officer in a blue overcoat, thrusting his right foot into the suspect's neck.

In a column about the fallout of these tape-recorded acts titled "Cops and media a little too cozy"—an ironic suggestion, considering that it appeared in *The Toronto Sun*, the closest thing the city had to a police blotter—Christie Blatchford wrote an account of what happened after the prone men felt the weight of the officer's shoe against his throat:

> At this point a second plainclothes officer . . . runs into the picture, and it is here where I find the second disturbing aspect of this story, which is the comfort level the police in this city enjoy with the media.

This officer then faces the camera and shouts, "Cut it off! Cut it off!" At which point, the cameraman appears to put the camera on the ground. . . .

Not surprisingly, the Metro police were contesting the SIU's involvement in the investigation of these apparent demonstrations of excessive force. During a press conference, Metro police spokesperson Mike Sale explained that the force usually dealt with allegations of police brutality on its own. Reading between the lines, this meant that Metro was of the opinion that the SIU had perhaps overstepped the parameters of its probe into the accidental shooting. When asked by reporters if the police chief had told the SIU to "butt out" of the brutality investigation, Sale said that the chief, David Boothby, was on vacation. Second, Sale said, the acting chief— who was none other than Steve Reesor, a reliable sign that he was being groomed for the job—and the head of the SIU had engaged in "a keen discussion" on the matter. In other words, the entire affair was reminiscent of the ego clashes and turf competition that Judge Archie Campbell had denounced in his now nine-month-old report.

—◦—

From the very beginning, Brian King had always been willing to give the Homicide cops the benefit of the doubt. Even with Keith Nobrega, he didn't want to automatically assume that Reesor and Raybould had intentionally concealed the statement of such an important witness to Baltovich's defence. But now he was really starting to wonder.

At about the same time that Nobrega had come forward to the defence, the police had been contacted by one member of a five-person group from whom they had taken statements in 1990, only a week after Elizabeth Bain's disappearance. These statements, like Nobrega's, had never been disclosed to Gatward and Engel prior to or during Baltovich's trial. King might have been able to forgive the oversight if what they'd had to say was inconsequential, but when Greenspan sent over copies of the 1990 police reports, King was outraged.

Mark Golombek and Jean Astephan had agreed to call the police when they'd read about the Bain disappearance in the news that summer. They had been in

Morningside Park with Jean's sister, Kathy, as well as her boyfriend, Kevin Benoit, and another friend named Marty Fortier on the evening of June 19. Back then they were all in their late teens. They arrived some time around 8:00 PM and a few of them tossed a Frisbee around in a playing field near the entrance of the park. After a while, they walked west into the park along a footpath and stopped near the first bridge they reached, where they sat in a grassy area and turned on the portable stereo the guys had brought along.

No one in the group could later recall precisely how long they had lounged there, enjoying the long June twilight, before they were startled by the high-pitched screams of a woman, one after the other, coming from the other side of the river. The woman was screaming in short blasts with everything she had, taking quick breaths in between, then letting go again, with such force that it sounded as if she was tearing vocal cords. It was so loud that it drowned out the heavy-metal AC/DC tape they were cranking out on the boom box. Fortier and Benoit ran down to the river to help, but the Astephan sisters said they didn't want to be left alone, so Golombek said he would stay behind. Fortier and Benoit kept sprinting along the edge of the river, stopping at a spot they figured was no more than fifty feet from the woman in distress. But moments after they got there, the screaming stopped. It had lasted maybe a couple of minutes. Fortier and Benoit started shouting across the river, which was too deep and fast for them to cross. There was a clump of trees growing atop the far bank and they figured the woman in distress was just a short distance in, but there was no response to their cries.

Just then a couple of guys about their age pulled up on mountain bikes and said they'd heard the screaming too. It was starting to get dark, and, despite the curiosity of the four young men now huddled together scanning the shadows beneath the trees on the opposite side of the river, it was getting increasingly difficult to make anything out. They lingered for a time longer before parting ways, the cyclists off down the path, and Fortier and Benoit back to their friends. In the second statement Golombek and Jean gave the police on July 18, 1990, they estimated it was 9:30 PM when they returned to the playing field near the entrance of the park. They said they hadn't seen anyone else leave the park before they did at around 11:00 PM.

As Brian King had done with his initial investigation into David Dibben's alleged recantation, he dispatched Ted Harpur to interview the five young people who had heard the screams. Harpur spoke first with Mark Golombek at his apartment on April 23. Golombek remembered that night in good detail (considering it was seven years ago) and how some of them had phoned the police after reading about Bain's disappearance from the park in the newspaper. An officer had returned his call, but he now recollected that this was mainly to confirm Golombek had been the person who'd phoned in the first place. When Golombek didn't hear back from them, he assumed—just as Nobrega had—that the police had found the screams unimportant and, consequently, Golombek had put the entire matter out of his mind until recently.

The next witness Harpur interviewed, Martin Fortier, was not nearly as useful as Golombek, as his memory of that evening was fairly limited. Harpur was hoping that Jean Astephan and Kevin Benoit, now a married couple, along with Jean's sister, Kathy, who was living with them, still retained at least as much as Golombek. However, when Harpur arrived at Benoit's apartment building for their 8:00 PM meeting, no one answered when he knocked on the door. Harpur called Benoit's phone number twice during the next half hour, but he kept getting an answering machine. Waiting in his car outside, Harpur saw a light come on in the apartment at 8:35 and could see people walking around through the window so he buzzed the intercom in the lobby of the building. But again, there was no answer. Nevertheless, Harpur got himself inside the building once again and made his way up to Benoit's apartment. As he stepped into the hallway on the second floor, Benoit walked out of his apartment, and Harpur identified himself. Benoit nervously told Harpur that he had been forewarned by the police (Benoit had been interviewed twice the previous summer by Detective Sergeant Brian Raybould and Detective Jake Poranganel) that a private investigator might be coming around to speak with him and his wife. According to what the officers had said, it would only complicate things if he or the Astephan sisters happened to use the wrong words or mix their times up and, therefore, it was in their best interest not to grant interviews to anyone.

More than once, Benoit apologized for not being more cooperative. He said he had a job with the United Parcel Service and was in line for a promotion. He had the feeling that his involvement in the Baltovich case might work against him. Harpur wasn't too hard on him. Benoit seemed like a caring person who was simply trying to do the right thing. Even though he refused to give a taped interview, he didn't seem to mind talking to Harpur without a tape recorder in his face.

The screams, as Benoit remembered it, were so loud that they drowned out his cries offering assistance. He also now felt that the two cyclists might have been responsible for the screams, as the woman had become silent just before they'd arrived on the scene. And, finally, as he had asserted during his interview with Raybould and Poranganel, Benoit told Harpur that he now believed one of the cyclists, a guy in his early twenties with dyed blond hair, had been Paul Bernardo. He was ninety per cent sure, he said.

After reading Harpur's reports, Brian King summarized his thoughts about the newly disclosed "screams-in-the-night" witnesses in a letter to Brian Greenspan. King felt that Benoit's assertion about one of the cyclists possibly being Bernardo was unlikely, as Bernardo was not known to have committed any sexual crimes with a male accomplice. King also believed that, if Greenspan introduced the "screams" evidence, key witnesses like Ruth Collins and Keith Nobrega would be called into question. Collins and Nobrega both said they had seen Elizabeth Bain well before the sky had begun to darken, which was when the screaming had started. "The reality of the situation," King wrote, putting his own spin on how to deal with Benoit and the others, "is that no one (other than the perpetrator/s), even the Crown, knows what happened to Elizabeth that night and every potential piece of evidence must be seen as important."

A few days after King had sent Greenspan this batch of reports in late May, Rob called him collect—the only way he could call anyone—at the office. He did this once every month or two, usually to get an update and to find out what was happening with the appeal. "Have they set a date yet?" was usually one of Rob's first questions. King was always careful about what he said as far as the fresh evidence went, as the prison had the right to tape-record their telephone conversations if they were so inclined. He didn't think Warkworth security had any interest in Rob, so King would pass on tidbits related to some of the key developments, but wouldn't go into any great detail. Rob understood that King would tell him what he felt he could, and Rob rarely asked him to elaborate.

But this time, King detected that Rob's superhuman patience with the delays was starting to wear thin. Rob figured it was almost two years since he'd last spoken to Brian Greenspan. He'd put calls in to Lisa Silver, the other lawyer at Greenspan's firm working on the appeal, but it was a rare day when he could actually get her on the line (and that didn't count the months when she'd been on maternity leave). Even when he did get through, there was never anything terribly conclusive she could tell him about when the appeal might be heard. King could empathize with all of Rob's frustrations—even he had a hell of a time getting Brian Greenspan to return his calls.

And if one were to go by what was being reported in the newspapers, Greenspan had been a busy man lately. In October 1996, Greenspan had successfully defended former national cycling coach Desmond Dickie against charges of sexual assault and touching for sexual purposes brought by three female cyclists who had trained under him. And Greenspan was also front and centre in the long-running legal wranglings involving "hockey czar" Alan Eagleson, who once was professional hockey's top player agent, as well as the former executive director of the National Hockey League's Players Association for twenty-four years. Eagleson had been indicted for racketeering by a United States grand jury in Boston, Massachusetts, on thirty-two counts of fraud and embezzlement, after which an extradition application had been made by the U.S. Justice Department. Greenspan was also advising him on eight criminal charges of fraud and theft in Canada, as well as a class-action suit filed by former players in U.S. Federal Court in Philadelphia, charging that Eagleson and the NHL had conspired against them.

"Look, Rob," said King. "The squeaky wheel gets oiled first. If you want action, you and your family are going to have to be more aggressive. Start getting everyone to call Greenspan every day until he takes the time to answer your questions. I'm just not in a position to put pressure on him like that."

Rob decided to take King's advice. Greenspan's receptionist was soon deluged with calls from various members of the Baltovich family, until, finally, Greenspan arranged a time to meet with Rob's brother Terry and his parents at his office in late June. The way Terry later described the conversation to him, Greenspan didn't believe the appeal would be heard before Christmas. It wasn't a shock for Rob to hear this, but it was definitely disconcerting—he wasn't sure if it was ever going to be heard. As for bail in the meantime, Greenspan didn't think it was remotely possible, even if they brought every new piece of evidence to the table. That said, he expected to set a date for the appeal in three months at the most. Rob wasn't optimistic, but even a date would be comforting news. Terry said that the meeting lasted for almost three hours, and Greenspan spoke at length about the Crown's attempt to stall things, which, so far, had been successful. He sounded quite upbeat when it came to the fresh evidence surrounding Bernardo—the family was quite bowled over when they heard some of it—but now felt that Keith Nobrega was the key to the appeal. Terry told Rob that Greenspan wanted him to call from Warkworth on July 2 to hear some of this for himself. Rob looked forward to wringing as much information from him as he could. He was getting the sneaking suspicion that Greenspan wasn't exactly broken up about the delays, and that the only reason the appeal hadn't yet been heard was because he simply wasn't ready.

—◦—

By July, the inquiry into the wrongful conviction of Guy Paul Morin had heard five months of testimony. With the tables now turned on the police investigators, Crown prosecutors, forensic scientists and numerous Crown witnesses who had targeted him for more than a decade, Morin sat solemnly at a table each day and watched on as his lawyer, James Lockyer, launched a prolonged attack, never wavering in its intensity, on the people and process behind his client's persecution. And Lockyer had plenty to work with.

One of two inmates who had testified (in exchange for leniency) to hearing Morin confess in prison had later recanted in a letter to his family, only to recant his recantation at the inquiry. It came as no surprise to Morin that the man had been diagnosed as a pathological liar. The second jailhouse informant, a man who had been convicted of molesting almost a dozen children, told the inquiry (at which he was represented by none other than Brian Greenspan) that, upon hearing Morin's weepy confession so many years ago, he had been so enraged that his urge was to break through the concrete cell wall like Superman and kill Morin. When the hypocrisy of his position was pointed out to him by Lockyer, he replied, "Sir, there is a big difference between assaulting children and killing them." What was even more astounding was that, two days later at the inquiry, one of the Crown attorneys who had prosecuted Morin declared he was "still inclined to think [the jailhouse informants] are telling the truth," even though Morin had been exonerated by DNA evidence two years earlier.

This display was outdone just one week later when retired police detective Bernie Fitzpatrick, one of the lead investigators responsible for Morin's arrest, refused to concede publicly that he had arrested an innocent man. "It is my opinion,"

Fitzpatrick said, under pressure from Lockyer for him to set the record straight. "I would just as soon keep it to myself."

Other highlights of the Morin inquiry included testimony that numerous witnesses, including Christine Jessop's mother and brother, had either altered or fabricated their evidence as a direct result of police pressure; fibre evidence used against Morin had been contaminated during its stay at the Centre for Forensic Sciences prior to Morin's first trial, a fact that his various defence lawyers had never been informed of until the inquiry; statements given to the police by people who lived near the field where Christine Jessop's remains had been found, claiming they had heard a girl's screams late on the night Jessop went missing (at a time when Morin's whereabouts were accounted for), were never disclosed to Morin's defence; retired Durham Regional police sergeant Michael Michalowsky, previously charged with perjury and obstruction of justice in connection with the Morin case, used the same controversial method to avoid testifying before the inquiry as he had to stave off the criminal charges—he declared he was too ill, both physically and psychologically, to defend himself; the testimony of police officers and acquaintances of Morin who perceived Morin's demeanour at various stages subsequent to Jessop's disappearance as either strange or uncaring was repeatedly used against him by the Crown; and, in a similar vein, Lockyer revealed that Morin was the first person in the history of Commonwealth jurisprudence against whom the Crown had argued that, by not having assisted in the searches for a missing victim's body, the accused had betrayed his guilt (a legal precedent to which one of Morin's Crown prosecutors reacted at the inquiry by conceding that Morin was in a catch-22 situation, for had he attended any searches for Jessop, that would have been used against him as well).

For the last two weeks of July, the disturbing revelations at the Morin inquiry were overshadowed by the fallout from the latest developments in the renowned case of David Milgaard, who had spent almost twenty-three years in various Canadian prisons for the 1969 rape and murder of Gail Miller, a twenty-year-old nursing assistant from Saskatoon. Milgaard, who'd been sixteen at the time of Miller's death, along with Morin and the Nova Scotian Donald Marshall, made up one-third of a select group that had become known as "The Three M's" because all three had been convicted of murders they had not committed. As a result, their stories, part murder mystery and part suburban nightmare, had been widely publicized throughout Canada. After he had served almost his entire life sentence, Milgaard's conviction was quashed in 1992 by the Supreme Court of Canada, which, in its decision, suggested Saskatchewan order a new trial. During the intervening years, however, Milgaard had attempted suicide twice, and, in 1980, fled to Toronto while out on a day pass, only to be shot seventy-seven days later by the police who recaptured him.

The Supreme Court had based much of its judgment on what had come to be known about a man named Larry Fisher, who had been arrested nine months after Milgaard had been found guilty in January 1970. While Milgaard awaited an appeal behind bars, Saskatoon police apprehended Fisher and charged him with three rapes that shared a number of similarities with the Miller attack. For example, all three rapes had involved the threat of a knife and had taken place in the weeks preceding Miller's. Milgaard's lawyers, who were busy being turned down by every appeal court available to them—including the Supreme Court—likely would have had far greater success defending their client had they known about Fisher, who had resided only one block from Gail Miller's home. But the Saskatoon police and prosecutors involved, perhaps realizing they had convicted the wrong man, not only failed to disclose anything about Fisher's arrest to them, they went to considerable effort to keep it out of the public spotlight. Instead of prosecuting Fisher in Saskatoon—where all of the rapes had occurred—he was allowed to plead guilty in Regina, several hours away, where the glare of publicity was nonexistent. Years later, when Milgaard's lawyers finally did hear about Fisher, all references to him had been removed from Saskatoon police files.

Although the Supreme Court had struck down Milgaard's conviction, it had not formally acquitted him. So when Saskatchewan's attorney-general decided not to pursue a new trial against him, Milgaard was unsatisfied with the way the courts had left his reputation in a state of limbo. Many Canadians still believed him to be a guilty man who had been set free on a technicality. Seeking nothing less than an irrefutable exoneration, Milgaard and his lawyers were inspired by the new DNA testing that had cleared Guy Paul Morin's name in 1995. The twenty-eight-year-old semen stains left on pieces of Gail Miller's clothing by her attacker were sent to a laboratory in England, where it was immediately concluded through comparison to blood samples that they belonged not to David Milgaard, but to Larry Fisher—who had for years denied responsibility for Miller's death.

As the Milgaard family rejoiced, the Saskatoon police force held firmly to the untenable ground it had occupied for almost three decades. A spokesman for the force, Staff Sergeant Glenn Thomson, told the press that, in spite of the DNA results, Fisher was not necessarily a suspect. "He's the same person he was yesterday," Thomson proclaimed. "Assuming it was Mr. Fisher's semen on the clothing, all that shows is that he was in contact with the victim. It doesn't say Mr. Milgaard didn't commit the murder. It wouldn't be fair to say this clears one person and implicates another."

When contacted by a reporter with *The Globe and Mail* for a response to the police spokesman's comment, Greg Rodin, one of Milgaard's lawyers, said, "This is the kind of mentality we're dealing with. It gives the public a perfect example of the craziness that has happened here." Given the Saskatoon force's past involvement in the case, it didn't come as a shock when, within days of the DNA results being released, the Saskatchewan government asked the Royal Canadian Mounted Police to take over the investigation. In contrast to the Saskatoon force's apparent doubt over the scientific findings—which estimated that only one other man out of 400 million shared the DNA extracted from the semen on Miller's clothing—the RCMP took just three days to take Fisher into custody and charge him with first-degree murder.

In the meantime, Kirk Makin, *The Globe and Mail*'s justice reporter, had written a front-page article on wrongful convictions titled "Police 'tunnel vision' gives no justice, critics say." Makin, who had published an exhaustively researched book about the Morin case more than two years before Morin's exoneration via DNA, had since covered the Bernardo trial, as well as the Morin inquiry, which was still a long way from over. In his article, Makin cited an alarming statistic from the United States, that "for every five inmates scheduled to be executed during the past 25 years—a total of about 325 individuals—one is exonerated before the execution."

Through interviews with Dianne Martin, a law professor at York University's Osgoode Hall law school in Toronto, and Reverend James McClosky, the head of a U.S. organization that had "helped exonerate 18 innocent men serving life sentences, including David Milgaard," Makin delved into a substantive analysis of the multiple elements that wrongful conviction cases tended to feature on both sides of the border, some of which is reproduced here:

- Construction of the case by inept investigators, particularly when a small force is involved;

- Ignoring or suppressing the existence of other strong suspects;
- Suppression of evidence that the defence would have wanted to use at trial to enhance an alibi or blunt the credibility of a prosecution witness;
- A pro-prosecution judge who undercut the defence.

Many wrongful convictions also feature evidence of a so-called jailhouse confession supplied by unsavoury and unreliable prison denizens who trade their testimony for favours.

In a minority of cases, investigators overtly framed suspects using duress to extract a false confession or threatened witnesses to get them to provide false evidence.

However, the U.S. Department of Justice concluded recently that the No. 1 cause of miscarriages of justice is bad eyewitness identifications. The finding backs up a study several years ago in which professors Michael Radelet, William Lofquist and Hugo Adam Bedau found that mistaken eyewitness testimony lay at the heart of 209 of the approximately 350 U.S. wrongful convictions they studied.

Quite unwittingly, civilian and expert witnesses can fall prey to the urge to provide the police with what they plainly hope to hear, Prof. Martin said.

"I think it is almost a Stockholm Syndrome," she said. "The witness wants to be part of the solution. They internalize this pressure and produce the testimony the team needs."

Meanwhile, the police believe they alone understand the true rules and realities of their insular world, Prof. Martin said. The ends of convicting bad guys quickly justify the questionable means.

"Many police officers are afraid the justice system won't get it right," she said. "So they gild the lily. They leave things out. They try to give the courts what they think they want. You add in pressure from the community to solve a crime, and I sometimes think it is amazing we get it right as often as we do."

Experts in wrongful convictions believe that although prosecutors are much less likely than police to cut corners recklessly, they nonetheless may have trouble at times standing up to investigators.

"They have to work with them, so they won't always ask the hard questions," Mr. McCloskey said. "They just take it and run with it."

According to the Radelet-Lofquist-Bedau study, the average wrongful conviction takes seven years to correct. They estimated that 23 men were executed in the United States before their innocence was proved. Eight died in prison.

Mr. McCloskey said the greatest misconception in the field of wrongful convictions is that the exoneration of a wrongfully convicted person is proof that the system has worked.

"In the Milgaard case, the system did everything it could to hide the truth and keep it from coming forward," he said. "The system was eventually unable to resist the force of truth. We kept coming back and coming back—for 23 years."

The reality is that police and prosecutors invariably fight such a process tooth and nail, he said, and rarely end up accepting even the most clear-cut exoneration.

"They are afraid of being embarrassed, humiliating their predecessor, or bringing the justice system into disrepute," he said. "It takes a lot of dedicated people to bring forward devastating new evidence for year after year in order to break down the walls."

If seven years was the average length of time it took to negate a wrongful conviction, then two young men convicted in 1992 of first-degree murder (as well as two counts of attempted murder) in a gang-style shooting spree at a restaurant in Toronto's Chinatown were about to beat the odds by about two years. In early September, the Ontario Court of Appeal quashed the convictions of Thanh Tat and Sonny Long and entered acquittals on all counts. (Rob, having grown tired of the library job several months ago, was now tutoring a class of inmates—which included Sonny Long—in English, geography and mathematics at Warkworth. After hearing the news about his case, Long skipped into class with a big smile on his face and declared, "I got acquitted!") The appeal court judge reversed the decision based on the testimony of the sole eyewitness to identify Tat and Long as the gunmen.

The witness, "initially very tentative," said the appeal court judge, "became firmer only after prompting and suggestion by the police officer." Reading about the acquittals in the newspaper, Rob not only took solace in the fact that Thanh Tat had been represented at his appeal by Brian Greenspan, but that the officer referred to so reproachfully was Homicide's Steve Reesor, now deputy chief.

—◦—

In the days following the family meeting with Brian Greenspan back in late June, Adele was nervously awaiting word from the hospital that had taken a biopsy from a tumour on one of her lungs. She'd suffered through a battle with breast cancer two years earlier, but the doctors felt the growth had been excised in time to prevent the disease from spreading. With a tumour now afflicting her lungs, Adele, who'd been smoking most of her life, knew deep down that the biopsy would reveal the inevitable. Within days, it did.

The doctors were hopeful, however, that by removing the bad lung tissue, the cancer could be properly eradicated and would not spread to any other organs in her body. The doctors said they would need to conduct a few more preliminary tests throughout the summer before operating on the lung in September. But by the middle of August, Adele's health had deteriorated significantly. She was having great difficulty breathing and was often overcome with terrible bouts of weakness. The latest tests indicated that the cancer had cropped up in the lymph nodes of her esophagus, and her doctors now thought it best to operate as soon as possible. Seeing Adele in a hospital bed, her breathing laboured and her energy sapped, Jim suggested that she might want to wait a few weeks and regain her strength before the surgery. But Adele said no. She wanted to get it over with. So, on August 21, a Thursday, surrounded by family, she was taken into the operating room.

Much to everyone's distress, Adele was slow to recover and was either asleep or incoherent for days. Doctors notified Jim the following Thursday that she had contracted pneumonia and that things had taken a turn for the worse. She was pronounced dead the next day.

Jailhouse Notebook (15)

*W*hen Paul called to say that the doctors had decided to operate on Mom sooner than expected, I applied for a day pass so that I could see her at the hospital beforehand. But the powers that be turned me down, mostly, I think, based on the fact that my mother had come to the institution for a visit the previous weekend. Looking back on that afternoon, I can't help remembering how well she looked. She looked as good as I'd ever seen her in the past seven years. She'd quit smoking and was happy, laughing, having a wonderful time. It is a beautiful memory but hard to reconcile with what happened a week and a half later.

The prison made arrangements for me to travel to Scarborough for the funeral. Two guards, both decent guys, accompanied me in an unmarked family van. Over the car radio the announcers were scrambling to cover the death of Princess Diana, who had been killed during the night in Paris. The more I listened to people evaluating Diana's life, the more I was reminded of Liz. Of course it seems absurd in so many ways to compare the two, but they were both intelligent, beautiful, shy, caring young women (was my own mother really much different?) who, despite a thousand blessings for which to rejoice, will be remembered above all else for their suffering. One part of the stirring eulogy delivered by Diana's brother, Earl Spencer, at her funeral this morning has stayed with me. "For all the status, the glamour, the applause," he said, "Diana remained throughout a very insecure person at heart, almost child-like in her desire to do good for others so she could release herself from deep feelings of unworthiness, of which her eating disorders were merely a symptom."

Diana's fragility, which her brother so eloquently described, moved so many, I suspect, because, as thousands of citizens congregate to mourn the essence of this "real" Princess of the People, we are just beginning to come to terms with how pervasive this mysterious brand of suffering truly is. It is the condition of the modern age.

I wasn't able to devote too much thought to these ideas on the way to the funeral, for it had been so long (five years!) since my last ride in a vehicle that I was car sick from the moment we started moving. So by the time we arrived at the parking lot of the funeral home, I took two steps out of the van and threw up all over the place. Thankfully, there was a suit and a clean pair of leather shoes waiting for me inside.

It was an incredibly exhausting, bittersweet day. Almost immediately, it was obvious that many of the people there had come to see me, as well as to pay their respects. I must have shaken at least two hundred hands at the reception out at Paul's house. People I haven't seen since my childhood. People my mom knew as a young girl whom I'd never met. My head was spinning. On the one hand, it felt good to be with my family and all kinds of friends I hadn't seen in such a long time, but I wish these greetings had been brought about for another reason. At times I felt so guilty, realizing I was enjoying myself.

At one stage of the afternoon, my dad told me that, three weeks earlier, he and my mom had signed some papers sent to them by an adoption agency. I have not yet written about this, but a few years before they were married, Mom and Dad had conceived a child out of wedlock, a baby girl, whom they had put up for adoption. This little girl, my sister, now a middle-aged woman, had recently made a formal request to meet her biological parents, and Mom and Dad had given the agency permission to release their names and address. Of course it is too late for Mom, but maybe meeting and getting to know his only daughter will give Dad the lift he now needs.

I've been talking to Dad on the phone a lot over the last few days. He's always been so reserved, his emotions held in check. But then, after Mom died, and I heard his voice crack, I lost it. I haven't cried since my conviction and I have often wondered if I had any tears left. But talking to him was pretty devastating, and I felt like I was crying out everything I'd held in for the last five years. I know how, during the days, it will be easy for Dad to distract himself. But at night, when you get into bed and you're all alone . . . I know a little what that's like and I wish he didn't have to feel that way.

Dad is racked with guilt because he thinks he should have tried harder to persuade Mom not to have the operation so soon (or maybe at all), but it was the one thing she felt might give her the chance to live long enough to at least see me out of prison. From a selfish point of view, this is another aspect of my sadness. My freedom was her last remaining wish. It makes me so angry. I can't even go home and take care of my father.

My thoughts go almost exclusively to Dad. I'm just hoping that, somehow, he can muster the strength to get through this, because I know it's going to be very difficult for him. Frankly, I'm not optimistic but, who knows, perhaps he'll surprise me. What makes things worse is that he is the type of man who ruminates and who will ponder for a long time what could have been done differently. Was it the hospital's fault? Was it his fault? Even last night on the phone he was angry enough to start asking why Mom had to smoke. He's letting all of these feelings out, which is good, but I don't want it to become a habit. From personal experience, I know how "what-ifs" can destroy you if you hold on to them for too long.

—◦—

Jim woke up the morning after Labour Day and washed up before putting on a pair of grey slacks and a light blue short-sleeved golf shirt with the logo of a government lottery corporation on the left side of the chest. By the time he got down to the store and opened up, it was quarter to ten. He felt exhausted and was hoping for a quiet morning so he could just sit down on the stool behind the counter and rest. Instead, it was the busiest morning he'd had in ages and he didn't take his seat on the stool once.

Paul came to pick him up around noon, and Jim closed the store for an hour while they drove down to McDougall & Brown to settle up the bill for Adele's funeral. Things slowed down for a while later in the afternoon and Jim sat down and peered out the front window into the first bright crisp afternoon of what would soon be autumn, while every minute or two the screen door in the back room rattled in the wind. He was thinking about Adele and how she was always chirping with Rob on the phone. And about how he would watch her at the kitchen table and laugh. How he would ask, "What are you guys talking about?"

And how Adele would lower the receiver away from her chin and say, "Oh, Jim. Nothing."

Then his mind turned to the guards who had been kind enough to take Rob for a drive by the house and how Rob had said over the phone from Warkworth later that night that he couldn't believe how much the little trees in the front yard had grown. Jim had offered to scoot down to the store and open up so Rob could have a little walkabout inside, but Rob said he didn't want to get the guards in any kind of trouble with their superiors. Their orders were to make one stop at the funeral parlour and another at Paul's for the reception—and that was it. So the guards parked the van in front and let it idle at the curb for a few minutes while Rob just stared out at the unlit store. Imagining this caused Jim to break into a little smile as he shook his head.

One of the guys from the tattoo shop next door walked in and asked if Jim had any gold model paint. The guy didn't bother waiting for Jim to look, he just walked behind the counter and checked out the little glass jars for himself. "Jim, I bet you're the only guy in Toronto who still sells this stuff," he said. Jim had yellow but not gold. "Oh, well. Take care, Jim." And he was out the door.

It was quiet again for a while and then a scruffy-looking guy came in and asked if Jim would check his lottery tickets. He was too drunk to read the winning numbers posted on the counter, so Jim fed his tickets into the machine. "It will start playing music if you're a winner," he said.

"Then sing me a tune, my friend," the drunk crowed.

The machine was spitting out the results on receipt-sized pieces of paper. Jim said, "Not this week, I'm afraid." Without letting it get to him, the guy threw the useless scraps in the garbage and made his way to the door, where he turned around and asked if there was a bank machine at the end of the block. Jim nodded.

"I need some money for a case of beer," he slurred blissfully, raising a hand good-bye as his right leg wobbily anticipated the sidewalk.

Alone again, Jim checked the time. It was almost seven. Rob had said he was going to call that evening, and Jim decided to lock up in a hurry and get home—didn't want to miss Rob. So he emptied out both cash registers and put on his blue windbreaker and his cap and hit the lights. Earlier, he'd put some trash in a Coca-Cola box and grabbed it on his way out. After locking the dead bolt on the front door, he turned and stepped down from the stoop onto the sidewalk. He walked to the bus stop on the corner, where he laid the Coca-Cola box atop the trash filling the metal waste container next to the plexiglass shelter. Then he walked—limped, actually, as his feet were giving him trouble again—back in the other direction, his head down against the heavy wind that had now turned cold. He'd left the car in a spot on his side of the street today, and cars were whizzing by on Kingston Road as he opened the door and lowered himself in behind the wheel. By now, his was the only vehicle left on the block. He rested his small carrying case down on the seat beside him and fastened his safety belt before fitting the key in the ignition. He let the motor run for a good thirty seconds as he waited for a clear opening to get onto Kingston Road so that he could ease his way up to the lights. There, he signalled a right-hand turn and veered north into the familiar neighbourhood, where he would soon be home, fixing his own dinner, waiting for the phone to ring and to hear the comforting voice of the automated operator. *You have a collect call from . . .* And then the sound of his son saying his name. *Do you accept the charges?* And Jim would press the number one button on his telephone, which, as he'd known for some time, was how you said yes.

An Afterword

More than four years have passed since I first met with private investigator Brian King to discuss the plight of Robert Baltovich. At the time, writing a magazine article about the case was all I had in mind. King, politely cynical, gave me the distinct impression that several others had preceded me with similar plans. Cutting the conversation short, he handed me eight thick volumes of court transcripts from Baltovich's preliminary hearing and told me to come back once I had read them through. The following week I returned, and he had the first ten volumes from the trial waiting for me. This routine continued until I had made my way through almost forty volumes of court proceedings.

Convinced that I had expressed sufficient interest, King finally led me to the small, windowless office whose sole purpose was to house the material he had amassed on "the Bain file." Fully aware that he would have no editorial control over anything I wrote, King gave me unlimited and unconditional access to everything that lay within that room: court transcripts, police statements, thousands of documents pertaining to King's investigation (including tapes and photographs), Robert Baltovich's notes, a copy of Elizabeth Bain's diary from 1990 (which had been entered as evidence) and reams of correspondence. From very early on in the case, King had seen his investigative role as equal to that of his role as historian. Without access to the wealth of information he and his staff had meticulously accumulated, this book—or, for that matter, any book about the Bain-Baltovich story—likely never would have been written.

As I balanced the considerable task of sifting through King's vault of files and completing my magazine projects, almost two years passed before I drove out to the Warkworth Institution for my first meeting with Robert Baltovich on December 18, 1995. By then, I had been commissioned to write a feature article about the case for *Saturday Night* magazine (published in October 1996), but was determined that a book would follow. Like Brian King, Baltovich had been on the receiving end of a steady stream of interview requests for years—from producers at national current affairs TV programs to criminology students seeking a good subject for their theses. With an understandable degree of reticence, therefore, he agreed to open his life to an inquisitive stranger with no guarantee that the final product would be any more palatable than what he'd grown accustomed to.

Since then, Baltovich has provided at least fifty hours' worth of interviews, a handful of them conducted at Warkworth, the rest over the telephone. Not only did he exhibit astonishing patience while responding to countless inquiries, he did so under especially trying conditions. For, as any reader who has made it this far already knows, he has been forced to endure an inordinate number of delays awaiting the hearing of his appeal—a series of numbing blows worsened by events back home, such as the death of his mother.

When it came time to deal with Baltovich's experiences in various correctional facilities, he made available his written memoirs, referred to in the book as his "Jailhouse Notebook." These entries give valuable insight into his character and show, above all else, that his sense of humour may have been his best ally in weathering this terrible ordeal. Regardless of one's stance on his innocence or guilt, Baltovich's generous participation in this book has clearly served to enrich it, and for that he is owed an unreserved debt of gratitude.

In addition to the many interviews granted to me by Brian King and Robert Baltovich, another fifty or so people patiently answered questions about the case, quite often on more than one occasion. It is worth noting, however, that a number of individuals who figure prominently in the story—Crown attorney John McMahon, Deputy Chief Steve Reesor, polygraph examiner Frank Wozniak, as well as Detectives Brody Smollet, Jake Poranganel and Miro Pristupa—chose not to comment on any aspect of the case. The reason each gave was the same: that it would not be appropriate for them to comment while Baltovich's appeal was still before the courts. It must be noted, though, that this principle failed to prevent Detective Poranganel from telling *The Toronto Sun* two days after Paul Bernardo's arrest that there was "no connection at all" between Bernardo and the disappearance of Elizabeth Bain, nor did it dissuade Detective Sergeant Brian Raybould from telling me in early 1996 that he wouldn't have to think twice about pointing a loaded gun at Baltovich's head and pulling the trigger, if the law only allowed him to. (A little more than two years later, in April 1998, Deputy Chief Reesor made it clear that his old partner would be granting no more Baltovich interviews, particularly with me.) As for the Bain family, despite two letters sent to Rick and Julita Bain, they have expressed no interest in answering any questions. Fortunately, each member of the Bain family gave extensive testimony at Baltovich's various criminal proceedings.

Baltovich's "Jailhouse Notebook" entries, as well as those selected from Elizabeth Bain's diary, have been subjected to a minor degree of editing. Baltovich and Bain possess strong and distinctive written styles, but, as one might expect, there were occasionally repetitious passages that needed to be trimmed or transposed for the sake of clarity. Great care was taken not to excise any expressions that could be interpreted as relevant to the case against Baltovich or to his defence. For the most part, these excerpts are virtually intact.

In a similar vein, material such as letters, reports, transcripts of court proceedings, monologues from interviews, John Secord's journal entries, interviews conducted by the police or Brian King, conversations with Baltovich and his family recorded secretly by the police, transcripts of television newscasts and talk shows, as well as newspaper articles and columns, allowed a few liberties. Quite often, these offerings have been slightly condensed, usually to avoid retelling facts or to eliminate confusing references. Again, my intention was not to cut passages to favour one side over the other, but to make it easier for the reader to make up his or her mind without getting too mired down in distracting details.

These days, books such as *No Claim to Mercy* fall into a literary domain categorized as creative nonfiction. They have also been referred to as true-life novels (or nonfiction novels). In this case, the adjective "creative" hints at invention, which appears odd attached to the notion of truth. If the evidence against Baltovich was more concrete, and each utterance and movement was not so crucial to our understanding of his state of mind, then the book might have sustained periodic attempts at fiction within the narrative. As it stands, the only passage in which a blatantly fictional construct has been employed is in Part 3, when Steve Reesor and Brian Raybould visit Jimmy's Smoke Shop. Of course, I don't know precisely what those officers observed during the few minutes they were in the store, but it couldn't have been much different from what I saw several years later. The dialogue and action that took place during this encounter, however, was based on Jim Baltovich's memory of that day.

One of the great challenges confronting anyone wishing to comprehend the Baltovich case is establishing the sequence of events, especially during the weeks before and after Elizabeth Bain's disappearance. Before starting to write *No Claim to Mercy*, I put together a detailed chronology of the story (a document that now exceeds 25,000 words in length), commencing the day Robert Baltovich and Elizabeth Bain first met. Not surprisingly, testimony periodically conflicted over the timing of certain events. Most of these key discrepancies in memory are pointed out in the book, but there were many less important ones; for the sake of a lucid narrative, I selected the most likely scenario based on the flow of action on the day or days in question.

It should also be noted that real names have been used throughout with the exception of Paul Bernardo's former girlfriends.

There are a number of sources not mentioned in the book that I would like to acknowledge. Robert Fulford's portrait of Scarborough and its history, "Going to Scarborough Fairest," which appeared in the November 1991 issue of *Toronto Life* magazine, was of tremendous value. Flashes of local colour—polyester and velvet paintings, for instance—were borrowed with kind permission. As for Scarborough campus itself, "Decade Book: 10 Years of Scarborough College" and the "1990 Scarborough Campus Master Plan" provided further background.

My account of the Atikian trial was largely based on Peter Cheney's in-depth reports for *The Toronto Star*. The articles of another *Toronto Star* reporter, Philip Mascoll, provided background on the Julie Stanton murder case, as did those by *The Toronto Sun*'s Robert Benzie. The small report that speculated (incorrectly) that two long, black bones found in Scarborough in the summer of 1996 "may be" Elizabeth Bain's was written by the *Sun*'s Ian Timberlake.

The photo line-up experiments of Dr. David Dunning, the Cornell University psychologist, were brought to my attention through an article, "Picture Imperfect," by Daniel Goleman, which *The Globe and Mail* picked up from the *New York Times* Service on January 21, 1995.

I relied on a chapter titled "Food: The Case of Death's Time" in Jack Batten's *Mind Over Murder: DNA and Other Forensic Adventures* for an engaging account of the Steven Truscott case.

Stephen Williams's book *Invisible Darkness: The Strange Case of Paul Bernardo and Karla Homolka* has been vilified by a number of critics, the most prominent among them being Maggie Siggins, whose review in *The Globe and Mail* inspired the headline: "A shallow look into pure evil." Toronto poet Lynn Crosbie, who recently published the widely praised yet controversial *Paul's Case*, a "fictional treatment" of the Bernardo tale, described *Invisible Darkness* as "by far the most subversive and intelligent" of the three Bernardo books on the market before hers. Williams himself deemed this "faint praise when one considers the dearth of quality and research to be found in the 'quicky' books that were churned out post-Bernardo trial by tabloid-tempered reporters." However one might feel about Williams's book, it is the best work of nonfiction we have on the Bernardo-Homolka affair and, as such, it was a useful source (in conjunction with hundreds of newspaper and magazine reports) for certain details about the Scarborough rapist investigation and the events that followed the capture of Paul Bernardo.

The section that concentrates on the media coverage granted to the Bernardo-Homolka story by "A Current Affair" and other, more local, outlets, was taken from an article I wrote for the July/August 1995 issue of *Saturday Night* magazine called "Murder, They Wrote."

Jeremy Foster's remarkable week-long journey as a suspected serial rapist arrested by the York Regional Police was based on a report by *The Globe and Mail's* Michael Grange. Equally astounding was the trial of ex-hypnotist George Matheson, which I had the opportunity to witness firsthand. I am also indebted to *The Globe and Mail's* court-reporting duo of Thomas Claridge and Donn Downey for their accounts.

Redrum the Innocent, Kirk Makin's take on the Guy Paul Morin story, came in handy on a number of occasions. Of particular interest were his passages on how suspected killers usually react to an arrest and interrogation, as well as his observations about Judge John O'Driscoll, who played a brief but important role in the legal odyssey of Regina v. Morin. To his credit, Makin has stuck with this marathon of a story, and I read his coverage of the Morin inquiry closely and with admiration.

Because most of those who assisted in the research for this book are identified within the text, I will not name them again here, except to offer a most sincere and heartfelt thanks to all those who generously took the time to speak with me. There are also many who should be acknowledged for their support behind the scenes: the staff at King-Reed & Associates, especially Dee Moore and Linda Williamson, who always made me feel at home; criminal defence lawyers Ted Minden, Earl Levy and Jeffrey Kerzner (as well as others who asked to remain anonymous) for kindly putting up with my questions; my literary agent and squash comrade, Bruce Westwood, of Westwood Creative Artists; Cynthia Good at Penguin Books, for her unwavering determination, and editor Meg Taylor for her thoughtful insight; the Canada Council's Explorations Program for its much-needed assistance in the past; Joyce Carol Oates and Paul Auster, who helped foster my love for writing and then, in good conscience, sent me off to spend my twenties in penury; and finally, but really foremost, Dianna Symonds, my talented and caring editor at *Saturday Night* magazine, whose encouragement, I am sure, has meant more to me than she knows.

For guidance of a more personal nature, I would like to thank my friends and family, currently extended from Barry's Bay, Ontario, to the Caribbean. My mate, Julie Mitchell, the first to read the entire manuscript, offered a good number of excellent suggestions. Special mention should be afforded to my grandmother, Ferne Finkle, my beacon of light and warmth in the crazed firmament of life. Without her, this book would be but a dream and, therefore, it is lovingly dedicated to her.

—◯—

Due to the unresolved state of the case against Robert Baltovich, readers of this book may well be left wondering what has happened to him. At the time *No Claim to Mercy* went to press, Baltovich's appeal date had not yet been set. I will continue to follow events closely, as it is my intention to write for a future edition of the book a final section on the outcome of the appeal. In the meantime, however, there are a number of noteworthy developments that have taken place since Adele Baltovich passed away ten months ago.

Within days of his mother's funeral, Paul Baltovich got a call from the older sister his parents had put up for adoption before they were married thirty-five years earlier. Her name is Charlene, the same name Jim and Adele had bestowed upon her the day she was born. Charlene's surname was now Weitzman, as she had married a man named Brian Weitzman in 1994. Her adoptive parents, she explained, had moved from Toronto to California in 1967, where Charlene had remained, settling in Saugus, a suburban community about thirty miles northeast of Los Angeles. She worked in the aerospace industry, as did Brian, which was how they'd met in 1990. Charlene apologized for not having tried to get in touch with Paul and his family sooner, but she'd just given birth to her second child, a son—she had a two-and-a-half-year-old daughter named Nicole—and her doctors had thought it best to put off any emotional reunions with her biological family until the pregnancy was over. Paul then asked what the boy's name was and when he'd been born. Charlene said her son's name was Adam and that he'd been delivered on August 29—the same day, as Paul pointed out with amazement, that Adele had died.

By mid-November, Rob was seeking a transfer from his tutoring job at Warkworth, which he was finding increasingly stressful; Rob was considerably more serious about teaching than some of his fellow inmates appeared to be about learning. (A few weeks later, he accepted a clerical position as a pay clerk within the institution.) As much as he was looking forward to a change in work, he was even more eager to meet Charlene, who visited Warkworth on November 12 with her husband, Brian, and daughter, Nicole, as well Rob's father and brother. Rob described the scene in his memoirs: "As I strolled into the visiting area, I recognized Brian from the pictures that had been sent to me. Oddly, I couldn't see Charlene anywhere. As I embraced everyone, Paul told me that Charlene would be joining us in a moment. A few seconds later, she walked in. As I smiled and approached, she began to cry. I gave her a big hug. Part of my delight was based on the feeling that someone who should have been a big part of my life had, up until that moment, been absent. But, as we hugged each other, I realized that another part of me felt as if I was holding on to a piece of my mother, one that had entered my life at the same time someone so dear had left. Now, it seemed, our family had been completed."

That same fall, Rob was paying close attention to news stories about a lawsuit filed by Paul Bernardo's former best friend, Van Smirnis. Smirnis had taken *The*

Toronto Sun to court, claiming that the $100,000 the newspaper had posted in reward money (in addition to another $300,000 apparently donated to the *Sun*'s reward fund) rightfully belonged to him. Clifford Lax, a lawyer representing the *Sun*, conceded that Smirnis was the first person to come forward with information after the *Sun* went public with its reward for information leading to an arrest and conviction. However, Lax argued that Karla Homolka was the driving force behind Bernardo's conviction, not Smirnis. He also pointed out that there was a small cluster of tips both before and immediately after Smirnis's. Arguing on behalf of Smirnis, lawyer Malte Van Anrep asked each police witness the same question during the course of their testimony: if the officers who interviewed Bernardo after Smirnis's tip had managed to get Bernardo's DNA test results right away—instead of ten months down the road—would Smirnis now be seen as a major player in the Bernardo arrest and conviction? Their answer was of considerable importance to Rob and his appeal, as Smirnis would still be an important witness with regard to the fresh evidence related to Bernardo. So Rob was relieved to learn that their answer, without exception, was yes. On November 21, Smirnis was awarded a relatively meagre $10,000 of the total reward offered (probably just enough to cover his legal bills). In his ruling, Mr. Justice James Kent deemed Smirnis's information as having "value at the time it was provided. Its value, however, would be considerably less than the total amount of the reward."

On September 25, 1997, two weeks before Smirnis's suit began to be heard, another legal proceeding, one far more crucial to the Baltovich appeal, was going on behind closed doors, away from the media spotlight that would soon be pointed in Smirnis's direction. For it was on that day that Keith Nobrega, the witness whose statement was unknown to Baltovich and his lawyers until four years after his conviction, travelled into downtown Toronto to be cross-examined on his affidavit. The Crown attorney upon whom this task had fallen, Shawn Porter, was familiar to me. I had seen him arguing on behalf of the Crown at various stages during the legal proceedings in the Bernardo case, and he had struck me as being quite young, maybe thirty, although I later learned he was several years older. Porter is a courtroom personality in the making, with his ruffled, thinning blondish hair, his slightly affected brooding manner, made bearable to his observers by his intelligence, not to mention the obvious pleasure he gains from having all eyes and ears trained on him, and by his unpredictable wit.

With Brian Greenspan present, Porter took Nobrega through the same story he had given Brian King over a year earlier. Eventually, Porter asked Nobrega about how, when he'd seen the Missing poster for Elizabeth Bain on Friday, August 24, 1990, it caused him to contact the Bain family. Nobrega explained that he'd had to work that weekend but that following his shift on Sunday afternoon, he'd driven down to Morrish Road, which was where the poster had indicated Elizabeth Bain's car had been found. He told Porter that he'd gotten out of his car and just stood there. "A funny thing happened," Nobrega said. "My hair started to stand up, like body hair, but that's beside the point. I stood there and I looked at the spot, then drove off and found a phone booth in the little strip plaza nearby."

"Pause there for a moment," Porter interjected. "What caused your hair to stand on end all over your body? What was there?"

"This is . . . I can't explain," said Nobrega. "This happens to me sometimes, you know, it's a funny thing. I've had experiences where my hair stands on end. I'm from Guyana—lots of funny things happen down there. I'm not going to get into that to explain this, but I'm just telling you what happened to me."

"Are you mildly psychic, sir?"

"Sometimes. I would say sometimes I am."

"Or fully psychic at other times?"

"At times I am, and I know at times I am, but this is not something that I can call on and reproduce."

"It's not something that you can call on at will," Porter said. "It's something that's visited upon you. And was it visited upon you that day?"

Nobrega explained that standing near the auto body shop on Morrish Road made him want to go to the phone booth and call the number on the poster. No one answered, and it bothered him until the following morning as he prepared for another shift at work. He told Porter he was feeling "agitated." "It was like something moving me," said Nobrega. "Go and get a hold of the Bains, phone this number right away."

To have a witness as potentially damaging to the prosecution as Keith Nobrega declare himself the recipient of psychic experiences, mild or otherwise, must have given Porter a rush of professional satisfaction equal only to Brian Greenspan's dismay. Nobrega, whose story was so important that it never travelled beyond a select group of Homicide investigators until it was too late, was now about to become the umpteenth person in this case whom a lawyer would attempt to discredit based on the fact that a strange, inexplicable feeling came over them when they visited one of the locations where Elizabeth Bain was last seen (or thought to have been). Considering the fact that Bain had still not been found, was it really that strange that Nobrega would get a "jump," as he described it, when he first saw her photo, or that the hair on the back of his neck stood up when he saw for himself the place where her car was found? Was it truly that peculiar for him to feel that way when he was quite possibly the last person, other than her attacker, to see Bain alive?

(Apparently, Nobrega's reaction was more common than Porter realized. On May 30, 1998, *The Globe and Mail* published an interview with former Metro Toronto Police Chief, William McCormack, who was flogging his book, *Life on Homicide*. When asked if he had ever seen a ghost, McCormack responded, "No. I've had many cases when the hair on my neck stood up. I couldn't explain it. I'm convinced there are people who have.")

Regardless, Porter could wait only a few minutes before returning, with a rather patronizing air, to the psychic issue. When Nobrega described how the photos of Elizabeth Bain would give him a jolt, even before he had realized she was the terrified-looking person he'd seen on the highway, Porter asked, "But is it a jolt or a psychic experience? Or both?"

"It's a jolt and a psychic experience," said Nobrega. "Something hits you, like if you got an electric shock and you don't know where it came from."

"A burst of other-worldly information that is now in your mind and you have to deal with it," Porter added. "Is that fair?"

"Well, let me explain something to you. Have you ever sat down in a crowded room and felt somebody looking at you? And you turn around and you see somebody looking at you? Have you ever had that experience?"

"All right," sighed Porter, well schooled enough to know that he didn't want to get into a discussion with Nobrega on this issue, particularly if he was going to equate "psychic" behaviour to such a common sensation. "Here's the problem," Porter said. "I'm not really in a position where we can engage in a dialogue. Maybe we can do that afterwards when we're not paying for this reporter guy. But, for now, if you could just describe the psychic experience you're having."

"This impression I got was like a burst of energy to my conscience," explained Nobrega. "Let's say you're walking along the road one night, a dark night, and suddenly you see that you just walked past an open manhole cover. You get a jolt, a shock, like that, you know like 'holy smoke.' It was that sort of electric effect."

So much for Martians, voodoo, time travel, predicting world crises, communicating with the dead, locating corpses for frustrated police investigators or whatever else Porter was hoping for. The issue of why Nobrega's statement was never disclosed to Baltovich's defence, it is worth noting, was never raised.

—◦—

Christmas 1997 was Rob's seventh in a correctional facility. Several weeks before the holidays, Rob had been informed that Brian Greenspan had handed over the assignment of getting the appeal to the stage that a date could be set to David Humphrey, Greenspan's law firm partner. Greenspan was reportedly juggling one of the heaviest caseloads in the province, the most prominent file belonging to former hockey impresario Alan Eagleson, on whose behalf Greenspan was negotiating a novel two-nation plea bargain related to his numerous fraud charges in Canada and the United States. (In early January, Eagleson pleaded guilty to three counts of fraud in each country and was ordered to pay $1 million in restitution and sentenced to serve an eighteen-month term at a correctional facility in Ontario.)

Although Rob was hopeful that Humphrey might expedite the appeal process, months passed, and by the end of March 1998, he was convinced that his lawyers were no closer to setting a date. His patience with Greenspan and Humphrey had run out. On April 1, Rob sent a stern letter to Humphrey filled with words like "completely unsatisfactory" and "entirely unacceptable." "For the past two years," he wrote, "I have consistently been told that the hearing of the appeal is imminent, only to be disappointed time and again. . . . The current state of affairs cannot and will not continue any longer. My family and I have begun seriously discussing the possibility of seeking representation elsewhere. Given what I feel has been unfair treatment by your law firm, this would serve the interests of the eventual success of the appeal and my physical and psychological well-being. I deeply desire that peace of mind that would come knowing that my counsel has my best interests at heart and at present I have grave doubts that my interests are being served by your firm. I am certain that many firms would jump at the chance to represent me, especially given the nature of the case and the strong grounds for appeal that exist."

When Humphrey received the letter, he and Sharon Levine, the lawyer who seemed to have taken the now-departed Lisa Silver's spot on the case, expressed their concern over the letter to Rob during a telephone conference call. They assured him they were doing all they could, and that Brian Greenspan was still overseeing the case. Rob just couldn't comprehend what was holding up the appeal. Well, they explained, the affidavit of Patricia Hood, David Dibben's cousin, had not yet been signed. And it seemed as though Janine Godsoe, the woman who had once introduced her ex-boyfriend Paul Bernardo to Elizabeth Bain, was no longer as agreeable to participating in the Baltovich appeal. Humphrey said they would have no choice now but to subpoena her so that she could be cross-examined as a hostile witness prior to the appeal—in Humphrey's view, Godsoe was that important to their case.

Given Rob's infrequent contact with Greenspan over the years, an article in *The Globe and Mail* two weeks after mailing his letter to David Humphrey filled him simultaneously with resignation and laughter. Apparently, Eagleson had put in a request with the authorities at the Mimico Correctional Centre in Toronto, where he was serving his sentence, for a pass to return home for Easter dinner. When his request was denied, Greenspan drove to Mimico and, as the *Globe*'s source inside the jail described it, demanded that Eagleson be treated "like a normal prisoner," for Eagleson had learned that other inmates had been granted similar passes. According to the source, Greenspan created "a major ruckus" and became so outraged that he insisted on speaking to the men in charge of the institution, both of whom were at home for the Easter weekend. For the first time that the source, a Mimico employee, could remember, the superintendent and the deputy superintendent both drove to the institution during their off hours, only to tell Greenspan, who'd threatened to hold a press conference to announce the mistreatment of his client, that Eagleson was still being denied a pass. For Rob, the lasting impression of this story was that Greenspan seemed to have a more proactive policy of communication with clients like Eagleson than he did with him.

A little more than a week after the story of Eagleson's "jail fracas" had hit the news, Steve Reesor's photograph was on the front page of *The Toronto Star*, beneath the banner headline "Deputy chief of police entangled in gun scandal." *Toronto Star* reporters Jim Rankin and John Duncanson broke the story of how Reesor, "the deputy chief in charge of the Toronto police force's firearms and property units used the gun unit to sell his own .38-calibre revolver." Reesor, who had sold the gun in early 1997, must have known it was illegal for gun registration unit officials to keep, sell, buy or barter firearms that passed through the unit.

Having received a number of formal public complaints about the firearms unit between 1993 and 1996, internal affairs investigators began examining the unit around a month after Reesor had used it to sell his privately owned .38 Smith & Wesson handgun. Internal affairs, the *Star* reported, alleged "that the firearms registration unit was running a guns-for-cash scheme that also involved falsifying federal gun paperwork." An internal audit of the unit had uncovered the fact that roughly three thousand items, including guns, knives and ammunition, could not be accounted for on the unit's computer system. By the spring of 1997, the internal affairs investigation resulted in more than ninety criminal charges against five civilian staff at the unit, all of whom were suspended without pay. Although none of the charges were connected to the gun Reesor sold, Rankin and Duncanson decided to call Toronto Police chief David Boothby to inquire about what disciplinary action had been applied to Reesor for his actions. Boothby said he'd told Reesor that it wasn't proper for police officers to sell their guns through the gun registry. "It was an error," Boothby told the *Star*. "He admits it and he has been counselled."

Two months earlier, Rankin and Duncanson had written a series of articles about the property unit, which was also under Reesor's command and also being investigated by internal affairs. Instead of missing guns, this time the two *Star* reporters were onto allegations "that items seized as evidence or recovered stolen goods" had "disappeared or been mishandled." One fairly typical example given was the story of a woman who had recently gone to the unit to claim a diamond ring, only to be told it couldn't be found and that she should come back later. "When she returned," wrote Rankin and Duncanson, "the ring had turned up. But when she attempted to slip it on her finger, it didn't fit. It had apparently been resized to fit a smaller finger, three sources in law enforcement confirmed."

Through its sources, the *Star* also obtained a photograph of the office belonging to the property unit's civilian manager, Leo Coelho, taken in the fall of 1995. Hanging on its walls were six framed limited-edition sports prints, featuring a number of professional hockey and baseball players—all of which were supposed to have been returned to their rightful owner months earlier. Another thousand prints that the rightful owner had been selling on consignment when the prints came into police possession were still missing. When Jim Rankin tracked down the man who had invested in those thousand prints, Rankin learned that he had never been directly informed that he could pick up the prints at the property unit. The *Star*'s sources inside the unit suggested that its staff were "instructed to make little or no effort to contact owners of items held there." As one insider described it, "The employees were told, in no uncertain terms, that unless somebody inquires about their property, they were not to take the time to notify the owners." The reason for not contacting owners was that, after ninety days, unclaimed items could be sold by the police at an auction. In 1996, the Metro Toronto police force made $249,103 in net revenue from auctions, up about $75,000 from the year before.

Rob Baltovich, it went without saying, read the articles about Reesor's troubles with no small degree of satisfaction. In the wake of Reesor's gun scandal, Rankin and Duncanson updated their reports on the property unit in early May with another banner headline declaring that the internal investigation of the unit had widened. When Rob read about how the *Star* had learned that a box of evidence from the Scarborough rapist investigation had been destroyed before Paul Bernardo had admitted to the crimes in late 1995, he wrote Rankin and Duncanson a letter in which he urged them to keep digging around. Was the evidence destroyed because it might have helped his appeal? Quite possibly not, but whenever Reesor was involved, Rob couldn't help being cynical.

Brian King, too, was caught off guard by the negative coverage Reesor was getting. King wondered if Reesor had seen it coming, for he'd run into Reesor around Christmastime at a fund-raising event for the Hospital for Sick Children hosted by a group of local Crown attorneys, and Reesor, in a most jovial mood, had seemed as though he had not a care in the world. Despite the surfacing of Keith Nobrega, as well as other key facets of the appeal, Reesor's opinion of Baltovich hadn't shifted, even slightly. He told King that he'd be willing to offer Baltovich a deal. Now that Baltovich had been incarcerated for almost seven years, Reesor said that he was ready to grant him parole if Baltovich disclosed the location of Bain's body. King was no longer sure whether Reesor's bravado came from an honest belief that Rob was a killer or a not-so-subtle form of self-preservation, the best defence being a good offence.

Nevertheless, few could have predicted the way Reesor's gun scandal would mushroom into a story of enormous proportions. The day after the Star broke the story, Rankin and Duncanson followed it up with a front-page piece touting the fact that the head of the Homicide Squad, Staff Inspector Ed Hoey, had also used the firearms unit to sell two guns for an acquaintance. Even former police chief William McCormack, who had retired in 1995, was expecting to be called as a witness in relation to an illegal gun sale being investigated by internal affairs. More than anything else, the *Star*'s revelations indicated that, if high-ranking officers such as Reesor and Hoey had used the firearms unit to sell guns, then the upper echelons of the police department had likely been aware that the unit was engaged in the illegal trade of guns. Instead of putting a stop to such activity, some police brass decided to take advantage of it.

But the issue that really caused the gun-scandal story to be tackled by just about every Toronto news source, instead of just the *Star*, was the way two of the five civilian employees originally charged in the scandal still faced the prospect of defending themselves in court while Reesor had merely been "counselled." Susan Eng, a former chair of the police services board and an avid gun-control advocate, announced her disapproval in the *Star*. "I think counselling—'Don't do it again, tsk, tsk'—is not enough. It seems to me that this is a lot more serious." Eng also said it "speaks volumes" about police culture that civilian employees were facing the heat even though senior officers condoned using the gun unit to sell firearms. "When caught," said Eng, "they just protect themselves. Just suppose you are an average civilian employee in the gun unit and a senior officer comes in and says, 'Here, take care of this for me.' I mean what are you, an idiot? And say, 'No I won't, because these are what the rules are.' This is where the public trust we have here breaks down. We have senior officers asking a civilian to breach the trust."

Concurring with Eng, the president of the union representing seven thousand members of the Toronto Police Force, Craig Bromwell, faxed a letter to Solicitor-General Jim Flaherty asking that the Ontario Civilian Commission on Police Services "commence an investigation into the actions of the senior command and certain departments within the Toronto Police Service." This request by the Toronto Police Association was, according to the *Star*, "unprecedented and stunned many in police circles." *The Globe and Mail* suggested that it signalled a "vote of non-confidence in [the] chief." Two days later, on April 29, 1998, Chief David Boothby held a press conference to announce that he was relieving Reesor of his duties as head of the property and firearms units pending an internal review regarding the sale of his gun. Reesor would maintain all of his other responsibilities as head of operational support command, Boothby told reporters. "I have said it before and I will say it again," said Boothby, who, at times, appeared shaken, "I have absolute confidence in Deputy Chief Reesor."

On May 12, two weeks after Boothby's press conference, Ontario's civilian police watchdog ordered the Toronto police services board to commence an investigation into the force's management discipline system. The Ontario Commission on Policing Services asked the board to report back to it in forty-five days. Police association president Craig Bromwell predicted this was the first stage in what could be a long battle to make the police hierarchy more accountable.

In the meantime, *The Toronto Sun*'s columnist Christie Blatchford had entered the fray. Blatchford, who claimed that Reesor had always struck her as "a very smart, good officer," admitted that, when news of Reesor selling his gun first went public, she didn't really understand why it was such a big deal. It wasn't until she looked into the matter that she changed her mind. What it boiled down to was that, simply by transporting his restricted handgun from his house to police headquarters downtown, where the sale of his gun had taken place, Reesor had committed an indictable offence under the Criminal Code. If an ordinary citizen was caught carrying a gun on the road without the required permit—which Reesor had not obtained—the maximum penalty, if convicted, was five years in prison.

"Common sense might tell us, aaah, so what if a high-ranking officer once moved his gun without a piece of paper?" wrote Blatchford at the end of her May 5, 1998, dispatch on Reesor. "But it was not an insignificant thing, and the most important aspect is that what would land the ordinary citizen in trouble, and perhaps even the uniformed cop, seems to have little effect on the brass. The police board does not have to be spoiling for a fight to make a few inquiries. It is my experience that in such small incidents there is often a larger story."

If there was one current story to which this philosophy of Blatchford's applied, it was the wrongful conviction of Guy Paul Morin. In early April 1998, the Morin inquiry concluded with the public release of Commissioner Fred Kaufman's 1,400-page report, which *The Globe and Mail*'s Kirk Makin described as "branding the Morin case a landscape of error and ineptitude." Kaufman's chief mandate was to make recommendations that would help prevent another wrongful conviction like Morin's, and the commissioner had few difficulties tabling an exhaustive list.

About a month later, in mid-May, Makin reported that the Ministry of the Attorney-General had assembled a committee to implement Kaufman's proposals. Ontario prosecutors agreed to adopt three of them immediately. The first directive was that prosecutors no longer address defendants as "the accused" but by their proper names. The second allowed defendants not being held in custody to sit beside their lawyers instead of in the isolated prisoner's box (as Baltovich had). The last related to the establishment of a special team of lawyers who would vet potentially unreliable Crown witnesses, such as jailhouse informants, before they were ever called upon to testify in court. More changes seemed to be on the way, but first there had to be a meeting between senior bureaucrats from all of the provinces to look into changes that involved "criminal procedures lying within federal jurisdiction." Who, one might ask, was the Ontario Crown attorney appointed to head the committee overseeing these crucial matters? None other than John McMahon, the man who had prosecuted Robert Baltovich.